OTHER BOOKS BY
MALCOLM MCCONNELL

MALCOLM McCONNELL

WITH

RESEARCH BY

THEODORE G. SCHWEITZER III

SIMON & SCHUSTER

NEW YORK LONDON TORONTO SYDNEY TOKYO SINGAPORE

INSIDE HANOI'S SECRET ARCHIVES

SOLVING THE MIA MYSTERY

SIMON & SCHUSTER
Rockefeller Center
1230 Avenue of the Americas
New York, New York 10020

DESIGNED BY BARBARA M. BACHMAN

Manufactured in the United States of America

10 9 8 7 6 5 4 3 2 1

Library of Congress Cataloging-in-Publication Data
McConnell, Malcolm.
    Inside the Hanoi secret archives : solving the MIA mystery / Malcolm
McConnell.
        p.   cm.
    Includes bibliographical references and index.
    1. Vietnamese Conflict, 1961–1975—Missing in action—United States.
2. Vietnamese Conflict, 1961–1975—Prisoners and prisons.   3. United
States—Foreign relations—Indochina.   4. Indochina—Foreign relations—
United States.   I. Title.
DS559.8.M5M4   1995
959.704'37—dc20   94-38692
                                                                                       CIP

ISBN: 0-671-87118-8

Photo credits: Photo 30 courtesy of F. C. Brown. All other photos collection of
Theodore G. Schweitzer III.

ACKNOWLEDGMENTS

MALCOLM MCCONNELL AND TED SCHWEITZER WISH TO THANK THE FOL-lowing persons, without whose advice and assistance this book would not have been written:

Former Secretary of Defense Melvin Laird; General John W. Vessey, Jr., USA (Ret.); General Robert C. Kingston, USA (Ret.); Major General John E. Murray, USA (Ret.); Major General John K. Singlaub, USA (Ret.); Colonel Albert F. Gleim, USA (Ret.); Colonel Glenn Nordin, USAF (Ret.); Captain Byron Wiley, USN (Ret.); Colonel James S. Hanke, USA (Ret.); Colonel Hayden B. Peake, USA (Ret.); Colonel Joseph A. Schlatter, Jr., USA; Lieutenant Colonel Frederick Caristo, USA (Ret.); Lieutenant Colonel John Haralson, USA (Ret.); Lieutenant Colonel Paul D. Mather, USAF (Ret.); Major Charles D. "Chuck" Melson, USMC (Ret.); Carlos Campbell; and Douglas Pike.

Commander Frank C. Brown, USN, shared his impressive private archive of POW/MIA documents. His insights were greatly appreciated.

B.G. "Jug" Burkett provided records and original research findings into the phenomenon of bogus prisoners of war. Harve Saal helped clarify the issue of fraudulent Special Operations veterans.

Robert K. Brown, publisher of *Soldier of Fortune,* gave assistance throughout the project.

Lieutenant Colonel Jack Donovan, USA, Lieutenant Colonel David L. Fredrikson, USA, and Lieutenant Colonel Charles D. Robertson, USAF, of the Joint Task Force/Full Accounting, Detachment 2, shared their experiences.

Former Soviet Air Force Captain Alexander Zuyev offered a unique perspective.

Major William Burkett, USA, Major Ralph Peters, USA, and Major Pete Johnson, USAR, of Task Force Russia, made important contributions.

Senator John F. Kerry, Frances Zwenig, William Codinha, Deborah De-Young, Bob Taylor, Larry Carpman, and Steve Gekoski of the Senate Select Committee on POW/MIA Affairs graciously assisted in this project.

Former Prisoners of War Admiral James B. Stockdale, Medal of Honor, USN (Ret.), James Warner, James Shively, Ronald Bliss, and Guy Gruters gave important assistance.

George L. Brooks provided wise insights on the case of Robert Garwood, as did former Marine Paul Olenski.

The following active and retired officers of the People's Army of Vietnam assisted the project: Lieutenant General Hoang Phuong, Senior Colonel Pham Duc Dai, Lieutenant Colonel Tran Thanh Hang, Lieutenant Colonel Bang Lam, and Major Lai Vinh Mui. Ambassador Ha Van Lau also provided assistance.

Lon and Gail Stickney shared the perspective of the American veteran returned to Vietnam.

Carol Emery McConnell and Brian Morgan were especially adept at locating documents buried in American archives.

"James Renaud" and "Peter L. Bogen" of the Defense Intelligence Agency's Operations Directorate made vital contributions to the book.

What may perhaps turn out to be the most significant advancement in the U.S. Government's negotiations with the Socialist Republic of Vietnam began developing in September 1992. Through the efforts of an American civilian under contract to the Department of Defense, wartime records from the Vietnam Central Military Museum were passed to the U.S. officials. Included in these materials were photographs of American wartime casualties and crashsites. This material clearly documented that the Vietnamese archives did indeed hold records that could most certainly help resolve the fates of Americans missing from that war.

—POW-MIA FACT BOOK
DEPARTMENT OF DEFENSE
OCTOBER 1992

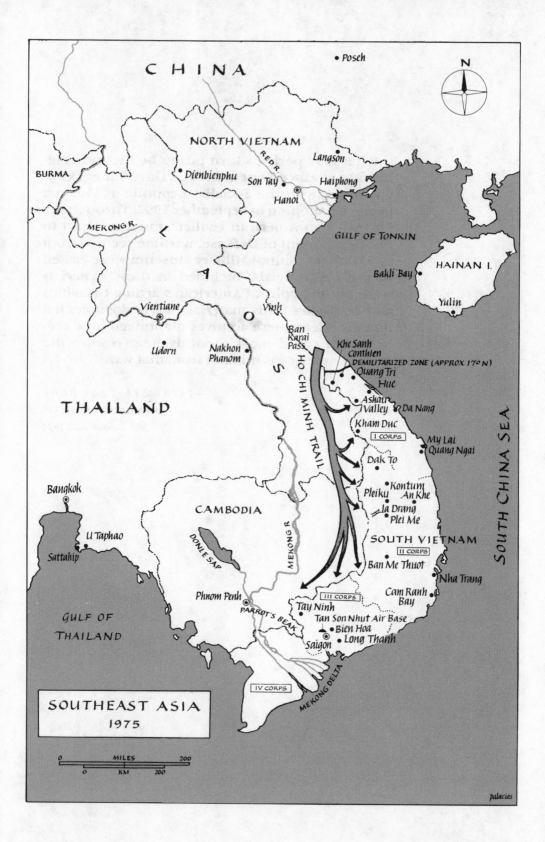

CHINA

• Poseh

NORTH VIETNAM

BURMA

• Langson

• Dienbienphu   Son Tay   Haiphong
                 ⊛ Hanoi

RED R.

GULF OF TONKIN

HAINAN I.

MEKONG R.

• Bakli Bay

• Yulin

Vientiane ⊛   Vinh

L   A   O   S

Ban
Karai
Pass

SOUTH CHINA SEA

Udorn   Nakhon
              Phanom

THAILAND

HO CHI MINH TRAIL

Khe Sanh
Conthien
DEMILITARIZED ZONE (APPROX 17°N)
Quang Tri
Hue

Ashau
Valley   • Da Nang

Kham Duc

I CORPS

My Lai
Quang Ngai

Bangkok
⊛

Dak To

CAMBODIA

Pleiku   • Kontum
           An Khe

Ia Drang
Plei Me

U Taphao

Sattahip

DON LE SAP

MEKONG R.

SOUTH VIETNAM

II CORPS

Ban Me Thuot

• Nha Trang

Phnom Penh
⊛

Cam Ranh
Bay

GULF OF
THAILAND

PARROT'S BEAK

III CORPS

Tay Ninh

Tan Son Nhut Air Base
Bien Hoa
⊛   • Long Thanh
Saigon

IV CORPS

MEKONG DELTA

SOUTHEAST ASIA
1975

0   MILES   200
0   KM   200

palacios

PREFACE

AT PRECISELY EIGHT ON THE BRIGHT, CHILL MORNING OF FRIDAY, October 23, 1992, George Bush strode onto the portico of the Rose Garden, followed by retired General John W. Vessey, Jr., Bush's personal emissary to Vietnam on Prisoner of War and Missing in Action (POW/MIA) affairs. Senators John McCain and John Kerry of the Senate Select Committee on POW/MIA Affairs flanked Vessey.

The President looked pale as he descended the steps to the rostrum and faced the television cameras. With the election only two weeks away, media pundits were predicting an upset victory by Bill Clinton, due in part to unexpectedly strong support for third-party candidate Ross Perot. Only a few Bush loyalists still managed to speak convincingly of a home-stretch rally. Bush himself was blandly optimistic. He seemed almost serene despite the chalky pallor and puffy eyes, the obvious signs of fatigue that he chose not to disguise with makeup on the campaign trail. Indeed, the last month of the race was the most energetic campaign anyone in the Washington press corps could recall having been undertaken by an incumbent president.

This early morning Rose Garden ceremony was a prime example of Bush's renewed energy. As soon as he finished here, he would board his Marine One helicopter for the brief flight to Andrews Air Force Base and begin another cross-country jet whistlestop tour that would take him to six cities over the next eighteen hours. Given that schedule, it was obvious that Bush considered this ceremony politically important. Most of the regular White House press corps, however—who didn't have access to helicopters—were already fighting the Beltway traffic, en route to Andrews and the press charter plane that would trail Air Force One.

But the Rose Garden was far from empty. "The usual suspects," a cameraman muttered, nodding toward the VIP guests grouped along the well-trimmed boxwood hedges. They had been dragooned from the bureaucracy to serve as camera fodder for the ceremony. Today they included senior military intelligence officers in beribboned uniforms, State Department officials, and an additional contingent of MIA families.

Half hidden in the VIP party, a lean, dark-haired man with smooth features and a quietly aloof manner stood anonymously between Ambassador Richard Armitage and an admiral. None of the reporters recognized the man. In his expensive silk tie and conservative pin-striped suit, the stranger appeared to be just another government executive summoned for this election-year ceremony. Had the Rose Garden media realized, however, that this man was not simply a bored observer, but rather the principal reason the President had organized this ceremony, they would have jostled closer to him, ready to pounce with notepads and minicassettes extended as soon as the President completed his brief remarks.

The man's name was Ted Schweitzer. He had just returned from Hanoi, where he had spent the previous seven months conducting research in the secret military archives of the People's Army of Vietnam (PAVN). What Schweitzer had uncovered in those dusty, mildewed offices of the Central Military Museum in the old French Citadel was probably no less than the key to the emotional mystery concerning the fates of 2,265 American servicemen still officially listed as Missing in Action since the end of the Vietnam War.

Schweitzer had been the principal agent of Operation Swamp Ranger, one of the most adroit and audacious espionage operations the U.S. government had launched since World War II.[1] Ostensibly a private researcher gathering material for a book on American MIAs, Schweitzer was actually a contract agent—officially a "consultant"—of the Defense Intelligence Agency (DIA) Operations Directorate. His assignment to Hanoi had been so sensitive that even his government travel orders were classified top secret.

President Bush began his remarks by noting that General Vessey and Senator McCain had just returned from Hanoi, where Bush had sent them to conduct extraordinary negotiations with the Vietnamese government. Bush added that resolving the nagging POW/MIA issue and achieving the "fullest possible accounting" of our missing men in Indochina, while leaving behind "the bitterness of war," had been his administration's consistent policy. Progress on this question, he stressed, had always been difficult.

But, Bush said, he was personally committed to solving the problem. "You see," he stated, leveling his gaze at the television cameras with his most sincere presidential expression, "for all of us, the POW/MIA issue is a question of honor, of oath-sworn commitments kept. . . .

"And then last summer," Bush stated, "we got our first glimpse of Vietnam's vast set of wartime archives."

He noted that the recent Vessey-McCain mission to formalize American government access to these archives—which included thousands of POW photographs, uniforms, and other artifacts, as well as detailed records—was the most "significant breakthrough" in the long POW/MIA stalemate.

"Hanoi has agreed to provide us with all—and I repeat, *all*—information they have collected on American POWs and MIAs," Bush emphasized, again gazing for effect into the cameras. "And today, finally," the President added, "I am convinced that we can begin writing the last chapter of the Vietnam War."[2]

Reporters standing on the dew-covered lawn exchanged speculative glances. The President of the United States had just publicly announced that the wary and intractable Communist government of Vietnam had formally agreed to provide *all* the information in their possession about Americans captured during the long war.

In the absence of this information, a storm of wild rumor and speculation concerning the MIAs had swirled for twenty years. A shadowy cottage industry had developed on both sides of the Pacific, with unscrupulous traders peddling dubious information and artifacts, ranging from counterfeit dog tags to questionable "live sightings" of prisoners still being held in Indochina, to blackened shards of human bones supposedly salvaged from downed aircraft. Recently, intriguing grainy photographs purporting to show middle-aged American POWs still in Communist captivity had surfaced—and had either been embraced as authentic, or dismissed as cruel frauds by advocates of opposing views within what is known as the MIA "community."

The conspiracy myth surrounding the Americans who remained missing after Operation Homecoming in 1973 had evolved to baroque intricacy. By 1992, there were thousands of zealots—in shifting alliances and grassroots volunteer organizations—who believed with cultlike fervor that hundreds of American POWs had been deliberately and callously abandoned in Indochina after the war, that there was a vast conspiracy within the armed forces and the executive branch—spanning five administrations—to cover up all evidence of this betrayal, and that the governments of Communist Vietnam and Laos continued to hold an unspecified number of living American POWs, despite their adamant denials of this charge.

And this zealous faith was not limited to a radical fringe. A public opinion poll conducted the year before by the *Wall Street Journal* and NBC News found that a startling 69 percent of Americans believed that U.S. prisoners of war were still being held in Indochina.[3] This disparate body of believers spanned the political spectrum. But they did have one politician of national stature who shared their view: Ross Perot. And if George Bush had any chance of winning the election in four weeks, he had to recapture a significant portion of the putative Republicans who now leaned toward Perot.

Announcing that his administration had found the solution to the intractable MIA mystery was a step in that direction.

IN RETROSPECT, THAT Rose Garden ceremony was obviously as much an exercise in political damage control as it was a revelation of the ultimate "breakthrough" on the MIA enigma.

Unraveling the layers of that mystery is the goal of this book.

INTRODUCTION

BAN KARAI PASS, NORTH VIETNAM

1245 HOURS, NOVEMBER 25, 1968

TWO AIRCRAFT SLASHED THROUGH THE NORTHEAST MONSOON CLOUD deck and rolled toward the notch of the mountain pass ahead. The laterite mud of the switchback road was a rusty orange against the deep greens of the jungle.

The two F-4 Phantoms, twenty-ton fighter-bombers, sixty feet from nose to tail, and almost forty feet across their swept-back wings, were painted the mottled green-and-tan camouflage of the Southeast Asia war theater. This was Grommet Flight, a photo reconnaissance mission of the U.S. Air Force 432nd Tactical Reconnaissance Wing flying from the Udorn air base in northeast Thailand. Grommet 01 was an RF-4C photo reconnaissance variant of the Phantom, the workhorse aircraft of the Vietnam War. Grommet 02 was an F-4D armed escort, the air superiority modification of the Phantom.[1]

The flight was fifty minutes outbound from Udorn and had just refueled from the Brown Anchor KC-135 airborne tanker above the Mekong River frontier between Thailand and Laos. After tanking, the aircraft had turned onto a northeast heading, crossed the narrow panhandle of Laos, and cut back on a sharp descending turn through the overcast above the Annamite Mountains of North Vietnam. Their orders were to photograph as much of the twisting laterite road—"Line of Communication 914" in military terms —as weather and enemy defenses permitted, all the way from the steep foothills to the east to the Ban Karai Pass itself, and then down the western slope of the high ridges into Laos.

This road was one of the principal tributaries of the Ho Chi Minh Trail, the skein of dirt roadways, footpaths, submerged bridges, and river fords that stretched all the way from the Mu Gia Pass in the North to the multiple termini in southern Laos, Cambodia, and South Vietnam.

To the Communist People's Army of Vietnam (PAVN), this narrow, snaking, bomb-pocked laterite road was Strategic Route 20 of the Truong Son, "The Long Mountains." It was one of the principal logistics corridors of the PAVN's Military Region 4. Protecting the road from air attack was the responsibility of the 280th Air Defense Regiment, a unit equipped with heavy machine guns, rapid-fire 37mm cannon, and radar-controlled 57mm antiaircraft guns.

To the U.S. Air Force, blocking "choke points" such as the Ban Karai Pass had become a major objective of the long war.

Grommet Flight's mission was meant to further that objective. The air war against the Vietnamese Communists was in its fifth year and perhaps its twenty-fifth evolution of strategy and tactics. These four years had been marked by periods of intense bombing, punctuated by pauses, which American military and civilian leaders sincerely believed would elicit appropriate responses from the Hanoi Politburo.

For much of that time, American air power had pounded the transportation system of North Vietnam. The tactical goal of the bombing had been to interdict the flow of Communist troops and military equipment from the North to the battlefields of the South. But the strategic rationale for the four years of bombing had been to convince the Communists that their war of aggression in the South was unwinnable, and ultimately too costly.

That strategy had failed.

Ten months earlier, Communist forces in South Vietnam had unleashed their Tet Offensive during the 1968 Buddhist lunar New Year. Although the subsequent two months of hard combat throughout South Vietnam had been a clear military defeat for the PAVN and its Vietcong auxiliary forces, the offensive's strategic objective had been met: The American people had been the ones convinced that the war in Vietnam was unwinnable.

In the wake of the Tet Offensive, Lyndon Johnson had addressed the nation on March 31. "I shall not seek, and I will not accept, the nomination of my party for another term as your president."

Johnson invited the North Vietnamese to participate in peace negotiations in Paris. He then declared that he had suspended bombing north of the twentieth parallel, in effect sparing North Vietnam's industrial and population centers. Just before the November presidential elections, Johnson had ordered a complete halt in bombing of North Vietnam as a belated gesture of support to his party's presidential candidate, Hubert Humphrey.

This had not helped the Democrats. Richard M. Nixon was elected president by a plurality of less than 1 percent on November 5, 1968. One of Nixon's few clear campaign strengths had been his "secret plan" to end the war in Vietnam.[2]

With the bombing of North Vietnam indefinitely suspended, American air power was concentrated on the Ho Chi Minh Trail in Laos and on the mountain passes connecting Laos and Vietnam. The bombing halt freed the PAVN to use the Vietnamese side of the mountainous frontier as a safe staging zone for reinforcements en route south. The U.S. Air Force now flew multiple daily reconnaissance flights over these passes to photograph truck convoys and troop formations preparing to enter Laos.

Always quick to seize tactical opportunities, the PAVN reinforced the defenses of these passes with concentrations of antiaircraft weapons. In the four weeks since the November 1 bombing pause, two RF-4C reconnaissance planes had been shot down in the region.

This was a grim prospect for Grommet Flight. The northeast monsoon stratus deck was broken today, but the cloud bases were only 3,000 feet above the twisted spine of ridges that flanked the Ban Karai Pass. The two aircraft would have to snake up the gorge from the northeast, clearly silhouetted against the overcast, well within automatic-weapon and antiaircraft cannon range.

"Cricket, Grommet zero one," the flight leader called their airborne command post, a C-130 transport orbiting above the Lao panhandle. "Rolling in to target."

"Roger, Grommet," the airborne commander replied. "Clear to target. Good luck."

Grommet 02, the escort, slid back to a trail position 400 feet behind the recon Phantom. The planes rolled in unison onto their right wings and fishtailed up the gorge. They held their speed just below 300 knots so that the RF-4C's powerful nose-mounted cameras could achieve optimum stereoscopic effect.

The two-man crew in the lead aircraft were preoccupied with their camera run. They definitely wanted to get usable imagery on one pass and not have to double back.

In Grommet 02, the thirty-eight-year-old pilot, Major Joseph C. Morrison, and his backseater in the tandem cockpit, First Lieutenant San D. Francisco, twenty-four, scanned the forested hillsides of the steep and narrowing gorge anxiously. They were approaching a hard right turn in the valley that would force both aircraft to bank and expose their bottom sections broadside to any enemy gunners hidden in the jungle. But so far there had been no red tracers glowing in the dull monsoon afternoon.

The crew of the lead aircraft had completed their brief camera-run checklist when they heard a startled call from Major Morrison.

"Flak." His voice was thick. "We took a hit . . . Mayday. We're going in."

Grommet 01's crew scanned their rear cockpit mirrors. There was no sign of the other aircraft. But the overcast sky behind them was laced with orange and red tracers of rapid-firing antiaircraft cannon.

The lead pilot hauled back on his control stick and advanced his throttles, throwing the big aircraft into a spiraling corkscrew climb away from the pass. He flipped his radar transducer to the Emergency position, and called a distress message on the Guard Channel monitored by Search and Rescue forces in Thailand.

"Mayday, Mayday. This is Grommet zero one. My two is hit and going down."

"Roger, copy," the somber voice of the Cricket aerial command post acknowledged. "Do you have a visual?"

The lead aircraft was still clawing for the protection of the overcast. Now incandescent pink cannon rounds sailed and wobbled toward the plane from the seemingly unbroken forest below. The pilot eased his throttles and rolled through a full circle, both crewmen scanning the ridges below. There was no sign of Morrison and Francisco's aircraft. It had simply disappeared. And there were no parachutes visible against the mottled green forest.

Then the pilots heard the sharp electronic ping of two RT-10 survival radio emergency beepers. The crewmen of Grommet 02 had ejected.

"I've got two solid beepers," Lead called.

The Cricket commander ordered the unarmed reconnaissance Phantom out of the area. Then Cricket contacted the Rescue 1 command post of the Search and Rescue headquarters at Udorn to announce the loss. With any luck, a Jolly Green Giant helicopter would recover the pilots before enemy troops found them.

TWENTY MINUTES LATER, the rescue flight consisting of a Sikorsky HH-3 Jolly Green Giant helicopter and four A-1E propeller-driven Skyraiders was en route from Nakhon Phanom air base, Thailand, seventy miles west across the Lao panhandle. Two Skyraiders, call signs Sandy 04 and 05, were the first aircraft on the scene. The Sandys used their automatic direction-finding radio compasses (ADF) to home in on the beeper signals coming from the jungle slopes almost a mile from the bomb-scarred dirt roadway that marked the pass.

The beepers were a good sign, but not actual confirmation that Morrison and Francisco were alive on the ground. Enemy soldiers might be using captured beepers to bait the Sandys into a flak trap. The chunky mottled-green Sandys hugged the forest roof, rolling and jinking to thwart enemy gunners as they roared toward the Ban Karai Pass, the heavy thud of their radial engines echoing off the limestone pinnacles and through the steep gorge.

Sandy Lead, the rescue commander, had steady beepers on Guard Channel. But he needed voice confirmation from the downed airmen before he would commit the vulnerable Jolly Green Giant helicopter to attempt a rescue. The Jolly's procedure would be to follow a Sandy to a survivor's site, call for the man to pop a smoke marker, then hover and lower a bullet-shaped jungle penetrator rescue sling by cable through the trees. Once the man was strapped in, the helicopter would winch him up and proceed to the other survivor.

That was the standard plan. It had succeeded hundreds of times in undefended stretches of the Lao mountain wilderness along the Ho Chi Minh Trail. But effecting that type of helicopter rescue in a heavily defended sector was usually impossible.

"Grommet zero two, Sandy Lead, copy?"

A panting, garbled voice broke through the static and the steady ping of the other beeper. The words sounded like, "Zero two Bravo." That would have been Lieutenant Francisco, Bravo being the designation for the back-seater.

Then the other beeper went silent and Morrison's voice, loud and clear, filled the Guard Channel. "This is zero two Alpha on the ground and moving." He sounded winded, as if struggling through the steep jungle. And he sounded scared.

The Sandy pilots now saw the reason for Morrison's fear.

The crushed, smoldering wreckage of the Phantom lay on the northern face of a ridge above the dirt roadway. Two orange-and-white parachute canopies were draped among trees halfway up the slope from the smoking debris. But less than 700 meters away, in a clearing on the north side of the track, thatched huts and slit trenches of an enemy military camp were clearly visible. As the Sandys careened through the pass, the pilots saw Communist soldiers trotting across the dirt road and into the forest below the wreckage.

The two Skyraiders wheeled in a tight turn, maneuvering back for a strafing run on the enemy troops. If the Sandys could lay down enough 20mm cannon fire and pound the roadway with antipersonnel cluster bombs, the Vietnamese soldiers might stay away from the survivors long enough for the Jolly to get in and snatch them.

But that optimistic scenario did not develop. After two strafing and bombing runs, Sandy Lead called in the Jolly. But when the helicopter approached from the west, dodging and banking among the limestone cliffs, the hidden enemy gunners who had held their fire now cut loose in unison.

"Break left!" Sandy Lead called the Jolly pilot.

The big jungle-green helicopter barely escaped the interlocking web of tracers that sailed up from hidden positions on either side of the gorge.

The rescue forces climbed for the overcast and headed west into Laos to regroup. The only chance of success was to bring in enough air support to maintain constant strafing and bomb runs around the survivors' positions and on the obvious antiaircraft sites, so that the Jolly could safely approach.

But while Rescue 1 at Udorn and the Cricket airborne command post were diverting fighter-bomber flights to the scene, the monsoon overcast thickened. The base of the cloud deck lowered until the pass itself was shrouded. There was no way fighter-bombers, even the nimble Sandys, could fly flak suppression in that weather.

The rescue attempt was suspended for the day.

0640 HOURS, NOVEMBER 26, 1968

A Cessna 02 forward air controller (FAC), call sign Nail 12, was on station just after dawn. He found a break in the overcast and cautiously spiraled down until he was free of the clouds. But the western valley and the gorge of the Ban Karai Pass were still covered by fog. The FAC flew his maneuverable light aircraft skillfully, using every possible terrain feature for shelter while he called for the Grommet 02 crew on the rescue channel.

After several calls, the FAC heard a strong beeper signal. The ADF radio compasses placed the beeper higher up the ridge than the survivors had been reported the day before.

"Grommet zero two, copy?"

"Zero two Alpha," Morrison called back.

Morrison gave a long beeper transmission while the FAC climbed to take an ADF bearing on the signal.

That was a necessary risk. The FAC had to have a good location if there was to be another rescue attempt by a Jolly Green. But he knew the enemy troops had direction-finding equipment of their own. The FAC told Morrison to sit tight, then called Rescue 1 to dispatch another Search and Rescue flight.

A force of two Jolly Greens and six Sandys, backed up by multiple flights of flak-suppression Phantoms, was on orbit in the overcast above the Ban Karai Pass within an hour of the FAC's call.

All that was needed now was a final ADF confirmation on Morrison's position and the first Jolly pass could be ordered.

"Grommet zero two, Sandy Lead, copy?"

There was no voice reply. There was no beeper.

The rescue force commander called again.

There was no reply.

After an hour of attempting contact with no reply, the rescue flight returned to base.

NOVEMBER 25, 1968, LEXINGTON, KENTUCKY

Peggy Morrison knew exactly what faced her when she saw the dark blue Air Force sedan pull into the carport of their suburban home. Every Air Force wife with a husband in the war zone dreaded this moment. The two officers approached her front door somberly. She was glad that her daughter, Cindy, and son, Jed, were already in bed.

It was Monday night in Arizona, already Tuesday morning in Vietnam.

The doorbell rang and she composed herself to face the inevitable.

MAJOR MORRISON AND Lieutenant Francisco were officially listed as Missing in Action. But given the circumstances of their loss, the Air Force considered it a strong possibility that they had been captured alive.

As of November 25, 1968, over a thousand American airmen were listed as Missing in Action in Indochina. No one knew how many had survived their loss and been captured alive.

Grommet 02 was the 132nd F-4 Phantom shot down out of a total of 1,757 aircraft lost in combat up to that point in the Vietnam War.

Before the war ended for the United States, another 1,962 fixed-wing aircraft would be lost in combat. And the rolls of the Missing in Action would swell inexorably.

PEGGY MORRISON WAS not to learn the true fate of her husband until almost twenty-four years later, when Ted Schweitzer's Operation Swamp Ranger brought home irrefutable evidence that he had died in enemy hands.

NOVEMBER 26, 1968, NEW YORK

That Tuesday morning, Dr. Henry Kissinger was called by President-elect Richard Nixon's campaign manager, John Mitchell. Kissinger had met with Nixon at the Hotel Pierre on Monday to discuss a possible appointment in the new administration. Now Mitchell was pleased to tell the brilliant young Harvard professor that the President-elect wanted Kissinger to serve as his national security adviser.

The successful conclusion of the peace negotiations with the Vietnamese that had begun in Paris was to be his first priority.

PART 1

CHAPTER 1

In the bleak winter twilight of Wednesday, December 13, 1972, President Richard Nixon's national security adviser, Henry A. Kissinger, was hunched in a narrow seat aboard an Air Force jet, 37,000 feet above the North Atlantic.

Kissinger was depressed. It had been just over four years since he had accepted Nixon's offer of the national security adviser position. But the war in Vietnam dragged on.

The jolting C-135 had left Orly Airport in Paris an hour earlier, bound for Washington. Before boarding, Kissinger had met in the VIP lounge with reporters covering the peace negotiations between the United States and the Democratic Republic of Vietnam (DRV).*

Kissinger's rapport with the press had been unusually good during the long Paris peace negotiations, which had reached an apparent stalemate in the past week. But tonight his attempts at sardonic humor had been strained.

His face was gray, his deep Mitteleuropa voice subdued. Kissinger told the reporters he was returning to consult with President Nixon, and that he and Le Duc Tho, his North Vietnamese counterpart, would "remain in contact through messages," then decide when and if another session of the Paris talks would be necessary.[1]

The reporters were perplexed. Only seven weeks before, on October 26, Kissinger had announced that he and Le Duc Tho had reached a complete agreement "in principle" on a nine-point draft accord presented by the Vietnamese to end the long Vietnam War.

This accord called for the United States to withdraw its remaining troops and advisers and for neither America nor the DRV to introduce any new weapons or troops into the South. Military commissions drawn from U.S., North and South Vietnamese, and Vietcong forces would coordinate a general cease-fire. An international control commission would supervise the disengagement in the field. The future leadership of South Vietnam would

---

* During the war, few Americans used the term Democratic Republic of Vietnam; the Communist North was generally called North Vietnam, and its military, the People's Army of Vietnam (PAVN), was almost always called the North Vietnamese Army (NVA) in official documents and news media accounts.

be decided through "genuinely free and democratic general elections under international supervision."

From the American perspective, the key point in the draft accord covered the exchange of prisoners of war and other detainees. All "captured and detained personnel" were to be released during the sixty days of the final U.S. troop withdrawal. This was explicit agreement by Hanoi and its Vietcong ally to release all American prisoners.

From the Vietnamese Communist perspective, Point 8 was critical. This called for the United States to contribute "to healing the wounds of war and to postwar reconstruction" in Indochina. Implicitly, this committed the United States to funding massive reconstruction projects, and in Hanoi's interpretation, to paying war reparations.[2]

On that bright autumn afternoon at the White House, Kissinger had been anything but somber and depressed.

"Peace," he had announced with uncommon grandiosity, "is at hand."

BY LATE 1972, America had become so disenchanted with the protracted military disaster in Indochina that the majority of the voting public and their representatives in Congress would have acquiesced to almost any face-saving expedient that allowed America to disengage. However, there was one political requirement that transcended expediency. No American president— even Richard Nixon, who would win one of the most decisive landslide victories in the history of presidential elections that November—had enough political power to extricate America from the Indochina quagmire before Hanoi agreed to return the country's prisoners of war.

Henry Kissinger, one of the most politically astute national security advisers ever to serve a president, was painfully aware of this link between Nixon's concept of an "honorable" settlement and domestic politics. He specifically warned Nixon that they had to thrash out an agreement with Hanoi in the Paris talks that winter or "pressures will build up domestically if we fail to reach an agreement or get our prisoners back."[3]

And in October, less than two weeks before the election, Kissinger had been confident that he had achieved a peace formula that met the politically acceptable criteria Nixon's concept of honor entailed.

THIS OPTIMISM WAS reflected in the Pentagon offices responsible for tracking American POWs and missing in Indochina. With an end to the war finally in sight, an overall review of MIA cases began in the Defense Department.

Case number 1329 was carefully scrutinized. Major Joseph Morrison and First Lieutenant San D. Francisco had disappeared into the jungle of the Ban Karai Pass almost four years before. Since then, there had been no better intelligence on their fates than the terse final Search and Rescue account:

"Radio contact was lost and could not be re-established. The parachute that had been visible the day before had disappeared. All efforts to re-establish contact with the crew failed."[4]

IN THE WEEKS between the optimistic October announcement and Kissinger's abrupt departure from Paris this December afternoon, the American and Vietnamese delegations had shuttled continually between the two negotiation venues: the American site in an elegant townhouse in suburban Neuilly and the DRV's villa in the bedroom suburb of Gif-sur-Yvette. And at each meeting it became increasingly clear to Kissinger that the Vietnamese Communists had, in fact, no intention of actually implementing the terms of the draft accord that both sides had greeted with such public optimism in October.

The loud, poorly insulated Air Force C-135 staggered through winter turbulence, fighting the westerly jet stream. To compound Kissinger's foul mood, he discovered that this elaborate airborne communications center lacked the capability to directly contact the White House. Any message Kissinger might have for his NSC assistant, General Alexander Haig, or for the President himself, would have to be relayed by Air Force radio telegram.

Kissinger chose not to exercise this option. The import of his message for Washington was too politically sensitive to pass through the labyrinth of military channels. Kissinger was convinced that almost four years of public and secret peace negotiations with the Vietnamese Communists—which included 174 tedious, acrimonious, ultimately futile plenary sessions at the glittering conference hall on Avenue Kleber—had ended in failure.

Aside from the tragic portents of this failure for both America and Vietnam, Kissinger felt a deep personal sense of betrayal and defeat.

Henry Kissinger had grown familiar with the Vietnamese Communist negotiating tactics during the four interminable years of the Paris peace talks. But he had never before met with such outright intransigence.

Since October, the Hanoi Politburo had decided that the United States was so desperate to achieve a cease-fire and complete its military disengagement, that the Communist side would not, after all, be obliged to grant the concessions found in the draft agreement. The Vietnamese Communists took advantage of the obvious rift that had developed between Saigon and Washington over the terms of the proposed cease-fire.

In Saigon, South Vietnamese President Nguyen Van Thieu, who had weathered the brunt of Hanoi's Easter Offensive in April and May only after a massive American aerial counteroffensive, now felt with some justification that he was being abandoned by his American ally.[5] Even though Hanoi had now dropped its demand that Thieu resign before any cease-fire could be implemented, the DRV's clear advantage in the draft accord was unacceptable to Thieu's government. Any agreement that would leave the Communist military infrastructure—including over 200,000 regular North Vietnamese troops—in place in the South, while ostensibly "free and democratic" elections were held, was tantamount to a death sentence for his anti-Communist regime.

But as Kissinger made clear to Richard Nixon, once the antiwar Young Turks of the 1972 congressional generation were sworn in to bolster traditional liberal Democratic leaders in both House and Senate, any vestige of "leverage" Washington still had over Hanoi would evaporate. If the White House wanted peace with honor, it was going to have to fight for it.[6]

Indeed, it was clear to all of Nixon's National Security staff that the last card they had to play was direct military pressure on Hanoi. But with only 27,000 American troops remaining in South Vietnam—most of them support personnel—that military pressure could only come from air power.

WHILE KISSINGER'S JET crossed the Atlantic, planners in the Pentagon were completing the warning order for that devastating use of this air power. A young Air Force lieutenant colonel named Richard V. Secord, attached to the office of the secretary of defense, helped prepare the message transmitted to the Pacific Command: "By order of higher authority, commencing on 18 December and continuing until further directed, you will make a maximum effort utilizing all assets currently assigned, including B-52s and Naval aircraft, to attack the following targets, which are validated for strike within a 48-hour period herewith. Further orders to follow."[7]

The targets in the plan—Operation Linebacker II—included for the first time Hanoi and Haiphong.

WHEN NIXON MET with Kissinger and his National Security advisers the morning of December 14 in the Oval Office, Alexander Haig led the faction that favored new air attacks into the North Vietnamese heartland. Although somewhat less bellicose than Haig, Kissinger concurred.

As Kissinger later stated in his memoir, "We had only two choices: taking a massive, shocking step to impose our will on events and end the war quickly or letting matters drift into another round of inconclusive negotiations, prolonged warfare, bitter national divisions, and mounting casualties. There were no other options."[8]

Nixon concurred.

KISSINGER'S VIEW OF this decision is insightful: "The B-52 bombing was in this sense *his* [Nixon's] last roll of the dice, as the March offensive had been Hanoi's—helpful if it worked; a demonstration to the right wing if it failed that he had done all he could."[9]

But even if the bombing campaign did fail and America was driven back to the negotiating table from a position of weakness, there still remained the problem of securing the release of American POWs from Indochina. The prisoners remained Hanoi's trump card.

North Vietnam's strength on the prisoner issue lay in the fact that only Hanoi knew exactly how many American POWs it held. Since the first American military and civilian personnel had been captured by the Vietnamese Communists in the early 1960s, it had been Hanoi's policy to keep their true number a closely guarded secret. However, when it suited the Politburo's strategic objectives, the Communists were willing to divulge fragmentary information on Americans in captivity. Thus, in December 1970, Hanoi gave Senator Edward Kennedy a list of 368 names of Americans who had been captured alive; the list included 339 said to be surviving prisoners, and 29 who had reportedly died in captivity.[10]

Almost immediately the Defense Department attacked the accuracy of this list on several grounds: First, the North Vietnamese roster did not include Americans captured by Communist forces in either South Vietnam or along the Ho Chi Minh Trail in Cambodia* and Laos. Further, the list did not contain Americans for whom there were reliable combat reports indicating they had been captured alive.

For example, neither Major Joseph Morrison nor Lieutenant San Francisco appeared on the list, although there was some evidence in the Search and Rescue forces' after-action report that the two airmen might have been captured alive.

Despite these discrepancies, the DRV delegation at the Paris peace talks continued to characterize the Kennedy list as "complete and final."[11]

The Pentagon officials most concerned with resolving the fate of American POWs and MIAs, however, dismissed Hanoi's 1970 list as a negotiation ploy. The Vietnamese Communists had a tradition of manipulating their Western enemies by treating POWs brutally, and in some cases, using them as quasi-hostages.

Certainly the experience of the French in the First Indochina War bore this out. Between 1945 and the cease-fire following the French military defeat at Dien Bien Phu in 1954, a total of 36,979 French Union forces, including mainland French, Foreign Legion, North African, black African, and Vietnamese colonial troops, were captured by the Vietminh. Only 10,754 prisoners—fewer than one third of the POWs captured alive—were returned to French control during the prisoner repatriations between July and October 1954. Sixty percent of the mainland French troops and Legionnaires died in captivity—from starvation, disease, and brutal treatment, including execution. It was later revealed that many French prisoners captured alive

---

* Because this narrative encompasses three decades, the name Cambodia, not Kampuchea, will be used throughout.

at Dien Bien Phu had died during the infamous death march through the Annamite Mountains that followed the defeat. The French African colonial prisoners fared slightly better. But almost 90 percent of the Vietnamese among the French Union POWs either died in Communist captivity or were not repatriated.[12]

Because most of the French Union POWs who disappeared were not Europeans, this blatant disregard for prisoner accountability, which had been a clear treaty requirement of the 1954 Geneva Accords, did not become a cause célèbre in the West.

However, the victorious Communist forces did use those surviving French POWs as bargaining chips to extract additional concessions from Paris at the Geneva peace conference. And Hanoi later manipulated the repatriation of skeletal remains of French troops who had died on the battlefields of Vietnam or in captivity in an even more blatant manner.[13] Bowing to pressure from Hanoi, successive French governments were forced to pay grossly excessive fees for the maintenance of war cemeteries in Indochina and for the processing of the remains of their dead for repatriation to France.

Now, almost twenty years later, as the Second Indochina War seemed to be winding down, Pentagon officials feared that a similar type of manipulation of the POW issue lay in store for the United States.

The specter of POWs as hostages had already appeared in a DRV proposal that came relatively early in the secret Kissinger–Le Duc Tho meetings. On August 16, 1971, the Communists proposed that both sides "produce the complete lists of military personnel and civilians captured during the war *on the day an agreement is signed*" (Emphasis added).[14]

The Communists were using the secrecy shrouding the number and identity of the American prisoners they held to pressure America into signing a cease-fire agreement.

And this tactic was effective. As of December 1972, Pentagon estimates of American POWs in the hands of the Vietnamese Communists varied, but the number was definitely higher than the 339 surviving prisoners Hanoi claimed. Casualty and intelligence officers in the uniformed services and analysts in the Defense Intelligence Agency (DIA) did not always agree in their interpretation of casualty reports for personnel lost in combat. But by mid-December, approximately 620 Americans lost across Indochina were listed as Prisoner of War by the Pentagon.[15]

Just under 2,000 more American military and civilian personnel were then carried on various Pentagon and State Department lists; they were almost equally divided between the two other missing-casualty categories: Killed in Action/Body Not Recovered (KIA/BNR) and Missing in Action (MIA).

The KIA/BNR category was self-explanatory, intended to cover cases in which there was sufficient evidence to believe that the person had died during the loss incident, but American forces had been unable to recover his remains.

The MIA category covered all the remaining cases, including unwitnessed aircraft losses at sea, in which there was insufficient evidence to determine the person's fate.

The total of approximately 2,000 Killed in Action/Body Not Recovered and Missing in Action cases at the end of ten years of American military action in Indochina matched the overall expectations of Pentagon casualty officers. Fifty-six thousand Americans had died on the battlefields of Indochina up to that point in the war. Over 8,500 U.S. aircraft had been lost by the end of 1972. But this figure was somewhat misleading; more than half the aircraft lost were helicopters shot down or destroyed on the ground in South Vietnam, incidents that usually did not result in missing men. And, in the 2,531 combat losses of fixed-wing aircraft up to that point, a large percentage of the aircrew had been recovered by Search and Rescue forces, were known to have died, or were believed to be prisoners of the Communists.[16]

(The MIA figures for Indochina were proportionally lower than America's missing in action casualties in World War II: 78,750; and the Korean War: 8,170. This was due to America's general military control of the South Vietnamese battlefield and exceptionally efficient Search and Rescue forces.[17])

Although the Nixon administration had skillfully used the POW and MIA issue to elicit political support for its conduct of the war, no senior administration official or military leader ever believed that as many as 2,600 Americans (the total of all three categories) had actually been captured alive.[18] However, the administration's campaign to rally American public opinion to the White House war policy and to put pressure on the Vietnamese Communists to better account for the American POWs they held—and implicitly to improve the treatment of these POWs—often exaggerated the number of prisoners in Communist hands. At one point, the Pentagon cited "sixteen hundred American POWs," and an administration-backed congressional resolution called on Hanoi to release the "fifteen hundred American servicemen" allegedly held by the Communists throughout Indochina.[19]

However, as the armed services and the DIA scrambled to establish an accurate list of "expected returnees" in the fall of 1972, the total of firm prospects never went much above 600; with the addition of "soft" possibilities—including men who might have somehow made their way ashore in North Vietnam from aircraft crashes in the Tonkin Gulf—the list temporarily rose as high as 1,100. But as Admiral Thomas Moorer, chairman of the Joint Chiefs of Staff from 1970 to 1974, later acknowledged, that high estimate was plagued by uncertainties.[20] Because the issue of total POW numbers was central to the Paris negotiations, however, the Defense Department kept all such estimates classified. But there were inevitable leaks to the news media. A December 1972 *Time* article, for example, described the plight of "the families of 554 U.S. prisoners of war in Indochina" who anxiously watched the Paris peace talks.[21]

(Years later, advocates of the theory that the Vietnamese Communists held back hundreds—or even thousands—of American POWs often refer to the obvious discrepancy between Hanoi's 1970 list of 339 surviving prisoners and the much higher classified 1972 Pentagon POW estimate lists.)

Any impartial examination of the MIA issue, however, must take into account that the 1972 estimates were based on flawed evidence. Accurate American intelligence on North Vietnam was woefully thin. Unlike during World War II, when the Allies had productive agent networks in Japan and Nazi-occupied Europe, and even in Germany—and had broken coded enemy radio transmissions—American intelligence operations on the ground in North Vietnam were a total failure. This was due in part to the fact that almost no pro-Western families remained in the North following the partition of Vietnam in 1954 and the subsequent brutal purges of "reactionaries" (including anti-Communist "stay-behinds" planted by the CIA) conducted by Ho Chi Minh's Communist government. Therefore, the American Military Assistance Command Vietnam/Studies and Observations Group (MACV/SOG) in Saigon, charged with developing intelligence on POWs, had no effective penetration agents in the North.[22]

This intelligence vacuum is one of the most important, but least understood elements of the entire postwar POW/MIA controversy. America entered the Vietnam War with inadequate information of North Vietnam's strengths and intentions. And, more than ten years later, America disengaged from Vietnam still lacking productive and accurate intelligence sources in the North.

A glaring example of this problem was the heroic, but abortive Special Forces POW rescue mission on Son Tay Prison on November 21, 1970. When Air Force CH-53 helicopters landed the rescue force in the heart of North Vietnam, the rescuers discovered the camp was empty. Later it was determined that the Son Tay Prison had been evacuated four months earlier. The Pentagon had risked dozens of its best and bravest troops on a virtual wild goose chase. To professional Special Operations officers, that heroic, beautifully executed, but ultimately flawed operation spoke volumes about America's inadequate intelligence resources in North Vietnam.[23]

The Pentagon had to depend on occasional defectors and a handful of American prisoners repatriated early for any reasonably accurate estimates of POW numbers in Communist captivity. These sources certainly confirmed that the 1970 list of 368 U.S. POWs captured alive was not complete. But the DIA and the Joint Personnel Recovery Center (JPRC) run by MACV/SOG were not able to provide Washington a larger, indisputably definitive list with which to challenge the Communist negotiators in Paris. (After the 1973 cease-fire, the JPRC was renamed the Joint Casualty Resolution Center or JCRC.)

Navy Seaman Douglas B. Hegdahl was one of three POWs repatriated early on August 4, 1969. He had memorized the names of almost 300 American POWs then held in ten (later eleven) separate camps in North Vietnam.

But these early POW releases were no substitute for a network of trained intelligence agents in Hanoi. This reality has been hard to accept by both left- and right-wing commentators on the POW/MIA controversy who cling to the belief that "American intelligence" was omnipotent, and that therefore Washington had to have possessed a complete list of Americans held captive by the Communists.

An examination of the historical record, which is now being opened through the declassification of wartime documents, reveals just how weak our POW-tracking effort was.

As strange as it now seems, the Defense Intelligence Agency often had to rely on newspaper and radio broadcast accounts from North Vietnam and the Eastern Bloc to verify that an American had been captured.

For example, the only indication that Major Joseph Morrison and Lieutenant San Francisco might have survived after radio contact was lost on November 26, 1968, was an article in *Quan Doi Nhan Dan,* the PAVN newspaper, which congratulated the people of Quang Binh Province for capturing "alive" two Yankee air pirates on November 25.

The MACV/SOG Command History for 1971–72 details the operations of the JPRC. This previously top secret document makes clear that the JPRC had painfully inadequate intelligence on the numbers and location of U.S. POWs held throughout Indochina, even though the unit had initiated an ambitious program of enemy prisoner and defector debriefing and a monetary-reward campaign to obtain detailed intelligence. The Command History notes that intelligence obtained from Indochinese sources provided "very little information [that] proved useful in the planning of PW recovery operations. Some information was valid, but was up to five years old. Often information was completely fabricated in the interest of monetary reward."[24]

But the Pentagon did have an impressive aerial and satellite reconnaissance capability. Powerful Keyhole satellites, as well as SR-71 Blackbird and U-2 reconnaissance planes, had photographed every suspected prison camp in Indochina.[25] And this effort was intensified following the embarrassing failure of the Son Tay raid. Reconnaissance photographs seemed to indicate that the PAVN had closed down outlying POW camps in North Vietnam, such as the Son Tay Prison, and consolidated all American POWs into three camps in Hanoi: Hoa Lo Prison, Cu Loc (the Zoo), and the Plantation (the summer villa of the former French colonial mayor of Hanoi).[26] Comparison of thousands of such photographs of Americans outside during exercise periods in these three prisons confirmed this indication.

But in May 1972, following the intense new bombing of North Vietnam in the wake of the PAVN Easter Offensive in the South, this surveillance revealed an ominous development. A long convoy of trucks took a large group of American POWs from Hoa Lo Prison during the night of May 13. The convoy delivered the prisoners to a previously unknown camp near the town of Lang So'n, 150 miles north of Hanoi, and almost directly on the

Chinese border.²⁷ The camp, a clump of squat stone buildings with orange tile roofs—built for the French Army—was in hilly, forested country prone to low clouds and mist, which made aerial reconnaissance difficult. The fact that the camp was inside the ten-mile "no-fly, no-bomb" zone buffering the Chinese frontier exacerbated this problem. But the import of the prisoner move was soon apparent. These prisoners were now definitely out of reach of any American rescue attempt. Moreover, the Vietnamese Communists could easily march them across one ridge and into China. Depending on the status of North Vietnam's expedient wartime alliance with China, the prisoners could be held there indefinitely as hostages to guarantee a favorable settlement at the Paris peace negotiations.²⁸

Hanoi was aware that securing the release of American prisoners was the cornerstone of President Nixon's "peace with honor" policy. In fact, one of Kissinger's chief subordinates, Ambassador to Laos William Sullivan, had remained behind in Paris to negotiate the final version of the Peace Accords protocol on the release of POWs, which Kissinger later described as "one of the most important documents for us."²⁹

It was conceivable that, even at this late hour, had the Hanoi delegation been generous and forthcoming during this negotiation of the POW protocol, the American side might still have capitulated and not unleashed the planned air offensive. But the Vietnamese Communists were not in a generous mood. The draft protocol they finally submitted on December 16 contained problematic clauses that Le Duc Tho had earlier agreed to delete. The most objectionable from the American standpoint linked the release of U.S. POWs to that of "civilian detainees" held by the Saigon government.

Many of these civilian prisoners in the South were in fact Communist military cadres from the North or members of the Vietcong infrastructure. Others were simply unfortunate people suspected of supporting Communist activity who had been swept up in dragnets that had been regularly cast by all the successive Saigon governments, beginning with the regime of President Ngo Dinh Diem in the 1950s. The South Vietnamese security services were often capricious in their pursuit of "Communists," and it was known that some police officials reaped a corruption bonanza by extorting bribes, both to preclude arrest and to secure release of bona fide enemy cadres and agents. This was a time-honored custom that dated back even beyond the Diem government to the French colonial period. Milking the antisubversive security program for graft had intensified during the Phoenix Program to destroy the Vietcong support base.³⁰

And after the multidivision PAVN invasion across the DMZ during the Easter Offensive, which was accompanied by a vicious parallel wave of Communist assassination and terrorism, the Saigon government's dragnets for subversives were cast even wider. American officials in South Vietnam estimated that Saigon held 58,000 Vietnamese Communist prisoners of war and an additional 80,000 civilian political prisoners who included an indeterminate number of Northern subversive agents as well as draft evaders, military deserters, and common criminals. Le Duc Tho's new demand that the United States somehow prevail on the Saigon government to guarantee the release of all these tens of thousands of military and civilian prisoners as a condition for the return of American POWs held by the Communists was neither practical nor reasonable.[31]

Understandably, this difficult negotiation soon reached a stalemate, and Ambassador Sullivan returned to Washington.

As NIXON WAS in a truculent mood following the Oval Office meeting, it was left to Kissinger to explain the failure of the Paris negotiations to the world. He met the White House press corps in the West Wing briefing room on the afternoon of December 16. After detailing the complete breakdown of the seemingly promising negotiations and citing Hanoi's obstructionist stance as the principal cause, Kissinger threw down the administration's gauntlet: "We will not be blackmailed into an agreement," he announced. He then emphasized the administration's position. "We want an end to the war that is something more than an armistice. We want to move from hostility to normalization and from normalization to cooperation."

Kissinger concluded by committing the United States to accepting the provisions of the October draft agreement. "We are prepared to maintain an agreement that provides for the unconditional release of all American and allied prisoners, that imposes no political solution on the other side, that brings about an internationally supervised cease-fire and the withdrawal of all American forces within sixty days."[32]

Although the White House tried to keep the details of its negotiating position secret, State Department and National Security Council staff members readily shared their frustration with the news media. This passage in *Time* was typical of these leaks, which were intended to show Hanoi that flexibility on the POW issue would bring an end to the fighting. *Time* quoted an anonymous White House staffer's summary of this policy: " 'One of the President's major considerations,' in resuming the bombing, according to one aide, was the conditions the North Vietnamese attached to the release of American prisoners of war. They welshed on the deal." To emphasize this point, the article added: "The P.O.W. issue proved to be the final blow. Nixon broke off the peace talks, warned the North Vietnamese that the bombing would resume if they did not soften their bargaining stance, and, when the North Vietnamese did not respond, launched his blitz."[33]

CHAPTER 2

THAT "BLITZ" WAS OPERATION LINEBACKER II, THE MASSIVE AERIAL bombardment of the Red River Delta and its cities.

THE BOMBING BEGAN on the night of December 18, 1972, Indochina time. With the exception of a Christmas pause, the Linebacker II campaign followed the same pattern for the next eleven days.

Two hours after sundown giant eight-engine B-52 bombers flying all the way from Andersen Air Force Base on Guam, or shorter routes from U Tapao in Thailand, approached their targets in three-aircraft "cells." These formations were shaped like arrowheads, with the three bombers separated horizontally by two miles and vertically in increments of 500 feet. This configuration allowed each bomber to cloak itself and its two wingmen in overlapping cones of Electronic Countermeasure (ECM) jamming from powerful onboard transmitters that smeared the enemy's radar picture of the formation. The cells flew in a long stream of three waves that approached Hanoi approximately five hours apart. The lowest B-52s maintained a bombing altitude of 36,000 feet, while the highest cells bombed from 39,000 feet.

Twenty minutes before the first bombers arrived, specialized tactical fighter-bombers hit targets around Hanoi to pave the way for the B-52s. Individual swing-wing F-111 bombers were the first to strike. They launched from Ta Khli air base, Thailand, just after dark. Using terrain-following radar, the F-111s snaked down the gorges of the cloud-covered Annamite Range and broke free of the low ceiling northwest of the city near the junction of the Black and Red Rivers. The F-111s accelerated to near-supersonic speed less than 500 feet above the ground and streaked toward their targets, the principal MiG fighter strips dispersed in the flat rice paddy countryside around Hanoi.

The F-111s were followed by other specialized fighter-bombers from Thai bases: F-105G and F-4C Iron Hand aircraft. These so-called Wild Weasels carried radar-homing Shrike missiles to attack the guidance systems of North Vietnam's dangerous surface-to-air missile (SA-2) defenses.

Additional electronic countermeasure EB-66 aircraft also preceded the B-52s. Then flights of F-4 Phantoms dispersed bulbous canisters of chaff:

millions of thin aluminum foil strips, cut to multiple widths and lengths, and designed to blind any SAM acquisition and guidance radars that managed to "burn through" the B-52 and EB-66 jamming.

When the first F-111 pilots broke free of the winter overcast inbound to Hanoi, they saw the entire capital district "lighted up like Las Vegas." Convoys of military trucks with headlights "blazing like strings of pearls" climbed the foothills southwest of the city. Locomotives and switch engines chugged across floodlit railyards. There were even blinking red obstacle lights on the city's two large radio antenna towers.[1]

As an F-111 screamed across Hanoi's western suburbs breaking windows with its low-altitude sonic boom, entire sections of the city suddenly went dark. One after the other, civil defense workers cut the power for a total blackout.

Fifteen minutes later, the first B-52s approached from the northwest. The bomber stream divided into three cells of B-52s, separated by twelve miles, beginning their dogleg approach to their targets: the enemy fighter bases ringing Hanoi.[2]

The initial reaction of the Hanoi district air defenses was confused. In his headquarters bunker at Bach Mai Air Base, PAVN Air Defense Forces commander Lieutenant General Hoang Phuong and his subordinates were bewildered by the scattered reports coming from the early-warning radar sites. The Americans' jamming and chaff were so effective that it wasn't until well into the first attack that the PAVN defenders realized they were actually facing waves of B-52 heavy bombers, not flights of smaller tactical aircraft. And the American countermeasures almost completely overpowered the Vietnamese altitude-finding radars.[3]

The first cells of B-52s were at their bomb-release points before the first SAMs were launched. To the American airmen, the scene was eerie and chilling. A bright moon lit the unbroken expanse of the cloud decks. Where the overcast was thinner, the bomber crews saw pulsing cascades of multi-colored flak bursts and gaudy streams of light cannon tracers probing soundlessly four miles below their flight level. As the SAMs were fired, the milky gray overcast glowed with swelling neon yellow donuts that expanded like incandescent smoke rings as the missiles accelerated through the clouds.

The first heavy bomber downed that night was a B-52G, call sign Charcoal 01. It was hit by two SAMs fired by the 59th PAVN Missile Battalion defending a sector north of the city. The bomber, flames streaming from its engines, pitched over, out of control, and careened down into the cloud deck. The huge aircraft crashed sixteen kilometers northwest of the city at 8:14 P.M. Hanoi time. The aircraft commander and the gunner were killed outright and the co-pilot was mortally wounded by shrapnel from the SAM explosions. But the three other crewmen managed to eject. They were captured by local militia soon after landing by parachute.

The capture of American airmen on the first night of the bombing was an important, but generally overlooked event. Historical accounts of Linebacker II have usually failed to note that the prisoner of war issue remained very much in the forefront of battle.

The treatment of these first captured B-52 crewmen was unprecedented. They were quickly brought before assembled members of the small international press corps in Hanoi, composed mainly of correspondents from Eastern Bloc nations. This was significant. During the previous eight years of the air war against North Vietnam, captured American airmen were presented to journalists only after the POWs had been carefully prepared for their appearance. This preparation usually entailed months of physical and psychological torture, meant to assure a suitable performance. Although these methods were brutal and crude, they had proved effective.

Now they were departing from this procedure. The surviving crew members of the first two B-52s shot down on the night of December 18–19 were presented to the Hanoi press corps almost as soon as they were brought to the city from their capture sites north and west of the city. The PAVN prison officials had not had time to brutalize these Americans into making elaborate propaganda statements. This was not necessary. There was a different purpose in presenting these shootdown survivors. Hanoi intended to demonstrate to the Pentagon and to the American public that the bombing campaign meant to secure the release of American POWs was only resulting in the capture of more American airmen.

This approach struck a resonant chord in the American news media. In an article on the newly captured B-52 crewmen, *Time* magazine noted with alarm: "If the new bombing continues, it seems a grim certainty that the POW-MIA count will climb still higher."[4]

Hanoi was making explicit the POWs' role as hostage, a tactic that had only been implied before Linebacker II.

But this new tactic had no effect on the Pentagon or the White House. The around-the-clock bombing of the Red River Delta continued.

Some bombs fell wide of their targets. One such notable bombing error occurred during a strike aimed at the Gia Lam railroad marshaling yard that actually hit nearby Gia Lam international airport.[5]

But the most tragic incident was the bombing of Bach Mai Hospital in Hanoi's southern outskirts on the night of December 22. A stick of 750 pound bombs, dropped from either an F-111 or a B-52, missed the Air Defense Forces headquarters at nearby Bach Mai Air Base and fell directly on the hospital's three-story patient wing. The building was demolished. Eighteen patients and hospital staff, including several newly qualified doctors who had volunteered to treat air raid victims, were killed. Fifty patients were wounded. Radio Hanoi quickly announced that the Americans had intentionally targeted the hospital in a campaign of "carpet bombing" meant to terrorize the city. The purpose of "this insane action," the broadcast concluded, was to strengthen the imperialists' negotiating position at the Paris peace talks.[6]

The civilian casualties in Hanoi gave the DRV yet another opportunity to play the POW card. After the thirty-six-hour Christmas hiatus in the bombing, Linebacker II began again with renewed ferocity. The American mission planners now employed better tactics by vectoring the bomber streams simultaneously from several directions, but American aircraft losses to SAMs continued to mount.

The Linebacker II bombing lasted three more days. The campaign had become a test of wills between the Nixon administration and the Hanoi Politburo. But there were other players in the drama. Ten days into the bombing, fourteen B-52s had been shot down over North Vietnam with a number of others crashing in Laos or Thailand. And the strain on the bomber crews had reached the point where veteran officers were beginning to crack. A number of airmen begged their flight surgeons to take them off combat status. Some refused outright to fly. One pilot, Captain Michael Heck, openly rebelled, taking his complaint against the flawed tactics to the press. As a decorated veteran of two previous combat tours, he made a strong case. Heck was court-martialed and drummed out of the Air Force within weeks of his rebellion.[7]

BUT THE QUESTION of whether the battle-weary airmen would continue to follow orders became moot on December 30. The White House announced that it was halting bombing of North Vietnam above the twentieth parallel in response to a North Vietnamese request that the Paris peace talks be resumed as soon as practicable. Henry Kissinger and Le Duc Tho would meet again in Paris on January 8. This breakthrough had stemmed from a secret diplomatic message from the Hanoi Politburo sent to the White House on December 26, which coincided with one of the biggest B-52 attacks of the campaign. In the message, Hanoi stated it was ready to resume a "serious negotiating attitude" and was willing to "settle the remaining questions with the U.S. side."[8]

The White House had won its gamble.

But the cost had been heavy. The American side had lost at least thirty-six aircraft in eleven days. (The Air Force chose not to list planes too badly damaged to fly again as "losses" in the Linebacker II campaign.) Ninety airmen were shot down over North Vietnam. Only forty-three were eventually repatriated.[9]

The Vietnamese losses were severe. Estimates of combined civilian and military casualties ranged as high as 3,000 dead, although the official DRV figure for confirmed civilian deaths was 1,318 in Hanoi and 305 in Haiphong.[10] The destruction to North Vietnam's military industrial base (rail-

yards, bridges, fuel dumps, and vehicle repair shops) was extensive. And
North Vietnam's air defense system, including SAM missile sites and radars,
was battered. American estimates of SAMs expended went as high as 1,000.
The PAVN maintains to this day that it only fired 300 SAMs during the
campaign.[11] But, whether North Vietnam had expended its SAM stockpile or
had instead suffered the destruction of its air defense system, the fact remains that the last missions of the Linebacker II bombing met little effective
resistance; none of the 150 aircraft attacking the Red River valley on December 29 was lost. Only twenty-three SAMs were fired that night and none
came close to American planes.

IN THE YEARS since that grim December, it has become a pillar of the American lore of the Vietnam War that Nixon's aggressive response to Hanoi's
recalcitrance "drove" the Communists back to the Paris negotiating table.
Conversely, the official Vietnamese interpretation of Linebacker II is that
the gamble of launching vulnerable B-52s against Hanoi's concentrated air
defenses was the last desperate gasp of the imperialists' failed strategy.[12] And
most military leaders in Hanoi today refuse to concede that they were forced
back to the peace talks by the bombing campaign.

In effect, both sides now claim victory.

Linebacker II has been transformed in Vietnamese official history into the
"Victory Over the B-52s." (This heroic name was given to a broad avenue
near Bach Mai Hospital in the south Hanoi district that was hit hard in the
December bombing. The avenue was renamed for a historic figure, Truong
Chinh, in 1993 in an effort to avoid needless anti-American provocation.)

These contradictory historical interpretations of the December bombing
epitomize the strong emotions that still prevail in both Washington and
Hanoi. A neutral observer would find historical merit in each of the two
positions. But even twenty years after the cease-fire, it is hard to find a
neutral observer among the government and military officials who led the
war effort in Washington and Hanoi.

Whatever interpretation is given to the two sides' linked diplomatic and
military strategies, it is clear that American prisoners of war were pawns in
this last military confrontation between America and Communist Vietnam.

CHAPTER 3

IN THE END, THE FINAL NEGOTIATIONS IN PARIS WERE AN ANTI-climax compared to the violent drama of December.

When Henry Kissinger and Le Duc Tho met again at Gif-sur-Yvette on January 8, their discussions advanced rapidly toward agreement. It was as if both sides recognized that the bombing had been a crude but effective means of forcing the peace talks back on track.

Although the Americans had hoped to return to the Paris negotiations armed with the implicit threat of renewed bombing, Congress had undercut the White House, just as Kissinger had warned in December. On January 2, 1973, the House Democratic caucus voted by a margin of two to one to cut off all funds for military operations in Indochina, provided Hanoi allowed our forces to safely withdraw and American POWs were released. This action eroded the credibility of the renewed bombing threat. And Kissinger had no brief from the White House to capitalize on the American military position by making unreasonable demands. Indeed, when he met with Nixon at Camp David just before returning to Paris, the President urged Kissinger "to settle on whatever terms were available."[1]

Within a week, these terms were settled. They were similar to those of the draft agreement of October 1972. But now, although both the Saigon government and the DRV would be allowed to replace worn-out military equipment after the cease-fire, the Communists would not be permitted to introduce new troops into South Vietnam. And the parties were bound from encroaching on the "sovereignty" of Cambodia and "neutrality" of Laos, a provision that, if observed by North Vietnam, would mean abandonment of the Ho Chi Minh Trail supply route.

These paper concessions by Hanoi, as well as relentless pressure from the White House and Kissinger's assistant, Alexander Haig, eventually convinced South Vietnamese President Thieu that he had no choice but to endorse the new agreement.

On the vital issue of prisoners of war, Hanoi mixed accommodation with rigidity. Le Duc Tho stubbornly held to his original position that the lists of prisoners would not be exchanged until the day the final agreement was actually signed by all parties. But the DRV relented on its insistence that the repatriation of American POWs be directly linked to the release of all military and civilian prisoners held by the South Vietnamese. Instead, all "captured military personnel and foreign civilians of the parties" would be returned and the last U.S. forces in South Vietnam would simultaneously withdraw during the sixty days following the cease-fire.[2]

The parties also agreed to provide each other information on missing in action personnel, to locate graves of dead MIAs, and to facilitate the repatriation of their remains.

Hanoi and its Vietcong ally, the Provisional Revolutionary Government (PRG), would now negotiate the release of Vietnamese civilians separately with the Saigon government. Although it was not noted in press accounts at the time, this decoupling of the Vietnamese and American POW releases gave the Saigon and Communist sides room for secret maneuvering, which probably involved bribes paid both by prisoners' families and the PRG. This arrangement was, in effect, a traditional Asian solution to the problem.

But Kissinger had accepted a staggered release of American POWs (to be matched by an incremental final withdrawal of the remaining U.S. forces in South Vietnam), which would run parallel to the first exchanges of Vietnamese war prisoners between the Saigon government and the Communists.

This left unresolved the critical question of American POWs held in Laos.

The Defense Department listed 317 American servicemen as MIA in Laos. (Separating the MIA and KIA/BNR categories was a dynamic process; as cases were continually reviewed, casualties were shifted from one status to another. Thus, a high total of 354 MIA cases in Laos had been reduced to 317 as the Paris peace negotiations reached their conclusion in January 1973.) Estimates of actual POWs in Laos also varied. The American intelligence community—including the CIA, which had better assets in Laos than the Pentagon—believed as many as forty-one Americans could have been held in northern Laos. But only a few of these men were known for certain to have survived their loss and to have been captured by either the Communist Pathet Lao or the North Vietnamese.[3]

During a private discussion in September 1972, Le Duc Tho assured Kissinger that there had been "very few" American POWs captured in Laos; he refused to elaborate. When Kissinger insisted that *all* American prisoners anywhere in Indochina be released after the cease-fire, Le Duc Tho replied that there were no U.S. prisoners in Cambodia. But all American POWs in Laos and Vietnam would be freed if the Americans resolved "the question of reparations."[4]

In January 1973, the DRV was slightly more forthcoming; they now assured the Americans that "all U.S. military and civilian prisoners in Laos shall be released no later than sixty days following the signature of the agreement," in other words, as part of the overall exchange of POWs.[5]

But the DRV refused to extend the provisions for the exchange of information on MIAs and the location of graves to Laos, even though it was common knowledge that PAVN (People's Army) forces, not the Pathet Lao, controlled areas where most Americans had been lost. (In fact, the DIA estimated that no Americans had been captured by the Pathet Lao since 1966.[6])

The DRV position was based on several factors. In principle, Laos was an independent country—that did not participate in the Paris negotiations—and the DRV had always refused to acknowledge that it had a well-established military presence along the Ho Chi Minh Trail in Laos. If Hanoi had been forthcoming about Americans who had been killed or died after capture and been buried along the trail, this would have opened that area of ongoing PAVN operations to American casualty recovery teams. Hanoi realized that such teams were primarily composed of Special Forces troops well versed in trail reconnaissance. The PAVN intended to continue to use the Ho Chi Minh Trail to complete the conquest of the South once the Americans had withdrawn. Therefore, opening Laos to MIA remains recovery teams was anathema.[7]

In reality, however, few knowledgeable Americans believed that a large number of Americans had been captured alive in Laos. Almost two thirds (61 percent) of the 1,200 American airmen shot down in Laos had been recovered alive through the effective and often heroic efforts of Air Force Search and Rescue forces operating from nearby bases in Thailand.

It was the consensus of American civilian and military officers that the Pathet Lao could have been holding a relatively small number of American POWs in caves around Viengxay, near Samneua, Communist headquarters in the mountain wilderness of northeast Laos. It was in these caves that intelligence reports had placed the three American POWs positively known to be in Pathet Lao hands: Air Force Captains David Hrdlicka and Charles Shelton, and civilian aviator Eugene Debruin.

Interagency intelligence discussions about possibly larger numbers of POWs in Pathet Lao hands were inconclusive. In one discussion in January 1973, American intelligence officers reported, "We have only six known prisoners in Laos, although we hope there may be forty or forty-one. We have known very little about the caves where they keep the prisoners in Laos. We just got the first photos of those caves recently and our impression is they are pretty big. We think they are holding more than six prisoners there."[8] Pentagon estimates confirmed the possible number of live POWs in Laos at forty-one.[9]

At this delicate endgame phase of the Paris negotiations, the American side chose not to press the issue of POWs in Laos before the cease-fire agreement was formally ratified. Kissinger and his team decided to wait for the list of prisoners that Hanoi would deliver the day the cease-fire was signed. Further, separate cease-fire negotiations between the surrogates of Washington and Hanoi in Laos, the Royal Lao forces and the Pathet Lao, were nearing conclusion. The National Security Council and the Pentagon believed that the small number of American POWs held in Laos would be included in the general prisoner release as the DRV had unofficially promised.[10]

With the knotty POW release issue resolved in principle, the question of American reparations and "post-war reconstruction" aid still remained. The Vietnamese were adamant that Kissinger provide "iron-clad assurances" of American aid to North Vietnam before the final agreement was signed. But in his last meeting with Le Duc Tho in Paris on January 23, Kissinger showed that he could be just as stubborn as the Vietnamese. "I told him that this could not be discussed further until after the agreement was signed," Kissinger stated in his memoir.[11] Thus, the POWs-as-hostage and the economic-aid-as-inducement remained linked to the signing of the final agreement, which theoretically bound both sides to its terms. Kissinger and Le Duc Tho initialed the agreement that day. The American secretary of state, William Rogers, and the foreign ministers of South Vietnam, the DRV, and the PRG were scheduled to sign the final agreement in a formal ceremony in the Paris conference center on January 27.

The peace agreement signing ceremony was completed with much fanfare beneath the crystal chandeliers of the conference center on a bright, chill Saturday in Paris.

That same day, military representatives of the DRV and PRG presented the American delegation with the two long-awaited lists of prisoners in their custody who were scheduled to be released in increments over the next sixty days. The two lists included a total of 586 American military and civilian prisoners held in North Vietnam and in PRG camps in the South, as well as an additional 55 said to have died in captivity, whose remains would be repatriated at an undisclosed later date.[12]

This total of 641 surviving and dead POWs accounted for by the Communist forces was close to the DIA's most recently refined estimate of 667 American military and civilian personnel thought to be in Communist hands.[13]

Significantly, there was no mention of any POWs captured in Laos.[14]

THE LIST DID not include the names of Major Joseph Morrison or Lieutenant San Francisco.

As Pentagon officials prepared for the difficult task of achieving a "full accounting" for all Americans lost in Indochina, incident case 1329 was forwarded to the new Joint Casualty Resolution Center (JCRC) in Saigon. Because both airmen were known to have survived the loss of their aircraft, it was assumed the Communists could, and perhaps would, readily account for their fates.

That assumption was incorrect.

· · ·

ALTHOUGH PENTAGON OFFICIALS and senior military officers were disappointed with this low total, they were not overly surprised. In a White House meeting of the Washington Special Action Group (WSAG), the high-level interagency task force working on the peace accords, two days later, Kissinger asked a representative of the Joint Chiefs of Staff for his opinion of the Communists' POW lists.

"It was pretty close to what we expected," the officer (whose name was redacted in the declassified transcript of the meeting) replied. "We're hoping for forty more on the list of those in Laos."

He referred to a third list of American POWs captured in Laos, which the DRV now promised it could obtain from the Lao Patriotic Front (LPF)—the Pathet Lao—under pressure from the U.S. delegation.

A WSAG Pentagon official added that most of those Americans named on the DRV and PRG lists had appeared in the U.S. estimates of possible returnees. But there were fifty-six men whom the Pentagon had carried as probable POWs who were not on the two lists.[15]

The White House intensified the pressure on the Vietnamese to produce the list of POWs captured in Laos. Kissinger's deputy, Air Force Lieutenant General Brent Scowcroft, passed word to the U.S. delegation in Paris the same day as this Washington meeting that Nixon had prepared a letter for DRV Premier Pham Van Dong detailing American plans for reconstruction aid. But Scowcroft said the letter would not be delivered until the DRV turned over the list of U.S. POWs captured in Laos. Le Duc Tho withheld the promised list at the next day's technical discussions. The U.S. delegation protested formally in a note, warning that the issue of economic aid depended on North Vietnam's accounting for prisoners captured in Laos.

Four days later, on February 1, the Vietnamese finally relented. National Security Council aide Colonel George Guay met a North Vietnamese counterpart and finally exchanged the Nixon letter on reconstruction aid for a list of American POWs captured in Laos. To Guay's chagrin, there were only ten names on this list, seven military men and three civilians.[16] (Two other Americans captured in Laos, Air Force Lieutenant Colonel Theodore Guy and Marine Corporal Frank E. Cius, were listed as South Vietnam captures by the Communists and scheduled for release by the DRV and PRG, respectively.)

When Guay expressed his astonishment at this small number—only a fraction of the 317 men then listed as MIA in Laos—the Vietnamese representative stated that these Americans were apparently the only U.S. prisoners captured in Laos on whom "they," the Pathet Lao, had information. This was a transparent charade. The American prisoners on the list had been captured in areas of Laos known to be controlled by the PAVN, not the Pathet Lao. Yet, in order to maintain the diplomatic fiction that the DRV was not operating in Laos—whose "neutrality" was protected by the terms of the new Paris Peace Accords—the Vietnamese Communists insisted that they did not have custody of the ten POWs. The Communist official promised, however, that the DRV was trying to verify the "existing situation" concerning American POWs held by the Lao Patriotic Front.[17]

The issue of using the promised postwar reconstruction aid as virtual ransom to win the release of American POWs held in Indochina has become a rancorous controversy since the war. Nixon administration officials, including Henry Kissinger, have consistently denied that the American side agreed to any specific amount of aid before the signing of the Paris Peace Accords.

This is technically true.

But President Nixon's secret letter to DRV Premier Pham Van Dong was delivered only four days after the Paris cease-fire accords were signed. Theoretically, the letter could have been delivered *before* the signing ceremony, had the Vietnamese Communists provided their lists of prisoners to be repatriated. Therefore there was clearly a linkage between the promised aid and the accounting for prisoners.

And Nixon's letter to the Vietnamese does specifically cite an aid amount: "Preliminary United States studies indicate that the appropriate programs for the United States contribution to postwar reconstruction will fall in the range of $3.25 billion of grant aid over five years. Other forms of aid will be agreed upon between the two parties." Approximately $2 billion in food and agricultural aid was also discussed, bringing total proposed American aid to over $5 billion.

The letter also promised that this reconstruction aid would be given "without any political conditions."

Nixon's message further proposed the creation of a Joint Economic Commission to develop the programs that would use this aid.[18]

Moreover, because Nixon's letter was hand-delivered to the Vietnamese Communists just days before the scheduled repatriation of the first contingent of American POWs on February 12, 1973, it is clear that the Vietnamese side considered the release of prisoners to be directly linked to the promise of a specific amount of aid.

Following the signing of the Paris Peace Accords, Kissinger prepared to visit Hanoi to discuss the practical details of implementing the peace agreement with the leaders of the DRV. One of the principal subjects of discussion was POWs and MIAs. After adjustments for inadvertent name repetitions, the number of American military and civilian prisoners scheduled to be released in increments now totaled 587 (including the ten men from Laos). During a visit to Beijing, Henry Kissinger had completed a separate negotiation for the release of two more Vietnam War POWs who had been captured and held in China: Navy Lieutenant Commander Robert

Flynn and Air Force Captain Philip Smith; they raised the projected POW release total to 589.[19]

But the Pentagon prepared an additional list of eighty persons—mainly downed airmen—who were still officially carried in the POW category, but who had appeared on none of the three Communist lists. Of these eighty cases, approximately twenty presented compelling evidence of survival after loss: Some men's photographs had appeared in the Eastern Bloc press; others had been publicly interviewed while in North Vietnamese custody.[20]

Kissinger arrived in Hanoi on February 10, accompanied by his Indochina expert, Deputy Assistant Secretary of State William Sullivan, the former U.S. ambassador to Laos. The American side immediately presented Le Duc Tho with a number of files on the most compelling of the POW cases. It was hoped that, if these men were still alive in Vietnamese hands, officially raising their cases in Hanoi might provide a face-saving expedient to the DRV to include the prisoners in the pending repatriation. This was a plausible ploy. It gave the DRV the chance to resurrect any surviving POWs who had been inadvertently *forgotten* on the original prisoner lists.

Kissinger pressed the DRV on the issue, trying to appeal to their common sense. He did not insist that the men had all survived their captivity, but he pushed the Communists for an accounting of their fates. "I called special attention to the nineteen cases where pictures of the captured had been published in the Communist press," Kissinger later noted. At the very least, he asked the DRV to supply more information on these men's fates.

But the Hanoi leaders would not budge: "Pham Van Dong replied noncommittally that the lists handed over to us were complete," Kissinger noted in his memoir.[21]

After rebuffing the Americans on the subject of POW/MIAs in the first meetings, the DRV demanded that Kissinger's delegation provide details on reconstruction aid. The American strategy was to spin out the issue of aid for as long as possible over the coming weeks and months in order to keep the positive aspect of their carrot-and-stick diplomatic démarche viable while assessing North Vietnam's compliance with the terms of the Paris Peace Accords. Rather than immediately deliver concrete proposals for postwar aid, the Americans directed the Vietnamese toward the planning of the Joint Economic Commission raised in Nixon's letter. This was the international equivalent of the old Washington gambit of studying a difficult problem rather than solving it. But the Vietnamese, bureaucrats par excellence, accepted the ploy.

Kissinger's delegation completed their discussions on the same day as the first release of American POWs, February 12, 1973.

MORE THAN 450 American POWs held in North Vietnam were scheduled to be released in three groups by the PAVN. These repatriations would coincide with releases by the Saigon government and the Provisional Revolutionary Government (Vietcong) in the South. A total of 120 American POWs in the South would be freed by the PRG, beginning with a group of twenty-seven turned over to U.S. officers at Quan Loi, north of Saigon. In the four days following this release, 4,000 Vietcong and PAVN prisoners would be repatriated to their own representatives in the Four-Party Joint Military Commission. In the North, American military and State Department representatives dealt directly with the PAVN.

The first prisoner release on February 12, 1973, in the North set the tone for the subsequent repatriations.

Prior to the signing of the Paris accords, the American prisoners in North Vietnam were consolidated into three camps in Hanoi: Hoa Lo Prison, Cu Loc (the Zoo), and the Plantation. Defying their captors' attempts to keep the prisoners disorganized, the Americans created their own military unit, the 4th Allied POW Wing, which reasserted a formal command structure among the once disparate prisoners.

The senior officers, including Navy Captains Jeremiah Denton and James B. Stockdale (later admiral), and Air Force Colonels Robinson "Robbie" Risner and John P. Flynn (both later promoted to general), managed to influence the terms of repatriation. They insisted that the sequence of release would be determined by a man's date of capture, not by rank or any Vietnamese concept of "progressiveness" that an individual might have shown during the years of brutal captivity.

Repatriated American prisoners were flown to Clark Air Base in the Philippines. They were immediately swept up in the elaborate military procedure dubbed Operation Homecoming.[22]

But as news accounts focused on the human interest aspects of Operation Homecoming—the men devouring cheeseburgers and milkshakes followed by multiple bowls of corn flakes in the Clark mess halls—there was a grimmer side to the repatriation process. Within hours of their arrival at Clark Air Base, the prisoners underwent carefully structured intelligence debriefings. One aim was to quickly obtain as much detailed information as possible about men still missing, especially those who might have been captured alive.

(The individual returned POW debriefings represent the richest single source of intelligence on the entire MIA issue. Unfortunately, unlike other classified wartime documents, these debriefings have never been made public and apparently are destined to remain classified indefinitely. When the Senate Select Committee on POW/MIA Affairs staff requested access to these Homecoming debriefings, the Pentagon refused to grant it. The official explanation for the continued classification was: "The former POWs were assured that under no circumstances would these recorded debriefings be released to anyone. The Department of Defense has and will continue to honor that pledge."[23] The apparent reason for this continued secrecy is that many of the ex-POWs being debriefed suffered deep emotional anguish as they frankly recounted the propaganda statements they were forced to provide the enemy after being broken by torture. This is understandable, but the continued shroud of secrecy surrounding the debriefing transcripts—and their factual information—has helped spawn a wave of myth and rumor in the postwar years.)

Some returnees were able to provide promising leads on the fates of the missing. Most of this information concerned cases in which crewmates had been separated during shootdown. Usually, the returned POW, when asking his Vietnamese guards about his crewmate, had been shown the man's flightsuit name tag, a helmet, or even his military identity card, and assured that the other man was still alive.

From these debriefings, the Pentagon obtained information on 156 servicemen who "may have died in captivity."[24]

The returned POWs also confirmed Pentagon fears that some of the men on the DRV and PRG died in captivity lists had been tortured to death or executed in retaliation for death sentences meted out to Communist prisoners by the Saigon government. At least five airmen held in the well-organized military prison system in Hanoi had died from torture: Navy aviators Kenneth Cameron, James Connell, and Walter Estes, and Air Force pilots Earl Cobeil and Edwin Atterberry.[25]

Injured surviving Linebacker II POWs gave details of the compressed torture sessions some had suffered in the desperate Communist attempts to force them into making propaganda statements within hours of capture. But despite these reports of brutality, the military debriefers concluded that the public display of these prisoners may have actually protected them. During the December bombing of Hanoi, Air Force counterintelligence officers had worried that B-52 crew members, who had never before been at serious risk of capture in Indochina, were now prisoners in Hanoi, where the Soviet military was known to have a large advisory mission that included GRU military intelligence officers. It was feared most of the aircrew members in sensitive specialties, including electronic warfare officers (EWO) and radar navigators, might simply disappear into Soviet military custody. But prisoner debriefings seemed to indicate that this had not been the case.

And the debriefers were surprised that no returning American military prisoners, even aviators with detailed knowledge of NATO strategy and tactics, reported having been interrogated by Soviet military intelligence officers in Hanoi. Only one American, a CIA officer whose name has never been released, reported any interrogation by a Soviet, in this case a civilian KGB officer, who contacted the American just before repatriation in early 1973.

(However, in 1991, a PAVN defector, Senior Colonel Bui Tin, testified before the Senate Select Committee on POW/MIA Affairs that "Cubans and Russians interrogated some Americans and treated them very badly." He said that these interrogations occurred "around December 1972," and were focused on Americans "with expertise in electronics."[26] Colonel Tin, who was deputy editor of the PAVN newspaper, *Quan Doi Nhan Dan,* in the 1970s, stated that he had no knowledge of any American POWs being transferred from Vietnam to the Soviet Union.[27]

(In 1992, members of Task Force Russia, a Pentagon investigative team researching evidence of Soviet involvement with American POWs from World War II, the Korean War, and the Vietnam War, received confirmation that Soviet intelligence officers were involved with interrogating American prisoners in Vietnam.[28] Retired former Soviet military officers who had served in Hanoi during the war told the American interviewers there was a "no-contact" order in effect that prevented Soviet personnel from direct interrogations of American POWs. One retired Soviet colonel stated, however, that a Russian officer sometimes sat behind a screen during interrogations of U.S. prisoners and passed questions to the Vietnamese interrogating the POW.[29])

After Operation Homecoming, the U.S. Air Force undertook a classified analysis of the captivity experiences of 322 returned Air Force POWs, which included a detailed examination of the types of information the North Vietnamese sought to obtain during interrogation. A total of 1,415 interrogation "incidents" were analyzed. During these interrogations, only a small percentage of questions dealt with strategically or tactically important military information. For example, only 2 percent of the questions concerned command structure in the POWs' units; 12 percent concerned aerial tactics; and only 7 percent of the analyzed interrogation sessions dealt with aircraft systems.[30]

One of the debriefing questions was, "Based on your personal experience, what were the captors' interests after the beginning of regular prison routine after the Fall of 1969?" (When the most severe propaganda-extraction torture decreased, following Ho Chi Minh's death on September 1, 1969.) Only 7.9 percent of prisoners were questioned about "aircraft or equipment." Fewer than 10 percent (9.5 percent) were questioned about "technical information on weapons systems or information systems." And only 2.7 percent were interrogated for "strategic information on war plans, nuclear capabilities, or strategic weapons systems."[31]

Clearly, the North Vietnamese were very interested in certain types of military information. But this was usually of an immediate tactical nature, not part of a more sophisticated collection effort. For example, A-6 Intruder pilot Red McDaniel was tortured soon after capture in 1967 to reveal which targets in Hanoi the Americans planned to bomb with their new television-guided bombs and missiles. But he was not asked to provide detailed technical information on the new weapons.[32] Air Force Colonel Norman Gaddis, captured in May 1967, was one of the most experienced senior officers to fall into enemy hands. He was tortured for information on theater tactics, not technical matters.[33]

However, the debriefers learned, there were several critical exceptions. In 1966, a Vietnamese interrogator presented Navy pilot Robert H. Shumaker a detailed list of thirty-five technical questions. The questions concerned aircraft antiaircraft warning systems and focused on such arcane matters as sensitivity to radar pulse repetition frequencies and bandwidths. Shumaker was certain no Vietnamese had written such complex questions. Moreover, the purpose of the questions was obviously to construct specific counter-measures in the acquisition and tracking radar of SAM antiaircraft systems. The Vietnamese did not build this equipment; they obtained it from the Soviet Union and its Eastern Bloc allies. Equally revealing was the tactic employed to extract this information from Shumaker. He was not tortured at that time. (Later, Lieutenant Colonel Tran Thanh Hang, a senior archivist at the Central Military Museum in Hanoi, told Ted Schweitzer that the Viet-namese guards liked Shumaker because he was a "quiet, nonaggressive young boy.") Instead, the interrogator offered to give him letters from his wife and mother, which were being withheld. And when Shumaker refused to answer the questions, he was not immediately "punished," the guards' euphemism for torture. Instead he was forced to stay seated on a stool for twelve straight days and commanded to "think deeply" on the offer.[34]

The primary responsibility of the Clark debriefers was to quickly obtain any concrete intelligence on Americans who the returned POWs believed might have remained in captivity.

And, although the debriefers gathered considerable information on men who might have survived their loss incidents, no returnee could identify any POW they believed had been left behind alive.[35] But many men speculated about crewmates or other POWs who might have died early in captivity. These widespread reports of brutal initial interrogation of prisoners who had been severely wounded or injured in their loss incidents alarmed the debriefers.

When the U.S. Air Force later analyzed the shootdown and captivity expe-rience of its returned POWs, it was confirmed that almost three quarters of them were injured or wounded during their loss or capture, and that almost all of these injured prisoners were subjected to mistreatment involving "sig-nificant pain" during the initial interrogation "before the start of regular prison routine."[36]

The Homecoming debriefers at Clark also learned that many of the pris-oners on Kissinger's list of eighty might have survived their first hours or days of captivity, only to be killed in the villages en route to Hanoi or during the first brutal interrogation at Hoa Lo Prison. The death from torture of wounded and injured men during their first interrogations could have ac-counted for the high ratio of MIAs to repatriated prisoners for North Vietnam shootdowns during the intensive Rolling Thunder bombing campaigns of 1966 through 1968.

Although such extreme brutality had not been inflicted on all the prisoners, systematic torture, the returnees told their debriefers, had been wide-spread. The primary purpose of the torture had been to coerce the Americans—especially senior officers—into making antiwar and pro-Communist propaganda statements, a process that often involved formal tape-recorded or written confessions to heinous war crimes such as the intentional bombing of schools, hospitals, and other purely civilian targets.

Beatings and rope torture were the most common methods. But the interrogators also employed ratchet-tightening "torture cuffs," manacles that bit into a man's arms and legs to produce intense, prolonged agony. These shackles were a relic of the French colonial jails, and some guards seemed to enjoy using them on Americans. In most cases, a prisoner could end the pain by "surrendering" to the interrogator, who would demand the man "show by your concrete acts that you are contrite." The concrete act was usually a war crime confession or anti-American propaganda statement.[37]

Prolonged torture was also used to break up clandestine prisoner communication networks, as punishment for infractions of camp rules, and in brutal retaliation for escape attempts.

One of the most savage periods of torture—which resulted in the death of at least one American, Air Force Captain Edwin Atterberry—occurred when he and Captain John Dramesi were recaptured following an attempted escape from the Zoo in Hanoi's southern suburbs in 1969. Dramesi nearly died at the hands of the sadistic interrogator known as the Bug, and he later reported to his debriefers that Atterberry was probably killed during this protracted torture.[38]

Although this post-escape "purge" had been extreme in its cruelty—men had the flesh literally flayed from their naked buttocks during weeks of flogging—most of the victims had survived. But the intelligence debriefers were equally alarmed at the reports of less systematic brutality, which most prisoners had experienced in one degree or another during the transport from their capture site to Hanoi. Almost every airman shot down in daylight reported being fired on while dangling in his parachute harness by the enemy on the ground—by regular PAVN troops as well as less disciplined militia. Most airmen who were initially captured by rural militia or villagers armed with farm implements or crude flintlocks reported vicious beatings. Many were saved from a massacre only through the intervention of regular PAVN soldiers.[39]

During the subsequent U.S. Air Force analysis of POWs' captivity experiences, it was determined that 6 percent of the surviving prisoners' injuries were caused by gunshot wounds.[40] It can be assumed that some percentage of airmen killed in their loss incidents were shot while descending in their parachutes.

But the returnees' accounts of torture and near-massacre were not their only grim reports. The debriefers learned of blatant, illegal collaboration by a small number of POWs, including two relatively senior officers.

The returnees undergoing the Operation Homecoming debriefings at Clark Air Base were incensed that the accused collaborators among them were not immediately arrested. Those accused fell into two groups.

Eight Army and Marine Corps enlisted men captured in the South had received special attention from the PAVN, once they were transferred to camps in the North. Although they had suffered the same arbitrary cruelty, short rations, and chronic illness common to all POWs held in the jungle camps, they were amply rewarded for collaboration once they reached the Plantation camp in the Hanoi suburbs. In return for extensive pro-Communist broadcasts on the DRV and the clandestine Vietcong radio stations, as well as similar written statements, these enlisted men received continual special favors. Their food was luxurious by camp standards, and in fact much better than the civilian diet in wartime North Vietnam. And they were allowed almost complete freedom of the camp exercise and sports yards. A few even helped the Vietnamese dig fighting positions and practice antiaircraft exercises after the Son Tay raid.[41]

By 1971, these enlisted collaborators had formed a Peace Committee and worked actively with the North Vietnamese on organized antiwar propaganda activities. When Air Force Lieutenant Colonel Theodore Guy, who had been captured in 1968 just inside Laos, was brought to the Plantation, he ordered these enlisted men to cease their collaboration, follow his orders, and obey the Code of Conduct. They rebuffed him.[42]

But the collaboration of these enlisted men was less troubling to the debriefers than the accounts of the activities of two career officers: Navy Commander Walter E. Wilber and Marine Lieutenant Colonel Edison W. Miller. They had engaged in the same types of activities as the Peace Committee enlisted men and received the same preferential treatment in return. What was more alarming to the debriefers was the fact that both Wilber and Miller had been senior squadron officers well versed in tactical and technical information before capture. If they had so obviously taken part in anti-American propaganda activities, it was feared, they might also have divulged all their military secrets.[43]

Much of the speculation about the level of military information extracted from American POWs, either under torture, or, in a few isolated cases, voluntarily, could be clarified if the Pentagon allowed better access to the 1973 POW debriefing reports. Unfortunately, the Pentagon will not allow the confidential transcripts of tape-recorded debriefing sessions to be redacted in such a way as to preserve privacy while providing concrete information.[44]

After the final prisoner release, Colonel Theodore Guy filed formal charges against the members of the Peace Committee. In his charging statement, Guy cited the men for disobeying lawful orders of a superior officer, disrespect to superiors, acting in conspiracy with the enemy, and aiding the enemy. Army Secretary Howard H. Callaway dismissed the charges against the Army men on the Peace Committee, noting that they had already suffered during years of "brutal conditions in South Vietnam." The charges against the Marines were also dropped, due to a technicality of military law that held that one branch of the armed services could not prosecute its members more severely than another. One of the Marine enlisted men accused, Sergeant Larry A. Kavanaugh, committed suicide just before the charges were dropped.[45]

Captain James Stockdale, the senior Navy ex-POW, also leveled similar charges against Wilber and Miller. But Stockdale added the specifications of mutiny and attempting to cause insubordination. Navy Secretary John W. Warner conducted a three-month investigation, but eventually dismissed the charges. Warner found that a court martial would unduly disrupt the lives of returned prisoners called to testify. But Warner forced both officers to retire.[46]

At the time, interest in the accused collaborators focused almost entirely on their conduct. But some intelligence officers noted an additional significant factor. The members of the Peace Committee, probably fearing court martial on repatriation to America, had petitioned the Vietnamese to help them obtain political asylum in socialist countries after the cease-fire. They had even filed formal applications for this asylum and were hopeful the process would be completed before the prisoner exchange. But the North Vietnamese disappointed them. The eight enlisted men were told they would have to be repatriated; if they left Vietnam directly for the Eastern Bloc, the Americans might use their defection as an excuse to "break the peace agreements." Their involuntary repatriation was a clear sign that the Vietnamese Communists clearly understood how seriously the American side took the issue of prisoner return. It would have been easy for Hanoi to allow these eight young Americans to remain in Vietnam and continue to participate in propaganda activities. But there was too much at stake in the cease-fire and complete withdrawal of American forces to risk by exploiting the propaganda potential of these eight men.[47]

(There was, of course, at least one live American who would remain behind in North Vietnam after the repatriation: former Marine PFC Robert Garwood. But by 1973, he was considered by the Vietnamese to be an officer in the PAVN, not a POW.)

Another indication that Hanoi had chosen to release all its surviving prisoners was the appearance of Bobby Joe Keesee among the returnees. Keesee was probably the most bizarre prisoner in Indochina. An Army veteran of the Korean War, Keesee had once flown a stolen airplane to Cuba and had been charged with other criminal activity. In 1970, he appeared in Bangkok, posing as a filmmaker. Keesee chartered a Bira Air Transport Cessna flown by two Thai pilots in Ubon, ostensibly to scout locations for a film in northern Thailand. But Keesee hijacked this aircraft and forced the crew to fly all the way across the war zone of the Lao panhandle, into southern North Vietnam, and land on a beach south of Vinh. He was last seen by the terrified

Thai pilots, dressed in a three-piece suit striding across the sand toward the muzzle flashes of charging North Vietnamese militia. The pilots managed to take off, but their plane was riddled by small-arms fire. Even though no American official was aware of Keesee's captivity, the Vietnamese Communists chose to release him.[48]

And still another indication that, for whatever reason, the North Vietnamese were not retaining prisoners was the case of Air Force Captain Charles F. Riess. He had been a forward air controller, flying an A-7 on clandestine missions over northern Laos. After being shot down on December 24, 1972, Riess was captured by PAVN troops (probably members of an Air Defense regiment supporting the Pathet Lao) and taken to Hanoi. Riess was separately held with the other POWs captured in Laos.[49]

As Operation Homecoming unfolded, the DRV stubbornly preserved the charade that the Lao Patriotic Front and its armed forces, the Pathet Lao, were responsible for all POWs captured in Laos. Hanoi maintained this facade up to the very end of the repatriation, despite repeated American protests. The North Vietnamese insisted that Pathet Lao, not PAVN officers control the release in Hanoi of American POWs from Laos, even though they had been captured by PAVN forces and held in North Vietnam. Hanoi announced that this small group would be released in a separate ceremony at Gia Lam Airport on March 28, 1973.

Had the Vietnamese Communists wanted to hold Riess after Operation Homecoming, it would have been relatively simple either to keep him in Laos or to keep him separate from the other Laos POWs in Hanoi. Once he was allowed to join the Laos group—the "Lulus," as they called themselves —he could not be held back without jeopardizing the cease-fire agreement. (However, activists still insist that Riess was kept separate from all POWs in Hanoi.[50] Riess himself refutes this.[51])

Two other members of this group were also indicative of Hanoi's apparent intentions. Lloyd Oppel and Samuel Mattix were young civilian workers with the Christian Missions of Many Lands. They were captured in October 1972 when North Vietnamese troops overran their mission station in the southern Laotian town of Keng Kok. Two of their colleagues, Evelyn Anderson and Beatrice Kosin, were murdered by the Communist soldiers. But Oppel and Mattix were marched all the way to Hanoi. They were held at Hoa Lo Prison, out of contact with other Americans, from December 6, 1972, until January 16, 1973, then taken to a rural jail for intensive interrogation. After the interrogators were satisfied neither man was an intelligence operative, they were returned to Hanoi. Had the Vietnamese chosen to hold these men after the cease-fire, it would have been easy simply to keep them in the rural jail.[52]

The last American POW repatriated from Vietnam was Army Captain Robert T. White, who was captured in 1969. He was not returned to U.S. control by the Vietcong (PRG) until April 1, 1973, a day after the last officially scheduled exchange. Captain White had *not* been on the PRG POW list. "They just plain forgot about me," White later explained. Obviously, had the Vietnamese Communists wished to hold him hostage, it also would have been easy for them to do so. White's belated repatriation reduced the Kissinger "discrepancy list" to seventy-nine.[53]

(In the years after the war, as the MIA controversy grew more rancorous, some activists discounted the importance of White's release by claiming that the PRG was not as cynical and manipulating as the North Vietnamese. This might have been true earlier in the war. But those who knew the political-military situation well affirmed that, by 1973, the PRG was under the complete control of Hanoi, and would not have released White without PAVN orders.[54])

Despite this evidence that the North Vietnamese had released all the American prisoners they held, there were other, more disturbing accounts from returned POWs that the Communists were withholding information about the fates of many other Americans who had probably survived their loss incidents. One troubling report from returnees who had been held at the remote Dogpatch camp on the Chinese border, for example, cited five or six American names scratched into the limestone blocks of the prison buildings. The returning POWs had seen the names on arrival in the camp in May 1972. But no one among the 209 prisoners had ever heard of these men. Later, when the Dogpatch prisoners were brought back to Hoa Lo Prison, the leaders of the 4th Allied POW Wing consulted their living "memory banks," prisoners charged with memorizing the names of every American ever reported in the PAVN prison system. That handful of names scratched on limestone blocks in the isolated camp did not correspond to any known prisoners.[55]

There could be no doubt that Hanoi held the answer to this riddle, as well as many of the other nagging mysteries surrounding the fate of more than one hundred men still listed as missing in action.

THE AMERICAN PUBLIC was not particularly interested in these mysteries in the spring of 1973. As news accounts of the torture suffered by American POWs appeared, public outrage against the Vietnamese Communists flared briefly. But stories of brutality in North Vietnam were matched—then quickly surpassed—in media reports of the horror endured by Communist POWs held in South Vietnam. Among the worst cases of abuse were hard-core Communist military cadres who had refused offers to change sides and assist the Saigon government's war effort. They had been held in the notorious "tiger cages" in the former French colonial prison on the island of Con Son, a dungeon reminiscent of Devil's Island. They had been shackled in these narrow pens, exposed to the elements, and kept on starvation rations for years.[56]

The net result of these disclosures was to further sour the war-weary American public on the Vietnam conflict. And those who had supported the American effort were unable to maintain a high moral position on the mistreatment of U.S. POWs, given the terrible revelations of brutality by our Saigon ally.

WHILE OPERATION HOMECOMING captured the attention of the American news media and public, a shadowy drama over the issue of POWs from Laos was unfolding.

Just before the signing of the Laos cease-fire in Vientiane, the permanent Pathet Lao representative, Soth Petrasy, told reporters that any release of American prisoners would occur in Laos, not North Vietnam. "If they were captured in Laos, they will be returned in Laos."[57] This was a direct contradiction of the agreement between Le Duc Tho and Henry Kissinger.

Under the terms of the cease-fire accord between the Pathet Lao and the Royal Lao forces, signed on February 21, 1973, a coalition government was to be formed within sixty days, and all prisoners—regardless of nationality—were to be released during that period. On the day of signing, Soth Petrasy told the American chargé, John Gunther Dean, that the Lao Communists did "hold foreign prisoners, including Americans."[58]

But Petrasy refused to elaborate.

During this time, the PAVN representative to the Four-Party Joint Military Commission supervising prisoner exchanges in Vietnam also began to hedge on Le Duc Tho's earlier promise to Kissinger that the DRV would guarantee the release of American prisoners from Laos. The National Security Council and the Pentagon had hoped that the Vietnamese and Laotian Communists had arranged a confidential, face-saving expedient by which the estimated fifty American prisoners held in Laos—the ten already on the DRV list, plus the possible forty-one held by the Pathet Lao in the cave complex near Samneua—would be released.

But as the incremental repatriations of Operation Homecoming proceeded, it became clear that any larger release of American POWs from Laos was not in the offing. Further, the Pentagon realized when the only other confirmed surviving Laos POWs, Marine Corporal Frank Cius and Air Force Colonel Theodore Guy (who had been held by the Vietcong and North Vietnamese) were released before the others on the list of ten—not by token Pathet Lao representatives—that the anticipated face-saving expedient had not developed.

The American embassy in Vientiane also reported that the Lao Patriotic Front would probably not be able to coordinate the release of any American prisoners they held—beyond those on the original DRV list—before the March 28 sixty-day deadline specified in the Paris Peace Accords. Ambassador G. McMurtrie Godley recommended that America concentrate on the release of those on the February 1 list, then determine "whether there are additional PW's to be repatriated, within the framework and time limits of the Laos cease-fire and military protocol."[59]

In other words, the embassy was suggesting a cautious approach, which would use the promise of American reconstruction aid to Indochina as an enticement to win the release of any U.S. POWs surviving in Pathet Lao captivity.

The first five weeks of the POW exchanges had been marked by tension and acrimony, as both Hanoi and Saigon sought to wring maximum advantage out of each repatriation. On several occasions, the United States had temporarily halted troop withdrawals from South Vietnam until the DRV confirmed arrangements for scheduled prisoner exchanges and provided final lists of POWs still awaiting repatriation.[60]

Hanoi and the PRG excelled at this type of posturing. Each time the United States threatened to suspend troop withdrawals, then relented, following a concession from the Communists, America's credibility—the much-touted "face" of Asian lore—was further eroded. The Communists' use of the remaining prisoners as de facto hostages, just as they had used French POWs, diverted attention from equally flagrant, and more militarily significant breaches of the Paris Peace Accords.

America did, however, have several arrows left in its military quiver other than suspensions of the troop withdrawals, which after all had little effect on the military balance in the South. Under the terms of the Paris accords, the United States was required to remove or detonate mines in North Vietnamese waters, including the completely mine-blocked harbor of Haiphong, North Vietnam's principal port. Over 11,000 magnetic and acoustical mines had been sown along North Vietnam's coast in May 1972. This mining had all but closed the DRV's ports to international shipping.

As the Communists dragged their feet on the arrangements for the incremental prisoner repatriations, the United States responded tit for tat, dragging out the mine clearing in a similar manner.[61]

And there can be no doubt that the North Vietnamese considered mine clearing a vital immediate requirement. The DRV planned to complete the conquest of the South, once American forces had withdrawn. And the PAVN needed replacements for the tanks and heavy artillery it had already dispatched down the Ho Chi Minh Trail. This heavy equipment could not be transferred from Eastern Bloc freighters onto barges, as lighter munitions and fuel had been after the American mining of the DRV's ports in 1972. Although the Chinese had sold the DRV a limited number of Type 59 battle tanks, the principal PAVN heavy tank at the time was the Soviet-designed T-54, which was supplied to the DRV by Warsaw Pact nations.[62]

Therefore, the North Vietnamese needed the port of Haiphong cleared of mines if they were to ever field another heavy conventional force in the South to replace their massive losses in the 1972 Easter Offensive.

And the American Navy and Marine Corps forces conducting Operation End Sweep—the clearing of mines from North Vietnam's three major ports —were under orders from the Joint Chiefs of Staff and the U.S. Pacific Command to match the pace of their operations with the DRV and PRG prisoner releases. For their part, DRV officials threatened the Americans that the release of POWs would "not go smoothly" unless all the mines were cleared by March 28, 1973. But the Americans called their bluff. On February 28, 1973, Commander-in-Chief, Pacific (CINCPAC) Admiral Noel A.M. Gayler ordered the mine clearing task force out of Haiphong anchorage after the North Vietnamese arbitrarily announced a delay in the next scheduled incremental POW release.[63] Mine clearing operations resumed following the next prisoner release, but were later again suspended when the DRV obstructed the repatriation process once more. This pattern continued until the completion of Operation Homecoming, and the subsequent determination by the Pentagon that the DRV had, indeed, released all surviving American and allied POWs.[64]

Closely watching the mine clearing, the DRV had to accept the reality that the last mines would not be cleared until all the POWs had been released. This was a critical factor in the overall POW-release issue, but the news media at the time—and certainly later POW/MIA activists—have largely ignored the importance of Operation End Sweep.[65]

The United States, of course, had another implicit bargaining chip: renewed bombing or possibly even offensive ground action. If the Vietnamese and Lao Popular Front refused to account for missing Americans or POWs still awaiting repatriation, the United States could have recommended offensive military operations.

Or so it seemed in principle.

In reality, every move America made in Indochina at this time was dominated by the deepening Watergate crisis in Washington. And this domination would intensify in the coming months. As evidenced by the January caucus vote, the Democratic majority in Congress was in near-revolt against the Nixon White House; if Nixon had not been impeached over Watergate, he probably would have been had he dared to break the cease-fire over the issue of POWs.

However, the U.S. military was ready to do just that. On March 22, 1973, with Operation Homecoming winding down, Chairman of the Joint Chiefs of Staff Admiral Thomas Moorer urgently cabled Admiral Gayler, ordering that the carefully orchestrated U.S. troop withdrawal be suspended again until Hanoi provided a final and full list of American prisoners held throughout Indochina. The American withdrawal, Moorer stated, should remain suspended until Hanoi facilitated the "release of all, repeat all, American prisoners held throughout Indochina."[66]

As the last American POWs were being released in late March, it became clear that—as Ambassador Godley had warned—the Lao Popular Front did not plan to repatriate any additional Americans beyond those on the original list; nor would the LPF formally account for those who had died in their captivity. This act of defiance—a final stab of salt into the festering wound of the Indochina military debacle—outraged Pentagon policymakers. On March 23, Air Force Lieutenant Colonel (later Major General) Richard Secord and Rear Admiral Thomas Bigley drafted an Action Memorandum that Acting Assistant Secretary of Defense (International Security Affairs) Lawrence S. Eagleburger sent to Defense Secretary Elliot Richardson. This message was incorporated into a memorandum that Eagleburger sent Nixon's National Security Adviser Henry Kissinger on March 28, the day before the final official prisoner exchange in Vietnam. The message stated that, "DIA concludes that the LPF may hold a number of unidentified U.S. POWs, although we cannot accurately judge how many."

Eagleburger's message recommended yet another series of carrot-and-stick actions to make the Lao Communists fully account for American MIAs. If they still refused, he recommended that "U.S. air strikes and Lao and Thai irregular offensive operations could be resumed in Laos in order to force the release of our prisoners in Laos." However, he softened this recommended "toughening of the U.S. stance" by noting that the position was made difficult "without a clear picture as to how many U.S. personnel are actually being held in Laos. The intelligence data available is voluminous but imprecise."[67]

Defense Secretary Richardson further softened the hard line by recommending to Kissinger that the LPF should be threatened with unspecified "direct United States action" (not air strikes) if they continued to stonewall. The LPF, he said, should be warned that "the U.S. will no longer play games with the POW issue in Laos. The LPF should be told that we know they hold U.S. prisoners, and we demand their immediate release as well as an accounting and information on all those who may have died." But rather than backing these hard words with the clear threat of a renewed bombing campaign, Richardson recommended a show of force through tactical aerial reconnaissance over Laos and a postponement in the withdrawal of the CIA's Thai Volunteer Forces in southern Laos.[68]

His recommendations reflected the prevailing political reality. Everyone knew that the rebellious Congress would not have acquiesced to any renewed military campaign—especially on the scale of Linebacker II—either against North Vietnam or Laos. The North Vietnamese were also well aware of this. As Kissinger testified years later before the Senate Select Committee on POW/MIA Affairs: "Hanoi sensed our leverage was rapidly eroding. A host of congressional resolutions made it clear that we would have no support for military action. . . . In response to my presentations [during meetings with the North Vietnamese], Le Duc Tho disdainfully read me editorials from the American press and speeches from the Congressional Record. . . ."[69]

This disdain was evident in the charade surrounding the release in Hanoi on March 28, 1973, of the last ten American POWs captured in Laos. Even though they had never been held by the Laotian Communists, Pathet Lao, not PAVN officers supervised their transfer to American military officials.[70]

With the big stick of renewed air strikes no longer a valid option, Kissinger was left only the carrot of reconstruction aid to entice the Indochinese Communists to provide a better accounting of our MIAs.[71]

And there can be no doubt that both the DRV and the Lao Popular Front saw the solution of the MIA issue linked to the question of postwar reconstruction and economic aid. When Senator Edward Brooke of Massachusetts visited Saigon, arriving from Laos on April 9, 1973, he told the staff of the American embassy that "The big chip in negotiating [the MIA and KIA/BNR cases] in these countries is aid. And the way we should play it now is that they won't get a dime unless we get full cooperation on the MIAs and BNRs." But Senator Brooke also commented that Southeast Asian officials had no concept of the political difficulty of funding an American aid program.[72]

However, just as congressional Democrats rebelled against renewed military action in Indochina, their Republican counterparts chafed at the prospect of rewarding the DRV and Pathet Lao with billions of dollars in aid. And overall congressional resistance to reconstruction aid only increased as it became clear that the Vietnamese Communists had no intention of abiding by the terms of the Paris Peace Accords.[73]

Even before the last prisoners were exchanged, PAVN reinforcements were streaming down the Ho Chi Minh Trail's skein of jungle supply lines, with long convoys of military vehicles even appearing in the more open, less mountainous western slopes of the Annamite Mountains. American intelligence estimated that at least 40,000 infantry troops, plus six armor regiments (with 300 tanks), and the equivalent of an entire Soviet-style artillery division (150 heavy howitzers) were transiting the western trail en route to heavily fortified staging bases in Laos and Cambodia. Even more alarming was the fact that these massive conventional forces were moving in broad daylight. The PAVN was plainly convinced that renewed American air strikes were no longer a threat. One frustrated military intelligence analyst told reporters that the Ho Chi Minh Trail now looked "like the New Jersey Turnpike during rush hour."[74]

The White House response was to express "grave concern" over this infiltration and to implicitly threaten renewed bombing on the scale of Linebacker II. "Based on my actions of the past four years," President Nixon warned, "the North Vietnamese should not lightly disregard such expressions of concern."[75]

The North Vietnamese did not even deign to reply to Nixon's warning.

If Nixon could not marshal congressional support for a military response to these flagrant breaches of the Paris Peace Accords, it was clear that he no longer had the political power to force the Indochinese Communists to provide a better accounting for American MIAs, especially those missing in the parts of Laos that were the PAVN's principal staging area for the renewed invasion of South Vietnam.

A TOTAL OF 591 U.S. prisoners of war were returned to American custody during Operation Homecoming: 566 servicemen and twenty-five civilians. (Bobby Joe Keesee and Captain Robert White, who were not named on the Communists' lists, were included in this total.)

On March 29, 1973, President Richard Nixon announced to the nation, "For the first time in twelve years, no American military forces are in Vietnam. All of our American POWs are on their way home."[76]

This was a message the American people had awaited for many years. One of the most painful chapters in our history had finally ended.

Or so it seemed.

CHAPTER 4

IN THE YEARS SINCE THE WAR, RICHARD NIXON'S STATEMENT BECAME synonymous with betrayal, in the view of those who believed America had knowingly abandoned surviving POWs in Indochina.

But the historical record does not support this interpretation.

Although it was clear to the American intelligence community that the Vietnamese and Laotian Communists could have definitely provided a much better account of the fates of many of our missing in action, the United States did not have confirmation of a single POW surviving in Indochina when Nixon addressed the nation.

Further, the North Vietnamese release during Operation Homecoming of Bobby Joe Keesee, the two young missionaries Oppel and Mattix, as well as Air Force Captain Charles Riess, was an indication that they meant to avoid any action regarding prisoners that would jeopardize the proposed postwar reconstruction aid program. Hanoi even passed up an attractive propaganda coup by not allowing the eight Peace Committee enlisted men collaborators either to remain in North Vietnam or to seek asylum in the Eastern Bloc.

(The presence of Robert Garwood in North Vietnam, living freely as a defector, was suspected by American intelligence, but never confirmed.)

And, although rumors have abounded, there has never been any verified attempt by either the Vietnamese or Lao Communists to use surviving American POWs as hostages to force the United States to fulfill its implied promise of postwar reconstruction aid to Indochina. Moreover, as events unfolded in the two years after the Vietnam and Laos cease-fires, it became clear that both the DRV and the LPF were willing to risk losing American aid largess by completing the conquest of their anti-Communist foes.

In the spring and summer of 1973, however, the question of surviving American POWs in Indochina remained an issue in Washington.

Dr. Roger Shields, who had headed the Pentagon's POW Task Force throughout the peace negotiations, reportedly disagreed with Deputy Defense Secretary William Clements on post-Homecoming policy. Clements advocated the position that all the "POWs" should be considered dead, and that the government should concentrate on resolving the fates of the MIAs. Shields believed that it was improper to solidify this position into official policy.

According to Shields, when Clements told him during an early April 1973 meeting that there were "no Americans alive in Indochina," he replied: "I don't believe that you can say that."

Clements, a senior political appointee, replied ominously: "You didn't hear what I said."

His implication, Shields believed, was that the issue of surviving POWs had already been settled as far as the Pentagon was concerned. Henceforth, the policy would be that all the survivors had been repatriated. Although Shields had no concrete information on live POWs, his experience had taught him that the Vietnamese and Lao Communists had manipulated the prisoner release issue to such a degree there was no way to be certain they had not held back prisoners.[1]

Shields met with President Nixon on April 11, 1973, for a brief, job-well-done session. Nixon told Shields that it would be "unfair and a disservice to MIA families to raise false hopes without justification."[2]

The next day, Shields held a press conference on POW/MIA matters. Responding to a reporter's question, he stated: "We have no indication at this time that there are any Americans alive in Indochina."

He pointedly added, however, that the Pentagon definitely did not consider the return of only ten POWs from Laos to be "a complete accounting for all the Americans lost in Laos." The United States would continue to press the governments of Indochina for a full accounting. "And we anticipate that, if any Americans are yet alive for some reason or another," Shields concluded, "we would be able to ascertain that through this process of accounting for the missing."[3]

So, by mid-April 1973, official government efforts shifted from recovering live prisoners to gaining a full accounting for the fates of the missing.

Following Operation Homecoming, 2,383 Americans remained officially "unaccounted for" in Indochina. They were divided into two main categories: 1,124 Killed in Action/Body Not Recovered (KIA/BNR) and 1,259 Missing in Action. By the end of 1975, this group was combined on a single "Prisoner of War/Missing in Action" (POW/MIA) list.[4]

But it was understood at the time that, for many, indeed for most of the servicemen and civilians in this combined category, there was no intelligence-based evidence that they had survived their loss incident.[5]

The total of 591 POWs released by North Vietnam and the PRG in 1973, plus the fifty-five known died in captivity cases, represented almost 70 percent of the "possibly captured" POW/MIAs actually named in Defense Department intelligence estimates for North and South Vietnam. So the U.S. government never suspected that the Vietnamese Communists had refused to release—for whatever motive—the *majority* of POWs they held, as has been alleged by some activists in the ensuing years.[6]

In fact, the post-cease-fire "POW" subcategory was never intended to indicate American prisoners known to be still remaining in captivity, but rather represented an estimate of men who had probably died or had been executed in captivity, and who had not appeared on Indochinese Communists' lists. After the last American prisoner was released, various classified lists of men known to have been captured alive or suspected to have survived their loss incidents were drawn up in the Department of Defense. As intelligence analysts debated which names should be included on these lists during the spring and summer of 1973, the total varied between sixty-seven and eighty-three.

But no senior official of the Nixon administration ever demanded that North Vietnam, the PRG, or the LPF release eighty-three live American prisoners. Almost everyone who reviewed the cases thought these men were dead.[7]

Unfortunately, reliable intelligence on this issue was woefully thin.

It was possible that several hundred of the combined POW/MIA category casualties might have been killed during their loss incident.

It was equally possible that they had been captured but not returned alive.

And it was also theoretically possible that many survivors among the missing men could have been held back by either the PAVN or the Pathet Lao.

The case for surviving prisoners was certainly stronger in Laos than in North Vietnam. If the North Vietnamese *were* holding several hundred POWs after the cease-fire for whatever motive—bargaining chips for reparations, hostages to leverage the release of Communist prisoners in the South—these prisoners would have to have been incarcerated in a secret, parallel prison system completely separate from the one in which the repatriated American POWs were held, one that had somehow escaped detection in the rigorous, long-term American satellite and aerial reconnaissance effort of the war. And, to this day, most returned American POWs who were held for years in North Vietnam do not believe that such a prison system existed.[8]

But it must be reiterated that the Pentagon simply did not have reliable intelligence on North Vietnam or Laos. By professional standards, "reliable" intelligence is information from a source that can be separately verified. For example, a satellite image of a structure that looks like a prison camp is confirmed to be so by a human agent, or vice versa. Vague rumors or agent reports of surviving POWs, which could not be independently verified, were not reliable intelligence. In the weeks after Operation Homecoming, when Roger Shields gave his press conference, no one in the American government had a list of live U.S. citizens positively known or strongly suspected to still be held by North Vietnam or the Pathet Lao.[9]

A month later, however, there definitely was at least one live American POW in Laos. His name was Emmet James Kay, a pilot with Continental Air Service, a CIA-sponsored air charter company that had been flying food, military matériel, and Royal Lao troops for years. On May 7, 1973, Kay's Pilatus Porter, a robust single-engine turboprop bush transport, was forced to crash-land on the Plain of Jars. Kay and his passengers, six Royal Lao soldiers, were immediately captured by Communist troops. On May 12, 1973, the Pathet Lao announced he was being held prisoner.

Kay was marched for a week to the Pathet Lao headquarters in the limestone cliffs of Viengxay, near Samneua. There he was held in one of the large caves that had drawn the attention of American intelligence the previous January. Kay encountered almost 300 Royal Lao and Thai mercenary prisoners in this cave complex. But he saw no other Americans.

A month later, Kay was taken by PAVN forces to Hanoi, where he received a medical examination, was obliged to sit through some propaganda sessions, then sent back to Viengxay. Although Kay's prison diet was spartan, his captors did allow him to receive regular food parcels, including canned meat and jars of Hawaiian poi, which Kay relished.[10]

Over the next sixteen months, the Lao factions squabbled incessantly over the composition of the coalition government, which delayed the final agreement on prisoner exchange. It was not until September 18, 1974, that Kay was turned over to the American embassy in Vientiane.[11]

During a news conference at Clark Air Base, Kay seemed relaxed and happy. He reiterated that he had been treated well in captivity. His Communist captors, Kay said, "always reminded me I was their only American captive and that I was a very important person."[12]

Kay also stated that the Pathet Lao had told him they had not taken other prisoners, but buried the bodies of any American aircrew near their crash sites.[13]

Kay's information seemed to be confirmed by the Royal Lao and Thai POWs repatriated from this cave complex. These POWs had not seen any American prisoners after the Vietnam cease-fire. One of the Thai prisoners, Chaicham Harnnavee, who was captured in 1965, said he had seen two American POWs during his captivity, but that they had been taken to Vietnam and freed during Operation Homecoming. He told reporters after his release that he had seen no other Americans since then, nor had he heard of any in Lao captivity.[14]

And none of the American POWs captured in Laos and repatriated during Operation Homecoming reported seeing unaccounted-for Americans in holding camps along the trail, prisoners who conceivably might have been kept behind in Laos by the PAVN. Further, wartime human and signals intelligence reports (which tended to be somewhat more reliable in Laos than in North Vietnam) on the three Americans known to have been alive as prisoners for several years indicated that they had died or were executed before the 1973 cease-fire.[15]

But, as with so many wartime events in Laos, the issue of surviving American POWs was certainly not cut-and-dried.

After Emmet Kay's return to the United States, rumors arose that he had secretly reported that the Pathet Lao told him they had many living American prisoners who had been transported to North Vietnam just before Kay reached Samneua.[16]

A Pathet Lao defector interviewed by the Defense Intelligence Agency gave a plausible account of visiting a cave near Samneua in March 1972, where he encountered several POWs, including three Americans. He stated that the prisoners were healthy and well fed. Because the POWs were allegedly kept in caves, however, it was impossible to confirm their captivity through high-resolution aerial reconnaissance photography.

In fact, the few wartime reconnaissance photos that show possible American POWs in Laos have been described as "the subject of furious disagreement" among intelligence officials and POW/MIA activists who saw them years after the war. These so-called volley ball photos seem to show twenty male Caucasians in a forest clearing, surrounded by Pathet Lao guards in black uniforms. In some views the Caucasians appear to be playing volley ball. But the Pentagon's photo analysts state that the pictures are inconclusive at best.[17]

Interpreting "overhead imagery" of possible POW camps and verifying human source reports on surviving American prisoners in Laos became a major undertaking for Joint Casualty Resolution Center (JCRC) officers in Thailand in the mid-1970s. At this point in the technical evolution of American reconnaissance satellites, the image resolution was such that skilled analysts could discern a Caucasian from an Asian in most photographs.[18]

Because American Special Operations Forces were not permitted to conduct ground reconnaissance patrols in Laos after the February 1973 cease-fire between the Lao factions, the JCRC focused on a more rigorous analysis of intelligence reports of possibly surviving American POWs.

In the process, the JCRC also systematically analyzed previously "jumbled" wartime casualty files and discovered a number of glaring errors in these reports. The worst problem concerned incorrect shootdown coordinates; during the war, some wingmen of missing aviators simply made their best guess about shootdown location. This was understandable: Perhaps they had been flying at high speed after a bomb run, on the opposite heading of the lost wingman. The margin of error in such cases could exceed thirty miles. Therefore agent reports of crash sites or airmen in parachutes often did not relate to "known" loss locations.

Despite this general confusion, American intelligence analysts received intriguing information on possible POW survivors in both Pathet Lao– and PAVN-controlled areas of Laos. The sources of this information were varied: satellite and aerial reconnaissance images, field reports from the Vientiane CIA station, and agents' reports ("humint") from indigenous-source networks run by experienced CIA field officers working out of American bases along Thailand's frontier with Laos.

According to one of these intelligence officers—who only agreed to discuss the matter on the condition of anonymity—there was "fairly voluminous" information on American POWs surviving in Laos during the 1974–75 period. But much of this information was of "low reliability."[19]

However, this officer saw certain elements in the human intelligence reports that, to him, indicated "almost conclusively" that Americans—other than Emmet Kay—had remained in Laos after April 1, 1973. These elements included similar sighting details by two or more agents from separate networks, who had no contact with each other. Some of these agent reports also contained clear or partially garbled names of possible American POWs, which correlated to men on the Laos POW/MIA list.

It can be independently confirmed that the wartime "tracking" of possible American POWs in Laos by intelligence officers was at least partially accurate. A recently declassified Central Intelligence Agency dispatch from the chief of station, Vientiane, to the CIA's Langley, Virginia, headquarters, sent on September 3, 1968, contained twenty-five names to be added to a "current list of POWs and MIAs in Laos." Among these names were four aviator POWs later released during Operation Homecoming: Frank Cius, Theodore Guy, Edward Leonard, and Walter Stischer.[20]

The remains of one pilot on the CIA list, Navy Lieutenant Commander Michael W. Wallace, whose RF-8G Crusader was shot down on the Ho Chi Minh Trail in March 1968, were later excavated from the crash site and positively identified at Central Identification Laboratory-Hawaii (CIL-HI).[21]

Agent reports and "live-sighting" accounts from defectors and refugees continued during the postwar years. A few initially seemed credible; others obviously were not. A good example of this frustrating pattern was the secondhand agent report that reached the DIA and JCRC in 1979. An American POW named "Ltc. Paul W. Mercland" was allegedly being held in a camp in Laos. There was no lieutenant colonel by that name listed as MIA. However, an Air Force major named Paul W. Bannon had been shot down near the Ban Karai Pass in Laos on July 12, 1969. The DIA speculated that the name "Mercland" might have been a distortion of "American," and that the report concerned Major Bannon.[22]

Bannon and his crewmate, First Lieutenant Peter Pike, were listed as MIA, category 4, which meant it was uncertain if the enemy had any knowledge of their fate. The circumstances of the loss indicated that the two airmen could have ejected, although no parachutes were seen, nor beepers heard. Like so many others, they simply vanished into the steep jungle mountains. No other agent report mentioned this garbled name.

Unfortunately, every other attempt made after the cease-fire to independently verify the disparate agent reports (including unconfirmed wartime reports) also resulted in failure. For example, an account of a stockadelike prison camp in a certain sector would not stand up to intense overhead reconnaissance surveillance. (It was posited that a substantial structure would be needed to keep American POWs alive for several years in the Laotian wilderness.) Equally, an intriguing reconnaissance image of such a structure could not be verified by agents' close ground surveillance. And this pattern persisted throughout the 1970s. "There was much more information than there was reliability," the intelligence officer now notes.

And agent photographs of possible American POWs working in northern Laos were soon positively identified as pictures of Frenchmen or other Europeans who had lived in the country for years. To compound the problem, scores of Soviet agricultural advisers and medical workers—surely a mixed blessing even for benighted Laos—began working in the region after the Pathet Lao takeover of the country in 1975.[23]

Despite repeated efforts, no agent managed to photograph a confirmed American prisoner.

This situation created considerable frustration among the American military and civilian intelligence officers in Thailand working on the problem. Many felt needlessly hamstrung because post-cease-fire rules of engagement meant they could not personally conduct ground reconnaissance to verify especially intriguing agent reports, as they had during the Vietnam War.

"I certainly believed that there were living American POWs in Laos," this officer states. "But we just could not prove it."

Retired Army Colonel Hayden Peake, who was the JCRC intelligence officer in 1974–75, however, does not share this officer's interpretation of the intelligence data on surviving POWs. Peake remembers most of these agents' reports as "badly flawed." He believes that the promise of reward money was the primary motive of the agents reporting live American POWs in Laos. In this regard, Peake's recollection is borne out by the earlier MACV/SOG experience in Indochina.[24]

Colonel Peake also felt at the time, and continues to believe, that the sophistication of indigenous agents was so low that they could not differentiate between the various European expatriates living freely in Laos—Soviets, missionaries, stay-behind Frenchmen from the First Indochina War, or Eastern Bloc advisers and technicians—and captive Americans. Further, Peake has no recollection of any correlation of "American" names in agents' reports with known Laos MIA cases.[25]

"Not a single case we analyzed," Peake notes, "came even close to relating to a living American." He continues to believe that a rigorous and neutral analysis of all the intelligence data available shows no surviving POWs in Laos.

However, Peake also feels strongly that it was a "stupid mistake" for the Defense Intelligence Agency and the JCRC to withhold classified casualty files from the family members concerned. He felt at the time that a careful examination of the loss incident reports would convince most family members that their loved one had not survived. But such an open examination of the classified casualty records was not an option at the time, given continuing wartime security concerns.

Others who examined the Laos POW intelligence data also had conflicting assessments. James Schlesinger, who served as director of the Central Intelligence Agency during Operation Homecoming, testified to the Select Committee on POW/MIA Affairs that he had a "high-probability assessment that people were left behind in Laos, and a medium-probability with regard to Vietnam."[26]

Retired Air Force Major General Richard Secord also testified to this committee that, based on extensive experience with intelligence operations in Laos, he believed POWs survived there "after Operation Homecoming."[27]

THE CONCLUSION THAT can be drawn from this ambiguous intelligence is that the United States never possessed conclusive proof of surviving prisoners held in Laos either by the Pathet Lao or the PAVN.

If there had been POW survivors in Laos, however, as time passed after Emmet Kay's release, the chances of their continued survival diminished. Most of the Laos MIA cases dated from the intense bombing of the Ho Chi Minh Trail in 1968 and 1969, which meant that POWs would have had to have survived in secret camps for five or six years to still be alive in the mid-1970s. There was a large clump of American MIA cases resulting from the disastrous Lam Son 719 incursion into Laos by the South Vietnamese in February 1971. But these cases almost all involved helicopter crews whose aircraft had suffered catastrophic shootdowns that left little chance of survivors. In fact, of the 354 Americans originally listed as MIA in Laos, the DIA later determined that a "significant number" should have been listed Killed in Action/Body Not Recovered.[28]

This DIA case review did not prove, however, that all or even most of the missing men in Laos had died before Operation Homecoming.

In some cases, obviously, there was little hope of resolution: If an aircraft crashed and exploded beneath the forest canopy on a remote mountain slope—on an overcast monsoon night—and there were no witnesses, the crew's fate was likely to remain forever unknown.[29]

But certainly there were other types of MIA cases in Laos, incidents in which the PAVN or the Pathet Lao probably had information. In the mid-1970s, however, when the chance of recovering any surviving POWs was still a practical option, the Indochinese Communists were in no mood to cooperate with the United States.

The mystery of possible POW survivors in Laos would not easily be solved.

AS THE DIA noted of the Laos casualty records, inaccurate after-action reports—either inadvertent or deceptive—produced a number of cases in which men who had been killed outright (KIA/BNR) were officially listed as MIA during the war. This disparity prevailed not only for Laos, but all of

Indochina. The subject of deceptive aircrew reports of shootdown survivors (when the airmen were known to be dead) that led to them being listed as missing has recently become public and controversial.

In February 1991, for example, retired Air Force Lieutenant Colonel Walter Stueck told the news media that it was an unofficial policy in his Search and Rescue squadron stationed at Nakhon Phanom, Thailand, for an aircrewman to state his preference of either being listed Killed in Action or Missing in Action if he were shot down and not rescued. The reason for the MIA preference was obvious: If a man was officially declared Killed in Action, his widow and family would receive a one-time payment of death benefits. However, if he was listed MIA, his wife and children would continue to receive his pay and allotments, plus government housing and military medical privileges, until the war ended and he was eventually declared KIA/BNR in a Presumptive Finding of Death (PFOD). Apparently, many men, especially those who were flying their second or even third combat tours in this seemingly endless war, were not above such quasi-official deception.

To prove his contention, Stueck referred to the MIA case of his squadron-mate, Lieutenant Colonel Richard A. Walsh III, an A-1J Sandy rescue pilot shot down on a Search and Rescue mission over the Ho Chi Minh Trail in Laos. Walsh was leading a group of four propeller-driven Sandys, including Sandy 03 flown by Stueck, to the crash site of an F-4 Phantom that had been shot down the previous night in the forested limestone-crag mountains northeast of the Lao village of Saravan, a logistic center on the western side of the Ho Chi Minh Trail.

As Sandy Lead, Walsh flew the first low-level reconnaissance pass over the survivor, a young Air Force lieutenant hidden beneath the forest canopy. Walsh was homing on the survivor's rescue radio beeper when the chunky aircraft took a direct hit from a 37mm antiaircraft round, nosed over, and crashed through the canopy to explode on the stony slope below.

Stueck, flying a thousand feet above, witnessed the entire incident. Yet, when the Sandy Search and Rescue pilots were debriefed, Stueck reported he was not sure if Walsh had survived because he had not seen the actual shootdown. According to the squadron's after-action report, there was a chance Walsh had survived. Walsh was declared MIA, not KIA/BNR as he should have been.

"I flat-out lied," Stueck told the press in 1991. "This is what Dick Walsh wanted," Stueck added, referring to Walsh's alleged preference of being listed as missing rather than dead in the event of a shootdown.[30]

After his statements to the press, the Air Force officially denied that such an unofficial policy could have existed. However, Stueck's contention was supported by two of his squadron-mates, and by an Air Force historian, who anonymously told the Associated Press that pilots in some units "were routinely asked their preference, and most selected MIA."[31]

If Stueck's contention is true, and this pattern of deception was wide-spread, then the original validity of the 1973 list of missing in action airmen is open to question.

Significantly, the post-cease-fire review of loss incidents undertaken by the JCRC, which carefully scrutinized after-action reports, quickly produced a substantial change in case status from MIA to KIA/BNR. Retired Army Colonel James S. Hanke was a JCRC intelligence officer in 1974. He states that the status of about 200 aircrew shootdown cases was changed from MIA to KIA/BNR in the first year after the cease-fire. "These were the most obvious cases," he adds, in which it was clear from the after-action report that the airman should have originally been declared dead, not missing. However, Colonel Hanke saw no evidence of blatant deception in these casualty reports.[32]

THE MYTH THAT "hundreds" of American missing were known to the government to have remained alive in Communist captivity in Laos grew inexorably after the cease-fire.

It was a natural human response among family members of men who had disappeared literally without a trace into the forested mountains of the Ho Chi Minh Trail to believe that their loved ones had somehow survived and were either being held captive or somehow evading capture beneath the impenetrable canopy of hardwoods. General Robert Kingston, the first commander of the post-cease-fire Joint Casualty Resolution Center (JCRC), personally encountered this heartbreaking faith early in his command. After a few months in Saigon, hobbled by the intrigues of the pro-Communist Four-Party Joint Military Commission—and the armed resistance of the Vietcong —Kingston had moved his headquarters to the American air base at Nakhon Phanom, Thailand, which stood on the banks of the Mekong River, the Thai frontier with Laos to the east. In the fall of 1973, Kingston was visited by the mothers of two American aviators who had been lost along the trail in Laos. They were strong-willed, middle-aged women, among the first of many MIA families who came to Southeast Asia following the cease-fire.

One of the mothers, trim and attractive with short gray hair, made her point forcefully. "General, we *know* our sons are alive."

"They were both tough and well trained," her companion added. "They survived. And we intend to find them."

The two mothers clung to a stubborn belief that their sons had evaded capture for years in the mountains of Laos.

From his headquarters windows, Kingston looked across the river at the somber green wall of the Annamite Cordillera rising into the haze. The chain of sharp ridges and plunging gorges, punctuated by sheer limestone pinnacles, formed the spine of the eastern Indochina peninsula. The mountains ran unbroken from the Chinese border a thousand miles to the north all the way to the Central Highlands of Vietnam, 600 miles to the southeast. This was the domain of PAVN's Group 559, the Truong Son Corps, which guarded and maintained the trail supply route from American air attack and the ravages of nature.

During one of his tours in Vietnam, Kingston had served as the senior adviser to the Army of the Republic of Vietnam (ARVN) Ranger Command. Some of these troops took part in cross-border reconnaissance and sabotage teams along the length of the mountainous trail. He knew that harsh landscape well.

But these two mothers had an almost religious faith that their sons were alive out in those mountains. Kingston suggested that, on their flight from Vientiane to Nakhon Phanom, a trip that would transit the Lao panhandle, the women observe the terrain below. In his mind Kingston could picture the tangle of interlocking ridges, so densely forested that the triple canopy seemed almost solid from the air, like the rippled, gray-green surface of a mossy boulder. Then, abruptly, the forest ended in a crazy jumble of bone-white limestone slabs, tilted like some ghost city in a science-fiction film. And everywhere man or nature had subdued the hardwood forest, unbroken thickets of thorny scrub jungle had spread in defiance of the prolonged American defoliation campaign.

Because of the chaotic relief, there were few streams in those mountains. Drinking water was scarce. Yet leeches were everywhere, as were mosquitos that carried an especially virulent strain of malaria. There were four species of deadly viper. And there were tigers. Then, of course, there was the enemy. For almost ten years America had bombed the trail and ambushed PAVN supply columns, killing and maiming tens of thousands. Prisoner debriefings revealed that PAVN medical services were primitive on the trail, and that rations were sometimes at starvation level. Also, there was never any salt, exacerbating the debilitating effects of the jungle heat. An experienced soldier like General Kingston knew the North Vietnamese would not, indeed could not, keep large numbers of American prisoners alive for long out in that cruel wilderness.

(In fact, by the end of the air war, Air Force survival and evasion instructors told their students that the enemy "did not take many prisoners in Laos."[33])

"Ma'am," Kingston said gently to the first mother, "on your way up here this morning, did you get a good look at that terrain?"

The two women stared at him, subdued.

Their confidence was shattered. During the three-hour trip over the Lao panhandle, the mothers had tried to follow Kingston's advice. The cumulative effect of gazing down at that merciless terrain had convinced them that the chances of their sons surviving were vanishingly small. The strong-willed woman with short, gray hair was convulsed with grief as she rode from the tarmac in a dusty jeep. In the VIP quarters, she grew hysterical. A flight surgeon had to sedate her. She spent the night in the dispensary. In the morning, both women, ashen and silent, left for Bangkok.[34]

The supposition that the PAVN could have maintained large hidden POW camps on the Ho Chi Minh Trail for years was not supported by reliable intelligence. Food had been in such short supply during the heavy trail bombing from 1968 to 1970 that PAVN troops transiting the trail were themselves occasionally forced to endure near starvation. And none of the surviving American POWs who were brought to North Vietnam along the trail ever encountered a sizable permanent prison camp. Nor did any South Vietnamese prisoners taken up the trail after the Communist offensive in 1972 see any sign of American captives.[35]

While the PAVN needed the trail to complete its conquest of the South, their presence on the ground kept JCRC teams from searching for MIA remains.[36] And, after the Pathet Lao gained complete control of the country in 1975, their adamant refusal—under pressure from the DRV—to allow JCRC teams into the area added to the aura of mystery surrounding those harsh mountains.

AFTER OPERATION HOMECOMING, while American MIA families either quietly accepted their grief or nursed their bitter frustration, most of the country turned its back on the Indochina nightmare.

Soon after Kissinger's last discussions with Le Duc Tho in the summer of 1973, the Yom Kippur War erupted in the Middle East and once more brought the United States and the Soviet Union to the brink of nuclear holocaust. From October 1973 until Nixon's resignation in August 1974, Kissinger was fully preoccupied with the Middle East crisis.

ON APRIL 30, 1975, the PAVN tanks finally rolled into Saigon.

The television picture of the squat T-54 battering down the ornate iron gates of Saigon's Presidential Palace was one of the quintessential wartime images—the U.S. Marines raising the Stars and Stripes on Iwo Jima's Mount Suribachi being another—that symbolized victory after an epic struggle. (It was later revealed that the Saigon tank photo had captured a reenactment, not the actual event.) But, unlike that heroic World War II photograph, the image of the Communist tank in the heart of Saigon epitomized an American defeat.

The tank photo appeared on America's television screens one day after the terrible footage of the last panicked evacuation of the American embassy. As the Huey lifted off the embassy helipad, a clot of humans hung briefly from its skids, making the helicopter seem like a crippled animal dragging its entrails. America's military impotence in Indochina was made tangible for the world to see.

Congress had easily thwarted the efforts of Gerald Ford's post-Watergate White House to unleash the only force that could have stopped the North Vietnamese juggernaut, American air power.

IN THE DEBACLE of the South's final collapse, over one hundred Americans —military deserters, missionaries, unofficial military advisers, civilian contractors, and miscellaneous adventurers—fell into Communist hands. With a few exceptions, these "civilian detainees" (the DIA's designation) were repatriated over the next eighteen months.

But in the chaotic period just before the fall of Saigon, an indeterminate number of Americans, including deserters and young civilian contractors, who had outstayed their jobs and their visas, piled onto the hundreds of crowded refugee flights leaving Tan Son Nhut Airport for the United States. When these flights landed at California air bases, the blacks and Caucasians were simply waved through immigration.[37] Therefore, an accurate count of Americans escaping Vietnam—or remaining behind to face possible Communist captivity—has never been possible.

What is significant about this Communist roundup of American civilian detainees was the eventual release of all but a few. POW/MIA activists after the war claimed that Hanoi had always planned to hold back American POWs to use as hostages in order to guarantee payment of Washington's promised reconstruction aid. But in April 1975, over a hundred Americans were captured, yet almost all were later returned alive to U.S. control, no ransom having been demanded or paid.[38]

The case of one of the detainees who died in captivity, retired CIA field officer Tucker P.E. Gougelmann, is also significant. Gougelmann was one of the agency's swashbuckling old Indochina hands, who had once commanded the Provincial Reconnaissance Units, the muscle of the Phoenix Program that attacked the Vietcong infrastructure after 1968. According to one account, he flew back to Saigon just before the fall of the city in April 1975, searching for four Vietnamese children he had adopted during the war. He had hoped to rescue them before the final Communist victory.[39]

Another version of the Gougelmann story has him retired and living in Saigon with his Vietnamese wife and children in April 1975. He is said to have refused to be intimidated into leaving Vietnam by the arrival of the victorious PAVN.[40]

In any event, Gougelmann was arrested in Saigon in June 1975.

Because the CIA failed to ensure that their South Vietnamese counterparts destroyed secret personnel and intelligence dossiers before Saigon was occupied by the PAVN, the Communists found a virtual treasure trove of information about CIA operations in South Vietnam. According to CIA officer Frank Snepp, who was in Saigon when the city fell, this was an "unpardonable mistake."[41] Gougelmann's name was either discovered in these files or was revealed by someone whose name the Communists plucked from the dossiers. He was reportedly interrogated by the KGB, pumped for information about possible other American stay-behinds and for the names of Vietnamese involved with the Phoenix Program. Although Gougelmann was a tough nut, he died in captivity a few months later, possibly from an overdose of opiates administered by his captors, following his final interrogation.

Another, younger CIA officer, workname "Lew James," was also captured in the collapse of South Vietnam. "James" was taken prisoner on April 16, 1975, when the coastal city of Phan Rang was captured by the PAVN. He was taken to Hanoi, brutally interrogated, and released six months later in October.[42]

Gougelmann's remains were returned by the Communists in September 1977 and positively identified.

Apparently, the information extracted from these two American intelligence officers, as well as from the scores of South Vietnamese former CIA agents and employees, took over a year for the Communists to process. Most American civilian detainees were not cleared for release until at least a year after the fall of Saigon.

TODAY, THOSE WHO maintain that the United States had the option of breaching the cease-fire between 1973 and 1975 to exert military pressure on North Vietnam and Laos to force the release of American prisoners, or at least to gain a better accounting for them, have obviously forgotten the prevailing political climate of those turbulent Watergate years and the subsequent disillusionment after the fall of South Vietnam.

By the summer of 1973, the White House was fully preoccupied with the Watergate crisis. And within a year, Henry Kissinger, the man who was best qualified to extract concessions from Hanoi, was himself under attack from a growing isolationist faction in Congress. Even as a successful secretary of state, Kissinger was the victim of incessant intrigues by his detractors.[43] It was not likely that he could have pressured the Vietnamese Communists into giving a "full accounting" of America's Indochina missing unless he could guarantee reconstruction aid. And he did not have that option.

In retrospect, it is clear that Hanoi's future negotiating position on the resolution of the MIA question was solidified within weeks of the 1973 cease-fire. The Communist leaders realized that—other than for mine clearing from North Vietnam's harbors—America had become militarily impotent in the region. Therefore, as Senator Brooke had told the staff of the American embassy in Saigon, America's sole remaining bargaining chip was postwar aid. Hanoi's leaders were well aware of this situation. The fact that the DRV had never intended to abide by the Paris Peace Accords did not shake Hanoi's resolve to extract payment from the United States for war damage, even though a considerable part of that destruction in South Vietnam's provincial cities was caused by the firepower of the PAVN during their final offensive in 1975.

From the American political perspective, of course, the question of reconstruction aid was rendered moot by the final Communist conquest of the South. On April 30, 1975, the day Saigon fell to the Communists, the State Department announced the extension of America's wartime trade embargo of North Vietnam (begun in 1964) to include the entire country. This act obviated any discussion of American economic aid to Vietnam for the foreseeable future.[44]

But the Vietnamese Communists still hoped to find some means of receiving this aid. On June 21, 1975, Premier Pham Van Dong wrote to twenty-seven members of Congress, specifically linking American contributions to "healing Vietnam's war wounds" with better cooperation on the MIA issue.[45]

His démarche was rebuffed out of hand. Although the United States would not provide reconstruction aid, Hanoi expected some other form of quid pro quo from America for every significant step in resolving the MIA issue.

This position would remain fundamentally unchanged for the next twenty years.

CHAPTER 5

BY THE END OF 1975, COMMUNIST FORCES IN INDOCHINA HAD CONsolidated their victories. The Communist North officially absorbed the South with the establishment of the Socialist Republic of Vietnam (SRV). The Khmer Rouge defeated America's surrogates in Cambodia and unleashed the unprecedented auto-genocide that became known as "the Killing Fields." In Laos the Pathet Lao easily overpowered their non-Communist coalition partners and established the Lao People's Democratic Republic on December 2, 1975. It appeared to many in America that the dire predictions of a domino effect following the defeat of South Vietnam had come to pass.

Certainly the remaining months of the Ford administration did not bring much progress on resolving the MIA issue. And when the U.S. and SRV delegations met in Paris in November 1976 to discuss the MIA accountability under the terms of the shattered Paris Peace Accords, the SRV position was that Vietnam could not implement the provisions of Article 8, which called for a full exchange of information on the missing, until the United States met its obligations to provide reconstruction aid under Article 21.[1]

In retaliation, the United States vetoed the Vietnamese application for membership in the United Nations. A stalemate ensued.

AS THE COMMUNIST governments consolidated their hold, the American public had to face the somber reality that its long, divisive struggle had ended in total defeat throughout Indochina, not simply in Vietnam.

Many Americans accepted the situation in Southeast Asia with indifference. Others, especially veterans of the war and families who had lost men in Indochina, went through a predictable emotional cycle of shock, disappointment, and, ultimately, refusal to concede that the bitter conflict had been fought in vain.

For some families of men still missing, this denial was to solidify into the fervent conviction that the Communists—who had so cynically broken the Paris Peace Accords—had further tricked the credulous Americans by withholding hundreds of POWs during Operation Homecoming. Further, this conspiracy theory postulated that high-level U.S. government officials were fully aware of this Communist treachery, but had chosen to ignore it by "abandoning" our surviving POWs in Indochina.[2]

Adherence to the theory of surviving POWs had its roots in the natural tendency of some families to continue hoping that their missing loved one would one day emerge from the jungle alive.[3] This fervent belief would eventually acquire many of the attributes of a cult: zealous adherents, a sense of persecution, and the conviction that its followers possessed knowledge not available to the public.

By the mid-1970s, grassroots movements were beginning in several parts of the country to champion the issue of allegedly abandoned POWs in Indochina. One of the earliest advocates of this cause was a conservative Chicago minister, the Reverend Paul Lindstrom. He had previously been active in a group called the Remember the Pueblo Committee, whose aim was to win the release of the Navy spy ship's crew held in North Korea in 1968. (Later, Lindstrom solicited funds for his Douglas MacArthur Brigade, a group of "ex-marines and European mercenaries" he hoped to raise to rescue American POWs from camps in Laos.[4])

Lindstrom achieved national prominence in autumn 1974, when he arranged a meeting in Mexico City between the mother of a missing Air Force officer and two purported Communist intermediaries. Mrs. Jean MacDonald of Chicago was convinced by Lindstrom that the two unnamed men in Mexico City had information about her son, First Lieutenant George D. MacDonald, the navigator of an AC-130 Spectre gunship shot down over the western branches of the Ho Chi Minh Trail in Laos on the night of December 21, 1972. Lindstrom told Mrs. MacDonald that the men he identified as "Southeast Asian Communists" could prove that her son was still alive.

In Mexico City, the men demanded payment ranging from $25,000 all the way up to $500,000 for tangible proof of her son's survival and to start the process of negotiating his release from Laos. They showed her a grainy photograph of a gaunt, bearded Caucasian, allegedly taken only three months earlier at an unspecified site in Laos. Mrs. MacDonald was convinced that the picture was indeed of her son.[5]

A widow, Mrs. MacDonald had no way to raise the money. She asked the agents for a letter in her son's handwriting to prove he had survived. They countered with an offer of a close-up picture, as well as her son's fingerprints. But they insisted on payment in advance.

She appealed for government assistance, demanding that action be taken to free her son from captivity. The DIA's Special Office for Prisoners of War and Missing in Action (POW/MIAs) investigated the matter. Every indication was that Lieutenant MacDonald's aircraft, Spectre 17, had suffered a catastrophic crash after a fuel explosion caused by direct hits from groundfire. Two of the enlisted crewmen manning the gunship's weapons in the cargo bay had managed to parachute to safety. But the rest of the sixteen-man crew were believed dead in the crash of the big four-engined aircraft. The State

Department's Prisoner of War Branch cautioned Mrs. MacDonald to pay no money and warned her to be cautious with Lindstrom. His actions in connection with MIA families were far from clear, and this apparent attempt to get money in Mexico City was alarming.[6]

Jean MacDonald received no further information from Lindstrom's alleged Communist agents.

(In February 1985, a JCRC team was able to excavate the crash site and retrieved a number of bone fragments. These burned and shattered bones were analyzed at the CIL-HI. Thirteen of the sixteen men on board Spectre 17—including Lieutenant George MacDonald—were positively identified, most through distinctive dental work. The crash site excavation was judged the first successful "negotiated return" field investigation in Laos. However, the MacDonald family and relatives of another airman, distrustful of the Pentagon, successfully sued the government to rescind the positive identification. But the government won its case on appeal. The MacDonald case was officially closed.[7])

As the groundswell of anger and frustration over allegedly abandoned POWs grew, particularly among veterans and MIA families, Congress reacted in a predictable manner.

Mississippi Congressman Sonny Montgomery, a conservative Democrat and decorated war veteran, created the House Select Committee on Missing Persons in Southeast Asia. Montgomery felt a strong sense of obligation to Vietnam veterans, who had been largely ignored by the war-weary country. Montgomery led two committee delegations to Indochina, meeting Vietnamese and Laotian Communist officials in 1975 and 1976.

Before these visits, Montgomery consulted Henry Kissinger for advice in dealing with the Communists. Kissinger recommended that the Montgomery Committee approach their discussions of the MIA issue with the Vietnamese "in the context of normalization" rather than strictly under the terms of the Paris Peace Accords, which, Secretary Kissinger noted, were now defunct.[8]

In all their meetings with the Indochinese Communists, therefore, Montgomery Committee members held out the promise of better relations with the United States—and implicitly, a lifting of the trade embargo—if the MIA issue was resolved.

For its part, the newly proclaimed Socialist Republic of Vietnam was adamant that no surviving American POWs remained in Vietnam. The Hanoi government continued to stress, however, that American reconstruction aid was a prerequisite to resolving MIA questions. But the Vietnamese did return three sets of MIA remains when Montgomery Committee members went to Hanoi in December 1975. This obvious use of American remains as the currency for quid pro quo exchanges between America and Vietnam set a pattern that would last for almost twenty years.

In one of the committee's widely publicized hearings, Assistant Secretary of State Philip Habib, who had been one of Kissinger's chief Paris negotia-

tors, testified that North Vietnam had always "bracketed the release of prisoners with what they described as 'U.S. responsibility for war damage in
Vietnam,' " into a single, indivisible negotiating point.[9] That continued to be
Montgomery's experience as regarded the release of POW remains. But
media accounts of this SRV position were interpreted by some as proof that
the Vietnamese secretly meant to ransom live POWs for Kissinger's promised
billions.

Montgomery, however, came to the conclusion that there were no surviving POWs in Indochina, either to be ransomed or to be somehow otherwise
"discovered" and freed following American concessions. He had given the
Communists ample opportunity to release prisoners who might have remained behind after Operation Homecoming. The Vietnamese and Laotians
made no offers.

NEVERTHELESS, THE ISSUE of Vietnamese ransom demands for live POWs was
to remain a controversy until the present day. During his deposition to the
Senate Select Committee on POW/MIA Affairs, former Secretary of State
Henry Kissinger directly addressed the question of ransom demands: "I
would not have been surprised at all if they had, three months later [after
the Paris Peace Accords], told us that they had just discovered 50 prisoners
and wanted $2 billion for them. But that did not happen."[10] The select
committee investigation later established that the issue of ransom was at
least discussed on two occasions during the first Reagan administration.

The first such discussion contains intriguing but inconclusive elements. A
Secret Service agent on the presidential detail approached the committee
through his attorney to state that he had overheard a conversation among
President Reagan, Vice President George Bush, National Security Adviser
Richard Allen, and CIA Director William Casey early in 1981 in the Roosevelt
Room of the White House. This conversation purportedly concerned an
"offer" from Vietnam transmitted through a third country, possibly China or
Canada, offering to ransom live American POWs for $4.5 billion.[11]

The committee took these allegations very seriously and began a thorough investigation. Unfortunately, they were unable to depose the Secret
Service agent under oath due to a Treasury Department determination that
such testimony would impair the ability of the Secret Service to guard the
President in the future. However, the committee was able to depose former
National Security Adviser Richard Allen. He at first recalled that there had
been such a discussion, but requested that he be allowed to review his
notes and diaries for that period. When Allen did so, he discovered that the
conversation had actually occurred on another occasion, when he discussed
rumors of ransom demands with POW activists, including Red McDaniel,
John M.G. Brown, and Representative Billy Hendon. Allen wrote the Committee: "It appears that my uncertainty during the deposition was justified,

and there never was a 1981 meeting about the return of POW/MIAs for $4 billion."[12]

Committee investigators scoured the files of the State Department, National Security Council, and the CIA searching for any evidence of such an offer. They found none. Select committee chief counsel William Codinha is adamant that this issue was investigated with great rigor. In order for such an offer to have circulated among the President's staff, the National Security Council, the Vice President's staff, and the executives of the Central Intelligence Agency, there would have to have been at least some paper trail or personal recollections. The committee discovered none. "A conspiracy to cover up such an offer," Codinha said in an interview, "would have involved at least several hundred people."[13]

Moreover, as he and other committee investigators have noted, there exists such a great financial incentive for retired military and government personnel with direct knowledge (and possibly documentary evidence) of such a sensational offer, that it is illogical none have come forward to sell their story either to the tabloid press and television or in book form.

The second offer allegedly occurred in 1984, and involved a Southeast Asian country, reportedly Indonesia. A man named I. Irving Davidson brought the offer to the NSC. Davidson said that a senior retired Indonesian general wanted to broker an offer from Vietnam to sell MIA remains and "possible live POWs." National Security Adviser Robert McFarlane took the offer seriously enough to dispatch his assistant Richard Childress to Vietnam to investigate the report. Childress later reported that the offer involved only MIA remains, not live prisoners.[14]

In 1992 select committee chief counsel William Codinha traveled to Southeast Asia and met with the retired general and his brother. The general stated the offer had been for remains only, but his brother remembered live POWs being offered for ransom. The general had a specific recollection that the Vietnamese wanted "several hundred million dollars" for the return of the remains of fifty American MIAs. Both men said they could reopen the channel to Vietnam for a discussion of purchasing remains, but neither spoke of live POWs.[15]

In retrospect it seems probable that this 1984 ransom offer concerned a substantial number of American MIA remains, possibly in the hands of active-duty or retired PAVN officers. It is improbable that such an offer could have been made without the knowledge and tacit approval of the Vietnamese Communist Party and state security apparatus.

IN DECEMBER 1976, the Montgomery Committee made its final report. Addressing a news conference, Montgomery announced his findings. "The sad conclusion is that there is no evidence that any of these missing Americans are still alive." He reiterated that his committee had reviewed all the available intelligence and had pushed the Indochinese governments to provide a better accounting for American MIAs. He was now convinced that no Americans remained alive in captivity in Indochina. "This is a final sad chapter to our involvement in Southeast Asia," Montgomery added.[16]

During the fifteen months of the committee investigation, the Pentagon had suspended the casualty status review process, which had been advancing inexorably toward Presumptive Finding of Death in almost every POW/MIA case. The committee now recommended that this review be resumed.

That recommendation was immediately attacked by the growingly vocal body of MIA activists. They were championed by Representative Benjamin A. Gilman, an upstate New York Republican who had served on the panel, but had rejected its conclusions. Gilman believed that Presumptive Findings of Death would relieve the Indochinese Communists of the responsibility of providing the fullest possible accounting for our missing men.[17]

ON OCTOBER 26, 1973, the U.S. Air Force officially changed the casualty status of Joseph C. Morrison, promoted to colonel since his loss, to Killed in Action/Body Not Recovered. (The casualty status of San D. Francisco, promoted to major after his loss, was changed to KIA/BNR in June 1978.)

BY 1982, THE armed services had finally overcome a stiff legal struggle with family members and issued Presumptive Findings of Death for every American missing in Indochina, with the exception of Colonel Charles Shelton, the Air Force pilot shot down over the mountain wilderness of northeast Laos in 1965. Shelton, promoted from captain after his loss, remained classified as a Prisoner of War—even though there was unusually good intelligence that he had not survived captivity—in an effort to assuage the politically active MIA family lobby.[18]

WITHIN WEEKS OF his inauguration, Jimmy Carter appointed United Autoworkers President Leonard Woodcock to head a commission to seek POW/MIA information from Vietnam and Laos, within the context of discussing "mutual relations."

When the Woodcock Commission visited Hanoi in March 1977, the Vietnamese turned over the remains of twelve American POWs. Again, the SRV adamantly denied that any living American POWs remained in Vietnam. But Hanoi promised to create an office to collect information on MIAs. The Vietnamese, however, stressed that the United States must take matching steps to focus on economic aid and reconstruction of war damage.

On March 24, 1977, the Woodcock Commission reported that there was "no evidence to indicate that any American POWs from the Indochina conflict remain alive." The Woodcock Commission's final report called for regular diplomatic discussions between Vietnam and the United States aimed at resolving the MIA issue and restoring relations. President Carter endorsed Woodcock's recommendations.[19]

During subsequent diplomatic discussions in Paris, the Vietnamese repeatedly raised the issue of the $3.25 billion promised in the secret Nixon–Pham Van Dong letter. When the American side refused to link the MIA issue to that specific aid package, the Vietnamese called a separate press conference to publicly link reconstruction aid with better cooperation on the MIA issue.[20]

Despite the lack of progress, the United States supported Vietnam's application to join the United Nations in July 1977.

On September 30 of that year, Vietnam returned thirty-three sets of remains, specifically linking this repatriation to the improved spirit of cooperation between the two countries.

Vietnam repatriated more than forty sets of remains in 1978, again citing the Carter administration's stated policy of normalizing relations.[21]

Then the promising situation was suddenly reversed. On December 25, 1978, Vietnam invaded Cambodia.

In retaliation, the Carter administration intensified the existing economic embargo against Vietnam early in 1979. And the newly prosperous nations of Southeast Asia were pressured to comply with both the spirit and the letter of the harsh trade restrictions. Even more damaging, International Monetary Fund and World Bank loans to Vietnam were now almost completely extinguished. And Japan, the principal non-Communist source of development aid, suspended its assistance indefinitely.

In February 1979, the People's Republic of China, sponsor of the Cambodian Khmer Rouge, retaliated by invading across Vietnam's northern frontier mountains.

The casualties Vietnam suffered in Cambodia and the subsequent border war with China in many ways eclipsed memories of the long war with the United States.

The situation worsened. Hanoi unleashed a pogrom against its sizable ethnic Chinese and Khmer minorities. The Politburo intensified the military draft and imposed draconian taxation, especially in the still relatively affluent former South Vietnam. Refugees swarmed out of Vietnam's myriad fishing ports in a seemingly endless flotilla of small boats. Many were ethnic Chinese, but a large proportion were southern Vietnamese who had welcomed PAVN troops as liberators in 1975.[22]

Gripped by this new struggle, Hanoi was not willing to seek better relations with the United States by diverting manpower and resources into an effort to resolve the MIA issue. Moreover, as the Carter administration appeared to favor the Khmer Rouge in the conflict, the Vietnamese Communists were not about to open their military archives to American investigators seeking sensitive and embarrassing wartime information on the fates of POWs, the disclosure of which could further isolate Vietnam on the international stage. And, from a tactical perspective, the PAVN was more opposed than ever to allowing U.S. military teams freedom of movement in the region to hunt for MIA remains.

Hanoi's leaders also convinced their weaker comrades and de facto allies in Vientiane to follow their lead. What little progress the JCRC had made in Laos was completely halted after the Vietnamese invasion of Cambodia. Clearly, resolution of the Laos MIA mystery would depend on an overall improvement of the Indochina situation. But such an improvement did not seem in the offing in 1979.

To those Americans charged with achieving "the fullest possible accounting" for Indochina MIAs—primarily the DIA's Special Office for POW/MIAs and the JCRC—this situation brought renewed frustration. Analysts knew that Hanoi possessed far more information on missing Americans than it had admitted; some speculated that the SRV could provide a good accounting for *most* of the approximately 300 bona fide MIA casualties that had occurred in populated regions of North Vietnam.

But Communist Vietnam's tentative overtures to the West had ended. Embroiled in Cambodia, threatened by the military might of China, Vietnam turned inward, drawing strength from an atavistic xenophobia and spartan resolve that had served it well through centuries of struggle.

The successors of Ho Chi Minh had accomplished his goal of reuniting Vietnam under the red banner of socialism. But the defeat of the South Vietnamese "puppets" and their American sponsors had been a Pyrrhic victory.

Vietnam was now more isolated than at any time in its modern history.[23]

PART 2

CHAPTER 6

NEAR MIDNIGHT ON THE BLUSTERY EVENING OF JANUARY 14, 1980, Ted Schweitzer stood on the deck of a Thai fishing boat 400 yards off the islet of Ko Kra. Overhead the northeast monsoon clouds churned by in the wind. Breakers smashed on the island's jungle headland fringed by a white coral beach. The Thai captain dropped his anchor and shut down the thudding diesel engine.

In the sudden quiet, Schweitzer could hear screams and indistinct shouts from the beach. He knew the island well. As a field officer for the United Nations High Commissioner for Refugees in Thailand, Schweitzer had journeyed out to this solitary islet three times in the previous few weeks to rescue Vietnamese boat people refugees from the Thai pirates who preyed on them.

This tide of refugees had swollen steadily during 1979, following the Vietnamese invasion of Cambodia.

To compound the refugee crisis in Indochina, tens of thousands of Cambodians—many Khmer Rouge combatants or their families—fled across the land border to Thailand.

As a newly appointed United Nations refugee officer, Ted Schweitzer found himself at the center of the largest forced migration of displaced persons since the Communist victory in China.

Normally when he heard that boat people had been stranded on Ko Kra, Schweitzer obtained assistance from the Thai Marine Police, who provided him a patrol launch. But after spotting dozens of half-naked boat people on the island during a helicopter patrol two days earlier, he had been unable to arrange the assistance of the regular police vessel.[1]

Schweitzer had also seen two Thai fishing boats, with the names and registration numbers painted over, which he knew belonged to a notorious Thai pirate gang. He realized that waiting for calmer weather would mean abandoning these refugees to the mercies of the pirates. The women and girls would suffer gang rape, the men would be beaten, and the entire group would be stripped and robbed of their meager possessions.

So Schweitzer hired a local fisherman to make the trip, paying the man $500 from his own pocket.

But the weather had been even worse than forecast and now the old fisherman prudently refused to venture into the rocky shallows until after sunrise.

As the half-moon slid behind the overcast, Schweitzer saw campfires flare on the beach. Again he heard women's screams, followed by hoarse bellows and laughter. The pirates were tracking down the Vietnamese refugee women in their hiding places and dragging them to the beach.

I have to do something, he thought. And, without further hesitation, he stripped to his undershorts and dived into the surging chill sea. He was a strong swimmer, but hadn't anticipated the power of the current, driven by the monsoon wind around the headland.

THE IMPULSIVE ACT was typical of Ted Schweitzer. A stubborn sense of purpose and dedication to causes he considered morally correct, if not indeed righteous, was a personal hallmark, as was independent action.

In the early 1970s, he was recruited as the librarian at the international school in Bangkok, Thailand. As with so many other young American men at that time, Schweitzer was immediately captivated by Southeast Asia. When his school contract ended, he signed on as a "media consultant," working for the Defense Department at Ramasun Station, the Army Security Agency's top secret intelligence-gathering post near the sprawling American Air Force base at Udorn in northeastern Thailand.

His job there was hardly cloak-and-dagger: He oversaw the station's sensitive secret archives. But during his tenure at Ramasun, he was dispatched on temporary duty to Phnom Penh and Battambang, Cambodia, to help salvage documents and cryptographic equipment from the American military mission, just before the capital fell to the Khmer Rouge. This dangerous assignment left a marked impression on Schweitzer. He was able to function well in the confusion of the besieged city. And he discovered that he had a previously unrecognized affinity for this type of adventure.

After eight years in Southeast Asia, Schweitzer had no intention of returning to the banalities of middle-class life in the American Midwest.

His fluency in Thai and French and his expertise managing computerized information systems helped him successfully compete for the field officer position with the United Nations High Commissioner for Refugees. But, typically, he chafed at the bureaucratic make-work in the main regional UNHCR office in Bangkok.

"I'm a *field* officer," he told Zia Rizvi, the UNHCR's senior man in Southeast Asia. "I'm not here to shuffle paper, but to help refugees. Send me to the field."[2]

Schweitzer was assigned to the port of Songkhla, living in a comfortable stucco house dating from the Portuguese colonial era. But his relations with the Thais here became strained when he rescued sixteen young Vietnamese refugee girls from a Songkhla brothel, owned in part by a local police official.

Despite warnings that the police were now reluctant to protect him, Schweitzer refused to remain safely on shore like a good bureaucrat when there were people who needed him on this island.

IT TOOK SCHWEITZER an hour to swim the 400 yards from the fishing boat to the island. He was exhausted when he finally hauled himself onto the base of a slippery rock cliff on the island's western tip. The current had swept him onto this dangerous landing place. The swell broke harshly across the exposed ledge, slamming him down repeatedly onto the jagged rock faces. Before he could struggle onto the rocky cliff, his arms and legs were slashed and ran with blood. Now he also had to think of his own survival, not just the plight of the refugees. The cliff was near vertical for over 200 feet. When he reached a ledge, he no longer had the strength to pull himself up.

Then he heard voices above on the clifftop. Schweitzer yelled. Two Vietnamese refugees descended toward the ledge. When the older man saw a battered, bleeding European, he exclaimed in English, "Oh, we are saved!" One of them took off his trousers and used them as a hoist to pull Schweitzer up.

After the refugees bandaged Schweitzer's legs with strips torn from a white shirt, they explained the situation. There were about eighty refugees on the island, the survivors of a capsized boat. They had been marooned there for over a week with no food and little water. Two days before, as the gale mounted, the Thai pirate boats had arrived and anchored in the sheltered shallows near the beach. The pirates had immediately attacked the refugees, killing several men with clubs and swords and driving the rest into the jungle. Then they had tracked down the women and girls and methodically begun an orgy of brutal rape.

Schweitzer had regained his strength by now. The two men who had found him led him down the reverse slope and through the jungle to a clearing where other refugees, thirty-five hungry, despondent men and boys, were huddled. Some had fashioned crude clubs and spears from tree limbs.

"We've got to help the women," he explained, his chest still heaving from exertion.

An older refugee, a man who had the quiet manner of an intellectual, shook his head in resignation. "They are too well armed."

Schweitzer shook his head. "They'll listen to *me*."

His attitude was a mixture of righteous confidence and ingrained naïveté that many he worked with mistook for arrogance. Schweitzer was more stubborn than arrogant. Tenacity was a common attribute among his Midwestern German family. This characteristic—and his affinity for adventure —would lead him into unusual situations over the next ten years.

Half threatening, half cajoling, Schweitzer managed to rally his improbable band to climb the jungle hill and approach the pirates' campfires. When they were within sight of the camp, Schweitzer strode forward alone into the flaring light. "I am a representative of the United Nations," he shouted in Thai. "Release those women."

He turned back toward the Vietnamese men and urged them forward into the firelight. They advanced cautiously.

Now the pirates leaped up from their tarps and blankets to brandish a motley collection of weapons—rusty pistols, lengths of pipe, knives, and axes. "Get back!" they shouted.

Schweitzer knew if they retreated now the pirates would chase them back down the beach and attack before they could reach the safety of the jungle. Again he shouted in his best gruffly authoritarian Thai. "If you kill these refugees, nobody will care." He paused for effect. "But I'm a UN officer. If you kill me, they'll look for me, they'll find me, and they'll hunt you down."

Schweitzer stood alone in the firelight, glaring at the pirates. A few tough young Thais swaggered toward him, but others appeared confused. A lean six feet, Schweitzer was smaller than many of the big Thai fishermen. And the look of fierce determination in his eyes—which he hoped masked the sudden onset of terror—made him appear even more menacing.

The pirates slowly backed down the beach away from him, and the Vietnamese refugee men surged forward, swinging their crude clubs and fists. The naked women and girls scurried into the elephant grass. Some of the young girls had been raped so violently that they could only drag themselves across the sand like injured crabs.

Then the pirates rushed to counterattack. In the wild melee on the beach, Schweitzer was clubbed over the head with a lead pipe, knocked to the ground and kicked unconscious.

When Schweitzer regained consciousness at dawn, his vision was blurred and he could barely stand upright. More alarming, his urine ran dull red from the kidney injury he had suffered in the night. But with the pirates gone, he managed to rally his refugees and form a human chain to swim them to the safety of the fishing boat anchored offshore.[3]

Over the next four months, Schweitzer made dozens of rescue missions to the offshore islands, saving over a thousand refugees. But twice more he had to physically confront the pirates, and again he was beaten and even stabbed.

By May 1980, his health seriously jeopardized, he reluctantly accepted a transfer to UNHCR headquarters in Geneva, where he underwent two emergency kidney operations. In 1983, the combination of kidney and spine injuries forced him to take a disability retirement from the civil service.

Schweitzer found himself prematurely retired, a beached, restless expatriate, living in the ersatz tropical luxury of the Florida Gulf coast. But he could not resist the magnetic pull of Indochina. Using his savings, Schweitzer founded the Southeast Asia Rescue Foundation, a nonprofit charity dedicated to assisting refugees and other needy people in Indochina. Schweitzer hoped to eventually establish a pirate-free sanctuary for boat people on the beaches of Thailand and Malaysia.

He was again motivated by a mixture of self-confidence and almost naive optimism. He firmly believed that the nations of the West cared enough about Indochinese refugees to establish an unprecedented quasi-governmental, multinational maritime patrol force in the South China Sea and along the coasts of Thailand and Malaysia. After several years of stubborn effort, however, his international force of refugee guardians remained an unfulfilled dream. Vietnamese boat people still plied the Gulf of Thailand in flimsy vessels and were still mercilessly plundered by Thai and Cambodian pirates.

So Schweitzer shifted his attention from the immediate problem of boat people refugees to the more fundamental issue of the desperate poverty in war-shattered Vietnam. If he could help improve economic conditions in Vietnam, he reasoned with typically grandiose confidence, perhaps fewer refugees would be forced by desperation to flee their country.

At the time, he had no way of knowing the nature of the bizarre odyssey on which he had embarked.

CHAPTER 7

BETWEEN THE INDOCHINESE COMMUNIST VICTORIES IN 1975 AND THE late 1980s, the United States sent four separate official delegations to Southeast Asia to seek information on MIAs. None of them achieved a significant breakthrough on resolving the issue.

Congressman Sonny Montgomery led his committee to Laos and Vietnam in December 1975 and August 1978; President Carter dispatched Leonard Woodcock to Hanoi in 1977; President Ronald Reagan sent Ambassador Richard Armitage to Vietnam on three occasions in the early 1980s to discuss MIAs; and Reagan named retired Chairman of the Joint Chiefs of Staff General John Vessey presidential special emissary to Vietnam on POW/MIA affairs in 1987. Following each group's travel to Indochina, the Vietnamese released a token offering of American MIA remains, but refused to cooperate further unless the United States offered concrete steps toward lifting the economic embargo and ending Vietnam's diplomatic isolation.[1]

Returning the remains of dead Americans—either POWs who had died in captivity, or men who were killed during their loss incidents—was the SRV's method of keeping the Americans focused on the issue without actually resolving it. Despite repeated denials, there can be little doubt that Hanoi used the return of American remains as a bargaining chip in a quid pro quo process they hoped would end with the embargo lifted and diplomatic relations restored between the two countries. In fact, it is possible to track the flow of the 381 confirmed American remains returned between 1974 and 1992 to chart the thaws and chills in the relations between America and Vietnam.[2]

After Carter intensified the economic embargo, following Vietnam's invasion of Cambodia, the trickle of American remains from Vietnam stopped completely for two years. When it began again in 1981, the annual total of repatriated remains averaged below ten until 1985, when thirty-eight sets of remains were returned.

Significantly, this largest annual repatriation of American remains since the cease-fire followed Richard Armitage's high-level diplomatic visits to Hanoi, during which both sides agreed to treat the resolution of the MIA question as a "humanitarian issue."

Armitage skillfully maneuvered the Vietnamese on this issue; personnel from Vietnam's Office for Seeking Missing Persons (VNOSMP) were flown to the Central Identification Laboratory in Honolulu (CIL-HI) to discuss "technical cooperation" in remains recovery. Even though all parties concerned realized the VNOSMP could not act independently, the front organization gave the Vietnamese a needed pretext to begin treating the MIA issue as a humanitarian, not a political-military problem.[3] One benefit of this improved situation was the resumption of joint Vietnamese-American excavations of American aircraft crash sites. This program had begun after the 1973 cease-fire, but had been quickly derailed by the wartime resistance of the Communists. Now JCRC teams could work directly with counterparts from the VNOSMP to try to locate remains at battlefield graves and crash sites.

Armitage and his Vietnamese counterparts also agreed to separately pursue the subject of economic aid and renewed diplomatic relations. This "expressed lack of linkage" allowed both countries to save face, and was the pivot Reagan used to name General Vessey the President's special emissary to Vietnam on POW/MIA affairs in April 1987.[4]

Although Vessey's mission to Vietnam began auspiciously, he would eventually encounter the same stubborn insistence that every positive step by the Vietnamese be matched by an American concession. To some Reagan administration officials watching Vessey's progress, this was proof that the Hanoi Communists were manipulating a patently humanitarian issue. But to officials of the Socialist Republic of Vietnam, it had been the Americans themselves who, through the terms of the economic embargo, continued to link improved relations between the two countries with progress on the MIA issue and other humanitarian questions.

So, despite public denials of linkage, the Vietnamese officials with whom Vessey dealt privately expected "progress" toward lifting the embargo and ending Vietnam's diplomatic isolation in exchange for each major step in resolving the MIA problem.[5] But they had not counted on the fact that Jack Vessey could be just as stubborn and patient as they.

President Reagan enlarged Vessey's humanitarian portfolio to include the power to negotiate the release of former Saigon officials and ARVN officers from reeducation camps, the emigration of Amerasian children of American servicemen, and the establishment of the Orderly Departure Program so that family members remaining in Vietnam could be reunited with their families in America. An old artillery man with a distinguished combat record —and a veteran trench fighter of internecine combat within the Beltway— Vessey stuck to his guns. He refused to discuss any issue other than MIAs and the three adjunct humanitarian questions.[6]

Vessey's stated goal was first to determine if any Americans remained alive and were held "against their will" in Vietnam. Next, he was to achieve the "fullest possible accounting" for all the 2,265 Americans officially unaccounted for after Operation Homecoming in 1973 and the fall of South Vietnam in 1975.

The Vietnamese, from Foreign Minister Nguyen Co Thach, down through every party and PAVN official with whom Vessey's delegations met, categorically denied that any American POW had remained in Vietnam after 1973. (The issue of Marine Private Robert Garwood, other stay-behinds, and deserters will be discussed below.) Vessey noted this official Vietnamese position but refused to officially accept it on behalf of the U.S. government. Instead, he concentrated on the MIAs.

Vessey and his team realized that the vast majority of these cases involved men who had not survived their loss incident. Between the mid-1970s and 1980, however, pressure from MIA families and their congressional allies had forced the Defense Department to add all the Killed in Action/Body Not Recovered cases to the new category "Unaccounted For." By December 2, 1980, DIA's "Unaccounted For" list had grown to over 2,500, the highest total at any time either during or after the war.[7]

This move had much more to do with Washington politics than with the realistic expectation that the reclassification would somehow resurrect American airmen whose bodies had been pulverized when their fighter-bombers, heavily laden with fuel and munitions, had collided with cloud-covered limestone pinnacles along the Ho Chi Minh Trail, or men who had sunk to the bottom of the Tonkin Gulf, still strapped in the cockpits of crippled Navy jets.

So instead of attempting the impossible by rigidly demanding that the Vietnamese account for every American on the expanded MIA list, Vessey negotiated an agreement that the two sides focus on a much smaller list of "Discrepancy Cases," an expansion of the list Kissinger had brought to Hanoi in February 1973. These were Americans who met certain specific criteria: They were either known to have been taken prisoner—some were photographed in captivity or positively identified by other American POWs—or they were observed by other Americans (often wingmen or Search and Rescue forces) to have been captured alive; another category was Americans lost under circumstances in which survival seemed likely or at least probable, i.e. men who were alive on the ground when the enemy overran their position.

Vessey adopted the DIA's "priority" hierarchy classification system for these cases. Category 1 was individuals known or suspected to have been POWs and so listed by their services, but who were not repatriated. Category 2 was individuals suspected to have survived their loss and have been taken prisoner. Category 3 was other cases where there was some intelligence that an Indochinese government should have known the man's fate.[8] And category 4 covered cases where it was unlikely the enemy had information.

As various offices of the Defense Department, including the DIA's POW/MIA branch, sifted through the MIA records on Vessey's behest, lists were compiled with varying totals. At one point the cumulative list of priority cases of all three categories reached almost 300. But, as Vessey was dealing with the Vietnamese Communists, he was most interested in cases in which Americans were lost under circumstances that suggested that the Vietnamese —not the Laotian or Cambodian governments—had additional information about their fates. And, because the Vietnamese Communists had controlled the areas in all three countries where most of these losses had occurred, Vessey would focus his efforts on Hanoi. Eventually, it was hoped, a larger, well-structured Defense Department effort could be mounted for Laos and Cambodia.[9]

Under this criterion, a priority list of 135 MIA cases was eventually established.

DIA CASE NUMBER 1329, the record of Major Joseph Morrison and First Lieutenant San Francisco, was on the "Vessey Priority List."

SINCE THE LATE 1980s, when General Vessey began to press the Vietnamese to help resolve these 135 MIA cases, confusion has grown concerning his discrepancy case list. The general public was not aware that no Laos cases appeared on the list, even though several of the most glaring discrepancies —men whose photographs as live POWs appeared in Eastern Bloc publications—were captured in Laos.

This category included three of the most famous POWs who remained unaccounted for after the cease-fire, men who were implicitly referred to in the Eagleburger-Richardson memorandum of March 28, 1973. Air Force Captain David L. Hrdlicka was an F-105 fighter-bomber pilot shot down in May 1965 over the rugged mountains of Samneua Province of Laos not far from the North Vietnamese border. He was seen by flight members circling above to have been led away by enemy soldiers. A year later, his picture appeared in the Moscow edition of *Pravda,* his hands bound, being prodded down a jungle trail by a soldier wearing a camouflage cape, probably a member of PAVN, not the Pathet Lao. Reliable intelligence reports indicated he died in captivity. But in 1990, because Vietnam stubbornly refused to acknowledge responsibility for American prisoners in Laos, Vessey did not include Captain Hrdlicka on the discrepancy list he took to Hanoi.

This policy also applied to the case of Air Force pilot Charles Shelton, lost in 1965, forty miles south of Hrdlicka's shootdown, and also photographed in captivity. The third man in this category was Eugene Debruin, a civilian C-46 cargo plane crewman, shot down in 1963, carrying supplies to anti-Communist guerrillas in the Lao panhandle. Both these men were reliably reported to have died in captivity, but the Vietnamese refused to admit any knowledge of the circumstances of their deaths.[10]

In fact, General Vessey's discrepancy list contained very few cases in which there was irrefutable evidence of Americans who had fallen into Vietnamese hands. Almost 80 percent of the list—105 cases—concerned ground troops lost in South Vietnam. Many were believed to have been captured by either Vietcong or PAVN troops and had probably died in captivity.

Of the twenty-eight North Vietnam cases on Vessey's discrepancy list, none were positively known to have been captured alive. But there was certainly strong evidence for capture in several of these cases.

Air Force Captain Bradley G. Cuthbert, for example, an RF-4C reconnaissance pilot shot down by a SAM missile in North Vietnam's Quang Binh Province in November 1968, was seen alive in his parachute by his crewman, Captain Mark Ruhling, who was captured shortly after reaching the ground. Ruhling was repatriated in 1973, but never saw Cuthbert alive on the ground. In August 1989, a team from the American JCRC were given one of Captain Cuthbert's dog tags by villagers near the shootdown site. They also reported rumors that Cuthbert had been hacked to death by woodcutters when he landed in the forest near their camp. The JCRC team could not locate a grave.

Although Vessey's Vietnamese counterparts professed no knowledge of such incidents, he and his colleague, General Robert Kingston, suspected that the PAVN had fairly accurate information on many such cases in which irate villagers killed downed American aircrew.[11] In fact, many of the North Vietnam discrepancy cases were similar to the Cuthbert incident, but lacked corroborating rumors of execution by civilians.

Using DIA and JCRC intelligence files, Vessey was able to determine several men on this list had probably died at the hands of regular or auxiliary PAVN troops, not ill-disciplined villagers.

THE CASE OF Major Joseph Morrison, Lieutenant San Francisco, and the loss of Grommet 02 was a prime example of this subcategory. Even though Hanoi had always stubbornly insisted that the steep Truong Son foothills just north of the Demilitarized Zone had been a depopulated wilderness during the war, both sides knew that the area had concealed a dense concentration of PAVN forces. And it was well established that Morrison and Francisco had safely ejected and parachuted into those jungle hills. Further, the after-action report made it clear that the wingman saw them land less than a kilometer from a fortified PAVN encampment. He had also seen PAVN soldiers jogging along the trails as the parachutes floated toward the earth. But the jungle was so dense that both airmen were able to evade immediate capture.

But to Vessey's and the JCRC's frustration, the Vietnamese had steadfastly denied for years that they had any knowledge of Morrison's or Francisco's fates, despite the evidence that both men had been surrounded by PAVN troops.[12] On August 4, 1987, the JCRC in Bangkok passed a detailed case narrative file—in effect a complete collection of everything the U.S. government knew about the loss of Grommet 02 on November 25, 1968—to the SRV embassy. This was one of the first transfers of such detailed American MIA case information to the Vietnamese following Vessey's preliminary meetings with Foreign Minister Nguyen Co Thach. The Vietnamese promised to take action on the case.[13]

Vessey's challenge in resolving such cases was twofold. First, he had to convince the Vietnamese that America had compelling evidence that Hanoi possessed records that could resolve the cases. Then, he had to persuade them that America wanted the information for purely humanitarian reasons, not to use as evidence to bolster claims of atrocities or war crimes.

He was not overly optimistic about his chances for success.

But for the first four years of his assignment, Vessey stubbornly concentrated on resolving these cases. He made it clear to the Vietnamese that the only way America would accept their assurances that no living American prisoners remained in Vietnam—or elsewhere in Indochina under Vietnamese custody—was to resolve the discrepancy cases. After considerable foot-dragging, Vietnam agreed to renew cooperation on the MIA issue and to focus on both the discrepancy cases and on locating documentation about American POWs listed as having died in captivity in either South Vietnam or in Communist captivity in adjacent Cambodia.

Meanwhile, Vessey also helped facilitate the repatriation of American remains, which the Vietnamese periodically "discovered," ostensibly in battlefield graves or at crash sites. This was a fiction to which Vessey was obliged to acquiesce in order not to rupture the accounting process.

However, both sides recognized that the discovery of most of these remains had in fact occurred years before. In many cases, the Americans had died or been killed in captivity and their remains kept in storage to be doled out as macabre bargaining chips.

Thus in 1987, eight sets of skeletal remains returned by Vietnam were identified as known American MIAs by the Pentagon's Central Identification Laboratory in Hawaii.

Now joint field surveys and excavations were conducted. American teams from the JCRC and the DIA's Stony Beach office in Bangkok joined Vietnamese counterparts to dig through crash sites in search of American remains and interview local Vietnamese who might have knowledge of shootdowns or other incidents in which Americans were lost. In some cases, it was suspected that the Vietnamese were "salting" crash sites with remains taken from storage.

In 1988, sixty-two sets of American remains were repatriated, some coming from crash sites, but many collected separately by the Vietnamese.

Lacking a modern forensic laboratory in Indochina, it was difficult for the American field teams to determine which remains were authentic new discoveries and which were contributed from a "warehouse" that DIA had information existed in Hanoi in the late 1970s. But detailed studies at the CIL-HI eventually separated the two categories. By March 1992, forensic anthropologists had studied 108 sets of remains turned over by the Vietnamese government. Twenty-eight of these sets showed evidence of having been kept in storage. This included bones sprayed with preservatives; other sets of remains showed signs of having been sanded in an effort to remove preservatives. The scientists also discovered that many bones showed little mineral depletion, unlike a skeleton left unprotected at a tropical crash site.[14]

Tran Vien Lac, a Vietnamese mortician who defected in 1979, had testified to congressional committees and informed the DIA during debriefings that he had helped process 452 sets of skeletal remains, which he was told were those of Americans. He worked on this project in Hanoi for two years beginning in 1975. Remains that had been processed, Lac said, were placed in storage to be released to the Americans as Hanoi deemed appropriate in order to gain concessions from the United States.[15]

The American position at the time was to accept these remains, whatever their provenance, as their return helped to close open MIA cases (including some on the discrepancy list) and ease the anguish of bereaved families.

But General Vessey, experienced JCRC investigators, and DIA analysts all recognized that digging up shattered aircraft wreckage at remote crash sites was not the optimum method of resolving cases like the loss of Grommet 02 and the disappearance of Morrison and Francisco. The Americans knew the Vietnamese Communist bureaucrats were meticulous recordkeepers. If any information existed on American MIAs, it would be found in Vietnamese military archives.

But the Vietnamese continued to deny that such archives existed.

By 1988, the situation had reached a stalemate.

FOLLOWING HIS RESIGNATION from the UN, Ted Schweitzer returned to Indochina in August 1988. He now focused his Southeast Asia Rescue Foundation on providing donated American medical supplies and equipment to Vietnam rather than on saving boat people. As he undertook this charitable work, he had no indication that he was about to become embroiled in the emotional cauldron of the POW/MIA controversy.

Schweitzer was received warmly by the Foreign Ministry of the Socialist Republic of Vietnam on his first trips to Hanoi. He was afraid that they might think that he was just another narcissistic American leftist, more interested in photo opportunities to demonstrate "solidarity" with heroic revolutionaries than in providing constructive assistance to a desperately isolated country.

But, in his typically forthright manner, Schweitzer told his escort from the Foreign Ministry, Ambassador Nguyen Can, "I'm no liberal. I voted for Ronald Reagan. I don't feel any guilt about the war. For me that's past history."

After that, Schweitzer found that the Vietnamese looked at him in a new light. They knew he had risked his life to ameliorate the plight of the boat people. But, more importantly, he came to Vietnam as a pragmatist bearing tangible medical contributions, not rhetoric.

And by the late 1980s, pragmatism was the watchword in Hanoi. Vietnam was in the throes of radical economic transformation when Schweitzer returned to Hanoi in July 1989 with several tons of medicines for a new pediatric hospital in Ha Nam Ninh Province.

Almost fifteen years after the Communist victory, the leaders of the party were reluctantly beginning to lead their country away from Communism and toward a free-market economy. This transformation did not spring from any ideological sea change among the stiff-necked, doctrinaire Tonkinese revolutionaries who had fought foreign imperialism for most of their lives. After the fall of Saigon, the party, led by its dogmatic leader Le Duan, set about dismantling all vestiges of quasi-independent commerce in the north and crushing the flourishing capitalism of the south. The later shift away from rigid neo-Stalinist control of the economy was a compromise born of reality.

During the Vietnamese Communist Party's Sixth Congress in December 1986, pragmatic reformers orchestrated a notable changing of the guard. The last elderly revolutionary colleagues of Ho Chi Minh stepped down to be replaced by younger, better-educated apparatchiks. For the first time, the party criticized orthodox Communist doctrine and took public note that mismanagement, corruption, and overcentralization had weakened the national economy.[16]

The policy of *doi moi,* "renovation," was initiated. Henceforth, industrial managers would be given greater control of their enterprises, privately owned small businesses would be tolerated, and joint ventures with Western private firms would be encouraged. Significantly, most of these reforms would be introduced in the south, then transplanted to the north.

In the most radical and far-reaching reform, farmers were allowed to lease their own land and sell surplus rice and vegetables on the free market once they had met a realistic government production quota. For the first time in the modern history of Vietnam, millions of peasants controlled the economic destinies of their own families, free of the domination of either absentee landlord or the omnipotent state. Cash flowed into the Vietnamese countryside. Food production increased immediately and the peasantry, numbering more than sixty million, began to flex its new economic power.

Once the party had crossed this ideological Rubicon, there could be no return to classical Communist control without the risk of a bloody peasant uprising.

By 1989, as the economic momentum of *doi moi* was building inexorably, the Warsaw Pact countries, led by the Communist German Democratic Republic, which had been Vietnam's staunchest political and economic supporters, were imploding. And the Soviet Union itself under Mikhail Gorbachev's leadership had traveled so far down the parallel roads of glasnost and perestroika that its future as a Communist superpower was clearly in doubt.

The practical result of this historical upheaval was a sharp reduction of Eastern Bloc military and economic support for Vietnam. Reformist party officials like the new Premier Do Muoi and his deputy, Vo Van Kiet, now spoke openly of a "mixed-economy" for Vietnam that would welcome foreign corporate investment and could coexist peaceably with its capitalist neighbors of the Association of Southeast Asian Nations (ASEAN).[17]

Unspoken in these events was the realpolitik of Vietnam's changed relationship with the Soviet Union. Gorbachev now depended on the West to underwrite the success of perestroika. In turn, the Western powers, led by the United States, exerted pressure on Gorbachev to steer Soviet client states away from aggressive policies. Vietnam, like Angola and Ethiopia, also felt a cool wind blowing from Moscow. Gorbachev made it clear that continued, albeit drastically reduced, Soviet economic support would depend on Vietnam's withdrawal from Cambodia. By midsummer 1989, Hanoi had begun the pullback of its occupation army. This retreat was a bitter tacit admission of China's hegemony. Hanoi's troops withdrew; China's ally, the Khmer Rouge, did not.

Vietnamese leaders realized the Soviet nuclear umbrella, anchored at naval and air bases in Da Nang and Cam Ranh Bay, which had shielded them from China since 1975, had become threadbare. Historically for Vietnam, isolation had always led to foreign domination. Their future security depended on forging alliances among the emerging economic giants of the Pacific Rim.[18]

For Vietnam, there was an unexpected positive side to the new power balance in Southeast Asia. Vietnamese military occupation of Cambodia was one of the three major issues of dispute cited by the United States for the continuing economic embargo, the other two being Vietnam's record of human rights abuses and lack of progress on resolving the MIA problem. By 1989, most of the 100,000 former Republic of Vietnam military officers and civilian officials had been freed from the harsh "reeducation" process and many had already left the country as part of the Orderly Departure Program.[19] That left the MIA stalemate as the single remaining obstacle to lifting the embargo.

Ted Schweitzer found himself the unexpected beneficiary of this outreach to the West. During his July 1989 visit, his Foreign Ministry hosts were unusually hospitable and accommodating. Instead of restricting him to the closely guarded ministry guesthouse near the Hoan Kiem Lake in central

Hanoi, they allowed Schweitzer to tour the city and its outskirts with only Ambassador Nguyen Can and his assistant, Duong Van Ngoc, as his guides.

At this stage of *doi moi*'s evolution, Hanoi was slowly emerging from the austere chrysalis of wartime Communism that had shrouded the capital for over three decades. But there were still very few private motor vehicles and even the rusting government Soviet Lada sedans and smoky GAZ-31 jeeps were sparse due to fuel shortages. Hanoi's broad, shady colonial avenues swarmed with bicycles. The stately French stucco villas and apartment blocks built in the 1930s had mildewed in the constant humidity of the Red River Delta and been so tainted by coal fumes that their facades were now a ubiquitous, muddy beige. But conditions were changing. When Schweitzer had first come to Hanoi eighteen months earlier, the people on the streets appeared almost as drab as the buildings. Because the shoddy Eastern Bloc clothing available in the three state-owned emporia was in short supply, most Hanoi citizens had been reduced to wearing faded green military uniforms or patched blue cotton workers' clothes. Most adult men wore the sun-bleached PAVN pith helmets issued to them as soldiers, giving the throngs of pedestrians an even more regimented appearance. Bright colors were extremely rare. Only bureaucrats and students from well-placed families stood out in their white shirts and black trousers. It seemed strange that a people who fostered such a deeply held distaste for the Chinese had been reduced to the bland style of Maoism.

The once colorful shops of French colon merchants lining thoroughfares like Hai Ba Trung or Trang Tien had been painted dull yellow and served as government offices or improvised apartments, with several generations of a family forced to live in a twenty-meter-square cubicle partitioned by woven bamboo screens or mildewed curtains. The only signs of the new experiments in free enterprise that Schweitzer had noticed on this first visit were the freelance bicycle tire repairmen that stood like sentinels on every corner and the thin rank of peasant women in black squatting by coal-fired tea braziers and soup cauldrons near the central railway station.

Reborn capitalism had not yet filtered up the bomb-cratered length of Highway One from the bustling street markets and private open-air restaurants of the south.

By the summer of 1989, however, private commerce was just beginning to transform Hanoi's drab facade. Now, on a few side streets, women tended simmering pots of aromatic broth, dispensing *pho ga* thick with chicken and rice noodles to hungry patrons.

A few street vendors even hawked cigarettes and tea.

During his subsequent trips to Hanoi, Schweitzer began to witness a startling transformation of the city. The street vendors slowly acquired gaudy pink-and-yellow running suits, transistor batteries, chewing gum, and cheap Chinese plasticware. Eventually, a few lucky teenagers had blue jeans and baggy T-shirts splashed with the bright logos of rock bands.

During this change, the government cut loose Vietnam's currency, the dong, from official supports; inflation soared briefly, but the black market sputtered and small private enterprise exploded. Slowly, cautiously, families began to spend their decades of clandestine savings in hoarded gold. A few of the chalky yellow storefronts on Hai Ba Trung had been refurbished to display Toshiba televisions and Honda motorbikes. But these luxuries were still beyond the reach of all but a few.

Walking back to his guesthouse in the quiet of hot summer nights, Schweitzer would see the hushed throngs of window shoppers who stood in silent, respectful ranks in the isolated crescents of light on the dark avenues, gazing at the bright shop displays, toward the glittering promise of *doi moi*'s future.

CHAPTER 8

ON THE HUMID, WINDLESS MORNING OF JULY 4, 1989, SCHWEITZER and his escort, Duong Van Ngoc, left the Foreign Ministry in the old diplomatic quarter of Hanoi, a district of handsome old villas with peaked tile roofs half hidden among towering flamboyant trees. They had just completed the inevitable long tea-drinking session that preceded the formal approval of Schweitzer's trip to the pediatric hospital in Ha Nam Ninh Province. They climbed into the ministry's rattling black Volga sedan and drove past the limestone bunker of the Ho Chi Minh Mausoleum. Even on this sweltering midsummer day, a long line of Vietnamese, most country people judging by their faded black clothes, or young conscripts, waited patiently to enter the monument.

The ministry driver honked his way through the bicyclists and turned left onto Dien Bien Phu Avenue. Through the overhead foliage, Schweitzer saw the gray stone shaft of the Cot Co watchtower, looming like a power plant smokestack over the vast walled polygon of military headquarters buildings, workshops, and barracks, collectively known as the Citadel. Behind those walls lay the heart and brain of Vietnam's powerful military establishment. Suddenly, above a rank of thick iron pickets, Schweitzer saw the gray, sharp-tipped cylinder of an antiaircraft SAM. The squat bulk of a T-54 tank was just visible through the iron grillwork.

He swung in his seat as the car passed, keeping the SAM in sight. "Why the missile?" he asked Ngoc. "I thought the war was over."

Ngoc replied in French. *"Bien sûr,* that war is over many years." He gestured through the rear window. "The missile is simply a display at the Central Military Museum. The Ministry of Defense is very proud of their collection. I can assure you it is *très historique."*

Having seen the SAM missile and tank in the museum courtyard, Schweitzer wondered what other military artifacts were on display. It certainly would be intriguing to get a look at the long war from the perspective of the People's Army of Vietnam. So, almost on a whim, Schweitzer blurted out, "Monsieur Ngoc, I would like to visit that museum."

The slight official nodded neutrally. The right side of his face and neck were a deeply rippled field of burn scars, as if napalm had eaten the flesh to the bone. "I will inquire with my ministry," he replied.

On July 12, Ngoc came to Schweitzer's room in the stifling ministry guest-house to announce that they were to visit the Central Military Museum at two that afternoon.

"We go directly there?" Schweitzer asked.

"Yes, of course."

Schweitzer was taken aback. Apparently there was to be no preparatory meeting during which a cadre of middle-ranking bureaucrats would lay the ideological groundwork for the visit.

At precisely two, Ngoc and Schweitzer climbed out of the little Russian sedan and entered the tall ornamental iron gate of the museum. The front courtyard was an incongruous mélange of well-landscaped flower plots punctuated by artillery pieces. The museum's administration building was bland gray, neoclassical with the typical deep column shade porticoes of the fin de siècle colonial period. Indeed, Ngoc told Schweitzer, the present-day museum had been built in the 1890s to be the headquarters of the French military signal corps for their entire Indochina colony.

They arrived in the middle of the afternoon rest period and the courtyard stood empty in the cloying heat. Schweitzer inspected the hulking tank that guarded the right flank of the administration building's entrance. As he had guessed, the placard in Vietnamese and English confirmed the tank was the T-54 from the 203rd Armor Brigade that had smashed through the gates of the Presidential Palace in Saigon the day the city fell, April 30, 1975. On this placard, the site of the victory was called the "Saigon Puppet Presidential Palace."

Glancing through open office doorways into the shadowy interiors, Schweitzer saw a few uniformed women officers working drowsily at desks, their long bolt-action rifles propped beside them. At this time, all PAVN personnel still carried weapons, a symbol of Vietnam's ongoing traditional state of vigilance.

Ngoc led Schweitzer around the left corner of the main building, into another wide courtyard paved with slate tile. Handsome flowering shrubbery and trees were interspersed with ranks of artillery pieces, armored vehicles, and the sinister finned gray tube of an SA-2 missile, poised at an acute angle on its launcher like a futuristic javelin. Although several of the military vehicles were Soviet- or Chinese-built and had seen combat with famous PAVN units, the majority were captured French, American, or South Vietnamese trophies.

The courtyard's centerpiece was the whitewashed concrete plinth on which was mounted a sleek aluminum MiG-21 interceptor. The shining jet fighter had a bright red engine-intake nose cone and bore the crimson serial number 4324 in broad red stenciled digits. But the most impressive aspect of this display was not the Soviet-built jet. A jagged, twisted heap of blackened and mottled-green aircraft wreckage was arranged in a seemingly chaotic rectangular heap at the foot of the concrete plinth: a junkyard jumble of debris that included ripped and shrapnel-riddled wing and tail panels, rusting jet engines, and sooty fuel tanks.

The arrangement of this debris was anything but random. Schweitzer read the identifying placards as he moved clockwise around the debris pile, recognizing as he did the pedagogical logic in this sequence. The first heap of torn aluminum was identified as a French "Hencat" fighter plane shot down on the Dien Bien Phu battlefield in 1954.

"They mean 'Hellcat,'" he muttered softly, so that Ngoc couldn't hear. Schweitzer had been in Southeast Asia long enough to know that finding error in an official text was the height of rudeness.

Subsequent placards identified debris from American fighter-bombers downed during the years of the long air campaign, and culminated with the principal trophy wreckage: a massive green slab of a B-52 bomber's tail and an equally bulky section of an F-111 swing-wing fighter-bomber. Both aircraft had been shot down during the Linebacker II bombing of December 1972. The placards stated that the B-52 had been downed by a SAM and the F-111, on December 22, 1972, by 14.5mm machine guns firing from the river embankment in central Hanoi.

This display had a barbaric but undeniably persuasive quality. It was almost as if the gleaming MiG-21, its nose adorned with fourteen red stars of downed American airplanes, was gloating above the mute, stacked tribute of its defeated foes. The monument also conveyed a less than subtle historical statement. Well-equipped foreign aggressors had thrown their best military technology against the stubborn will and determination of Vietnamese socialism, only to be smashed like foundered vessels on a rocky shore.[1]

"Our air defenses were very strong," Ngoc commented in a neutral tone, his scarred face and neck glistening with sweat. It was impolite to gloat overtly. But the skillful agitprop of the display spoke for itself.

This theme was repeated in the arrangement of the captured armored vehicles. The first was an American-built half-track of World War II vintage, "Seized in the battle destroying the French Mobile Regiment No. 100 at An Khe, June 1954." On the flank of the half-track's armored hood, a white stenciled announcement confidently proclaimed that the antifreeze had been tested to a temperature of thirty below zero. *That* useless information, Schweitzer mused, could have hardly reassured the hapless Legionnaires as they jolted through the choking heat and laterite dust of the central plateau, straight into the jaws of yet another well-laid Vietminh ambush.

Walking the rank of war trophy vehicles, Schweitzer noted that the sequence was again meant to be virtually a monument to the arrogant folly, the hubris, of the foreign aggressors. There were armored personnel carriers and self-propelled howitzers belonging to the "U.S. Puppets." Two had been captured on the "Southern Laos Front." Mounted on a low concrete stand beside this captured armor was a Soviet PT-76 amphibious tank that had also fought in the Lam Son 719 battles in Laos in February 1971. This defeat of the ARVN assault on the PAVN's main supply route in Laos had been a major setback in the American policy of Vietnamization of the war.

Schweitzer paused. He was unprepared for such a frank and tangible admission that the PAVN had fought with well-equipped conventional forces along the Ho Chi Minh Trail in the Lao panhandle. Until then, he had seen no tangible contradiction to the official Hanoi wartime line that lightly equipped "volunteers" had crushed the clumsy ARVN armor units. When the implication of this display was considered with that of the Soviet MiG-21 and the SAM and Soviet radar van, the long-held official North Vietnamese position that it had fought a low-technology peasant's war against America's well-equipped surrogates in the South was badly undercut.

Perhaps, he thought, this museum might in fact be "very historic," as Ngoc had asserted.

The next exhibit was the large Battle of Dien Bien Phu display housed in its own indoor amphitheater at the rear of the courtyard. Entering the wide, dimly lit room, Schweitzer was struck by the amphitheater's uncanny resemblance to the topographical exhibit at the Gettysburg Battlefield museum. This similarity extended right down to the colored lights flashing and snaking along the trenchlines as the scratchy melodramatic French soundtrack recounted the destruction of the colonial paratroopers in May 1954. The tall, intricately detailed mural on the far wall chronicled each phase of the French defeat, from their initial occupation of this isolated valley in the misty mountains on the Lao frontier, to the destruction of the flying boxcars making the last futile attempt at air-drop reinforcement of General Henri Navarre's beleaguered garrison.

Leaving the Dien Bien Phu display, Ngoc and Schweitzer were now joined by a pleasant, round-faced woman in her thirties, Lieutenant Colonel Tran Thanh Hang. She introduced herself as the senior museum curator and archivist. Ngoc, who translated, explained that Mrs. Hang, as she preferred to be addressed, was a respected PAVN officer who knew the museum's collection better than anyone. "She has served here for many years," he added.

They followed a group of red-neckerchiefed schoolchildren into the modern concrete exhibition hall that linked the two French colonial buildings. Now a thin young colonel named Que, one of the museum's deputy commanders, joined them.

This room was dedicated to the "American war," Mrs. Hang explained. Colonel Que remained silent, his face blank, as if he were a neutral referee at a sporting match. But Schweitzer sensed that the officer was closely scrutinizing him.

The most prominent feature of this hall was the wide ceiling-high photo mural of the Ho Chi Minh Trail on the far wall. At the side, a map detailed the tangled skein of supply routes that ran the length of the Truong Son—the Long Mountains—as the Vietnamese called the Annamite Cordillera.

Schweitzer was again impressed. The map accurately depicted each of the major supply bases and rest stops along the trail's multiple routes, a vast logistical system that Hanoi had stubbornly refused to acknowledge for decades. The sites of important engagements with American Special Forces teams and ARVN commandos were highlighted, as were the locations of SAM missile batteries at such notable choke points on the trail as the Mu Gia and Ban Karai Passes, the Ban Loboy Ford, and the major PAVN logistics base at Sepone. And the map's legend gave detailed information on the location of major PAVN units during the period between 1959 and 1975 when the trail was the main infiltration and supply route south. Here was another accurate depiction of historic events, not simply propaganda.

Along the base of the photo mural, which was a montage of black-and-white pictures of the trail's construction and defense, a unique array of military artifacts was displayed. Schweitzer was not surprised to see one of the famous trail bicycles with its crude wooden cargo racks and handlebar extensions that permitted one soldier to trundle a 200 kilo load of rice or munitions up and down the mountain trails.

But the unique artifacts were the American listening devices and seismic probes that had been air-dropped by the thousands along the trail's myriad tributaries. They were bullet-shaped, with a petal-spread of stabilizing fins, designed to penetrate the ground, leaving a twisted plastic antenna disguised as a sapling or a vine above the surface. The probes broadcast the thump of footsteps or the vibration of truck tires to American aircraft orbiting above. These were relics of McNamara's Wall, as the elaborate electronic surveillance network was derisively known in the U.S. military. The system was designed to provide detailed information on enemy troop and supply movements so that U.S. bombers could be precisely guided to their targets. Like so much else in the U.S. arsenal, the sensor system appeared effective in American laboratories, but was almost useless on the Indochina battlefield.[2]

Ngoc translated the display's Vietnamese caption that explained how the troops of the Truong Son Corps would unearth the seismic probes and sling them in tree branches far away from the active supply routes so that the devices would swing in the wind striking trunks and branches and transmitting bogus seismic signals.

"Our men had to adapt," he said, avoiding any obvious hint of scornful pride.

Colonel Que remained silent.

Next they turned to the displays of uniforms and equipment taken from captured American airmen. Now Schweitzer noted a sudden veiled tension in the bland faces of his two escorts. They stood before a large elaborate display of American equipment, dominated by a mannequin dressed in a U.S. Air Force flight suit, nylon web survival vest, and white flight helmet. These were not impersonal vehicles or munitions, but the actual uniform and equipment stripped from a downed American airman who might have been either dead or alive. The display also featured blowups of previously published news photos showing U.S. pilots, stripped to their T-shirts and boxer shorts, hands above their heads, prodded at bayonet point past crowds of screaming, irate villagers. In one display case, a whole collection of flight helmets was arrayed like coconuts in a market stall.

Schweitzer leaned closer. There were other personal items, signal mirrors, pen flares, pocketknives, and handwritten flight logs displayed on a backdrop of parachute cloth. One flight helmet caught his attention. It was Fiberglas with paired Kelly green stencil silhouettes of an F-105 fighter-bomber on the crown. At the helmet's forehead peak was a small plastic strip identification tag bearing the name "Risner."

"May I see this?" Schweitzer asked.

"Of course," Mrs. Hang replied, shifting her rifle to her left hand and passing the helmet to Schweitzer.

Schweitzer hefted the helmet in his hand, feeling the ruts and gouges in the otherwise smooth Fiberglas, proof of a hard landing. Actually touching this helmet was strangely moving. Lieutenant Colonel Robinson "Robbie" Risner had been shot down in September 1965 not far from Hanoi. He had been one of the leaders of the American POWs and had been repeatedly tortured to extract propaganda statements. His suffering and heroism as a prisoner had been well publicized. Handling Risner's actual flight equipment transformed his almost legendary heroism into a believable human experience. This was like trying on Joe DiMaggio's fielder's mitt or swinging Babe Ruth's bat in the Baseball Hall of Fame.

Now Schweitzer leafed through a flight log of a Navy pilot. The last entry noted a "good launch" from an aircraft carrier in October 1967. The printed block for the time of flight-deck recovery was blank. The plane never returned to its ship. There were similar documents in the display case.

Schweitzer felt like an intruder, but neither Colonel Que nor Mrs. Hang seemed concerned as he examined these artifacts. Since Operation Homecoming in 1973, the American POW story had reached epic proportions in both military literature and popular entertainment depictions of the prisoners' ordeal. But Schweitzer realized that there was—given Vietnam's isolation—almost nothing known about the extensive and sometimes sensationalized POW literature from the Vietnamese perspective. Perhaps the Hanoi government was uninterested in the entire episode and the scattering of documents, equipment, and clothing in these museum cases here was all they had collected from the almost 600 American POWs who had survived captivity. But he knew over 8,000 American fixed-wing and helicopter aircraft had been shot down during the long war. About half these aircraft losses resulted in casualties, which included men killed, captured, or missing in action. And he was aware that at least a thousand airmen remained officially unaccounted for.[3]

Then, glancing to his left, he saw another glass-topped case in which the laminated identity cards of hundreds of captured South Vietnamese soldiers and marines were displayed. He wondered if the museum had similar material on American prisoners in storage.

"Is this your entire collection on the captured Americans?" Schweitzer asked before considering the full implication of his question. But even as he spoke he realized he was seeking sensitive information, in effect probing the extent of PAVN information on men possibly still listed as MIA.

But Mrs. Hang replied in a forthright, positive tone. As Ngoc translated, she explained that the Central Military Museum in Hanoi, its counterpart in Ho Chi Minh City (formerly Saigon), and several regional military museums had in fact a "very complete" collection of uniforms, equipment, and personal effects from the Americans captured during the war.

"We have carefully listed all this," Mrs. Hang said, pointing vaguely out the open exhibition hall door toward a row of shuttered offices half hidden beneath the second-floor shade portico of the rear building. "We have never lost any captured enemy documents or other items."

Her words were crisp, almost dogmatic, spoken in the manner Schweitzer had come to recognize as an authorized statement. From his experience, the Vietnamese could be courteous but vague to a maddening point when they wanted to avoid commitment. But when authorized by their leaders to speak for the government, they were brutally frank. And Mrs. Hang had just revealed that "nothing" taken from the American prisoners had been lost.

Now Schweitzer was blunt. He pointed toward the glass case of ARVN identity cards. "Do you also have some like these from the Americans?"

Mrs. Hang nodded firmly. "We have everything."

"May I take pictures?" Schweitzer already had his camera raised.

Again she glanced at Colonel Que, who again nodded. "Of course." Mrs. Hang stepped aside, allowing him to shoot a series of close-ups on the POW artifacts.

Schweitzer had no idea if former American POWs realized their helmets and flight equipment were on display. He decided to photograph the material from several angles and to shoot close-ups of any name tags or ID plates, hoping these pictures might somehow aid the resolution of the MIA issue.

Mrs. Hang helped by arranging several helmets, survival vests, and logbooks on the glass-topped display case. Schweitzer shot one roll of film and loaded another. Then she unfolded two U.S. military "blood chits": white silk panels displaying the American flag above an appeal for assistance with reward promise, written in Asian languages, which downed aircrew carried. The panels now bore two serial numbers, that of the original blood chit, identifying the airman, plus a PAVN museum acquisition number.

Mrs. Hang disappeared for a few minutes, then returned with a thin sheaf of blue-gray cards. These cards were from her rich archives. She explained that the museum was the repository of all captured enemy artifacts as well as documents relating to captured enemy personnel. This museum, she said, maintained records on each American POW, detailed documents and photographs describing their capture, as well as the maps, logbooks, ID cards, and all other pieces of military equipment the enemy had with him at the time of capture. The museum, she added, also kept records of all the known crash sites of enemy aircraft in Indochina.

Standing in the musty display room, Schweitzer realized that this museum was markedly different from a similar American establishment. Rather than merely being an institution of popular culture, as in the West, the Central Military Museum was primarily a professional research and intelligence facility, a unit of the PAVN General Political Directorate. Its public education and propaganda roles were secondary to its principal function as a secure repository of wartime documents and artifacts.

Schweitzer took a series of close-ups of the cards, making sure the hand-written Vietnamese script and the Romanized block letters of the airmen's names were in sharp focus.

While he worked, Colonel Que watched in thoughtful silence from beside the case.

Back in the central courtyard, Schweitzer shot another half roll on the placards identifying the American aircraft debris surrounding the MiG-21 on its concrete plinth. He wasn't sure of the value of these photos, but he understood that they might be of some comfort to the families of the downed airmen who hadn't returned. And there had definitely been something in Mrs. Hang's manner and the colonel's silent acquiescence that indicated an unusual openness. He had heard vague political gossip among other foreign aid donors in Hanoi that the new official economic policy of *doi moi* was to be followed by an "openness" campaign, *coi moi,* just as glasnost had followed perestroika in the Soviet Union. Perhaps he had just witnessed a demonstration of this openness.

CHAPTER 9

SCHWEITZER RETURNED TO THE UNITED STATES IN LATE SUMMER 1989. At the urging of his State Department Humanitarian Affairs contact, Michael Marine, Schweitzer called the Defense Intelligence Agency to announce that he had pictures and information on the Hanoi museum that might be of interest to the government. On September 26, 1989, he was invited to meet the head of the DIA's Special Office for POW/MIAs, Army Colonel Joseph A. Schlatter, Jr. Schlatter interviewed Schweitzer in the agency's crowded, poorly air-conditioned offices in the E-Ring of the Pentagon.

Schlatter was a tall, thin officer in his mid-forties, whose friendly, precise manner seemed more typical of an academic than a decorated combat veteran. Schweitzer was taken by the man's guileless demeanor.

"Thanks for coming in," Schlatter said. "What can we do for you?"

Schweitzer handed over a selection of color prints that showed the helmets and flight equipment lined up on the display case. Then he spread the close-ups of the record cards on Schlatter's desk.

Schlatter studied the logbook in the corner of one picture and the pilot's helmet with the owner's name stenciled on it in another shot.

"The curator, Mrs. Hang, says she's got tons of this stuff," Schweitzer added, "and ID cards too."

Joe Schlatter looked up and gazed at Schweitzer with a serious expression, as if measuring his integrity. "May we keep these?"

"Sure," Schweitzer replied. "I've got the negatives, if you want them."

Now Schlatter hunched over a photo of the aircraft wreckage display. It was a shot of the placard for the F-111 wreckage. "How much of this plane is intact?"

Schweitzer tried to explain the debris he had photographed, turning the pictures at angles to re-create the display pile.

"All of this is very helpful," Joe Schlatter said, stacking the pictures. "We'll make sure they get to the right people."[1]

Schlatter then asked a series of soft-spoken but precise questions about Schweitzer's visit to the museum and the conditions under which he took the pictures. Although Schlatter's manner was relaxed, indeed diffident,

Schweitzer was aware that he was being probed. He answered accurately, leaving out nothing important.

"They've got a hell of a lot of material, Colonel Schlatter," Schweitzer concluded. "I definitely got the feeling they, well . . . *wanted* me to know this."

Schlatter nodded without speaking. Good military intelligence officer that he was, he gave no indication of how much the DIA already knew about the museum.

(Schweitzer would later learn that, although the DIA's Special Office for POW/MIAs knew of the museum's displays of captured uniforms and equipment, the agency did not know the extent of the museum's collection, nor did it then have information on any large prisoner-record archives.)

"When do you plan to go back?" Schlatter asked.

"As soon as I can put together all the medical supplies and equipment on my list," Schweitzer said, patting his battered briefcase. "I depend on donations, you know."

Schlatter pursed his lips and made a brief note. "Well, Ted," he said in the same quiet voice, "maybe we can help you out with some of your travel expenses in the future."

"Thanks," Schweitzer said, promising to contact Schlatter after his next visit to Hanoi.

As he descended the long escalator to the Pentagon Metro station, Schweitzer had no way to judge if his pictures would be of any real value to the government.

SIX MONTHS LATER, Schweitzer was back in Hanoi. On March 27, 1990, he met with the museum director, Senior Colonel Pham Duc Dai.

The colonel was a decorated PAVN veteran in his early sixties, a thin, almost frail-looking officer with wispy graying hair. But this initial impression of frailty, Schweitzer realized, was misleading. Colonel Dai's thin frame was wiry, tempered by four decades of war. And the colonel's physical toughness was at least equaled by his intelligence and willpower.

Schweitzer soon discovered that Dai's seemingly innocuous assignment as director of all military museums in Vietnam was actually a position of considerable power and responsibility. Because, in Vietnam, national history was the history of protracted war, military museums in Hanoi, Haiphong, Ho Chi Minh City, and Hue, as well as military "houses of tradition" in smaller towns, were an important department of the PAVN's General Political Directorate (GPD), one of six main directorates that report directly to the cabinet of the PAVN commander-in-chief. In the West, military history offices were separated from sensitive intelligence archives. In the PAVN, Colonel Dai's branch of the General Political Directorate combined both functions.

Moreover, Schweitzer learned, during the Vietnam War, the GPD shared responsibility for American POWs with similar departments of the Ministry of the Interior.

This General Political Directorate's prestige in the PAVN was unmatched. In fact, it was the Army's oldest institution and considered the "keystone" of the entire military structure. Any officer seeking advancement in the PAVN had to serve an apprenticeship in the GPD. Colonel Dai had spent his entire career in this important directorate, with combat service in both the French and American wars as a political officer.[2] As a senior colonel, he held a rank equivalent to an American brigadier general.

Colonel Dai had obviously studied Schweitzer's background. Their initial meeting was a stilted affair over tiny tea cups in the museum's formal reception room—an echoing high-ceilinged hall cluttered with massive and uncomfortable teak banquettes and high-backed chairs. Clearly Dai was probing both Schweitzer's sincerity and his politics. The first formal introduction was followed by several meetings over the next week.

As a young Vietminh soldier, Dai had been a guard at the Buoi Lycée in Hanoi where his future commander, General Vo Nguyen Giap, had once taught history. Dai's French had a soft Tonkinese accent, but was otherwise fluent. As with most Vietnamese officials, he preferred speaking his native language through an interpreter—usually his GPD subordinate, Major Lai Vinh Mui—but often spoke to Schweitzer directly in French, a language that younger PAVN officers in attendance did not understand.

"What is your particular interest in American prisoners?" Dai asked on their third meeting.

By now Schweitzer was accustomed to the circuitous manner of doing business that prevailed in the Vietnamese bureaucracy. He replied with an honest but suitably vague explanation. "Many American families of missing men would like more information on their loved ones."

"We have considerable information," Dai said in a flat, direct manner, evocative of Mrs. Hang's earlier positive admission.

Schweitzer waited for more. But Colonel Dai remained silent, chain-smoking the long British 555 filter tips from the Bangkok duty-free shop that Schweitzer had presented as a traditional "tea cup" gift. The sun broke through the cloying Hanoi overcast and flooded the museum courtyard with warmth. Dai was arthritic from years spent sleeping in the cold monsoon mud of the Truong Son.

"The sun is warm outside," he announced, rising from the teak bench. "We'll go out and drink beer."

There was a small wooden gazebo refreshment stand set among bitter orange trees off the side courtyard. Dai led Schweitzer to one of the tiny wrought-iron tables and offered a low wicker chair. Over cold cans of Saigon 333 Beer, without prodding from Schweitzer, the colonel made a strange declaration. The museum, he said, was the central repository for *all* the official records on every American, living or dead, who had fallen into PAVN custody during the long war.

"So you have detailed records, Colonel?" Schweitzer asked, trying to retain a neutral tone. He was excited. For some reason this veteran political officer was volunteering information on an extremely sensitive subject.

"We have everything," Dai replied. He pointed toward the rear of the building, indicating a raised concrete walkway that connected the old French structure with the mildewed concrete modern building that housed the main exhibit hall. The walkway led to a large, padlocked steel door on the modern building's second floor. "There we maintain records on every American who was captured."

"All the records, Colonel?"

Dai nodded abruptly and again rose. *"Venez avec moi."*

He led Schweitzer past the smelly latrine block and up a staircase to the second floor. Crossing the concrete walkway, Schweitzer got his first glimpse inside the warren of buildings and pathways of the actual Citadel—Vietnam's Pentagon—the long rectangular military quarter that stretched all the way to Ly Nam De Street, which was the boundary of Hanoi's Thirty-six Streets, the precolonial Old City.

Dai unlocked the steel door's heavy padlock and led Schweitzer into a dusty anteroom. Using another key, the colonel opened a plain green filing cabinet and removed a narrow ledger book with a red-cloth cover. The ledger was embossed with a tarnished gilt title and the large gold star of the PAVN.

"This is the central record index," Colonel Dai explained. "We can call it the Red Book." He opened the cover and thumbed through the pages, which were dense with blocks of handwritten numerical columns.

Examining the Red Book over Colonel Dai's shoulder, Schweitzer could make little sense of the cryptic entries.

The colonel patiently explained the complex index system as he flipped through the pages. The first seventy-six pages contained file numbers for photographic, artifact, and document records relating to the "Resistance War," the struggle against the French. The next seventy pages indexed records from what he called the "War of Independence" against America and its "puppets" in the Saigon government.[3] And the final section dealt with the Cambodian expedition and the Chinese border war.

Colonel Dai opened the Red Book to page 139. He translated the handwritten inscription at the top of the page, noting that the upper and lower blocks of numerical columns listed photographs and documents, including records on Americans shot down and captured during the Linebacker II bombing of Hanoi between December 18 and 30, 1972. There were over a hundred separate numerical entries on this page alone. But they were simply anonymous numbers, the photographs bearing a cryptic "P." before each four-digit entry. Schweitzer could make no sense of the system.

Then Colonel Dai deciphered the index. He tapped the first four-digit number in the document index block, 4926. "This is the shootdown record of an American aircraft."

Laying the open Red Book on a dusty table, he unlocked another filing cabinet and removed a bluish gray rectangular pasteboard record card from a thick stack of similar documents. The card was a printed form headed with the title, "Acquisition Card" *(PHIÊÚ KIÊ'M KÊ)*. Like the Red Book index, the card was handwritten in a neat Vietnamese cursive and bore the number 4926 in the upper-right-hand corner. Even though he wasn't fluent in Vietnamese, Schweitzer could see that this was the record of the shootdown of an F-111A at 2100 hours on the night of December 22, 1972. The aircraft had been destroyed near Hiep Hoa in the Hoa Binh section of Hanoi, a riverfront quarter.

Colonel Dai translated, noting the site of the crash and the unit that had captured the two American aviators.

"Who were they?" Schweitzer asked.

Dai went to the filing cabinet and produced another gray pasteboard card, which he handed Schweitzer.

"Sponeyberger, Robert D.," Schweitzer read, "Captain, USAF." He turned the card over. "Wilson, William W., Lieutenant, USAF."

He wondered if these men had survived. Then Colonel Dai answered his unspoken question.

"Both officers were released in 1973."[4]

Schweitzer leafed backward through the pages all the way to the early bombing campaign against North Vietnam in 1964 and 1965. He found the index page listing the records from August 5, 1964, to April 4, 1965. Colonel Dai produced record cards for shootdowns in this period. One gave details on the first American aviator POW, Navy Lieutenant, JG, Everett Alvarez, Jr., who had been shot down near Haiphong. A second card chronicled the shootdown and capture of an Air Force F-105 pilot, Carlyle Harris, who had been lost south of Hanoi.

Now Schweitzer sat on a stool and turned the Red Book pages slowly, trying to estimate the number of entries and gain some sense of the size of the archives they indexed. Colonel Dai obliged by periodically handing Schweitzer a record card with the details of a reference shootdown and capture. At one point Dai unlocked the door to an inner room and returned moments later with an armful of albums and a paper-wrapped packet.

"We have many photographs," Colonel Dai said in a neutral tone. He handed Schweitzer an album with a stained gray cover, open to a page on which small black-and-white prints were mounted. Dai watched silently for the American's reaction.

The pictures were shocking. They showed the mangled body of a dead pilot clad in a dark flight suit lying supine on a crude canvas stretcher. The man's left leg had been nearly severed by a deep, wedge-shaped wound that had obviously cut major arteries. In death, the face was smooth. Schweitzer noted the handwritten caption: "Waters, Samuel Edwin, F-105D, 13-12-66."

Another small print was the close-up of a dead pilot lying in trampled liquid mud, his arms above his head as if in surrender, a white flight helmet emblazoned with a clean American flag resting incongruously in his fingers. "Nelson, Richard C., 3-6-68," Schweitzer read.[5]

"We also have these," Colonel Dai said, handing Schweitzer a stack of military identity cards.

The top ID card belonged to the first POW, Everett Alvarez. On some cards the lamination was buckled by heat and moisture. Others were pristine.

"How many do you have?" Schweitzer knew he could ask frank questions in this stuffy little archive, isolated from other PAVN officers.

"We have records on every man who came under our control," Colonel Dai replied without hesitation.

"Everyone?"

"Every man," Dai confirmed. "Those who lived, and those who died."

Schweitzer felt a new rush of excitement. He breathed in deeply despite the small room's cloying dust. There had been thousands of neat entries in the Red Book, all written with a fine-nibbed fountain pen. Each of those four-digit index codes referred to a photograph, a captured American serviceman, an American's ID card, a piece of equipment or identifiable scrap of wreckage. Obviously this was not a neat, logical master index in the linear Western sense. Rather, it followed Vietnamese methods, which were an amalgam of traditional mandarin archives and the strict bookkeeping of French bureaucracy. Even though the Red Book index itself did not provide a clear chronology of aircraft shootdowns and captured Americans, Schweitzer realized that the index might be the key that unlocked the MIA mystery.[6]

"May I photograph these?" Schweitzer asked cautiously.

"Of course." The colonel smiled now, displaying his tobacco-stained teeth. He opened one of the photo albums on the low, dusty table.

Schweitzer flipped his camera selector switch to Flash and began to shoot.

When Schweitzer finished shooting, Colonel Dai carefully returned the photo albums and record cards to their proper cabinets, double-checked the locks, then locked away the Red Book. Leaving the museum later that day, Schweitzer had two more rolls of exposed film.

A WEEK LATER, on April 10, Schweitzer passed through Bangkok. He had developed his film and took a set of prints to André Sauvegeot, an old friend and resident Vietnamese expert at the American embassy. Sauvegeot had spent years working for the U.S. military mission during the war. He was probably the most fluent American Vietnamese speaker in the region. Now he was on contract to the State Department running his own listening post out of the Bangkok embassy political section. When one of the periodic American MIA delegations traveled to Hanoi, Sauvegeot was always the official interpreter. He was blade-thin and energetic and spoke with a habitual rapid-fire intensity.

"How the hell did you get *these?*" Sauvegeot asked, fanning the color prints across his desk.

"Colonel Dai put the books on the table," Schweitzer deadpanned, "and I pointed my camera and pushed the button."

"Come with me." Sauvegeot sprang from his desk, clutching the photos, and was already out the office door before Schweitzer could turn and follow.

Sauvegeot led Schweitzer to the embassy snack bar where they encountered none other than Colonel Joe Schlatter and his assistant, Gary Sydow, who had just arrived in Bangkok to confer with the Stony Beach office, the local DIA POW/MIA intelligence-gathering post that had been activated eighteen months earlier.

Schlatter greeted Schweitzer warmly.

"I've got something for you," Schweitzer said.

The four men trooped back out of the snack bar and up to Sauvegeot's second-floor office. After closing the door, Schlatter studied the pictures.

"How many of these pictures does the museum have, Ted?" Schlatter finally asked.

"Thousands," he answered, flipping through the prints to the shot that revealed the corner of the Red Book beside the albums on the table. "There's *thousands* of entries in this index."

"No kidding?" Schlatter shook his head.

"There were several filing cabinets in the first room," Schweitzer explained. "And when Colonel Dai opened the door, I saw a bunch more in the second room. It's a regular archive."

Schlatter and Sydow were staring at him. Then Schlatter spoke. "When are you coming back to the States?"

"Next week."

"There are some people in Washington I'd like you to meet," Schlatter said in his quiet, diffident way. "We'll get you a ticket from Florida."

UNKNOWN TO SCHWEITZER, the U.S. government, through the presidential emissary on POW/MIA affairs, General Vessey, was negotiating the establishment of a permanent DIA office in Hanoi, specifically charged with investigating Vietnamese military archives for information on American prisoners and missing.

And Schweitzer had just presented the first proof that such an archive existed in Hanoi, proof that would refute even the most adamant and persistent denials of the Vietnamese government.

IN LATE APRIL 1990, Colonel Joe Schlatter sent Schweitzer to meet representatives of the DIA's Operations Directorate, which was housed in a newer building off Rosslyn Circle across the Key Bridge from Georgetown. There was nothing diffident or overtly friendly about these officers. They were cool and businesslike as they asked Schweitzer a series of detailed questions about his background and dealings with the Vietnamese.

"What do you want from the government?" one of the operations officers asked bluntly. He was overweight and pasty white, his close-cropped hair prematurely gray. Like his two colleagues, he wore a well-tailored pinstripe and gleaming loafers. To Schweitzer, he looked like a senior corporate executive.

"Nothing, really," Schweitzer replied. "Joe Schlatter mentioned that you ... the government, might help with my travel expenses in return for photos from the museum."

The three men gazed blankly at him. Finally one handed a printed form across the metal desktop. "These are some forms we want you to sign."

Schweitzer carefully read the printed pages. One was a Privacy Act release that would allow the government access to his military record. The second was an agreement not to divulge details of this meeting. And other documents informed him of the penalties involved with breaching the Espionage Act.

What the hell am I getting into? Schweitzer wondered as he signed each page.

"Be sure your Social Security number is correct," one of the officers coaxed.

"And your date of birth," the gray-haired officer echoed.

SEVERAL MONTHS PASSED and Schweitzer heard nothing from the DIA. When he tried to reach Joe Schlatter, a secretary informed him that the colonel had finished his tour as head of the POW/MIA office and had been reassigned to Japan. Schweitzer abandoned any vague ambition he had harbored about working for the government in some intelligence capacity. But he did not forget about the PAVN museum.

He returned to Hanoi in December 1990 with another load of medical supplies. As soon as he finished the delivery formalities, he sent word to Colonel Dai that he was back. Dai invited him to have lunch at the museum on the afternoon of Thursday, December 6, 1990.

The habitual Hanoi winter drizzle had broken and the sun warmed the museum courtyard. Schweitzer and Colonel Dai sat in the shade of the bitter oranges and ate from a tin tray of spicy barbecued lamb and goat from the officers' mess in the nearby Citadel. Schweitzer made no mention of his contacts with the DIA. This was not simply prudence; he was convinced that government interest in him had ended with Joe Schlatter's reassignment. He and Dai chatted vaguely about the museum's archives and the interest of the American public in the MIA issue.

Then Colonel Dai nodded sharply, indicating he was shifting the conversation from polite small talk to more serious matters. "So, our collection is very valuable, *n'est-ce pas?*"

Schweitzer gnawed on a gristly hunk of goat meat and drank some beer before replying. He was being probed. If he had learned anything after almost twenty years in Southeast Asia, it was patience. He waited.

Finally, Colonel Dai approached a clear point of departure. "A scholar could write an interesting book based on these archives." He politely doled out the remaining beer from the can before opening a fresh one.

Schweitzer drank in silence, then nodded. "Yes, Colonel, most interesting."

"Would you like to write such a book?" Colonel Dai asked almost brusquely.

Although he knew nothing about writing, Schweitzer recognized that access to these detailed archives—which he was being offered to further some complex and involuted Vietnamese policy—would indeed give him the opportunity to help solve the MIA riddle and repair relations between America and Vietnam. It was an opportunity he would not pass up.

That afternoon, one of the GPD officers typed out a contract between Schweitzer's Southeast Asia Rescue Foundation and the Central Military Museum, which granted Schweitzer exclusive rights to research the museum's archives, to photograph and copy any material he saw fit, and to produce a book based on the museum's collection. Colonel Dai, however, required that the use of the museum's archives not be "detrimental to the interests and honor of the People's Army of Vietnam and the Socialist Republic of Vietnam, as well as not be detrimental to the friendship of the people of the Socialist Republic of Vietnam and of the United States of America."

Schweitzer had no idea how restrictive this caveat would be, but he realized that once he had somehow photographed or otherwise copied all the vast museum archives, there would be little the Vietnamese government could do to protect its honor and interests, if in fact this material threatened those vague concepts.

The third clause of the contract required Schweitzer's foundation to pay a fee for photographing and retrieving archives and translating records, which would be determined on a case-by-case basis. Finally, the net profits from any book would be shared between the foundation and the museum. After working in post–*doi moi* Vietnam for several years, Schweitzer understood that it was not at all unusual for a major organization of the Communist state such as the PAVN to enter into profit-making enterprises with foreigners. Indeed, one of the basic tenets of Vietnam's "renovation" was that state institutions must eventually stand alone and produce their own revenue. Already, he knew, the PAVN was conducting joint ventures in fish processing, logging, and construction with foreign companies. He assumed that this strange publishing project was a similar attempt at free enterprise by the General Political Directorate.[7]

But at the same time, he knew that very little in Vietnam was as simple or direct as surface appearances indicated.

Seated at his stained plywood desk, Colonel Dai dutifully stamped the contract with his seal and signed it for the government of Vietnam.

Schweitzer gave the colonel a smudged carbon copy and folded the original into his briefcase. He believed he had obtained the key that would unlock one of the darkest enigmas of the Vietnam War.

But as he walked out into the thin December sunlight, past the mute aircraft wreckage and trophy vehicles, he really had no firm idea how he could exploit that key.

ON AUGUST 9, 1989, the JCRC and Vietnamese Office for Seeking Missing Persons (VNOSMP) excavated a crash site in Quang Binh Province. The overgrown aircraft wreckage was in the steep jungle hills above the rutted switchback turns of old Strategic Route 20. The joint team positively identified the wreckage of an F4-D, Number 66-7523. It was Grommet 02. Both ejection seats were missing. Villagers reported vague rumors of American graves in the area. But none were found. No one questioned had ever heard the names Morrison or Francisco.

CHAPTER 10

TO AN OUTSIDER, THE DIA'S GAMBIT OF CONSIDERING SCHWEITZER, a well-intentioned volunteer, as a secret agent to survey Hanoi's classified military archives might have seemed an ill-conceived, indeed, a desperate ploy.

It was in fact a tacit recognition by the Defense Department that seventeen years of American efforts to gain the cooperation of the Vietnamese on resolving the MIA issue were now mired in stalemate, and destined for failure. Frustration was widespread among the officials in Defense, State, and the National Security Council charged with resolving this stalemate during President Bush's tenure. The Vietnamese had controlled the issue during and after the war, which made developing a coherent policy especially difficult for senior American bureaucrats. These men were used to hatching and pursuing their own policy initiatives, the established means of accruing power in Washington.[1]

But it was Hanoi, not Washington, that had set the rules and continued to direct the play in this particular competition. And, by 1990, it was beyond dispute that the missing in action issue had metamorphosed far beyond a humanitarian question, into a test of wills between stubborn men in Hanoi and Washington. In effect, there were bureaucrats in Washington intent on using the MIA issue as a means of finally subjugating their old foes, the Vietnamese Communists; and there were members of the Hanoi Politburo and military leadership equally determined to concede nothing to the Americans.

General John Vessey hoped that his focused approach on resolving the most blatant MIA discrepancy cases might break the willful logjam and start a process of rapid resolution of the issue. But to do so, he needed access to the Vietnamese military archives.

On Vessey's trips to Hanoi between 1987 and 1990, his agenda included expanding joint field operations and acquiring more concrete information on the fates of over seventy category 1 discrepancy cases. He pressed Foreign Minister Nguyen Co Thach to provide PAVN wartime records on American prisoners.

"If your country is adamant that no live Americans were kept in captivity after 1973," Vessey told Thach, "you should be able to provide records from your archives that show this."

Thach was evasive. "Our records are not good," he explained. "They're not at all as well organized as you would expect."

On his next visit, Vessey again pushed the issue of archives. They were vital, he said, in resolving the discrepancy cases.

"Many of our archives have been destroyed by termites," Thach now replied.

On a third occasion, General Vessey again focused on the need for American access to Vietnamese military archives that contained records on U.S. prisoners.

"These archives remain classified," Thach finally conceded. "It is against our law for foreigners to see them."

By now, Vessey had seen the sampling of index cards that Schweitzer had given to Colonel Schlatter, and had heard a description of the Red Book index in the Central Military Museum. So Vessey knew that the Vietnamese did have extensive archives. And he suspected their detailed prisoner records would reveal widespread mistreatment, including systematic torture to extract propaganda statements—which was already well documented in the large popular POW literature in the United States. But there was probably also evidence of arbitrary executions, which were definitely not documented. He doubted that the Vietnamese would willingly open these archives.

By mid-1990, Vessey's mission to resolve the highest priority discrepancy through access to the Vietnamese archives had reached a stalemate.[2]

IN THE WINTER of 1990–91, Ted Schweitzer was in the United States, still hopeful that he could find government or private backing for his "book," the research project he hoped would resolve the nagging MIA mystery. He had formed a tentative plan of action on the best means of copying the secret prisoner archives that Colonel Dai had shown him. Schweitzer realized that, whatever Dai's authority, it would be inappropriate simply to wade into the records of the museum, drag the files out of the dim, musty rooms to a sunlit table, and photograph them. He had a better idea.

Schweitzer's training as a professional librarian had coincided with the onset of the computer-database revolution. He had closely followed the evolution of this technology. The best way to copy both the archives and artifacts (including ID cards and photographs) in the museum collection would be to scan and simultaneously index them with a computerized optical scanner and database program, which would produce near-photographic quality indexed digital images, but would not have the blatant espionage stigma of photographing each page or object with a camera. Moreover, optically scanning the records would make him appear more scholarly and less a snoop—or worse, an actual intelligence agent, which at this point he clearly was not.

Schweitzer had suggested this approach to the DIA, but after Schlatter's reassignment from the POW/MIA office, no one seemed interested in pursuing the matter. For several months, Schweitzer was passed aimlessly around the bureaucracy, obliged to relate his unlikely tale of access to secret Vietnamese archives all over again to a series of incredulous officials in a series of reinventing-the-wheel sessions. His last meeting was in December 1990, with Lewis Stern, a mid-ranking, but well-placed Pentagon civilian.

Stern did not encourage Schweitzer. "We could never fund anything this . . . *irregular,*" he said.

Schweitzer left the Pentagon, convinced his brief, abortive career as an ad hoc intelligence agent was over.

ON JANUARY 22, 1991, during the thirteenth joint crash site investigation in northern Vietnam, the VNOSMP team leader told his American counterparts from JCRC that he had "found some information concerning the case of Major Morrison and Lieutenant Francisco" while researching the records of the Quang Binh Air Defense Forces. The records showed that an F-4 had been shot down on November 25, 1968, and had crashed almost directly below the place it had been hit. The 57mm antiaircraft battery had been stationed near the village of Cau Lang. The aircraft crew consisted of a major and a lieutenant. A man who was the leader of the Thuong Trach village people's committee during the war reported that all the civilians had been moved out of the area; therefore, only PAVN personnel stationed there would have witnessed the shootdown and the subsequent search for the aircrew. The joint investigation team was told by other villagers that the graves might be located near the kilometer 54 marker on the switchback road. The team found no graves.

DESPITE THE DISCOURAGEMENT from bureaucrats, Schweitzer remained convinced that he held the key to the MIA enigma. And he was also certain that some American publisher would be eager to fund the project that unimaginative bureaucrats had rejected.

But Schweitzer's optimism was almost immediately dampened. He discovered that the POW/MIA issue had evolved into a thriving cottage industry, which included a number of sensational rival books, some already under contract to publishers, others circulating among publishers.

One of these projects, *Kiss the Boys Goodbye,* by Monika Jensen-Stevenson, a former *60 Minutes* producer, and her husband, veteran war correspondent and historian William Stevenson, was subtitled "How the United States Betrayed Its Own POWs in Vietnam." It drew heavily on questionable sources to expand the prevailing conspiracy theory that large numbers of Americans remained captive in Laos after the war, and that some had been transferred from Indochina to the Soviet Union.

(A detailed, well-documented refutation of *Kiss the Boys Goodbye* was written by the Defense Intelligence Agency POW/MIA office [reputedly by analyst Robert Destatte]. A copy of this report is available in the records of the Senate Select Committee on POW/MIA Affairs in the National Archives.[3])

Another competing book was *Soldiers of Misfortune,* by journalists Jim Sanders, Mark Sauter, and R. Cort Kirkwood, which traced Soviet and North Korean deception in retaining American prisoners in their control after World War II and the Korean War. The book also made more sensational, highly speculative assertions that Soviet and Chinese intelligence officers had handpicked certain specialized American POWs for transfer out of Indochina during the war. As with the Stevenson book, these assertions were based on questionable sources.[4]

But the books were newsworthy and seemingly authoritative. And none of the books made any mention of a central POW archive in Hanoi. Instead, the authors concentrated on the more lurid aspects of the question: proving the existence of secret prison camps in Laos or tracking down American POWs who had allegedly been transferred to the Soviet Union during the war and were still languishing in the vestigial Gulag.

Further, Hollywood had cashed in on the emotional MIA issue. The popular Chuck Norris "MIA" movies jostled for business in the video stores with more equally improbable films, such as *Uncommon Valor* and of course the blood-and-guts *Rambo* blockbuster. A quiet, serious middle-aged man in a rumpled sportcoat like Ted Schweitzer, who claimed to have direct access to top secret Vietnamese archives, was no competition for Sylvester Stallone in a bloody headband, gripping a blazing machine gun in his naked bulging arms.[5]

What was most frustrating for Schweitzer was the knowledge that he had direct access to the information that would definitely help solve the MIA mystery.

Since 1973, the Vietnamese government had stubbornly denied that they had any additional information about prisoners who had not returned in Operation Homecoming. But Schweitzer now had reason to believe that these cases were indexed in the Red Book, which meant that their complete records existed *somewhere* in the PAVN archives.

For ten months, Ted Schweitzer's clumsy, unfocused book proposal, "All That We Left Behind," made the rounds of New York publishers. Schweitzer hoped that the POW ID cards, the aircraft identification plate, and the authentic sample PAVN prisoner record card he carried with him to show editors would somehow convince them of the book project's potential. But these arcane artifacts merely confused editors, who believed they were being asked to fund some type of an obscure military encyclopedia. Schweitzer's book project was rejected by each publisher he contacted.

He had hoped to receive a book advance adequate to purchase computer optical scanning equipment to copy the entire PAVN POW archive, including all the ID cards, dog tags, personal papers, and—most importantly—the Red Book index, as well as all the detailed PAVN prisoner record cards, which Colonel Dai had shown him in Hanoi.

By now Schweitzer had made a practical plan for the scanning equipment and computers he would need to successfully copy all the museum POW archives and artifacts under the relatively primitive conditions of Hanoi, where drenching humidity, baking heat, and regular power failures prevailed. One of the best optical scanners then available was made by Fujitsu. It required sophisticated software run by a powerful computer. But if he was going to be certain to obtain clear copies of handwritten documents (which were often mildewed and stained record cards), Schweitzer would need more computer power for image enhancement. And the best way to record such imagery was on optical disks, which would require their own database software and computer support. And somehow this whole system had to be tied together with a reliable software operating system into a functional, transportable package.

He estimated the cost for this system at somewhere between $75,000 and $100,000. And he had no guarantee, other than his contract with the PAVN museum, that the enterprise would succeed.

ON JULY 22, 1991, the joint American-Vietnamese MIA investigation team visited the PAVN Military Region 4 Museum in the city of Vinh. They were presented with the historical logs of the 280th Air Defense Regiment. Document 1462 listed American aircraft losses in November and December 1968. On a handwritten ledger entitled "American Air Pirates Killed and Torn Apart," entry 14 listed the names and serial numbers of Major Joseph C. Morrison and First Lieutenant San D. Francisco. The investigators were told that this roster was reserved for those dead American aviators who were so badly mangled or burned in the crash of their aircraft that no remains were recovered.[6]

The Vietnamese were unable to explain how two men who had safely ejected from their crippled aircraft and had spoken by emergency radio to Search and Rescue forces had become "torn apart."

BY AUTUMN 1991, it became obvious to Schweitzer that no publisher was willing to risk a book advance on a potential wild goose chase. Moreover, most experienced editors thought it unlikely that the Vietnamese Communists would have granted access to these sensitive archives to a well-meaning private researcher, when the combined energy of the entire U.S. government—open and covert—had been unable to gain this access during almost twenty years of protracted negotiations.

"Can you guarantee success?" an editor asked him. "How can I convince my publishing board that the Vietnamese have chosen *you* to give all this information when they've rejected everybody else?"

Schweitzer unfolded the dog-eared contract and handed it across the man's desk.

The editor, a middle-aged veteran of Sixth Avenue publishing intrigues, frowned over his half-framed glasses. "Not good enough," he said, handing back the creased paper.

Schweitzer recognized the near-impossible task he faced, trying to find a publisher. But he also realized that the Vietnamese were about to initiate a breakthrough in the stalemate, and they seemed to have chosen him as the conduit.

And he knew that officers like Colonel Dai, who held the key to the MIA mystery, had only recently been forced to concede the intensity of America's obsession with this issue. To the Vietnamese, the Second Indochina War— what the Americans called *the* Vietnam War—was merely one of a series of engagements in their long struggle for independence and what they considered their rightful hegemony over the eastern Indochina peninsula. A man like Colonel Dai had first seen combat as a teenager in the resistance to Japanese occupation during World War II. He had fought as a young soldier against the French at Dien Bien Phu, then for years in the "War of Independence" against the Americans and their South Vietnamese allies. Then, only a few years after the fall of Saigon, Dai had led troops into Cambodia for the most bitter jungle campaign against the brutally efficient Khmer Rouge. But within weeks, the PAVN was fighting the Chinese on Vietnam's northern frontier in pitched, large-scale conventional battles that dwarfed any combat he had seen in the South.

Men like Dai, and his counterparts in the Politburo, the Ministry of the Interior, and the Ministry of Foreign Affairs, had little patience with America's stubborn demands for a "full accounting" of its missing men. Since 1945, uncounted thousands of Vietnamese had disappeared behind prison doors—North and South—never to appear again. During the late 1950s, South Vietnamese President Ngo Dinh Diem had ordered the execution of an estimated 10,000 Communist cadres in the South. In the same period, DRV President Ho Chi Minh approved the execution of at least that many "reactionaries" as part of his collectivization campaign. Most had suffered hideous, unrecorded deaths.[7]

Yet the Americans insisted Hanoi account for every American missing in Indochina.

The years of American engagement in Indochina, roughly 1965–75, Schweitzer now saw, were *not* the momentous turning point in Vietnamese history that they were for most Americans, but simply a difficult period on the long continuum of war that began with Ho Chi Minh's Communist underground in the 1920s.

During these six decades of almost nonstop war, the Vietnamese people, both North and South, had suffered over one million killed. Their casualties included more than 300,000 men and women missing in action. In fact, there were over 100,000 families in the Socialist Republic of Vietnam that had officially listed at least one relative on the Vietnamese MIA rolls.[8]

So these hard-bitten veteran officials could not easily empathize with America's agony over a relative handful of missing men. But Schweitzer understood his country's preoccupation. Our engagement in the long Indochina War had a bitter legacy: It was the first war we lost.

Maybe, Schweitzer mused, making the rounds of New York publishers, I'm in a unique position to bridge the gap in empathy and understanding between the two countries. Despite the rejections, he remained determined to see his project through. Schweitzer recognized that his selection by the Vietnamese as a conduit of sensitive information represented a face-saving Asian expedient, which contained a convenient escape hatch of denial, should the information he uncovered prove too embarrassing for the PAVN. The Vietnamese were preparing a trial balloon for flight, and they wanted him to climb aboard the rickety basket. But he simply could not afford the price of the ticket.

In desperation, he turned to Texas billionaire Ross Perot, who had donated generously to various efforts to win the freedom of American POWs allegedly still held in Indochina. Perot's involvement with the POW/MIA issue went back to 1969, when he financed and led an intense public relations campaign designed to focus international attention on the plight of American POWs in Indochina. Perot's efforts, which included the creation of a grassroots public-awareness organization, United We Stand, in the 1960s, were his debut on the national political scene.[9]

Schweitzer's contacts with Ross Perot dated to the mid-1980s, when Perot was at the height of his obsession with Richard Armitage, one of Schweitzer's friends from the Vietnam War. Perot was a fervent believer in a bizarre conspiracy theory—one of several to which he subscribed—that Armitage had led a renegade American intelligence operation that had imported tons of heroin into the United States from the Golden Triangle of Southeast Asia.

"Mr. Schweitzer," Perot had said with his familiar twang during one phone conversation, "I have information that Armitage was the head of this drug trafficking by American intelligence agents."

"No way, sir," Schweitzer had responded. "I know Richard Armitage. Look, he might have fooled around with women and booze in Saigon and

Bangkok, just like a million other servicemen out there, but definitely not with dope. I know Richard far too well. He would *never* have screwed around with heroin."

"Well, Mr. Schweitzer," Perot had snorted. "You're either lying, or naive."

Now, six years later, Schweitzer managed to gain a telephone audience with Perot. Schweitzer outlined his unique access to the Red Book and the other museum documents. He was about to make his appeal for funding when Perot interrupted.

"All this information is all about men who are dead?" Perot asked.

"Yes, sir."

"You've got no information on men still alive?"

"No, I do not. I—"

"Well," Perot snapped. "I find that all very interesting, Mr. Schweitzer. But those men are all dead, and I don't care about them. The ones *I* care about are the ones still in those bamboo cages over there."

Schweitzer received no funds from Perot.

IN OCTOBER 1991, Schweitzer visited his old friend and superior officer, Brigadier General Harry C. "Heinie" Aderholt, USAF (Ret.), at his Florida office. Aderholt, a legendary Air Commando officer, had spent years in Southeast Asia during the war. He still had good government connections. After Schweitzer showed Aderholt the materials from Hanoi and explained his frustrations trying to gain backers for the project, Aderholt picked up the phone and called Ambassador Richard Armitage at the State Department.

"Rich," General Aderholt said. "You remember Ted Schweitzer from Thailand. He's got something very interesting here, and I want him to come up and see you. This could be important."

"Send him up anytime," Armitage replied. "Have him call me when he gets in town."

Schweitzer left for Washington that afternoon.

Richard Armitage then held an ambassador-level post as the White House special envoy to the new Commonwealth of Independent States (the former USSR). Schweitzer knew Armitage well from the 1970s in Southeast Asia and from his later refugee-rescue days. He hoped the experienced official could advise him where next to seek discreet government backing. Armitage had been the assistant secretary of defense for international security affairs during the Reagan administration, which might have partially explained Ross Perot's obsession with toppling a powerful figure. A Naval Academy classmate of Marine Lieutenant Colonel Oliver North, Armitage had served in Vietnam and elsewhere in Southeast Asia as a naval officer and later civilian official.

As a key foreign policy official of the first Reagan administration, Armitage had traveled three times to Vietnam on the MIA issue. In February 1984, he had led a delegation to Hanoi that had wrested a formal agreement from the Foreign Ministry to accelerate the pace of MIA accounting efforts through clear and logical practical steps. Under his forceful persuasion, the Vietnamese agreed to focus on the most easily accessible discrepancy cases: men lost in the Hanoi-Haiphong corridor. The Vietnamese also agreed to try to locate "easily recoverable remains," which was probably diplomatic fiction for remains already in their possession. Richard Armitage was goal-oriented, however, and did not care where the remains came from as long as they were recovered.

Armitage was a tight-lipped political tactician, used to obtaining results in sensitive negotiations. (He later led the American team that negotiated the withdrawal from major military bases in the Philippines.) It was perhaps Armitage's background as a tough player of international political hardball that first earned him the wrath of Ross Perot.[10]

Ted Schweitzer met Armitage at his State Department offices early on a bright October morning. As usual the stocky, bald official had already been at his desk for several hours.

"What have you got for me, Ted?" Armitage held out his hand.

Schweitzer handed over several U.S. Air Force ID cards, three photographs of battered American pilots in muddy flight suits—obviously airmen who had just been captured—and two gray rectangular pasteboard index cards, cut to the metric size of the old French colonial filing drawers. The cards' information was in Vietnamese, written on both sides in a variety of hands, the small crablike characters completely filling the available space.

Armitage glanced at the photos and ID cards, then put on his reading glasses to study the record cards. He read both several times before looking back up at Schweitzer. Now Armitage's expression was intense.

"Ted," he asked, "you don't read Vietnamese, do you?"

Schweitzer shook his head. "No," he began in his earnest manner. "I'm working on it—"

Armitage interrupted. "But you *do* understand what you have here?"

Ted nodded. "They're POW records."

Armitage held up one faded gray card. Its file number was 392. The card's central data block was filled with neat handwritten Vietnamese notations in cursive script, which had a flowing but crisp quality, indicative of a fine-nibbed fountain pen, rather than the smeared ballpoint lettering commonly seen in Southeast Asia.

"Four slash nine slash nineteen sixty-five," Armitage read, noting the date of the incident. "F four-C."

He continued to read slowly, frowning when he encountered an unfamiliar word. Then he came to the middle of the card in which the names of the two American aviators were printed in capital letters of the Roman alphabet. "Branch, James A., Captain. Jewell, Eugene M., First Lieutenant." Armitage continued reading, sometimes moving his lips to help comprehend an unfamiliar Vietnamese military expression. He shook his head, his lips pursed. "They even note the type of radar directing the guns that shot this plane down."

Armitage read the reverse side of the card and most of the second document before looking up to again gaze levelly across his half-frame glasses at Schweitzer. "Captain Branch and Lieutenant Jewell were shot down in Nghe Tinh Province just north of Vinh. They were on a strafing run and were hit at low altitude. This is the first confirmation of their deaths. We should be able to recover some remains."

"I guess that's worth something," Schweitzer said quietly.

"You better believe it, Ted."

Armitage spun in his chair, picked up a telephone, and called Principal Deputy Assistant Secretary of Defense for International Security Affairs Dr. Carl Ford. Officially, Ford was a career Defense bureaucrat. But Washington insiders knew he was actually a high-ranking career CIA officer, the agency's permanent liaison at the Pentagon, the man who orchestrated sensitive matters involving the uniformed services and the intelligence community.

"Carl," Armitage said, "I've got a guy here I want you to see immediately."

Schweitzer walked through the autumn sunshine to the Foggy Bottom Metro station, then took the subway across the river to the Pentagon. Carl Ford ushered him into his spacious office in the Pentagon's E-Ring and offered a welcome cup of coffee. Like Armitage, Ford became completely absorbed in the Vietnamese record card. A stocky man in his forties with a close-clipped beard and deep-set eyes, Ford appeared more a reclusive professor than one of the most powerful intelligence professionals in Washington. As he read, he absently chain-smoked Camels.

Ford's reading knowledge of Vietnamese was rusty, but adequate for the task at hand. Several times as he read, he pursed his lips as Armitage had and muttered.

When Ford finished reading the cards, he spoke with the soft assured manner of a college dean. "Ted, this is definitely a valid project. We're going to make sure that it is supported. Even if there's only a one percent chance of success, we have to back it."

Schweitzer breathed in deeply, listening intently. He realized that this was the first indication of truly high-level support.

Ford continued in a confident manner. "If anybody can do this, we can. Richard's already behind it, and the two of us will go see Secretary Cheney together."

Schweitzer felt a rush of excitement.

"Just make a list of what you need, Ted," Ford said.

"Well . . ." Schweitzer began. "I'm going to need some computer equipment."

"Within reason," Ford said, "that really should not be a problem."[11]

CHAPTER 11

TED SCHWEITZER'S UNEXPECTED SUCCESS IN SECURING GOVERNMENT support did not mean that the DIA's Special Office for POW/MIAs, the branch of the bureaucracy most concerned with the issue, had suddenly changed its mind about the merits of his project. In fact, the office, and the entire analytical division of DIA, would remain hostile to and skeptical of Schweitzer.

Rather, the obvious receptiveness that Richard Armitage and Carl Ford had shown him was an indication that the Bush administration was under increasing pressure to achieve a breakthrough on the emotionally charged issue before the 1992 election, then only thirteen months away.

Even though no senior official in the Pentagon or the intelligence agencies believed that surviving American POWs remained in Indochina so long after the war, the Bush White House had to battle a much different public perception. The confusion surrounding the American disengagement from Indochina and the subsequent myriad live-sighting reports helped spawn one of the most persistent myths in modern American history.[1] As noted above, twenty years after the Vietnam War, 69 percent of the people surveyed in a *Wall Street Journal*/NBC News poll believed American POWs were still being held in Indochina.[2] This was a perception any Republican president seeking reelection with support from the party's conservative wing would have to overcome.

Seen in this context, the decision to use Schweitzer as its primary agent to penetrate the inner sanctum of the Vietnamese archives was just one of several new parallel initiatives that included a diplomatic "Road Map" of steps toward lifting the trade embargo, plans for expanded JCRC field investigations in Indochina, renewed efforts by veterans' and MIA family groups, an accelerated schedule of Vessey-delegation activity, and the ambitious investigation by the newly installed Select Committee on POW/MIA Affairs of the United States Senate.

The Road Map for normalizing relations between America and Vietnam was an astute policy maneuver hatched by the senior executives of the Inter-Agency Group. In April 1991, the IAG convinced Vietnam to accept the Road Map plan that would measure the SRV's cooperation on the POW/MIA issue, and stabilization of Cambodia, through a series of benchmarks—or "gates" in Washington jargon—eventually leading to the lifting of the trade embargo and the restoration of diplomatic relations.[3]

Although the Road Map remains classified, and the SRV has never officially acknowledged its acceptance of these conditions, it became clear almost immediately after Hanoi leaked a copy of the document to *The Nation,* Bangkok's leading English language newspaper, that Vietnam intended to follow the Road Map.[4]

The first phase called for Hanoi to influence its surrogate government in Phnom Penh to accept an international peace settlement in Cambodia. Hanoi was also obliged to "accelerate" cooperation on resolving "as fully as possible all remaining POW/MIA cases with a target of completing the work in the next 24 months and longer if the U.S. determines it would be helpful to achieving the fullest possible accounting."[5]

Road Map phases two, three, and four established a clear quid pro quo by which America matched every specific concession by the Vietnamese (and their Cambodian allies) with a specific U.S. concession. These included gradual steps toward lifting the embargo, such as the reestablishment of telecommunication links between the United States and Vietnam and the granting of exceptions to the embargo for U.S. commercial firms to meet "basic human needs," including contracts on medical and agricultural projects. When "substantial progress" on diplomatic and MIA problems had been demonstrated during the two-year period between 1991 and the end of 1992 (a time frame clearly geared toward the presidential election), America would open a diplomatic liaison office in Hanoi and invite Vietnam to establish one in Washington. Finally, when Washington and Hanoi agreed that all previous pledges of progress toward resolving the POW/MIA issue had been met, the United States was prepared to approve International Monetary Fund loans, establish full diplomatic relations, and lift the remaining strictures of the embargo.

It was clearly in Vietnam's interest to comply with the Road Map. Obviously, the SRV would have to demonstrate visible dramatic progress on the MIA issue, not merely make grudging and obscure concessions as in the past. Ted Schweitzer's unusual access to the secret archives of Hanoi's Central Military Museum did not seem so bizarre when examined within the context of the SRV's compliance to the Road Map. Solving the MIA mystery had acquired new political importance, and the White House intended to earn political capital from any breakthroughs.

UNTIL 1991, THE DIA's central role in the slow, frustrating investigation of the MIA issue had remained basically unchanged for two decades. Despite chronic criticism that the agency's POW/MIA office was indifferent to the needs of MIA families, that it was inefficient, and that it was burdened with a "mind-set to debunk" valid intelligence on live American POWs still in

Indochina, the DIA's lead agency position had never been seriously challenged.[6] Now the DIA was forced to concede that it was no longer the only game in town.

Most of the criticism of the office from both the public and Congress concerned its inadequate effort to find concrete answers about missing men, especially those who fit into one discrepancy category or another. This effort was especially ineffectual when examined in the light of the Reagan administration's imprudent 1982 declaration that resolving the MIA issue was a matter of the "highest national priority."[7] Even conceding the inflated rhetoric of the first Reagan White House, it was ludicrous to describe the Defense Department efforts to resolve the MIA mystery—which basically involved business as usual by the DIA office for five years after Reagan's statement—in such heroic terms. If in fact resolving the issue had been assigned the highest priority by the national intelligence community, hundreds of highly skilled professional analysts and case officers, supported by a technical and administrative staff numbering in the thousands, would have been assigned to the effort.

This simply did not happen.

The staff of the DIA's Special Office for POW/MIAs did grow slowly during the Reagan administration—but remained fewer than thirty—and never swelled to the size adequate to meet the intelligence collection and analysis requirements it faced. In the Joint Chiefs of Staff ten-year operations plan for 1973–82 (which governed the allocation of funding and personnel resources for intelligence activities), POW intelligence activities were assigned priorities 49 and 56, well below sociological data (priority 16), and below exploitation of physical environment (priority 46) and civil defense (priority 48). This low priority led to a commensurate anemic allocation of resources, including the timely satellite imagery by the most sensitive observation platforms (Talent-Keyhole "real time" reconnaissance satellites) necessary to trace refugee reports of live Americans held captive in Indochina. The fact was that almost no senior Pentagon officers or civilian officials believed there were live POWs in Vietnam or Laos, so no one would authorize the permanent allocation of scarce resources to this line of investigation.[8]

And it was a full four years after President Reagan's statement that the DIA officially listed the POW/MIA issue as its number one priority. And that was an "exception to policy" bordering on naked political deception.[9]

The truth was that the office was badly understaffed, anemically funded, and poorly organized during most of its post-cease-fire operations.

After the massive exodus of Indochinese refugees in the late 1970s, the DIA office intensified the processing of "live-sighting" refugee reports—under considerable pressure from the National League of Families and its allies in Congress. Altogether, the DIA processed over 15,000 refugee statements between the fall of Saigon and 1991.

More than half were so-called dog tag reports: a refugee's claim that he or she possessed or had seen a military identity tag of an American military man, who might or might not be missing. Almost 4,000 of the refugee reports concerned wartime crash and grave site information, most of it in the south, and most were already noted in DIA and JCRC records. There were also about 3,000 hearsay reports of live American "prisoners." But most of these were eventually determined to involve either American deserters (about twenty-four in number) or Soviet and Eastern Bloc technicians who arrived in South Vietnam after the fall of Saigon.[10]

These secondhand refugee reports had to be viewed in the context of their sources. In North Vietnam, both peasants and city dwellers habitually referred to all Caucasians as *lien-so,* "Soviet," while in the South, villagers saw all white foreigners as *my,* "American."

However, 1,672 refugee reports were firsthand sightings of live Americans. But, under analysis, only fifty-seven remained validly "unresolved" by 1991.

During the 1980s, the POW/MIA office was twice carefully scrutinized, once by senior DIA officers and again by an independent task force.

In a 1985 memorandum to the agency's executives, Navy Commodore Thomas A. Brooks, DIA's assistant deputy director for collection management, presented the details of his in-depth review of the office. He criticized "particularly sloppy" operations in the late 1970s, which continued into the 1980s. Brooks cited poor recordkeeping, which included "mixed-up, loose papers, undated scribbled analyst notes, misfiled papers, etc." He also noted poor follow-up on live sightings that should have immediately stimulated "tasked imagery" by reconnaissance satellites and aerial photography. Another serious defect Brooks noted was the failure of the office to employ the most basic analytic tools, such as the commonly used pattern analysis system of plotting source reports on maps and trying to draw conclusions from the resulting concentrations.[11]

(The intelligence technique of pattern analysis was well established by the 1950s. However, the subsequent advent of high-speed computers greatly enhanced the efficacy of this technique. In the case of American MIAs in Indochina, pattern analyses using electronic databases should have been a major element of the DIA POW/MIA office's analytical work during the twenty years since the American withdrawal from Vietnam. But because the issue was not one of the agency's "national priorities," the office did not develop the powerful computer software and multifactor MIA database necessary to perform sophisticated pattern analyses until recently.

(The DIA now officially reports that it is actively using pattern analysis to compare refugee live-sighting reports with database information on MIAs.)

But Commodore Brooks found no basis for the allegation that the office was gripped by a mind-set to debunk reliable reports of live American prisoners. He noted that the analysts had been deluged by "so many fabrications for so long that their first subconscious reaction is, 'This is just more of the same garbage.'" Commodore Brooks conceded that most of these reports were in fact worthless. However, he stated the obvious: Some live sightings could have been valid and should have been followed up on a much more professional basis. If that were to be accomplished, Brooks concluded, the office had to receive more funding and personnel and so did the DIA-backed JCRC effort in the refugee camps of Southeast Asia, particularly in the form of skilled polygraph operators and interpreters to better verify live-sighting reports.

Brooks added that the DIA had to pay better attention to its image. Agency officers needed to be perceived as "open-minded, objective professionals who take this business very seriously and are willing to talk to anyone who might be able to provide us information." This included the "lunatic fringe" of disreputable con men who had been preying on MIA families for several years.

In his detailed list of recommendations to improve the MIA office's future operations, Commodore Brooks included the following intriguing task: "Put a Reservist to work doing a study on the backgrounds/common denominators of the couple of dozen MIAs who were known to have been captured alive but who never showed up in the prison system." It is significant that in this classified internal document Commodore Brooks did not raise the issue of hundreds of additional missing Americans who might have fit into this category. At most, Brooks implied, the Indochinese Communists should have been able to provide information on a "couple of dozen MIAs" who were known to have been captured alive but subsequently disappeared. By studying their backgrounds for any common denominators, Brooks was suggesting that this group might include military specialists who could have been targets for especially intense interrogation, or for transfer to the Soviet Union or China, North Vietnam's two principal allies.[12]

Another interesting element of this recommendation was the call to put a reservist on this important assignment. This was a tacit admission that the office was so understaffed that a regular analyst could not be spared. Indeed, with an authorized strength in 1985 of only eighteen people—military and civilian of all ranks (the staff was then being expanded to twenty-eight)— the office could hardly be considered the lead unit of an endeavor that was supposedly America's highest national priority. (By 1993, the reorganized POW/MIA office had a staff of 170.)

Less than a year after the Brooks memorandum (and a subsequent comprehensive in-house DIA review of the office led by Air Force Colonel Kimball Gaines), a Pentagon task force led by retired Air Force Lieutenant General Eugene F. Tighe, Jr. (a former DIA director), recommended a "complete overhaul" of the agency's POW/MIA office. But the task force found "no evidence of a cover-up by DIA."[13] Moreover, the group's report noted that it was "self-evident that a large number of MIAs may never be properly accounted for."[14]

Because the six-man Tighe Task Force and its six-man Senior Review Panel were composed of distinguished retired military officers (including former POWs Lieutenant General John Flynn and Brigadier General Robbie Risner) as well as senior civilian intelligence officials eminently knowledgeable on the issue, their conclusions were considered authoritative.

But even as the Tighe Task Force's report (classified secret in 1986, declassified in 1992) absolved the DIA's POW/MIA office of charges that it had abetted a cover-up of abandoned American prisoners in Indochina, the document sparked a controversy that reverberates with acrimony to the present day.

General Tighe was personally convinced before the group began its work that American POWs had been abandoned in Laos and Vietnam after the fall of the South in 1975. As DIA director in June 1981, he had testified before the House Subcommittee on Asian and Pacific Affairs that, although the agency had no evidence to support refugee reports of live American POWs in Southeast Asia, it was his personal judgment that "American servicemen are alive and being held against their will in Indochina."[15] This was his only such statement as DIA director. However, after retirement, General Tighe had been vocal about this personal belief in statements to the news media.

But Tighe realized that most of his task force colleagues did not share his belief. In fact, during the conference on the final draft report on May 27, 1986, former JCRC commander General Robert Kingston, a review panel member, challenged Tighe about statements he had made on television. "Gene," Kingston asked, "are you still telling people you have unequivocal evidence that we left prisoners behind?"

Tighe backed down. "I never said that," he replied. "And if you heard that, I was being misquoted."

Kingston had personally seen and heard Tighe make this statement on a nationwide television show. How the hell can you misquote yourself? he wondered.

(It is of interest to note that Ross Perot, also a member of the Senior Review Panel, rarely attended its meetings and was not present for this review and approval session.)

During that May 27, 1986, meeting, the task force members sharply debated the wording of a key conclusion. General Tighe suggested the following: "DIA holds information that establishes the strong possibility of American prisoners of war in Laos and Vietnam."

But members objected. Kingston noted that they had seen no evidence to support such a statement. He and Major General John Murray suggested a compromise, which was accepted: "DIA holds information that establishes the strong possibility of Americans in Laos and Vietnam."

The members understood "Americans" to refer to voluntary stay-behinds: deserters, civilian contractors gone native, converts to Vietnamese religious sects, overzealous missionaries, and Americans involved in drug trafficking.

It had always been accepted that there were scores of AWOLs and deserters, including escaped stockade and brig prisoners, loose in the criminal underworld "twilight zones" of South Vietnam's cities at the end of the war. Indeed, when U.S. Military Assistance Command, Vietnam headquarters in Saigon held a general muster in November 1972, 350 troops could not be accounted for. As the U.S. role in the war wound down, some Air Force enlisted men had simply taken empty seats on planes bound for America, thus effecting unofficial "transfers" out of the war zone. But totaling the irregular Air Force departees and the deserters who sought asylum in April 1975, the Pentagon could not reach the figure of 350 who did not make the general muster.[16]

Many of the in-country deserters later voluntarily returned to American control as Saigon fell in April 1975. Estimates of their numbers varied greatly. The official estimate by the U.S. embassy in Saigon was as low as twelve. But unofficial speculation put the number of deserters in South Vietnamese cities as high as 300. As Communist forces closed in on Saigon, an undetermined number of Americans in civilian clothes, many with Vietnamese dependents, came forward. Commenting at the time, an American State Department official stated: "We aren't asking questions. If an American wants to go home, we'll get him home."[17]

But in a final version of the task force report that General Tighe edited that summer, this crucial conclusion had been reworded to read: "DIA holds information that establishes the strong possibility of American *prisoners of war being held* in Laos and Vietnam" (emphasis added).[18]

General Robert Kingston was incensed that the rewritten conclusion made its way back into the report after he had approved a "final" version that did not include this sensational charge. In December 1986, Kingston wrote DIA Director Air Force Lieutenant General Leonard H. Peroots to express his grave concern about this matter. Kingston noted that the draft report he had signed "has been significantly altered," and that none of the panel members was informed of the changes. Peroots told Kingston that the Tighe Task Force had not been an official DIA entity, and that any changes made in the final version had been made by Lieutenant General Tighe himself, not the DIA.[19]

Kingston's fellow task force members, retired Army Major General John Murray and retired Air Force General Russell Dougherty, also mentioned these changes to Peroots. Murray was troubled by the replacement of the word "Americans" with "prisoners of war being held."[20]

The conclusion flew in the face of the long-held official denial that such information existed. Although the report was classified, news of the finding soon leaked. And over the intervening years, this allegation has continued to spark controversy.

What has never been revealed, however, is the fact that the controversial charge was *not* in the original report approved by the six working members and the six members of the Senior Review Panel.

Years after the Tighe Task Force report, General Kingston remains indignant that POW conspiracy buffs continue to cite the document—a draft of which he had approved in good faith—as proof that American POWs survived after the fall of Saigon. He is especially galled that Tighe's "editing" gave the impression that the board and the senior review panel—which included former POWs, and the former JCRC commander (Kingston himself) —unanimously approved the controversial conclusion.[21]

However, this controversy was not the only blow the DIA suffered at the hands of an insider.

ON THE MORNING of Tuesday, February 12, 1991, Army Colonel Millard A. "Mike" Peck, a trim, sandy-haired officer whose youthful appearance concealed his almost twenty-nine years in uniform, strode into the offices of the director and executive director of the Defense Intelligence Agency. The sealed envelopes he presented contained a memorandum entitled "Request for Relief."

Mike Peck had been the head of the DIA's Special Office for POW/MIAs for only seven months. Now he was resigning as chief of the office, and also requesting an expeditious retirement from active military service.

With a Distinguished Service Cross, three Silver Stars, the Purple Heart with two Oak Leaf Clusters, and the proverbial chestful of lesser medals, Colonel Peck was among the most heavily decorated soldiers of the Vietnam War.[22]

During three combat tours in Vietnam, beginning as a young Special Forces lieutenant on an A team in the Central Highlands, Peck had established an outstanding reputation of courage and dedication to duty.

But now Mike Peck was tossing in the towel.

Or so it seemed. Actually, because DIA's executives were overburdened with the pressing business of the Gulf War, Peck's resignation sparked no immediate response.

Finally, six weeks later, on March 28, 1991, Peck finally tacked a copy of the resignation memo to his office door and walked out.

Peck's memorandum made sweeping allegations of gross misconduct, including a possible cover-up among the government officials who had managed the MIA issue for the past twenty years. He also accused Ann Mills Griffiths, director of the National League of Families of American Prisoners and Missing in Southeast Asia, of blatant interference in the intelligence process. The memo cited "unscrupulous people in the government, or associated with the government" who manipulated the entire POW/MIA issue for "personal or political advantage."

In Peck's memo, the DIA office had been used as a "toxic waste dump," where his overburdened staff were habitually deluged with make-work and disinformation (including a variety of false leads), in order to keep the entire sordid "mess" safely "out of sight and mind." The mind-set to debunk, Peck wrote, "is alive and well. It is held at all levels, and continues to pervade the POW-MIA Office. . . ."

Coming from a man with Peck's combat record, these accusations were impossible to ignore.

Peck's memo stated that, based on his personal experience, "it appears that any soldier left in Vietnam, even inadvertently, was, in fact, abandoned years ago, and that the farce that is being played is no more than political legerdemain done with 'smoke and mirrors,' to stall the issue until it dies a natural death."

In his final paragraph, "A Farewell to Arms," Colonel Peck stated he was resigning "to avoid the annoyance of being shipped off to some remote corner, out of sight and out of the way, in my own 'bamboo cage' of silence. . . ."

Peck's bitter memorandum provided more ammunition for those who believed that arrogant politicians and bureaucrats (including DIA executives) had somehow been both indifferent to the plight of our Indochina MIAs for decades, yet had also been active, longtime members of an elaborate conspiracy to conceal the true fates of these missing men.[23]

As with the Tighe Task Force controversy, however, there turned out to be both less and more to Colonel Mike Peck's action than news media accounts revealed.

First, there was confusion about Peck's "resignation": the pinning of the accusatory tract to a public door, just as Martin Luther had nailed his Ninety-Five Theses to the door of the Wittenberg Cathedral. It appeared initially as if a last straw had dropped within the murky confines of the Pentagon, spurring this hitherto well-disciplined and courageous officer to his final gesture of self-sacrifice.

Following this line, most of the news media portrayed Mike Peck as the ultimate whistleblower.

Peck's memo became another article of faith for POW/MIA activists, proving that a wide-ranging government conspiracy existed to cover up the crass abandonment of our missing men after 1973.

But inside the Pentagon, the men whom Peck had accused of "high-level knavery" quickly counterattacked. Within days of Peck's dramatic walkout, Defense Secretary Dick Cheney had ordered a formal management inquiry, led by Ronald J. Knecht, special assistant to the assistant secretary of defense for command, control, communications, and intelligence. Knecht's team of investigators worked for two months. The team conducted two long interviews with Colonel Peck, during which he was asked to produce evidence to support his charges, or to provide an indication where the inquiry might turn to find such evidence.

Details of the inquiry team's findings were made public on January 28, 1992, in a report to the Senate Select Committee on POW/MIA Affairs.[24]

The Knecht report's most damaging revelation was that the resignation memorandum that Colonel Peck submitted on February 12, 1991, was in fact an empty gesture. Four days earlier, on February 8, DIA Director Lieutenant General Harry E. Soyster had informed Peck that his performance was unsatisfactory and that the Pentagon would find him a new assignment more in line with his skills as a Foreign Area officer (Peck's area of expertise was Western Europe). In Soyster's opinion, Peck was "a good officer in the wrong job." Because Peck spoke French and had cross-trained with the French military, Soyster proposed that he be transferred to a senior liaison position with the French Army in Germany. But Peck told Soyster that he did not want to leave the Washington, D.C., area.

Four days later, Peck delivered his memo to Soyster.

Although Peck was one of the most decorated heroes of the Vietnam War, he had no experience in formal intelligence analysis or in management of intelligence production activities.[25] His DIA experience was mainly in channeling already acquired current intelligence to the Pentagon's Joint Staff. Peck had a six-week overlap with his predecessor, Colonel Joe Schlatter, in June and July 1990. But, according to the Knecht report, three months later in October, the DIA's senior executives and other Pentagon officials realized that "Colonel Peck was just not getting the job done. . . ."

The report makes clear that Mike Peck, the epitome of the courageous, action-oriented combat officer, was ill-suited to the faceless drudgery and repetitive legwork—not to mention the intra-Pentagon diplomacy—that were inherent in the position. Peck was a romantic—some claim a quixotic —figure, cut from similar but less glittering cloth as that of another brave young officer who had shone brightly in war but foundered on the shoals of the postwar bureaucracy: Colonel T. E. Lawrence ("of Arabia").

Indeed, Mike Peck's self-image was that of a swashbuckling lone wolf, leading Special Operations in pursuit of the ultimate Truth that lay at the heart of the MIA enigma. He made references to the word "Crusade" while describing his motivations and actions in his "Request for Relief" memorandum.

With his distinguished war record, boyish good looks—and reportedly active libido—Mike Peck was also known as a ladies' man. A profile in the *Washington Times* described him as "the bird colonel who lifts weights to fool his biological clock, boasts a stable of British sports cars, collects machine guns, and keeps women on a string."[26] These idiosyncrasies had a certain impact both on Peck's tenure as chief of the office and his subsequent actions.

Some of the most bitter acrimony of the "Request for Relief" memo was aimed at Ann Mills Griffiths, director of the National League of Families. Peck accused her of actively sabotaging intelligence investigations and of trying to dominate DIA policies. He found her a meddlesome outsider intent on "jerking around" those trying to pursue initiatives that could resolve the POW/MIA problem. Obviously, Peck did not enjoy having Griffiths as a colleague.

The Pentagon inquiry team found Peck's allegations concerning Ms. Griffiths to be without foundation, but noted that she was a "tough and demanding" representative of her constituents, POW/MIA families.

This was technically true. However, there was also anecdotal evidence that Griffiths had indeed meddled in POW office business, and that she viewed her position on the Inter-Agency Group as entitling her to direct access to DIA analysts whenever she wished. And she was not in the habit of seeking the approval of the office director when she wanted information on a case. Once, she reportedly ordered an entire section of analysts to work throughout the Fourth of July holiday weekend so that she would have material she wanted for a league meeting.[27]

Other directors had accepted Ann Mills Griffiths as a permanent, politically powerful Washington icon with whom they had to deal if they wished to run the POW/MIA office. Mike Peck chose to challenge her privileged position.

And the fact that Griffiths was a rather unadorned middle-aged woman with whom Peck had to relate on a purely professional level was also a factor. According to the Knecht report, Peck told one senior official that Griffiths was "the first woman he had met that he could not control."[28] Moreover, Ann Mills Griffiths told Knecht's inquiry team that *she* was displeased that Mike Peck had made romantic overtures to members of MIA families and to women on her own office staff.

These charges might well have simply been Pentagon "corridor sniping," as one experienced civil servant has commented. And there was no doubt a personality conflict of monumental proportions existed between Peck and Griffiths.

But a personality conflict had nothing to do with Peck's substantive charges: that the U.S. government had covered up information about abandoned POWs and was actively discouraging efforts to find the truth about these men's fates.

In Peck's memo, he cited "persistent rumors and innuendoes of a government conspiracy, alleging that U.S. military personnel had been left behind" in Indochina. But in the "Conclusions" section of his memo, Peck cites no evidence of such a cover-up. Instead he blames "high-level knavery" that manipulates and controls the entire issue to "obfuscate the question of live prisoners." He repeats that, based on his experience, soldiers in Vietnam were "in fact, abandoned years ago. . . ."

When questioned by the Pentagon's inquiry team, however, Peck was unable to cite any evidence to support this serious allegation, but again referred to persistent rumors.

Colonel Peck's memo notes that he had planned to revamp the office to "aggressively pursue innovative actions and concepts" to renovate the live-sighting process and thus refurbish "the image and honor of DIA." The Knecht report makes clear that Peck's innovative approach would have been "very operationally oriented," and would have included rescue operations in Southeast Asia, which Peck wanted to personally lead.

Further, Mike Peck intended to convince his superiors that America's goal should be to force the Vietnamese government to admit their culpability (or prove their innocence) in holding American POWs after 1973. He wanted to use a Special Operations A Team to kidnap members of the Vietnamese Politburo and coerce them to reveal the truth.[29] Only then, Peck said, would the resolution of the issue truly be a matter of highest national priority for the United States.

Peck reiterated to Knecht's inquiry panel that the best way to follow up on a live-sighting report would be to send U.S. military teams immediately into the nations where refugee live-sighting reports indicated Americans might still be held.

Yet Peck also told the inquiry team that it was largely a waste of time for his analysts to follow up on these reports because any American POWs kept back by the Communists would be in a secret prison system. And in these same interviews, Peck contradictorily stated his opinion that there were no American prisoners left alive, and that we must force the Vietnamese to provide the details of their deaths.

(The staff of the Senate Select Committee on POW/MIA Affairs tried repeatedly to subpoena Peck for a sworn deposition on his various allegations. But, as Committee Chief of Staff Frances Zwenig stated, "No matter how hard we tried to serve Mike Peck [the subpoena], he successfully eluded us."[30])

On March 21, 1991, Peck told journalists during a briefing in the office of New Jersey Congressman Richard Zimmer more or less the same thing. When queried by a reporter about live POWs in Southeast Asia, Peck replied, "Nah, they're all dead."[31]

It was in fact Peck's statements during this March 21 meeting in Congressman Zimmer's office that precipitated his walkout a week later. In addition to stating the opinion that any Americans remaining in Indochina after the U.S. withdrawal were now dead, Peck told the reporters that it was possible the U.S. government had "abandoned" servicemen after the 1973 cease-fire.

Then he commented on Operation Desert Storm and the liberation of Kuwait. "Big deal," he said. "We went in and beat up on a third-world country. They're giving ticker tape parades for guys who went in there and shot the enemy in the back. I fired more rounds myself in Vietnam than the whole Army did in the Gulf."[32]

According to Ronald Knecht, this attack on the U.S. forces who served in Operation Desert Storm was the "last straw" for General Soyster. He immediately transferred Peck out of the DIA and back to the Army, a career-crippling transfer. Only then did Mike Peck affix the memo to the door of the POW/MIA office.

Unlike T.E. Lawrence, who disappeared into obscurity after the debacle of the Versailles Conference, Colonel Mike Peck went on to take an active role in the ongoing POW/MIA controversy—but eventually he too disappeared, into the obscure corridors of the conspiracy theorists.

WEDNESDAY, NOVEMBER 6, 1991, was the first day of public testimony before the Senate Select Committee on POW/MIA Affairs. And the very first witness was another intelligence community insider who appeared to break boldly from the official line that no American POWs had remained in Indochina after Operation Homecoming. Garnett E. "Bill" Bell, Jr., was the head of the U.S. POW-MIA office in Hanoi, a branch of the JCRC. A former infantry reconnaissance NCO and member of roving intelligence teams with multiple tours of combat duty in Vietnam, Bell had been one of those American soldiers for whom the long war and its aftermath had been the dominant factor of their careers, if not their lives themselves. Indeed, Bell's personal life had been marred irreparably in April 1975, during the chaotic final days of Saigon, when his wife, Nova Lynne, a volunteer worker, and their son, Michael, were killed during the crash of the giant C-5A transport carrying Vietnamese orphans out of the country.

After joining the Military Intelligence branch, Bell specialized in Indochina, and became a warrant officer. Fluent in Vietnamese, he was rightfully considered one of the military's true experts on the country. After the cease-fire, Bell had worked first for the DIA, specializing in Vietnam, then for the JCRC, investigating MIA cases.[33]

He testified to the select committee that, between 1973 and 1975, the United States had received reports "that Americans were still being held, but they were unconfirmed."

But, when Bell was assigned to the DIA in the mid-1970s, he added, he began receiving evidence that confirmed these initial reports. This evidence hardened after he retired from the military and worked for the JCRC in Bangkok as a civilian in the 1980s.

"After we began to interview refugees . . . I think we can say that [POWs remained in Southeast Asia after 1973] with certainty now," Bell told the senators.

When asked how many might have been left behind, Bell answered, "Possibly ten or less."

His testimony was the first by any American speaking in an official capacity to state categorically that there had been live Americans still "being held" after 1973.[34]

POW/MIA activists immediately seized on Bell's statement, stressing the certainty of his testimony that Americans had remained in captivity, and downplaying the small estimated number: ten or fewer.

What the public did not learn during the next thirteen months of the select committee investigation were the details of Bill Bell's informed opinion on this subject. That was delivered during his long deposition to committee investigators in a closed room on Capitol Hill the next day. In this exacting discussion of the issue of live American prisoners, Bell stated that his certain knowledge of Americans held captive after Operation Homecoming was actually more in the order of a virtually certain probability, based on a combination of intelligence data, including extensive debriefings of Indochinese refugees.

He explained that the development of the discrepancy case list in the 1980s produced information that two American POWs in South Vietnam might have remained in captivity in a camp in Tay Ninh Province, near the Cambodian border, after April 1, 1973. Another investigation suggested that "five individuals," two blacks and three Caucasians, had been reported in that same camp in 1974. And a third refugee report indicated two more Americans, including a suspected voluntary stay-behind, McKinley Nolan, were in a second camp in 1974.

So, in the late 1980s, Bell said, he and his JCRC team members came to the conclusion "that there was a total of seven Americans who were still there in 1974."[35]

Bell added that he had long suspected the Vietnamese, especially the Vietcong, held back a small number of prisoners as part of their "general pattern" of dealing with POWs. Their tactic, he said, would have been to use the Americans as hostages to gain the release of the most important of their own civilian prisoners being held by the South Vietnamese. He reported that American POWs held in the South had been exchanged for Vietcong prisoners during the war, a fact that had never been admitted by the American government.

But Bell could provide no information whether or not the Vietnamese Communists ever tried to use these hypothetical hostages to win release of their own important prisoners from the South Vietnamese government. After 1975, of course, the issue was moot; Saigon's prisons were emptied by the victorious People's Army (PAVN). Any Vietnamese prisoners still alive were released.

Bell further explained that there was absolute proof that the Vietnamese held two suspected American drug smugglers whose boat had foundered in Vietnamese waters in 1978. But they were released in 1979. And these were accused criminals, not POWs.

(Bell was referring to James Paul Cotton and Eric Stephen Ingram, who were held for approximately a year and released in 1980.)

The only airman POW among the ten possible American captives Bell believed with "certainty" had been kept back after 1973 was Navy Lieutenant Clemie McKinney, an F-4E radar intercept officer shot down in 1972. McKinney's remains were repatriated in 1985 and positively identified by the Central Identification Laboratory in Hawaii (CIL-HI) in 1988. (His family still disputes the identification and the Presumptive Finding of Death that preceded it.)

A refugee source reported to Bell that he observed a black American prisoner being chased by PAVN soldiers in the Cua Viet area of Quang Tri Province in the late 1970s. The refugee saw the American hide under a bridge and the PAVN soldiers shoot him in the leg, delivering a fatal wound. Then the soldiers pulled the dead man from the water and dragged the body away. The remains CIL-HI identified as McKinney were missing a portion of the right leg. Bell also stated that the forensic anthropologist told him, after examination of the remains, that the date of death "could not have been prior to 1975."

Bell believed the refugee report related to Lieutenant McKinney, and promised to provide the Senate investigators with a copy of Clemie McKinney's casualty file. There is no record that he did so.

(However, the casualty record of Lieutenant Clemie McKinney indicates that he was Killed in Action/Body Not Recovered on April 14, 1972, during the PAVN Easter Offensive in Quang Tri Province. His Phantom F-4E, flying from the USS *Kitty Hawk,* took a direct antiaircraft hit while on a bombing run and "was observed to continue its dive until impact. No ejections were observed." Under these circumstances, the report continues, "successful ejection would have been virtually impossible."[36])

Bell was unable to provide any further information on Americans who possibly might have survived up to the present day.

Given the caveats and the level of informed speculation (the case of Lieutenant McKinney), which Bell honestly and frankly admitted during his deposition, it is clear that he had reached his estimate of approximately ten live American "prisoners" held in Vietnam following the cease-fire only after a long and deliberate process of professional analysis. This type of certainty—a significantly high degree of probability, to use intelligence jargon—did not, however, amount to smoking-gun proof that either the North Vietnamese or the Vietcong had held back large numbers of American POWs to use as bargaining chips in various post-cease-fire negotiations.

Therefore, Bell's highly publicized testimony was hardly the sweeping, explosive revelation—ostensibly a shocking embarrassment to the U.S. government—that it has come to represent among POW/MIA activists. Rather, Bill Bell, a cautious, experienced analyst, was speaking honestly on the record, revealing everything he knew and not venturing into imprudent speculation.

But his testimony to the committee provoked unexpectedly dramatic repercussions. Certainly Bill Bell was not the first knowledgeable American official to offer the opinion that Americans had remained in Vietnam after Operation Homecoming. But he *was* the first to state in an official capacity (as opposed to a clearly identified personal opinion) in such a public forum that he could say with "certainty" Americans had remained in captivity after 1973.

The various critics of government POW/MIA policy viewed Bell's testimony as a courageous and selfless action, which was sure to elicit disapproval, if not punishment, from his superiors in the Pentagon.

But Bell's statement on the ten possible POWs remaining after 1973 was hardly a revolutionary act. It would, however, become the kernel of yet another conspiracy myth within months of his testimony.

Just before the first committee hearings, General Vessey and the Pentagon had secured agreements from the Indochinese governments on improved cooperation on POW/MIA matters, which included greatly increased access to American field investigators. In response, Secretary of Defense Dick Cheney activated the Joint Task Force/Full Accounting (JTF/FA). The Pentagon planned to set up substantial JTF/FA field offices (task force detachments, in military nomenclature) in Hanoi, Vientiane, and Phnom Penh. These detachments would be supported by an administrative office in Bangkok and be part of the Pacific Command (CINCPAC), headquartered in Honolulu. The new JTF/FA would replace the Joint Casualty Resolution Center, of which Bill Bell was the temporary-duty office head in Hanoi.

Launching a new "joint" command was an unprecedented step in the fall of 1991, the period that has come to be known as the official end of the Cold War. Elsewhere in the U.S. military establishment individual armed service commands and joint units were being rolled up and abolished. So the creation of JTF/FA was a real windfall for the Pacific Command.

The three task force detachments would each be commanded by an O-5 level officer (lieutenant colonel or Navy commander) with several other new O-5 and O-4 slots in each unit, which would also provide new slots for senior NCOs. Further up the food chain, the JTF/FA created positions for yet more field-grade officers, as well as two new jobs for flag officers, a one-star and a two-star. As the rest of the military was shrinking, CINCPAC's empire was waxing fat.

All this would have a direct bearing on Bill Bell's fortunes, and on his future place in the POW/MIA issue.

When Bell returned to Hanoi following his testimony and deposition, he learned that the planned deployment of JTF/FA was definitely proceeding. He was far and away the most knowledgeable American field investigator, and since he was a relatively senior civil servant (the equivalent of military O-5 rank), many of Bell's supporters optimistically assumed he would be given the command of the Hanoi JTF/FA detachment. Bell himself hoped that he would be promoted to a senior executive service rank and appointed as the operations officer for Indochina, reporting directly to General Needham, the JTF/FA commander at CINCPAC in Honolulu.[37]

But Bell had apparently not considered the intramilitary ramifications of the new organization. As leading a detachment would be equal to battalion, squadron, or ship command, an absolute requirement en route to general's or admiral's stars, it was absurd to hope that the Pentagon would deprive a promising young officer of such a plum assignment by giving it to a civilian intelligence squint (and former enlisted man to boot). And the J-3 operations slot for the JTF/FA was reserved for a senior field-grade military officer, who would have review responsibilities for subordinate officers' efficiency ratings.

Nevertheless, Bell continued to lobby for a senior position in the JTF/FA chain of command. He seemed confident that when his unique experience became known, Pentagon leaders would promote him to this responsibility.[38]

But when it seemed that the Hanoi detachment command was going to an infantry lieutenant colonel named John Donovan (who happened to be a protégé of General Needham), that Bell would be sent to Bangkok, and that there would be no promotion to the senior executive service, Bell was crestfallen.

Bell soon became an icon, like Colonel Mike Peck, for those who firmly believed the United States should have been able to force the Vietnamese to reveal every scrap of information they possessed about American prisoners, no matter how embarrassing or damaging it might be to improved relations between the two countries.

Many who believed America could wring the truth from Vietnam also believed that only Bill Bell (not General Vessey, a skilled negotiator, nor his colleague, General Kingston, who had years of experience in clandestine operations) was skilled enough and experienced enough to master these wily Asian Communists.

Within two years of Bell's controversial testimony, he retired from government service, following news reports of yet another transfer, this time completely out of Indochina and back to the expanding warren of the JTF/FA's home bureaucracy in Honolulu. The fact that he had become a supernumerary in the uniformed service–dominated Joint Task Force was rarely discussed in the news media.

The Senate Select Committee on POW/MIA Affairs, however, did investigate Bell's allegations and found that he remained a "key player," although not a prominent figure in the JTF/FA.

Although many are convinced that Bell's chances as a civilian of landing a senior position in the JTF/FA chain of command were about as good as the proverbial snowball in hell, it is also true that Vietnamese officials found him a potential threat to their efforts to control access to their archives as a tactic in the ongoing Road Map negotiations with the United States.

Bell's fluency in the language and experience as a translator during the prisoner-exchange negotiations in 1973 made him problematic for the SRV officials, who wished to extract the maximum advantage for the minimum concessions during the negotiations with the Americans. And the fact that Bell had a near-encyclopaedic knowledge of the most troubling MIA cases made it almost impossible for his Vietnamese counterparts to hide or distort the facts of any case he was investigating. In addition, Bell's background in combat intelligence units in the South during the war tainted him with the stigma of a prisoner interrogator (torturer), which is ironic, considering that the PAVN's General Political Directorate (which led the technical negotiations with the Americans in Hanoi) was the parent unit of their own side's brutal prisoner interrogators.

For these reasons, the Vietnamese were not displeased to see Bell replaced. And removing his uniquely valuable knowledge base from the Hanoi investigative effort certainly did diminish the program's effectiveness.

Once no longer in Vietnam, the radical POW/MIA activists placed Bell on their roster of martyrs, beside Colonel Mike Peck and General Gene Tighe.

CHAPTER 12

MUCH OF THIS INTRIGUE AND ACRIMONY WAS STILL NASCENT IN THE late fall of 1991 when Ted Schweitzer finally came in from the publishing wilderness and acquired government sponsorship for his unique research.

In December, Schweitzer found himself the object of intense interest from the American intelligence community. Carl Ford introduced Schweitzer to a series of rather humorless gentlemen he took to be CIA officers. With a certain amount of reluctance, Schweitzer turned over all the documents and artifacts in his possession so that they could be analyzed for authenticity. (He imagined stoop-shouldered technicians in white lab coats inserting microscopic shreds of the museum record cards into computerized mass spectrometers.)

Then he was asked to sign more release papers that would permit a rigorous "controlled debriefing," bureaucratese for a polygraph interrogation to test agents' motives. These polygraph examinations are never fun: The examiners—who exuded transparently bogus bonhomie—probed his personal life and habits, as if Schweitzer had surrendered any right to privacy when he signed the release forms.

When Schweitzer explained the progress of the operation to his mentor, Richard Armitage, the gruff ambassador shook his head. "Listen, Ted, I've seen deals like this before. The Pentagon is full of douche bags who'll try to derail this project. If any of them come out of the woodwork, let me know and I'll fix it."

Armitage's offer of direct, personal intervention to protect Schweitzer and to insure the success of his project was more than bravado. Schweitzer knew that the stocky, balding troubleshooter consistently produced results for the White House.

As assistant secretary of defense for international security affairs, Armitage had earned a reputation as a workaholic of legendary proportions. To prepare for Defense Secretary Caspar Weinberger's daily 8:00 A.M. world situation briefings, Armitage normally woke at three, and was in his office by four, in direct personal phone contact with military leaders and civilian officials in each of the planet's trouble spots that might be discussed at the meeting.

When other, more plodding assistant secretaries dutifully made notes to assess one of the ongoing crises, Armitage's habitual reply was: "I already called the minister of defense (or commanding general) and he assures us the situation is stable. Our ambassador agrees."

Armitage lived by the credo that bureaucratic caution and inertia were inexcusable. He was a rarity in Washington (or any other national capital): a truly dedicated civil servant who believed in doing whatever was necessary (within the bounds of legality) to help the president who had appointed him achieve his goals.

The success of Schweitzer's project had become one of the goals of the Bush White House. Therefore, Armitage would apply his full intellect and vigor to help achieve that success.

Armitage explained that the President wanted to help Schweitzer in any way the administration could without jeopardizing the historic entrée Schweitzer had made in Hanoi. And, although Schweitzer realized that a breakthrough on the stalemated POW/MIA issue would bolster Bush's re-election campaign in 1992, Armitage made it clear that the President also had a personal stake in breaking the stalemate. As a young Navy pilot in World War II, Bush had been shot down and almost captured by the Japanese, in an area where enemy troops regularly executed captured American aircrew. Bush's interest in the MIAs of the Vietnam War had a "There but for the grace of God . . ." quality to it.

But there were wider geopolitical considerations, Armitage explained. American-Vietnamese relations were at a pivot point. The collapse of the Soviet Union and Vietnam's other Eastern Bloc allies had not only deprived Hanoi of economic support, but also of Soviet military protection from China. Increasingly, Vietnam was isolated and becoming desperate to secure new allies. The Hanoi government saw the United States—with its large corporations eager to expand in Asia, and its powerful Seventh Fleet—as its potential savior.[1]

But the POW-MIA issue remained a critical stumbling block to better relations. It was probable, Schweitzer was told, the PAVN "book" research contract was the subtle means that Hanoi's leaders had chosen to break this stalemate, while maintaining their sense of honor.

"Your country needs you on this one, Ted," Armitage had told him in his most persuasive manner.

Schweitzer was now committed to working secretly for the government. In exchange for their support, he pledged to share whatever information he obtained with them on a confidential basis.

In one intense week, Schweitzer was fingerprinted, photographed, then obliged to sign another bewildering array of secrecy agreements, all of which bound him to follow orders under threat of the criminal sanctions of the National Security Act of 1947, "as amended." It was when he signed one extremely sensitive secret agreement, which gave the government carte blanche to tap his phones and to delve into all of his personal affairs, that

Schweitzer realized the irreversible nature of his involvement with U.S. intelligence.

What Schweitzer did not initially realize was that his arrival on the scene ignited another of the internecine firefights of the intelligence bureaucracy's endless turf wars. As Carl Ford, a senior CIA career officer, was now serving in Armitage's old fiefdom as principal deputy assistant secretary of defense for international security affairs, he and Armitage decided the Pentagon's Defense Intelligence Agency should fund and manage Schweitzer's unusual project. But the DIA balked at the prospect. The agency, especially its Special Office for POW/MIA, had been badly used by exotic volunteer amateurs in the past two decades.

To hard-pressed DIA bureaucrats, aiding Schweitzer was a no-win situation: If his project was successful (due to the machinations of the Vietnamese Communists), it would make the frustrating failure of DIA's twenty-year effort at resolving the issue even more apparent; if Schweitzer failed, and worse, was exposed as an incompetent amateur agent on the DIA payroll, the agency would be seen as squandering government funds while grasping at ridiculous straws.

Up to then, Ford and Armitage had neatly sidetracked that bureaucratic quagmire by having the Central Intelligence Agency fund Schweitzer's operation and administer his initial screening and professional training. Once Schweitzer was safely "signed in," however, Director of Central Intelligence Robert Gates, who outranked the heads of the other intelligence agencies, executed one of the masterful bureaucratic power plays for which he was renowned inside the Beltway. POW/MIA affairs, Gates ruled, were the responsibility of the DIA. Schweitzer's project concerned only this issue. Therefore, the DIA would fund and manage Schweitzer's operation. To make sure the DIA complied efficiently, Gates let it be known that the President took a personal interest in the success of Schweitzer's project.

IN JANUARY 1992, Schweitzer was assigned a full-time case officer from both the CIA and the DIA's Operations Directorate. The DIA case officer was a taciturn and sardonic chain-smoking Army colonel who went by the work name James Renaud. It was Renaud who continued Schweitzer's accelerated training in the tradecraft of clandestine operations. For several hectic weeks, Renaud and Schweitzer became inseparable. Renaud taught him how to use a variety of telephone, fax, and telegraphic emergency codes and signals, which he could employ from Hanoi to convey surprisingly detailed information, ostensibly in a manner that would protect the content of his message. Schweitzer had to memorize the location of several dead-drop message delivery sites in various Southeast Asian cities.

Now officially on the U.S. Air Force payroll, but secretly working for DIA's Operations Directorate (a smaller clandestine service parallel to its better-known CIA counterpart), Schweitzer and his operation were given the secret designation "Swamp Fox." But within days, the operation was renamed "Swamp Ranger" because the original name had been used for an earlier project. Schweitzer was then given his official cover story and assigned his new work name, "Francis Marion" (the Revolutionary War hero known as the Swamp Fox). Schweitzer spent three days learning and convincingly regurgitating this cover story to Renaud's exacting satisfaction.

If pressed by the Vietnamese, Schweitzer was to reluctantly admit that Ambassador Richard Armitage, his "friend in the White House," had secured government funding for Schweitzer's computer equipment—because the government wanted to see Schweitzer's book published as soon as possible.

That was it. He was to admit nothing more.

But while discussing the subject of the book cover story, Carl Ford now told Schweitzer that the many secrecy agreements he had signed officially prevented him from *ever* writing about or profiting from his activities as part of a covert operation.

"Oh, shit," Schweitzer swore. "You mean after all this, I can never write my book?"

"That's the way things are," Ford replied. "I'm afraid you're stuck now."

Schweitzer thought a moment. He just couldn't walk away from the opportunity to help resolve this agonizing issue, and he knew the chances of convincing a publisher to fund the project were almost nonexistent. "Well, okay . . ."

"We can talk about the book later," Ford added to soothe Schweitzer's frustration.

But Schweitzer was beginning to feel trapped. Despite the excitement of the espionage-craft training, replete with "brush-pass" document-exchange meetings in hotel lobbies and multiple car swaps in the shadowy garages of suburban malls, Schweitzer sensed that his trainers and handlers had little real understanding of the challenge he faced in Hanoi. And he was coming to realize that Hanoi was at least as faction-ridden as bureaucratic Washington. Who would protect him if the Vietnamese equivalent of Richard Armitage's hypothetical jealous bureaucrat "douche bag" attacked?

Armitage and Ford knew how difficult Schweitzer's mission would be. His first weeks back in Vietnam would be extremely delicate, Carl Ford told him. If the PAVN realized he was returning to Vietnam as a secret Pentagon intelligence agent, the Vietnamese might suddenly close off access to the museum archives, or even destroy sensitive records before they could be scanned. Worse, discovery of the full extent of his government sponsorship might permanently sour American-Vietnamese relations at this critical juncture.

"If you fail, Ted," Ford warned, "I'll probably get fired."

(It has since become clear that the Bush administration did, in fact, invest considerable political capital in Schweitzer's project, which was seen as the only practical means of forcing the obstinate Vietnamese into a fait accompli admission that they possessed much more extensive and better organized POW archives than they had previously admitted. Almost as soon as Carl Ford realized the potential of Schweitzer's access to the museum archives, he told Congress that the Pentagon's International Security Affairs division was about to take advantage of "new opportunities" that had just been identified in Southeast Asia.[2])

Schweitzer also understood the danger of failure. He had worked hard to win the trust of the PAVN and he knew Colonel Dai and his superiors would feel a personal sense of betrayal if it was suddenly revealed that Schweitzer was cooperating secretly with American intelligence.

On the other hand, Ford assured him, the potential benefits of the operation offset "any risk."

If Schweitzer could quickly scan the key museum archives—especially the critical Red Book index—and deliver that data to the DIA, the important first round of the battle would have been won. The Vietnamese could never again claim their POW/MIA records were scanty, badly organized, and inaccessible to American investigators: If they insisted on falling back on their previous duplicitous patterns, the Americans could cite them for breaking the terms of the Road Map agreement.

"*Any* risk?" Schweitzer asked. "What about my ass? If the PAVN finds out I'm working directly for U.S. intelligence, they could throw me in jail. I'm going out there to do research on prisoners, not become one."

"Don't worry," Ford soothed. "The Vietnamese like you."

ONCE THE CLUMSY preliminaries had been completed, Schweitzer was ordered to assemble his optical scanning and computer system. "Buy what you need," he was told.

"Don't go ape shit," Renaud said, "but money is not an issue here."

Suddenly, the lack of funding that had plagued him for two years was solved. Now he faced an equally serious problem: He had to complete the design and successfully assemble a complex, but "deployable" optical scanning and data-indexing and storage hardware system—plus test and debug the intricate software to run it—that would stand up to the climate and Third World conditions of Hanoi. Until then, this scanning system had simply been an abstract paradigm that might someday, somehow, become available. Now his new superiors told him he had a month to "get the show on the road."

But to Schweitzer's amazement, he received almost no practical help with this problem from his case officers and trainers in the warren of drab, anonymous offices strung through Washington's sprawling Virginia suburbs. The men he dealt with used computers only for word processing and data retrieval. And the government's "cludgy" old Wang work stations and IBM

Federal Systems databases were dinosaurs that would have been considered comically obsolete in private industry.

For months, Schweitzer had envisioned a truly state-of-the-art scanning and storage system for Operation Swamp Ranger. But the worldly, hard-boiled intelligence professionals were woefully lacking in this area of expertise. There were, of course, world-class computer experts in the technical directorates of the CIA, DIA, and National Security Agency. But these people were engaged in highly classified projects that precluded granting Schweitzer access to their laboratories and work rooms.

In any event, Renaud added, he had already sounded out these experts in a manner that would not breach operational security. "They say the system you're planning can't be built."

Schweitzer understood their skepticism. Practical optical scanning was a new technology; in early 1992, desktop optical scanners capable of reproducing mountains of documents with near-photographic quality, which could then be digitally stored and indexed, were rare. In the entire U.S. government, the FBI was the only agency that was using this technology in a practical application, but their equipment was large and cumbersome, and the software to run it was not available for use outside the bureau.

"Just buy what you need," a CIA case officer named Tony told Schweitzer. "Put it together and make it work. You're the expert."

The case officers imposed a few conditions, however. First, the equipment had to be "sterile," devoid of any invoices or warranties that could be used to trace it back to the U.S. government. So, before he even began to assemble his unique scanning system, Schweitzer had to obtain a collection of pro forma invoices from unsuspecting distributors in Singapore by fax and DHL courier. Second, he had to pay cash for each piece of hardware and software. The procurement funds came in bundles of very slightly used $100 bills, no two with sequential serial numbers, and none with any marks whatsoever. And the purchase prices had to be at tax-free government rates. But the vendors would not be obliged to submit competitive bids, which was normal procedure in government procurement.

Schweitzer began his quest in the well-stocked computer stores of the northern Virginia suburbs. The merchants, some Middle Eastern and South Asian immigrants, were used to meeting the demanding requirements of the high-technology "Beltway Bandit" consultant firms that fed at the rich contract trough of the nearby Pentagon. But none of these merchants had ever assembled a system that fit Schweitzer's complex requirements.

The optical scanner itself—a piece of equipment resembling a bloated desktop photocopy machine—did not present a problem. The then current state-of-the-art machine was the Fujitsu 3096, which could be upgraded with image enhancement in order to successfully scan the often faint and faded handwritten museum record cards and indexes. The normal industrial application for this scanner linked it to a large mainframe computer with a huge memory. This was because optical scanning of handwritten documents devoured up to one megabyte of memory per document page.

"I want to be able to scan tens of thousands of pages of handwritten documents," Schweitzer explained to a perplexed and dour Iranian in Rosslyn, midway between Georgetown and the Pentagon. "And I will be working in a very remote area, on 220 volt current, fifty hertz, which is often unreliable."

The man frowned so energetically that his bushy eyebrows almost knitted.

"Oh, yeah," Schweitzer added, "my data storage system will have to be small enough to transport as airline baggage. In fact, all the hardware will have to be."

"Sir," the merchant said, "you cannot do this."

Schweitzer received the same reply from two more merchants. They would all be willing to come to his office and install an optical scanning system, coupled to a mainframe computer the size of a refrigerator. But none could envision a system that Schweitzer could carry with him to some unspecified corner of the Third World, which would meet both his scanning and data storage requirements.

In mounting frustration, Schweitzer badgered Renaud to arrange a contact with the FBI technicians that ran their optical scanning system.

"No way," Renaud replied in his terse, sardonic manner. "We go over there and start asking questions, the whole operation will come unglued."

He had a point. The Federal Bureau of Investigation was notoriously jealous of its turf, and quick to undermine competitors for scarce funding, especially for innovative technology.

This setback only stiffened Schweitzer's determination to succeed. He had promised Richard Armitage and Carl Ford that he would deliver, and he was not about to quit so easily. The challenge reminded him of the task he had faced establishing the big refugee camp on the Thai-Cambodian border in only seven days. At least, he mused, there wasn't some asshole television correspondent blocking the way of the water tankers.

But there were at least a few recalcitrant bureaucrats in the Pentagon woodwork who placed unnecessary obstacles in Schweitzer's path, just as Armitage had warned. While Schweitzer was still wrestling with the scanner hardware problems, a lowly but strong-willed DIA bureaucrat in an administrative support section let it be known that he objected to the "irregular nature" of the expenses Schweitzer was beginning to accrue. The bean counter seemed to resent Schweitzer's presence as an outsider. Henceforth, the man stated, he would process no further fund requests from Swamp Ranger—which looked like a bastard child neither embraced nor rejected by the CIA or the DIA—until higher authority clarified the nature of the project.

Schweitzer went to Carl Ford for help before calling in Armitage's heavy artillery.

"I'll take care of it," Ford muttered, clamping a smoldering Camel in the corner of his mouth and reaching for the telephone.

When Schweitzer visited the administrative section a few days later, the surly bureaucrat had been replaced. Schweitzer learned that the man had been called to Ford's office and severely reprimanded. To make his point, Ford appended a statement to the official's latest efficiency report, a terse, scathing indictment of the man's attitude and comportment. (A few months later Schweitzer learned that the offending bureaucrat had opted for early retirement.)

Heartened by this support, Schweitzer soldiered on in his struggle to assemble a workable scanning and data storage system.

He went to another small computer store in Rosslyn. A Toshiba representative had recommended this store as a good source for reliable optical disk storage drives. And it was this type of memory system that Schweitzer now sought. Optical disk data storage is similar to the more familiar compact disk recording system for sound and video. For Swamp Ranger, the merits of optical disk storage were numerous: Each rewritable optical disk had a full gigabyte of storage capacity. Shaped like six-inch square pancakes, the disks could only be accessed by a Panasonic laser drive, so that there was little danger they could be inadvertently damaged or overwritten by Vietnamese uninitiated in the exact access procedure. And with such an optical disk drive linked to his scanner, Schweitzer would have a virtually unlimited data storage capacity, provided he brought with him enough of the expensive disks.

But he had to somehow tie together—"integrate" in computerese—with electronic connections and facilitating software the scanner, a control console, the optical disk drive, and at least one backup storage and retrieval system.

He explained his requirements once more to this sympathetic store owner, a striving Middle Eastern immigrant.

"Have you got a really good, hardworking computer hacker who can work with me?"

"I do, sir," the man replied.

That afternoon, Schweitzer met a young man from Lebanon named George. Schweitzer studied George's face. He was in his mid-thirties and had the earnest, slightly bemused appearance often seen in creative systems engineers.

"We will build you your system, Ted," George promised after they sat for an hour in a hotel coffee shop, sketching various designs on paper napkins.

As Schweitzer had hoped, George proved to be both diligent and energetic. He had not yet been corrupted by clock-watching, benefits-conscious American work habits or short-sighted attitudes.

"What're you doing with a raghead?" one of the case officers asked. "Can't you find an American to work with?"

"Nope," Schweitzer replied. "I can't."

George and Ted Schweitzer became close friends. They shared a common passion: problem solving. This was fortunate; there was no shortage of problems.

Schweitzer and George set up shop in a pair of adjoining fourth-floor rooms of the Americana Motel in Pentagon City. In one room they pushed the beds and armchair to the corner and installed two broad rectangular banquet tables to form a long, L-shaped workspace. Then Schweitzer began peeling off $100 bills from the stack of operational funds he had signed for. George provided the hardware at the specified price. The profits on the sales were his only salary.

Within a week, Schweitzer's operational funds were lighter by $20,000, but they had the main hardware components of the system in place on the motel room tables.

The centerpiece was the Fujitsu optical scanner, which had been upgraded with the very latest sensitivity modules. This was linked to a powerful but relatively compact hybrid personal computer control console, which George had assembled from component parts that included the most powerful central processing unit chip then available, an Intel 486 DX. George also installed the largest available RAM memory and hard drive in this PC, which would serve as the control console. At this point in its evolution, Schweitzer's scanning system was an ingenious, but relatively straightforward application of advanced computer technology.

But he also had to meet another, tougher requirement beyond the daunting task of scanning and indexing thousands of handwritten documents and military artifacts in the secret Hanoi archives. Schweitzer's case officers had warned him that Colonel Dai's General Political Directorate initiative might actually have been a freelance operation lacking the support of the Politburo. Therefore, Schweitzer might initially be allowed to scan sensitive documents, only to have the disks with his stored data confiscated, once the news of his unprecedented operation reached senior party hard-liners. Schweitzer saw at once that he would need a clandestine method of preserving each day's harvest of scanned data, so that he could safely deliver at least some new material to his case officer in Bangkok, should the hard-liners prevail and quash the PAVN enterprise.

In the virtually hundreds of computer magazine articles Schweitzer had consulted, he had read about a new magnetic tape backup memory system produced by an innovative small company called Valitek, located in the mini–Silicon Valley of western Massachusetts. The beauty of this system was that the user could store up to 150 megabytes of digital data (which represented 150 pages of scanned museum archive documents) on a single cheap audio cassette available at any drugstore or Radio Shack.

And this led to the Valitek system's other attractive attribute. Schweitzer realized he could use standard commercial music cassettes, anything from a classical orchestra to a Madonna tape, to store digital data from the archives. His plan was simple. He would leave the first few tracks of these cassettes untouched, then record data on top of the later selections. Any Vietnamese counterintelligence officer examining Schweitzer's cassette collection would simply hear fifteen minutes of Beethoven's Fifth or "Material Girl," followed by the chaotic rustling of meaningless digital noise, which fit the pattern of many cheap pirated rip-off music cassettes available on the streets of Asia.

If the tape backup worked, Schweitzer mused, his system would become as truly "spy-friendly" as he hoped.

Schweitzer called Valitek's young president, Bill Kenney. After explaining he was involved in a sensitive government project overseas, Schweitzer asked how much Valitek's magnetic tape backup would cost.

"I'll send you one free," Kenney said. "If it works out for you, and I'm sure it will, tell your friends about it."

The small, robust tape memory backup arrived at the Americana the next day by Federal Express, and George patiently attached the equipment to the dense skein of looping cables connecting the various components of the scanning system.

They were ready to test the "full-up" system. This first trial was a disaster. Nothing worked. The various components would power up, but none of them could communicate with the others.

With stoic patience, George spent two eighteen-hour days carefully replacing the complex web of connecting cables so that he was finally certain the hardware was at least physically connected. Finally the separate units were capable of communicating in the hissing gibberish of digital bits and bytes.

The next morning, Schweitzer and George, both unshaven and groggy from sleep deprivation, began to sort through the babble of the software patchwork quilt they needed to weave together to make the system function. Schweitzer had chosen a powerful new database program called File Magic that was recommended for large government storage and retrieval systems. The program worked under the Windows manager program, which meant the appended software for the other components had to be so adapted. This was not easy.

Two weeks passed in a blur of hardware and software crashes, hours on long-distance vendor assistance hotlines, and frustrating near-victories, which inevitably ended in blank screens or terse, mocking program warnings: "This file cannot be read," or, "Your hard disk cannot be accessed."

One of their worst days came when George tore back the shrink wrap of a factory-new software disk for the Cornerstone ultra-high-resolution monitor and installed the program on the main console hard drive. Luckily, he had earlier installed a security program designed to detect the insidious Michelangelo computer virus that was then infecting systems throughout the world. The Michelangelo virus was designed to activate on the artist's birthday, March 6, of that year. And when it activated, Michelangelo destroyed the entire memory of an integrated system.

As George hit the Enter key, the screen flashed and the room filled with a nagging beep.

"Virus detected," Schweitzer and George echoed, their voices stricken.

"Let me handle this," George whispered.

He knew that programs infected with the Michelangelo virus that came in sealed factory packages could be especially virulent. With the utmost care, he removed the offending disk, and used the virus checker to inspect every segment of the hard drive. It was almost ten o'clock that night before George was satisfied that their carefully constructed software assembly had not been infected.

By the next week, George and Schweitzer achieved their first major breakthrough: The hardware of the system was fully integrated, each unit now compatible with the others without further enervating crashes. Two days later, they were almost convinced that the software assembly, woven together with scores of small "patches," was functional.

But after repeated trials, the system stubbornly refused to cooperate. George refused to accept defeat. Hunched over the console, the screen filled with a confusing storm of bizarre programming symbols, George struggled through one entire night, subsisting on sweet rolls and large Styrofoam cups of coffee.

Schweitzer fell asleep in a nearby straight chair. George woke him to the light of a sleety March dawn.

"It's working," the young engineer said.

Schweitzer rose, shook the sleep from his head, placed one of the handwritten museum cards on the scanner's glass face plate and lowered the lid. Half an hour later, he was convinced George was right. The entire system worked flawlessly on repeated trials. Each of the storage matrixes, the PC hard drive, the optical disks, and the tape backup could be accessed by the other to sort and swap data. And equally important, the hard copies produced by the laser printer were indeed of near-photographic quality.

Schweitzer held up one of the American military identity cards Colonel Dai had provided, comparing it to the hard copy of the scanned original. Every minute detail was reproduced legibly.

Their long struggle with these obstinate machines had ended in success.

With the system working, Schweitzer had to set up the password security system he had designed for use in Hanoi. He realized that Vietnamese counterespionage officers would be capable of probing his computer files unless they were "locked" by password-only access. He chose variants of the word "Hilton" for the three password gates he installed in the program. This was a reference to the Hanoi Hilton, Hoa Lo Prison, where many American POWs suffered years of brutal captivity.

On power-up, the screen now flashed: PASSWORD. Entering HILTON accessed the software. The password MILTON opened the word-processing program, and RILTON was needed to unlock individual files. Schweitzer reasoned that, should his cover story fail, and professional interrogators from the Ministry of the Interior pressure him for the passwords, he could always mutter "Hilton" in a slurred voice and still be certain they could not fully breach the system's security screen.

TWO DAYS LATER, Schweitzer prevailed on the case officers to bring one of the reclusive computer experts from the intelligence community to inspect the system. This was more than a courtesy visit. Schweitzer needed the man's advice on how to configure the subject fields of the scanning software. He knew, of course, that the Pentagon was vitally interested in any names of missing Americans or POWs, but he also realized that the dates of incidents in the museum records would be of major concern. However, the Vietnamese method of dating—day, month, and year—conflicted with the DIA method, which, for example, would list 670318 for March 18, 1967.

After a brief discussion, Schweitzer and the CIA systems engineer agreed on common scanning fields.

Finally, Schweitzer felt bold enough to ask this expert's opinion of the system that he and George had worked so hard to assemble.

"What do you think of it?" Schweitzer patted the scanner with an almost paternal pride.

The older engineer beamed with admiration and shook his head. "Man," he said, glancing at Schweitzer and the case officers, "this is one slick piece of work. We don't have anything like it."

THAT AFTERNOON, TONY arrived with a group of burly young men in ski jackets. Ted and George had disassembled the entire scanning system and Tony's team carefully packed it into anonymous brown cardboard boxes for overseas shipment. Schweitzer watched anxiously as his precious hardware was loaded into a featureless white van in the parking lot below. Then the van left.

Schweitzer now received orders to report to the Ambassador Hotel in Bangkok and be ready for work on Monday, March 16, 1992.

In intelligence parlance, Swamp Ranger had become operational. Schweitzer was about to step through the looking glass.

CHAPTER 13

DESPITE SCHWEITZER'S ACHIEVEMENT IN MASTERING HIS COMPUTER problems, there was still bureaucratic reluctance to support Operation Swamp Ranger among some elements of the DIA. Several experienced officers in the POW/MIA office and DIA analysts assigned to the new Joint Task Force/Full Accounting remained wary of Schweitzer. To them, this freelance project—which promised access to archives that the Vietnamese had claimed for twenty years did not exist—seemed highly questionable.

For almost twenty years, the DIA had been tricked, cheated, pilloried, and otherwise abused by the collection of publicity-hungry POW activists, scandal-mongering writers, unbalanced, self-appointed adventurers, and outright con men who comprised this lunatic fringe. In many ways, the unrelenting assault on the DIA by these opportunists and zealots resembled similar campaigns by the conspiracy buffs dedicated to unearthing the "truth" about the assassination of John F. Kennedy or exposing the alleged forty-year government "cover-up" of visits by extraterrestrials in Unidentified Flying Objects.

However, where the assassination conspiracy advocates and UFO cultists represented only a minor irritant to the Justice Department and the Pentagon, the scam artists and self-righteous fanatics of the POW/MIA movement were capable of much more serious mischief. In fact, to many veteran officers in the DIA and JCRC the POW/MIA lunatic fringe were as much an obstacle as the Vietnamese Communists to the "fullest possible accounting" for the missing.

The process was insidious. It began in the late 1970s and gathered momentum through the 1980s. A loose network of retired military officers, failed politicians, Southeast Asian anti-Communist "resistance fighters," and unscrupulous professional fund-raisers in the United States unleashed a campaign of disinformation and deception that did more to confuse the POW/MIA issue and raise the level of acrimony than any other group during or after the war.

Although their tactics differed, these so-called activists' basic positions were essentially identical: They claimed to have hard evidence—often described as "intelligence data"—that *proved* as many as several hundred American POWs remained alive in Communist captivity in Indochina. When pressed hard (which was rare), the activists rehashed the frustrating and contradictory agents' reports and reconnaissance imagery from the mid-1970s Laos intelligence operations. But the activists found the inconclusive data to be rock-solid evidence of surviving POWs.

The corollary to this assertion was that the U.S. government was fully aware of these prisoners' situation, but refused to render assistance; therefore, only courageous private efforts could free the remaining POWs before they died, succumbing to the brutal conditions of their prisons, which were usually described as "bamboo cages" in some unspecified jungle region of Vietnam or Laos.

(The image of the American POW held in zoolike bamboo cages was so pervasive that few people questioned its authenticity. Most Americans assumed that all POWs were kept in such cages. In reality, a relatively small number of U.S. prisoners held in the South were imprisoned in bamboo cells or cages, usually as a punishment for some infraction of camp rules, or to coerce them into making propaganda statements. Most of the POWs in those camps slept in huts, often with their feet in wooden stocks. However, one American POW, Ernest C. Brace, a captive of the Pathet Lao and PAVN for seven years in Laos, was in fact held for most of that time in a classic bamboo cage. His description of this terrible captivity is wrenching: "My tall six foot frame eventually became paralyzed under the strain of being forced to exist inside a four foot high cage that decreased to two feet at the opposite end."[1]

(Following the immense popularity of the 1978 film *The Deer Hunter,* the bamboo cage image became fully ingrained in the American consciousness. Bamboo cages became common fund-raising devices with POW/MIA activist groups. One of the most notable examples was the bamboo cage used by a veteran named Al Ziegler for his widely publicized hunger strike near the Vietnam Veterans Memorial in 1989. Ziegler, who lost almost thirty pounds in the first month of the hunger strike, told the news media: "As I deteriorate, so do the men in Southeast Asia waiting to come home."[2] Like many activists, Ziegler apparently saw fit to exaggerate his military record. He described himself as a "tank commander" in Vietnam, when in fact he had served in a heavy equipment maintenance organization, not a combat armor unit.[3])

If one accepted the thesis that hundreds of Americans languished in these bamboo cages years after the war—and there was voluminous, skillful propaganda produced to convince potential contributors of its validity—then the donation of $25 or $50 or even $500 to these courageous private rescue operations would seem a small price to pay to secure the freedom of those wretched American servicemen who had been abandoned by their own government.

As this campaign gained momentum, the competing private rescue groups produced increasingly flamboyant claims in their fund-raising efforts. This in turn generated publicity, which stimulated the shoestring, poorly organized Indochinese resistance groups in exile in Thailand to fabricate even more sensational "intelligence" on American POWs, whose prisons were usually claimed to be located in the particular area of interest of the resistance group possessing the "evidence." Armed with this dubious intelligence data, the American activists would publicly badger the DIA to analyze the evidence, and when the long-suffering agency was pressured by Congress to rise to the bait and inevitably refute the dubious claims, the activists had further grist for their propaganda mills that the American government in general was actively involved in a cover-up, and the DIA was crippled by the "mind-set to debunk."

There were several net effects of this self-perpetuating disinformation cycle:

The private rescue groups had a continual supply of ostensibly plausible "intelligence" of live American POWs in Indochina. This resulted in renewed successful fund-raising campaigns.

The Southeast Asian resistance groups were rejuvenated and given a modest new source of income to replace their generous wartime funding by American intelligence.

A small group of private adventurers—including Vietnam "veterans" of dubious pedigree—gravitated to Indochina and conducted a series of failed comic-opera POW rescue missions.

Marginal congressional figures such as Billy Hendon and John LeBoutillier, who championed the private POW rescue groups, achieved stature beyond their brief tenure as legislators.

And the DIA (and JCRC) wasted untold time and effort extinguishing the endless sensational brushfires started by these activists.

Air Force Lieutenant Colonel Paul D. Mather was one of the JCRC's longest-serving officers, having joined the unit in 1973 and remaining with it until 1988. For almost ten years of his tenure, Mather charted the increasingly audacious machinations and sometimes outright fraudulent deceptions of the lunatic fringe. In "The MIA Story in Southeast Asia," a monograph Mather wrote while a research fellow at the National Defense University, he describes the impact of these groups on the U.S. government's slow but determined effort to reach the bottom of the MIA mystery. One of the most insidious of the "extremely counterproductive" effects of the private rescue efforts, he notes, was the intelligence contamination of Indochinese refugees. In order to produce plausible evidence for their fund-raising efforts in America, private rescue groups—or their Asian accomplices—sometimes salted refugee camps with purloined wartime MIA records, including photographs of missing men. The resulting "live-sighting reports" had to be diligently analyzed by the understaffed JCRC. And always, often after hundreds of wasted man-hours, the reports were proven bogus.[4]

Another serious negative result of these private efforts was the stimulation of the efforts by refugees and resistance groups to recover the remains and artifacts of missing American servicemen from crash sites in Laos and remote areas of Vietnam. Once the word spread in the refugee camps that rich Americans were literally paying fistfuls of green dollars for bones, scraps of aircraft wreckage, and melted shreds of nylon parachute harness, the unofficial excavation of crash sites accelerated. And, as in other spontaneous private enterprises in Indochina, a brisk trade in counterfeit artifacts and documents quickly developed.

One such attempted deception in November 1987 involved an Israeli "businessman" in London, who represented some unnamed colleagues in Thailand who claimed they could negotiate the release of American POWs from Vietnam through Cambodia. As bona fides, the Thais gave the Israeli photos of a gaunt, unkempt Caucasian man standing in a thicket of elephant grass, holding beneath his chin the front page of *The Nation,* from Bangkok. This familiar hostage verification technique was meant to prove the man had been alive after the date the paper was published. The Israeli contact stated that a ransom of $1.2 million would procure the release of all the Americans in this group.

(In this regard, the scam was a latter-day variant of the 1974 Mexico City con-game run on the hapless mother of Lieutenant George MacDonald.)

But when the JCRC and DIA investigated the case in Thailand, they discovered the man in the picture was an American named Charles Strait, a former Air Force enlisted man who had married a local woman and settled in Thailand in the 1970s. Strait readily admitted that he had been recruited by some "entrepreneurs" to pose as an American POW. With this scam exposed, the Israeli and his Thai colleagues disappeared.

However, the lesson of this incident was that the flamboyant offers of reward money made by private American POW rescue groups were obviously the stimulus for the fraudulent photo. In fact, one such group, the American Defense Institute, led by former POW Captain Red McDaniel and former North Carolina Republican Congressman Billy Hendon, circulated a photograph in 1987 among Indochinese refugees, in which a group of eight congressmen were shown standing at a table stacked high with bundles of currency totaling $1 million: a reward to be paid to the first Asian to bring forward a living American prisoner. Later, flyers announcing this reward were floated across the Mekong River from Thailand to Laos and launched by balloon from a vessel in the South China Sea to be carried by prevailing winds into Vietnam.[5]

For years afterward, repeated fraud attempts by refugees—several involving doctored photographs of living American "POWs"—continued to plague American MIA investigators in Indochina.

And in turn, these bogus reports of living prisoners became "evidence" that stimulated further fund-raising efforts by exploiters among the American activist groups.

By the mid-1980s, the pool of potential donors to these private rescue groups had shrunk, probably as a result of oversolicitation by the competing fund-raisers, as well as the general frustration and disappointment that none of the flamboyant claims of live POWs had borne fruit. In response the groups escalated their rhetoric.

And this escalation resulted in shameless emotional blackmail, often aimed at MIA families and the unsuspecting, patriotic middle class who supported them.

For example, Operation Rescue (not connected to the anti-abortion group), headed by a self-promoting retired Air Force lieutenant colonel named Jack Bailey, claimed in an October 17, 1986, solicitation letter: "Must raise $13,671.71 by Friday, October 31 or vital intelligence gathering missions might have to be stopped." Bailey noted that without these missions "there's no hope for the return of POWs and MIAs captive in Vietnam." Unless the person contributed immediately, Bailey boldly wrote, "an American serviceman will die in the jungles of Vietnam."

The Skyhook II Project, headed by a former one-term Republican congressman, John LeBoutillier, wrote in an undated solicitation letter: "We're close to making contact with an American POW who has been alone since his fellow prisoner died of natural causes less than a year ago. That effort could fail for lack of funds. Please be as generous as you can as soon as you can."

An undated solicitation brochure from the American Defense Institute circulated in the mid-1980s cited a "key source in the Defense Intelligence Agency" for "overwhelming" evidence from satellite photos and communications intercepts that "approximately one hundred POWs still remain." LeBoutillier's Skyhook II also cited a highly placed Pentagon source (probably the Tighe Task Force) as "verifying that Americans are still being held captive in Southeast Asia under incredibly cruel conditions." Earlier, LeBoutillier's group had cited eyewitness refugee reports of Americans "starved and clad only in filthy rags . . . kept chained in tiny bamboo cages . . . made to work like animals pulling heavy plows . . . forced to toil from daybreak to nightfall in steaming tropical heat . . . kicked and beaten constantly just for their guards' amusement."[6]

The Skyhook II Project also quoted unnamed European sources, "two Swedes on business near Hanoi" and a "West German diplomat," as more reliable eyewitnesses who saw living American prisoners in both Vietnam and Laos. Supposedly the Swedes "ran into a chain-gang of men slaving on a road." These slaves then yelled, "We are American POWs. There are many of us here . . . many of us. Tell America not to forget us." The German diplomat supposedly saw a similar group in Laos. When asked who they were, the diplomat's cruelly cynical Lao guide "laughed and said, 'They are American POWs leftover from the war.' "[7]

The thrust of these appeals was clear: Unless the donor contributed generously, American POWs abandoned after the war—who were still languishing in cruel captivity—would die.

This emotional extortion was similar to the successful fund-raising ploy of televangelist Oral Roberts, who once gravely announced to his electronic congregation that an apparition of Jesus Christ several hundred feet tall had warned Roberts that he would "call me home" (i.e. Roberts would die), unless he raised several million dollars.

If nothing else, the private rescue groups, and the professional telemarketing consultants they hired, were observant and adaptive; what worked for Oral Roberts also worked well for them.

It is significant that the prevailing imagery of the refugee reports and the "eyewitness" accounts by Europeans in the fund-raising appeals consistently describe gaunt, brutalized American POWs being used as slave laborers in "chain gangs" or pulling heavy plows in rice paddies. If even some of these reports were valid, it meant that identifiably Caucasian prisoners were consistently exposed to America's sophisticated aerial and satellite reconnaissance technology.

Simply stated, from the mid-1980s onward, America's air- and space-borne reconnaissance "platforms" were so powerful that they could identify distinctive racial features (height and limb length) of individuals photographed against a suitable background: the caked mud of a dry rice paddy, the reddish hue of a laterite road. So, by claiming in their fund-raising materials that there were thousands of reliable eyewitness reports of perhaps hundreds of Americans kept as field slaves by Lao and Vietnamese Communists, these groups were also implying that the leaders of America's intelligence community—plus all the senior military officers and civilian Pentagon officials who regularly viewed aerial and satellite reconnaissance photos of Indochina—were part of a massive and ongoing cover-up to perpetuate the enslavement of our abandoned POWs.

As has been noted, the satellite imagery available in the early 1980s identified suspected Caucasian prisoners at a detention camp in Laos. If there had been "hundreds" of such sightings from across Indochina, as some groups claimed, the U.S. government cover-up of this information would have been massive.

Defendants of Captain Red McDaniel and former Congressman John LeBoutillier have stated that these two honorable men might have been overzealous in their fund solicitations, but they were not cynically deceptive. That may be true. Certainly Red McDaniel elicited sympathy. He had the unfortunate distinction of being the returned POW who had survived the longest and most intense period of torture: several uninterrupted weeks of flogging in 1969 at the hands of the sadistic Cuban interrogator called "Fidel" in Hanoi's Cu Loc Prison (the Zoo). Some who knew McDaniel stated that McDaniel himself was not motivated by greed. However, the fact that there have been four McDaniel family members working full-time at the

American Defense Institute, plus two others part-time, could lead one to question some of the motivation behind the institute's aggressive fund-raising.

Whatever McDaniel and LeBoutillier's motives, however, the emotionally charged "evidence" cited in the two groups' materials provided powerful ammunition for the growing body of critics who believed the U.S. government was actively engaged in a cover-up of the embarrassing truth that America had knowingly abandoned hundreds of POWs in Indochina.

It is also interesting to note that the field slave image of the abandoned POW, who "toiled" all day and was chained all night in a "bamboo cage," matched the dramatic image of fictional POWs in such popular films as *Uncommon Valor, Missing in Action,* and, of course, *Rambo.* These movies, which appeared from 1983 to 1985, were commercial successes in America and Southeast Asia. In what U.S. Military Academy professor Elliott Gruner calls "an unprecedented cycle of POW/MIA rescue scenarios," the movies evoked emotional responses in both Asian and American audiences.[8] Many young Americans, particularly those with only sketchy memories of the Vietnam War, believed the adventure films were some type of docudramas, which represented historical events. This popular view of the brutal captivity endured by allegedly abandoned American POWs was echoed in the fund-raisers' emotional appeals.

In Thailand, the films were popular for another reason: Indochinese refugees and Thai opportunists also accepted the veracity of the POW-as-slave image. The JCRC noted that following the release of these films, this imagery became common in both refugee live-sighting reports and fraudulent secondhand reports that Thai con men tried to parlay into successful ransom negotiations.[9]

And the acceptance in America of the myth that the wily Lao Communists were still holding an indeterminate number of American POWs, which became widespread in the wake of these films, prepared the ground for even more audacious fraud by the worst of the scam artists, both American and Asian.

Probably the most notorious such individual was retired Air Force Lieutenant Colonel Jack Bailey. His Operation Rescue had been seeking gullible donors for years. Bailey settled in Southeast Asia after retiring from the Air Force in 1969. By 1981, he had acquired a decrepit old coastal freighter, the *Akuna,* which had been involved in the smuggling trade in Thailand. Bailey solicited funds, claiming that he ran the *Akuna* as a rescue vessel to save Vietnamese refugee boat people from Thai pirates. Ted Schweitzer encountered Bailey during this period, when Bailey tried to pressure the UNHCR into paying exorbitant fees for a relatively small number of refugees Bailey's vessel had brought into the port of Songkhla, where Schweitzer was the senior UN officer. Schweitzer refused and Bailey took his pathetic load to Singapore.

That was one of the few fruitful rescue attempts that the *Akuna* conducted. The ship remained at anchor for years, even though Bailey continued to successfully solicit funds for fictional rescue exploits on the South China Sea. It is noteworthy that Bailey even claimed to have carried out a heroic one-man confrontation with armed pirates who were slaughtering prisoners on an island, an exploit eyewitnesses dispute. It is probable that he had heard of Ted Schweitzer's heroism on Ko Kra and simply expropriated it as his own.

This would have been in character. Bailey, who claimed to be "one of the highest decorated American fighting men of any war" (two Purple Hearts, a Silver Star, and a personal citation from the president of Korea), also stated that he had served as a jet fighter pilot in Korea and had later flown 256 combat missions in Vietnam. All of this was a lie. He had never served overseas during the Korean War; his one tour in Vietnam had been as a ground support officer, not a pilot; he had been awarded only one Purple Heart, and he had never been awarded a Silver Star, nor any personal decoration by the president of Korea.[10]

Apparently emboldened by his success at acquiring donors, Bailey launched his most flagrant deception in July 1991. For years he had had in his possession photographs of a man he called in his fund-raising appeals "Major X," an alleged American POW being held in the inevitable bamboo cage in Laos. The pictures showed a clean-shaven middle-aged Caucasian in a blue polo shirt standing in some type of rural Asian bamboo structure and also kneeling at what appeared to be garden work. For several months, Bailey used the Major X photos in Operation Rescue's fund-raising appeals, stating that the man appeared to be a surviving POW who had been held for almost two decades not far from his crash site in Laos. The same fund-raiser showed a "Major Y," a robust, bearded Caucasian in his late thirties wearing a military shirt and blue-jean shorts, standing with two hill tribesmen near a bamboo hut.[11]

Then Bailey raised the ante by contacting the family of a missing American, Captain Donald Carr, a former Special Forces officer who had been lost in the crash of an OV-10 Bronco reconnaissance plane in southern Laos in 1971. Carr's family in East Chicago, Indiana, was dumbfounded by the photograph. Indeed, the picture seemed to be a remarkably close likeness to Captain Donald Carr, taking into consideration the passage of time. What was most remarkable were the same animate dark eyes and unusual protruding ears.

"That's Don," Carr's brother Matthew exclaimed when he saw the pictures. "I'm positive."

Carr's former wife, Carol Collins, had the Bailey pictures compared with earlier pictures of her husband by Colorado State University forensic anthropologist Dr. Michael Charney. He announced that the man in the Bailey photo was definitely Donald Carr.

Jack Bailey capitalized on the unexpected luck. He held a news conference in which he appealed for funds to conduct further intelligence gathering. And he basked in the sudden publicity. He was, after all, the first activist to furnish indisputable evidence that there were live American POWs in Laos. For the moment, the news media ignored Bailey's questionable record with the Akuna, and Jack Bailey rode a wave of media-generated success. He held a Pentagon investigation team at bay with vague promises that he would soon reveal all he knew about "secret" POW camps in Laos, where several of the alleged prisoners whose photographs had appeared in Bailey's publications were held captive.

Then several enterprising reporters and the DIA conducted an intensive investigation that revealed without question that the man in the photo was not Donald Carr, but Guenther Dittrich, a German smuggler of exotic birds who had indeed worked in Thailand, but was now awaiting trial on smuggling charges in Frankfurt. Carr's former wife went to Germany and confirmed that Dittrich was the man Bailey had originally called Major X. The notorious bamboo cage in the photos was exactly that; but it was a cage of a bird export company in Bangkok, which Dittrich had visited several years before.

"We'd all been had," Carol Collins later said.

Bailey denied the photo was a fraud. He claimed that the Dittrich episode was part of an elaborate government plot to discredit him, and that Carr could be alive.[12]

Despite this well-publicized debunking, Bailey retains many supporters among the hard core of true believers in the POW/MIA activist community. And these supporters refuse to accept the indisputable proof that the other Caucasians identified as live POWs in Bailey's publications were actually European aid workers and missionaries.[13]

Bailey and his enterprising colleagues were not the only hoaxers to almost succeed with elaborate live-POW photograph scams.

In August 1990, American officials in Phnom Penh, Cambodia, began receiving reports of three living American POWs still in captivity who were available for ransom. As with most such reports, the informant, a Cambodian student, claimed to be an intermediary for a Vietnamese guard who would turn over the prisoners when the ransom was paid. In this case, the student mentioned the $2.4 million reward reputedly offered by the U.S. government.

After several months of fruitless negotiations, it was determined that the garbled names that the Cambodian contact gave could be correlated to Air Force Major John Robertson, shot down over North Vietnam in 1966; Navy Lieutenant Larry Stevens, shot down over Laos in 1969; and Air Force Major Albro Lundy, Jr., lost in Laos in 1970.

The Cambodian intermediary also provided some equally garbled biographical information on the three alleged POWs, which contained some valid data, but which was basically gibberish of the type usually provided by Asians with a poor understanding of English. Although the men's dates of loss were correct, the information on their wives and family members was nonsensical. For example, both Stevens and Lundy were said to have wives named "Sweet Mary," and Major Robertson's mother, Phyllis, was listed by the intermediary as "Rpoesioner," and Stevens's mother, Gladys Leona, had become "Russiver Lumerriper."

The DIA concluded that a con game was under way. As in other cases, the Cambodian scammers had apparently obtained the names and dates of loss of the three men from a handbill that had been circulating for several years in Indochina. This handbill contained a wartime picture of each of the servicemen, as well as artistic renditions of how they might appear years later. Even though given this evidence of fraud, the DIA did not pursue the matter vigorously.

Then the other shoe dropped. In November 1990, Xerox copies of a grainy black-and-white photograph were faxed to a Cambodian refugee in California, then Xeroxed and forwarded to the families of Robertson, Stevens, and Lundy. The photo showed three middle-aged, mustachioed Caucasian men, seeming to hold a rectangular white sign with the word "PHOTO" and the date "25-5-1990" followed by the characters "NNTK! K.B.e-19." There was no doubt that the three middle-aged men in the picture bore a striking resemblance to the three airmen; more significantly, the faces of the three alleged prisoners looked a great deal like the artistic renditions of how the Americans might appear after twenty years of captivity.[14]

The impact of this photograph was more sensational than the appearance of Bailey's Donald Carr picture. The Robertson-Stevens-Lundy picture appeared on the front pages of major newspapers and made the cover of *Newsweek* in July 1991. Red McDaniel and the American Defense Institute exploited the picture to the maximum in their fund-raising activities. And, although there was no flawed forensic confirmation as in the Carr photo, the relatives of two of the men depicted publicly announced the photos did indeed portray their loved ones.

Once more the long-suffering DIA had to divert its resources from legitimate remains-recovery operations to track down the origin of yet another elaborate scam. A year later, DIA investigators from the Stony Beach office in Bangkok finally traced the picture to old Soviet magazines at the former Soviet Cultural Center in Phnom Penh. After several false starts, the DIA investigators were eventually able to locate the original photograph of the three mustachioed men in a 1923 edition of *Soviet Life* magazine in the mildewed archives of the National Library in Phnom Penh.

Commenting on this phenomenon in an editorial, the *Washington Post* pilloried the "unscrupulous crooks [who] have spread disinformation and perpetrated hoaxes that have made it extremely difficult for government investigators" trying to achieve a full accounting for missing Americans.[15]

Despite this harsh debunking, however, the photograph of the three al-leged live prisoners continues to be accepted as a valid relic among POW/MIA true believers and is still being used as a fund-raising tool by several private rescue groups.

UNFORTUNATELY FOR THE DIA and JCRC, American POW rescuers did not limit themselves to scams and fund-raising. A few actually undertook private covert operations into Communist-controlled Laos in search of living Ameri-can prisoners.

The best known (most notorious to the DIA) of these figures was former Special Forces Lieutenant Colonel James "Bo" Gritz, a relentless self-pro-moter who organized several well-publicized private commando missions to search for live POWs deep inside Communist Laos.

Bo Gritz is sometimes regarded as the model for the movie character John Rambo, the muscular, heroic loner who takes on both the wily Asian Communists and the treacherous, cowardly American bureaucrats who man-age the ongoing conspiracy to hide the truth on live POWs.[16]

Gritz had been active in grassroots veterans' POW/MIA activist groups in the late 1970s. Based on the adulation he received from those groups (which involved embellishment of his already admirable war record, according to some sources), Gritz organized his first abortive POW rescue attempt, Operation Velvet Hammer, in the spring of 1981. This was a bizarre affair. It was allegedly a highly covert operation, but Gritz and his motley associates quickly blew the cover of their training camp in Florida and squandered the large fund of privately donated contributions without ever fielding a rescue force in Southeast Asia.[17]

One contributor who was taken in by Gritz's charismatic promises of concrete action by "seasoned, professional military men" was George L. Brooks, one of the founders of the National League of Families and the father of missing Navy airman Lieutenant Nicholas G. Brooks, who was lost in Laos in 1970. (His remains were brought to the U.S. embassy in Bangkok by Lao resistance fighters in 1982; they were later positively identified by CIL-HI.) George Brooks mortgaged his home to provide Bo Gritz $30,000 for this dubious operation. Years later, Brooks remains bitter and scornful about Gritz and other "scammers."[18]

Despite this fiasco, Gritz continued to successfully cultivate donors, often implying secret high-level government support for his activities. During this period Gritz would sometimes also show both critics and potential donors a letter allegedly written by the deceased deputy director of the DIA, Army Lieutenant General Harold Aaron. The FBI later determined that this letter was not authentic. However, Gritz did manage to convince some low-level Pentagon officials that he could provide usable intelligence data from Indo-china. While official approval of covert support for Gritz was pending, he was provided some travel funds, a long-range camera, as well as communications and other equipment—explicit, albeit limited, government sanction of his activities—which Gritz exploited to great effect.

ACTUAL EVENTS IN Southeast Asia during this period helped Gritz's efforts at fund-raising and self-aggrandizement. In December 1980, the CIA and DIA in Thailand received what has been called "perhaps the most compelling and multiple-source intelligence ever made available" to analysts and policymakers of "possible" live American POWs still in captivity. This intelligence data included overhead imagery—Keyhole satellite and SR-71 photographs—as well as reports from an indigenous agent "with unusually good access" of possibly thirty or more American POWs working at a remote detention camp in a narrow mountain valley in central Laos, approximately fifty-five miles east of the Lao-Thai border.[19]

The primitive facility was near a slash-and-burn farming village called Nhommarath on some Lao maps. Analysis of reconnaissance imagery by the CIA concluded that this was definitely a "detention camp," surrounded by an outer "stockade-type" fence and a similar inner fence enclosing a smaller area of huts. Two guard towers, an automatic weapons position, and a trench revealed the camp to be a military establishment, not a defensive enclosure of farmers. Further, because the four-meter-high outer stockade fence blocked the view of the surrounding hills, and the position of the guard towers allowed observation inside the compound but not of the surrounding area, and because the facility was not built on a nearby hilltop, the CIA was convinced that "this facility is for the detention of personnel." The CIA determined that the camp had been built between April 1978 and September 1979, and occupied in December 1980.[20]

This was the camp that another source had earlier described as the captivity site of "Ltc. Paul W. Mercland."

To further interest the analysts, a "third country" radio intercept (probably from an American-sponsored Thai intelligence facility) revealed a Pathet Lao message that could relate to the movement of American POWs from the southern town of Attepeu to the camp that same month.

What made these reports most intriguing were reconnaissance images that showed agricultural implements that appeared to be too long for short Asian prisoners; shadows cast by people in the camp enclosure also appeared too long for those of Asians. And there were also reasonably clear images of "tall people inside the fence, and short people outside."[21]

Even more enticing were images of what appeared to be the number "52" and possibly the letter "K" marked out among rows of crops in an agricultural plot inside the inner compound of the camp. The number 52 could have related to captive B-52 crewmen, or possibly to fifty-two prisoners. The letter K was given to U.S. aviators to use as a ground distress signal. Again, however, analysts could not agree if these were actual human-crafted foliage digits (and the letter K) or "artifacts" of the imaging process.

A January 6, 1981, CIA spot report described the "K," but later, more rigorous CIA analysis did not confirm the existence of the letter. However, this later analysis definitely did confirm "what appears to be the number 52" in the crop area. "Each numeral is 1–2 meters wide and 3 meters high." Moreover, the CIA noted: "The location of the numerals is such that they most likely cannot be seen from either of the two observation towers because of trees located in the line of sight."[22]

A retired Navy SEAL officer, who saw the actual satellite images while on the staff of the Pentagon Joint Special Operations Command, is adamant that the digits marking "52" were "clear and unmistakable."[23]

That distress signal could have been made by American POWs surviving from the war, or it could have been the work of resourceful Asian prisoners who hoped it would spark an American rescue attempt.

The CIA led a joint covert operation to quickly train a Lao mercenary reconnaissance team to investigate this detention camp. The team, numbering about thirty men, was given long-range cameras (some with infrared film for night photography) as well as scrambled radio equipment. These Lao irregulars managed to infiltrate the area of the detention camp and to take a wide range of photos of the inmates.

But analysis of the photos did not reveal any Caucasians. Before a second, more extensive field reconnaissance could be mounted, Bo Gritz's activities in Florida spawned a press leak on the real special operation in Laos, and all further efforts were canceled.[24]

The single most promising sighting of possible live American prisoners had ended in frustrating failure.

(The validity of these possible POW distress symbols eventually evolved into an unquestioned article of faith among POW/MIA activists. In a March 1994 article in *The American Legion* magazine, Mark Sauter and Jim Sanders mixed quotes and information from the 1981 spot report and the later, more definitive CIA analysis to make it seem "possible that the letter 'K' followed the '52.' "[25]

(Interpretation and verification of purported POW distress signals has been the subject of rancorous controversy among activists in the intelligence community for years. One of these sets of symbols was discovered in 1988 in a dry rice paddy near the town of Samneua in northern Laos, the area where American POWs were known to have been held during the war. A large "USA" measuring eleven by four meters, followed by a smaller possible "K" was reported by CIA analysts on December 3, 1988. Later, more exhaustive agency analysis confirmed the human artifact nature of the letters USA, but was equivocal about the letter K. The analysis noted that the USA letters were of more recent origin and concluded the "markings were man-made."[26]

(But when a DIA team visited the area in November 1992, they found a farmer and his teenage son who stated that the boy had made the USA symbol, fashioning the letters after the markings on an envelope the family had received from relatives in the United States. The boy said he had made the giant letters by burning piles of rice straw after the harvest.[27] Even though the DIA has rigorously investigated the Lao family's background, activists still feel the agency site inspection was part of a cover-up.[28]

(Another intriguing set of alleged POW distress signals was discovered on the roof of an obvious new prison built near the North Vietnamese coast north of Haiphong after the Communist conquest of South Vietnam in the summer of 1975. American reconnaissance imagery revealed "a unique alternating light and dark pattern" in roof tiles installed during repairs. This pattern could be transposed into the Morse Code symbol for K, the well-established downed-airman distress signal.[29]

(However, more complete analysis by the DIA revealed that this prison was in fact a reeducation camp that held former South Vietnamese prisoners through the 1970s. Interviews with men released from this camp revealed no knowledge of Americans held there.[30]

(In 1994, the Lao government finally allowed a JTF/FA team to inspect the stockadelike camp near Nhommarath, the subject of the abortive 1981 rescue raid. By then, DIA photo analysts had determined that the "52" and "K" seen in satellite imagery "were probably not man made." Also, supplementary debriefings of former Royal Lao Army officers who had been held in the camp in 1980 and 1981 indicated that there had never been American POWs held there.[31])

THE PUBLICITY SURROUNDING the abortive 1981 official covert operation gave credence to private efforts such as Gritz's. Moreover, Gritz still had the support of members of the National League of Families, including Ann Mills Griffiths, who reportedly used her membership on the Inter-Agency Group to pass along intelligence information and target data to Gritz.[32]

A year later, Gritz found other supporters among the Hollywood glitterati, including Clint Eastwood and *Star Trek's* William Shatner. In November 1982, Gritz launched Operation Lazarus, his only actual armed ground operation in Indochina. His "command" included a small group of Vietnam veterans (some with bogus credentials) and POW/MIA daughters. Gritz established a headquarters on the Mekong River, Thailand's border with Laos. The American women and some men running the group's radios remained in Thailand. On November 27, Gritz, accompanied by three Americans and a group of Lao resistance fighters, crossed the Mekong into Laos near the Thai frontier post of That Phanom. Within days they confronted a rival Lao resistance band and immediately returned to Thailand, where they were arrested for illegal border crossing. After a minor media circus of a trial,

Gritz and his group were declared persona non grata and expelled by the Thai government.

Despite this setback—or probably using it as shelter from unglamorous reality—Gritz continued to claim that he had indisputable "evidence" of live American POWs in Laos and that he could lead a better-organized (implicitly better-funded) covert operation to secret prison camps in Laos.

Commenting on Gritz's activities, the National Security Council scornfully summarized his contribution: "Throughout his years of involvement, Mr. Gritz contributed nothing of value to the POW/MIA issue. In fact, his activities have been counter-productive."[33]

Like Jack Bailey, Bo Gritz was undeterred by such adversity. He continued to remain active in the POW/MIA community and pursued publicity as energetically as he did contributions. In 1984, Gritz obtained the Air Force Academy class ring of a dead American hero, Air Force Captain Lance P. Sijan, who was posthumously awarded the Medal of Honor for evading capture for six weeks in the mountains of Laos, then stubbornly resisting the interrogation by his Vietnamese captors. Gritz got the ring from a Lao intermediary and attempted to convince the Sijan family to hold a gaudy Las Vegas press conference to publicize the ring's return. Implicit in this manipulation of a family's emotions was Gritz's indirect plea for money from the Sijans to cover the "expenses" he had accrued in obtaining their son's ring.[34]

Bo Gritz is currently a perennial candidate for president of the United States and has managed to maintain a small cultlike band of dedicated followers.

Notwithstanding the emotional trauma Gritz's activities has inflicted on MIA families, his activities could have been considered an amusing minor footnote to the overall issue of Americans missing after the Vietnam War. But Gritz became the idol of an even more devious rogue named Scott Barnes, who parlayed his involvement in Gritz's activities into an entire separate chapter in the overall POW/MIA myth.

Scott Barnes, a burly, short-tempered young man, graduated from high school in southern California too late for the Vietnam War. He enlisted in the Army and was trained as a stockade guard, but was discharged after only sixteen months. The Army cited both "failure to meet acceptable standards for continued military service" and "poor attitude; lack of motivation; lack of self-discipline" among other weaknesses as the reasons for Barnes's discharge. After serving several years as a uniformed officer on various southern California police forces, where he was disciplined for improper conduct, Barnes joined up with Bo Gritz and went to Southeast Asia. He obviously enjoyed the netherworld of would-be American mercenaries milking the POW rescue racket.

But Barnes eventually proved too flaky for Bo Gritz to accept. Barnes was involved in the abortive reconnaissance mission (Operation Grand Eagle) meant to precede Gritz's actual foray into Laos, Operation Lazarus. Barnes joined a five-man team of Gritz operatives and went to the Thai-Lao border to await a contact from the Lao resistance. The man never appeared; the group quarreled and split up.

Barnes surfaced a few years later having written a sensational book, *BOHICA* (Bend Over Here It Comes Again), a "memoir" of this fiasco, which had now evolved into a secret government-sponsored prisoner search foray into Laos.[35]

In the book Barnes claimed that he had been recruited for secret American intelligence operations while an Army enlisted man—which would conveniently explain his poor conduct separation from the Army. (In this account, Barnes elevated himself from a failed stockade guard to an undercover military intelligence agent and former Green Beret with unspecified combat service in Southeast Asia.) As a member of a secret team, Barnes revealed in his often lurid narrative, he had been sent into Laos to locate American prisoners, photograph their prison camp, and bring this evidence out to his case officers in Thailand. But he supposedly rebelled when he was issued assassination weapons and told his mission was now to "liquidate the merchandise," murder the hapless American prisoners so that their existence would not embarrass the U.S. government.

Barnes wrote of heroically swimming the river frontier between Thailand and Cambodia on his infiltration mission. This would have been difficult as the Thai-Cambodian frontier is a land border.

Barnes also referred to personal contact with DIA director Lieutenant General Eugene Tighe, who coordinated the reconnaissance and assassination operation. Tighe called this "hogwash."

But the most disturbing allegation of *BOHICA* concerned the "true" motive for the dastardly prisoner assassination order, which Barnes refused to obey. His team, Barnes wrote, had been ordered to kill Americans held captive in Laos because these prisoners were actually bogus POW rescuers who had in fact infiltrated Laos to plant fraudulent Yellow Rain samples as evidence of Soviet chemical warfare. This deceitful web was so convoluted that even Barnes originally had a hard time sorting out the details in his media statements.[36]

In addition to these incredible intrigues, Scott Barnes used *BOHICA* as a vehicle to add to the lurid legend of U.S. officials in Southeast Asia who were allegedly deeply involved in narcotics trafficking. It was apparently this part of the narrative that first brought Barnes to the attention of Ross Perot. Barnes's accounts of deceitful American intelligence officials secretly involved in drug trafficking (i.e. Perot's old nemesis Richard Armitage) closely matched the billionaire's penchant for conspiracy.

All this would have been of little general interest had Barnes not again surfaced in the summer of 1992, this time as an unofficial security adviser to Ross Perot during his first period of active candidacy for the presidency. In a dramatic July announcement, Perot withdrew from the campaign, charging that undisclosed sinister forces in the Bush camp planned to disrupt his daughter Carolyn's wedding by releasing a scandalous altered photo of her, reportedly in a lesbian embrace.

"I had reports that there was a plan to embarrass my family," Ross Perot told a nationwide news conference.

What he did not reveal was that the origin of those reports was none other than Scott Barnes. And Perot, whose loyalty is said to run as deep as his vindictiveness, refused to find fault with Barnes. In fact, there is evidence that Ross Perot fully accepts Barnes's accounts of high-level conspiracies involving abandoned American POWs in Indochina.[37]

"Barnes is credible and knows what he's talking about," Perot told the press.

Had Perot not dropped out of the campaign early—only to reemerge as a candidate in October—he would have undergone more rigorous media scrutiny and might not have fared so well in November. And some analysts are convinced that the significant percentage of the November vote Perot garnered deprived George Bush of reelection and won the race for Bill Clinton. Therefore, it can be argued that the phony POW rescuer Scott Barnes exerted a negative influence far beyond the circle of the Rambo wannabes who haunt the lunatic fringes of the POW/MIA issue.

For his part, Scott Barnes continues to stir up mischief and adamantly defends his contrived background. When Army Chief Warrant Officer-4 Steve Gekoski, an investigator for the Senate Select Committee on POW/MIA Affairs, checked into Scott Barnes's background, he encountered a web of cleverly forged official documents that seemed to substantiate many of Barnes's lurid tales. It was only through patient legwork—Gekoski was a twenty-year veteran of the Army's Criminal Investigation Division—that Gekoski was able to disprove all of Barnes's claims of having been a secret government agent. But Gekoski does pay Barnes a grudging back-hand compliment: "He's the most devious and clever manipulator I've ever encountered."[38]

Barnes is obviously as audacious as he is devious. In his sworn deposition to the Senate Select Committee, Attorney Neal Kravitz confronted Barnes with a true copy of his military discharge papers, which contained the official statement of poor performance that led to Barnes's separation from the Army.

"Have you ever seen that document before?"

Barnes replied: "This document? No. This document is a fraud. Not a bad one, but it's a fraud."

Kravitz then compared the true discharge paper to the one that appeared in Barnes's book, *BOHICA*. The two documents were important because they presented concrete proof that Barnes had not been tapped for secret agent training as a young soldier, but rather had been drummed out of the

Army for discipline and attitude problems. And lacking this alleged covert intelligence training, the entire elaborate fictional house of cards he had created would come tumbling down.

But rather than concede the indisputable fact that the discharge paper that appeared in the book was a forgery, Barnes counterattacked, charging that the U.S. government was party to a "continuing cover-up."[39]

Scott Barnes has been described as a pathological liar with a streak of grandiosity. In this regard, he is not the only such mischief-maker among POW/MIA activists. While Barnes is one of the principal sources in Monika Jensen-Stevenson and William Stevenson's flawed book *Kiss the Boys Good-bye,* a self-proclaimed former POW named Larry Pistilli plays a similar role in the Jim Sanders et al. book *Soldiers of Misfortune.*[40]

Pistilli's tale of wartime heroism is almost as exciting as Barnes's account of postwar intrigue. Pistilli told the authors of *Soldiers of Misfortune* that in the fall of 1965 he was assigned to the I Corps region of Vietnam "working on special, classified, missions," when, after some rather cinematographic heroism, he was captured and taken to a camp in North Vietnam near Dong Hoi. There, he said, English-speaking Soviet and Chinese Communist interrogators selected American POWs for transport to China or the Soviet Union. Pistilli claimed to have escaped from the camp with three other Americans during an air strike and fought their way back to American units in the South after "some frantic hand-to-hand combat."

Once back among friendly forces, however, Pistilli and his comrades were subjected to a brutal "classified debriefing," in which American intelligence officials used brainwashing techniques similar to those of the Communists.

Pistilli's account of this secret Soviet-Chinese operation (which would have been a unique example of military partnership between the two Communist giants at that period) has been widely cited as proof of a separate covert prison system in North Vietnam.

But there are problems with Pistilli's account. He never served in Vietnam in any capacity, either in a regular unit or on a classified operation. Pistilli's military service lasted from August 3, 1964, to July 31, 1967. His only overseas duty was as an auto communication equipment operator with the Army's 57th Signal Company in Korea.[41] Pistilli had never served in combat, never been a prisoner of war. His heroic account cited in *Soldiers of Misfortune* is an outright lie.

Even though Pistilli had been debunked by 1992, two of the authors of the book continued to defend his credibility, albeit somewhat indirectly. Describing the alleged secret Eastern Bloc prison camp in North Vietnam, Mark Sauter and Jim Sanders wrote in their second book, *The Men We Left Behind:* "A third American [Pistilli] claims to have escaped from this facility, but his veracity cannot be verified."[42]

Had the authors bothered to query the National Personnel Records Center in St. Louis, they certainly would have been able to verify Pistilli's well-documented mendacity.

Another bogus POW, Samuel Kim, even went so far as to have a memoir of his imaginary captivity published and well reviewed as a nonfiction book, *The American POWs.*[43]

The problem of bogus POWs spreading lurid accounts—which become widely accepted tenets of the overall POW/MIA lore—is not limited to Larry Pistilli and Samuel Kim. Richard Burns, a therapist at the Department of Veterans Affairs (VA) Medical Center in Gainesville, Florida, has recently noted that phony POWs, many who claim to have been part of secret Special Operations units, are a common feature in what he calls the "wannabe syndrome" of fraudulent Vietnam veterans.[44] It should be noted that former prisoners of war receive priority treatment from the VA, thus there is an incentive to make false claims. When B.G. "Jug" Burkett, co-chairman of the Texas Vietnam Veterans Memorial, began investigating claims of self-described Vietnam POWs, he found that 26 percent of the people carried on the rolls of the American Ex-POW Association, a private group in Arlington, Texas, were in fact bogus. Some of these fake POWs were relatively harmless men who used the period of their alleged captivity to cover difficult times in their military service (usually stockade or brig time). But others, like Pistilli, caused problems beyond their immediate circle of family and friends.

Phony Vietnam War POWs are the source of some of the most grotesque POW tales, which seriously debase the historical record by Ramboesque claims of fictitious savagery on the part of their Communist captors. (These phony POWs are apparently not satisfied with the well-documented cruelty of the Vietcong and North Vietnamese captors.) For example, two veterans cited in the book *Vietnam Wives: Women and Children Surviving Life with Veterans Suffering Post-Traumatic Stress Disorder,* by Veterans Administration clinical psychologist Aphrodite Matsakis, Ph.D., make baroque claims about their captivity. One, a veteran called Bob, said he had been tortured repeatedly during nine months of captivity by the Vietcong. He also claimed to have been put back on combat duty following the end of his captivity. (It is unspecified whether he was rescued or escaped.) And once back in the war zone, Bob supposedly "inflicted those same horrors on as many VC as he could find." (Dr. Matsakis does not explain when Bob lost both his legs to below-the-knee amputations.)

Fred, another self-described POW Dr. Matsakis treated, "was sexually abused by Viet Cong guards during his six months as a P.O.W. After he was released, he sought to kill his abusers, but they could not be found."[45]

The Defense Intelligence Agency confirmed that neither of these cases was authentic: No American held captive by either the Vietcong or NVA was returned to combat duty. The DIA also stated that there had been no reports of sexual abuse by Communist captors in Indochina, inflicted on either male or female prisoners. When the author queried Dr. Matsakis about this discrepancy, she replied that the POWs cited in the book were "composites of several men in order to insure confidentiality."[46]

Taken individually, the lies, forgeries, tall tales, distortions, and exaggerations of the fund-raising scammers, the Rambo wannabes, and the bogus POWs are relatively harmless. It can be argued that gullible people who contribute to patently questionable causes (be they the Reverend Oral Roberts or Lieutenant Colonel Jack Bailey) have more money than sense.

But, taken collectively, this massive duplicity has formed a mosaic of deceit, half truth, and exaggeration that has completely distorted the underlying reality of the POW/MIA situation and has seriously eroded the effectiveness of the U.S. government agencies charged with resolving the issue.

PART 3

CHAPTER 14

TED SCHWEITZER REACHED THE AMBASSADOR HOTEL IN BANGKOK LATE on the steamy night of March 15, 1992. The long flight out from Washington was uneventful. Tony, his CIA case officer, escorted the computer equipment via Europe. James Renaud, of the DIA, traveled alone to Bangkok. The truly clandestine part of the operation had begun.

At Bangkok's hectic Don Muang Airport, Schweitzer squared his shoulders and entered the line of weary tourists and Thai families trudging toward the glass-fronted immigration counter. Then, as trained, he forced himself to relax and fiddled distractedly with his dangling camera and carry-on bag—just another middle-aged American business traveler transiting one of the busiest airports in Asia. In his hand he clutched a plausibly worn passport bearing his photo and the name of Francis Marion.

The bored young Thai immigration clerk stamped Schweitzer's passport without even glancing up.

Schweitzer managed several hours of jet-lagged sleep in the chill air-conditioning of his eleventh-floor room in the Ambassador. Then he awoke and stared out his window at the smoggy dawn. The six lanes of Sukhumvit Road, Bangkok's main commercial arterial, were already clogged with yellow Toyota taxis, open-backed jitney buses, pickup trucks, and Honda motorbikes. Almost ten million Thais now lived on the expanse of coastal plain between the airport and the mouth of the Chao Phraya River. The rather quaint Asian town of interlocking khlong canals and gilded dome wat temple complexes that Schweitzer had first known in the early 1970s had given way to a sprawling warren of mid-1970s concrete and 1980s-boom high-rise towers. The major khlongs had been filled in and paved in an effort to reduce traffic congestion. But the new roads only increased the volume of vehicles in the city; and with the traffic came the humid smog, as well as the incessant bedlam of honking horns.

"Welcome home," Schweitzer said to the waking city. For indeed, Bangkok was more his home than any town in America.

But the sleepy neighborhoods of old teak-slab houses shaded by banyan trees he had known as a younger man had disappeared beneath the relentless juggernaut of prosperity. Sipping his strong Thai coffee, Schweitzer watched the flow of traffic mount inexorably as the sun rose through the pall of tan smog. Soon the heat would drive him back into the air-conditioning.

He was surprisingly well rested and only slightly nervous. In his last contact with Renaud on the plane, the case officer had confirmed the original plan: Schweitzer was to check into the hotel and stay in his room, while Renaud and his unseen colleagues conducted a routine countersurveillance sweep to make sure no one was following Schweitzer or paying undue attention to his room. At this stage of his evolution as a clandestine agent, Schweitzer had boundless faith in his handlers' competence. He assumed they executed their operations with the same flawless skill and efficiency such professionals always seemed to accomplish in spy novels and movies.

Watching the trucks and swarming taxis, Schweitzer recognized that Thailand's explosion of prosperity during the previous two decades was a direct but unexpected result of the long Vietnam War. America had used Thailand as the staging base for its protracted bombing of the Ho Chi Minh Trail in North Vietnam. American construction companies had built the multibillion-dollar highway system that led north and east from Bangkok to the huge air-base complexes at Ubon and Udorn, where he had served during the war years. Support bases like Korat had sprung up in the dusty, once impoverished interior. The wild frontier country of the northeast had been opened to commercial exploitation when bases like Nakhon Phanom and its satellites were hacked out of the scrub jungle of the Mekong flood plain.

For over ten years, hundreds of thousands of American servicemen who flew and supported the roller-coaster bombing campaign lived in Thailand and spent their generous salaries on the necessities of life and the pleasures of the flesh. Bangkok itself became the major R&R ("rest and recuperation") center for American forces in Indochina. The commercial sex industry that brought both untold prosperity and the unprecedented scourge of AIDS to the city evolved during the Vietnam War.

But above all it was the long bombing campaign from Thai bases—plus the overgenerous American economic and military aid channeled through Thailand's oligarchy that secured the use of the air bases—that lifted the country from minor Third World status to its undisputed position as one of Asia's commercial powers.

Schweitzer would always remember the endless droning convoys of flat-bed munitions trucks trundling along the web of wide American highways, carrying the raw matériel of war to the bases. Day and night the trucks rolled north, the dull green cylinders of 750 pound bombs lashed in orderly piles like so many ingots of pig iron en route to steel mills.

Sipping his coffee in the swelling heat, Schweitzer had a sudden bizarre insight. Just as Thailand's explosive prosperity had been an unexpected offshoot of the long Vietnam War, the MIA situation and its ongoing repercussions were actually a strange type of industrial accident. For years,

America sent fast but clumsy fighter-bombers—that had been designed to penetrate the rear echelons of the huge Soviet Army on the plains of central Europe—into the limestone gorges of the Truong Son, pitting one Phantom or Crusader against a lumbering Soviet-built GAZ truck or a clutch of bicycles slung with rice bags or burdened with mortar shells in canvas pouches. Month after month the American jets unloaded their bombs with assembly-line regularity; year after year the Vietnamese replaced their losses in men and vehicles and continued the relentless drive south. In the North, the bombing campaign was ostensibly more sophisticated, with valuable "logistical complex" targets prevailing. But the net results were the same as along the trail.

Men flew their tours. Some were shot down and rescued, others shot down and captured, others still simply disappeared.

And today, teams of American investigators and their Indochinese counterparts mined those crash sites like prospectors, hoping to strike a treasure lode in this latest evolution of the Vietnam War's strange industry.

But he knew the answers to the MIA mystery did not lie among all the jungle-choked crash sites of the Lao Panhandle or the steep ridges of Tonkin. The real mother lode of information that would solve the mystery of our missing men lay behind locked doors in Hanoi.

That night, Schweitzer's sleep was interrupted by the phone.

"Go to the room next door," Renaud said.

"Next door?" Schweitzer was momentarily confused.

"Next door," Renaud repeated patiently. "Room eleven twenty-seven. There's a Do Not Disturb sign on the door."

Schweitzer cautiously entered the empty corridor and knocked on the door of Room 1127. A sleepy James Renaud opened the door slowly. Inside Schweitzer found all the boxes with his optical scanning and storage system.

Before leaving Washington, Schweitzer and the DIA had agreed that it was vital to set up and test the scanning system in this Bangkok hotel, to be sure it had survived overseas shipment, before venturing into Hanoi where spare parts were unavailable.

All that night, Schweitzer fought jet lag to patiently assemble and connect his equipment, working from the wiring plans that he and George had written. At ten that evening, with the tropical moon high over the city, Schweitzer powered up the system to test it.

The screen of the main console remained black, devoid of even a blinking cursor or password prompt. Schweitzer's face popped with sweat, despite the air-conditioning. He checked his cables and powered up the equipment once more. The screen remained black.

"Son of a bitch," he whispered. Somehow the equipment had been damaged in transit, even though Tony had assured him it would be handled "like the crown jewels."

James Renaud returned later that night.

"I'm screwed," Schweitzer said, pointing to the useless collection of equipment.

"Well," Renaud said with typical irony, "maybe you are. But I can tell you one thing for sure. You ain't gonna get another forty thousand bucks to replace this stuff."

"Okay," Schweitzer replied stubbornly. "I understand. I'm just gonna have to fix it."

Operational rules precluded bringing any local computer technician into the hotel room to actually observe this elaborate scanning system. At best, Schweitzer could carry individual components to a workshop for bench tests. But that process could take weeks and, in the end, not result in the proper diagnosis of the full system.

Instead, Schweitzer opened his tool kit and began to disassemble the main console's central processing unit. He had never done this before, but had seen George modify the guts of the personal computer. George was on the other side of the planet, unfortunately.

After a delicate, nervous hour of work, Schweitzer had the CPU's case open and the motherboard and hard drive exposed. Suddenly he saw an obvious problem. One of the expansion cards George had added to the CPU—a rectangular green maze of chips, condensers, and semiconductors, bristling with vulnerable solder connections and looped polychrome angel-hair wiring—seemed to be ajar. Schweitzer delicately reseated the card in its slot and patiently reassembled the system.

He turned on the personal computer. The screen rippled with the blue-and-yellow manufacturer logo, then blinked to the dark gray matrix. The welcome challenge PASSWORD greeted him.

"Thank God," Schweitzer whispered as he typed HILTON on the keyboard.

FIVE DAYS LATER, Ted Schweitzer was again at Don Muang Airport. He nervously shepherded a small convoy of porters pushing baggage carts down the stifling jetway to the door of the Vietnam Airlines Tupolev TU-134 transport, the thrice-weekly 1:30 P.M. flight from Bangkok to Hanoi. On the carts were the eleven bulky cardboard cartons of his scanning system. Schweitzer had paid a generous excess baggage fee and convinced the normally inflexible airline staff to allot him six empty seats in the Soviet-built airliner's cramped business-class compartment.

Now, wielding a fistful of Thai baht bills as incentive, Schweitzer supervised the placement of each box of computer equipment before taking his own seat and strapping in.

He was damp with sweat in the stuffy cabin. But at least he was on the final leg of his trip. Glancing out the window, he saw the Thai baggage handlers laboring in the shimmering humidity, slamming suitcases into the cargo hold of the battered aircraft.

He breathed deeply. In the next few days, he would either be successfully installed as the first American clandestine agent ever inserted into Hanoi, or he would be in some kind of trouble, the nature of which he did not care to contemplate at that moment.

"Something to drink?" the stewardess mumbled listlessly.

"I would love a cold beer," Schweitzer replied with heartfelt sincerity.

CHAPTER 15

As the drafty Tupolev airliner reached its maximum cruising altitude of 7,000 meters above the parched brown plains of northern Thailand, the reality of the endeavor Ted Schweitzer had embarked on was beginning to sink in. He shivered. Maybe it was just his sweaty shirt drying in the suddenly chill cabin. In any event, he was on his way to Hanoi, the capital of Communist Vietnam, carrying optical scanning and computer equipment, ostensibly a dedicated scholar bent on unearthing historical truth. The fact that Schweitzer was actually an agent of the Defense Intelligence Agency assigned to penetrate a secret military archive in Hanoi seemed to lose substance as he sipped his Saigon 333 beer and gazed down at the muted beige foothills of the Annamite Range that spread northeast of Vientiane, indistinct in the haze.

The mountain spine of Indochina was shrouded by overcast, the remnants of the northeast winter monsoon. But north of the Mu Gia Pass, the cloud deck broke and Schweitzer gazed down at the lush greens of the Tonkinese highlands, and on to the spreading paddies of the Red River Valley. In a moment of illogical fear bordering on panic, he struggled to remember the confusing babble of word and number codes, the cryptic alarm signals, and all the other alien liturgy of espionage tradecraft that James Renaud had drilled into him in the previous frantic weeks. None of this, of course, was in writing. A good spy committed such basic procedure to memory. But now Schweitzer's memory was failing him.

Then he remembered Renaud's patient counsel: "Don't try to remember too much at any one time. Don't get too spooky. You *are* exactly what you say. You're not playing a role."

That was called living a legend, a basic tenet of a clandestine operation. The only way the Vietnamese would ever discover Schweitzer was working for the DIA was if he revealed it. There was not a single piece of paper, not a hastily jotted address or emergency phone number, in all his baggage that linked him to the U.S. government. He was Ted Schweitzer, private citizen, erstwhile relief worker, now scholar. He did have a valid contract to write a book on American POWs. The People's Army of Vietnam had invited him to conduct this research. He was not breaking any law, as long as his American government sponsorship remained secret.

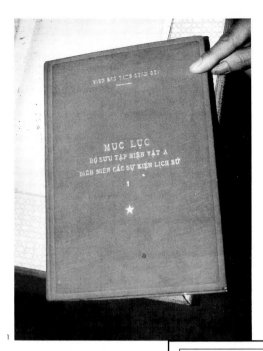

Central Military Museum POW Documents

The Red Book index of documents and holdings of the Central Military Museum of the People's Army of Vietnam (PAVN), Hanoi. This index has been described as the Rosetta Stone of the MIA mystery. Ted Schweitzer's electronic scanning of the index was the first major success of Operation Swamp Ranger.

Page 119 of the Red Book index, which covers documents and photos relating to the air war in North Vietnam from June 1965 to December 1968. This is a reproduction of the original document electronically scanned by Ted Schweitzer. The English captions were added by Schweitzer. The significance of this page is that the document does not include acquisition card 3805, which relates to Major Dean A. Pogreba, an Air Force F-105 pilot shot down near Hanoi in 1965.

119.c: Other events in the North 6 - 1965 to 12 - 1968.   119

c- Các sự kiện ở miền Bắc từ 6.1965 đến 12.196⁰ :

1. Âm mưu mà địch :   119.1: Conspiracies of the enemy.

2695   3050

119.2: Defeating the American War of Destruction in the North (1965-1968).

2- Đánh thắng cuộc chiến tranh phá hoại mà đế quốc Mỹ ở miền Bắc 1965- 1969.

a- Ở Quân khu Thủ Đô :   119.a: The Capital Military Region.

P.5975   P.5977   P.5980   P.6015   P.6135   P.6529

3270   3271   3852   4293   4992   4796   4798   4957 —
4874   4911   5057   5668 — 5669 — 5670 — 5671   5672 —
5673   5674   5675   5676 — 5677   5678 — 5679 — 5680 —
5763   5764 —

b- Ở Quân khu 1 : The First Military Region.

P.5585   P.5596   P.5701   P.5704   P.5582   P.5583   P.5584   P.5585
P.6334

BRUCH

390   398   411   412 —   516 —   555   465 —   772 —
839   869   1074 — 1150   1163 —   1168   1514 — . 1518 —
1519   1744   1960 — 2792   2604 —   2656   2860 —   2866 —
2886   2901   2932   2933 —   2942   3113 —   3189 —   3555 —
3518 — 3819   3820 — 3850 — 3947   4004   4157 —   4770 —
4790   4791   5162 — 5165 — 5800 —

PHIẾU KIỂM KÊ

Số đăng ký: _3805_
Số lượng hiện vật: _2_

Số hồ sơ : _3805_	**Tên gọi và nội dung lịch sử hiện vật**
Hồ sơ gồm : _Hồ sơ lớn_	
5 biên bản tự lập ;	_Giấy chứng minh và công ước Giơ ne vơ._
	Của tên thiếu tá giặc lái máy bay Pogreba bị bắn rơi và
Nguồn gốc ngày sưu tầm	_chết tại miền Bắc Việt Nam (Thanh hoá)._
_8.69_	
	Bởi bản đồ. 5/10
Tài liệu kèm theo hiện vật	_DEAN, ANDREW POGRERA., MAJ. (Thiếu tá), USAF, Bởi thẻ đ. 21847/0FFIE_
	và F1050 số ngày 05 tháng 10, năm 1965
	Chết chưa tìm được hài cốt
Phân loại sưu tập	
_A3,4,5_	
_B2,3,5_	
_C4-15_	

Museum acquisition card 3805 (both sides): Major Dean Pogreba. Although not listed in the central index, this acquisition card and Pogreba's military identity card and Geneva Convention card are held by the museum. Pogreba is an MIA whose remains have never been returned. Schweitzer's scanning of these documents and the photographs of Pogreba's military cards were the first proof that he had fallen into enemy custody in 1965.

Số đăng ký _3805_

GHI CHÉP TỪNG HIỆN VẬT

Tờ số: _____

Tên hiện vật	Số lượng	Chất lượng kỹ thuật Sáng chế	Kích thước trọng lượng	Tình trạng hiện vật	Số chất liệu	GHI CHÚ
Giấy chứng minh	1	Bằng bìa cứng ly Typo mực xanh bên ni lông trong, xung lệ Anh	6,5 x 9,5	Cũ sờn một chút	Gỗ số 20/1	
Công ước Giơ ne vơ	1	Giấy trắng in và đánh máy mực đen bên ni lông trong suốt C-125 526 64b	6 x 9,5	Cũ rách một đường ở góc trên	Gỗ số 20/x	

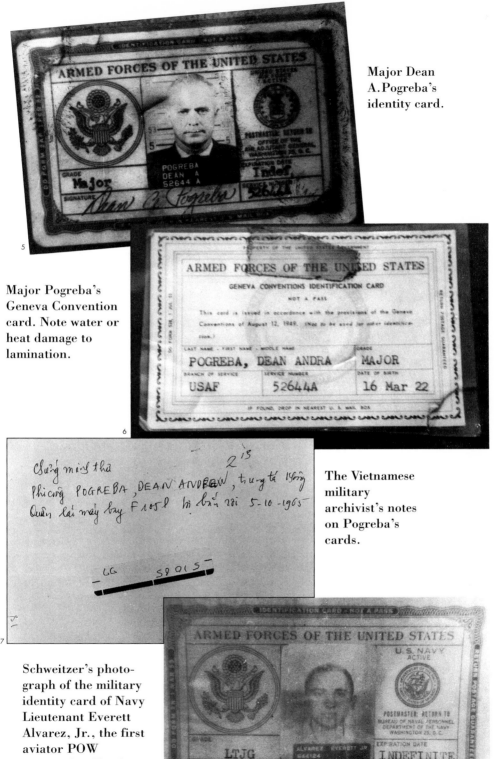

Major Dean A. Pogreba's identity card.

Major Pogreba's Geneva Convention card. Note water or heat damage to lamination.

The Vietnamese military archivist's notes on Pogreba's cards.

Schweitzer's photograph of the military identity card of Navy Lieutenant Everett Alvarez, Jr., the first aviator POW captured in North Vietnam, in August 1964.

5. Chiến thắng chiến tranh phá hoại bằng không quân
của đế quốc Mỹ ở miền Bắc từ 5-8-1964 đến 5/1965:
a. Trận đầu tiên: 5-8-1964:

P.2631	P.2632	P.2633	P.2634	P.2635	P.2636	P.2637	P.2638
P.2639	P.2640	P.2642	P.2643	P.2644	P.2645	P.2646	P.2647
P.2650	P.2651	P.2652	P.2653	P.2654	P.2655	P.2656	P.2657
P.2658	P.2659	P.2660	P.2671	~~P.5662~~	P.5640	P.5642	P.5643
P.5644	P.5647	P.5646	P.5647	P.5648	P.5649	P.5650	P.5651
P.5652	P.5653	P.5656	P.5658	P.5659	P.5660	P.5662	P.5663
P.5664	P.5665	P.5666	P.5667	P.5668	P.5669	P.5670	P.5671
P.5672	P.5673	P.5720	P.5721	P.5738	P.5739	P.5793	P.5794
P.5795	P.5796	P.5867	P.5981	P.5976	P.5978	P.5991	P.6297
P.7796							

58	74	133	191	250	261	286	296
430	523	623	658	~~786~~	~~1070~~	~~1418~~	~~2870~~
~~3083~~	~~3102~~	696	721	722	786	916	986
989	1070	1108	1145	1146	1147	1149	1217
1241	1242	1255	1256	1257	1258	1269	1346
1383	1418	1510	1511	1615	1620	1958	1959
2036	2037	2038	2202	2371	2476	2477	2478
2613	2683	2797	2857	2869	2879	3083	3102
3811	3850	3853	3941	4003	4082	4114	4135
4501	4817	7012					

The Red Book index page listing photographs of American prisoners
and their equipment captured between August 1964 and August 1965.
Although Schweitzer scanned every page of the Red Book and was
allowed to scan documents and photographs pertaining to almost all the
entries, the Vietnamese withheld approximately ninety-five documents
relating to events during the height of the air war. This signifies that
they have more material in their archives than they have admitted
to the Americans.

Museum photo of Lieutenant Alvarez on the day he was captured, August 5, 1964. The Vietnamese mixed such innocuous propaganda photos with truly significant documents on missing Americans.

10

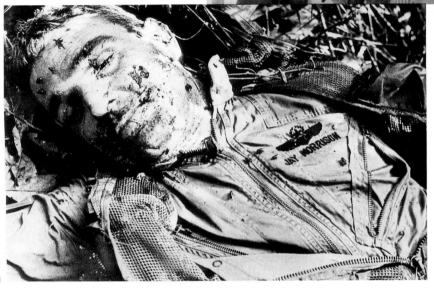

11

Photo of Major Joseph C. Morrison, an MIA Air Force F-4 pilot shot down on November 25, 1968. He was killed by PAVN forces the next day following a brief evasion. Morrison's remains have never been recovered. This photograph of Morrison's body was one of eleven such photographs Schweitzer obtained showing the bodies of dead airmen about whom the Vietnamese have never before revealed information.

12

Photo of identity cards of Major Morrison and his backseat pilot, Lieutenant San D. Francisco. The Vietnamese told Schweitzer that Lieutenant Francisco had also been killed attempting evasion. But they revealed no photo of his body.

PHIẾU KIỂM KÊ

Số hồ sơ : 2863 Hồ sơ gồm Phiếu bảo quản hiện vật số 6907	**Tên gọi và nội dung lịch sử hiện vật** Mảnh máy bay Tang vật của chiếc máy bay A4 E thuộc Hải Quân Mỹ bị quân ta ta bắn rơi tại nông trường Sao vàng Thanh Hóa ngày 25-6-1965
Nguồn gốc ngày sưu tầm	MONGILADI PETER NMN JR Trung tá hải Quân Chỉ chức đóm đóm
Tài liệu kèm theo hiện vật	
Phân loại sưu tập	

13

Museum acquisition card 2863, Navy Commander Peter Mongilardi, a Killed in Action/Body Not Recovered aviator for whom the Vietnamese denied any knowledge since 1973, and Mongilardi's military identity card. Note possible ballistic damage, but no bloodstain.

14

Photo of the remains of Air Force Major Marvin N. Lindsey, an MIA since 1965. His remains have never been returned, and the Vietnamese had previously denied any knowledge of his fate.

Photograph of Navy Lieutenant Lee E. Nordahl, an MIA since 1965. He is clearly receiving medical treatment in this photograph, yet the Vietnamese had previously denied any knowledge of his fate. His remains have never been returned to American custody.

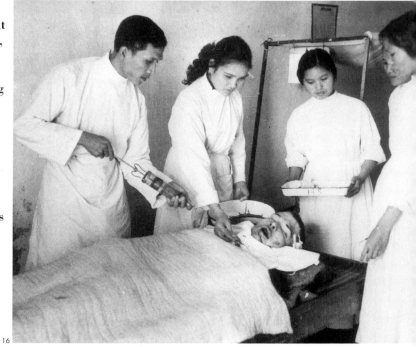

Photograph of the remains of Air Force Captain John W. Seuell, an MIA
F-4 pilot shot down in 1972. The Vietnamese had previously denied any
knowledge of Seuell's fate, as well as that of his crewmate, Major James
A. Fowler. This picture was the first evidence of Seuell's death.

VIỆN BẢO TÀNG QUÂN ĐỘI

PHIẾU KIỂM KÊ

Số đăng ký: 3816
Số lượng hiện vật: 2

Số hồ sơ: 3816
Hồ sơ gồm: Một tấm
lai ngày 14-8-1969
(biên bản tư liệu)
Nguồn gốc ngày sưu tầm
8.69

Tài liệu kèm theo hiện vật

Phân loại sưu tập
A9, 3, C, 2
B5, 2, a, v; B2, 3, 5.
G4. 15.;

Tên gọi và nội dung lịch sử hiện vật

Chứng minh thư và Công ước Giơnevơ
Của tên đại úy Mỹ Mellor Fredric, giặc lái máy bay Mỹ bị quân và
dân ta bắn rơi tại Mộc Châu ngày 13-8-1965.
Sơn La

Mellor, Fredrick   lái máy bay F-103
Chết, chưa tìm thấy hài cốt.

18

Museum acquistion card 3816, Air Force Captain Fredric M. Mellor, a reconnaissance pilot shot down over North Vietnam and missing since 1965, and Mellor's identity card. Mellor was known to have survived the shootdown. His name appears on General Vessey's "Last Known Alive Discrepancy List." Despite this proof that the Vietnamese know his fate, his remains have never been returned.

IDENTIFICATION CARD - NOT A PASS

ARMED FORCES OF THE UNITED STATES

UNITED STATES
AIR FORCE
ACTIVE

DEPARTMENT OF THE AIR FORCE

POSTMASTER: RETURN TO
HQ USAF (AFCAS)
WASHINGTON 25, D. C.

GRADE
Captain

MELL
FREDF
AO 30653-t

EXPIRATION DATE
INDEFINITE

SIGNATURE
Fredric M Mellor

SERVICE NUMBER
A03065346

IF FOUND, DROP IN NEAREST U. S. MAIL BOX

RETURN POSTAGE GUARANTEED

DD FORM 2AF 1 MAR 59

19

(*Above and opposite, top*) Air Force identity card of Captain
Richard J. Mallon, an F-105 pilot shot down in southern North
Vietnam in January 1970, and the downed F-105's equipment. The
remains of Mallon and his crewman were returned by the Vietnamese
after the war. Wartime reports indicate Mallon was captured alive.
This is substantiated by the photograph of both men's undamaged
parachutes, pistols, and survival equipment. This may be tangible
evidence of what the Vietnamese told Schweitzer was their "darkest
secret": that a number of American prisoners were executed at the
time of their capture, enroute to Hanoi, or during interrogation.

22

The flight helmet of Lieutenant Colonel Robinson "Robbie" Risner from
the PAVN Museum.

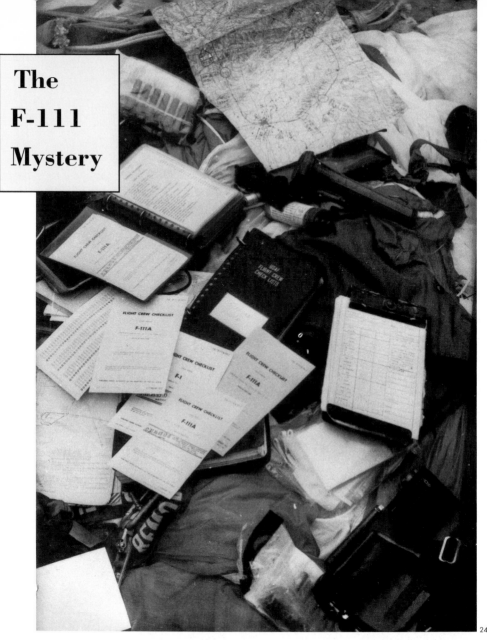

The F-111 Mystery

PAVN photograph obtained by Schweitzer of the flight equipment removed from the escape capsule of the U.S. Air Force F-111A shot down on the night of December 18, 1972, during the first phase of the Linebacker II bombing of Hanoi. The photograph clearly shows sensitive flight manuals as well as maps and personal equipment of the two MIA aviators, Lieutenant Colonel Ronald J. Ward and Major James R. McElvain. These manuals and their personal equipment are in near-perfect condition, showing no fire or water damage or bloodstains; further, the parachute nylon and riser in the upper left corner of the picture is proof that the escape capsule parachute deployed. However, until the DIA obtained the photograph of Major McElvain's remains, the Vietnamese refused to admit they had knowledge of these men's fate.

The escape capsule of the F-111A shot down four days later on December 22, 1972. The pilots in this shootdown, Captain Robert D. Sponeyberger and Lieutenant William W. Wilson, were captured alive and repatriated in March 1973. This is evidence that, given the condition of Ward's and McElvain's flight equipment, their escape capsule also landed intact.

The Quest for Remains

26

27

(*Above and opposite, top*) Photographs of purported American skeletal remains offered for sale to Ted Schweitzer by a Vietnamese "private citizen" in Ho Chi Minh City (Saigon) in 1993. Although the government of Vietnam has officially barred such transactions, private individuals continue to sell American remains with quasi-official military approval. Schweitzer arranged forensic examination of these remains before purchase. They were determined to be non-American.

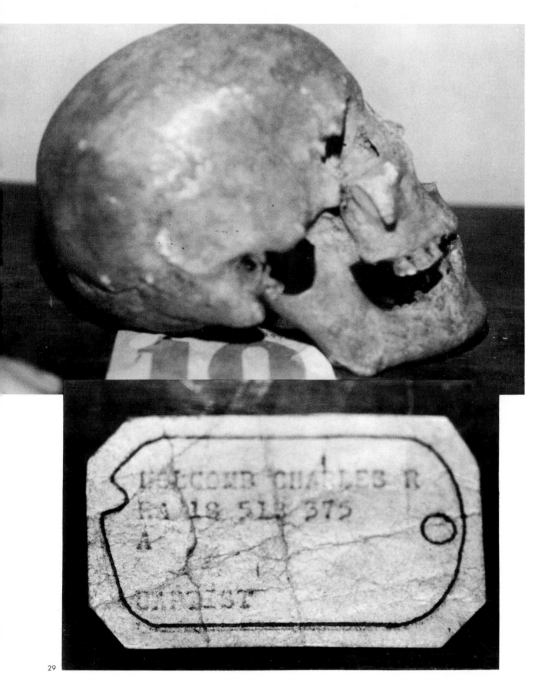

29

A tracing of the dog tag ostensibly belonging to a dead soldier's bones. This dog tag, however, was for Charles R. Holcomb, who returned alive from the war.

Capture in Laos

A wartime photograph taken by a helicopter crewman of the capture of two unidentified American airmen in a roadside clearing on the Ho Chi Minh Trail in Laos. Note the PAVN soldier atop the rockpile, center ; the two American aircrew, one kneeling, one standing; and the two other PAVN soldiers. Ted Schweitzer was told that a number of Americans captured in remote areas such as the Ho Chi Minh Trail died or were killed before reaching Hanoi.

As Schweitzer silently repeated this comforting mantra, he began to relax. He speculated yet again on the motives of the Vietnamese officials who had invited him on this bizarre mission. There was no doubt that the Socialist Republic of Vietnam wanted to normalize relations with the United States. And the Bush administration had made it clear through the State Department's Road Map drawn up the previous spring that, once the Cambodian political and military situation had stabilized, future progress on normalization would depend on Vietnamese cooperation on the missing in action issue. Even though Vietnam had not officially ratified the Road Map, Hanoi had followed its provisos in disengaging its army from Cambodia and helping achieve a viable political solution to that tortured country's problems. And it had been the Vietnamese government that leaked the text of the confidential Road Map to the Thai press, so that each concrete cooperative step on the MIA issue could be publicly acknowledged and used to set the stage for a reciprocal American concession in the carefully orchestrated quid pro quo process.

Schweitzer had read the agreement in *The Nation,* one of Bangkok's English language newspapers, the previous fall. He now had come to realize that his selection as an unofficial conduit of information was part of the shadowy diplomatic exchange between Hanoi and Washington. According to the Road Map, Vietnam was to continue helping resolve the "highest priority discrepancy cases of Americans last known alive," facilitate the "rapid repatriation of American remains readily available to Vietnam," and help implement a two-year program that would include "productive joint investigations and cooperative research activities."[1]

Obviously the Vietnamese viewed his book research as a suitably neutral and comfortably face-saving method of opening the door to their vast POW archives, the existence of which they had steadfastly denied for almost twenty years. But if this was their motive in choosing Schweitzer, the choice undoubtedly meant that the PAVN and its party superiors in the Politburo believed that he was indeed a private scholar, and certainly not a trained intelligence agent. As in so many of their dealings with the West, indirection bordering on intricate deception undoubtedly shaped this particular "cooperative research" activity. The Vietnamese probably intended to provide Schweitzer with the minimum information necessary to qualify for a positive reciprocal Road Map gesture from the United States, a niggling process they hoped would end with the lifting of the trade embargo.

The Vietnamese were masters at such diplomatic charades. As a relatively small nation, they had a long tradition of extracting concessions from more powerful nations based on elaborate, ostensibly conciliatory agreements, which they had no intention of honoring.

The Paris Peace Accords of 1973 were probably the best example of this process. Clearly the Vietnamese Communists had no intention of abandoning their conquest of the South when they signed the accords. Indeed the

Communist members of the various cease-fire teams never acted as peacekeepers, but were rather the thinly disguised fifth column of the ulti- mately victorious PAVN. In fairness, the Paris Peace Accords were a mutually deceptive exercise: When Richard Nixon and Henry Kissinger promised at least $3.25 billion in reparations, they no doubt realized the aid stood little chance of winning congressional approval. But both sides had participated in the elaborate "peace with honor" charade because it brought short-term positive benefits. America could disengage its forces in relative safety. The Vietnamese Communists could regroup and resupply for the final campaign free of the threat of renewed American air attack.

Now, nineteen years later, America and Vietnam were parties to another elaborate, multiclause diplomatic agreement that, when successfully imple- mented, would restore normal relations between the two countries and resolve the MIA mystery that had festered since 1973.

As Schweitzer pondered his strange role in all this, he suddenly pictured the ornate lacquer boxes and silver filigree work that was the quintessence of Tonkinese art. Some of the antique lacquer chests he'd seen in Hanoi were so richly layered and meticulously detailed that they appeared massive, almost ponderous. Yet when he had lifted the chests, he'd discovered they weighed almost nothing. The seemingly thick walls were paper-thin. And the intricate silver filigree turtles—the cultural totem of the Tonkinese— found in every Hanoi art gallery presented the same illusion. They looked chunky and dense. But they were hollow, feather-light.

The Vietnamese were masters of such convoluted illusion. Schweitzer now had a nagging fear that Colonel Dai and the PAVN General Political Directorate might have conceived of his research in the museum archives as just such an exercise in trompe l'oeil. They might have intended to throw him a few crumbs, make some welcome dollars in the process, then send him home. But Schweitzer was confident, in fact determined, that he could obtain much more.

Before leaving Washington, Carl Ford had told him, "Get us that damned Red Book, Ted."

Schweitzer now understood the critical importance of that document. Once in American hands, the Red Book could be used as the wedge to pry open the entire treasure trove of POW archives he knew existed. If he could successfully scan the entire Red Book index of POW document holdings —and deliver his computer file safely to James Renaud in Bangkok—the Vietnamese could just not stubbornly refuse to give access to the thousands of documents listed in the index at some future evolution of the Road Map's diplomatic ballet.

The Tupolev jolted through broken clouds. The green width of the Red River delta opened ahead. They were descending into Hanoi's Noi Bai Air- port.

· · ·

As PLANNED, SCHWEITZER held back for several minutes fussing with his clumsy assembly of cartons, so that the throng of eager French tourists, Japanese businessmen, and overseas Vietnamese passengers could surge down the boarding stairs ahead of him. He had been taught not to stand out in crowds. "Don't be first, don't be last, and never volunteer for anything." But that was going to be difficult, lugging several hundred pounds of computer equipment. Luckily, his escort from the Foreign Ministry, Miss Doan Thi Ngoc Lan, greeted him at the foot of the stairs. "Welcome back to Vietnam, Mr. Swisg-er," she said, mangling his name as most Vietnamese did.

In the quiet but precise manner of so many women officials in Vietnam, Doan Thi Ngoc Lan quickly organized a team of porters and a baggage cart. Five minutes later, they had cleared passport control and customs and were loading the boxes into a surprisingly clean minibus.

The bus driver honked his way through the airport crowds and onto the rough concrete highway astride the narrow dike that cut due south through the pastel green paddies of spring rice toward the Red River bridges and Hanoi.

"You had a pleasant flight?" Miss Lan asked.

She was simply making small talk, as expected, but Schweitzer thought he noted a strained edge in her voice and manner. No, he cautioned himself silently. Don't start getting paranoid.

The driver used his horn like a battering ram to scatter the ubiquitous overloaded bicycles, three-wheeled cyclos, and the occasional battered Honda motorbikes that plied the two-lane road. They passed through the drab industrial suburbs of Gia Lam that had been heavily bombed during the Linebacker II attacks. Two decades after the war, there was little evidence of bombing. The Eastern Bloc concrete prefab apartment blocks and light-industry complexes built in the 1980s already looked shoddy and run-down, the facades cracked and stained with the pervasive mildew of the river bottom.

This close to the city, Schweitzer noticed, there were many more of the buzzing Honda 90cc motorbikes. At $2,400 per bike, the noisy Hondas were tangible proof of the new prosperity engendered by the *doi moi* economic reforms.

Still honking incessantly, the minibus driver rolled onto the old French-built span across the Red River, which was now called the Chuong Duong Bridge. The iron trestle span and the Paul Doumer Bridge further upstream had been the frequent targets of American bombing and had only been successfully cut toward the end of the war by tactical aircraft using the new laser-guided bombs. Halfway across the river, the bridge passed over a wide tongue-shaped gravelly island that was almost covered by a dense warren of small cinderblock houses and shops. This was Hanoi's newest *arrondisse-ment,* O Quan Chuong, the most recent "gate" to Hanoi's traditional center, the Thirty-Six Streets. This teeming neighborhood had begun as a squatter settlement, and had quickly evolved into a working-class quarter housing more than 100,000 people.

Schweitzer grinned as they passed above the hive of narrow lanes and rusty corrugated metal roofs. His first assignment as an intelligence agent had involved this neighborhood. In 1989, when he had made his first con-tacts with the DIA office in Bangkok, one of the officers had asked a favor.

"Next time you're in Hanoi," the man said, "how about checking out a sighting report we had on a stay-behind deserter named Nolan."

"Well . . . I guess so," Schweitzer had agreed, not hiding his reluctance.

"It shouldn't be hard," the officer assured him. "He's a black guy, sup-posed to be living under the Doumer Bridge in a little shantytown."

On Schweitzer's next trip to Hanoi, he had searched for the "little" squat-ter village under the bridge and had discovered instead the densely popu-lated quarter of O Quan Chuong. If there was a black American deserter from the Vietnam War living down there, it certainly would not have been easy to find him. The incident left an impression on Schweitzer: The level of understanding of the realities of contemporary Vietnam on the part of the American intelligence officials charged with resolving the MIA issue was ridiculously poor, and hopelessly outdated. That gravelly island under the bridge had no doubt been a small squatter camp right after the war. But almost twenty years had passed. This was Asia; populations grew; cities expanded. If there had been any American POWs held back after the war, tracking them based on the knowledge level that particular officer's informal tasking had revealed would not have been easy.[2]

Schweitzer had since learned that the status of McKinley Nolan had been one of the most nagging unresolved cases confronting the DIA in the years since the war. In 1967, Nolan had been a young black private with the 1st Infantry Division stationed in War Zone C, the rubber plantation district northwest of Saigon. Against regulations, he had married a local girl, an ethnic Cambodian. Nolan went absent without leave on November 9, 1967, disappearing with his wife. Originally listed as MIA, his status was later changed to the DIA's "AA" category: deserter. Nolan appeared in Hanoi during the war where he reportedly volunteered to participate in propa-ganda broadcasts. Admiral James Stockdale, one of the senior American POWs, called Nolan a U.S. defector who provided the female English-speak-ing propaganda announcer known as Hanoi Hannah with tape recordings meant to encourage other Americans to defect.[3]

After the 1973 cease-fire, Nolan was reportedly sighted at a coffee planta-tion in northern Cambodia, using the name Buller. A subsequent CIA report (probably based on a refugee live sighting) described Nolan as alive and healthy as late as 1978.[4] That had probably been the source of the DIA Bangkok officer's request to Schweitzer to investigate the shantytown under the Doumer Bridge.

The problem of accounting for American stay-behinds had dogged the DIA's effort at achieving a full accounting for missing Americans since before the fall of Saigon. This was because the status of these men could not be easily determined. During the war there were several hundred AWOLs and deserters living in the cities of South Vietnam, particularly in Saigon, Da Nang, and the largest city in the Mekong Delta, Can Tho. Many of these young men gravitated to underworld "twilight zones" and became involved in drug trafficking, black marketeering, and other crime.

Reportedly, 268 deserters took advantage of the unofficial amnesty proclaimed in the last frantic days of April 1975 before the fall of Saigon. They were flown to California and processed out of the armed services through the Oakland Army Base after receiving general discharges.[5]

Because some of these deserters were reportedly involved with passing low-level intelligence to Vietnamese Communist forces, and did not take advantage of the April 1975 amnesty, they were not listed as "civilian detainees" by the DIA after the fall of South Vietnam. As already noted, over a hundred American citizens, contractors, and others married to Vietnamese, missionaries, and at least two active or retired intelligence officers, did fall into Communist hands in 1975. Some of these Americans reportedly found their own way out of Vietnam after the Communist takeover. Many of this category were reportedly not counted in American MIA totals.[6] But all those known to the U.S. government (registered by American consular officials) have been accounted for since the war.

There remained an estimated twenty-odd Americans of indeterminate category: some deserters, some volunteer stay-behind collaborators, like McKinley Nolan.[7] Some of these men may have once been bona fide POWs who "crossed over" while in captivity. Why they were not repatriated during Operation Homecoming as were other alleged collaborators in Hanoi has not been determined. Further, there definitely were other Americans imprisoned by the Vietnamese Communists after 1975 on criminal charges of drug-trafficking and gun-running. The combination of these categories of Americans has badly confused the general MIA issue, and the live-sighting report situation in particular. As a result of this confusion, since the late 1970s all U.S. government pronouncements about possible live Americans remaining in Communist Indochina have identified MIAs as those being "held against their will."[8]

There certainly was a historical precedent for such stay-behinds. During the First Indochina War, hundreds of French troops and some non-French Europeans from the Foreign Legion crossed over to the Vietminh side. Many of these men were young Germans with leftist sympathies who had been first caught up in the maelstrom of World War II, then forced by circumstances to serve in the Legion. One, a German named Schroeder, was reportedly "adopted" by Ho Chi Minh, and took the name Ho Chi Long.[9] Called "international combatants" by Vietminh propagandists, most of these shadowy figures remained in Vietnam for years after the war.[10] One Ukrainian, Platon Skrzhinsky, deserted from the Legion soon after arriving in Vietnam to fight for the Vietminh. He was given the Vietnamese name Than, "Loyal One."[11]

(At present, members of the Clinton administration knowledgeable about MIA matters believe that any Americans living freely in Vietnam are probably deserters. Deputy White House Chief of Staff Roy Neel commented after attending a briefing on MIAs at Pacific Command Headquarters in Honolulu that there were probably no American POWs still alive in Indochina. Neel, a Vietnam veteran, commented that any living Americans in Vietnam "were deserters." He added, "I would not be at all surprised if you went back to Vietnam and you would find Americans living there who went over [deserted]."[12])

SCHWEITZER'S TASKING TO try to locate Nolan led him to an interesting revelation. Nobody in DIA ever asked him for information about possible live POWs in Vietnam during his trips back and forth, bringing medical supplies to Hanoi. Later, during his direct contacts with Richard Armitage and Carl Ford, neither official told him to be especially alert for any information on live American prisoners. This was significant. Armitage had led the Reagan administration's first delegations to Hanoi in the early 1980s, which resulted in Vietnam publicly embracing the concept of resolving the MIA issue as a humanitarian matter. Ford was a senior career CIA officer and longtime member of the Inter-Agency Group, Washington's principal experts on the issue. Both men were as "read in" as anyone could be. But neither had given him any indication there were live American prisoners of war in Indochina.

Both, however, had stressed the importance of his mission to finally penetrate the Vietnamese military archives to determine, if possible, the fates of those men who did not return.

CHAPTER 16

THE MINIBUS CARRYING SCHWEITZER AND MISS LAN, ITS HORN STILL bleating, pulled onto Trang Tien Street and scattered the rank of cyclos parked before the seedy, state-owned Dan Chu Hotel. Schweitzer carefully supervised the unloading of his boxes. Here amid the throngs of bicycles and pedestrians in the center of Hanoi, he felt comfortably at home. He dismissed his earlier apprehension on the airplane as an inevitable bout of first-mission nerves.

Miss Lan sat with Schweitzer in the hotel dining room and made polite small talk, informing him that she would escort him to the museum early Monday morning. She offered to take him on a tour of Dong Xuan Market the next day.

Inspecting his predictably dingy room, and finding no obvious rats in residence, Schweitzer set about unpacking. Miss Lan's offer to spend her free time with him was unusual. A "honey trap"?

Schweitzer dropped the lid of his suitcase.

No, he thought. That's just paranoia.

MISS LAN'S MINISTRY of Foreign Affairs minivan deposited Schweitzer at the Central Military Museum just before nine on the clear spring morning of March 30, 1992. He had spent a restful weekend. The bad nerves were behind him, and he was eager to get to work.

But when Major Lai Vinh Mui, the younger General Political Directorate officer assigned as Schweitzer's interpreter, greeted him, Mui was somber and taciturn.

"Come into this office," he said coolly, leading Schweitzer to a narrow room off the arched portico at the rear left-hand corner of the main museum building. The narrow room was musty-smelling, the walls colored a milky aqua with chalky tinted lime wash. The tall windows facing the courtyard equipment exhibition, dominated by the triumphant MiG-21 on its concrete plinth, were covered with cheap print blue drapes.

Colonel Dai, his deputy, Colonel Nguyen Van Quan, and another GPD officer Schweitzer recognized as a Colonel Nguyen Van Tich, head of the museum's archives section, sat at an L-shaped table arrangement, as if members of a court martial. Despite the heat, they wore brown wool uniforms, the tunics buttoned. Major Lai Vinh Mui's wife, Lieutenant Colonel Tran Thanh Hang, the senior woman archivist, sat stiffly to one side. As Schweitzer entered the room, he was immediately struck by the tense atmosphere. There were none of the usually ubiquitous tea pots and cups, no water glasses, ashtrays, or the other common accoutrements of Tonkinese hospitality.

Colonel Dai shook Schweitzer's hand stiffly, a cold perfunctory gesture. The other officers gazed at Schweitzer through half-closed eyes, their lips pursed. He recognized this expression as distaste bordering on contempt.

"Asseyez-vous," Dai said in French, pointing to a single rickety plywood chair that stood isolated at the center of the angle formed by the L-shaped tables.

Schweitzer swallowed, his mouth suddenly dry. *What the hell is going on?*

Major Mui took his place beside Colonel Dai and began to translate a long, staccato statement. Dai, like a presiding judge, was presenting a rehearsed summary of Schweitzer's contacts with the museum. Colonel Dai emphasized that Schweitzer had presented himself as a "private citizen research scholar." In conclusion, Dai asked Schweitzer to confirm that all these facts were true.

"Yes, of course," Schweitzer said, trying to smile and also offer an expression of sincere puzzlement.

But his ploy did not lessen the tension in the small room. Dai opened a gray pasteboard folder and removed several glossy eight-by-ten-inch photos, the American-size format. He handed them to Schweitzer.

Gripping the pictures, Schweitzer felt his hand begin to tremble, but he managed to steady his grip. The photos were indeed familiar. They were copies of the shots he had taken almost two years earlier as Colonel Dai spread museum records, American military identity cards of POWs, and the Red Book index on the table of the musty anteroom of the museum's second-floor secret archive. These were the pictures that eventually convinced Richard Armitage and Carl Ford to ramrod the authorization for Operation Swamp Ranger through the Washington intelligence bureaucracy.

Schweitzer felt his face flush with heat. He fought a moment of dizziness and nausea, as Colonel Quan moved to block the door. These pictures were supposedly classified top secret, as was every other aspect of his operation. *How the hell did they get copies back here?*

Colonel Dai provided the answer as Mui translated. "These photographs were brought to us from the American intelligence office here in Hanoi," Dai said coldly, referring to the new Joint Task Force/Full Accounting (JTF/FA) detachment that had arrived in Hanoi in March.

Schweitzer had been briefed on the JTF/FA operation before returning to Indochina. This Pentagon unit had supplanted the Joint Casualty Resolution Center MIA operation that had functioned since 1973.[1] The Hanoi detachment was commanded by an energetic young infantry lieutenant colonel named Jack Donovan, the officer whom JCRC investigator Garnett "Bill" Bell had disparaged the previous autumn. Bell, now based in Bangkok, not Hanoi, found himself merely providing investigative support for the military detachment in Hanoi. This JTF/FA unit did have an experienced civilian analyst from the DIA in its complement, a colleague of Bell's named Robert Destatte, thus Colonel Dai's derogatory reference to the detachment as the American "intelligence office."

"Robert Destatte first took the photographs to the Foreign Ministry and accused them of withholding important records," Dai said. "He has demanded that we provide everything. He was very rude and caused us many problems with the ministry."[2]

Dai was chain-smoking 555 cigarettes now, speaking in rapid, brittle bursts of words, almost too quickly for Mui to translate.

"Then Garnett Bell," Dai continued, not disguising his anger, "who we know is an intelligence officer, brought us several pictures." He pointed rudely with his thumb at the fan of photographs in Schweitzer's lap. "He demanded to see our archives."

As Dai paused now for Mui to translate, Schweitzer could see the old colonel positively twanging with rage. As soon as the translation ended, Dai spoke gruffly: "How did Destatte and Bell get these pictures?"

Schweitzer knew he was flushing, but breathed evenly and dispersed his tension by shaking his head slowly and frowning. "I . . . I really don't know."

He tried to recall all the good advice James Renaud had given him to prepare for such unexpected emergencies. But Schweitzer could not think clearly. Instead his mind was churning with a chaos of bizarre speculations. Those pictures were meant to stay within the DIA Operations Directorate "compartment" that supposedly isolated Operation Swamp Ranger from the analysts in the agency's POW/MIA office. Schweitzer had been assured that his operation was a secure "second-channel" effort, completely independent of the JTF/FA. He was supposedly working for Carl Ford, who in turn supposedly reported only to the secretary of defense, the national security adviser, the CIA, and to the President. Renaud had assured him that his identity as a clandestine operative would be a closely guarded secret, both to guarantee his safety and to bolster the success of the operation.

"How did Destatte get these pictures?" Colonel Tich demanded.

Again Schweitzer shook his head. "I just don't know."

"How did American intelligence obtain these photographs?" Colonel Quan snapped, speaking for the first time.

Again Schweitzer bungled through a noncommittal answer. He tried to stand up, but Major Mui put a hand on his shoulder. The April morning sun now flooded the courtyard. The room became stifling, but no one offered Schweitzer a cup of tea or even a glass of water. Again and again, each officer posed the same question.

"How did American intelligence get copies of your pictures?"

Mui coldly described the JTF/FA analysts as having been arrogant and rude in their demands that the museum turn over all the archives from which Schweitzer had obtained these documents. Schweitzer could imagine the scene: For years the PAVN had denied the existence of such detailed POW records. Now they had been caught by surprise, indeed, ambushed by the same indignant Americans whom they had long deceived. Worse, these confrontations had occurred following a formal visit by presidential emissary General John Vessey, who accompanied the new JTF/FA delegation to Hanoi, giving the American military team the cachet of his prestige. The new JTF/FA had planned to push rapidly and forcefully ahead to resolve as many MIA cases as possible in a relatively short period of time. To do this, they expected complete access to Vietnamese military archives, including those of the PAVN museum.

But Schweitzer knew that the Vietnamese wanted to continue to closely control access to any sensitive records, keeping the American investigators ignorant as to the full contents of the archives. The sudden and unexpected demands by Bell and Destatte had punctured this defensive PAVN shell.

From Schweitzer's experience with Vietnamese officials, such surprises were anathema. This incident was a classic loss of face. Although Westerners bandied about that hackneyed term lightly, it was a very serious matter for men like these PAVN officers. They had been caught in a lie by Americans they considered inferior in rank and status. This calamity would probably sour any future relationship between the PAVN's General Political Directorate and the JTF/FA. Schweitzer understood the gravity of the situation, and now recognized that he had to completely isolate himself from those JTF/FA analysts who had sparked this unfortunate and dangerous incident.

Sticking to his tactic of claiming complete ignorance, Schweitzer hoped this would deflect the questions to other aspects of the problem. But he soon recognized he was dealing with skilled interrogators. Patience was their long suit. All morning, as the temperature in the narrow blue-washed room mounted insufferably, the three male officers asked the same basic question: How had photographs that Schweitzer had assured them would only be shown to private American publishing firms found their way into the hands of DIA officers?

Four hours later, Schweitzer was allowed to go alone to the tiny café tables on the shady terrace and eat a hurried bowl of noodles. Then the interrogation began again. He now fully recognized the nature of his predicament. His passport and visa were at the hotel reception desk, which everyone knew was controlled by the security forces of the Ministry of the Interior. All his computer equipment was stacked in boxes outside on the portico, guarded by a glum soldier.

If the Communist government of Vietnam wished to treat him with real malice—and, in the process, damage the nascent reconciliation between the two countries—they had a variety of options. They could arrest Schweitzer as a spy, using the book contract and the purloined photographs of secret documents as convincing evidence. Or, they could simply cancel his visa, confiscate the expensive computer equipment as evidence in an espionage investigation, and completely derail this secret second-channel attempt to crack open the PAVN archives. Or, in a more sinister manner, Hanoi could arrest Schweitzer as a common criminal, using any manner of planted contraband, clap him into jail, and there sweat the truth out of him, using techniques at which he knew they excelled. He did not imagine for a moment that he would be capable of maintaining his legend, strapped to an interrogation table in a windowless room at the Ministry of the Interior.

Eventually the afternoon sun shifted from the blue drapes and the room cooled slightly. But still the questions continued.

"We must learn how it was possible that American intelligence got possession of your photographs," Dai persisted. "Nothing can proceed until we know that."

Schweitzer continued to shake his head in an unconvincing display of disbelief.

"I just don't know."

WHEN THEY DROVE Schweitzer back to the Dan Chu Hotel it was almost dark. He wanted to buy a $40 bottle of Black Label scotch of questionable pedigree and drink it alone in his room in a vain attempt to escape from his predicament. But Schweitzer knew he had to get word to the DIA of this pending disaster. So instead of getting drunk, he sat down at his Toshiba laptop computer and typed out a fax message to James Renaud, using the commercial cutout address of a "publishing company" in the Washington area.

> **Dear James:**
>   **As I really don't know you that well, I hope you don't mind my addressing you as James. Perhaps I should have said Dear Mr. Renaud . . .**

This was the prearranged danger signal. By expressing his confusion over the manner of salutation, Schweitzer was alerting the DIA that both he and the operation were in grave jeopardy. He explained the situation:

> **I had quite a shock this morning when I met with Colonel Dai of the museum and Major Mui of the political department, who showed me copies of many of my own pictures, which I took during my previous visits to Hanoi. Colonel Dai told me that he was given these "secret" photos by a Garnett Bell two or three days ago, during the week of 22–29 March 1992. Ac-**

cording to Colonel Dai, this Garnett Bell apparently has additional documents of mine, which he also intends to share with
PAVN.

Schweitzer paused at his computer keyboard. He had to be very careful not
to inadvertently reveal to the Vietnamese counterintelligence types he was
certain would read this outgoing fax that he was familiar in any way with
DIA personnel. So instead of imploring James Renaud to rattle cages at the
DIA, Schweitzer adopted a tone of injured indignation, which he hoped was
convincing:

> **I'm afraid I don't know just what to make of this unhelpful
> development, but I consider these photos and documents to
> be my personal property, and I consider this to be a dangerous
> breach of publishing confidentiality, which I intend to pursue
> in the courts with my legal editor upon my return. I trust that
> you might advise the senior editor now.[3]**

He carried the page down to the reception desk and waited while the
middle-aged woman clerk in a rather threadbare silk Ao Dai dress sent the
fax message. Certain that the message had been received at Renaud's fax
machine, Schweitzer retrieved his original and trudged back up the dim
staircase to his room.

He was depressed and angry, wary that he had become a pawn in some
shadowy and convoluted internecine struggle within the American intelligence community. And there was still a sour knot of fear lying below his
churning anger. It was one thing to bandy about the romantic James Bond
term "clandestine operation" while undergoing make-believe training exercises in the sterile shopping malls of the northern Virginia suburbs. But it
was something altogether different to contemplate the reality of a clandestine operation turned bad while sitting on the lumpy edge of a Russian-
made bed in the Dan Chu Hotel in Hanoi. In the next few days a number of
bad things could happen, the least of which might be the loss of his computer equipment and his expulsion from Vietnam.

Schweitzer really did not want to contemplate the more disastrous scenarios. He rose and went down to the musty dining room. It was better to let
the scampering rats divert his attention than to sit up here alone worrying.

But even after two cans of 333 Beer and a plate of bland rice and greens,
Schweitzer was still burdened with angry fear.

And that fear was beginning to swell to uncomfortable and strange proportions. Had the DIA itself intended all along to offer him up as some kind
of sacrifice? Did his handlers all the way from James Renaud back through
the original CIA officers Carl Ford (the "publisher") had assigned to work
with him actually have hidden, Byzantine motives in conducting this opera-

tion? And if so, why? What could be the possible purpose of the government —which had spent so much money and taken so much trouble to train him —in betraying him?

That night, Schweitzer lay awake for hours, listening to the gibbering rats in the ceiling panels, gnawing on these unanswerable questions.

SCHWEITZER'S FAX WAS read with alarm in the DIA's Operations Directorate. James Renaud, his case officer, had just returned on the grueling eighteen-hour flight from Bangkok. He was jet-lagged and tense, and in no mood for this news.

He knocked once on his supervisor's door, then strode in and handed the officer a copy of Schweitzer's message.

"Emergency signal in the first paragraph," Renaud said, tapping the page. "Our boy's in trouble. He's calling for help, and I sure as hell don't blame him."

As Renaud's superior scanned the message, his dark, chunky face became rigid with anger. "I'll take care of it."

Renaud shook his head. "What the *fuck* do those people down there think they're doing?" He pointed in the direction of the DIA's POW/MIA office two floors below. "They're messing with an agent in jeopardy in a dangerous denied area. Schweitzer might think he's a good buddy of the Viets, but they'll cut his balls off and serve 'em for breakfast if they think he's a spy."[4]

"I *will* take care of it," the officer repeated impatiently.

Renaud recognized that there was a major bureaucratic flap brewing. If the intelligence analysts assigned to the JTF/FA had intentionally compromised a recruited agent on a duly authorized clandestine operation, it would be a breach of the National Security Act. If they had maliciously tried to "burn" such an agent who happened to be an American citizen and who had the full backing of the Pentagon E-Ring (Carl Ford) and of the President himself, it was simply foolish. Renaud saw that his boss intended to pursue the matter, as soon as he left the room, but he felt compelled to ask one final question, a breach of professional etiquette in the need-to-know world in which they both operated.

"Were those assholes in JTF/FA read in on the operation?" Renaud asked imprudently. "Did they know who Schweitzer was?"

"If they didn't," his superior replied, "they certainly should have. And if they did know, then they're in real trouble."

That afternoon, James Renaud met with Tony, the CIA case officer who had handled Schweitzer's preliminary training for Operation Swamp Ranger. After Renaud explained what the JTF/FA analysts had done, Tony shook his head in angry disbelief.

"If those guys were in CIA," he said, "they'd be in jail right now."

(James Renaud later told the author his own feelings on the near-fatal compromise of Schweitzer's operation. Speaking of the JTF/FA analysts who took Schweitzer's photographs and documents to the PAVN museum, Renaud said: "I would have shot the sons of bitches."[5]

(The Defense Intelligence Agency will not discuss this incident. And it was never established that Bell or Destatte were aware of Schweitzer's position or appreciated the possible impact of their actions. However, in James Renaud's fax message to Ted Schweitzer in Hanoi dated April 8, 1992, Renaud states: "Be assured we share your concerns and, like you, consider release of your photos a breach of rights of authorship. Our legal department is working diligently in an attempt to discover who made the copies of your originals and how they were released."[6] Renaud was using the "publishing" firm as a descriptive cover for the DIA Operations Directorate. His statement implies that the actions of the JTF/FA analysts could be a breach of agency policy. Later, Garnett Bell denied that he ever showed any of Schweitzer's photographs to Colonel Pham Duc Dai. Bell also stated that he was unaware of Schweitzer's employment by the U.S. Government or his role in a clandestine operation. However, Bell did concede that "someone associated with the museum" could have "observed" these photographs in Bell's Hanoi office. Bell added that his office was then located in the Interior Ministry guesthouse and was open to "either suspected or confirmed [Vietnamese] intelligence" officials. Bell also later confirmed that at some time during his tour of duty as an MIA official in Indochina, he was told by superiors to avoid contact with Ted Schweitzer and not to refer to him in conversations with the Vietnamese.[7])

ON THE MORNING of Tuesday, March 31, Schweitzer was again shown to the single chair before the L-shaped tables. The questions began in the same staccato monotone. But now they showed Schweitzer photocopies of the acquisition cards detailing document holdings on POWs that Schweitzer had used to gain backing for his operation.

"How did the American government obtain these documents?" Colonel Dai persisted.

"I just don't know." Schweitzer's voice sounded hollow in his own ears.

"The men who brought us these photographs and documents are intelligence officers," Colonel Quan said. "How did they get these things?"

At no point had these officers directly accused him of being an intelligence agent. But the implication was obvious. If he was playing a double game, they would consider him a spy.

Colonel Dai tried a new approach to penetrate Schweitzer's facade of innocence. "If you are a writer," he said with obvious disdain, "what have you written?"

This was a tough one. Then Schweitzer remembered he had several reprints of the *Reader's Digest* "Drama in Real Life" article describing his terrible encounter with the Thai pirates while saving Vietnamese refugees on Ko Kra Island. He opened his large aluminum briefcase, dug through the papers, and handed two of the reprints across the table.[8]

"You wrote this?" Dai asked.

Schweitzer nodded. "I worked with the writers. It's my story, and it has been printed around the world."

The officers seemed impressed. But they were not convinced of his bona fides.

The questions continued as the sun again heated the room. Schweitzer was tempted to play the role of the indignant, unfairly accused American benefactor, who had done so much to help Vietnam and now was being pilloried. That might have worked. But he realized he would be dooming the operation if he used this ploy.

Instead he attempted deception. Returning from the stinking latrine at the Citadel side of the museum compound, Schweitzer took his chair and spoke eagerly.

"You know," he exclaimed, as if the thought had just occurred to him, "I think I might know what happened."

He let Mui translate and paused, watching the PAVN officers unsuccessfully try to hide their sudden interest.

"Do you remember an American prisoner named Larry Guarino?"

The officers nodded.

U.S. Air Force Major Lawrence Guarino was one of the best known of the repatriated POWs. An F-105 pilot in his forties, Guarino had been shot down in the mountains west of Hanoi on June 14, 1965. Like so many other captured American aviators, he had almost been killed by the irate villagers and provincial militia who captured him. At Hoa Lo Prison in Hanoi, Guarino had immediately antagonized his guards by insulting the GPD subwarden and interrogator Major (later Colonel) Nguyen Van Y (pronounced "ee"), who was known as "the Rabbit." When the Rabbit had called him a "dirty, rotten criminal," Guarino had replied contemptuously: "I am a major in the United States Air Force. I demand some respect and proper treatment."[9]

That was the beginning of Guarino's eight-year acrimonious relationship with his captors. During his captivity, Guarino suffered the brutal torture and indignities inflicted on the most rebellious and "unrepentant" senior officers among the American POWs. But even after being temporarily broken by torture, he always remounted his obstreperous resistance to authority. Schweitzer knew the Vietnamese hated Guarino, and probably would have killed him had he not been such a well-known prisoner.

Guarino had circulated the manuscript of his POW memoirs among publishers in New York while Schweitzer was making the rounds of editors with his own unsuccessful book proposal.[10] Schweitzer heard the book had indeed been published by a small house, but doubted the Vietnamese knew the details of Guarino's project.

Now he spun a detailed story of how Guarino had actually visited the same publishing houses in New York where Schweitzer had left his book proposal, which, he added, had contained copies of his museum photographs and documents.

"It must have been Larry Guarino who stole my photographs from one of the publishers," Schweitzer concluded in what he hoped was a tone of sincere indignation.

"How would Guarino do this?" Colonel Tich shot back.

Schweitzer began an explanation of corrupt practices among capitalists in New York.

Now Colonel Tich interrupted. "How would Guarino contact American intelligence?"

Schweitzer shook his head. "I don't know for sure, but isn't Guarino a retired Air Force colonel?"

He knew that Guarino—who was a combat veteran of two wars and long captivity—was now safe in Florida, while Schweitzer was in danger here in Hanoi. Schweitzer felt that Guarino would not blame him for using his name in this manner.

The PAVN officers nodded as if accepting this explanation.

Schweitzer avoided studying their faces too openly. But he sensed that his alibi had taken root.

Now that he had established a plausible cover story, Schweitzer slowly elaborated on it. Over the next two days, the panel of officers continued to probe him. Schweitzer did not risk expanding the story beyond manageable limits. Insisting that he did not know any details, Schweitzer suggested that possibly "Time-Life" publishers in New York might have shared the photos and documents with Guarino. If they had, he could only surmise that Guarino had taken them to "Washington." After that . . . Schweitzer shrugged and opened his hands, indicating he could advance the speculation no further.

On the fourth morning of interminable questioning, he was almost convinced the officers had accepted his explanation. Colonel Dai had left the room, and even Quan, who had seemed the most skeptical, now nodded his understanding as Schweitzer worked his way through the scenario for perhaps the fiftieth time. But, after returning from another visit to the latrine, Schweitzer was frustrated when Colonel Tich led the discussion back to square one.

"We just cannot understand how these American intelligence officers obtained your photographs," Tich said, as if he had not heard any of the previous two days' discussion.

Schweitzer was tempted to force the issue, to stand up, tell them all to go to hell, stalk out, and try to recoup his passport. But he hesitated. This was some kind of a test, he realized. These General Political Directorate officers were obviously determined to be absolutely certain that he was not involved with an American intelligence operation.

This realization sparked significant revelations. Carl Ford and Schweitzer's trainers, including James Renaud, had speculated on whether Colonel Dai's initiative in opening the archives to Schweitzer had been a purely PAVN enterprise, or if they were acting at the behest of the civilian party leadership in the Politburo. Now Schweitzer realized that access to the museum POW archives was almost certainly an operation compartmented within the Army, probably within the leadership of the GPD. If senior party leaders had been involved, there would have been at least one civilian investigator from the Ministry of the Interior among his interrogators.

This meant that the General Political Directorate, the "keystone" of the PAVN, which reputedly harbored some of the country's most pragmatic reformists, had probably launched this initiative independently. Schweitzer could not hope to fathom their motives. But he had been dealing with Vietnam long enough to realize nothing was ever simple or straightforward in this country. Every intricate trompe l'oeil lacquer chest contained a hidden nest of even more deceptively ornate boxes.

All he knew for certain at this stage was that the General Political Directorate of the People's Army had intended to use him as a conduit of information, which they firmly intended to control. Conversely, if they really wished to open their archives exclusively to Schweitzer, they did not intend to share the material with the JTF/FA, the official representatives of the American government, which they had disparaged this week as a virtual nest of spies.

Perhaps they saw Schweitzer as a direct conduit to the American people.

This would explain their marathon effort to ascertain any connection he might have with American intelligence.

Schweitzer decided that he could do no more to convince his interrogators. Either they would have to accept his story or reject it. He opted for a melodramatic counterattack. Standing and shaking his head in pseudoanger, he raised his voice for the first time that week.

"I'm not interested in your views on this matter," he said. "The truth is, Guarino has destroyed my book project. And I'll deal with him when I get back to Florida."

His outgoing fax of Monday evening had probably already been translated and circulated among a select group of counterintelligence officers, which no doubt included at least one of the men facing him across the rickety plywood tables. If so, they would have read of his threat to take legal action against the JTF/FA officers for a breach of copyright. His indignation would be all the more believable.

"Please sit," Colonel Dai said. He muttered to Lieutenant Colonel Tran Thanh Hang and she obediently disappeared to fetch a tin tray of Saigon 333 beer and the clinking accoutrements of the traditional hospitality tea service that had been withheld all week. "Nothing has been ruined," Dai soothed.

Schweitzer sat down, straining to keep a triumphant smile from his face.

* * *

THAT AFTERNOON SCHWEITZER learned that there was, as should have been expected, a very practical side to this accommodation. With Mui translating, Dai and his two colleagues laid out the financial conditions they now expected Schweitzer to meet in order to complete his unprecedented research. The earlier tentative payment schedule they had agreed on was "no longer acceptable," Mui explained.

Schweitzer wrote careful notes, made a show of calculating his available funds, then gave tentative agreement.

"Of course I'll have to write my editor for his confirmation," he said.

Pending authorization from the DIA—which he was confident would be forthcoming—Schweitzer promised to pay the museum more for its services than under the terms of his 1990 contract. Although the fees he agreed to were virtually chicken feed compared to the profligate excesses of most intelligence operations, he knew these cash payments in American dollars represented a fortune to officers of Dai's generation. They were the men who had fought a forty-year struggle and were now nearing a retirement of penury in the topsy-turvy new world of *doi moi*.

The initial fees for professional service of approximately $12,000 that Dai would divide among his colleagues represented more money than these officers had probably ever possessed. Added to that, the increased office rental and supplemental payments for clerical staff and security guards needed for the scanning operation meant that the senior officers would be able to share the largess with their subordinates, without having to deplete their own windfall. Finally, the increased fee from $2 to $4 for each page of documents successfully scanned provided an incentive for Colonel Dai and his colleagues to bring forward most if not all of their voluminous holdings of POW records.

The total increases in the new payment schedule almost doubled his original estimate from $25,000 to $49,000. Schweitzer was confident the DIA would approve this new payment schedule, *provided* he could scan the Red Book and demonstrate the potential of his operation.

Colonel Dai told him that he could unpack his computer equipment in the morning and begin scanning the Red Book on the morning of Saturday, April 4, 1992.

That night Schweitzer sent another fax to James Renaud's commercial cutout, carefully listing monetary terms of the agreement. In this message, Schweitzer was able to summarize the essence of the GPD initiative:

I shall have an exclusive agreement granting unlimited access to the document collection of all Vietnamese military museums and will scan the Army Museum document collection in its entirety. They will share this information with no one else

during the life of the project, except the US MIA Team [JTF/FA], who will be given limited access to specified files only. This was their [PAVN] stipulation, not mine.[11]

For better or for worse, the PAVN had chosen to disregard the spirit of "cooperative" archive research stipulated in the Road Map and to focus their efforts on Schweitzer's research, while limiting the access of the official American investigators from the JTF/FA. At this stage, he had no definitive information on why the PAVN had opted for this procedure.

(Despite this blatant departure from the quid pro quo exchanges of the Road Map process, the Vietnamese had benefited from American rewards generated by tangible cooperative acts by the Socialist Republic of Vietnam. In September 1991, for example, the Bush administration announced a direct grant of $1.3 million to help Vietnamese military veterans and civilians disabled in wars.[12] A month later, General Vessey returned to Hanoi and met with the new premier [a purported moderate], Vo Van Kiet, and the new foreign minister, Nguyen Manh Cam. Premier Kiet promised "unconditional cooperation" in resolving the MIA issue.

(That month, Secretary of State Baker offered concrete steps toward normalization with Vietnam, citing Vietnam's positive attitude on the Cambodian peace settlement. In the same period, the PAVN turned over a section of an eighty-four-page Air Defense Forces registry of American aircraft lost in North Vietnam's Military Region 4, which straddled the old Demilitarized Zone.[13]

(General Vessey returned to Hanoi in January 1992, leading a military delegation, which included the CINCPAC officers responsible for the new Joint Task Force/Full Accounting. His delegation's primary purpose was to gain access to PAVN archives and to receive Vietnamese authorization to deploy multiple teams of official American archive researchers. Although the Vietnamese did turn over the rest of the Military Region 4 Air Defense Forces document, they did not agree to a more extensive system for American investigations of PAVN archives.[14]

(On March 4, 1992, Assistant Secretary of State Richard Solomon led a delegation to Hanoi to discuss progress on implementing the Road Map. The Americans then announced the U.S. Agency for International Development [USAID] would provide small-scale humanitarian aid to Vietnam, based on the SRV's "increased efforts to resolve the POW/MIA issue."[15]

(This was the status of the quid pro quo exchanges under the Road Map when Ted Schweitzer arrived in Hanoi.

(The official American position on access to PAVN archives remained that the SRV had agreed to grant complete and exclusive access to these records to the JTF/FA.)

Unaware of all these quasi-diplomatic exchanges, Schweitzer was left to speculate why he was being given full access to the files while the JTF/FA

212][MALCOLM McCONNELL

was not. There was probably a combination of reasons, he guessed. It was true the museum officers resented both Bill Bell and Robert Destatte because of their backgrounds in military intelligence during the war. And the fact that both men were fluent in Vietnamese, while Schweitzer could so far read and speak only some of the language, certainly meant that he was less of a security hazard around their sensitive military archives than Bell or Destatte. But undoubtedly the most important consideration was Schweitzer's ability to pay $50,000 in cash, or even more, directly to the General Political Directorate, depending on the number of documents eventually scanned.

But the PAVN's assessment of his motives, his ultimate purpose, and his character was also a factor, Schweitzer speculated. They no doubt believed he was a well-intentioned do-gooder, unskilled in the finer points of an intelligence investigation, who could be easily controlled and manipulated. At this stage of the game, the PAVN intended to construct one of their ornate lacquer boxes, beautiful to behold, but hollow and lacking of substance.

So be it, Schweitzer thought. He intended to beat them at their own game.

CHAPTER 17

SCHWEITZER'S OPERATION SWAMP RANGER WAS NOT THE ONLY TARGET of intrigue in Hanoi. Although Vietnam had officially accepted the Pentagon's new Joint Task Force/Full Accounting with promises of "full cooperation," it soon became clear that the PAVN was at best a reluctant participant in this effort.

The brouhaha over the photographs with which JTF/FA officers Bill Bell and Bob Destatte had challenged the museum staff was only the proximate irritant. More fundamentally, the PAVN's General Political Directorate deeply resented being placed in a subordinate role to the Ministry of Foreign Affairs and the Ministry of the Interior in dealings with the Americans.

Having started operations under strained and unfortunate circumstances, the JTF/FA detachment commanded by Lieutenant Colonel Jack Donovan tried to forge ahead in difficult circumstances. But Donovan was aware that his Vietnamese counterparts were waging a shadowy guerrilla campaign of resistance, beneath the public mantle of full cooperation. Nothing was easy for the American team. It would eventually take months to receive authorization to erect a television satellite receiving antenna at the "Ranch," the walled housing and office compound below Ho Tay Lake in western Hanoi that the detachment occupied that spring. This was perhaps a minor irritant, but to the Americans, who were forbidden from "fraternizing" with the Vietnamese, and generally restricted in their movements, access to Western television was an important morale booster.[1] To the distrustful Vietnamese bureaucrats, however, retaining control over all aspects of this American military team's operations in their country took precedence over hospitality.

This type of petty bickering evolved into an underlying relationship of distrust, bordering on chronic harassment. The American military team, which had been welcomed with great fanfare, now often found itself stymied in trying to accomplish even the most routine functions. There were endless administrative meetings with the detachment's Vietnamese liaison representative, Ho Xuan Dich, of the Vietnamese Office for Seeking Missing Persons (VNOSMP). Making progress during this period, Donovan later frankly admitted, was "extremely difficult."[2]

Nevertheless, he and his men plugged ahead as best they could. Donovan had served in combat during the Vietnam War as a young Marine. He had seen heavy fighting along the DMZ, an experience that inured him to hardship. Like his JTF/FA superior, Brigadier General Thomas Needham, Donovan was neither smooth nor diplomatic. But Donovan understood his role was to keep pushing ahead and eventually produce tangible progress through the resolution of MIA cases.

The detachment's responsibilities included joint field investigations, archive research, and investigation of live-sighting reports of Americans.[3]

The Vietnamese viewed each of these responsibilities through a bifurcated perspective. On the one hand, the SRV government was committed to "full cooperation" with the Americans to recover MIA remains at crash sites and from battlefield graves, to open relevant archives to the Americans, and to give JTF/FA live-sighting investigators free access to the entire country, including its extensive prison system. So it was imperative that the Vietnamese publicly demonstrate they were assisting the JTF/FA detachment to fulfill its mission. If the SRV openly thwarted these American efforts, Vietnam could expect no positive reciprocal steps under the terms of the Road Map agreement. And the Pentagon had made a point that it was "firmly committed" to following the Road Map policy, even though Vietnam had not officially ratified the agreement.[4]

But neither the Vietnamese civilian bureaucracy controlled by the Communist Party nor the PAVN intended to completely relinquish control of MIA matters, including access to remains, crash sites, and battlefield graves —and, particularly, access to classified military archives. Rather, the SRV at this period followed a policy of making public displays of cooperation while stringently controlling the practical results of any official American investigation.

Thus when young American troops arrived to conduct field investigations, the Vietnamese made sure the events received maximum publicity. Members of the international press corps in Southeast Asia found themselves courted by both the SRV and the Pentagon to cover such compelling media events as joint crash site investigations in the Vietnamese hinterland at which sweating young American soldiers dug side by side with their PAVN counterparts, sifting through the wreckage of the Phantom or Intruder that had been shot down before these young men were born.[5] These digs made good television, but they produced few tangible results.

THE NATIONAL LEAGUE of Families of American Prisoners and Missing in Southeast Asia has been a consistent critic of Vietnam's widely publicized cooperative relationship with the JTF/FA. The league has pointed out that, although numerous expensive site excavations have been conducted, "the extensive joint field activities in Vietnam have brought few results. . . ."[6]

The league has also documented compelling evidence that most accessible crash sites and known battlefield graves in Vietnam have probably already been excavated, and that any available MIA remains had been removed and placed in storage either in Vietnamese government or private hands.[7] In 1992, for example, only six sets of remains recovered at crash sites or unilaterally located by Vietnamese were positively identified as known American casualties.

BEYOND BENEFICIAL PROPAGANDA, there were other obvious reasons why the Vietnamese Ministry of Foreign Affairs and the VNOSMP encouraged the joint field investigations. The crash site excavations had already become a lucrative source of funds for the Vietnamese before the JTF/FA arrived. And when the administrative discussions produced a payment schedule that far exceeded Vietnamese expectations, the SRV was more than pleased. Under the terms agreed on, Vietnamese laborers working with Americans on the excavations would be paid from $20 to $40 per day. In a country where the average peasant earned less than that per month, this was an attractive incentive to concentrate on field investigations.

The Vietnamese authorities, not the Americans, supervised the actual disbursement of payment, so the possibility for corruption among these authorities was obvious. Beyond the payment of laborers, the field investigations offered other financial benefits. Because American teams were only allowed in Vietnam during scheduled "iterations," travel time to remote sites was a key issue. The Vietnamese were eager to arrange transportation via government-chartered Soviet-built Mi-8 helicopter. As with any helicopter operation, the fees were high; reportedly $4,000 per flight hour.

(DIA case officer James Renaud later stated that the cost of recovering one set of forensically verified American MIA remains through the JTF/FA system in 1992 and 1993 averaged around $1 million. This cost included labor and transportation fees paid to local authorities. His estimate was echoed by others. Journalist and historian Neil Sheehan cited the figure of $1.7 million per set of recovered remains in an analysis of the POW/MIA issue he wrote for *The New Yorker* in 1993.[8])

By the summer of 1992, the Vietnamese civilian authorities who supervised the JTF/FA's activities encouraged the Americans to continue field excavations, while the PAVN was actively discouraging JTF/FA investigators from penetrating too deeply into military archives.

Meanwhile, Air Force Lieutenant Colonel Charles D. Robertson, on loan from the Department of Foreign Languages at the U.S. Air Force Academy, proceeded to doggedly investigate live-sighting reports for the JTF/FA. Robertson, a low-key but determined officer, was stubborn enough to match even the most recalcitrant Vietnamese bureaucrat. Eventually, he was able to inspect every labor camp, jail, and prison at which earlier refugee reports had placed Caucasians. Robertson struck a "dry hole" at each of these facilities. But he persisted in his efforts, and carefully logged each foray, so that critics among the American activists could not claim the JTF/FA was ignoring these avenues of investigation.[9]

The well-publicized joint field investigations did manage to conceal the fact that the PAVN had virtually closed the door to the JTF/FA's archive investigators. Where the last of the JCRC-sponsored archival research had produced promising leads both in Hanoi and elsewhere, the General Political Directorate now made it extremely difficult for official American researchers to pursue those avenues of inquiry.[10]

ON THE MORNING of Saturday, April 4, Schweitzer had his scanning office— the same narrow corner room where he had undergone the severe questioning—set up at the Central Military Museum. As Major Mui supervised the installation of the new air conditioner and voltage stabilizers, he told Schweitzer that the senior GPD officers were now convinced that he was not a spy. They believed that American intelligence would never allow officers from an overt operation, the JTF/FA, to blatantly betray a clandestine operative. Bell and Destatte's actions had only reinforced Schweitzer's bona fides with Colonel Dai and his colleagues.

Or so it seemed.

Schweitzer did not waste time comforting himself with this reassurance. It was entirely possible that the General Political Directorate believed Schweitzer was in fact a highly placed spy, and that they had decided to proceed with the archive scanning because his operation promised to pay more money directly to the PAVN than did the JTF/FA effort. Although the JTF/FA operation, with its elaborate crash site investigations, promised to generate millions of dollars over the next several years, that money would be paid to civilian ministries, which meant the People's Army would not receive its due.

Further, by limiting JTF/FA access to the museum archives, and concentrating on Schweitzer as the sole conduit, the PAVN could more easily control the flow of documents. No doubt that was one of their major considerations.

Once he had the Red Book scanned, Schweitzer realized that it would then be especially important for him to scan the maximum number of PAVN documents, from as broad a spectrum of the archives as possible, so that DIA experts in Washington could subject the Vietnamese holdings to the full rigor of intelligence analysis.

Although he was not fully versed in the fine points of such analysis, Schweitzer recognized that experts could learn a great deal from both the types of documents the Vietnamese delivered and those they chose to withhold. If there were chronological breaks in the documents made available for scanning that coincided with particularly sensitive MIA cases, it could be surmised that the PAVN had decided to withhold information on those cases.

Successfully scanning the Red Book central index of museum POW document holdings would be the first critical step in this process.

Coaxing the elaborate electrical power supply into life, Schweitzer put the optical scanning system through a full cycle, using an American military ID card and a museum document as test objects. Colonel Dai, Major Mui, and his wife, Lieutenant Colonel Tran Thanh Hang, watched with unfeigned curiosity as the Fujitsu scanner hummed, the chalky green glare of the xenon lamps leaking from the edges of the cover. The strange clicks and buzzes of the optical disk data storage drive seemed to fascinate them. Schweitzer punched in a command on the keyboard and the image of the document appeared on the monitor's large screen.

"Not in color?" Mui asked, like a little boy disappointed in his new bicycle.

Schweitzer grinned. Since his last trip to Vietnam, the karaoke craze that had already swept through most of Asia had exploded in Hanoi. It seemed that every other grubby storefront and teahouse was now dominated by a huge color monitor and echoed with the off-key tones of an amateur singer crooning the lyrics of a sentimental Vietnamese love song as the computer-generated lyrics scrolled across the screen, superimposed on a gauzy, saccharin video.

"No color, but the scanned image does make a good copy," Schweitzer explained.

He typed in another command and the laser printer whirred. A crisp copy of the scanned document slid into the paper bin. Dai and Mui held up the original and the scanned copy. Except for the obvious difference in paper, the two were identical.

"Like a photocopy machine," Mui said, sounding slightly disappointed.

"Almost the same thing," Schweitzer replied. They did not understand the difference between his optical scanning system, which allowed the images to be stored in a digital format—adaptable to database retrieval techniques—and a simple Xerox machine. For the moment, it didn't matter what they understood, as long as they provided the documents.

Mrs. Hang jingled a ring of heavy keys and left the office to fetch the Red Book from the second-floor secure archives. She returned a few minutes later casually carrying the narrow ledger book with the faded red-cloth cover. Schweitzer immediately recognized the ornate embossed title and gilt star. This was without question the same index Colonel Dai had shown him almost two years before.[11]

Mrs. Hang handed Schweitzer the book and he leafed through it. Even with the new air conditioner running, he caught a whiff of mildew exuding from the cover. Yet the handwritten pages themselves were in excellent condition. Schweitzer knew that the new foreign minister, Nguyen Co Thach, had told General Vessey many of Vietnam's POW archives had been destroyed by termites. Schweitzer fanned the pages. There was certainly no evidence of termite damage to this vital index. That was because the index had been stored in a metal filing cabinet all these years. And, he suspected, this was the case for any truly important military archive. The Vietnamese were such compulsive recordkeepers that they would never sacrifice key documents to termites through negligence.

While the scanner and optical disk storage systems ran through their test cycle, Schweitzer paged through the Red Book. Renaud had warned him that the initiative by the PAVN might be an elaborate deception. Schweitzer could be allowed to examine the index, but not actually to scan it. Or Colonel Dai might allow him to scan the index, but not to leave the country with the scanned data in his possession. So, at a minimum, he had to gain a reasonably detailed overview of what the book contained as quickly as possible.

The 208 handwritten pages were numbered with rubber-stamped numerals, which in some cases had badly faded. The last half of the index seemed to be written in a clearer hand than the first hundred pages.

The basic format of the entries was the same throughout the book. A brief summary of the document holdings was written horizontally across the eight vertical ledger columns. And the individual photographs and related documents were identified by number in two blocks within the ledger columns, the upper group bearing the designation "P." referring to photographs, and the lower-block four-digit numbers identifying documents.

With Mui translating, Schweitzer perused the Red Book, trying to get a feel for the museum's vast archives it indexed.

Page one did indeed go back to the very beginning of the PAVN. This entry was entitled "Establishment of the Indochinese Communist Party, the Political Line and the Military Doctrine of the Party (1930–1945)." These entries ran through page eleven. Schweitzer was surprised to note that pages twelve and thirteen were blank, as if the archivist had left room for additional entries as they might be required. He made a note to scan every page of the book, even if some were blank. That way no one back at DIA could accuse him of ignoring vital material. And, he mused, there might well be entries in invisible ink that could later be detected.

Page fourteen was the title entry for "Collection A2," which covered the "Resistance Movement Against French Colonialism and American Intervention, 1945–1954." He flipped pages until he came to page sixty: "People's War in Different Zones in the Winter-Spring Attack in 1953–54, and the Dien Bien Phu Campaign." As expected, there were scores of entries for this monumental battle. But on page sixty-five, the section for "Returning the Prisoners of War" listed dozens of photographs, but only one document. If that was all they had on French POWs, he thought, what could he expect on American prisoners? This section again ended with two blank pages.

The heart of the book, as far as the DIA was concerned, began on page seventy-six: "Collection A3: The Resistance Against America (1954–1975)." The first pages of this section dealt mainly with the formation of the PAVN and its support for the "Patriotic Forces" in South Vietnam. But Schweitzer noted on page ninety-three there was a section of document holdings on the "Ap Bac Victory." This was the 1963 battle in the Mekong Delta where American advisers and their units in the Army of the Republic of Vietnam (ARVN) suffered their first major defeat. The battle was significant because three American helicopter crewmen were killed, and five helicopters, including one of the new UH-1C Huey gunships, were destroyed.[12] Schweitzer found it interesting that the PAVN had ten photographs and five original documents in its holdings in Hanoi for a battle that was supposedly conducted by purely Southern-led guerrillas.

On page 101, Schweitzer found his first evidence of holdings on American POWs. Under entry 101.c, "The North Bay Events (Defeating the Maddox) 3-8-1964," he found listings for the first American air actions against North Vietnam after the Tonkin Gulf incident in which the destroyer U.S.S. *Maddox* reported being attacked by North Vietnamese torpedo boats.

Schweitzer made a note on his pad that the documents and photographs beginning on page 101 would be of special interest. Indeed, page 103 of the index made it clear that the museum had extensive holdings on the American air war in the North. The entry entitled "Fighting Against the American Air Forces in Vin-Dong Hoi-Vinh Linh" for the summer of 1965 had scores of documents listed.

"Mui," Schweitzer asked, trying to sound casual, "how many of these documents concern prisoners?" Mui shrugged and asked Mrs. Hang. She leaned over the book, running her finger over the entries, then spoke.

"Many," Mui translated. "Hundreds."

On page 105 Schweitzer was surprised to find a long listing of documents pertaining to North Vietnamese actions in Laos: "Fighting for the Laos Revolution (1961–1965)." For decades, Hanoi had strenuously denied that its forces had given anything but "fraternal" and minor technical support to the Communist Pathet Lao. Yet here were entries for documents that detailed dozens of battles in which major PAVN units participated.

The Rolling Thunder bombing campaign between 1965 and 1968 had been extremely well documented. Schweitzer stopped counting when he had reached 140 documents on index page 121 alone pertaining to this campaign. The Linebacker II bombing campaign was equally well documented. Index page 139: "Defeating the Air Force B-52 Attack by the American Imperialists: 18-30-12\1972" listed almost 200 photo and document holdings.

Eyeing the dense swarm of four-digit numeral blocks on these pages, he was keenly aware that each represented an original PAVN document or photograph never before seen by Americans. Many were reports from military units that had captured American POWs. Other acquisition entries represented prisoner artifacts such as identity cards, flight equipment, and personal possessions. At the very least, if he could optically scan all these pages and deliver them to the DIA, the Vietnamese could never again deny they had extensive archives.

Schweitzer tapped his pencil on the columns of entry blocks. "And how many of these concern prisoners, Mui?"

Mrs. Hang glanced at the page. "Most of them."

On page 143 Schweitzer found one of the key entries he was searching for: "The Return of Prisoners of War to the Enemy." There were forty-five photographs listed and twenty-two documents.

The index entries ended on page 208: "Diplomatic Relations with Cambodia, 1975–1985."

Schweitzer lifted the top of the optical scanner and laid the Red Book facedown on the glass.

"As we say in America, Mui," he joked, "the best place to begin is at the beginning."

Mui smiled politely but saw nothing amusing. "We say the same."

THE ACTUAL SCANNING of the Red Book took only two days. And on the second day, Schweitzer forced himself to take a long, beery lunch break with Mui and Dai under the lychee trees at the refreshment gazebo in the museum courtyard. Following Renaud's instructions, he did not want to appear overly eager to grab and run. That would have triggered alarm bells among the counterintelligence types that were undoubtedly watching him closely.

Even with the long lunch and a short nap to sleep off the Saigon 333 beer, Schweitzer had successfully scanned all 208 pages of the Red Book by late afternoon on the second day. Mui, Mrs. Hang, and Colonel Dai alternately hovered at his elbow, taking turns to supervise the procedure. But Schweitzer soon realized none of them fully understood the complexities of the digital scanning process. They still saw the optical scanner as some type of photocopy machine that was somehow connected by wires to the computer monitor. But they did not appear to understand that, once scanned and preserved in the system's multiple redundant data storage banks—the hard disk of the CPU, the optical disks, and the Valitek tape backup—the scanned images would be easily transportable in a variety of modes.

As they prepared to close the office that evening, Schweitzer lightened the mood by joking with the dour old PAVN pensioner assigned the plum job of sleeping in the curtained alcove, posing as a "guard." Schweitzer cautioned the old soldier to keep a close watch, but make certain not to touch any of the equipment. Schweitzer made grotesque buzzing sounds and mimed electric shock, a display that had the pensioner laughing and even drew a wide smile from the austere Mui.

While performing this act, Schweitzer slipped the plain white magnetic tape cassette out of the Valitek drive, dropped it into his briefcase, and inserted a fresh tape. He made a show of running the system through a permutation or two, using the keyboard powerball to flip the Windows icon rapidly across the monitor menu in a diverting display of complex technology.

"There," Schweitzer said, powering down the system. "We're finished for today."

Mui did not even glance at Schweitzer's sturdy aluminum briefcase as they closed the office door.

That night at the Dan Chu Hotel Schweitzer sent another coded fax message to James Renaud's commercial cutout number in the Washington area. Noting that the museum holdings contained documents on "virtually the entire history" of the PAVN and that the museum's collection "may be even more encompassing and valuable than I had thought," Schweitzer requested that the fees paid for specific services be raised from his first estimate. These increases were virtually small change for the DIA, but requesting them from his "publisher" made it appear that Schweitzer did not have access to unlimited funds.

He then spun a yarn about shopping for a beautiful tropical bird in an outdoor market, a diversion he and the unsuspecting Foreign Ministry escort, Miss Lan, had actually taken on Sunday. Schweitzer described finding a "very beautiful bird with many beautiful feathers."[13] This was the prearranged word code to notify the DIA that the Red Book was in good condition, had many pages ("feathers"), and that he had successfully scanned the entire index and had the images safely stored. To make sure there could be no confusion in this message, Schweitzer said he believed the bird to be a blossom-headed parakeet *(Psittacula roseata)*. This was the agreed-upon signal that the document he had scanned was in fact the original handwritten Red Book index, not a doctored copy.

Before returning to the museum the next morning, Schweitzer prepared two extra tape copies of the scanned Red Book digital data.

For one copy, he used a Walkman and his portable stereo tapedeck to transfer the Valitek data onto a commercial cassette of Lorrie Morgan's popular album *Something in Red.* He hoped that James Renaud would appreciate the irony. After blocking the no-copy ports on the Lorrie Morgan cassette, he erased the music and transferred the data onto it. In the Walkman earphones, he could now hear only the chaotic hiss and click of the digital data.

It was impossible that any Vietnamese customs inspector at Noi Bai Airport —or anyone else in Southeast Asia—would have the hardware and software needed to retrieve this data, should they take the unusual step of confiscating this innocent music cassette.

That was one secure backup.

For the next, he dismantled the actual Valitek cassette by unscrewing the plastic top. Then he rolled the magnetic tape into a tight spool the diameter of a U.S. quarter coin. He had already decided where he would carry this "ultimate" backup. His Reebok sneakers were suitably scuffed and stained by the detritus of Hanoi streets to virtually fade into nonexistence. Using a razor blade, he cut a narrow slit into the thick padded tongue of the left shoe. The tight spool of magnetic tape, secured by a snippet of Scotch tape, fit into the tongue padding without leaving a bulge. He closed the slit with superglue. When he squeezed the Reebok tongue, he felt nothing unusual.

That morning at the museum, he casually laid a copy of the original Valitek data tape in its labeled plastic box on the table beside the tape drive. The plastic cassette box lay undisturbed for several days, obviously not an object of attention for the museum staff. Schweitzer was now convinced he could safely smuggle to Bangkok the spool of backup tape hidden in the tongue of his sneaker, even if Vietnamese customs confiscated the music cassette and the primary repository of the scanned data, the optical disk.

And, if he were successful, his primary assignment would have been accomplished in a relatively straightforward manner—if he didn't consider the de facto sabotage by the JTF/FA analysts and the grilling he had endured by the GPD officers.

Miss Lan accompanied him to Noi Bai Airport on the afternoon of April 22, 1992. He had laid the ground for this sudden trip to Bangkok by feigning computer trouble. Manipulating his complex software, he disabled one of the utility programs in the DOS matrix, so that he could not access the optical disk drive. This glitch Schweitzer blamed on a faulty card in the CPU. When he opened the case of the central processing unit and displayed the bewildering array of chips and semiconductor boards, Mui stepped back as if in alarm.

"This is the one I'll have to replace in Bangkok," Schweitzer said, pointing to a pop-in circuit board, "unless you think I can find one here in Hanoi."

Mui shook his head. "I don't think so."

Even with Miss Lan running interference through passport and customs control, Schweitzer was sweating with fear at the airport. When he lay his aluminum briefcase on the chipped concrete inspection bench, he also set two packs of State Express 555 filter tip cigarettes beside the case.

"I don't smoke," he said. "So I don't need these."

The customs inspector slid the cigarettes into the pocket of his uniform tunic and chalked a clearance mark on Schweitzer's unopened case.

Forty minutes later, he was on the Thai Airways Airbus, bumping down the rough taxi ramp for takeoff. Schweitzer did not actually relax until the plane crossed the Mekong River and entered Thai airspace.

Thai customs, of course, was no problem.

When Schweitzer checked into the Ambassador Hotel as Francis Marion, it felt perfectly normal to be using a cover name. James Renaud had cautioned him not to lower his guard because Bangkok was a known hub of the Vietnamese intelligence services. So the transfer of the optical disk with the scanned Red Book data would be conducted in an "operational manner."

After sunset, Schweitzer strolled down Sukhumvit Road, dressed in a flowery shirt, lugging his laptop computer, just another sightseeing businessman. He also carried a small, nondescript imitation-leather portfolio, which held the optical disk, sealed in its flat plastic box.

Following instructions, he doubled back twice to purchase postcards and a pack of gum from the tourist kiosks along the wide, smoggy boulevard. This was meant to flush any foot surveillance. He detected none.

At Siam Square on Rama I Road, Schweitzer made a show of videotaping the gilded pagoda near the Intercontinental Hotel. He then entered the park and walked up a gravel path beneath flamboyant trees to a park bench. There he encountered James Renaud. Schweitzer was astounded by the case officer's disguise. He looked like an aging hippie in his greasy long-hair wig, dark granny glasses, and grubby tie-dye T-shirt.

Without speaking, Schweitzer sat on the bench and consulted his pocket guidebook. Renaud, also silent, stood and walked slowly away along the path, carrying Schweitzer's plastic portfolio.

He left behind his identical bag. Schweitzer hefted it in his hand and strode off in the opposite direction. On the corner of Phayathai Road, he caught a taxi back to the hotel. As expected, the bag he had exchanged in the brush pass contained a torn scrap of yellow notepad with a few jotted words: "Room, 9:00 p.m."

In the time it took the taxi to reach the hotel, Schweitzer knew, Renaud would have handed off the disk to one of his colleagues. Maybe this was an overly elaborate James Bond charade, but Schweitzer was reassured that Renaud was insisting on high professional standards. After the fiasco of the JTF/FA analysts almost sinking the entire operation before it began, Schweitzer did not want any slip-ups here in Bangkok.

At nine that night, seeing the Do Not Disturb sign on the knob, Schweitzer knocked on the appointed door of the safe house hotel room, which would only be used for this particular meeting.

James Renaud, absent his hippie wig and granny glasses, opened the door cautiously. The two men smiled broadly as they shook hands.

"Damn!" Renaud drawled. "You actually pulled it off."

"I did what I promised," Schweitzer said proudly. "But those bastards from JTF/FA almost got me strung up by my thumbs."

Renaud stopped smiling. He sat at the room's teak desk, his notebook open, taking notes while Schweitzer recounted the details of the first two weeks of the operation in Hanoi. His voice was tight with bitter anger when he described the snafu with the photographs and documents.

"They've called those boys down to Bangkok for a little come to Jesus talk," Renaud explained.

"No bullshit?" Schweitzer was beginning to learn that in this business, the truth was a malleable commodity, twisted as need be to meet contingencies.[14]

"That's what I understand," Renaud said.

Schweitzer knew there was no way to verify or refute this reassuring information.

"Anyway, you got the goods out," Renaud said, trying to dilute the tension. "Was there any hassle at customs?"

Schweitzer shook his head. "No problem at all. And I always had my backup."

He proudly cut open the tongue of his Reebok sneaker and extracted the tight spool of magnetic tape.

"Pretty slick," Renaud agreed, taking the tape. "But didn't I warn you about getting too spooky? They hung Nathan Hale for less than that."

Schweitzer admitted this ploy could have landed him in a Hanoi jail cell had he been detected. "But I didn't want to mess up when I promised Armitage and Carl Ford I'd deliver the goods."

"Well, you delivered them. What are you going to do for the next act?"

Schweitzer explained that he intended to copy all the thousands of museum document cards relating to the air war and American prisoners. "If I work hard, I can get the job done in a few months."

Renaud reminded Schweitzer he was on a six-month contract with a ninety-day progress review. "We've got the Red Book earlier than we anticipated, Ted," he explained. "That should help smooth things in D.C. Go on back to Hanoi and keep working. I'll try to get the extra money you need authorized."

Schweitzer explained that he would need more than money to successfully probe the museum's archives for information on important MIA cases.

"Get me the hot cases," he told Renaud. "I'll concentrate on them."

Although Renaud was less than optimistic that the DIA Special Office for POW/MIAs would cooperate with Schweitzer's operation if it meant that the Vietnamese would continue to stonewall their own analysts in Hanoi, he reassured Schweitzer that the agency's Operations Directorate would support him in any way it could.

(In fact, Renaud quickly recommended that the DIA provide Schweitzer with a " 'short list' of critical PW cases," an additional $25,000, and that the agency approve the operation for the full six-month contract.[15])

Schweitzer returned to Hanoi two days later, carrying a new pop-in board and a bulging plastic sack of airport duty-free gifts for his Vietnamese associates.

CHAPTER 18

WHILE SCHWEITZER WAS IN BANGKOK MEETING WITH HIS CASE officer, five members of the Senate select committee arrived in Hanoi for a three-day visit. The delegation was led by the chairman, Senator John F. Kerry, and the Republican vice chairman, Senator Bob Smith. Senators Hank Brown, Charles Grassley, and Charles Robb completed the delegation. With the exception of Grassley, the senators were all Vietnam veterans. The Hanoi visit was part of a ten-day trip around Indochina, a normal enough fact-finding mission, heavy on well-publicized contact with local officials and public ceremony.

Kerry and Smith, however, intended the direct meetings with Vietnamese officials to be more than ceremonial. They wanted substantive actions from the Vietnamese that would dramatize a new atmosphere of openness and cooperation on the POW/MIA issue.[1] Up to that time the select committee had thoroughly explored the historic record on the issue through testimony and depositions of a large number of witnesses, and was embarked on the most active professional investigation ever undertaken. Yet the political profit of this exhaustive effort had so far been negligible. Both leaders of the committee needed concessions from the Vietnamese that would justify their work.

But, like the members of the JTF/FA, the senators received quintessentially bland and vague promises of improved cooperation from Foreign Minister Cam and Defense Minister Lieutenant General Doan Khue with whom they first met. As always, the Vietnamese side was adamant that there were no American POWs either in captivity or living freely in Vietnam.[2]

In a break from tradition, the committee delegation also met with Interior Minister Bui Thien Ngo, who controlled all prisons in the country. He also promised the full cooperation of his ministry, but, to the senators' frustration, was just as vague as his ministerial comrades had been.

On the second afternoon of the delegation's visit, they were taken to the Central Military Museum. Colonel Dai and other GPD officers escorted Kerry's party past the MiG-21 plinth and the savage trophies of wrecked American aircraft into the modern central exhibit hall where they were shown uniforms and flight equipment of captured American airmen.[3]

The seemingly most substantive portion of the visit was the meeting with

Communist Party General Secretary and former premier Do Muoi and the Deputy Minister of the Interior Le Minh Huong. Do Muoi, an energetic and unusually forthright leader from peasant stock, expressed surprise that American investigators had told the senators they were having difficulty gaining access to PAVN archives. He gave his solemn promise that members of the JTF/FA would have unlimited access to whatever place, persons, or records they believed relevant to resolving the POW issue "in 1992."[4] Do Muoi actually challenged the senators several times to tell him personally what the committee needed and wanted from Vietnam to resolve this question. He made a very persuasive presentation. Even experienced politicians like Kerry and Robb were impressed by Do Muoi's apparent sincerity.[5]

To demonstrate his good will, Do Muoi gave permission to JTF/FA investigators to cross Vietnam's border into neighboring sites in Laos, if Lao authorities also agreed. The senators welcomed this tangible new sign of cooperation as dramatic evidence of a true breakthrough on the issue.

Then Do Muoi reiterated the official line that no American POWs had been kept after Operation Homecoming in 1973. That was to be expected at such a ceremony.

If he had stopped there, the meeting would have been an unblemished success. But Do Muoi continued. He adamantly denied that the Vietnamese government or military had ever stockpiled and stored remains of American POWs in a warehouse. This assertion, which had been graphically disproven by both forensic evidence amassed at the CIL-HI and by public testimony of the Vietnamese defector Tran Vien Lac, known as the "Mortician," was transparently false and certainly tarnished Do Muoi's credibility.[6]

When the senators mentioned JTF/FA's desire to begin using American helicopters in field investigations, rather than the poorly maintained Vietnamese Mi-8s, Do Muoi and his colleagues refused to consider the request. Playing to possible war guilt in some members of the delegation, the Vietnamese officials suggested that the distinctive sound and image of American helicopters would probably provoke "negative reactions" among rural people. Do Muoi's officials did not discuss the high cost of chartering the Vietnamese helicopters nor mention how the charter fees were eventually allocated.

On April 21, the day the delegation arrived, the senators told the Vietnamese they wanted to visit Thanh Liet Prison, at a crossroads town twenty kilometers south of Hanoi. American POWs had been held there during the war. And since 1984, several refugee live-sighting reports had indicated Americans might still be held in the prison. When Lieutenant Colonel Charles Robertson, JTF/FA's live-sighting investigator, had requested permission to inspect Thanh Liet Prison several weeks earlier, the Vietnamese Ministry of the Interior had refused. Now the committee delegation was given access and drove south along old Route 1 in a small convoy of minibuses. But when they arrived at the prison on the afternoon of April 22, the camp commander restricted the senators to the small section of the prison where American POWs had been held during the war. Kerry placed angry phone calls to the Ministries of Foreign Affairs and the Interior to protest. After some heated palaver on the phone lines, the senators were shown through all the rooms in the prison. They found no evidence of Americans having been held there since the war.[7]

This confrontation produced useful press release copy and video footage. It seemed to dramatize both the resolve of the select committee and the fundamental spirit of cooperation by Vietnam's leaders, which had combined to overcome bureaucratic foot-dragging.

The only untoward incident during the congressional visit to Hanoi occurred when the committee motorcade slowed to cross the railroad tracks near the intersection of Dien Bien Phu Avenue and Trang Thi Street. A man on the sidewalk threw a chunk of brick that smashed the windshield of the lead minibus. Senator Charles Robb, a former Marine infantry officer, leapt out of the second car and chased the man through the startled crowd. Robb is tall and husky; he clearly terrified the unidentified rock-thrower. Luckily, the ubiquitous young Interior Ministry security guards stationed along the motorcade route caught the man before Robb did, thus preventing the type of occurrence diplomats describe as "especially unfortunate." Embarrassed escorts from the Ministry of Foreign Affairs told the delegation the rock-thrower had been "crazy in the belly." By this, they meant the man was drunk.[8]

When the delegation returned to Washington at the end of the month, Chairman John Kerry proudly announced what would later become known as a "breakthrough." Speaking at a press conference, Kerry stated, "We are no longer knocking on the door; that door is open. And the question is whether we're going to be allowed now to walk through room-to-room, basement and attic, and be able to find the answers to our questions."[9]

The day after the delegation returned to Washington, the Bush administration announced that it was making an exception to the trade embargo to allow American sales of foodstuffs, medicines, medical and hospital equipment, and other items that met "basic human needs." The Bush administration also waived restrictions on nongovernmental charitable organizations to operate in Vietnam.

State Department spokeswoman Margaret Tutwiler said the decision was made "in response to Vietnam's strengthened commitments to take positive actions on POW/MIA issues," as well as Vietnam's support for a political settlement in Cambodia.[10]

In the media coverage of the committee visit to Vietnam were no reports of the PAVN's plans to restrict the JTF/FA's access to their archives, while trying to channel carefully selected material through the unusual conduit of Ted Schweitzer's ostensible book research project.

THE BRIEF HANOI spring quickly gave way to the languid heat and humidity that cloaked the Red River Delta for six months of the year. But Ted Schweitzer was determined not to allow the weather to provoke the languor and procrastination among the museum staff that he had encountered in his previous summer trips to Hanoi. To his surprise, however, Colonel Dai's people seemed eager to move directly into the long, plodding task of scanning the thousands of documents in the archives indexed in the Red Book, which concerned the American air war.

But even with this obvious willingness to work, the tedious and painstaking nature of the job slowed progress.

They began by consulting the printed copy of the Red Book that Schweitzer had produced with his scanning system. After some discussion, Colonel Dai and Mrs. Hang agreed that the documents on the air war began with those listed on index page 101: "The American Imperialists Fight Against the North (1961–1965)."

The next morning, Mrs. Hang brought a large pile of documents from those listed on page 101. They were mainly page-size gray pasteboard museum acquisition cards, some covered with dense handwritten notes, others with only a few brief entries. Schweitzer arrayed the documents in numerical order, checked them against the printed index page, then made a list of those missing. Mui verified the tally and gave Mrs. Hang the list to try to track down the absent documents. She returned with another pile of cards that afternoon. But still, some were missing. She retreated to the second-floor archive to search them out.

"You'll have to come back in the morning," Mui explained.

Mrs. Hang took the stack of documents that Schweitzer had neatly arrayed in numerical order to lock them up for the night.

The next morning, she carried the documents back to the scanning office. Now all but two or three items on the index page had been located. Schweitzer began his scanning, making sure the copying sequence exactly matched the index listing.

As Mui and he worked, Schweitzer often paused to ask for a quick summary translation of the information on the documents. James Renaud had reminded him that this unprecedented operation might be "terminated" at any time by the Vietnamese government. So Schweitzer tried constantly to determine the nature of the material in the archives, in the event he was not permitted to remove the scanned data from Vietnam.

In the initial batch of documents, there was considerable material on the first American POW in North Vietnam, Navy Lieutenant, JG, Everett Alvarez,

Jr., shot down on August 5, 1964, flying an A-4C Skyhawk during the first retaliation raids following the murky Tonkin Gulf incident. Schweitzer scanned nine documents that dealt with Alvarez from the entries on page 102: "The First Battle (5-8-1964)." And he was pleased when he also found several documents on Alvarez's fellow Navy pilot, Lieutenant, JG, Richard C. Sather, who had been shot down and reported killed in the same raid. Sather's remains had been repatriated in 1985.[11]

Alvarez lived through over eight years of captivity and was among the first American prisoners repatriated during Operation Homecoming in 1973.

Schweitzer realized, of course, that granting access to the records on these two American casualties cost the PAVN nothing. Neither was a controversial case. But the fact that such detailed records existed for American prisoners had never been confirmed. As Schweitzer lay the bluish gray document acquisition cards onto the glass face of the optical scanner, he realized that every step he now made was an unprecedented stride into uncharted territory.

But working through the initial documents those first two weeks back in Hanoi, Schweitzer noticed a pattern emerging. At the close of the day, there were always a few documents missing from his numerically ordered stack of material to be scanned in the morning. This meant Mrs. Hang had to carry the entire stack back to the second-floor secure archive for safekeeping overnight, a procedure that conveniently provided the General Political Directorate adequate time to carefully scrutinize the material.

Schweitzer realized that a hidden review must have occurred each night up in that musty archive. Some mornings Mrs. Hang would appear late to explain that she was having "difficulty" locating certain documents. Schweitzer learned to judge the sensitivity of the material by the length of time Mrs. Hang was closeted away on the second floor. He assumed there was another entrance to the archives from the staff offices in the wing of the modern annex building he had never visited.

From his discussions with James Renaud, Schweitzer knew that DIA analysts might eventually be able to determine the types of information the Vietnamese did not want to divulge from the pattern of documents Mrs. Hang was "unable to locate." So he chose not to protest that a few records listed on each Red Book page were missing at this stage of the operation. And, to be fair, Mrs. Hang was eventually able to produce almost all of the documents listed in the index. As Renaud had predicted, the prospect of being paid $4 per page of documents successfully scanned provided the proper incentive to "expedite the declassification review" the PAVN undertook each night.

In Bangkok, James Renaud had given Schweitzer an informal list of several "hot" MIA cases and told him to gather as much information as he could from the archives relating to them. These were not suspected live POWs languishing in Vietnamese prisons, but rather cases for which the DIA believed the Vietnamese definitely had more information. Some were on General Vessey's list of 135 discrepancy cases. Others were not. Schweitzer was certainly willing to investigate any leads that arose during the scanning process. However, he discovered that undertaking this scrutiny always disrupted the assembly-line procedure he had established.

By now, Schweitzer wrote most of his reports on computer disk, which he hand-carried to Bangkok. He was confident that the Vietnamese could not break the altered variant of the word-processing program in which the messages were written. This channel gave Schweitzer a better opportunity to describe his progress and problems than the commercial fax messages he had been using since March. In one computer disk message sent in late June, Schweitzer complained to James Renaud that this attempt at impromptu field analysis was too disruptive. Trying to match shootdown records with MIA cases often proved frustrating.

One fragmentary record described an F-4 Phantom shot down south of Vinh at an undetermined date in June 1966. Several days later, the badly decomposed body of an American pilot washed ashore and fishermen buried it on the beach, then reported the incident to their local militia chief, who in turn wrote a report for the village People's Committee of the Party, who, in their turn, wrote a report for the local Air Defense Forces commander. These documents eventually found their way to the museum. But the most important element of information from the American perspective, the name of the dead pilot who washed ashore, was missing.

Schweitzer and Mui spent a hot, aggravating afternoon trying to attach a name to this body. Eventually they decided it was probably either Navy Ensign Harry Belknap, a Phantom radar intercept officer, or his pilot, Lieutenant, JG, Lawrence Nyman. But they could not be certain. In effect, the afternoon was wasted because Mrs. Hang came to collect the unscanned documents before they could continue their real work.

Commenting to Renaud on the effect of this amateur document analysis, Schweitzer cautioned: "I have to get moving and continue scanning, or I'll never get finished. The detailed analysis will have to be done in Washington. It is now late June, and I'm not even half finished scanning."[12]

Schweitzer realized that a case such as this could only be resolved by a JTF/FA investigation on the scene, to interview the fishermen who had buried the dead American, and to try to locate the grave. But he also realized that several typhoons had swept the coast since the war, and a shallow, sandy grave on a beach had probably been destroyed. This was indeed a frustrating business.

But, as the work progressed through the weeks of cloying summer heat, Schweitzer did try to keep an informal tally of POW and MIA names that appeared in block Roman letters on many of the scanned documents. By mid-June, he had encountered only names of prisoners repatriated during Operation Homecoming or men listed as Killed in Action/Body Not Recovered, some of whose remains were later repatriated.

Major Mui and Mrs. Hang seemed to be chafing under the ceaseless drudgery of the process. Although Schweitzer's corner office was air-conditioned, the rest of the museum was not. The windowless upstairs archive beneath the concrete roof of the new museum annex must have been a humid oven at night. This probably accounted for the drop in "missing" documents as the full heat of the Hanoi summer bore down.

But the drudgery was slowly producing results. During one of Schweitzer's regular checks of the documents being scanned against MIA records, he encountered a shootdown report for February 18, 1966. The handwritten document noted that a U.S. Navy A-6A Intruder had been hit by groundfire and crashed in the mountains, forty-four kilometers west of Hanoi. Both airmen had been killed in the crash. Report Number 3044 was detailed, listing the tail number of the A-6A as VJ 5N105. The line noting the fate of the airmen, Lieutenants, JG, Joseph V. Murray and Thomas A. Schroeffel, read: "Killed, bodies not yet recovered [from wreckage]," (chêt, chua tìm thâng hāo côt).[13]

Schweitzer's official MIA list noted that the February 18, 1966, shootdown had resulted in two Killed in Action/Body Not Recovered casualties, who were in fact Lieutenants, JG, Joseph Murray and Thomas Schroeffel. Their remains had never been returned by the Vietnamese. Yet here was the first indication that the Vietnamese had concrete information on the dead airmen's bodies. Schweitzer realized as he scanned the document that, at the very least, the Vietnamese could no longer continue to deny they had records on this incident. Hopefully, when confronted with the information, they would lead the JTF/FA investigators to the crash site to recover these remains.

(The scanned images of these handwritten documents were so sharp that they were later to be verified as authentic contemporaneous wartime entries, rather than later forgeries. Schweitzer had this requirement in mind when he insisted that the Fujitsu scanner be augmented by the latest image-enhancement technology.)

There were over one hundred documents concerning shootdowns listed on Red Book index page 119, "Defeating the American Air War of Destruction in the North (1965–1968)." And it took almost a week for Mrs. Hang to "locate" all of them. But Schweitzer persisted. Finally, she delivered every document listed, including an acquisition card for an Air Force first lieutenant named Donald W. Bruch, an F-105D Wild Weasel pilot, shot down near Hanoi in April 1966 and listed as Killed in Action/Body Not Recovered.[14] The acquisition cards for Bruch's documents and flight equipment could be later used to determine the location of his grave, if in fact his remains had not already been exhumed and stored as negotiating capital by the Vietnamese government.

But to Schweitzer's surprise, Mrs. Hang also delivered an acquisition card, number 3805, that was *not* in the Red Book index, but which fell between documents number 3355 and the next entry, 3818. This was the card for the museum acquisition of the military ID card and the Geneva Convention card of Air Force Major (later Colonel) Dean Andrew Pogreba.

Schweitzer's DIA casualty list noted that Major Pogreba had been shot down northeast of Hanoi flying an F-105D on October 5, 1965. He had been the Lead pilot of a five-aircraft strike, call sign Mercury. Their target had been the Lang Met highway bridge near the borders of Lang So'n and Ha Bac Provinces, about forty miles south of the Chinese border. During the strike, the weather was poor, with low broken clouds. Antiaircraft fire was intense and the flight was forced to jink violently to avoid 37mm fire and radar-controlled 57mm flak. While the flight was approaching the target, at least three surface-to-air missiles exploded nearby. Pogreba's wingman, Captain Bruce G. Seeber, watched him roll in to the target, deliver his bombs, then pull away into the clouds. His last radio transmission was: "Mercury Lead heading one-one-four degrees." This southeast heading was the proper vector for the flight rally point over the South China Sea. But when the surviving flight members reached the safety of the rally point, two of the aircraft were missing, Pogreba's and Seeber's.[15]

Seeber was shot down and captured almost at once. Injured, he was taken to Hanoi's Hoa Lo Prison, but was not told of his wingman, Major Pogreba's, fate. To further confuse the situation, Chinese Communist radio announced the capture of an American pilot named Dean Pogreba that day. In 1973, during his post-release debriefing, Seeber reported that he believed Pogreba had crashed near his own aircraft and had probably been killed. The JCRC had repeatedly requested information on Pogreba during the twenty years since the war. But the Vietnamese Communists had consistently denied any knowledge of his fate.[16]

Now Schweitzer had located an official Vietnamese military record that stated unequivocally Pogreba had been killed in the shootdown of his aircraft on October 5, 1965. Acquisition card number 3805 noted that Pogreba had "died in the crash of the [F-105] airplane." *(Bãi tòa tò li F105).* Further, the record confirmed that Pogreba's plane had crashed at Latitude 2130 North and Longitude 10621 East, very close to the officially estimated loss coordinates. The record noted that Dean Andrew Pogreba had been "killed but the body not removed" from the crash site.[17]

BY 1992, POGREBA'S case had become a cause célèbre to POW/MIA activists. Retired Air Force Brigadier General Thomas Lacy made sensational public disclosures in 1990. Lacy, a former fighter pilot who had held responsible command positions before retirement, had later become active in the POW/MIA issue. He announced that he had secretly gone to Vietnam in the late 1980s, traveling on a "diplomatic passport" (the provenance of which he did not explain).[18] Lacy then contacted Dean Pogreba's widow and presented the shocking news that he had personally encountered Pogreba, who was alive and well, and living in a prison camp north of Hanoi. When reporters pressed Lacy for details, he refused to provide any more, stating that he would be placed in "trouble" with the U.S. government if he did so.[19]

Pogreba's widow was skeptical. However, Dean Pogreba's son, Larry, was more receptive to Lacy's bizarre account than his mother. "It's a plausible story," Larry Pogreba told the press. "I want to believe Lacy."[20]

When General Lacy later gave a sworn deposition to the Senate Select Committee on POW/MIA Affairs, his testimony not only reiterated the claim that he had encountered Dean Pogreba alive in Vietnam more than twenty years after his loss, but also that he had encountered other live American prisoners.[21]

By way of background, General Lacy testified that he was aware of several secret operations during the Vietnam War that had resulted in large numbers of Americans lost as Missing in Action. He cited a hitherto unreported operation in which the U.S. put "Marines" into the Mu Gia Pass in North Vietnam. (Lacy did not explain why the North Vietnamese chose to cooperate with the United States by also keeping this operation secret.) He added that it was his opinion that all the secret operations had resulted in approximately "5,000 or 6,000, maybe more that were left in Vietnam after the Paris Peace Accords and Operation Homecoming."[22]

General Lacy further strained the credulity of the committee staff counsels by describing his association with Major Dean Pogreba. According to Lacy, he was aboard the Navy airborne command post over the Tonkin Gulf near North Vietnam on October 5, 1965, the day Pogreba was shot down. Lacy stated that he heard radio intercepts of a Chinese MiG shooting down Pogreba's F-105. Then, Lacy added, a daring Special Forces mission was inserted to get Pogreba "out of the prison camp in China." This operation succeeded, Lacy said, but was pinned down in North Vietnam, despite air cover for the team and numerous resupply missions. Incredibly, Lacy told the committee staff that this group remained active in enemy territory for two years before capture.

Staff Counsel William Codinha asked: "Are you saying they resupplied these guys in the field for two years?"

Lacy replied: "Yes, sir."

"Without picking them up?" Codinha pressed.

"Yes, sir," Lacy replied.[23]

In other testimony during the deposition, Lacy stated that he had also encountered a live American POW who had been secretly returned from

Indochina, Air Force Captain Tommy Gist. Lacy testified that Gist was being treated for drug addiction (the morphine habit having been induced by the Vietnamese Communists) in an Oklahoma City Veterans Administration hospital, where Lacy said he met Gist. According to Lacy, he himself had been drugged and kidnapped in Colorado by unknown sinister agents and secretly flown to Oklahoma to be "interrogated."[24]

Lacy's account of finding Dean Pogreba—a gray-haired old man—during a mission to Vietnam as a secret presidential emissary in January 1989 was equally bizarre. Lacy stated that he had met with retired Communist leader Le Duc Tho to locate living American POWs. When questioned by committee counsel William Codinha about the bureaucratic mechanics of this secret mission, Lacy stated that he submitted his expense vouchers directly to Ronald Reagan and was reimbursed in cash by the President.[25] (Apparently these strange transactions occurred before Reagan left office on January 20, 1989. Lacy also testified that Howard Baker, whom he described as a White House official, had been present at a 1985 Oval Office meeting with Reagan. Senator Bob Smith, the committee vice chairman, who was observing the deposition, gently corrected Lacy on an obvious error: Baker had been Senate majority leader in 1985, not White House chief of staff. The retired general admitted that he often confused names.[26])

Lacy then described going to a prison camp at a place called Bao Ninh, thirty miles northeast of Hanoi. There he encountered Pogreba and three survivors from the five-man Special Forces team that had rescued Pogreba from China and had embarked on the purported two-year odyssey of evasion through the Annamite Mountains in the mid-1960s. Lacy stated that he had demanded that these prisoners be released, but that the Vietnamese refused.[27]

When asked to provide documentary evidence of these secret missions, General Lacy stated that his secret records had been stolen out of his house in the spring of 1989.

Senator Smith, after reminding Lacy that he was testifying under pain of perjury, told the retired general, "What you're saying right now is a real bombshell if you're telling the truth."[28] Smith continued to stress that Lacy was under oath, giving him ample opportunity to change his testimony. Lacy stuck to his strange story.[29]

Smith and attorney Codinha later discussed the deposition testimony at great length. Codinha stated the obvious: The retired Air Force general had provided no credible evidence whatsoever. Senator Smith agreed. Lacy's bizarre account of having been drugged and kidnapped, then taken to a VA hospital where he encountered a secretly repatriated POW, completely undercut his tales of serving on clandestine prisoner rescue missions to Hanoi. None of General Lacy's weird testimony was entered into the committee's final report.[30]

General Lacy's disjointed deposition could well have remained simply a baroque sidebar to the committee's massive investigation had the testimony not been seized upon and exploited by activists, who saw in the bizarre story confirmation of the more radical MIA conspiracy theories.[31] Perhaps the most sensational exploitation was conducted by Michael Van Atta, a self-described private "covert action" operative who chaired the Live POW Lobby of America. Van Atta's newsletter, *The Insider,* written by "a group of current and former intelligence officers," had a field day with General Lacy's testimony.[32]

In order to lend credence to Lacy's story, Van Atta breathlessly revealed that he "had been provided with a lead to obtain a copy" of Lacy's deposition.[33]

Van Atta did not tell his readers that the transcript of the Lacy deposition had always been openly listed in the public record inventory of the select committee records available to any researcher at the National Archives in Washington.[34]

To further muddy the already turbid Lacy waters, Van Atta concluded that the general had probably "operated in the same envelop" (in the same manner) as the Iran-contra operation, funded by the National Security Council through "off-the-books" means.[35] Van Atta chose not to relate Lacy's fanciful account of being drugged and kidnapped from his home in Colorado, and then secretly flown to the VA hospital in Oklahoma. Instead, Van Atta concentrated on Lacy's tale of meeting the drug-addicted, secretly repatriated POW, Captain Tommy Gist.[36]

The bogus atmosphere of intrigue surrounding the Lacy deposition intensified through the circulation of a newsletter from the National Vietnam P.O.W. Strike Force, one of the most radical activist splinter groups. The organization reproduced a letter from Mike Curry (a member of the group and a nephew of Major Dean Pogreba) to the DIA. Curry called the April 2, 1992, Lacy deposition "secret testimony...recently unearthed by our organization in a remote corner of the National Archives."[37]

Curry repeated Lacy's most bizarre charges, then added that "the word on the street in POW/MIA family circles is that General Lacy is living in luxury at taxpayer expense under the Federal Witness Protection Program just to keep embarrassing information from public view. Who authorized this and why?"[38]

As an MIA family member, Mike Curry's faith in Lacy's testimony might have been understandable.

But Michael Van Atta's use of the deposition seemed more cynical. He and his group had a record of melding shards of truth with rumor to produce sensational but plausible-sounding "intelligence" reports. Claiming to be current or former intelligence officers was part of his group's facade. In fact, Michael Van Atta had never been an intelligence officer. His military record showed that he had served nine months in Vietnam (March to December 1969) as an infantry sergeant squad leader.[39]

For years, Michael Van Atta was one of the most strident voices claiming that abandoned American POWs had survived in Indochina at least until the late 1980s.[40] He tried to organize a "Private 'Delta Force' " reminiscent of Bo Gritz's farcical efforts, which he hoped to insert into Laos to rescue American POWs reportedly held in caves, including one guarded by a tank.[41] And on frequent trips to Southeast Asia Van Atta had often resorted to distortion, rumor mongering, and half-truths similar to his sensational report on the Lacy deposition to give the impression he and his colleagues were on the verge of freeing live Americans.

In an especially egregious case, Van Atta stated that he had encountered "sources" in the Ministry of Defense in Vientiane, Laos, who "admitted that they had direct, first hand contact with live American POWs after the Vietnam war ended in 1973." Van Atta then described one American POW alive in Samneua in 1974. He did not reveal, however, that this man was Emmet Kay, who was later released.[42]

Ironically, Schweitzer's attempt to clarify the fate of Major Dean Pogreba later itself became exploited in a similar manner. In Van Atta's newsletter, *The Insider,* of December 1993, for example, he cited an intelligence report "which identified Pogreba (and nine others) as prisoners of war based upon data found in a Hanoi Army Museum on an optical computer disc."[43] The newsletter clearly distorted this information. Nowhere in any data, documents, or artifacts scanned by Ted Schweitzer in the PAVN museum and stored on optical disk was there any reference to Pogreba being a POW.

By May 1993, the DIA had completely lost patience with Michael Van Atta and his "Insiders." The agency challenged Van Atta to, in effect, fish or cut bait regarding typically florid allegations he had made concerning one of his team's "covert action" trips to Vietnam. Van Atta had written that the team, working out of a hotel in Hanoi, had traveled to a "heavily guarded facility" and had been "able to uncover evidence that some Americans were still in Vietnam and in fact several members of the team saw first hand, at a distance, what they believed to be some live Americans."[44]

Charles F. Trowbridge, Jr., the deputy director of the DIA's Special Office for POW/MIAs, wrote Van Atta a long letter challenging him to document this and other such allegations. After demanding that Van Atta provide full descriptions of these Americans, Trowbridge asked:

> **Did the team approach the Americans; was contact actually made with the Americans; what was stated between the Americans and the team? If the team did not approach the Americans, please explain why a team that traveled to Vietnam to look for**

**American POWs would have done nothing when it spotted
what it believed to be Americans?**[45]

Neither Michael Van Atta nor any member of his group replied to the challenging questions in Mr. Trowbridge's letter.[46]

CHAPTER 19

As Schweitzer slogged through the tedious process of document scanning with the museum staff, he became convinced that there probably were very few shootdowns in the Red River valley and the densely populated surrounding areas of Vietnam's northern provinces that had not been documented by the PAVN. The detailed records on the February 1966 A-6 shootdown of Murray and Schroeffel, the precise location of Pogreba's crash site, and scores of similar meticulous documents were evidence that the Vietnamese military—through its ascending echelons of authority from village militia to the headquarters of the Air Defense Forces—carefully logged every American aircraft downed within its zone of authority. In many cases, Schweitzer scanned into his computer multiple pages listing the serial numbers of various twisted and burned scraps of aircraft component and flight equipment recovered by village militia.

This painstaking attention to recordkeeping was most pronounced in the PAVN's Military Region 1, which included Hanoi. Moving south, the level of detailed documentation tapered off slightly, but was still voluminous.

But when Schweitzer requested documents listed on Red Book index pages 126, 127, 133, and particularly from pages 133 to 135, which covered many aspects of the long war along the Ho Chi Minh Trail, Mrs. Hang seemed troubled.

That afternoon Colonel Dai summoned Schweitzer to his office and reminded him that the "book contract" only concerned the air war over the North.

"But I'm interested in all aspects of the war with the Americans," Schweitzer said. He recognized that this might be an attempt to wring more money from his generous sponsors in America. But he was mistaken.

Colonel Dai produced his copy of the December 6, 1990, book contract and pointed to item number one, which committed the museum to make available to Schweitzer "the historical materials relating to the Air War in North Vietnam."[1]

"We only have authority to release information on this subject," Dai explained in French.

The matter was closed. At this stage of the operation, Schweitzer was nervous about pressing too hard for fear he would reveal his true intentions. But he realized the subject of American losses in Laos was a delicate one.

Colonel Dai, however, soon made it clear that the PAVN could be flexible on the release of sensitive MIA information from any region of Indochina where Vietnamese Communist forces had fought, provided that the Americans approached the General Political Directorate on its terms. During a series of ostensibly informal discussions over tea cups and cans of beer under the museum lychee trees, Dai laid out a proposal of the resolution of the MIA problem that would circumvent the official American JTF/FA effort.

Schweitzer realized that the PAVN, especially the GPD, deeply distrusted the official American MIA-resolution effort. Dai and other PAVN officers had told Schweitzer that the American MIA office was an officially sanctioned nest of spies, bent on prying military secrets that had nothing to do with the MIA issue from their archives.

The smoldering resentment of American methods flared into an open breach in July during a field investigation of a crash site in Kontum Province in the central highlands of southern Vietnam. PAVN officers angrily told Schweitzer that the JTF/FA archivist and interpreter, Robert Destatte, had accused Vietnamese soldiers of planting skeletal remains of an American airman in the wreckage. Apparently this confrontation had occurred in the presence of local officials and rural laborers who had been hired to help with the excavation.

As someone who had worked in Southeast Asia for twenty years, Schweitzer saw the significance of the confrontation. It was entirely possible that either PAVN officers or local villagers had indeed salted the crash site with remains that had been previously exhumed and kept in storage. If that were true, then the act was a combination face-saving expedient and an effort to produce a "successful" crash site excavation.

From the American perspective, such tampering with evidence irreparably damaged the procedures of forensic anthropology they had been ordered to employ.

To the Vietnamese, however, these digs, like so much in their lives, were public ritual. This particular ritual was meant to demonstrate cooperation between the two countries and the humanitarian concern of the PAVN, the local government, and the villagers involved. Agitprop was a cherished Vietnamese Communist tradition. Tangibly dramatizing "cooperation" was a vital element at this stage of the expanded JTF/FA field investigations. For Destatte to employ aggressive "tactics" by accusing them (probably with valid cause) of using the crash site investigation for propaganda purposes was both incomprehensible and needlessly antagonistic to the Vietnamese. If Destatte had a problem, Colonel Dai implied, he should have worked out a solution with his Vietnamese counterparts in private. Any public display of antagonism, from the PAVN perspective, had to be met with a suitable counterattack.[2]

That counterattack came almost immediately. Two young members of the JTF/FA investigation team were seen to make an obscene gesture at a statue of Ho Chi Minh in a village near the crash site, Dai reported. And the aggressive act had been "witnessed" by agents of the Ministry of the Interior, the state internal security apparatus. This "outrage" was seized upon as an example of belligerent American tactics. The PAVN lodged a formal protest. The incident quickly escalated, with angry exchanges in the field and in Hanoi.

The net result was that the two offending Americans were expelled from Vietnam. The tension, mutual acrimony, and suspicion of the JTF/FA by the Vietnamese mounted. It was difficult for Schweitzer to know for certain whether the two incidents were directly connected, but he knew enough about the Vietnamese by now to believe they were.

As is usually the case in such incidents in Vietnam, there were both political-social elements and more practical matters at stake. The Americans were publicly punished for provoking a loss of face among the Vietnamese over the remains-planting accusation. And, on the practical level, the punishment of expelling the two Americans escalated the tension between JTF/FA and the Vietnamese government to the point where the issue of planted remains was no longer important.[3]

(Lieutenant Colonel Jack Donovan, commander of Detachment 2, JTF/FA, later confirmed that the regrettable incident involving the two Americans had occurred. Although he would not divulge details, he stated that "members of the Defense Department team in central Vietnam" did things that were contrary to U.S. government policy. These actions were "embarrassing to Vietnam." Donovan also confirmed that the incidents occurred at a time when there were still strong suspicions of the Americans among many Vietnamese officials.[4])

This suspicion was strongest among old-guard Communists and their allies in the Ministry of the Interior. With *doi moi* flourishing, the Soviet empire—Vietnam's staunchest political, economic, and military supporters—collapsing, and increasing numbers of prosperous overseas Vietnamese returning home to do business, state security officials were terrified of foreign-instigated anti-Communist agitation.

Therefore the incident with the JTF/FA team in the former South Vietnam was especially unfortunate. There was already incipient paranoia at the Ministry of the Interior, with many officials convinced American agents were about to trigger a counterrevolution. These fears focused mainly on the southern half of the country, the former Republic of Vietnam.

(Nine months later, in May 1993, Dao Quang Ho, a respected Buddhist monk, committed suicide by self-immolation in protest of state repression of religion.[5])

Discontent among southern Christians and independent Buddhists who refused to accept state control over religion was spreading in the south. And university students, normally the pampered junior elite of socialist Vietnam, were staging protests in support of religious and political freedom. Such actions would have been unheard of before *doi moi*.

A few weeks after the incident with the JTF/FA personnel, a former South Vietnamese Air Force officer named Ly Tong, who had returned to Ho Chi Minh City, ostensibly to invest in private business, hijacked a Vietnam Airlines flight from Bangkok. Tong forced the pilot to circle low over Ho Chi Minh City while he dropped bundles of leaflets calling for a popular uprising against the Vietnamese Communist Party. Tong then ordered the pilot to fly south toward the Mekong Delta where he parachuted from the airliner. He was arrested and eventually sentenced to twenty years in prison.[6]

Such disorder was anathema to the party and its internal security apparatus. Experienced political operatives such as Colonel Dai tried to avoid being contaminated by any possible association with subversive activity. And the fact that hard-liners, acting from a variety of motives, chose to tar the official American MIA investigation office, the JTF/FA, with the brush of subversive agitator, both complicated and inadvertently assisted Schweitzer's operation.

Now Colonel Dai proposed an unusual method of breaking the deadlock.

He explained that he was the senior political officer and director of external affairs for the Vietnam Veterans Association (VVA), the officially sanctioned group that represented the interests of millions of former PAVN soldiers. These PAVN veterans, he said, controlled much of the information on American MIAs lost throughout Indochina. They knew the locations of battlefield graves.[7] They had marked their maps with the locations of crash sites. But these men were no longer in the army. The only practical way they could be contacted was through the VVA.

Dai suggested that a senior American, perhaps Senator John Kerry, contact the Vietnamese government to propose that the Vietnam Veterans Association become the official conduit for delivering information on MIA cases to the U.S. government.

"All information?" Schweitzer asked.

"Yes, of course," Dai replied, "everything."

The implication was clear. Not only would the VVA provide access to its veterans who had knowledge of American MIA cases, but Dai and his colleagues would use the organization to deliver the General Political Directorate's massive archive of documents and artifacts.

Dai assured Schweitzer that the project had the approval of the president of the VVA, General Song Hoa, a retired lieutenant general named Tran Van Quang, and of the party general secretary, Do Muoi.

As Dai sketched out the VVA project, Schweitzer assessed its scope. The PAVN was proposing a completely separate parallel effort, an elaborate third channel that would require a massive staff and budget. Offices would be established in PAVN museums and houses of tradition throughout Vietnam.

PAVN veterans would be interviewed in those offices and would lead American investigators to the graves of buried Americans.

An important element of this program, Dai emphasized, would be a joint Vietnamese-American veterans commission. American members would provide information about Vietnamese MIA cases from U.S. military and intelligence archives. This would make the entire effort much more palatable to hard-liners who distrusted the JTF/FA. Dai explained that many old-guard GPD officers (no doubt himself included) viewed the presence of the JTF/FA as an embarrassing breach of sovereignty that had been imposed on Vietnam by the inequitable terms of the Road Map policy, which itself was seen as simply an extension of the unwarranted American trade embargo. He added that common PAVN veterans were also bitter that American soldiers had come to Vietnam demanding information about a relative handful of missing men when the PAVN's MIA rolls numbered over 300,000.[8]

Colonel Dai's audacious proposal completely circumvented the JTF/FA operation that Do Muoi and the government had so enthusiastically endorsed during the April meeting with the delegation from the Senate Select Committee on POW/MIA Affairs.

Was Dai lying about the party's support?

Schweitzer had no way of assessing the truth in this quintessentially Vietnamese proposal. Dai was either suggesting a unique and practical way to solve the MIA mystery or he was proposing another complex scam, a racket to divert money from serious investigations. Schweitzer realized the offer had elements of both.

It was clear that Dai's VVA proposal had several goals.

First, if the project was actually implemented, the VVA would have found at least part-time work for tens of thousands of unemployed veterans.

But, if this rather implausible panacea did not materialize, Schweitzer recognized, at least the VVA leadership would have been seen to try.

And from this effort, they would have demonstrated that it was the General Political Directorate of the PAVN—not the VNOSMP, or its civilian cadres such as Ho Xuan Dich from the Ministry of Foreign Affairs—that controlled the key to resolving the American MIA mystery.

It was now also obvious that, sooner or later, the U.S. government was going to have to deal directly with the PAVN on the GPD's terms, if any real progress was going to be made toward the fullest possible accounting the American government sought.

IN JUNE 1992, Major Mui approached Schweitzer at the museum with a sensitive proposition. Mui said he had been contacted by former PAVN soldiers who had the remains of at least one American Special Operations soldier who had been killed in Laos in June 1967. Mui's contacts wanted to sell the remains of Master Sergeant Billy Ray Laney, a Green Beret who had been aboard a U.S. Marine Corps CH-46 helicopter taking off with a mixed American and South Vietnamese Special Forces team from a ridge overlooking the Ho Chi Minh Trail fifteen miles west of the South Vietnamese border. The big twin-rotor helicopter did not burn on crashing in the tall rain forest. Three of the South Vietnamese troops made their way back to the original landing zone and were recovered by American search parties the next day.[9]

Only one American, Sergeant First Class Charles Wilklow, was rescued. He stated that several South Vietnamese and American survivors, both wounded and uninjured, probably had been killed when North Vietnamese Army troops threw grenades into the helicopter wreckage. But it was later determined that at least two of the Americans were captured alive. Marine Corporal Frank Cius was one of the handful of "Laos" POWs released in Hanoi in 1973; Green Beret Master Sergeant Ronald J. Dexter, captured with Cius, died in captivity six weeks later.

Sergeant Billy Ray Laney was last seen alive sprawled on the deck of the helicopter with a broken back.[10]

Mui explained that the former PAVN soldiers had "carried the bones back with them from the South." He added that they also had Laney's dog tags and ID card.

Schweitzer made a careful note of this and explained that he would try to get the word to Americans who might be interested in the information.

This was the first concrete indication that the PAVN General Political Directorate was in contact with "retired" officers or men who had American remains they wanted to sell. Coming after Colonel Dai's proposal that American veterans deal directly with the Vietnam Veterans Association, under PAVN sponsorship, the offer seemed to be yet another tangible example of what the General Political Directorate could provide if they were properly handled.

"Many people know you are working with us," Mui told Schweitzer. "These soldiers brought this information because they hope to make a little money."

Mui's implication was clear: Under Vietnamese law, it was illegal for citizens to possess remains of war dead.[11] But almost no one observed the law, and Mui stressed that other PAVN soldiers had "much more information" about MIA remains. These PAVN soldiers had fought in the South and in Laos. They had buried dead Americans, then later retrieved their remains and brought them back to the North.

"They know the bones are worth money," Mui added.[12]

A few days later, Mui approached Schweitzer to announce that the PAVN soldier also had the remains of another victim of the June 1967 Special Operations helicopter loss, the pilot, Marine Captain Stephen P. Hanson.

Schweitzer considered the new offer valid, and a confirmation of the earlier proposal to sell remains of Sergeant Laney. It was unlikely that someone perpetrating a fraud would have had enough information about the

1967 helicopter shootdown to associate the names of these two victims, and claim that both their remains were available. What made this new offer especially significant was that the incident occurred in Laos and involved PAVN trail security forces, possibly from Army Group 559. This meant that the soldier who had contacted Mui might well have other information about American MIAs lost in that part of Laos.

Schweitzer and Mui discussed the amount of money the man might want for all the remains that had been recovered from this crash site. Mui did not name a specific amount, but Schweitzer gained the impression that an offer ranging between $1,000 and $5,000, depending on the actual number of remains, would be acceptable.[13]

"That's a lot less than one million per set," Schweitzer said to himself, jotting a note on his pad after Mui had left the museum office.

He duly filed his report to the DIA, but did not receive instructions on how to pursue this matter at that time.

In southern Vietnam at this time, traffic in dubious MIA bones and relics was mounting. Criminals raided cemeteries to retrieve bones and skulls—a terrible breach of Buddhist doctrine, which places great emphasis on the sanctity of village graveyards and ossuaries. In March 1990, Vietnamese police found one cache of almost 400 sets of skeletal remains in the storeroom of a shop in Saigon; forensic tests revealed none was American.

Police also caught an enterprising villager who had built a press to stamp out reasonably authentic-looking American dog tags. The man used names and serial numbers from wartime American military files. But the names and numbers were often garbled, and none of the dog tags purportedly belonging to missing Americans referred to a valid casualty.[14]

The trade in bogus dog tags continued unabated despite occasional crackdowns by Vietnamese police. By early 1992, police had arrested eleven people who had hoarded a total of 742 complete or partial sets of remains. Examination by forensic pathologists revealed that none was American (Caucasian or Negroid).[15]

Street vendors peddled *mia* to tourists in most of the cities of the former South Vietnam. Prosperous and enterprising vendors also sold ersatz Zippo lighters and grainy photocopies of ID cards, all allegedly belonging to missing Americans.

In a variation of the ID card scam, criminal dealers in both Hanoi and Saigon circulated an ID card, with the data partially blacked out, that purportedly belonged to an American who had been transferred to the USSR. Ted Schweitzer traced the serial number to an actual American POW, Air Force Captain Robert F. Waggoner, who was shot down in 1966 and repatriated during Operation Homecoming in 1973.

But such elaborate frauds were far less common than the burgeoning street trade in forged dog tags and other dubious MIA artifacts.

(This author bought one "MIA" dog tag on the Saigon riverfront in February 1993. The vendor, a smooth-talking English speaker, guaranteed that the remains of the missing man, Robert E. Sutton, could be found in a village in Tay Ninh Province. The vendor finally reduced his asking price of $10 down to $1. There is no Robert E. Sutton listed among American dead or missing in Southeast Asia.)

The DIA was obliged to analyze almost all the myriad dog tag reports that arose over the years in Indochina and among refugees. According to Garnett Bell, the veteran analyst, the DIA had elaborate wall charts that traced the progress of a particular dog tag from one owner to another. When photocopies of dog tags or ID cards were involved, the DIA had to analyze them to see if the same machine had been used.[16] The amount of time wasted on these frauds was unfortunate, in view of the short staffing the DIA Special Office for POW/MIAs suffered until recently. But had the agency not performed this level of rigorous investigation, activists would have yet more grist for their cover-up mill.

As more American tourists, including returning veterans, came to Vietnam in the early 1990s, the audacity and ingenuity of the bogus MIA-remains peddlers increased. Some dishonest Vietnamese, too young to have personal memories of Americans, believed any returning veteran was a potentially gullible buyer for bogus MIA remains.

The case of Lon and Gail Stickney of Seattle, Washington, was typical of this situation. Lon Stickney had flown CH-47 helicopters in Quang Ngai Province during the war. He was returning to Vietnam for the first time in twenty years to show the country to his wife, Gail. At the Pacific Hotel in Da Nang, a maid approached the Stickneys with a small plastic bag containing a collection of human hair, teeth, and bone fragments. With the bag, she presented a small card with the words "Diaz, USMC" inscribed on it. The young woman swore these were the remains of a Marine killed during the war.

Lon Stickney was outraged. His unit had suffered heavy casualties in the war; he did not appreciate being accosted in this manner. He seized the startled maid by the arm and led her to the hotel desk where he insisted the police be summoned. After considerable shouting, denials, and general excitement, the woman was led off to jail. The Stickneys and their driver departed the next day for the north.[17]

When this incident was recounted to Ted Schweitzer, he commented that the woman and the policeman that arrested her were probably members of the same bogus MIA-remains ring. After the Stickneys checked out of the hotel, Schweitzer suggested, the maid was no doubt back on duty with the plastic bag containing her grisly wares in her pocket.

(There was no missing American in Indochina named Diaz.)

But there was a long history of both private Vietnamese citizens and the government of the SRV using American MIA remains for financial and political gain. Indeed, the skeletal remains of Americans killed in the war had become an established, if macabre commodity of barter by the time Ted Schweitzer set up operation in the Hanoi museum. Tran Vien Lac, the Vietnamese mortician who defected in 1979, testified that he personally had processed 452 sets of remains, most of which he believed to be those of dead Americans. It was established with some certainty that these remains were stored by the Vietnamese government, possibly in a "warehouse" in Hanoi.[18] By the end of 1992, Vietnam had repatriated over 300 sets of remains, which had been forensically verified as American MIAs by the CIL-HI.

However, American MIA investigators could not be certain how many more sets of remains the Vietnamese still held. General John Vessey tried to estimate the total number of remains that could have fallen into enemy hands in North Vietnam. In what he called his "sensibility check," Vessey laid out a plausible formula in testimony to the Senate select committee. He stated that it was well known from Vietnamese records that Air Defense Forces, militias, or local people recovered dead Americans from aircraft seen to crash. The bodies were buried nearby, then exhumed within a few years.

Vessey asked the Air Force what percentage of peacetime crashes produced remains. He was told about 70 percent. Using that percentage as the maximum wartime probability, he estimated that 70 percent of those crashes might have been observed. He then estimated that 70 percent of the observed crashes resulted in identifiable remains buried in graves that were accurately marked and not subject to erosion by mountain torrents and scavenging. This calculation resulted in an estimated probability of less than one quarter of the KIA/BNR shootdowns in North Vietnam producing remains.[19] Since there were approximately 300 well-documented KIA/BNR shootdowns in North Vietnam, Vessey's estimate suggested that these losses would have rendered approximately seventy-five sets of remains recoverable by the SRV government. If accurate, the estimate meant that most of the easily recoverable remains in North Vietnam had already been located.

But the fact that the mortician had presented credible evidence of a much larger number of remains in government hands suggested that Vietnamese recovery efforts had been widespread and efficient throughout the war zones of Indochina.

The total projections for recoverable American MIA remains depended on loss circumstances. In 1977, the Defense Department briefed the Woodcock Commission that no more than 1,339 missing Americans throughout Indochina were expected to be accounted for. But in many of these cases the Pentagon believed no actual remains would be recovered. Some of the aircraft had been lost over water, while others had been observed to have exploded in fireballs when hit by enemy groundfire or missiles. And the Pentagon further estimated that 772 of the 1,339 MIA incidents had occurred in remote areas and might not have been observed by the enemy.[20]

By 1992, there were still 1,053 Americans unaccounted for in South Vietnam. Most were ground troops lost in small-unit actions in remote areas. Depending on the nature of reports from witnesses, some were listed as POW/MIA and others as KIA/BNR, but most informed military experts believed the vast majority of these cases were men whose bodies were left behind on the battlefield. Retired Army General Robert Kingston described the difficulty of recovering the remains of such casualties in remote areas:

> **As a battalion commander, 1st Battalion, 35th Infantry, 25th Division, out of Pleiku, along the Ia Drang Valley along the Cambodian border in MR-2, we came across a number of skeletal remains. I'm talking 20, something like that. We took the dog tags, left them there.**
>
> **I had helicopters. I could have picked them up and brought them back to base camp. Nobody told me. During the Korean War, I had a similar experience.**[21]

FROM THE SUMMER of 1992 onward evidence accumulated that the Vietnamese government was no longer withholding hundreds of stored MIA remains as they had in the past. The fact that the repatriated remains up to that point correlated to many—but by no means all—of the crash sites in heavily populated areas was significant.

Further, after July 1992, when the DIA authorized Ted Schweitzer to explore the clandestine purchase of MIA remains (circumventing both American policy and Vietnamese law), the retired PAVN officers who purportedly held dozens of MIA remains were unable to produce more than one forensically verified set. The U.S. government decision to use Operation Swamp Ranger in this manner was not an attempt to supplant the stalled JTF/FA field investigation effort, but rather to complement it with an investigation to determine if in fact PAVN sources, either active-duty or retired, had stockpiled significant numbers of MIA remains.

Had Schweitzer been able to purchase remains from several of the sources that approached him through the General Political Directorate, this would have indicated a significant unofficial "warehouse" still existed. At that point, the secretary of defense or the White House would have intervened to bring such a flagrant breach of Party General Secretary Do Muoi's promise to provide full cooperation in resolving the MIA question to his attention.[22]

Schweitzer eventually reached the conclusion that there were probably still scores of remains in remote crash sites, especially in mountainous areas of northern Vietnam and Laos. But other, less remote crash sites had probably already been "mined" by rural people trying to recover gold and platinum from the electronic circuitry of the crashed aircraft. Vietnamese officers told Schweitzer that a twin-engined American fighter-bomber or attack plane such as an F-4 or A-6 contained about $5,000 worth of precious metal. It took exhausting and painstaking work to extract the gold and platinum from the wreckage. But to destitute villagers with no other source of money, the job payoff was worth the work. And these crash site miners also occasionally found skeletal remains in the wreckage, an added bonus.

Schweitzer later learned that there were also a number of remote battlefield graves, many along the Ho Chi Minh Trail, that had not been well documented by PAVN forces during the war. Remains from remote crash sites and graves could probably only be recovered through slow and diligent efforts by the JTF/FA—provided their budget allowed for financial inducement adequate enough to bring forward PAVN soldiers with knowledge or wartime documents listing the crash sites or graves.[23]

As Ted Schweitzer continued his clandestine research operation and burrowed deeper into the General Political Directorate, it became clear that most of the authentic American MIA remains that the government in Hanoi had kept in storage in earlier years had now been repatriated. There were definitely more sets of remains stored in Vietnam, he believed, but no longer in a central government warehouse. That winter Schweitzer testified before the Senate Select Committee on POW/MIA Affairs that the officials who once had custody of warehoused remains had retired and possibly taken the remains with them when they left government service.[24]

But, by the summer of 1993, after months of frustrating negotiations with PAVN officers and private Vietnamese, Schweitzer became convinced that they either did not have the remains that they claimed, or that they were toying with him. In March 1993 he wrote the DIA that remains in "private" hands "constitutes the real crux to the problem and mystery for us here in Vietnam. I believe there are definitely remains in the hands of individual Vietnamese and/or groups of Vietnamese. The question is, do these individuals have a connection to the central government or do they actually represent the government's policy in some way?" Schweitzer concluded by stating, "I am becoming more and more convinced that the central government could play a larger role than they do in resolving these cases more quickly. I am becoming more and more convinced that there is some sort of policy to motivate us to lift the embargo via the enticement of these remains."[25]

IN THE HOT summer of 1992, however, the PAVN was still determined to demonstrate to Schweitzer the wealth of untapped information in its archives. And Mrs. Hang must have been ordered to provide as much information as she could within guidelines.

At the end of one stifling July afternoon—the air conditioner made little impact on the blanket of humid heat—she turned to Schweitzer.

"Do you want some very good material?" she asked, Mui translating.

Up until then Mrs. Hang had not taken an overly forward role in the project. But Schweitzer knew she had contacts not only here at the museum, but throughout the warren of General Political Directorate offices in the surrounding Citadel.

"Sure," he said, trying not to sound eager.

"Tomorrow morning," she said.

The next day, Mrs. Hang arrived early in the cool of the morning. Schweitzer was waiting as promised. She opened a green pasteboard folder and produced a thin deck of American identity and Geneva Convention cards. The first two cards she handed Schweitzer to examine were Major Dean Pogreba's Air Force ID card and Geneva Convention card. Then she handed across the cards belonging to Major Joseph Morrison and his back-seater, Lieutenant San Francisco. Mrs. Hang made a point of returning the other cards to the document folder.

Although the PAVN had handed over a few American ID cards to JCRC investigators in the 1980s, the documents had usually referred to so-called BB or NR cases, men listed as Killed in Action/Body Not Recovered, or whose remains had already been returned. Now Schweitzer was presented with personal documents of priority MIA cases.

He had been in Asia for enough years to realize he was being offered valuable material for a price. This was a test, probably arranged by Colonel Dai to see how valuable such material was in terms of hard cash dollars. Schweitzer also recognized that the test was also meant to determine the depth of his "publisher's" pockets; by now, he feared, Dai and his GPD colleagues suspected he was more than a simple scholar under contract to an obscure publisher.

James Renaud and the DIA had authorized Schweitzer to pay for such material. This was not misguided and inappropriate generosity. Paying for purloined sensitive information was a time-honored part of clandestine operations, the bread-and-butter of similar DIA projects worldwide. The agency had given him a sliding scale of value, with "XX" MIA cases (the DIA casualty designation for men missing as of 1973) such as those of Pogreba, Morrison, and Francisco being the most valuable.

Schweitzer opened his aluminum briefcase, unscrewed the false bottom of a can of shaving cream and removed a tight roll of new $100 bills. Counting carefully, he lay down $400 in cash for each of the six cards. Mrs. Hang and Mui seemed satisfied. Schweitzer scanned images of both sides of the cards, then lay them on a clean tan dustcloth and photographed each of them with his new Nikon camera.

"If you have any more material such as this," Schweitzer said, "I'm sure my publisher would be happy to pay for them."

Mui and Mrs. Hang exchanged silent glances. Schweitzer saw that his cover as an independent scholar was probably frayed beyond repair. But, as James Renaud had predicted, earning this kind of money was an enticement that these PAVN officers were not about to reject.

Using word code, Schweitzer managed to fax news of this development to James Renaud's commercial cutout in the United States. Renaud replied with several faxed messages on the letterhead of his dummy publishing company. In each of these messages, the first paragraph contained a hidden number code that incorporated a prearranged four-digit base number that was activated working backward from an intentionally misspelled word. In these messages the key words included "brightem," "qualety," and "comming." Working the cipher, Schweitzer obtained the reference numbers for the cases the DIA wanted him to concentrate on.

His first priority case numbers were M130, Major Joseph Morrison, and F055, Lieutenant San Francisco. Over the next several days, Mrs. Hang produced many more artifacts from the two airmen, including their Defense Department immunization certificates, government driver's licenses, the inspection cards from their parachutes and life preservers, and even a crisp, unfaded $20 bill one of the pilots had carried with him on the day they were shot down over the Ban Karai Pass in 1968. Schweitzer scanned and photographed each artifact.

Schweitzer felt a wave of sadness as he stared into the tanned young faces on the identity cards. Major Morrison was a fit, handsome man in his thirties, a strong determined jaw, a confident combat officer, a fighter pilot who no doubt believed himself invincible. Lieutenant Francisco's face was more open, less worldly. His dark hair was short, his eyes wide-set, guileless. Shooting his pictures at different F stops and shutter speeds, Schweitzer noted that the cards were unblemished and showed no evidence of water- or bloodstains, or any damage by heat.

But when he asked for records on the cases, Mrs. Hang seemed nervous. "Those men are dead," she said. "I have seen pictures. They are dead."

She told Schweitzer that these artifacts had not come from the Central Museum but from "another office" of the PAVN. He assumed this was somewhere in the Enemy Proselytizing Department of the General Political Directorate, which he knew to be another repository of POW records.

"I would like to photograph material like this from other Americans for my book," Schweitzer told her.

She slipped his payment into her folder. "That will be possible."

Schweitzer knew that within the Vietnamese Communist system officials such as Mui and Mrs. Hang worked within a collective group, which is sometimes described as a "cell" in the West. Hers was headed by Colonel Dai. Any money Schweitzer paid them was no doubt being shared with other people. In that regard, the labor collective in Vietnam had partially supplanted the traditional family that, for centuries, had shared any income and savings among its members.

To demonstrate that Colonel Dai's cooperation had the full blessing of his superiors, Lieutenant General Nguyen Nam Khanh, deputy director of the General Political Directorate of the PAVN, visited the museum on July 23. He watched closely while Schweitzer, Mui, and Mrs. Hang demonstrated the document-scanning procedure. Dai hovered behind the general, trying to look unflustered. Schweitzer saw that one of the formal rituals of approval that were such an important part of Vietnamese life was taking place. General Khanh was a member of the Central Committee of the Communist Party, and despite his formal rank of lieutenant general (three stars), had in fact considerably more power than four-star generals outside the GPD. His presence here in this office, while PAVN officers assisted an American in the copying of documents from a secret archive, was meant to dramatize in an unmistakably explicit manner that Schweitzer's work was fully authorized by the GPD.

Turning to leave, the general spoke at length to Colonel Dai. Mui whispered a running translation to Schweitzer.

"This work is very important to the Army and to Vietnam," General Khanh said. "You should help Mr. Schweitzer in every way you can. He is a friend of the Vietnamese people."

When Colonel Dai returned to the office, he was smiling broadly, revealing his long, tobacco-stained teeth. "Before you go to Bangkok again," he told Schweitzer, "we will give you something very significant to show your publisher."

THE NEXT MORNING Mrs. Hang came in alone and seemed eager to speak with Schweitzer as soon as Mui arrived to translate.

"Do you want me to bring you photographs of Americans?"

Schweitzer had no idea what she was offering. Given Colonel Dai's promise, he was expecting "significant" MIA records. His priority tasking was documents and POW artifacts, not photos. He looked at the stack of documents she had brought with her and realized the work they represented, then considered what possible use photographs might be to his project.

"Photographs take up too much of my computer memory," he said, pointing to the scanner. "I'd rather stick with these documents."

As he was preparing for his trip to Bangkok later that week, however, Mrs. Hang arrived carrying several black-and-white photographs of different sizes.

"These are interesting," she said.

The first two photos she lay on Schweitzer's desk showed an American in a sweat-soaked tropical flight suit, sprawled supine, obviously dead, on a hillside of trampled elephant grass and scrub palm. One picture was a full-length view of the man's body and included his bare left foot. The picture must have been taken after the Vietnamese soldiers had removed his prized jungle boots. The second picture was a close-up. Someone had unzipped the nylon mesh survival vest to reveal the man's name embroidered beneath his muted pilot's wings on the left breast of the flight suit.

"Jay Morrison," Schweitzer read. "That's Major Joseph Morrison. Jay is a nickname." Schweitzer swallowed. This was the first picture of a dead American MIA that the Vietnamese had ever released. The picture was indeed *significant*.

Mui and Mrs. Hang nodded somberly. They were subdued, studying the pictures, as if forced to commit a breach of etiquette.

Schweitzer examined Major Morrison's face. The eyes were not quite closed. He seemed about to doze off into a peaceful sleep. His forehead and cheek were flecked with dried blood from the sharp blades of elephant grass and thorn vines. But there were no obvious wounds on the body.

Schweitzer lay the pictures of Morrison to one side.

The next picture Mrs. Hang presented showed another distressing scene. A young Caucasian, completely covered with a stained white sheet, except for his swollen head, lay on his back on a crude operating table. The young man's eyes were closed, his lips battered and swollen. Four Vietnamese medical workers in white smocks hovered over the patient. One guided a tube into the man's throat, half hidden beneath the sheet. Another medical worker pumped a large primitive glass cylinder syringe, moving liquid through the tube.

The young man was either already dead and being embalmed, or near death and receiving a transfusion.

Mrs. Hang explained this was a photo of Navy Lieutenant, JG, Lee Nordahl.

Schweitzer consulted his casualty list. Lieutenant Nordahl had been the co-pilot of an RA-5C Navy reconnaissance mission shot down near the coastal town of Hong Gai on December 20, 1965. The remains of Nordahl's pilot, Guy Johnson, had been repatriated in 1977. But despite repeated requests for information, the Vietnamese had denied any knowledge of Nordahl's fate. He was one of the priority MIA cases James Renaud had tasked Schweitzer to investigate.

"He is alive in the picture," Mrs. Hang said, "but a short time later, he died."

Later, when Schweitzer discussed the Nordahl case with Major Mui, it was clear that the Vietnamese were very nervous about releasing this photograph.

"Lieutenant Nordahl died in the hospital," Mui said. "But in the photo, you see that he is alive. A doctor can tell you that."

Schweitzer again examined the Nordahl photograph. The swelling of the young man's head was ominous, probably indicating a skull fracture. Given the primitive conditions of North Vietnamese hospitals, Nordahl's death had probably been inevitable. Still, Mui's anxiety about the picture was unmistakable.

"If someone in your government wanted to exploit this case," Mui explained, "it would be easy. There is no denying the man is alive in the hospital. But . . . because of confusion in the war, my government did not report later that Nordahl was dead. But he did die."

Schweitzer recognized the Vietnamese dilemma. POW/MIA activists could claim the picture was the smoking gun, proving that Nordahl had indeed survived capture and was among the hundreds of living POWs that America had callously "abandoned" in Indochina in 1973. This photograph could be distorted to *prove* Lieutenant Nordahl had been sent to the Soviet Union, to the caves of Samneua, Laos, or perhaps was still living in a dungeon beneath Ho Chi Minh's tomb.

Surely, Schweitzer thought, the PAVN must have had more pictures of POWs who had survived capture but later died. The General Political Directorate was using the Nordahl photograph as a trial balloon, to assess how the American government would treat this case. If the DIA did not use "tactics" to exploit the obvious discrepancy between Nordahl's true fate and Vietnam's twenty-seven-year denial of any knowledge of the case, the PAVN would be prepared to turn over similar photos of other sensitive cases.

Following Mui's request, Schweitzer put the Nordahl photo into his passport folder. The Vietnamese insisted that he not mix this extremely sensitive picture with the others.

The Nordahl case epitomized the value of Operation Swamp Ranger. If America's goal was to solve the MIA mystery, the General Political Directorate was willing to cooperate by closing all the cases in which they had knowledge, even the most sensitive ones. But the Vietnamese would insist on doing this in a confidential, back-channel manner, so that they would not be forced to officially account for the lies and deception that had shrouded the issue for so many years.

BY MID-JULY, Schweitzer had obtained pictures of seven dead Americans. Six were MIA cases, including Joseph Morrison, and one was a KIA/BNR case, Navy Lieutenant Edward Dickson.

These pictures were all of high quality, taken, he was told, by "Army photographers" during the war. The images he was being shown were all in focus and properly exposed, indicating a professional using good equipment. Moreover, several of the shots of dead airmen were accompanied by other pictures of the man's survival and flight equipment neatly stacked near his body. These were not spontaneous "combat" photographs, but rather the product of a well-organized program of documenting American casualties. The Morrison picture, which had been taken in a remote mountainous area far south of Hanoi, indicated that the casualty documentation program had been operating at least throughout the four PAVN military regions of North Vietnam and probably in adjacent areas of Laos.

In several of the pictures, the dead American airmen had been already placed on bamboo stretchers and stripped of their boots and flight suits. In others, the photographer had apparently arrived soon after the dead man was discovered.

One of these photographs showed Navy Lieutenant Gilbert A. Mitchell, an A-6A bombardier-navigator shot down near Haiphong on March 6, 1968. He was sprawled on his back in a shallow impact crater of oozing mud, which covered his lower body. Twisted, mud-caked wreckage protruded from the crater. But the Vietnamese had smoothed the muck away from Mitchell's face and placed his white flight helmet, emblazoned with the U.S. and South Vietnamese flags as well as a heart, beside his head. Like Morrison, the young aviator seemed to have slipped into a tranquil doze.

The photos of Air Force Captain John W. Seuell, shot down in June 1972, showed him in a white T-shirt, his flight suit having been removed from his upper body. Seuell lay in a scrub jungle clearing, a PAVN soldier leaning over him. His limbs showed signs of fracture and rigor mortis, indicating the photographer had reached the site several hours after the man's death. There could be no doubt that he was dead. An accompanying photo showed Seuell's parachute canopy bundled loosely beside his boots and survival equipment.

By now, Schweitzer had also either purchased outright, photographed, or scanned the military identity cards of eleven MIA and four KIA/BNR cases.

One of these cards belonged to Navy Lieutenant Bruce C. Fryar, an A-6 Intruder pilot lost in Laos in 1970. This was a well-known case. Fryar's bombardier-navigator, Lieutenant Nicholas Brooks, was the son of George Brooks, one of the founders of the National League of Families. Their plane had been shot down just after sunset on the Ho Chi Minh Trail in Laos, just west of the Ban Karai Pass. Fryar's Navy wingman and the Air Force forward air controller both saw two good parachutes descend into the forest among the towering limestone pinnacles that marked this section of the trail. And one of the downed Intruder crewmen was observed lying immobile on the ground, still in his parachute harness. A heroic attempt by a Search and Rescue helicopter crew to retrieve this airman was driven off by heavy groundfire.[26]

In 1982, men calling themselves "Lao Resistance" fighters delivered the skeletal remains of Lieutenant Brooks to the American embassy in Vientiane. They said they had no knowledge of Lieutenant Fryar's fate. But now the PAVN, which had complete military control over that portion of Laos, was tacitly admitting that it had taken Fryar under its control, either alive or dead.

Schweitzer recognized that delivering Fryar's identity card was an unmistakable signal that there was much more information on Laos MIA cases in the PAVN archives.

Beyond these photographs and ID cards, his list of scanned PAVN documents that revealed concrete evidence with the potential of resolving MIA cases now totaled in the hundreds.

He was pleased at this unexpected bounty and realized that the relatively small outlay of money that he had spent so far—in comparison to the vastly larger expenditures by JTF/FA—had produced proportionately a much better return.

Schweitzer had found a relatively cheap pipeline for his clandestine second-channel operation to tap a well of documents, photographs, and POW artifacts that potentially could resolve the vast majority of remaining MIA cases.

Schweitzer realized that this handful of photographs of dead American MIAs would resolve only a few of the outstanding cases. But he also recognized that the geographic and chronological distribution of the pictures, which showed casualties that had occurred between 1965 and 1972 from all across North Vietnam, provided an unmistakable message from the General Political Directorate. This collection of materials was a greatly expanded analog of the photos and record cards he had been given in 1989.

And, as the Fryar ID card from Laos made clear, the PAVN was using this sampling of documents, photos, and artifacts to send an explicit signal that they had much more of this material available.

It was as if General Khanh and Colonel Dai were saying: "The answer to the MIA mystery is in our hands."

Schweitzer was now convinced that the key to resolving the entire MIA issue lay within the limestone walls of the Citadel, not at jungle-choked crash sites scattered across the length of Vietnam and Laos that were being so dramatically scoured by the JTF/FA.

Certainly, there were many MIA cases in which an aircraft had crashed at sea, unobserved in foul weather or darkness, or had flown into a steep trackless ridge along the Ho Chi Minh Trail and disappeared beneath the impenetrable roof of the triple-canopy forest. But in all the other cases in which American aircrew had come down in areas under Vietnamese Communist control, the PAVN, with its tradition of meticulous recordkeeping, had undoubtedly documented the loss and the recovery of living or dead American airmen.

This was the true significance of these representative specimens of MIA case photographs and identity cards.

Colonel Dai and his GPD colleagues had explained to Schweitzer the position of PAVN progressives on the MIA question. This element of the PAVN, which included the GPD, was now ready to resolve the MIA issue. These middle-aged and younger officers—Dai being one of the oldest— unlike their more doctrinaire superiors of General Giap and Le Duc Tho's generation who had fought the French for independence and led the PAVN in the long war against the Americans, viewed the world from a pragmatic perspective.

But Dai and his colleagues made it clear the PAVN wanted this resolution of the issue to proceed on their own terms. They told Schweitzer the PAVN did not want the American government to seize on this first release of truly sensitive material and use it as a pretext to increase the JTF/FA's pressure on

Vietnam to provide a "full accounting" of the MIA issue as America defined that term.

Writing to case officer James Renaud, Schweitzer described the development: "This first round of information will be a test as to results. If it only produces additional 'negative pressure,' it will be the last round." He cited the Morrison-Francisco case. While providing Morrison's picture, the PAVN did not offer Francisco's, even though it was reasonable to assume that both men had been photographed on the day they were killed.[27]

The PAVN wanted their new cooperation on resolving the MIA problem to produce tangible reciprocal positive actions by the U.S. government. They were not about to suddenly open the doors to their secret archives without first extracting the type of quid pro quo benefits they had become accustomed to since the Bush administration instituted the Road Map process. But Schweitzer believed the General Political Directorate of the PAVN was in fact committed to a resolution of the issue.

The motives of these younger, more pragmatic, officers were based on several factors: First, their goal was to end Vietnam's diplomatic and economic isolation, which had become severe after the collapse of Communism in Eastern Europe and the Soviet Union. A major negative offshoot of this isolation was that Vietnam was now deprived of the Soviet nuclear shield, which had previously blunted Chinese hegemony in the oil-rich South China Sea. Vietnam needed a replacement for that shield. The only power that could counterbalance China's huge military force was the United States. And the only way to elicit American support was to end the trade embargo and restore diplomatic relations by resolving the MIA issue.

These Vietnamese officers believed that the Bush administration, which had hammered out the practical, step-by-step Road Map policy, offered the best hope of achieving these goals.[28]

But at this stage, even the progressive element of the PAVN resisted offering full cooperation to the official American MIA investigators of the JTF/FA. As Colonel Dai had earlier made clear, the General Political Directorate distrusted and disliked the American military and civilian officials assigned to Hanoi. Moreover, Schweitzer recognized, the JTF/FA had become isolated within the political fiefdom of the Ministry of Foreign Affairs and the Vietnamese Office for Seeking Missing Persons (VNOSMP). The PAVN's General Political Directorate, which held all the important MIA documents and artifacts, was struggling to wrest control of the issue from the civilians.

Schweitzer now found himself caught up in a murky power struggle that involved at least two Vietnamese factions and the official American MIA office. He had always made it a point to act in a friendly manner to his Vietnamese contacts and to publicly accept their assurances that they wished to resolve the MIA issue for humanitarian reasons. In this regard, his DIA case officers encouraged him to ingratiate himself openly to the Vietnamese as a way of gaining their confidence. Now, however, with the JTF/FA teetering on persona non grata status, Schweitzer's close contacts with the General Political Directorate of the PAVN placed him in an unsought opposing position to his American colleagues.

He had become in fact the good cop in an accidental good cop, bad cop scenario.

Or at least he wanted to believe the situation was inadvertent. But the level of acrimony and intrigue in Hanoi was so intense that, when tired or discouraged, Schweitzer sometimes believed that it was possible he was being manipulated as part of a larger, unseen megaoperation in which both the Swamp Ranger program and the JTF/FA were simply pawns. If that were the case, the Vietnamese were also being squeezed to channel their best information in his direction by the unacceptably aggressive "tactics" of the JTF/FA.

But in the end, Schweitzer was forced to remember that this was Southeast Asia. No matter what unseen political machinations prevailed, money was still the dominant factor in most endeavors. And Operation Swamp Ranger provided him with enough funds to meet the needs of the various cells, collectives, and regional factions within the General Political Directorate that controlled the truly important MIA information. By now, he had many of these officers on his operational payroll. He was spending more money than they had ever dreamed possible, but he was receiving documents and other vital MIA information the Vietnamese had denied for decades existed.

And, under *doi moi,* such free enterprise was officially encouraged. The People's Army, like other government institutions, was, after all, eventually meant to become more financially self-sufficient. All I'm doing, Schweitzer mused, is helping them meet their quota a little early.

Schweitzer knew that, if he could continue along this track, he could eventually deliver everything these shadowy PAVN officers possessed.

But that would take time. And time was an issue. This was an election year, and George Bush was doing badly. With Ross Perot hovering about the presidential campaign, the MIA issue had become politically important. From his most recent discussions with James Renaud, he knew just how eager the DIA was for a "breakthrough." Schweitzer recognized that, whatever progress he made with the Red Book index, scanned POW and MIA documents, and this latest batch of photos, his work would undoubtedly be exploited by the White House for political gain before the November election.

IN JULY, JUST as Bush's clumsy and overconfident reelection campaign was beginning to come unglued, he was publicly jeered when he addressed the annual convention of the National League of Families of American Prisoners and Missing in Southeast Asia.

Bush had tried vainly to placate the noisy agitators. But they belonged to a rebellious splinter faction of the league and subscribed to all the lurid beliefs of the most radical live POW advocates. He finally lashed out at a young journalist of vague accreditation who had begun heckling him from the rear of the room even before the MIA families began their chant of "Liar!" Finally, Bush's left fist jutted forward and he jabbed his index finger at the heckler. "Sit down," Bush shouted, "and shut up!"

That night, the network newscasts, which would have normally ignored the convention, ran C-SPAN tape of the President's outburst. To the chagrin of his campaign managers, Bush's anger was incorrectly described as having been vented at MIA family members frustrated by years of government indifference and ineptitude. The image of Bush losing his composure and lashing out at decent, concerned American citizens was one of the indisputable negative landmarks in his disastrous campaign.[29]

One irony hidden by this political embarrassment was that the day before the fiasco, Bush had ordered the immediate declassification and release of over a million American documents relating to the emotionally charged issue. This announcement was intended to be the highlight of his appearance before the League of Families.[30]

But the shouting incident completely eclipsed this positive step. Bush's campaign staff was becoming frustrated about the stalled MIA issue. They were desperate for some tangible progress in Vietnam that would make headlines before the election.

SCHWEITZER NOW DISCOVERED just how desperate the administration had become to achieve such visible progress.

Mui reported that a strange American civilian had appeared at the museum. He was reportedly a hulking man with thick dark hair and an almost incomprehensible southern American accent. He wanted to buy pictures of American airplanes shot down during the war. Schweitzer's anxiety level rose a notch.

The next day, the museum staff reported that the man's name was Eugene Brown and he was from North Carolina, supposedly a Vietnam War buff who was collecting photographs for a book. Schweitzer's anxiety ratcheted even higher.

Within a week, Gene Brown was working with Colonel Nguyen Van Tich, head of the museum archives. Now Brown's ostensible amateur interest in wartime photographs extended to pictures of American POWs. Mui reported nervously that Colonel Tich was selling a number of photographs to the American at high prices.

Worse, Mui noted, Colonel Tich had not yet shared the money with the members of his cell and with his comrades in the so-called Nghe Tinh Group. This was an informal network of officers from Nghe Tinh Province in central northern Vietnam, the ancestral home of Ho Chi Minh, and the Communist heart of the country. They were considered an elite hard core of military revolutionaries and provided mutual support to their comrades similar to that of the alumni of service academies in the armed forces of Western nations.

This breach of group ethics focused unwanted scrutiny on Colonel Tich. Apparently, Brown was now under Ministry of the Interior surveillance. But Tich's Nghe Tinh connections initially kept him out of trouble, probably after he was obliged to share Gene Brown's largess with his comrades.

(Gene Brown proved to be an unpaid "walk-in," operating without DIA control. The loose operation, called Druid Smoke, was meant to collect POW and MIA photographs in Hanoi. The DIA's authorization to exploit Brown is an indication of just how desperate the Bush administration had been to achieve a breakthrough before the November presidential election.[31])

CHAPTER 20

AFTER TWO BRIEF TRIPS OUT OF VIETNAM, TED SCHWEITZER RETURNED
to complete the document-scanning operation at the Central Military Museum in September 1992. By now, he recognized that he had been granted access to most, but certainly not all the documents relating to American POWs that were listed in the Red Book index.

He was certain that unseen PAVN officers were scrutinizing the gray pasteboard record cards that he carefully assembled in numerical order each afternoon to be scanned in the morning. He neatly stacked these documents and secured the bundle with rubber bands in a precise manner. Then in the morning the stacks would arrive missing the rubber bands, the documents jumbled and out of sequence. On at least four occasions, he noted that record cards on his numerical list of the previous afternoon were missing from the morning's stack.

When he asked Mrs. Hang about this, she feigned ignorance, insisting he had made a mistake in his list. Schweitzer did not press the issue. That would have provoked a confrontation that would have resulted in a loss of face for either him or the museum. It was clear, however, that whoever was scrutinizing the documents he selected was removing those considered embarrassing, sensitive, or simply too valuable to be given up at this stage. Even though the American government felt time pressure, the General Political Directorate was not in a precipitous rush to see the resolution of the MIA problem.

Schweitzer now kept an informal log, tracking which documents were being withheld. Some of this censorship was not sinister. On index page 137 of the Red Book, for example, a report on the leadership of the party had inadvertently been included in documents on the defenses against American air attacks between 1969 and 1973. Mrs. Hang caught the error and removed the document. That was understandable.

But by carefully reviewing his lists, Schweitzer determined that there was a consistent pattern of withholding documents from the listings on other index pages dealing directly with the American air war in the North, and by supposition, with American casualties. Of the more than 400 documents listed on Red Book pages 102 to 105, which treated the early phases of the air war, nineteen had been withheld.

All the approximately 500 documents concerning the war in Laos, including the air defenses along the Ho Chi Minh Trail, indexed on pages 106 to 118, had been withheld. Clearly the PAVN was not about to open its secret archives on Laos at this time.

The exclusion of seventy-six documents dealing with the air war in PAVN Military Regions 1 through 4, which included all the provinces of North Vietnam, was troubling. He was allowed to scan almost a thousand of these documents, many of which revealed information on MIA cases for the first time. But Schweitzer could only guess at the contents of those that had been withheld.

The selective withholding of records was not unique to the Central Military Museum in Hanoi. In 1991, JCRC investigators visited the PAVN museum in Vinh. They were given an excerpt of the museum's index, then allowed to examine the actual registry book, which was similar to but much less extensive than the Red Book. The American investigators found that "a number of items mentioned in the register excerpt did not appear in the register." Further, they found gaps in the register where items they had already examined were not listed. The JCRC team suspected that the ostensibly official document they had examined was not the original, but a replica that had been selectively recopied from an original. The JCRC team was also disturbed to find that certain documents of potentially high interest listed in the register were not made available for examination.[1]

But Schweitzer was certain that the Red Book index he had scanned was a handwritten original. There were no gaps in pages, although there were certain sections that ended with several blank pages. As noted, to be sure he had not inadvertently missed anything important in the Red Book, Schweitzer scanned all 208 pages.

In total, ninety-five museum record cards, not including those dealing with the war in Laos, South Vietnam, and Cambodia, had been withheld from the approximately 2,000 documents he successfully scanned between April and September. The documents withheld were less than 1 percent of the records he was permitted to copy.[2]

On the other hand, Schweitzer had been given several dozen records, including the documents on Major Dean Pogreba, that had *not* been listed in the index. Those additions had no doubt been part of the GPD's effort to demonstrate the importance of its archives in order to entice the American government away from its dependence on the civilian-dominated VNOSMP.

Nevertheless, the missing documents were troubling. There could be a number of reasons for this systematic withholding of records.

Maybe the officers that controlled those documents had not been satisfied with the share of the payments they were receiving from Colonel Dai and simply decided to withdraw valuable records and save them as a nest egg to be independently sold later.

Or there could have been a general policy not to release records that documented American prisoners dying or being killed in transit from their capture site to the central PAVN prison system in Hanoi. Certainly, the General Political Directorate seemed eager at this point to use their cooperation as a means to expedite the resolution of the MIA issue to the point that the United States would agree enough progress had been made in the Road Map agenda that the economic embargo could be lifted. Documents that revealed American "air pirates" had been hacked or beaten to death by irate villagers—or ill-disciplined PAVN troops—would undoubtedly be seen as antithetical to improved relations between Vietnam and the United States. To the Vietnamese Communists, historic truth was flexible.

Another, more troubling possibility was that Colonel Dai and his GPD colleagues had meticulously culled hundreds of sensitive records. These documents might have dealt with Americans who had been captured alive and shunted into the hypothetical secret, parallel prison system that was so prominent in the conspiracy theories of radical POW/MIA activists in America. Or some of these records might have documented the handover of American POWs to Soviet or Chinese intelligence operatives.

These were possibilities that could not be ignored.

However, by sampling the content of the material in the batches of documents he was permitted to scan, he did not find obvious chronological gaps that included dates on which large numbers of American aircraft were lost in incidents that produced MIAs.

Certainly, the bulk of the Red Book documents did not seem to be riddled with obvious gaps. Schweitzer came to believe that the ninety-five missing records could not possibly have contained information about the hundreds of American MIAs who activists claimed had disappeared alive into Communist captivity. More likely, these records dealt with some of the twenty-eight MIA cases from North Vietnam on General Vessey's Last Known Alive Discrepancy List, the bulk of which concerned MIA cases in South Vietnam. The missing records also probably documented cases in which injured or wounded American prisoners died during their initial interrogations, either in the disparate military regions or in Hanoi itself. Certainly this was information that the General Political Directorate of the PAVN was not eager to reveal until the American trade embargo had been lifted.

Schweitzer's suspicion that the PAVN would not reveal any truly defamatory information on its treatment of American captives until the trade embargo was lifted and diplomatic relations were at least partially normalized was confirmed that summer.

During the two years that Schweitzer's "book" project had been developing in Hanoi, he had been introduced to Colonel (formerly Major) Nguyen Van Y, the GPD officer who served as the Hoa Lo Prison interrogator known as the Rabbit. They met several times to discuss the information in PAVN archives on American POWs.

Colonel Y recognized that he had become a detested figure in the United

States, based on the accounts of those returned American POWs who had suffered so grievously during the interrogations Y had supervised. He felt that this demonization had been unfair. His country was at war, he now rationalized, the United States had unleashed a savagely destructive bombing campaign, and Y's assignment had been to wring the maximum propaganda value out of those unfortunate Americans who had been captured by the Vietnamese.

It had been Colonel Y who was charged by the General Political Directorate to maintain the detailed records on every American prisoner in PAVN custody in North Vietnam. Each American POW had in effect his own "201"-type personnel file. These were known as the Blue Files, so named from the ubiquitous blue-gray pasteboard covers favored by the PAVN. Depending on the length of a man's captivity, his Blue File might number hundreds of pages and include everything from detailed medical reports (including estimates of physical damage inflicted during torture), to thorough biographic notes, to copies of all the propaganda statements the man had been forced to write. The Blue Files also contained old-fashioned reel-to-reel tape recordings of many of the brutal interrogation sessions.

The last time Schweitzer and Colonel Y had discussed the Blue Files was that July. Earlier, Y had promised to share the Blue Files with Schweitzer at some unspecified time in the future. Now Schweitzer asked the dour, taciturn officer if he was ready to honor that promise. Implicit in Schweitzer's question was the offer of a generous cash payment for each of the Blue Files Colonel Y turned over.

"No," Y replied. "I keep control of all Blue Files. It is not yet time for you to have them."

Schweitzer tried to reason with the officer, again making it clear that these files would be a very "valuable" part of his book.

But Y became impatient, and Schweitzer did not press his point. Colonel Y was probably one of the few officers in the General Political Directorate for whom money was not an irresistible enticement.

"Maybe I will keep the Blue Files," Y said. "Maybe I will write my own book."

That was the last time Schweitzer discussed the Blue Files with Colonel Y, but at least he had confirmed that these important records still existed.

Schweitzer was trying to estimate the actual extent of detailed PAVN records on American prisoners and MIAs, beyond the documents he had scanned and the relatively small quantity of photographs and identity cards he had so far been provided. More than ever he recognized that the PAVN probably had information on the great majority of Americans who had been lost in North Vietnam and the areas the Communists controlled in Laos, Cambodia, and South Vietnam.

· · ·

ONE AFTERNOON, DRINKING tea with Colonel Dai, Schweitzer was given a dramatic example of the extent of this information. Sitting on the tiny rattan chairs beneath the museum's lychee trees, Dai launched into one of his familiar accounts of the long war in the South. The tea cups gave way to cans of beer, and Schweitzer realized he was being offered valuable information.

Dai explained that in 1967 he had been a political officer in a ground combat unit attached to the PAVN 3rd Division. His unit was operating in the coastal Binh Son District of Quang Ngai Province, a pro-Communist stronghold, best known for the atrocity of the My Lai massacre. Dai and a small group of PAVN regulars were bivouacked in a rural hamlet on the banks of one of the many meandering rivers that separated the coastal paddy fields.

On April 21, 1967, they were rousted from their afternoon sleep by an alert sentry who smelled the distinctive mosquito repellent used by American soldiers. Earlier, the sentry had watched some Americans paddling a sampan past the village, but they had been well out in the stream and posed no threat. This new group were on foot.

Dai grabbed his weapon and slid into a hiding hole behind the clay fireplace of the village house in which he had been sleeping.

The American soldiers, four tired young men in sweat-soaked fatigues, ambled into the village. When they had passed Dai's hiding place, PAVN soldiers lying in ambush cut them down with a short burst of fire from their AK-47 assault rifles.

Dai took command of the situation. Beyond the nearby paddy dikes and bamboo groves, he heard helicopters flying low, no doubt already searching for the four stragglers. If the aircraft spotted the dead Americans, their battalion stationed across the river, the Song Tra, would encircle the village. Dai's unit would have no escape route.

So, while Dai's force slipped away, the villagers submerged the bodies of the dead Americans in the river. A group of village children conducting the normal evening task of washing their water buffalo sat on the bodies to keep them weighted down, while American helicopters and foot patrols swept the area.

The U.S. patrol that entered the hamlet had been brutal, determined to find their missing comrades. When they threatened to execute an old man, one of the village women, Ba Hao, said that she had seen four Americans in a sampan and then heard a burst of fire from an ambush site further down the river. The patrol left to encircle the supposed ambush position.

After dark, the villagers dragged the bodies of the four Americans out of the shallow water and buried them on the opposite bank. The next day, when Dai's unit returned to the hamlet, he was given the Americans' identity cards, which he turned over to higher PAVN authorities. Dai cautioned the village Communist cadre to rebury the Americans so that their bodies would not be discovered and provoke deadly retaliation.[3]

"This was war," Dai repeated. "We had no choice."

Schweitzer consulted his chronological casualty list for MIA cases in South Vietnam in April 1967. Dai's report described the well-known "Mangino Four." Specialist Fourth Class Thomas A. Mangino was the senior American soldier. He was accompanied on a combat patrol that afternoon by PFCs Paul Hasenbeck, David Winters, and Daniel Nidds. They were members of a battalion from the 196th Light Infantry Brigade of the Americal Division. The afternoon of their death, patrol members in a sampan had just tied up to a dock on the river when they heard a burst of AK-47 fire from around the bend in the stream behind them. They assumed Mangino's team had exchanged fire with a sniper. But, twenty minutes later when Mangino and his men had not returned, helicopter and ground sweeps were ordered. Mangino and the other three soldiers were never located. They were listed as Missing in Action and eventually entered on General Vessey's Discrepancy List as DIA case number 0646.

What Schweitzer found significant about this grim incident was that the village woman's cover story of the four missing American soldiers paddling a sampan had now been incorporated in the official American casualty records and had even been included in the incident report in the Vessey list.[4]

At the same time Dai was revealing his detailed knowledge of the fate of the Mangino Four, investigators from the JTF/FA were in Quang Ngai Province interviewing villagers. Although the American investigators received hearsay reports of the men's deaths, no one came forward to reveal their graves.[5]

Now Colonel Dai told Schweitzer that he could lead American investigators to the graves, and in so doing, resolve four nagging MIA cases.

"There are many stories like this among Army veterans," Dai explained.

This message was meant to persuade the American government that it was wasting its time with the VNOSMP and should concentrate its efforts with the PAVN, and by extension, the Vietnam Veterans Association.

"We can convince the villagers to reveal their secrets," Colonel Dai added.

He explained that, in areas such as Quang Ngai Province, where the occupation by American troops and their allies, the South Koreans, had been especially harsh, villagers would never cooperate with the JTF/FA unless convinced by the PAVN to do so.

"I visited My Lai after the atrocity," Dai told Schweitzer. "There is still much hatred there."

To Schweitzer, Colonel Dai's revelation about the Mangino Four was more than just a gripping account of desperate combat. Over a thousand of the 2,265 Americans still unaccounted for in Indochina (both MIA and KIA/BNR cases) were in South Vietnam. Detailed knowledge of these men's fates, as Dai suggested, probably still resided among villagers from the regions where the men were lost and among Vietcong and PAVN veterans who held the Americans prisoner and eventually buried their remains.

Reaching this disparate group of witnesses and convincing them to talk would not be an easy or straightforward task. Dai was correct in suggesting that PAVN officers with combat experience in the South, both active-duty and retired, had the moral authority needed to obtain this information. But, given the fact that the JTF/FA was lavishing money on Vietnamese civilians through the funnel of the VNOSMP, it was not reasonable to expect Dai's colleagues to perform this complex mission gratis.

Vietnamese peasants might be less sophisticated than their compatriots in the big cities, but they certainly saw when there was money to be made.

If, in fact, there was more information available on the location of American MIA graves in the South, the fates of several hundred American airmen missing in the North remained a mystery. And Schweitzer knew that enigma had to be at least partially resolved before any American administration risked lifting the trade embargo and restoring diplomatic relations with Vietnam.

Schweitzer began to focus on Major Mui, with whom he was now developing a close relationship, if not an actual friendship. Mui was too young to have served in combat against the Americans in the South. He had traveled widely for a Vietnamese, having been trained in Russian and English for six years in the Soviet Union. Now he was the chief English interpreter for the PAVN's General Political Directorate. But this position entailed more than just the technical process of translation from one language to another. Mui was expected to analyze the information he translated and provide substantive guidance to his GPD superiors. In this capacity as a senior adviser, Mui had direct access to all the generals in the powerful directorate. And this access allowed Mui to serve as clear conduit for whatever information the GPD wished Schweitzer to receive.[6]

Equally important, at age thirty-eight, Mui was young enough to be flexible in his outlook. Although he had earned membership in the Communist Party at only thirty-one, he was not a doctrinaire Communist. Mui often told Schweitzer that the party he believed in was more a nationalist institution than a branch of international Communism. Perhaps this pragmatism was instilled in Mui by his stay in the corrupt and crumbling Soviet Union, an experience that would have disillusioned even the most idealistic young Communist.

Schweitzer now pressed Mui to help resolve one of the most sensitive and nagging unanswered questions of the MIA mystery: Did the Vietnamese Communists turn over American POWs to the Soviet, Eastern Bloc, or Chinese military assistance missions operating in North Vietnam during the war? Were American prisoners transferred from Indochina to the Soviet Union, as so many American POW/MIA activists had charged?[7]

Schweitzer repeatedly emphasized to Mui that, until that question was answered, there would always be lingering suspicion of the Vietnamese among many Americans.

As Schweitzer hoped, Mui had thought about this issue himself and recognized its importance. He began making discreet inquiries among his most knowledgeable colleagues in the GPD.

One afternoon in mid-September, Mui appeared with another officer at the museum. Colonel Dai and Mrs. Hang were out of town, searching for documents and American identity cards that Schweitzer had requested. Mui had chosen this opportunity to introduce Lieutenant Colonel Nguyen Van Thi, a GPD officer, to Schweitzer at the museum. They sat under the lychee trees drinking tea as the day cooled and the bicycle traffic on Dien Bien Phu Avenue faded after the midday rush hour.

Like many Vietnamese, Thi looked younger than his years. The fact that he wore the collar tabs of a lieutenant colonel also meant little. Intelligence officers rarely displayed their true rank. He explained that he had served his entire career in the GPD and was familiar with all aspects of the American MIA issue. Now he wanted to address the sensitive question of American prisoners who might have been sent to the Soviet Union.

"The Russians were constantly pressuring us to turn over American prisoners during the war," Thi explained. "They felt we had an obligation to meet their needs because of all the aid they gave us. But we never released any prisoners to them."

Schweitzer made notes as the man spoke, so that it would be clear there was a record of this conversation. "How could you resist giving the Russians what they wanted?" Schweitzer prodded. "Didn't you depend on them for weapons? What about your SAMs?"

Colonel Thi smiled. "We had the Russians, and we had the Chinese. They were very jealous of each other. If one applied too much pressure, we turned to the other country."

This was plausible, Schweitzer concluded, but certainly not definitive proof.

"I find it difficult to imagine you could resist years of pressure from the Russians. Didn't you at least give them one American?"

Thi shrugged and let his face go blank, a quintessentially Vietnamese expression bordering on disdain. "I cannot guarantee that the Russians didn't steal *one* American prisoner. But I can tell you what our policy was."

Schweitzer made a note. But before he could continue this line of questions, Thi spoke.

"Giving American prisoners to the Russians is not our darkest secret." His voice became slow and precise, just as Colonel Dai's did when making a didactic, officially sanctioned point. "Our government does not want America to know that our darkest secret is that we killed many American prisoners in cold blood. They were tortured to death in prison, or simply killed outright from fear they would try to escape. And our leaders are afraid to admit this. They were tortured to death here in Hanoi. And they were killed in other parts of the country. That is our worst secret in the MIA affair."

Again Schweitzer made slow, deliberate notes, but Lieutenant Colonel Thi did not object. "How many died?"

"Perhaps hundreds," was all Thi would say.

"Many Americans have suspected this," Schweitzer said, trying to keep the dialogue open.

But Nguyen Van Thi now became reticent. He would not be drawn out. His revelation was obviously one of the "significant" pieces of information that the General Political Directorate was offering Schweitzer.

"Perhaps our leaders would be more willing to discuss this issue, if we knew there would be no reprisals from Washington."

Schweitzer jotted another note. He was being asked to relay a message: A guarantee of amnesty might result in more detailed information about the fates of the Americans killed after capture.

"Vietnam will never accept war crimes trials," Thi said adamantly. "Our own people have suffered many atrocities in the war."

That was their fear, Schweitzer saw: humiliating war crimes trials presided over by their former enemy.

"It's usually the winner that calls for war crimes trials," he noted.

"People in Washington can promise one thing, then do another," Thi said.

(Vietnamese officials Schweitzer dealt with continued to voice fears of war crimes trials focused on the issue of Americans killed in captivity. As the civil war in the former Yugoslavia intensified, they pointed to press accounts of continuing American calls for international war crimes tribunals as proof that the United States would raise the issue with Vietnam.[8] Schweitzer was unable to convince his contacts that American-mandated war crimes trials in Vietnam were totally improbable.

(On the other hand, the fear voiced by Vietnamese officials about such future trials could also have been a convenient ploy to avoid discussing in detail a deeply embarrassing matter. For decades, the official Vietnamese Communist line has been that American prisoners were treated humanely. Admitting that large numbers died under torture or were murdered by ill-disciplined troops or frenzied mobs would amount to a serious loss of face, a calamity to be avoided at all costs in East Asia. An example of the Asian reluctance to make such admissions can be seen in the painful Japanese dilemma over the embarrassing issue of captive Asian "comfort women" during World War II. It was only with great reluctance, and almost fifty years after the war, that the Japanese government admitted to the practice.[9])

Lieutenant Colonel Thi now reminded Schweitzer of the accusations and acrimony that had been hurled at the PAVN by the Americans in the JTF/FA in the name of "cooperation."[10]

Over the next few weeks, Schweitzer discussed the issue of Americans killed after capture with other PAVN officers. Colonel Dai described a typical such incident. Once, on the Ho Chi Minh Trail, PAVN troops captured an American pilot as soon as he landed by parachute. The airman's wingman orbited low over the clearing. American Search and Rescue forces, including the heavily armed A-1 Sandy propeller-driven fighter-bombers, could be heard approaching. The PAVN forces dashed up the slopes for cover, trying to drag their American captive with them. But the man refused to run, expecting to be rescued.

"If a prisoner refused to run," Dai explained, "our men had no choice. They had to shoot him down. It was the heat of battle."

Dai said there were many such brutal incidents on the trail.

But after Nguyen Van Thi's revelation, other PAVN officers were reluctant to discuss further the death of Americans in captivity. However, they did grudgingly reveal that rural militias, especially in heavily bombed areas, often lost control of the local villagers and American prisoners were murdered.

Schweitzer duly reported to the DIA all such ostensibly frank admissions.

Perhaps the PAVN's General Political Directorate was being completely honest with him, a breach of the deception that had prevailed for more than twenty years. But it was equally possible that the entire revelation of Vietnam's "darkest secrets" was just another elaborate deceit, an especially complex and ornate lacquer box that held a hollow core of lies.

Whatever the degree of truth in these revelations, they tended to confirm similar information obtained during the debriefings of returned American prisoners, which pointed to widespread mistreatment of newly captured Americans, especially in heavily bombed areas of North Vietnam's southern provinces.

One of the most notorious cases of this brutality was that of Navy Lieutenant Ronald W. Dodge, an F-8E pilot shot down in May 1967 west of Vinh in Nghe Tinh Province. Dodge ejected safely and landed on the ground, but was surrounded by PAVN troops. His last words on the survival frequency were, "I'm breaking up my radio." That September, *Paris Match* published photos of Dodge, his head bandaged, surrounded by armed militia and an angry mob of Vietnamese villagers. He never made it north into the central prison system. For years the Vietnamese denied any knowledge of his fate. But his skeletal remains were eventually repatriated and positively identified in 1981. The U.S. government was certain Dodge had either been murdered by the village mob or died under interrogation before reaching Hanoi.[11]

As already noted, most American POWs who survived capture and were repatriated have mentioned either being fired on while descending by parachute, or while evading on the ground. Many of these returned POWs have also stated that they narrowly avoided execution at the hands of outraged villagers or ill-disciplined troops.[12]

In addition, the JCRC has received a number of refugee witness reports of Americans executed by PAVN troops, militiamen, or villagers. One account was typical. In November 1973, a refugee from Quang Binh Province, North Vietnam, witnessed an American F-4 Phantom shot down. One of the crewmen landed near a hilly village called Chanh Hoa. Village militiamen found the airman hiding in a bamboo grove. He was dragged into the village center where the militiamen beat him to death with hoes and clubs. The JCRC has tentatively connected this report with the loss of either Air Force Captain Victor J. Apodaca, Jr., or his crewmate, Lieutenant Jon T. Busch. (This case has special significance because Apodaca is the brother of Delores Apodaca Alfond, a leader in the National Alliance of Families for the Return of America's Missing Servicemen, the private POW/MIA splinter group that broke away from the larger National League of Families, and which maintains there are large numbers of living American POWs still in Indochina.) Busch's remains were returned to an American delegation headed by General John Vessey in 1988.[13]

This type of savagery has been attributed by some to the understandable spontaneous rage of rural people who were subjected to years of bombing, as the American air campaign attempted to interdict Communist supply lines from the southern provinces of North Vietnam over the mountain passes into Laos and down the Ho Chi Minh Trail.

That may have been the case. But intense Vietnamese Communist propaganda that demonized American aviators as "air pirates" and American ground forces as cruel and rapacious barbarians also contributed to the atmosphere of hatred in which an unknown number of American captives were massacred. This type of North Vietnamese and Vietcong propaganda intensified after the My Lai massacre in March 1968. A typical Communist radio broadcast of that period described American forces as ruthless butchers that flooded Vietnam's rivers with blood. It called upon all Vietnamese to slaughter Americans "in order to avenge our people, to wash out insult to our nation and save your pride and your own life. . . . Point to American heads and shoot!"[14]

(It is noteworthy that the Communist propaganda calls for vengeance for American atrocities became most shrill following the discovery of widespread atrocities by Communist forces during their occupation of the South Vietnamese city of Hue during the 1968 Tet Offensive. At least 2,000 South Vietnamese civilians [and some foreigners] were executed by Communist forces in Hue, a coldblooded slaughter that dwarfed the carnage of the My Lai massacre. But Communist officials are reluctant to this day to concede the extent of this atrocity.[15])

American airmen captured south of Hanoi and moved slowly north often experienced repeated ritual beatings and public displays of punishment during their transport. Survivors reported that this treatment, apparently meant to channel the people's rage toward the enemy, sometimes went beyond the bounds of ritual abuse and became truly dangerous. It can be surmised that many who did not survive were killed during such sessions of ritual punishment. In this regard, the public display of prisoners and their agitprop punishment sessions were an established tradition among Vietnamese Communist forces. This treatment was meted out to French POWs during the First Indochina War both before and after the fall of Dien Bien Phu.[16]

Often it was only the intervention of a well-disciplined regular PAVN soldier or more senior militia noncommissioned officer that prevented mob slaughter of a captured American.[17]

But there were other documented cases during the war in which even regular PAVN troops or main force Vietcong units publicly tortured to death or executed captured Americans. During one such incident in August 1967, an American Marine helicopter crew answering a distress call observed fifty Vietcong soldiers torturing four wounded American prisoners on an isolated beach south of Da Nang. American forces intervened and scattered the guerrilla force with heavy losses to the Communists. Two of the prisoners were rescued alive, but two had already died.[18]

American prisoners captured in South Vietnam and held in jungle camps also reported similar brutal treatment. In April 1968, Marine Private First Class Earl Weatherman, who had defected to the Vietcong and was held prisoner, witnessed the execution of a fellow POW who had attempted escape.[19] And the case of Army NCO Harold G. Bennett was probably the best known execution of an American prisoner. Bennett was captured in December 1964 and held in jungle camps in South Vietnam. On June 24, 1965, Radio Hanoi announced that Bennett had been shot in retaliation for the execution by the South Vietnamese of a well-known Vietcong prisoner, whose nom de guerre was Tran Van Dong.[20] (Schweitzer later obtained Harold Bennett's identity card and was able to confirm that he had been executed in the South. But, as Schweitzer was leaving Hanoi on a trip to Bangkok carrying Bennett's ID card, his PAVN escorts requested he return it because the artifact was considered "too sensitive" for release at that time.)

Torture of prisoners by village mobs or guerrilla forces in the South were terrible aspects of the long war. The PAVN leadership could claim with some justification that these were regrettable but atypical incidents. Senior PAVN officers still maintain that the ill treatment of American captives ran completely counter to established policy, which was to amass as many American POWs as possible to use as de facto hostages in the negotiated end of the war. PAVN troops, either regular or militia, who blatantly disobeyed orders to keep Americans alive, were allegedly punished.[21]

But the PAVN has long refused to publicly discuss the fates of many Americans who were known to have survived the cruel *étape* from their shootdown site to Hanoi relatively uninjured, but who were killed in some manner once in the central prison system. One such notorious case was the death of Air Force Captain Wilmer "Newk" Grubb, a reconnaissance pilot shot down over Quang Binh, North Vietnam, in January 1966. His capture was announced by the New China News Agency, and several propaganda statements, one in Grubb's own voice, were broadcast by Radio Hanoi in February. That same month, photographs of Grubb appeared in Eastern Bloc publications. He was shown to be in good health except for a leg wound. But in 1970, the Communists announced that Grubb had in fact died on February 6, 1966, "as a result of injuries in [his] crash."[22]

Many American POW experts believe that Grubb was one of a number of prisoners who died under torture during attempts to extract increasingly more dramatic propaganda statements. As already noted, all American aviator prisoners arriving in Hanoi between 1966 and 1969 were subjected to brutal interrogation, no matter how badly they were wounded or injured. It is reasonable to assume that many did not survive this treatment. One who came close to dying until his true identity was recognized was Navy Lieutenant Commander (now Senator) John S. McCain II. McCain was shot down over Hanoi in October 1967, and although seriously injured, was almost murdered by militiamen after he was dragged from Truc Bach. Despite his critical condition, McCain was tortured in Hoa Lo Prison by the interrogators known as the Bug and Pig Eye. McCain believes he would have died early in captivity from this treatment.[23] Only after his captors discovered McCain was the son of the admiral commanding U.S. forces in the Pacific was he given adequate medical treatment.

McCain's treatment was far from unique. Almost three fourths of the returned U.S. Air Force POWs later evaluated stated they had been wounded or injured on arrival in Hanoi yet were subjected to "significant pain" during torture used in their initial interrogation sessions.[24]

Given the fragmentary information available from returned POWs and from public disclosures of information excerpted from still classified POW debriefing reports, it is clear that "hundreds" of American POWs could have been tortured to death, as Lieutenant Colonel Nguyen Van Thi reported to Ted Schweitzer. These deaths need not have occurred in a secret parallel prison system, as some have suggested.

The interrogation center just inside the entrance of Hoa Lo Prison, separately known to POWs as Heartbreak Hotel and New Guy Village, was large enough that newly arrived POWs undergoing brutal initial interrogation could have been kept separate from their fellow captives. If these new arrivals died under torture and their bodies were removed, their presence might never have been noted even by POWs held in the nearby cellblock known as Little Vegas.[25]

Returned POW James H. Warner knows of at least two newly arrived prisoners who were killed by the PAVN interrogator known as the Bug. One, Warner believes, was Navy Lieutenant, JG, Walter O. Estes, a Phantom backseater captured in November 1967. He was known to have arrived alive in Hanoi and was interrogated in the Heartbreak Hotel area of Hoa Lo Prison by the Bug and his sadistic enlisted man subordinate known as "Straps and

Bars" (a reference to the torture implements he used). Warner believes that an unknown number of other POWs could have been killed under torture in this section of Hoa Lo Prison during the years of the most brutal interrogation for propaganda statements—1966 to 1969.[26]

Public accounts have described the deaths under torture of at least four American POWs, two by the Cuban interrogator known as Fidel, who brutalized American prisoners at Cu Loc Prison camp in Hanoi in 1967 and 1968. This Cuban military officer and his assistant, "Chico," were reportedly originally in Hanoi as English instructors. Intelligence reports recount that they volunteered to take part in a training exercise to learn the most effective methods and techniques for extracting information and propaganda statements from American prisoners. The goal of the program was to gain the complete submission of a selected group of Americans. Extreme torture was alternated with improved treatment. When one prisoner, Air Force Captain Earl Cobeil, resisted the Cubans, he was tortured to the point of insanity and eventually died under interrogation.[27]

The widespread authoritative accounts of American prisoners, who were already in precarious physical condition, suffering extreme torture substantiate the statements Nguyen Van Thi made to Ted Schweitzer about the PAVN's "darkest secret."

And an analysis of the DIA POW/MIA casualty records further substantiates the accounts Schweitzer heard from PAVN officers concerning the execution of many American prisoners either while evading capture, or soon after they were taken captive. For example, comparing the number of "XX" category (Missing in Action) and "NR" (Negotiated Remains Returned) cases in North Vietnam for the three years between 1967 and 1969 with the number of surviving returned American POWs lost in North Vietnam for this period, an interesting pattern emerges. Approximately one third as many American shootdown casualties became Missing in Action or were positively known to have died (from forensic identification of their returned remains) than survived captivity and were repatriated. Yet most of the "XX" category had reportedly managed to eject from their crippled aircraft. This indicates that approximately 200 might have survived the initial loss incident, only to have died in the hands of their Vietnamese captors.[28]

If this were true, and the Vietnamese had records of these deaths, Major Mui's fears of American retribution were understandable. And if documents revealed that a significant number of these Americans died under torture, as Mui stated, the fears of the Hanoi leadership might have been justified. Certainly, had this information on widespread torture deaths been made public in 1992, generally positive American attitudes toward the rapprochement with Vietnam might have changed.

A further analysis of the official American casualty records, however, seems to indicate that most of the Americans killed on the ground might have died before they were taken to Hanoi for intensive interrogation. The author conducted a detailed survey of the Defense Department's POW/MIA casualty lists, trying to determine if there was a relationship between the location of loss and the eventual fate of the casualty case. The fates of hundreds of aircrew shot down in North Vietnam and Laos were compared. In order to determine if certain "specialist" aircrew from highly sophisticated aircraft might have been separated after capture (and possibly shipped to the Soviet Union, as some activists have asserted), the loss-location-fate analysis was broken down by aircraft type. Two standard authoritative casualty record lists were used in combination: the DIA's *U.S. Personnel, Southeast Asia (and Selected Foreign Nationals),* dated February 1, 1990; and *Citizens and Dependents Captured, Missing, Detained or Voluntarily Remained in Southeast Asia, Accounted for or Unaccounted for, from 1-1-61 Through 79/10/11,* dated October 11, 1979.

Of the total of 523 F-4 Phantom fighter-bomber aircrew lost in North Vietnam before Operation Homecoming, 175 survived captivity to be repatriated. Seventy-six percent of those F-4 crew survivors (133) were shot down above latitude 20 North, the target areas of the Red River valley known to American mission planners as Route Packages 5 and 6. The remains of seven F-4 aircrew have been returned by the Vietnamese; all are from Route Packages 5 and 6. Of the 231 F-4 aircrew listed as MIA, only thirty-two were shot down in the Route Packages 5 and 6 area above latitude 20 North. Eighty-six percent of the F-4 Phantom crew MIA cases were shot down south of Route Packages 5 and 6.

A total of 103 F-4 Phantom fighter-bombers were lost in Laos. Only two of these aircrew survived captivity and were repatriated. The remains of one lost F-4 airman were returned. One hundred of the 103 F-4 crewmen lost in Laos are listed as MIA.

Forty-six A-4 Skyhawk pilots survived captivity and were repatriated. Twenty-seven of them were lost in Route Packages 5 and 6, while another twelve were lost near coastal cities of North Vietnam. Thirty-seven A-4 Skyhawk pilots remain MIA. Two thirds of these cases occurred below latitude 20 North.

This pattern holds for F-105 pilots shot down over Laos. All nineteen who were not rescued remain MIA or KIA/BNR. Six A-7 pilots were lost in Laos. Only one survived captivity; the other five are missing. All five A-4 Skyhawk pilots lost in Laos and not rescued are listed as MIA or KIA/BNR.

A total of 107 A-6 Intruders were shot down during the war. Sixty-seven of their crew are still MIA. Of these, fifty-three were lost below Route Packages 5 and 6 in North Vietnam, or along the Ho Chi Minh Trail in Laos.

Of the twenty-six A-6 Intruder aircrew who survived captivity and were returned, nineteen were shot down in Route Packages 5 and 6. The three negotiated remains returned for A-6 crewmen all involved men lost near Hanoi and Haiphong.

Significantly, many of the surviving prisoner A-6 crewmen were bombardier-navigators, whose specialized technical training reputedly made them targets of any secret Soviet dragnet that had been cast to siphon away important American prisoners.

Perhaps the most famous missing A-6 crewman is Navy Lieutenant James Patterson, Captain Red McDaniel's bombardier-navigator. Although their plane was lost above latitude 20 North, the shootdown occurred in the jungle mountains west of Hanoi. McDaniel believes that his crewmate, Patterson, was taken to the Soviet Union, where he is still alive (according to McDaniel).

In 1985 the Vietnamese turned over Patterson's military identity and Geneva Convention cards to American MIA investigators. Then, in December 1990, JCRC field teams interviewed witnesses who stated that the same militia unit that captured McDaniel shot Patterson to death. His buried remains were said to have been dug up by animals.[29]

The pattern that emerges from this analysis is that the fate of an airman lost in North Vietnam or Laos during the war was much more a function of the loss location than of the aircraft flown or the man's aircrew specialty. Simply stated, the closer to Hanoi a man was shot down, the better his chances of surviving as a prisoner until the end of the war. Conversely, the further from Hanoi, the more likely the man would disappear as a Missing in Action casualty.

The definitive reasons for this pattern will not be determined without better cooperation from the Vietnamese Communists. However, two factors seem significant. First, villagers or militia in heavily bombed areas, isolated from the stricter discipline of the capital region, no doubt vented their hatred of Americans on their captives more freely than did Vietnamese troops and civilians further north. Secondly, the fact that most men who survived their shootdowns were probably wounded or injured made the long trip to Hanoi perilous, especially if they were given a brutal initial interrogation in the provinces.

But it should be recalled that DIA analysts had long suspected that a small number of airmen with critical technical specialties might not have been repatriated, even though they were known to have been captured alive.[30]

But the actual fates of these missing men—if in fact known—will only be revealed when the government of Vietnam and the PAVN eventually decide to divulge all the information in their massive archives.

CHAPTER 21

THE REVELATIONS OF LIEUTENANT COLONEL NGUYEN VAN THI AND OTHER General Political Directorate officers are interesting, but can only be confirmed by exhaustive archive research and an ambitious program of witness interviews. Those projects will take time, and a much better atmosphere of mutual trust between America and Vietnam.

The GPD's admission of the "darkest secrets" should certainly not be taken as proof positive that no American POWs were transferred from Indochina to the Soviet Union or its Eastern Bloc allies during the war.

For now, however, this is a matter that can only be assessed using the scarce credible information available. And, as with so much else in the larger POW/MIA issue, there has been considerably more heat than light generated on the "Moscow bound" mystery.

Did the Vietnamese turn over American prisoners, especially men with valuable strategic and technical information, to the Soviets?

It is counterintuitive to believe that the large Soviet military assistance program in Indochina during the war—which is now known to have included an active KGB and GRU military intelligence component—was not tasked by Moscow to obtain technical information on American weapons and tactics. This tasking would have focused on new aircraft and weapons that were sometimes deployed to the Vietnam War theater before arriving in the frontline NATO units arrayed against Warsaw Pact forces in Europe. For Soviet military intelligence officers in Indochina *not* to have exploited the information bonanza the American POWs represented would have been tantamount to dereliction of duty.

Every senior American military officer, active-duty or retired, interviewed for this book agrees on this point.[1]

And since the collapse of the Soviet Union, former Soviet officers have confirmed earlier investigative reports that the USSR was heavily involved in the Indochina war.[2] Just before the demise of the Soviet Union, perestroika had reached the point that veterans groups in Moscow were granting Western reporters access to their previously secret Soviet Vietnam Veterans Association, a group of aviators and Air Defense Force, artillery, and GRU military intelligence officers who had performed fraternal "internationalist" duty in Indochina.[3] And despite continued Vietnamese government denials that the

Soviet presence during the war had been minor, recent interviews by American MIA investigators in Russia indicate this presence was large and well organized.[4] Given recent confirmation of this hitherto murky direct Soviet military involvement in the Vietnam War, the question of Moscow's exploitation of American POWs for intelligence purposes becomes clearly relevant.

Moreover, recent revelations of secret Soviet exploitation of American POWs captured during the Korean War requires a serious historical examination of the Indochina-MIA question to focus on the Soviet connection. For years, the Soviets steadfastly denied that they had exploited American POWs during the Korean War. Then, after the collapse of Communism in the USSR, the U.S.-Russian Joint Commission on POWs/MIAs, established to investigate the Soviet-MIA connection, and the Pentagon's investigative support group to the commission, Task Force Russia (TFR), made major breakthroughs on the Korean War MIA mystery.

In November 1993, the Pentagon released a startling document prepared by Task Force Russia, which had been integrated into the Defense POW/MIA Office (DPMO), a new entity that had also absorbed the DIA's Special Office for POW/MIAs. The document, entitled "The Transfer of U.S. Korean War POWs to the Soviet Union," was written by the Joint Commission Support Branch, Research and Analysis Division. Although the Defense Department raised the caveat that this report—which consisted only of "working papers" —had not been confirmed by the Russian co-chairman of the commission, retired General Dmitri Volkogonov, the Pentagon's intent was to publicize the commission's exhaustive and revealing research on this sensitive matter.[5]

The study was the result of extensive interviews of former Soviet officers who had served with Korean Communist forces in the 1950s, with former officers of the State Security Ministry, and with former guards and inmates of Gulag labor camps. Commission researchers also scoured Soviet military and intelligence archives when permitted to do so. The conclusions of the report were shocking:

> **The Soviets transferred several hundred U.S. Korean War POWs to the USSR and did not repatriate them. This transfer was mainly politically motivated with the intent of holding them as political hostages, subjects for intelligence exploitation, and skilled labor within the camp system.[6]**

The report details the rail and sea shipment routes of these unfortunate American POWs to Siberia and then on to Gulag camps in the Komi-Perm National District of the Russian Federated Republic.

The most relevant section of the report for the Indochina experience concerned what Pentagon researchers called "The Soviet Hunt for F-86 Pilots." During the Korean War, the newly introduced F-86 Sabre Jet fighter was the only combat aircraft that had a practical radar gunsight. This technology gave the F-86 a marked advantage over its Soviet rival equivalent, the MiG-15.

To obtain this advanced American technology, secret Soviet Air Force intelligence teams in Korea were tasked to seize captured American F-86 pilots and transport them to the USSR. Using clear statistical analysis, the Pentagon researchers showed that, although most American pilots who survived the harsh life in North Korean and Chinese prison camps were repatriated, there is "almost blatant evidence" that highly skilled F-86 pilots were an exception.

A total of fifty-six F-86 Sabres were shot down during the war, resulting in an estimated forty-seven pilots surviving their loss incidents. But only fifteen F-86 pilot POWs and one pilot's remains were repatriated during the prisoner exchanges in 1953. Thirty-one F-86 captured pilots had disappeared in North Korea.[7]

The Pentagon investigators in Russia discovered strong evidence that these thirty-one American pilot POWs were among the estimated total of 200[8] American prisoners transferred from Korea to the USSR.[8] The Soviets also had a well-organized equipment collection program that eventually transferred a large quantity of American hardware, including a largely intact F-86, to the USSR.

Some of these pilots were interrogated for technical information by the MGB (the predecessor of the KGB) and others by GRU military intelligence. Others were turned over to the Sukhoi and MiG aircraft design bureaus to assist in developing new Soviet fighters and aircraft weapons systems. Still other American aviator POWs (including B-29 radar operators and bombardiers) were shipped to special prison camps within large Soviet military research centers such as the MGB facility at Sary-Shagan to help develop Soviet surface-to-air missiles that could overpower American electronic countermeasures.[9]

Russian sources told the American investigators that, once the POWs were made to realize that they had been irrevocably absorbed into the Soviet Gulag system, they were persuaded to cooperate by a combination of coercion and extended privileges, which included better food and liquor dispensed in "special houses" within the larger camp complex or intelligence center. These prisoners were assigned Slavic names and no record of their captivity as American POWs could be found in former Soviet archives. As former U.S. ambassador to the Soviet Union Malcolm Toon, co-chairman of the joint commission, noted in his transmittal letter to this report, "There is no doubt that further research is essential." This was indeed an understatement. The secret archives of the intricate state security and military intelligence apparatus of the former Soviet Union are so vast and compartmentalized that they hid a large, well-organized prisoner transfer and exploitation program for four decades.[10]

The particular relevance of the Korean War POW transfers to the Indochina war experience is twofold. First, as noted, Soviet security agencies were so closed to outside scrutiny that they managed to effectively keep the prisoner transfer operation secret from foreign espionage penetration. Secondly, the methodical exploitation of advanced American military technology logically indicates that the same pattern of operational conduct by Soviet civilian and military intelligence agencies would have prevailed eleven or twelve years later during the Vietnam War. In other words, if Soviet intelligence viewed American aviators and their equipment as a resource to be exploited in Korea, why wouldn't American POWs in Vietnam have been viewed in the same light?

The answer, however, is not as simple or straightforward as it might seem. The North Korean Communists were a completely docile surrogate of the Soviet Union. And, during the Korean War, the Chinese Communists cooperated fully with their Soviet allies. As the Pentagon study indicates, Chinese military intelligence teams had no qualms about turning over American prisoners to their Russian colleagues. One former Chinese officer, Shu Ping Wa, told the Americans that he had personally handed over three American airmen to the Soviets. "The Russians wanted the pilots," Shu explained.[11]

But the Vietnamese Communists were, by most historic accounts, more independent than either the North Koreans or the Chinese. Further, by the mid-1960s, the great schism had divided the Chinese and the Soviets so that Vietnam could often effectively play one side against the other while attempting to maintain a degree of national sovereignty that had been beyond the reach of the North Koreans during their war.

When the new Soviet premier Aleksei Kosygin met with Vietnamese Communist leaders in Hanoi in 1965, he offered more military aid on the condition that the Vietnamese accept Soviet rather than Chinese policy guidance in their conduct of the war. The Vietnamese rebuffed him in reportedly "stormy" negotiations. One of Kosygin's advisers described the Vietnamese Communists as a "bunch of stubborn bastards."[12]

However, the Democratic Republic of Vietnam did depend to a large degree on Soviet technology for its vital air defense system. By 1967, there were already 800 members of the Soviet Air Defense Forces serving in Vietnam.[13] With Soviet aid, North Vietnamese missile defenses grew inexorably to become one of the most formidable systems in the world by the end of the war. Therefore, it is difficult to accept the more simplistic Vietnamese assurances that Vietnam had successfully rebuffed every insistent Soviet request for access to American prisoners by threatening to play their China card. And it cannot be denied that the Soviets desperately needed a better understanding of the new American aircraft and weapons systems that became operational during the Vietnam War. Several of these aircraft played a strategic and tactical nuclear weapons delivery role in NATO war plans. They included the F-4 Phantom, the A-6 Intruder, the F-111, and, of course, the Strategic Air Command's B-52 intercontinental strategic bomber.

(However, some retired American intelligence officers believe that John Walker, the Soviet Union's spy in the U.S. Navy, could have provided much of this technical intelligence, beginning in the late 1960s, through his access to the secure code rooms of fleet aircraft carriers.)

To meet their intelligence needs, the KGB's First Chief Directorate, responsible for scientific and technical intelligence, and the GRU reportedly launched an elaborate operation to recover American military technology and weapons systems from Southeast Asia. A large volume of American high-technology matériel eventually reached the First Chief Directorate's Department T research institute in Moscow.[14] Arguably, this bonanza of American equipment, which included almost-intact cockpits of advanced aircraft, could be best exploited with the assistance of knowledgeable American prisoners. And since it is known that the equipment was taken to Moscow, it might be assumed that at least some American POWs followed.

Despite the logic of this argument, American researchers from Task Force Russia and the joint commission have not found it easy to investigate Soviet exploitation of American Vietnam War POWs. The problem has not been with the Russian leadership. Boris Yeltsin and the Russian co-chairman of the Joint Commission, General Dmitri Volkogonov, have consistently pledged their full cooperation. Volkogonov reported evidence that 119 American POWs of the Germans in Europe during World War II were held in the Soviet Gulag after the war. By 1992, most were dead, but those still in Russia were not "currently being held against their will."[15]

Yeltsin himself told the Senate Select Committee on POW/MIA Affairs that his government had found evidence of American prisoners from World War II and the Cold War held captive until recently in the Soviet Gulag.[16] He also stated that documents have been unearthed indicating "several U.S. citizens" taken prisoner during the Vietnam War had been held in the USSR.[17]

But, when Task Force Russia later tried to follow up leads in the Russian Ministry of State Security (the successor of the KGB) archives, they frequently found themselves rebuffed when the sensitive subject of Vietnam War transfers was raised. The reception given American investigators by the Russian Army GRU military intelligence archivists was even colder. One American officer working as an interpreter for Task Force Russia, Army Reserve Major Peter C. Johnson, described his Soviet counterparts as a "group of sullen ex-Bolsheviks," who consistently "stonewalled us."[18]

There could be a number of reasons for this lack of cooperation. Certainly members of the former Soviet security services were among the *nomenklatura* elite of their Communist society, and many tend to blame the demise of the Soviet Union on intrigues by Western intelligence agencies. There-fore, these Russian officers were often loath to cooperate with their victori-ous former rivals. Moreover, unlike the retired MGB and GRU officers (and Interior Ministry Gulag guards) who cooperated with the Americans on the investigation of Korean War POW transfers, many of the leaders of the GRU and Russian Ministry of Security (ex-KGB) who might have direct knowledge of Vietnam War transfers are still on active duty and much less likely to reveal secrets than their retired colleagues.

Further, some of the aircraft, strategic weapons procedures, and tactics that would have been exploited by transferring U.S. prisoners from Indo-china to the USSR still play a role in American military war planning. And many Russian officers continue to view NATO and the West as their principal opponents.

Nevertheless, official American investigators from both the joint commis-sion (Task Force Russia) and the Senate select committee have hammered away on the issue of Soviet exploitation of American POWs in Indochina. And eventually these investigators achieved tangible results. Al Graham, a Senate select committee investigator, found evidence that the Soviets did in fact interrogate American prisoners in Vietnam as well as other evidence indicating that "at least a few U.S. POWs may have been transferred to the Soviet Union."[19]

Interviewing members of the Soviet Vietnam Veterans Association, Al Gra-ham and his colleagues were able to determine that Soviet intelligence officers took an active, but indirect role in technical interrogations of Ameri-can POWs in Vietnam. Observing a "noncontact" rule, these Soviet officers reportedly sat behind screens during interrogation sessions meant to extract technical information from lists of questions they had prepared. This prac-tice was no doubt the source of the sophisticated written technical question-naires reported by returned POWs such as Navy Commanders Robert Shumaker and James Mulligan.[20]

(It should be recalled that at least one returned American POW, former Navy pilot James Warner, now an attorney, believes that a small number of collaborators among American prisoners in Hanoi were capable of divulging a relatively large amount of critically important tactical and strategic informa-tion.[21] Now that it has been confirmed that the Soviets had an active technical interrogation program in Hanoi, Warner's opinion acquires new relevance.)

Colonel General Vladimir Abramov, who commanded Soviet forces in Vietnam during the war, told committee investigators that the Vietnamese had provided him with a detailed report on every American airman held prisoner. He also stated that this information might have been forwarded to Moscow. However, in his second interview on June 1, 1992, General Abra-mov abruptly denied having made these statements. It was assumed that he had been coerced to change his statement by Russian security officials.[22]

Clearly, retired and active-duty Russian military intelligence officers and members of the former Soviet security services have more information about the exploitation of American POWs during the Vietnam War than they have publicly admitted to date. But, after the bloody events of the counter-coup in Moscow in October 1993, it became clear that Russian President Boris Yeltsin needed the former Soviet security services (GRU and Ministry of Security) more than they needed him. It is likely that they will resist further admissions for the reasons stated above, and that the relatively weak power of the Russian presidency will be insufficient to pressure these officers to reveal more, no matter how adamantly the American Defense Department protests.

In the face of this resistance, some private American groups have tried to circumvent the government in Moscow and appeal directly to Russian citizens. Accuracy in Media, the conservative watchdog group, placed an advertisement in the Russian newspaper *Nezavisimaya Gazeta (Independent Gazette)* offering a $100,000 reward for information leading to the discovery and release of any survivors of the Soviet shootdown of Korean airliner KAL-007 or "any American military personnel from Vietnam, Korea or from World War II who have been kept as prisoners by the Soviet Union."[23] This and other similar ads might well have sparked much of the cooperation on the Korean War prisoner exploitation and the limited information on the Vietnam War interrogation of American POWs by Soviet officers.

To date, however, no reward money has been paid and no surviving American POW has been found on Russian soil.

But common sense indicates that at least a few American POWs may have been transferred from Indochina to the Soviet Union for intelligence exploitation. Unfortunately, as with the equally tantalizing issue of American POWs held after the war in Laos, there has been widespread irresponsible speculation on the "Moscow bound" prisoner-transfer issue.

The general pattern of this activity has been to incorporate scattered and inconclusive intelligence reports into plausible theories masquerading as definitive proof that American prisoners were transferred from Vietnam to the Soviet Bloc.

What makes such accounts compelling to activists is that they are built on credible evidence that the Soviet Union definitely did detain American prisoners after World War II, during the Cold War, and of course, as recently revealed, during the Korean War. Unfortunately, while some accounts are accurate for the earlier incidents, they slide into unsubstantiated speculation and sensationalism when they treat the Vietnam War.

John M.G. Brown's recent book *Moscow Bound* has been criticized for this shortcoming. Brown relies on solid documentation for proof of Soviet exploitation of American POWs in the 1940s and 1950s, but uses less rigorous standards to support his thesis that large numbers of American POWs were siphoned away from Indochina to disappear into the Soviet Gulag.[24]

In a similar manner, the section on Indochina in *Soldiers of Misfortune* relies on discredited sources to document the transfer of American POWs to the USSR during the Vietnam War. One of the more disreputable of these sources is the bogus escaped "POW" Larry Pistilli. Although Pistilli is cited as having been a shadowy Special Operations commando who escaped from a prison camp near Vinh run by Soviet and Chinese officers, his actual military record proves that he never served in Vietnam, but was rather a radio repairman in an Army signal company in Korea.[25]

Advocates of the Soviet POW transfer theory continued to rely on Pistilli's wild tale as proof that Soviet and Chinese interrogators selected American POWs for transfer out of Vietnam.[26] Once such *proof* enters the POW/MIA activist fund-raising and newsletter system, however, it tends to acquire the validity of historic truth. And when Pentagon investigators debunk fabrications such as Pistilli's, this in itself gives credibility to the false accounts among the more extreme conspiracy theorists. In this regard, the phenomenon is analogous to similar episodes in the endless John F. Kennedy assassination investigations.[27]

Unfortunately, there appear to be even more Larry Pistillis circulating at the grassroots level of the POW/MIA activist movement than achieve national prominence. Retired Air Force Colonel Ben Pollard, who was a POW in Vietnam for six years and is a former president of the group NAM-POW, an association of former prisoners, states that the phenomenon of bogus Vietnam War POWs is widespread. Pollard also believes that these frauds greatly distort the historic record.[28]

Colonel Pollard's assessment is borne out by the record. Texas Vietnam Veterans Memorial Fund co-chairman B.G. Burkett has uncovered bogus escaped POWs similar to Larry Pistilli in many parts of the United States. One of the most ludicrous is Joel Jay "Doc" Furlett, who claimed to have escaped from Son Tay Prison and crawled across North Vietnam dragging a wounded comrade on his back, winning a chestful of valorous decorations in the process. Furlett's record reveals he had never served in Vietnam, and in fact, had spent less than a year in the Navy, all at the Great Lakes Naval Training Center in Illinois.[29] Yet Furlett was lecturing widely to student groups on his POW experience until he was debunked.[30] When confronted with his actual record, Furlett claims that the documents from St. Louis referred to a cousin of the same name and that Furlett's true service record had been altered in a vast conspiracy by the federal government and chemical companies to punish him for exposing the dangers of Agent Orange, the defoliant used in Vietnam.[31]

Such bogus POWs, often claiming to have been psychologically traumatized by their experience, are becoming a well-known phenomenon among mental health professionals treating veterans.[32] They would be a relatively harmless phenomenon if it weren't for the distortion of the historic record that invariably results from their deception.

The mischief caused by such deceptions is difficult to assess. But it is known that such lies have helped perpetuate an important POW/MIA sub-myth generally known as the "Black Cowboy" theory, which in turn is often connected to Moscow-bound allegations. Various groups and individuals, including retired Air Force General Thomas Lacy, have suggested that several thousand "black" (secret) Special Operations soldiers and agents were lost as either POWs or MIAs in Indochina.[33] Given the supposedly sensitive nature of these men's assignments, some theories hold that they were transported in large numbers to the Soviet Union, where attempts were made to "turn" many against their country.[34] The Pentagon and retired senior officers of obvious integrity familiar with the issue adamantly deny that there were American Special Operations forces or civilian agents lost in Indochina but not carried on official lists.[35]

In 1992, the Moscow connection acquired a new and sensational dimension when retired KGB Major General Oleg Danilovich Kalugin made widely publicized allegations that Soviet intelligence officers had interrogated American POWs in Vietnam years after all were supposedly released during Operation Homecoming. Kalugin was a convincing figure, fluent in English and dapperly dressed in expensive suits. He barnstormed the American talk-show circuit promoting the CNN book on the failed August 1991 Communist coup that triggered the final collapse of the Soviet Union. Kalugin was also searching for a publisher for his memoirs of the KGB.[36]

The charge that American POWs underwent KGB interrogation in Vietnam after the war was the most controversial of several revelations Kalugin made during his media tour. Specifically, Kalugin alleged that a former colleague, Colonel Oleg Nechiporenko, interrogated at least three American POWs in Hanoi between 1975 and 1978.

This sensational allegation was seized on by many who suspected that not only had Vietnam retained American prisoners after the war, but also that Hanoi had helped the Soviets exploit them. Advocates of this view connected Kalugin's assertion to the testimony of PAVN defector Bui Tin, who had told the Senate select committee that Soviet officers had interrogated American prisoners with expertise in electronics "around December 1972."[37] It appeared that Kalugin was providing smoking-gun evidence that linked Soviet involvement with live POWs after the war.

However, when Colonel Oleg Nechiporenko was interviewed on NBC-TV's *Today* show, he contradicted Kalugin, stating that he had interviewed only one American, and that was before Operation Homecoming in 1973. On his second trip to Vietnam in 1976, Nechiporenko added, he was "only working with some information," not in direct contact with Americans.[38]

It is possible that both Kalugin and his colleague were telling the truth as they recalled events. The U.S. government has always conceded that one American POW, reputedly a CIA officer, was interviewed by a KGB officer just before Operation Homecoming in 1973. Further, it is known that a CIA officer who used the work name Lew James was captured in the town of

Phan Rang during the collapse of South Vietnam in April 1975. James was taken to the North and brutally interrogated before his release at the end of October that year. The CIA stated that James was not interrogated by the Soviets. But relevant information extracted from James's interrogations could have been provided to Nechiporenko a few months later in 1976.[39]

Although it is possible that Kalugin was telling the truth, the U.S. government has no record of any American POWs returning from Vietnam after Operation Homecoming. And records indicate the last of the civilian detainees taken in the fall of Saigon returned in August 1978.[40]

Czechoslovak defector Major General Jan Sejna, who fled to the West in 1968, is also highly regarded among those trying to establish proof of prisoner transfers to the Soviet Union from Indochina. General Sejna testified in a Senate select committee deposition and stated in interviews that he had personal knowledge of as many as ninety American POWs transferred to the Soviet Union via Prague in the mid-1960s. Sejna also alleged that he had information about secret medical experiments conducted on American POWs in Korea.

However, Sejna avoided open testimony to the committee.

And when Sejna's allegations were made public, the Pentagon sought to undercut his statement. In a declassified formerly secret memorandum provided to committee investigators, the CIA commented on Sejna's background and assertions. The memo noted that he was a political officer attached to the Czechoslovak General Staff, whose specialty was Communist Party matters. During his post-defection debriefing, Sejna reportedly admitted he had no hard information on intelligence matters.[41]

A comprehensive review of CIA files on Sejna, furthermore, "revealed that, at no time did Sejna tell the CIA about U.S. POWs, a hospital in Korea, medical experiments on U.S. POWs, or about U.S. POWs having been moved from Indochina to the USSR in any timeframe."[42]

In addition, the memo noted Sejna's specific response to inquiries about POWs during his post-defection debriefing. The document provided an excerpt from the tape-recorded debriefing of March 23, 1968:

Debriefer: Have you heard about our prisoners who are there in Vietnam? How many are there and where are they?
Sejna: No. No, I have not heard anyone talking about it. (*Ja jsem neslysel nikoho o tom hovorit.*)[43]

Another allegation of an East European–Soviet connection emerged in 1993, but was quickly refuted. Declassified State Department telegrams from 1967 revealed that an East German lawyer, Wolfgang Vogel, offered to facilitate an exchange of American Vietnam War POWs undergoing medical treatment in East Germany for Communist spies imprisoned in the West. But when contacted by journalists, Vogel admitted that he was mistaken and that no American POWs were held in East German hospitals. General Markus Wolf, head of East German foreign espionage, also told journalists that there were never any American POWs held in East Germany. And the list of American POWs supposedly available for exchange names men who were held in North Vietnam and repatriated during Operation Homecoming.[44]

One of the best known adherents of POW transfers to the Soviet Union is retired U.S. Air Force Senior Master Sergeant Jerry Mooney, an enlisted intelligence analyst who performed three tours of duty with the National Security Agency and was engaged in signals intelligence surveillance at various times during his career. Mooney has repeatedly alleged that he had seen intelligence data that a number of American prisoners in Indochina fell into Soviet hands and were transported to the Soviet Union.[45] Mooney stated under oath in an affidavit that U.S. intelligence analysts tracked certain downed American aviators under the category "MB (Moscow Bound)." He also stated that an extensive cover-up ("a Bamboo Curtain") existed within the U.S. government as part of a conspiracy to abandon Americans who might have fallen into Soviet hands. He felt this was particularly relevant to the fate of the crew of an EC-47Q electronic intelligence aircraft shot down over Laos on February 5, 1973, a week after the signing of the Paris Peace Accords.[46]

But when Mooney testified before the Senate Select Committee on POW/ MIA Affairs, he denied any direct knowledge of a "Moscow Bound" route for American POWs from Indochina to the USSR as he had often earlier alleged. He testified that he "saw no evidence that they [American POWs] went to the Soviet Union." He added that he believed they had been taken there, but could provide no conclusive proof.[47]

Mooney's two-day deposition to the Senate Select Committee on POW/ MIA Affairs is even more revealing than his testimony in open hearings. Questioned by Committee Chief Counsel William Codinha, Mooney admitted that his "Moscow Bound" and "China Bound" lists had been unofficial documents, in effect personal musings written in a notebook, which had been based mainly on speculation, not substantive intelligence data.[48] In 1992, Mooney was able to offer the Senate select committee a "reconstructed list" of those missing Americans he considered to have been Moscow or China "Bound," in 1972, but he admitted under questioning that this reconstruction had not been based on any official intelligence data, but rather on "about four and a half years of thinking about it."[49]

Nevertheless, Mooney is quoted in speculative accounts in which he provides plausible-sounding information supposedly based on extensive signals intelligence intercepts that detail prisoner transfers to the Soviet Union, citing dates, places of embarkation, and aircraft type.[50]

Another former American noncommissioned officer with a background in intelligence, Barry Toll, also made dramatic allegations about POW transfers to the Soviet Union. Had he been able to substantiate his assertions,

Barry Toll would have become famous, and in the process unearthed a truly monstrous conspiracy meant to cover up the abandonment of hundreds of American POWs in Indochina and the transfer of many of them to the Soviet Bloc.

Barry Toll arrived on the POW/MIA scene in the summer of 1992, when he contacted Senator Kerry, chairman of the Senate Select Committee on POW/MIA Affairs. Toll sent Kerry a long statement detailing sensational charges that the highest levels of the American government had been aware of up to 340 American POWs held in Laos after Operation Homecoming in 1973. He also accused the Pentagon's highest intelligence offices and the Nixon and Ford White Houses of suppressing concrete information on flights from Indochina in which American POWs were transferred to the USSR and the Soviet Bloc between 1973 and 1975.[51]

What made Toll's dramatic accusations significant was the fact that he had served as an intelligence staff sergeant in an elite unit assigned to the World Wide Military Command and Control System's Airborne Command Post, under the Commander-in-Chief, Atlantic, at Langley Air Force Base, Virginia, from June 1973 until July 1975. The team on which Toll was a junior member was one of several charged with around-the-clock duty to administer the "Doomsday" orders under the Single Integrated Operational Plan (SIOP) in the event of nuclear war. In this capacity, Toll's team allegedly received sensitive, high-level intelligence from U.S. government sources worldwide. These intelligence bulletins were part of daily updates to be used in strategic decision-making in the event of sudden nuclear war.[52]

Barry Toll claimed that he "personally saw, distributed and briefed high-ranking officers of the Joint Staff, on intelligence reports, analyses and operations regarding the transfer of U.S. POWs and/or MIAs from the custody of North Vietnamese or Laotian authorities through Soviet Bloc nations, or directly into the USSR."[53]

Toll further stated that it was "the considered opinion of the Joint Chiefs of Staff and the entire U.S. intelligence community" that there were an estimated 290 to 340 U.S. POWs alive in Laos after Operation Homecoming. He stated that he specifically recalled this information, as well as reports on the transfers of U.S. POWs to the Soviet Bloc, was included in the President's Daily Intelligence Briefing agenda on more than one occasion between 1973 and 1975. Toll said he personally recalled up to five occasions when American intelligence agencies tracked the "real-time movements" of Soviet and Eastern Bloc aircraft carrying American POWs out of Indochina.[54]

He provided detailed descriptions of these flights, which he said included diplomatic courier trips and on two occasions used the presence of an East European ambassador to North Vietnam as cover for the transfer of American POWs. And on one occasion, he said, the U.S. military made an attempt to intercept and force down one of these aircraft believed to be carrying

American POWs out of Indochina. But the plane "fled into Soviet air space at the approach of U.S. intercept aircraft, and the attempt was abandoned."[55]

Toll stated that it was his knowledge of the cover-up of these events by the American intelligence community and two presidential administrations that drove him to request immediate relief from duties that resulted in his discharge from the Army in August 1975.

In view of these sensational charges, the Senate select committee assigned one of its most capable and experienced investigators, Army warrant officer Steve Gekoski. He was a Criminal Investigation Division special agent at Fort Meade, Maryland, who had handled many sensitive cases involving the National Security Agency, espionage, and counterintelligence.[56]

Gekoski patiently tracked down most of Toll's former enlisted and officer colleagues. None of these officers or NCOs recalled seeing any of the message traffic that Toll claimed described surviving POWs or transfers of prisoners from Indochina to the Eastern Bloc or Soviet Union.[57]

Gekoski's investigation also revealed that Toll never mentioned the alleged conspiracy as the reason for his request for discharge from the Army. Rather, Toll had gone Absent Without Leave (AWOL) from his duty station during the period July 3 to 9, 1975. This was a serious infraction for someone in his position, which was covered by the military's Personnel Responsibility Program (PRP). Personnel serving under the restrictions of the PRP, who include those responsible for strategic nuclear weapons and extremely sensitive intelligence, are automatically suspended from duty and subject to criminal investigation for infractions such as going AWOL. It was clear that Toll's period of AWOL would have disqualified him from further service on the SIOP Battle Staff.[58]

Gekoski further discovered that Toll was under active investigation by the Defense Intelligence Agency before having gone AWOL. Although the DIA did not reveal the exact nature of this investigation, Gekoski surmised that it was connected to Toll's increasingly unstable behavior. Toll's emotional problems, Gekoski discovered, had come to a head in the summer of 1975. As a combat veteran of the Vietnam War, Toll had been treated for "a traumatic war neurosis" before July 1975, and had manifested symptoms of that disorder when interviewed by an Army psychiatrist after requesting release from military service.[59]

Attorney J. Lawrence Wright, who represented Barry Toll on the AWOL charges that led to his discharge from the Army in 1975, clearly recalled the incident in correspondence to the Senate select committee, which included a sworn affidavit describing the events. Wright, a former combat infantry officer in Vietnam, wrote committee investigator Robert Taylor that Toll's "reasons for wanting to leave the Army were complex," and might have included national security "and maybe even POW/MIA issues." However, Wright found these points irrelevant to his client's case, which concerned a smooth and unencumbered discharge. Wright confirmed that Toll was under investigation by the Defense Intelligence Agency at the time.[60]

In his affidavit, Wright also stated that Toll was particularly affected by the fall of South Vietnam to the Communists and the Khmer Rouge victory in Cambodia, which precipitated the notorious genocide. Wright cited Toll's "overwhelming belief that the Administration was lying to the American people," and noted that Toll "said he could no longer serve in the military. More precisely, he could not continue as part of the direct Chain of Command."[61] Wright also noted that another reason for Toll's request for a discharge "had to do with secret documents and transmissions that Staff Sergeant Toll had seen but could not disclose to me."[62]

It is unlikely that Wright would have forgotten detailed accusations about multiple transfer flights of American POWs from Indochina to the Soviet Union, if in fact Toll had discussed this with his military counsel as he later claimed while defending his position.[63] Toll also claimed to have discussed this issue with a number of relatives and prison psychologists. (In 1976, Barry Toll was arrested for conspiracy to smuggle cocaine and served two years in state and federal prisons in Michigan.[64]) Committee investigators Steve Gekoski and Robert Taylor were unable to corroborate Toll's assertions with any of the sources he cited.[65]

During Steve Gekoski's and the select committee counsels' exhaustive investigation of Barry Toll, they encountered some other unusual aspects of Toll's background. Among these was Toll's statement that convicted Soviet spy John Walker, then a retired Navy warrant officer, might have tried to recruit Toll for his espionage ring. Toll later pursued the Walker spy ring allegation by contacting the FBI in September 1986, offering to provide information about Walker. In a phone conversation on September 11, 1986, Tampa, Florida, FBI Special Agent E.S. O'Keefe, Jr., spoke with Toll about this matter. Toll stated that he left the U.S. Army after "flipping out" and receiving psychiatric treatment. Toll also told O'Keefe he actually had no information that John Walker had ever tried to recruit him, "or otherwise engage him in his [Walker's] espionage ring."[66]

(Toll also later began telling journalists and claiming on computer bulletin boards that he had been on secret reconnaissance missions as a member of the elite covert operations branch of the American military in Vietnam, MACV-SOG, and had served as an intelligence officer at the American embassy in Bangkok.[67])

Gekoski eventually reached the conclusion that Barry Toll was a deluded self-promoter, possibly motivated by a desire to create a smokescreen of sensational charges to disguise the true circumstances of his discharge from the Army and his later drug conviction. This inference was bolstered during one interview when Toll gave Gekoski a disjointed and rambling account of his service on the Battle Staff of the Airborne Command Post. Toll said that he had received calls directly from Richard Nixon while the president was "dead drunk," ordering Toll to prepare for an immediate nuclear attack on the Soviet Union.[68]

During his deposition to the select committee, Toll did not reiterate this particular bizarre charge. But he did discuss equally strange events. Toll stated that during the 1973 October War in the Middle East, the Airborne Command Post staff received repeated messages from members of President Nixon's cabinet "telling us not to obey a nuclear execution order from the president." This, Toll testified, was "virtually treasonous and unconstitutional, but this was the pervasive atmosphere of circus and theatrics going on in the Nixon administration."[69]

Even though Barry Toll continues to be one of the most consistently cited "intelligence experts" among radical POW/MIA activists, select committee Vice Chairman Senator Bob Smith, not a man to shy away from controversial figures, has distanced himself from Toll. Commenting on Toll's revelations, Senator Smith said: "It was a single source thing. I don't rule it out." But Smith concluded, "Without documents, it's very hard."[70]

Select committee investigator Robert Taylor, however, feels that Toll's allegations have not been fully investigated. The CIA denied committee investigators access to its Executive Registry Files, which would have contained message traffic that Toll claimed described the POW transfer flights. And the agency's President's Morning Briefs were made available only in executive summary form for Senators Kerry and Smith.[71] Nevertheless, retired intelligence officers familiar with these matters state that the summaries of White House morning intelligence briefs that the two senators were shown would definitely have contained references to POW transfer flights, had they been tracked.

Toll became one of the new stars in the activists' constellation of martyrs, men who had tried but failed to expose the vast government conspiracy to hide the shameful truth that America had knowingly abandoned hundreds of prisoners in Indochina. (By the summer of 1993, Barry Toll and Colonel Mike Peck were appearing together as members of a new activist splinter group called Valor, whose objective was to present their revelations of this conspiracy to the American public.[72])

THE FACT THAT there have been several dubious attempts to document Soviet abduction of American POWs from Indochina should not be cited as proof that such a program never existed. Many bona fide intelligence experts believe that the Soviet Union and its Eastern Bloc allies did in fact remove some American prisoners from Indochina during the war. But because no conclusive evidence of this has emerged in the former Soviet Union, these experts also believe that the program was probably small and highly compartmentalized.

Army Major Ralph Peters of Task Force Russia stated that his unit had only found a few shadowy indications—not documentary evidence—that "perhaps one, two, or three very high-skill" American POWs had been taken from Indochina to the Soviet Union.[73] But he added that there was ample evidence that the Soviets simply did not have the same degree of leverage over the North Vietnamese Communists as they had over the North Koreans.

Peters's Task Force Russia colleague, translator-interpreter Major Pete Johnson, confirmed Peters's view that the evidence was sketchy at best. But Johnson said the number of "high-skill" American POWs who might have been abducted by the Russians from Indochina could have totaled as many as ten. However, he stressed, there was simply no concrete proof of this. And Johnson was convinced that the new Russian Ministry of Security was destroying embarrassing files on POW/MIA matters.[74]

If this is true, the United States may never discover the actual fate of any American prisoners who were taken to the Soviet Union from Indochina to be exploited by the Soviets.

Army Major William Burkett, whose responsibilities for the new Defense Prisoner of War/Missing in Action Office (DPMO) include ongoing investigations in former Soviet archives, further confirms Peters's and Johnson's assessment that "a very small number" of high-skill POWs *might* have been transferred from Indochina to the Soviet Union. He states that the DPMO "has not completely ruled out the possibility that some prisoners were transferred." However, Burkett adds, American investigators have not yet unearthed any direct evidence of such transfers. But the Americans are now asking "much more pointed questions" of the former Soviet security services, including non-Russian organizations in the former Soviet republics. He is hopeful that this line of inquiry will eventually bear fruit.[75]

Former Soviet Air Force fighter pilot Alexander Zuyev believes that Soviet military intelligence exploited American POWs from Indochina in the Soviet Union. Zuyev was a pilot in the first Soviet Air Force regiment to become operational with the MiG-29 Fulcrum advanced fighter.

While undergoing combat-readiness testing with his fighter regiment at the large Soviet Air Force base at Mary in Central Asia, Zuyev asked a nuclear weapons officer the origin of the unique dual-channel-code arming procedure for tactical nuclear bombs. The officer told him that the Soviet forces had adopted this system in the 1970s from similar American techniques.

"The American methods, we obtained from several U.S. Air Force 'guests,' nuclear-qualified pilots our fraternal Socialist comrades in Vietnam provided us during that Imperialist war."[76]

Zuyev questioned the officer to be sure these exploited American POWs had actually been taken to the Soviet Union, not just interrogated in Vietnam. The officer assured him that they had been transported to the USSR.[77]

In 1989, Zuyev defected from his base in Soviet Georgia, flying a MiG-29 to Turkey.

Given this specific reference to an officer and a unit who had such detailed information, the United States intelligence services or civilian POW/MIA investigators should be able to make direct, focused inquiries with the GRU on this matter. And the American government should use every means at its disposition to obtain answers.

CHAPTER 22

By LATE SEPTEMBER 1992, TED SCHWEITZER HAD SUCCESSFULLY scanned and stored in his database several thousand documents and photographs relating to the American air war in North Vietnam. More than fifty of these documents contained specific information about missing Americans. Often the records bore the grim notice: "Killed, body not yet recovered from wreckage."

In addition, he had obtained multiple photographs of eight dead Americans previously listed as MIA and one of a KIA/BNR case. He also had scanned and photographed military ID and Geneva Convention cards for these men, as well as for another ten MIA cases. These records, photographs, and artifacts spanned both the geographic and chronological dimensions of the air war in North Vietnam. Even though the number of photographs and artifacts was relatively small, the existence of such definitive and detailed information signified that, without question, the PAVN controlled much more elaborate archives than they had ever admitted.

Schweitzer had also purchased over 3,000 additional photographs from other Vietnamese sources during this period. Many of them were stock propaganda shots, simply transferred from the military photo morgue of the Vietnam News Service. The DIA understood that purchasing these innocuous pictures was a way of spreading some of the "publisher's" largess among the museum's GPD colleagues while simultaneously providing the Vietnamese with a suitably convincing matrix in which to insert important photos such as those of Morrison.

Some of the propaganda pictures showed predictable scenes of village militia grouped in heroic poses around the wreckage of American aircraft.

Other pictures, however, were much more significant, although the Vietnamese might not have recognized the nature of the information they were divulging. Pictures of the carefully stacked flight and survival equipment of an American F-105 pilot shot down in March 1967, Captain Joseph J. Karins, Jr., indicated that he had landed safely by parachute. The tropical Air Force flight suit was not bloodstained. The parachute canopy was billowed in a manner suggesting it had been fully deployed, and there was no fire damage to the empty boots or other personal equipment. Yet Karins had not been repatriated in 1973. In 1988, his remains were returned following a visit to Vietnam by General Vessey's delegation. The Vietnamese provided no explanation of the circumstances of Karins's death. Yet this photograph indicated that he might have been among the executed victims of the "darkest secret," which Nguyen Van Thi had revealed to Schweitzer.

Although the Vietnamese might have believed they were selling a gullible American worthless photographs, many of the pictures revealed important information about the treatment of missing American airmen.

Schweitzer realized that thorough scrutiny of all these thousands of pictures by skilled analysts at the DIA might reveal considerably more information about the circumstances of death of many Americans whose remains had already been repatriated, as well as provide evidence that the Vietnamese might still possess the remains of some missing airmen. In fact, a debate arose within the DIA over the potential value of such pictures. Some members of the Operations Directorate believed that there was much to be gleaned from photos such as that of Karins's captured equipment and clothing. But a faction among the analysts of the Intelligence Directorate discounted the value of these pictures, possibly from not-invented-here jealousy.[1]

The DIA's Special Office for POW/MIAs certainly found the Swamp Ranger pictures and documents (as well as those from the smaller, parallel Druid Smoke effort) to be valuable. But finally obtaining this sampling of important material after so many years of adamant denial that it existed angered and outraged many of the intelligence analysts.

In analytical notes on the photographs of Major Joseph Morrison's body, and the pictures of Morrison and his crewmate, Lieutenant Francisco's, identity documents the DIA prepared for further negotiations with the Vietnamese, the agency noted bitterly that "we requested information on the fate of Maj. Morrison and 1st Lt. Francisco at least 11 times." These requests began at the first Four-Party Joint Military Commission meeting in April 1973 and spanned almost twenty years of contact with the Vietnamese Communists, including an April 1991 meeting between General Vessey and Vietnamese Foreign Minister Nguyen Co Thach (Nguyen Manh Cam's predecessor). The JCRC also conducted four field investigations of the Morrison-Francisco case. On one list of graves of U.S. pilots in PAVN Military Region 4, Morrison and Francisco were listed under the category "Air Pirates Killed and Torn Apart," which implied there were no remains available.[2]

The analysts' bitter conclusions could have been an overall commentary on the long-held Vietnamese policy of denying Americans readily available information on MIAs:

- We have now located a photograph showing Maj Morrison's remains and showing material effects belonging to both Maj Morrison and 1st Lt Francisco.

- This is one of the most troubling photos we found.
   —Clearly the Vietnamese government has known the fate of both these men since the time of their loss.
   —Because Maj Morrison's family was not given these photos earlier, his loved ones have suffered years of uncertainty.
   —Maj Morrison's family wants very much to bring his remains back to the U.S. for burial.
   —1st Lt Francisco's family has urgent questions as to his fate.[3]

This was a direct challenge to the Vietnamese to deliver Joseph Morrison's remains and to reveal details of Lieutenant Francisco's death.

In using Schweitzer and Operation Swamp Ranger as the conduit to deliver the photographs of Morrison dead on the jungle mountainside and the pictures of the two airmen's personal possessions, the PAVN had tacitly—but confidentially—admitted that they had controlled both sets of remains in 1968. Clearly any implementation of the "full cooperation" that Party General Secretary Do Muoi had promised the Kerry delegation in April would, at a minimum, entail meeting the requests in this revised negotiation document.

Colonel Dai, however, had repeatedly warned Schweitzer that belligerent wording such as these notes in the revised Morrison negotiation folder—"aggressive tactics"—would be met with equally aggressive countertactics. The PAVN General Political Directorate was determined that this accounting would be made in a manner that did not entail an unacceptable loss of face. They were adamant that transfers of relevant MIA information could only continue through Schweitzer's back-channel conduit.

But the Pentagon's POW/MIA office and the JTF/FA it supported did not take this PAVN requirement into consideration. The official American researchers seemed determined to rub the General Political Directorate's collective nose in their past duplicity. This was a mistake that would prove disastrous. The official American response to the initial Operation Swamp Ranger "product" would soon lead to the closing of the effective back channel that Schweitzer and the DIA's Operations Directorate had so skillfully opened.

In the revised negotiation analysis of the Swamp Ranger photograph of Lieutenant Gilbert Mitchell, the DIA noted that the Vietnamese had earlier mistakenly identified repatriated remains of Mitchell as those of his crewmate, Lieutenant Commander Richard Nelson. But this clear photograph of Mitchell's intact body in the muddy crater showed that both sets of remains "were under your control at the loss site." The negotiation folder notes concluded:

- We have these obvious concerns:
  —We are disappointed the Vietnamese have not given us this photo before, along with information associated with it.
  —It is unfortunate also that the Vietnamese have not returned the remains of LCDR Mitchell, which were apparently stored as LCDR Nelson.[4]

This reference to stored human remains was intended to set the official record straight as to this flagrant contradiction to publicly stated Vietnamese policy. Further, the message would serve as formal notice that the U.S. government expected these and other sets of remains to be repatriated.

The tone of frustrated indignation continued in subsequent negotiation folder notes based on the Swamp Ranger and Druid Smoke photographs.

The photograph of Air Force Major Marvin Lindsey, who was shot down south of Hanoi in 1965, was troubling. In the revised negotiation document based on this picture, the DIA reminded the Vietnamese that Americans had requested information on the case repeatedly since 1973, including six discussions during periods of allegedly increased cooperation, which involved technical discussions between the JCRC and the VNOSMP on resolution of MIA cases for humanitarian reasons. Lindsey's crash site had been identified and witnesses interviewed, who stated his body had been buried nearby.

Then documents appeared indicating Lindsey had been captured alive, but the VNOSMP rejected this analysis. The Swamp Ranger photographs of Lindsey, however, did support the analysis that he had been alive on the ground, but subsequently shot. He is shown lying on his right side, his flight suit unzipped, his T-shirt soaked with blood from apparent bullet wounds to the thorax. Since he was not wearing a parachute harness or survival vest, it was possible that Major Lindsey had been shot after capture.

Once more, evidence analyzed from the photographs and documents Ted Schweitzer had obtained from the PAVN tended to confirm the "darkest secret" assertion that a number of Americans had been killed by Vietnamese forces before they reached the central prison system in Hanoi.

"Please help us to understand your past reluctance to share relevant photographic and other documentary evidence with us," DIA analysts wrote in the revised Lindsey negotiation folder notes. They concluded with an open challenge: "Considering the extensive wartime effort made to document the death [sic] of American casualties, as evidenced by these photos, we are unable to understand your inability to repatriate the remains of Major Lindsey."[5]

The Swamp Ranger photographs and detailed records from the PAVN museum archives documented beyond any doubt that Vietnam had withheld information about American MIAs for years, and clearly had more information about the disposition of MIA remains than it had ever previously acknowledged.

Some of the most intriguing photographs and documents obtained during Operation Swamp Ranger concerned the loss of advanced F-111 strategic bombers and the fate of their crews. Eight of the controversial, swing-wing bombers were shot down over North Vietnam during the war with the loss of crewmen captured or missing.[6] Four of these losses occurred during the Linebacker I and II operations in 1972. Earlier F-111 losses often involved failure of the terrain-following radar equipment that allowed the planes to fly "nape of the earth" missions. Despite technical problems, the F-111 was the most advanced operational combat aircraft flying in 1972. Obviously the Soviets were interested in gleaning as much technology as possible from the F-111s shot down in Indochina.[7]

When Ted Schweitzer had first reported an F-111 wing among the aircraft wreckage surrounding the concrete plinth of the triumphant MiG-21 display in the PAVN museum, the DIA had tasked him to discreetly search the slab of debris for any serial numbers on subcomponents. The wing was identified as part of the wreckage of the F-111 crippled by groundfire over central Hanoi on the night of December 22, 1972.

This aircraft had been flown by Captain Robert Sponeyberger and Lieutenant William Wilson. They managed to fly on one engine to the mountains fifty miles west of Hanoi, where they ejected. Their aircraft was equipped with a modular escape capsule, basically a detachable cockpit in which both crewmen remained strapped while descending under a single large, cargo-type parachute. Although both airmen evaded the enemy for several days in the jungle hills, they were eventually captured. Both were repatriated during Operation Homecoming. Schweitzer obtained several PAVN records documenting the shootdown and capture of Sponeyberger and Wilson.[8]

Later in 1992, investigators from Task Force Russia photographed an F-111 escape capsule on display at the Moscow Aviation Institute. The capsule's serial number had one obscured digit that could have referred to either the Sponeyberger-Wilson aircraft or to an F-111 shot down in Laos near North Vietnam on November 7, 1972. This plane had been flown by Air Force Majors Robert M. Brown and Robert D. Morrissey.

Although the DIA analysis of the Brown-Morrissey crash indicated that their plane's escape capsule had not separated and that both men were considered "poor candidates for survival," their fates had been the subject of considerable speculation among POW/MIA activists since the late 1980s.

Former Air Force intelligence NCO Jerry Mooney had reportedly tracked the capture of Brown and Morrissey through radio intercepts and also received information that they had been flown to the Soviet Union.[9] After his retirement from the Air Force, Mooney seemed to acquire more and more detailed information about specific radio intercepts he had analyzed more than fifteen years before. However, as noted, when asked under oath if his "Moscow Bound" speculation had been part of official American intelligence community analyses, Mooney equivocated and admitted this had been only personal conjecture.[10]

Nevertheless, the DIA considered it important to determine whether the Moscow F-111 escape capsule came from the November 7 or the December 22, 1972, F-111 shootdown.

The thousands of documents Schweitzer had obtained from the PAVN archives included detailed records of several F-111 losses. One was the October 17, 1972, shootdown over Hoa Binh Province, in which Captain James Hockridge and Lieutenant Alan Graham had been killed. Their remains were repatriated in 1977. Among the artifacts from this incident Schweitzer photographed were military ID cards belonging to the two airmen. Both were fire-damaged, as were other documents recovered from the escape capsule.[11]

One intriguing photograph from the seemingly unimportant Swamp Ranger collection showed the assembled contents of an F-111 escape capsule. Airmen's personal kneeboards (used for navigation and communications notes), flight manuals, flashlights, and a tactical aerial navigation chart were displayed against the folds of a large parachute. The personal equipment, flight manuals, and documents were in pristine condition. They bore no sign of fire or water damage; none were bloodstained. It was initially thought that this was material recovered from Wilson and Sponeyberger's F-111 escape capsule. But then a DIA analyst noted the date on the back of the picture: "18-12-72 F-111A 233."

This correlated to the December 18, 1972, shootdown of the F-111A flown by Air Force Lieutenant Colonel Ronald Ward and Major James R. McElvain. Their bomber, call sign Snug 40, was lost the first night of the Linebacker II bombing, after attacking the Hanoi International Radio complex. Snug 40 had "skied" down the Annamite Mountains from the west, flying at near-supersonic speed, but using terrain-following radar to maintain an altitude of less than 200 feet above ground level. After dropping their bombs, Lieutenant Colonel Ward made his scheduled radio call at 8:53 P.M. (2053 hours): "Snug four zero, off target."[12]

At 9:00 P.M., the 7th Air Force Joint Rescue Co-ordinating Center relayed a normal report that Snug 40 was over water. This shifted Search and Rescue responsibility to naval units in the Tonkin Gulf. But when the aircraft failed to return to its base in Thailand, a review of the radio communications could not clearly determine whether Snug 40 had actually crossed the coast, or if the crew had simply called their intention of doing so.[13]

Search and Rescue efforts were fruitless. No emergency beepers or personal radio distress calls were heard from the crew. However, SAR forces were busy that first night of the Linebacker II bombing, tracking crippled B-52 bombers.

Over the years, the JCRC requested information on Ward and McElvain from the Vietnamese, but received no response.

Now this single picture of undamaged personal and flight equipment from an F-111 escape capsule raised the clear possibility that the two men had ejected and landed unhurt on the ground. Unlike the material from the Hockridge-Graham aircraft, these items were completely unblemished. Most revealing were the airmen's kneeboards, flashlights, and small items from survival vests. It was improbable that this was a photograph of the Sponeyberger-Wilson escape module's contents. They would not have left behind flashlights, maps, and survival ration pouches while they evaded capture in the mountains.[14]

Again, the Vietnamese had either inadvertently revealed more information than they had intended, or were trying to pass a veiled message, via Schweitzer, that they did indeed have answers to many of the darker aspects of the MIA enigma, and were now willing to reveal them.

Later, the DIA's Operations Directorate seized on this opportunity. Based on the evidence pointing to the possible survival of Snug 40's crew, American investigators pressed the Vietnamese for more information. A photograph showing Major James McElvain dead in an open coffin, still in his flight suit, was quietly passed to the DIA. The Vietnamese did not provide a similar photograph of Colonel Ward. Neither officer's remains has been repatriated.

Schweitzer's Operation Swamp Ranger had proven beyond all doubt that the Socialist Republic of Vietnam possessed vast archives on captured and missing Americans, a stockpile of their artifacts, and probably scores, if not hundreds, of MIA remains.

The response of the Bush administration to this revelation was dramatic.

BY LATE SEPTEMBER, the PAVN General Political Directorate was dealing with Ted Schweitzer as if he were an unofficial American ambassador. Although both Schweitzer and the Vietnamese maintained the polite fiction that he was a private citizen engaged in scholarly research, Colonel Dai was authorized to use Schweitzer as a conduit for important messages to Washington. Dai told Schweitzer that Do Muoi and the party leadership would favorably consider a U.S. government approach that would shift the resolution of the MIA issue from a purely American endeavor to a "common" effort that would also address the question of Vietnamese missing in action.

He urged Schweitzer to inform Washington that the time for such an initiative was at hand. Senior Vietnamese, including the recently appointed Foreign Minister Nguyen Manh Cam, the director of the ministry's Americas Department, Le Van Bang, and Ambassador to the United Nations Trinh Xuan Lang would all be in New York for the start of the new General Assembly session. "The approach should be made at the U.N. in New York," Schweitzer advised the DIA on September 29, 1992.[15]

Armed with the knowledge that the Vietnamese government expected a conciliatory démarche from the Americans to be made at the United Nations, Secretary of Defense Dick Cheney and Acting Secretary of State Lawrence Eagleburger consulted with National Security Adviser Brent Scowcroft and President Bush. They agreed that an approach would be made to the Vietnamese.

But it would not be a conciliatory gesture.

After thoroughly briefing the Senate Select Committee on POW/MIA Affairs on the Operation Swamp Ranger finds, the White House turned matters over to Cheney and Eagleburger. They invited Foreign Minister Nguyen Manh Cam and his assistant Le Van Bang to a meeting at the State Department on October 8, 1992.[16] The Vietnamese clearly expected a fence-mending session, long on expressions of mutual respect, but short on practical details.

No sooner had the Vietnamese delegation arrived, however, than the American side invited them to inspect a display of documents and photographs neatly arrayed on a wide mahogany table. The photographs of Major Joseph Morrison and the other dead Americans were attached to the revised negotiation folder notes, which challenged—indeed, demolished—previous Vietnamese claims that their information on missing Americans was sparse and disorganized. The printout of the entire Red Book index and a selection of pertinent PAVN record cards, including a dozen that revealed detailed information about American MIA cases, were a stark testament to the actual extent of Vietnamese archives.

The photographs and documents were evocative of courtroom evidence exhibits in a well-crafted case. There was nothing the Vietnamese could say that would refute this mute testimony of their government's long duplicity.

This was not a congenial meeting. These senior American officials coldly reminded Foreign Minister Cam that Party General Secretary Do Muoi had solemnly promised full cooperation on resolving the MIA issue as quickly as possible. Implicit in this promise had been a major breakthrough to be publicized before the November presidential election. That promise had been made in April. Now it was October.

The Americans did not offer any concessions or any of the traditional encouraging quid pro quo steps toward easing the economic embargo. Rather, they left the unmistakable impression that, in the face of this overwhelming evidence of long-standing Vietnamese deceit, it was Hanoi's turn to make a major concession.

The Vietnamese delegation retreated to consult in private. Le Van Bang phoned unofficial American advisers, including a Washington lobbyist, and a member of a veterans organization friendly to Vietnam.

"What do we do?" Bang asked one American. "We don't know what they want."

"Why don't you ask them to come to Vietnam to talk about it?" one American adviser suggested.[17]

Foreign Minister Cam and Le Van Bang formally invited presidential emissary General John Vessey to Hanoi to discuss the full extent of the Vietnamese archives on American MIAs.

THE DIA HAD prudently ordered Ted Schweitzer out of Hanoi and down to Bangkok two days before this Washington confrontation. Unaware of the developments in Washington, he believed that the trip was just another debriefing session. He was wrong.

"I'm afraid the agency is not renewing your contract," James Renaud said. He handed Schweitzer a form to sign that guaranteed he would not divulge sensitive details of any ongoing intelligence operations.

"You're making a bad mistake to fire me now," Schweitzer told Renaud. "Things are just beginning. I've hardly got my foot in the door and now you're slamming it shut."

"I just follow orders, Ted," Renaud replied.

Schweitzer signed as ordered, but would not let the issue rest. He tried to call Richard Armitage, but discovered he was on an official mission to Russia. Next Schweitzer called the chief of staff of the Senate select committee, Frances Zwenig.

"They're making a mistake firing me now," he explained. "I'm just getting into the really good material."

Frances Zwenig promised to raise the issue immediately with Loren Craner, an acquaintance on the National Security Council, the son of a former POW.

Schweitzer returned to his own hotel room and had almost fallen asleep when the telephone rang again. It was Loren Craner, Zwenig's contact on the NSC.

Craner listened to Schweitzer's problem, then replied succinctly. "Don't leave your room. Someone will get back to you before five A.M. your time."

At exactly 4:50 A.M., the telephone rang once more. It was James Renaud. "Who the *hell* did you call in Washington?" He sounded amazed. "I just had my ass chewed up and spit out over a satellite line. I'll be right over."

This was a breach of procedure. Case officers did not ever visit agents in their hotel rooms.

Renaud arrived a few minutes later looking sweaty and harassed, having had no sleep either. "I understand I might have exceeded my orders. It appears that you're not exactly terminated."

"What the hell does that mean?" Schweitzer was frustrated. Was he fired or not?

He snatched up the phone and called Craner at his NSC office. "It's still not clear whether or not I'm still under contract."

"Let me talk to your man there," Craner said.

Renaud took the phone. His face flushed, then went pale. "Yes, sir. I understand, sir. Absolutely, sir." He hung up.

Smiling now, Renaud shook his head. "You are definitely *not* terminated," he said, as if reciting verbatim orders. "You are still an official U.S. government consultant."

"Okay," Schweitzer said. "I'm going back to Hanoi then."

Renaud shook his head. "You can't do that. At least not right now. Something's happening. This is not a real good time for you to be in Hanoi."

Schweitzer was not mollified. "Well, I *am* going back. That's where my job is. My agents up there are relying on me. And I've got to make sure they're okay with all of this shit going down."

GENERAL VESSEY'S DELEGATION, which included Senator John McCain, who was a member of the Senate Select Committee on POW/MIA Affairs, Deputy Assistant Secretary of State Kenneth Quinn, and JTF/FA commander Brigadier General Thomas Needham, left for Hanoi on October 15. They reached Hanoi on October 17. The next day they met with Deputy Foreign Minister Le Mai in the ministry's ornate conference hall. The Vietnamese side had used the week between the Washington confrontation and this meeting to prepare their revised policy. It amounted to a capitulation. Before the formal meeting began, Vessey and McCain conferred with Le Mai, who assured them that Vietnam would sign any agreement the Americans proposed.[18]

The American delegation was amazed at the rapid progress of the formal discussions. There were none of the turgid hours of indirection and empty rhetoric that had marked earlier discussions. The green tea hardly cooled before Le Mai was detailing the Vietnamese proposal: The Socialist Republic of Vietnam was in the process of collecting widely dispersed documentary evidence and artifacts concerning American POWs and MIAs. All this material would be assembled in the Central Military Museum in Hanoi and made available to the JTF/FA. Vietnam was prepared to sign a formal agreement to that effect immediately.

"Immediately?" General Vessey asked, straining to suppress his amazement.

"As soon as an agreement can be written," Le Mai affirmed.

Vessey then suggested the delegations split up into teams to draft the agreement and the separate memoranda of understanding that would detail the mechanisms to implement it. By that afternoon, the teams were at work. General Needham led the team drafting the military provisions, while Assistant Secretary Kenneth Quinn worked with his Vietnamese counterparts to structure the language of the formal agreement.

The next morning, both sides signed the agreement and related memoranda.

In a joint communiqué, the two sides noted that Vietnam had provided "important information" on resolving MIA cases. In response, "The United States will move more rapidly toward normalization of relations."[19] Both sides saw the Road Map leading into the final stage of the long negotiations.

The Vessey delegation left Hanoi on October 19, less than forty-eight hours after they had arrived.

Thanks to Schweitzer's Operation Swamp Ranger, they had accomplished more in those two days than any other American negotiators had in the previous two decades.[20]

ON RETURNING TO Hanoi, Ted Schweitzer was immediately drawn back into his strange role as an unofficial senior diplomat. He was granted a ceremonial meeting at the Central Military Museum with one of the last surviving members of the revolutionary pantheon, General Vo Nguyen Giap, the victor of Dien Bien Phu and the chief architect of North Vietnam's ultimate victory in 1975. Schweitzer posed for pictures with the smiling old warrior. Giap, never having been one of Ho Chi Minh's favorites, had been shunted even further from the centers of power in recent years. But he was still brought forth on occasions such as this to greet especially important foreigners who were considered "friends of Vietnam." They're throwing holy water on me, Schweitzer thought.

That afternoon, Colonel Dai and Major Mui met with Schweitzer behind closed doors at the museum to discuss these latest dramatic developments.

The Socialist Republic of Vietnam, they explained, wanted to do as much as possible to resolve the MIA issue in order to help President George Bush win reelection. Vietnam was afraid of an unknown politician like Bill Clinton, who suddenly seemed a serious challenger to Bush, and would prefer to help the current administration so that the quid pro quo steps of the Road Map could continue on schedule. Under this scenario, Bush would win reelection, the embargo would be lifted, and Vietnam would finally share all its information on American MIAs, including, implicitly, its darkest secrets. The specter of Ross Perot winning the White House was so distasteful to the Vietnamese that they did not even mention him to Schweitzer, although he realized Perot's presence on the fringes of the campaign had contributed to the willingness to sign the new cooperation agreement with General Vessey.[21]

When Schweitzer received word that he was requested to attend the formal White House ceremony on October 23, at which President Bush planned to announce the new agreement between the United States and Vietnam, Colonel Dai and Major Mui were clearly impressed. In an Asian Communist country that placed such emphasis on hierarchical authority, only those of great power would be invited to attend such a prestigious ceremony.

On the morning Schweitzer was to leave Vietnam, Dai gave him a message for President Bush that he said came directly from Vietnam's senior leaders.

"You can tell President Bush that he can announce to the American people that Vietnam has agreed to release all its documents on American prisoners and missing," Dai said, speaking slowly and distinctly, so that Schweitzer could write down every word of Mui's translation.

"*All* documents?" Schweitzer asked.

"Vietnam has agreed to turn over all, I repeat *all* documents on American prisoners and missing," Dai patiently emphasized.

Schweitzer wrote his instructions carefully.

Then Dai spoke again, and Schweitzer resumed taking notes.

"Trying to find an end to the MIA affair is not easy," Dai said. "The Vietnamese government cannot even agree on the price of rice. How can they agree on something as complicated as relations with America? But the war is over. How many years of futile war did you fight with Vietnam? How many years of embargo have you had with no result?" Searching for words, Dai turned to parable as he often did. "Can you pressure your own son to obey you against his will? Can you order your daughter to marry a man she does not want? America cannot come to Vietnam and order us to deliver this document or that record. Tell us what information you need, and we will provide it in our own way. Eventually, we will provide everything."

Schweitzer dutifully wrote Dai's words.

"President Bush can phrase this in any way he desires," Dai continued. "Vietnam will support whatever the President tells the American people on this point."

Dai paused until Schweitzer had finished writing and closed the cover of his notebook.

"The only secrets that we will not reveal," Dai added, speaking softly, "are the details of men who died under torture."

The stuffy office was silent a moment.

"But we want to help President Bush win reelection," Dai concluded.[22]

SCHWEITZER DID NOT have much time for a formal debriefing when he finally reached Washington's northern Virginia suburbs on Thursday, October 22, 1992, after almost thirty hours of continuous travel from Hanoi. But he did tell James Renaud the Vietnamese message for President Bush.

"That kind of message traffic is way the hell over my pay grade," Renaud said.

He was right: The latest Vessey mission to Hanoi had already sparked the interest of the news media. Important political considerations were now involved with every aspect of the issue.[23]

Renaud contacted his superiors in the DIA's Operations Directorate. The consensus of the Defense Department was that this was a National Security, not an Intelligence matter. Therefore, Schweitzer was instructed to relay the message himself directly to National Security Adviser Brent Scowcroft.

To do so, Schweitzer was escorted to the White House just before seven on that bright, chilly Friday morning. Anonymous young men in dark pin-striped suits escorted him from one office to another in the Old Executive Office Building just west of the White House proper. Finally, he was told that General Scowcroft was already briefing the President in the Oval Office, but that Loren Craner would carry the message to him. Schweitzer opened his notebook and read the words, making sure Craner copied them verbatim.

Then Schweitzer joined his old friend Richard Armitage, General Colin Powell, and the throng of guests who were assembling for the ceremony in the Rose Garden.

SCHWEITZER STOOD IN the front row of guests beside Richard Armitage on the lawn, flanked by an admiral from the DIA. Three groups of MIA families, women in middle age with grown children, completed the row. At exactly 8:00 A.M. President Bush led his key national security advisers out the Rose Garden door of the Oval Office and onto the portico steps where the rostrum stood. General Vessey was at Bush's right. Senators John McCain and John Kerry, and Brent Scowcroft trailed Vessey.

McCain was ruddy-faced and chunky, his hair a premature stone white. Only his quick blue eyes were youthful. He had survived five and a half years' captivity in Hanoi, much of it in solitary confinement. As co-chairman of the Senate select committee, McCain brought both the needed cachet of bipartisanship and the moral authority of an ex-POW sincerely concerned with the fate of his missing comrades. John Kerry had commanded a Navy assault boat on the Mekong twenty-five years earlier. He was tall and lean in an almost painfully angular way, as if his acerbic manner had seared the flesh from his lanky frame, leaving behind a kind of bony armor.

Bush was just as tall as Kerry. But the President looked old this morning, tired and drawn. The campaign was not going well. Schweitzer wondered if the soft-spoken young aides had managed to convey the Vietnamese message to Scowcroft in time for Bush to incorporate it in his formal remarks.

President Bush thanked General Vessey and Senator McCain for their work in Hanoi and added that the presence of Senators Kerry and Smith emphasized the bipartisan nature of the effort to achieve the fullest possible accounting for Americans still missing in Indochina. This was an obvious attempt to downplay the election-eve nature of the ceremony.

"Early in our administration," Bush said, "we told Hanoi that we would pursue a policy that left behind the bitterness of war, but not the men who fought it. Our approach was called the 'Road Map.' "

By the time Bush reached the meat of his remarks, his voice had warmed and rang with conviction. "For all of us, the POW/MIA issue is a question of honor, of oath-sworn commitments kept. It's a nation's test of its own worth, measured in the life of one lone individual."

He noted that General Vessey's persistent and steadfast efforts had been "the toughest task he has ever faced."

But that effort had finally been rewarded. "We vowed to follow every lead," Bush said. "And then last summer, we got our first glimpse of Vietnam's vast set of wartime archives."

Ted Schweitzer and Richard Armitage exchanged a quick glance of satisfaction.

President Bush explained that Vessey and McCain had just reported on their successful mission to Hanoi. "I'm pleased to announce this morning," Bush said, "that our policy has achieved a significant, a real breakthrough."

Now Bush paused so that his words could be readily bracketed by silence into neat soundbites for the network microphones and cameras. Bush, normally a lackluster stump speaker who jumbled his syntax, seemed to have been transformed this cool fall morning into an accomplished orator.

"Hanoi has agreed to provide us with all—and I repeat, *all*—information they have collected on American POWs and MIAs." Schweitzer watched the reporters writing fast to catch all of the President's words. He felt his own worn leather-bound notebook in his suitcoat pocket, in which the same phrase was written. Politics was indeed a strange business, Schweitzer mused.

And the political nature of this ceremony was obvious. Bush's campaign was in trouble less than two weeks before the election. The MIA issue, which Ross Perot had long claimed as his personal property, was part of the problem. The confrontation with Foreign Minister Cam and Le Van Bang that led to the "breakthrough" agreement just signed in Hanoi had been motivated by Bush's sinking campaign poll numbers. He had to trump Perot with his own MIA card, and in so doing, highlight Clinton's weakness in military affairs by dragging Vietnam back to the front pages.

The fiasco of the shouting match with MIA relatives during the disastrous July meeting of the National League of Families still haunted the Bush campaign. Indeed, in September, three former Republican secretaries of defense had testified under oath to John Kerry's Senate select committee that a small number of American prisoners might have been inadvertently abandoned to the Communists in Laos at the time of Operation Homecoming, following the 1973 Paris Peace Agreement.[24] Further, three former sub-cabinet-level Reagan administration officials intimately familiar with the wartime MIA issue, including Ambassador Richard Armitage, testified during those hearings that the United States had knowledge of "Americans" alive in Indochina after the war.[25]

All these developments had raised the MIA cauldron from a disgruntled simmer to an angry boil.

But then Schweitzer realized that this ceremony, which had certainly sprung out of political expediency, actually transcended politics. The relationship between America and Vietnam would never be the same after this morning. Using the words of the message that the Vietnamese had asked Schweitzer to convey to the White House, the President had just committed the Socialist Republic of Vietnam to providing *all* the information on American missing held in their vast archives. The genie was out of the bottle. Vietnam might continue to drag its feet, but it could no longer simply stonewall by releasing meager dribs and drabs of information.

Bush's voice remained strong, his cadence measured. From where Schweitzer stood, Bush certainly did look and sound presidential. "And today, finally," he added, "I am convinced that we can begin writing the last chapter of the Vietnam War."[26]

After Bush left the Rose Garden to board his helicopter to Andrews Air Force Base and another hard day on the campaign trail, the reporters trooped toward the adjacent White House briefing room for a news conference with General Vessey and the two senators.

"Hell of a story," a veteran *Washington Post* reporter muttered to a colleague from a television network.

The TV correspondent nodded as they joined the throng crowding the brick walkway. "I'd like to know how anyone ever got into those archives. *That*'s the real story."

As the two newsmen chatted, the VIPs filed past them to climb the low stairs, past the Oval Office, and into the West Wing. In the crush, Ted Schweitzer bumped shoulders with the *Post* reporter.

"Excuse me, sir," Schweitzer said in his quiet manner.

The reporter never even glanced at him.

GENERAL JOHN VESSEY had served in three wars and had been one of the country's most successful chairmen of the Joint Chiefs of Staff. He had won a battlefield commission on the Anzio beachhead and a Distinguished Service Cross in Vietnam. But his last years of active duty had been spent in a different, less obvious type of combat along the shores of the Potomac. He knew how to handle a press conference.

Vessey told the reporters that two days before in Hanoi the Vietnamese had described his mission as the "turning point" in solving the long MIA mystery. The Hanoi government would now collect all material on American POWs and MIAs from their military archives, place it in museums, and make it available to American investigators.

For over five years, Vessey said, he had been seeking access to those archives, but had been consistently rebuffed by the Hanoi government. The Vietnamese had always stressed that their laws prohibited foreigners from entering military record rooms and added that, in any event, their archives were not well organized.

Then last fall, the U.S. Defense Department—which had official jurisdiction for POW/MIA affairs—began to receive "some material," which came from "private sources who had been permitted into the Central Army Museum in Hanoi."[27]

Keeping his cards close to his chest, Vessey explained that this material was "obviously very valuable," and that its acquisition by the Pentagon triggered the chain of events leading to the historic breakthrough. Once the Defense Department had been able to verify the authenticity of the photographs and, more important, the detailed records from the Hanoi army museum, the Vietnamese could no longer claim that their archives were meager and inaccessible. In early October, Vessey explained, Secretary of Defense Dick Cheney and Acting Secretary of State Lawrence Eagleburger summoned Vietnamese Foreign Minister Nguyen Manh Cam to Washington and confronted him with the material. He was forced to admit that Vietnam had in fact extensive records that could resolve the unknown fates of many, if not most, Americans missing in action.

Although Vessey did not elaborate on Foreign Minister Cam's sudden reversal, the veteran journalists in the press room who had served in Southeast Asia during the war, such as Don Oberdorfer and Thomas Lippman, recognized that Cam's action was quintessentially Vietnamese. For almost 3,000 years, the Vietnamese have viewed themselves as a people threatened by larger powers. The long history of Vietnam is replete with intrigue and deception directed toward the outside, dating from the revolt of the Trung Sisters against the Chinese in the first century A.D. to the United States in our own time.

Vietnam had the great misfortune of lying on one of the most volatile geopolitical fault lines of the Cold War. East and West had made war in Vietnam for thirty years. This bitter history hardened the xenophobic resolve of the Vietnamese Communists. To most senior military and party officials in Hanoi, truth has always been a tactical weapon. As American historian Stanley Karnow aptly stated, this history has left the Vietnamese "inured to duplicity."[28]

Answering reporters' questions about the "private American" who had first obtained the material, General Vessey identified him as Ted Schweitzer, "an historical researcher who was in the museum in Vietnam with their agreement, getting material to write a book." Vessey added that Schweitzer had found "other material that pertained to this issue," had copied it, and given it to the Pentagon.

Asked if the U.S. government had paid Schweitzer for the photographs and documents, General Vessey assumed the neutral expression of a veteran poker player and shrugged. "Some," was all he said.

THE WHITE HOUSE now began a series of carefully orchestrated leaks about Ted Schweitzer's role in Hanoi. In the next two days—while James Renaud employed all his best tradecraft to shield Schweitzer from overly inquisitive reporters—journalists friendly to the Bush administration were secretly given access to Schweitzer before Renaud whisked him out of Washington and back to Southeast Asia.

The television and press accounts based on those interviews were positive but somewhat limited in scope because most reporters could not find Schweitzer to interview him. This media coverage offered tantalizing hints of a colorful espionage adventure involving a lone scholar who had ostensibly outwitted the wily Communists in Hanoi while under the control of American intelligence.[29]

Schweitzer was correctly described as a former UN refugee officer and professional librarian who had gained access to the Hanoi military archives as a result of humanitarian missions to Vietnam delivering donated medical supplies. His recruitment by the DIA as the primary agent of Operation Swamp Ranger, and his success at electronically scanning Vietnamese POW documents—ostensibly under the noses of the disapproving Hanoi Politburo—were also outlined.[30]

News accounts stressed the almost 5,000 photographs of American POWs, dead and living, that Operation Swamp Ranger and a smaller, parallel effort, Operation Druid Smoke, had harvested from Hanoi archives. Because the White House and Pentagon limited access to Schweitzer, however, reporters were not allowed to conduct follow-up interviews. If they had, the critical importance of the *documents* Schweitzer had electronically scanned—as well as the frank statements from the Vietnamese on the fates of hundreds of MIAs he had reported to the DIA—would have made headlines.

However, one important administration source, Principal Deputy Assistant Secretary of Defense Carl Ford—who had implemented Operation Swamp Ranger—did allude to the importance of the documents. "At one point," Ford told *Time,* "I suddenly thought, wow, the Rosetta stone of the MIA issue."[31]

IN LATE SEPTEMBER, the family of Major Joseph Morrison had received a phone call from the Pentagon. Two officials would like to visit the Morrisons in Tucson. There were new developments in Jay Morrison's case.

Jed Morrison, a banking executive now in his late thirties, agreed to receive the Pentagon delegation in his home. The Morrison family gathered there. Waiting for the men from Washington to arrive, Jed nervously rearranged furniture in his living room, while his sister, Cindy McClanahan, her husband, and Jed's wife watched.[32]

Peggy Morrison sat stiffly in an armchair, staring out the wide window to the curved suburban drive along which the officials' car would approach. It had been twenty-four years since Jay Morrison's F-4D Phantom was shot down over the steep jungle slopes of the Ban Karai Pass. She understood that the men from the Pentagon were bringing final evidence of her husband's death. This would be closure to the long nightmare of uncertainty. But their visit would also extinguish any vestige of hope. And she dreaded seeing the pictures of his body.

When the two officials arrived, they presented an anonymous manila folder, containing photographs and documents Schweitzer had obtained, which confirmed Major Morrison's death in North Vietnam at the hands of the enemy the day after his aircraft was shot down. Cindy Morrison McClanahan and her brother, Jed, stood and spoke at the same time. "I want to see the pictures."

Peggy Morrison remained in her chair, torn by anguish as she watched her two children take the folder of photographs into a bedroom and close the door. Peggy knew she should be with her children at this moment, but she could not bear to see pictures of her husband's body if he had been mutilated. Finally she asked, was Jay mangled? Had rigor mortis set in?

The officials explained the photographs had been taken soon after death. Jay Morrison's body was intact, unmutilated.

Jed and Cindy came out of the bedroom, their faces red and constricted, their eyes moist. The pictures, they said, were graphic, but not grisly.

Peggy Morrison went to the bedroom and sat on the bed. Slowly she examined each photograph, starting with those of the wreckage and flight equipment. Finally, she gazed at the picture of her husband sprawled supine on the jungle hillside. She noted the expression of peaceful determination in her husband's half-closed eyes. He had died quickly.

For almost twenty-four years, Peggy Morrison had assumed Jay had been killed evading capture and had thus been spared the ordeal of captivity. That knowledge had comforted her. But now, gazing down at his face on that Vietnamese mountainside, she silently asked him, "Why, oh why didn't you choose to be captured?"[33]

The morning passed. The Morrison family began the slow process of absorbing their grief. The pleasant, mundane necessities of life reappeared to buffer their emotions. Now they could begin to prepare for the next stage. Perhaps one day soon the Vietnamese would agree to return Jay Morrison and Lieutenant Francisco's remains to American control.

BEYOND BRINGING CLOSURE to the Morrison family, the photographs and documents concerning the loss of Grommet 02 on November 25, 1968, and the fate of its crew, also put to rest one of the more lurid of the myriad speculations generated by POW/MIA activists since the war. For whatever motive, retired Air Force Sergeant Jerry Mooney had earlier exploited the Morrison-Francisco shootdown to highlight his alleged encyclopedic knowledge of the enemy's sinister intrigues involving American prisoners. Mooney purportedly had detailed information that Major Morrison and Lieutenant Francisco had been captured alive and exploited as slave laborers in a secret underground military complex in Quang Binh Province. Mooney's baroque speculations had become an important element of the vast POW/MIA conspiracy lore.[34]

But the Operation Swamp Ranger photographs and documents completely discredited Jerry Mooney's claim.

CHAPTER 23

FOLLOWING THE WHITE HOUSE CEREMONY, TED SCHWEITZER'S MEDIA contacts were limited to two carefully orchestrated interviews, one with *Time*'s Bruce Van Voorst, the other with correspondent Jim Walker of ABC, George Bush's nephew.[1] While the DIA basked in the rare glow of favorable, albeit controlled, publicity, James Renaud made certain that Schweitzer did not contact anyone else in Washington who was not read in on Operation Swamp Ranger.

But, in yet another of the operation's many ironies, Schweitzer was encouraged to maintain his contacts with the PAVN's General Political Directorate. He called Major Mui at prearranged contacts at least ten times in the next few days, so that the GPD could be kept fully abreast of the developments in Washington. While reporters from the *New York Times* and the *Washington Post*—as well as eager producers from *Inside Edition* and *Hard Copy*—were scouring the banks of the Potomac for this colorful secret agent, he was holed up in a room at a suburban Embassy Suites hotel, consulting with his Vietnamese counterparts. Colonel Dai and his colleagues were better informed on these events than the American reporters of major newspapers, who had covered the POW/MIA beat for years.

And, just as the DIA enjoyed the good press, the General Political Directorate reveled in their media image as the Vietnamese group most responsible for the historic "breakthrough."

SCHWEITZER ARRIVED BACK in Hanoi the weekend before the American presidential election. Major Mui and Miss Lan from the Foreign Ministry met him at Noi Bai Airport. From a telephone call to Mui the week before, Schweitzer knew that he would not be dragged off the airliner and shot on the spot as a spy. Indeed, Mui had assured him that, as far as the PAVN General Political Directorate was concerned, the White House ceremony and the media revelations of the Red Book and MIA photographs had been exactly what the Vietnamese military had wanted.

But Miss Lan seemed tense and was decidedly cool toward Schweitzer. In the minibus jolting through the swarms of bicycles along the highway to the city, she turned away and muttered, "I am so disappointed with you."

Schweitzer tried to soothe her with some empty platitudes about trying to "do what is best for both our countries," but she remained aloof.

But when Mui joined Schweitzer at his guesthouse, the atmosphere changed completely. Mui produced a copy of the Tokyo edition of *Time* magazine and opened it with a flourish to Bruce Van Voorst's full-page story. Beneath the bold headline "The Truth at Last," the story's center column was dominated by a color picture of Ted Schweitzer shaking hands with Colonel Pham Duc Dai.[2] The implications of the headline and photo layout were unmistakable: A daring American operative and a forward-looking and resolute group of Vietnamese officers had joined forces to open the "hidden archives" of the Central Military Museum, which contained a "major cache of meticulously maintained and documented accounts of missing American service personnel."[3]

If the General Political Directorate had hired a skilled New York public relations firm, it could not have obtained better publicity.

"So, Ted," Mui said with mock sternness, which dissolved into a grin, "you are the famous Swamp Ranger."

Schweitzer held up his hands in token surrender. "Don't believe everything that you read in the American press."

Like most Vietnamese of his generation, Major Mui was a pragmatist. He was not inclined to dwell on the past. His role in winning positive recognition in America for the General Political Directorate had brought praise enough from his superiors.

When Mui and Schweitzer met the next morning with Colonel Dai, the normally reserved old political officer was cheerful and guardedly optimistic. He explained that the coup of orchestrating the "breakthrough" of the White House ceremony had, as intended, solidified the GPD's position at the center of the MIA issue. But he warned that there were "many elements" in both the PAVN and the civilian ministries that were jealous of him and the museum staff. Unfortunately, the American MIA office in Hanoi seemed to be siding with those elements intriguing against Dai.

The General Political Directorate, Dai said, was still in the position of a "defensive goal tender." But he said he and his superiors were about to go on the offensive. "The championship match is beginning now," the old colonel said, wagging his finger. The PAVN intended to wrest control of the MIA negotiations from the civilians. It was Colonel Dai and the General Political Directorate that had conceived of the second-channel approach, which the American Pentagon had exploited through Schweitzer's operation. This was now shown to have been a proper policy. It was, after all, the army in general, and the GPD in particular, that possessed all the information on missing Americans. It had been stupid to have ever delegated the resolution of the MIA question to civilians.[4]

As had now become his habit, Schweitzer absorbed this information with more than one grain of salt. He had become aware of just how convoluted and intricate Vietnamese deceptions could be. Indeed, officers like Colonel Dai seemed to spend much of their time engaged in elaborate charades meant to shield their true goals and motives. Again, the image of the ornately layered lacquer box rose in Schweitzer's mind.

As if to demonstrate this pervasive Potemkin Village element, the director of the VNOSMP, Ho Xuan Dich, paid a courtesy call on Colonel Dai at the museum that very afternoon. On one level this was a ritual of obeisance: the mandarin paying homage to the warrior. In the past, Colonel Dai had always been convoked to the Ministry of Foreign Affairs; Dich had never deigned to visit the museum. Dai was obliged to make a reciprocal gesture.

He did so in a typically dramatic fashion. While drinking tea in the museum's formal reception room, Dai noted, almost in passing, that he understood Dich's brother, Dung Quang Chinh, had disappeared as a PAVN soldier fighting in the South in 1966. Dich confirmed that his family had received official notice that his brother had died in December 1967, but had no more information. Colonel Dai made a show of questioning Dich about his brother's unit, then after a suitable pause, announced that Dai had in fact documents here at the museum that listed the exact location of his brother's grave in Quang Ngai Province.

Dich seemed sincerely appreciative. Recovery of his brother's remains and their interment in the family ossuary in the north was a heavy responsibility, which Dich as the surviving son bore personally.

On one level, this exchange appeared to be a chance beneficial episode, two elderly Vietnamese men, a soldier and a bureaucrat, interacting in a purely human manner. But at a deeper level, Schweitzer realized, Dai's gesture had been a demonstration of power. The GPD controlled vast stores of information, not just about American MIAs, but also about thousands of missing Vietnamese soldiers. And now that the PAVN was assuming its proper position of prominence as the element of Vietnamese society that controlled the MIA issue—and, implicitly, that would receive the major share of available American money—officers like Dai could afford to act benevolently.[5]

Making notes on this incident, Schweitzer repeated his silent mantra: Nothing in Vietnam is ever simple or straightforward.

WORD OF GEORGE BUSH'S defeat reached Hanoi on the morning of Wednesday, November 4.

Although officially neutral, senior Vietnamese officials did not try very hard to hide their disappointment. "The majority of Vietnamese leaders wanted Bush to win the election, and most thought that he would win," an anonymous bureaucrat told the *Washington Post*. "That's why we gave the American side all those documents on the POW/MIA issue."[6]

This disappointment was centered on the uncertainty over whether the incoming Clinton administration would continue to follow the Road Map established by the Bush State Department and Pentagon. By optimistic Vietnamese reckoning, the quid pro quo process had been scheduled to culminate with the lifting of the U.S. trade embargo and the establishment of diplomatic relations in May 1993, when Cambodian elections were scheduled.

Now this optimistic scenario had been shattered by the fickleness of the American electorate.[7]

At the PAVN museum, where the GPD had assumed such a central role in the Road Map process, the officers Schweitzer encountered seemed uncertain of what reaction to the Bush defeat would be proper. They asked him if the vote was final, if there were no appeal process. Democracy was a mysterious process. Sudden reversals of political power were a frightening spectacle.

Within days, President-elect Clinton sent Vietnam a message that his administration would not be weaker than the Bush White House when it came to negotiating the MIA questions. Clinton gave his first post-election speech on Veterans Day, November 11. He called for a "final and full" resolution of the POW/MIA issue. Although Clinton praised Vietnam for opening their archives, he emphasized that he would continue the Bush policy of refusing to normalize diplomatic relations with Vietnam as long as it was "suspected of withholding information." To the loudest applause in the speech, Clinton stated, "I won't rest until this issue is resolved. We must have as full an accounting as is humanly possible."[8]

THE RITUAL OF anointing the GPD and the Central Military Museum as the prominent Vietnamese institution to resolve the MIA issue continued. JTF/FA commander Thomas Needham, newly promoted to major general, arrived in Hanoi to facilitate the implementation of the latest agreement signed by Vessey's delegation in late October.

With much fanfare, investigators from Detachment 2, "the Ranch," set up shop in the Central Military Museum, where they proceeded to examine American POW artifacts. Pictures in a front-page story in the *New York Times* showed JTF/FA researchers photographing and cataloging objects such as boots and flight equipment belonging to American POWs. In the pictures, the Americans are using laptop computers and tripod-mounted close-up lenses to detect faint serial numbers on bits of equipment. The operation appeared to be rigorous and highly professional. Detachment 2 commander Lieutenant Colonel Jack Donovan is quoted in the story describing the new open-access agreement as a "breakthrough." In the same tone, Donovan noted, "I've heard this described as the biggest development since 1973 in terms of accounting for missing Americans."[9]

(The museum staff was not impressed by the JTF/FA's technology. Major

Mui asked Ted Schweitzer: "Why don't they have digital scanners like you do?")

A few days before the American military investigators arrived with their computers and cameras, Colonel Dai informed Schweitzer of a major modification to the Vietnamese agreement to turn over all materials concerning missing Americans to the JTF/FA. Dai implied that, following the defeat of George Bush, Vietnam had now decided to deal only with Senator Kerry and his Senate select committee. Kerry was scheduled to lead a delegation to Hanoi in mid-November. The documents mentioned in the agreement with General Vessey would be turned over to Kerry, and the JTF/FA would simply be informed of what had been released.

Under this policy, which Dai said had been jointly approved by the Ministries of Defense, Foreign Affairs, and the Interior, the General Political Directorate through Colonel Dai would have total authority concerning the release of all documents and artifacts in Vietnamese hands throughout the country.

"This decision was made at the highest levels," Dai had told Schweitzer, indicating that the sudden reversal in the October agreement had been approved by both party and government leadership.[10]

The purpose of this abrupt shift was to extract the maximum political advantage from the minimum acceptable concessions. The Vietnamese viewed Senator Kerry and his committee as representing America's new political leadership: President-elect Bill Clinton and the Democrats. Following their own traditions of intrigue, the Vietnamese wanted to curry favor with the new power structure in Washington. Making Kerry the public recipient of the "breakthrough" documents would focus attention on the image of cooperation, while avoiding the practicalities of substance. In contrast, any documents, photographs, and artifacts of major relevance to solving MIA cases turned over to the JTF/FA would simply disappear into the black hole of the DIA, to be slowly chewed and digested by the analysts.

Vietnam wanted dramatic gestures that would provoke reciprocal dramatic concessions from both the lame-duck Bush administration and the incoming Clinton White House. So Hanoi planned a dual course: the masquerade of full cooperation with the JTF/FA, coupled with the release of selected documents to Kerry's committee.

This intricate policy seemed to bear immediate fruit. In a move that began before the November 3 election, the Treasury Department lifted a provision of the trade embargo, permitting Vietnam to receive U.S. dollar payments for telephone calls made by Vietnamese Americans in the United States to their homeland. This concession appeared minor, but it permitted Vietnam to collect $2 million that had been held in an escrow account. The State Department also announced it was sending a relatively high-level delegation to Vietnam to discuss direct aid for "humanitarian needs." This was the first such delegation at the deputy assistant secretary level since the abortive

Kissinger talks after Operation Homecoming in 1973. Given the stubborn refusal of the United States to discuss such issues before "full cooperation" from Vietnam on the MIA issue was achieved, the move signified to the Vietnamese that the Road Map was still functional.[11]

With the means of collecting payments for telecommunications established, AT&T quickly signed an agreement with Vietnam to establish direct-dial telephone links between the United States and Vietnam's five largest cities. This was a major step toward ending Vietnam's international isolation, as AT&T controlled many of the Far Eastern satellite communications circuits that carried direct phone and data links between Vietnam and the United States and Europe.[12]

There were still several major hurdles to cross before the trade embargo could be lifted, however, the United States–led freeze on International Monetary Fund development loans being among the highest. But the political and military leadership in Hanoi clearly recognized that major "breakthroughs" on resolving the MIA issue, such as the sequence of dramatic events that began with Operation Swamp Ranger and culminated in the Rose Garden ceremony in October, were the key to progress.

And it became equally clear that Vietnam's leaders viewed John Kerry as a major player in this process. Colonel Dai and his GPD colleagues consulted Ted Schweitzer about Kerry's influence with the new administration. Schweitzer did not know much in this regard, but commented that Kerry was smart, attractive, and ambitious. Some of the PAVN officers seemed to make much of the fact that Kerry had been an antiwar activist.

"Yes," Schweitzer conceded, "but don't forget, he fought in combat as a Navy officer in the Mekong Delta first. He wasn't a draft dodger like Bill Clinton."

This left a certain amount of confusion among older officers like Colonel Quan and his Nghe Tinh group colleagues, including Colonel Tich. To them, Clinton and Kerry appeared to come from the same generation and political subset of their party. The fact that Kerry was a New England liberal who had risen to power in the old Kennedy-O'Neill machine in Massachusetts, while Clinton was New South and ostensibly a New Democrat, was meaningless to them. Indeed, Schweitzer realized that there were very few people in Hanoi who had even a gross understanding of American politics. To the Vietnamese, the term "party" connoted factions and intrigues; Clinton and Kerry were assumed to be in the same faction.

But the Vietnamese leadership underestimated Kerry's resolve. Even with his background as an antiwar activist, he was an experienced attorney determined to allow the investigation his committee had begun to run its full course.

When Kerry returned to Hanoi on November 16, accompanied by Senators Thomas Daschle and Hank Brown, he carried with him a letter from President Bush to Vietnamese President Le Duc Anh, which promised "reciprocal actions" toward lifting the U.S. trade embargo, provided Vietnam continued to offer true cooperation in solving the MIA problem. This conciliatory gesture was widely publicized.[13]

But there was another letter related to the committee delegation visit that remained unpublicized, and which demonstrated that Kerry was interested in concrete results, not just propaganda displays. On November 2, he and committee co-chairman Bob Smith sent the Vietnamese government a long, detailed request for specific information meant to achieve "specific results" in the areas of live-sighting reports, priority discrepancy cases, U.S. MIA remains, and wartime documents and photographs. There was nothing vague in this request. Kerry and Smith cited chapter and verse, drawing upon the DIA's tentative analysis of the Red Book and related secret documents Ted Schweitzer had recovered from PAVN archives. Their letter also made explicit demands for information on the remains of MIAs who were pictured in the Swamp Ranger photographs. "Seizing on the opportunity provided by the recent opening, we would like to bring back to the American people concrete evidence of the benefits that will come from our evolving new relationship," the letter stated.[14]

The enclosures to the letter did not represent the political softball the Vietnamese had anticipated. One demanded information on sixty-three names from the "Vessey II: Last Known Alive" list, while another asked for the prompt return of the remains of thirty-seven Americans officially listed by the Vietnamese as having died in captivity. The documents the committee requested included twelve important records indexed in the Red Book. Among them were the detailed reports of downed American aircraft from the major Air Defense Forces commands in North Vietnam during the war.[15]

It was now impossible for the Vietnamese to deny these records existed. Thanks to Operation Swamp Ranger, everyone from Secretary of Defense Cheney to Foreign Minister Cam, to the swarms of DIA analysts in windowless bullpens in northern Virginia had taken note of these and scores of similar vital documents.

Significantly, the Kerry-Smith letter also requested a meeting with Colonel Dai and Ho Xuan Dich, and asked that they be allowed to speak directly to the American people to explain the progress made to date.[16]

Kerry's letter caused consternation among the Vietnamese, who immediately consulted Schweitzer for advice. The most sensitive issue was remains. Even though the PAVN had records of grave locations for some of those who died in captivity in southern Vietnam, the Army had not collected all these remains.

In fact the only set of remains they could immediately locate were those of Navy Lieutenant Michael J. Allard, whose ID cards Schweitzer had recovered. But Allard was a KIA/BNR case. A retired PAVN officer had allegedly sold the remains to an overseas Vietnamese who could now deliver them for a fee. But if the PAVN took custody of the remains, it would appear that they had been in official storage. The GPD proposed a typically convoluted compromise: Schweitzer would pay a reasonable "reward" to the unnamed person who held Allard's remains, then they would be turned over to the JTF/FA detachment just before the Kerry delegation arrived. The PAVN would say that unknown parties had simply brought the remains to the museum. In this manner, everyone would be satisfied.[17]

Schweitzer passed on the proposed compromise to his case officer. But the Vietnamese were not able to deliver the remains. This development set a frustrating pattern. Over the next nine months, Schweitzer was repeatedly offered remains of American MIAs, often listed by name with a correct date and place of loss. He had been authorized by the U.S. government to pay well for these remains, as part of a concerted effort to determine the extent and location of any possible new quasi-official "warehouse." But each time he came close to recovering remains, the proposed deal collapsed.

Senator Kerry's delegation arrived at Noi Bai Airport on the morning of November 16, 1992. Accompanied by JTF/FA commander Major General Thomas Needham, the senators went directly to a government conference hall and met with Deputy Foreign Minister Le Mai. Kerry did not spend much time on diplomatic pleasantries, but immediately opened his November 2 letter to the enclosures and began discussing the importance of the documents to the overall resolution of the MIA question. Without committing his government, Le Mai promised that the request would be given serious consideration.[18]

Attempting to downplay the importance of documents and enhance the significance of field investigations, Ho Xuan Dich, head of the VNOSMP, told the senators that many American missing had been buried in remote areas, "and maybe the people who buried them have died, too."

But Kerry ignored this ploy. "A larger question," he said, "is about when you had somebody who was at a prison site and they died."

Dich tried to parry this unusually blunt statement. He made an allusion to directors of hospitals in which patients die, who could not be expected to bury the dead bodies themselves. "Senior commanders of military units cannot pinpoint where someone dies."

Dich was fighting a rear-guard action to keep the thrust of the MIA investigations within his civilian group, and away from the PAVN.

But Senator Tom Daschle now took up the offensive, noting that POW artifacts, such as dog tags, combat equipment, and weapons, "aren't buried. If they were made available, they would help clarify" the fate of many missing men.[19]

The meeting ended with both Le Mai and Dich promising to act quickly on the requests for documents. "Any request, any question you raise," Le Mai said, "we will give the clearest possible answers."[20]

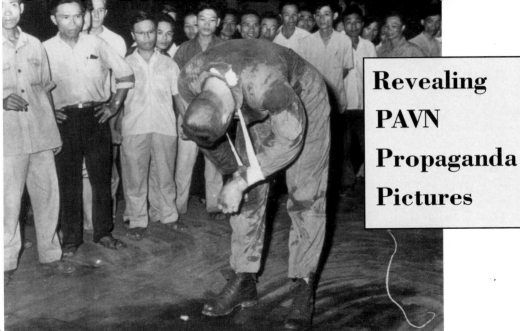

Captured American Air Force pilot James D. Kula, and Kula being paraded before an angry crowd in Hanoi on July 29, 1972. Note the armed guards in the truck. Without the protection of such guards, Ted Schweitzer and the author were told, some newly captured American airmen were killed by irate Vietnamese civilians. Kula was returned alive in 1973.

Air Force Captain Robert J. Sandvick, captured near Hanoi in August
1966. Note the well-armed local militia, one of whom carries an
American World War II vintage Thompson submachine gun. Due to the
presence of the PAVN photographer, Sandvick was not ritually beaten at
this time.

Capture of Navy pilot Lieutenant Commander Robert H. Shumaker, February 11, 1965, near Vinh, North Vietnam. Note the regular PAVN soldier armed with a folding-stock AK-47. Other aviators captured in this heavily bombed region were not so fortunate.

35

Capture of Air Force Sergeant William A.
Robinson, September 20, 1965, by North
Vietnamese militiawoman Buu Chinh.
Robinson was a crew member on a Jolly
Green Giant rescue helicopter shot down
over North Vietnam. He was released from
captivity in 1973.

36

The North Vietnamese stamp featuring the capture of Sergeant
Robinson. This stamp commemorates the two thousandth American
aircraft shot down over North Vietnam in 1967.

37

U.S. Navy pilot Commander Harry T. Jenkins being taken to
interrogation in Hanoi's Hoa Lo Prison (the "Hanoi Hilton").
He was shot down in November 1965 and released in 1973.

An unidentified U. S. Air Force B-52 bomber crewman after
capture in Hanoi during the Linebacker II bombing campaign,
December 1972.

Capture of
U.S. Navy
pilot
Lieutenant
Charles D.
Stackhouse,
April 25, 1967.
He was
released in
1973.

39

40

Capture of an unidentified American airman in November 1967.
The regular PAVN soldier at the right carries an AK-47, while the
militiawoman at the left has a French rifle.

Propaganda parade of American POWs through
central Hanoi, July 6, 1966. Even though the
prisoners were heavily guarded, many were
beaten by civilian spectators. Such displays and
ritual beatings of POWs in smaller towns and
villages resulted in some deaths, Vietnamese
officers now privately admit.

"Mining" Crash Sites

An armed Vietnamese village woman picks through the wreckage of an F-4D Phantom shot down on June 23, 1968, near Vinh, North Vietnam. The two crewmen, Lieutenant Colonel Donald Casey and Captain James Booth, were never repatriated, nor were their remains returned, yet the aircraft wreckage was relatively intact compared to truly catastrophic crashes. Note that the engine being dismantled by the militiawoman did not suffer a meltdown through massive fire damage. Downed American aircraft represented a virtual gold mine to the Vietnamese. Approximately $5,000 worth of gold and platinum could be recovered from the engines and avionics of these aircraft.

43

Recovering potentially valuable engine components from a downed American fighter-bomber.

44

Mining an American crash site. If human remains were recovered years after the war, local peasants often hoarded them, believing American recovery teams would pay for these remains.

Breaking up the
jet engines of a
downed American
aircraft in the
search for gold.
Note the antique
musket rifle
carried by the
barefoot
militiaman.
Both Vietnamese
are members
of hill tribes.
The crash was
probably near
the Mu Gia Pass
on the Ho Chi
Minh Trail.

45

46

A more sophisticated mining operation
conducted by PAVN regulars in the
jungle of North Vietnam.

The PAVN Museum and Ted Schweitzer's Activities in Hanoi

47

Ted Schweitzer working on documents with PAVN Senior Colonel Pham Duc Dai, winter 1993.

Schweitzer working with PAVN Major Lai Vinh Mui, winter 1993.

48

49   Schweitzer working at the console of his optical
scanning system in the PAVN museum, Hanoi.

50   Senator John F. Kerry, chairman of the Senate Select Committee on
POW/MIA Affairs, during the ceremonial transfer of Colonel Dai's
wartime diary at the PAVN museum, November 18, 1992. Major Mui
translates for Colonel Dai, and André Sauvegeot, former U.S.
embassy officer, Bangkok, translates for Kerry.

Kerry and Senator Hank Brown examining Colonel Dai's diary with Dai.

Senator John McCain and staffers of the Senate Select Committee on
POW/MIA Affairs at the Central Military Museum, Hanoi; the PAVN
T-54 that captured the Presidential Palace in Saigon is their backdrop.

53

Ted Schweitzer with Senator Kerry and Colonel Dai at the Central
Military Museum, Hanoi. At Schweitzer's right is Major Mui's wife,
Lieutenant Colonel Tran Thanh Hang, the senior museum archivist.

54

Ted Schweitzer in Hanoi with PAVN General Vo Nguyen Giap,
Vietnam's greatest military hero. At Giap's right is Lieutenant
Colonel Bang Lam, a PAVN military photographer and artist.

The letter from President Bush to Vietnamese President Le Duc Anh that Senator Kerry brought with him explicitly presented the prospect of lifting the economic embargo. "We are at a critical juncture," Kerry told reporters. "We are definitely on a road leading to normalization." Referring to President Bush's letter, Kerry said, "The President may be in a position, if we get adequate cooperation and we can speed this process up, to make positive moves with respect to the embargo."[21]

THAT AFTERNOON SCHWEITZER received a call from Major Mui, "inviting" him to come to the museum. He had been in Hanoi long enough to realize the word "invitation" was tantamount to a direct order. Schweitzer left his guesthouse immediately.

Colonel Dai and Mui greeted him rather formally and led him to Dai's closed office at the rear of the museum. The government of Vietnam, Dai explained, had an important offer to make Senator Kerry. They realized the senator had made requests for specific information, which the PAVN was now trying to assemble in order to make a formal presentation when the Senate committee delegation visited the museum in two days. Some of the documents were available, others were not. However, the government of Vietnam was concerned with a more important issue.

"You know about the Lao Files and the Blue Files?" Dai asked.

Schweitzer nodded, "I've been told about the Blue Files."

In previous weeks, Major Mui had described the Blue Files in some detail. They were essentially "201"-type personnel records on each American POW held by the Vietnamese during the war. Named for the ubiquitous blue-gray pasteboard jacket, each file contained daily prison records on each prisoner. The files included items such as photographs—some showing the bruises and scars of torture—letters from the prisoners and from their families, and copies of signed war crime confessions and other propaganda statements. The Blue Files also held medical records, which would clearly document the brutality to which many of the prisoners had been subjected. But audio tape recordings of interrogation sessions were perhaps the most sensitive items in the Blue Files. If Nguyen Van Thi was correct, some of these tapes recorded the sound of men being broken under torture.[22]

Mui had explained that the JTF/FA had been pressuring the PAVN for months to turn over the Blue Files. But Vietnam was reluctant to do so, fearing that the brutal and gruesome content of some of the files might be leaked to the American news media and cause a sudden hardening of public opinion against Vietnam in the United States, just when the PAVN second channel to resolving the MIA issue was developing so well.[23]

"The Lao Files are different," Colonel Dai added. "We have good records for Americans killed or captured along the supply route you call the Ho Chi Minh Trail. These records come from our army groups that served and fought there for years. They are complete." Again, Dai was engaging in the ritual of reciting instructions from his superiors, while Schweitzer took careful notes in order to relay the message to the American government.

"These Lao Files can solve many of your MIA cases," Dai stated.[24]

"How many?" Schweitzer asked.

"Many," was all Dai would say.

Now Dai detailed a plan that had been approved "at the highest levels of our government."

Schweitzer was asked to contact Senator Kerry before the select committee members met with Premier Vo Van Kiet the next afternoon at one-thirty. Schweitzer was to inform Kerry that Vietnam was offering a confidential arrangement to expedite the "breakthrough" process toward normalizing relations. If Senator Kerry asked Vo Van Kiet for the Lao Files during this meeting, the Vietnamese would release them to Kerry's delegation immediately. This would be a very positive and newsworthy event, dramatizing the success of the new PAVN channel to important MIA information.

But there was one important "condition" to the release of the Lao Files, Dai said. The Vietnamese government asked that America, through Senator Kerry, not ask for or even mention the Blue Files until sometime after the trade embargo was lifted and normal diplomatic relations had been established between Vietnam and the United States. When those conditions had been met, Vietnam would release all the Blue Files, including those that documented the deaths under torture of American POWs.[25]

Schweitzer closed his notebook and left Colonel Dai's office. Walking back through the museum courtyard, past the trophies of aircraft wreckage and armored vehicles, he realized just how important Colonel Dai's proposal was. Vietnam was counterbidding, raising the ante from the sweeping request for documents in the Kerry-Smith letter. Once again, the PAVN and the party resented what they considered inflexible diktats from the Americans.

As Colonel Dai had warned, America could not force Vietnam to comply with each demand. But Vietnam was willing to resolve the MIA issue on its own terms. Instead of releasing still secret detailed military records from its Air Defense Forces in North Vietnam, the PAVN would provide the Lao Files, which might solve as many as one hundred MIA cases. Then, when the embargo was lifted and diplomatic relations established, Vietnam would quietly turn over all the Blue Files, which would finally resolve the question of how many American prisoners the PAVN actually had captured. The Blue Files would also reveal the "darkest secrets" of these men's fates.

And once this information was known, the details contained in the documents Kerry's committee had requested would amount to supplementary, not pivotal information.

However, Vietnam was not addressing the sensitive question of remains in this dramatic offer. And Schweitzer realized that no American government would ever reestablish diplomatic relations unless it was convinced the Hanoi leadership had made every effort to return American MIA remains still in quasi-official hands.

SCHWEITZER HAD LUNCH with Senator Kerry's delegation at noon on Tuesday, November 17, 1992. They met in the dining room of the Pullman Metropole Hotel. The hotel had recently been refurbished and was the sole oasis of Western luxury in Hanoi. The three senators (Kerry, Daschle, and Brown), Schweitzer, and committee staff director Frances Zwenig shared a quiet round table in the ornate older section of the dining room. Schweitzer was seated directly across from Kerry and next to Zwenig.

The other two senators let Kerry take the lead while he questioned Schweitzer about the nature of his work with the PAVN. Schweitzer answered honestly and, under this questioning, revealed details of Operation Swamp Ranger that he had never shared with anyone outside the Operations Directorate of the DIA. But as Schweitzer spoke, Kerry's face grew rigid with impatience. His long fingers drummed on the linen tablecloth and he eyed Schweitzer coolly with an expression bordering on contempt. Clearly, the senator was not impressed by clandestine operations. Finally he interrupted to express the opinion that there was no need for secrecy in anything Schweitzer was involved in.

"The Vietnamese have promised to open their archives," Kerry said. "They will do so, if we maintain consistent pressure." Kerry was apparently referring to President Le Duc Anh's promise of full cooperation the day before.

Kerry was not asking Schweitzer's opinion, he was delivering an inflexible dogma. The meeting was not going well.

Speaking carefully and slowly, Schweitzer now outlined the major points of the proposal Dai and Mui had offered on behalf of their government. Vietnam, Schweitzer said, was prepared to turn over the Lao Files immediately, if Senator Kerry requested them during his afternoon meeting with the premier.

Kerry nodded impatiently. But his contempt for such intrigue was no longer veiled.

"We can't have anything under the table here," he snapped. "We have to put all our cards on the table, and so do they."

Schweitzer waited for Kerry to finish speaking, then continued as if he had not heard Kerry's words. The Lao Files would be delivered to Senator Kerry, but no one on the American side should even mention the more sensitive Blue Files. When the embargo was lifted and diplomatic relations established, Vietnam would supply the Blue Files. They certainly could not deny these records existed because they knew Schweitzer was going to discuss them with the select committee delegation, and also report to American intelligence on this matter.

Kerry asked only a few terse questions. He exchanged meaningful glances with Frances Zwenig, but did not acknowledge that he had accepted the proposal. However, Schweitzer was certain that Kerry and Senator Daschle had fully understood the nature of the Vietnamese offer. Unfortunately, Senator Brown, who was not feeling well, had excused himself early from the lunch.

Before Schweitzer could discuss the offer further, the two senators and Frances Zwenig rose and climbed the low stairs out of the dining room to the lobby where they were immediately surrounded by their Vietnamese and American entourage.

Schweitzer returned to the museum to await word of the meeting's outcome. Late that afternoon, Major Mui arrived at the museum. He looked pale, grim, and disappointed. The meeting had been a disaster. Instead of responding to the confidential Vietnamese offer, Mui had been told, Kerry had asked Premier Vo Van Kiet to immediately release all documents on American POWs, including both the Lao Files and the Blue Files.

The Vietnamese had sensed betrayal, Mui said, and the premier, who had been prepared to turn over the Lao Files in the meeting, now retreated to vague statements about the need for "inquiries" as to the location of such documents.

"Can't you do anything?" Mui asked.

Since returning from Washington, Schweitzer had noted that the Vietnamese had come to consider him an important member of the Bush administration, someone with direct access to the decision-makers in the Pentagon and White House. Once more, they were viewing America through the perspective of their own society.

"I told Senator Kerry what he should do to obtain the Lao Files," Schweitzer explained. "But I'm afraid I don't have any control over him."

"The Army of Vietnam does not take orders from American senators," Mui said coldly, referring to the lists of rigid demands in the Kerry-Smith letter.

(The author later determined that Major Mui's report on this matter was only partially correct. Frances Zwenig's detailed contemporaneous notes of the delegation's meetings reveal that Senator Kerry did indeed ask Vo Van Kiet for both the Lao Files containing Ho Chi Minh Trail shootdown records as well as individual "prison records," his term for the Blue Files. Although Zwenig's notes do not describe Vo Van Kiet's response, her record of the delegation meeting with President Le Duc Anh clearly indicates that the president promised to turn over the Lao Files. But in fact, the first of the Lao Files was not turned over until the next summer.[26]

(DIA case officer James Renaud remembers Schweitzer's field reports on the proposal to use Senator Kerry as a conduit for the release of the Lao Files, as part of a confidential understanding that would also include the release of the Blue Files at some point after diplomatic relations between the two countries were established.[27])

THE NEXT MORNING, Foreign Minister Nguyen Manh Cam turned over to the Kerry delegation five of the most important military records on the list of twelve documents requested in the Kerry-Smith letter. These records included reports of the 350th Air Defense Division and detailed lists of downed U.S. aircraft in the four provinces of North Vietnam that had borne the brunt of the long bombing campaign. Although the release of these documents was one of the most notable achievements of the "good-cop, bad-cop" campaign combining Operation Swamp Ranger and the JTF/FA, the ceremony was not highlighted in news media accounts of the select committee delegation visit.[28]

That afternoon, the Kerry delegation visited the Central Military Museum, accompanied by several reporters and a camera crew from ABC-TV. Colonel Dai, dressed in his best woolen uniform, escorted the senators and the news media through the museum. There were plentiful "visuals" to please the cameramen and press photographers. Dai virtually shoveled piles of intriguing American POW artifacts toward the senators across the freshly polished glass tops of the exhibit cases. The delegation was shown Social Security cards, driver's licenses, survival manuals, and photographs of young women whose long hair and miniskirts evoked the turbulent 1960s. In the museum armory, the senators were led past racks of captured American M-16 rifles and M-60 machine guns. They were allowed to handle the pistols of captured American pilots that had been laid out on a wide wooden artifact drawer.

Then in a well-staged, ritualistic demonstration of cooperation and openness, Colonel Dai handed Senator Kerry the battered black-and-gold flight helmet that Senator John McCain had worn in October 1967 when he ejected from his crippled Skyhawk and parachuted into Ho Tay Lake in Hanoi's northern suburbs. Colonel Dai also presented Senator Kerry with the stained and mildewed war diary Dai had carried as a major in Quang Ngai Province in 1967. The diary contained a detailed description of the ambush in the riverside hamlet where the Mangino Four had been killed.[29]

When reporters pressed Lieutenant Colonel Jack Donovan, the Hanoi JTF/FA detachment commander, to comment on Vietnam's long history of deception on MIA matters, he answered more like a skilled diplomat than the thick-witted infantryman that activists had called him. "We're delighted with this new cooperation. I'm too busy to worry about the past."[30]

After the museum visit, the three senators, accompanied by JTF/FA head General Needham, were given a guided tour of the Citadel. They were the first Americans allowed inside the walled PAVN headquarters since twelve of the most intransigent POWs were held there in a cellblock known as Alcatraz during the war. The PAVN guides pointedly showed the Americans several underground bunkers and bomb shelters. This was to refute claims by some activists that surviving American prisoners were still held in such dungeons within the grim Citadel walls.

THE NEW NEGOTIATIONS between the United States and Vietnam did not take place in a vacuum. Indeed, events in Asia were rapidly overtaking both countries' policy positions and rendering them obsolete.

Three days after Bush lost the election, Japan announced the resumption of aid to Vietnam after thirteen years' suspension that began with Vietnam's invasion of Cambodia. Japan also announced a formal agreement to lend Vietnam $370 million of long-term loans at negligible interest rates. Although Japan had agreed to delay the announcement of the policy shift until after the American election, the move diluted much of the impact of the U.S. trade embargo.[31]

Economists believed the Japanese move also signaled its intention to resist continuing American opposition to development loans to Vietnam from the International Monetary Fund, the Asian Development Bank, and the World Bank. It was Tokyo's well-established policy to use such loans as risk-deferment tools for Japanese corporations investing in potentially lucrative Southeast Asian markets. Cash-rich banks and corporations in Taiwan and Singapore were certain to follow the Japanese lead.

"The embargo is dead," a European ambassador in Hanoi told the *Washington Post*. He said it was only a question of "weeks or months" before the U.S. would be forced to lift trade sanctions.[32]

These economic moves no doubt bolstered the confidence of Party General Secretary Do Muoi and Premier Vo Van Kiet that Vietnam could manipulate American public opinion by making significant concessions on the release of MIA information, while still withholding sensitive and embarrassing records detailing the deaths of large numbers of American POWs in captivity. But the Vietnamese leaders still could not be certain that the incoming Clinton administration would not modify the Road Map by adding unacceptable demands that Vietnam institute sweeping internal political reforms leading to Western-style democracy. In fact, they had reason to worry. One of Clinton's important unofficial foreign policy advisers, Democratic Senator Bob Kerrey of Nebraska, a Vietnam veteran and Medal of Honor, had advised Clinton that such reforms should be an important facet of the new administration's policy toward Vietnam.[33]

To further complicate matters, Vietnam was struggling to find its way in the radically altered geopolitical landscape of Southeast Asia following the collapse of the Soviet Union, its principal shield against China. Since 1989 when the terminally crippled Gorbachev regime effectively withdrew support from Vietnam, China had relentlessly asserted its hegemony over the South China Sea and the surrounding region. China had fortified outposts on Woody Island in the Paracels Group, establishing a naval choke point for shipping transiting the South China Sea to and from the Gulf of Tonkin. Under the guise of customs inspections to prevent smuggling, China had proceeded to embarrass Vietnam by seizing more than twenty-four Vietnamese ships en route from Haiphong to Hong Kong. Some of the vessels and crews were kept prisoner for months in direct violation of international shipping laws.[34]

This Chinese pressure was meant to demonstrate its military superiority over Vietnam and to reinforce Chinese territorial claims to the Spratly Islands 600 miles to the south, which were also claimed by Vietnam and several of its neighboring countries.

After the American withdrawal from its large military bases in the Philippines, China proceeded to fill the power vacuum by acquiring a significant force of advanced, long-range strike aircraft and interceptors from Russia. In addition, China launched a credible blue-water naval force of modern guided-missile frigates, equipped with the latest East European technology. Vietnam had no air or naval forces that could compete with this new Chinese arsenal.[35]

Therefore, to the Vietnamese, the lifting of the U.S. trade embargo represented only one facet of a vital two-step policy goal. The leaders in Hanoi wanted full American diplomatic recognition and a tangible American business presence in Vietnam as quickly as possible, so that the United States would have a valid investment to protect from destabilization or direct military threat from China.[36]

Beginning about this time, Vietnamese leaders repeatedly assured visiting American business executives and journalists that Vietnam fervently desired a renewed American military presence in Indochina. "We want the American Navy back in Cam Ranh Bay," retired Ambassador Ha Van Lau, one of General Vo Nguyen Giap's principal aides in the battle of Dien Bien Phu, told the author.[37]

And if one aspect of this goal was the home-porting of an American aircraft carrier battle group in the beautiful deep-water harbor of Cam Ranh Bay, another was definitely the reestablishment of large American petroleum companies in Vietnam's offshore oil fields. Mobil Oil had explored the offshore fields just before the collapse of Saigon in 1975. Since then, Vietsovpetrol, a joint Vietnamese-Soviet venture, had exploited the field. But the primitive 1950s-vintage Soviet oil rigs were doing serious damage to the rich White Tiger field, allowing seawater to seep into the oil strata and pollute the crude. Moreover, the Russians were unable to effectively explore the nearby fields.

Vietnam needed modern exploration and production technology. The Mobil Corporation had retained all the original seismic survey and exploration maps. Vietnam wanted Mobil back.[38]

The Bush White House, of course, was well versed in all these complex diplomatic and economic variables. The nascent Clinton administration was not. It was the consensus of Bush and his senior advisers that the screw could be tightened several more turns to force further MIA concessions from Vietnam before ending the embargo.

AFTER CONSULTATION WITH Defense Secretary Dick Cheney, Acting Secretary of State Lawrence Eagleburger, and National Security Adviser Brent Scowcroft, President Bush reached his decision in mid-December. His administration would not lift the American trade embargo against Vietnam. Instead, the White House announced on December 14 that Bush had issued an executive order that allowed American corporations wishing to do business in Vietnam to sign contracts, hire employees, rent offices and plant facilities, and conduct commercial research, all in preparation for conducting business, once the U.S. embargo was lifted. This gesture was described as coming "within a whisker" of ending the trade embargo.[39]

But the White House statement made it clear that this gesture was, in turn, intended to provoke another reciprocal act from the Vietnamese in the long quid pro quo process. Vietnam was urged to facilitate the "rapid repatriation of all recovered and readily recoverable American remains." This was a clear reference to MIA remains in quasi-official hands. But the White House also applauded the Vietnamese efforts to recover American remains from private citizens.[40]

To stimulate increased Vietnamese cooperation on remains recovery, Bush was sending Senator Kerry back to Vietnam yet again, this time accompanied by his hard-line Republican co-chairman, Senator Bob Smith. They were carrying another message from Bush, this one to Communist Party General Secretary Do Muoi, urging him to intervene personally on the remains issue. Bush presented the possibility that the embargo might be lifted, should Vietnam suddenly "discover" a significant number of American MIA remains.[41]

But Kerry and Smith's whirlwind trip struck a dry hole. Do Muoi and the Hanoi Politburo were not flexible enough to respond before the Bush presidency ended.

Responsibility for ending the embargo through the resolution of the nagging MIA question had now shifted back to Hanoi and onto the new administration of Bill Clinton.

PART 4

CHAPTER 24

IN HANOI, THE END OF THE BUSH ADMINISTRATION AND THE inauguration of President Bill Clinton coincided with the Tet lunar New Year. Tet 1993 was one of the most joyous New Year's celebrations in recent memory. No Vietnamese troops were serving in combat. Hotels in Hanoi and Saigon—only bureaucrats still called it Ho Chi Minh City—were crowded with foreign business executives. International investment money was pouring into the country. And everyone expected the U.S. trade embargo to be lifted before the United Nations–sponsored elections in Cambodia later that spring.

The wide, shady boulevards of Hanoi buzzed with new Honda motorbikes and a growing number of small Japanese sedans. This Tet holiday was marked by opulent displays. On almost every street corner, vendors sold potted tangerine trees, carefully pruned so that the slender branches bore miniature fruit, a costly luxury, but a sure harbinger of good luck for the new year. The private grocery and produce market in the arcade between Hai Ba Trung and Thoung Kiet Streets was laden with pyramids of gleaming apples, stacks of fat navel oranges, mounds of dragon fruit from the southern coast, plastic tubs of candied lychee, and true luxuries such as pickled carp and smoked duck. While a few American tourists cautiously photographed the mildewed ocher walls of Hoa Lo Prison only a block away, the citizens of Hanoi literally turned their backs on the past and thronged into the market, clutching thick rolls of 5,000 dong banknotes.

Twenty-five years after the bloody disaster of Tet 1968, the streets of Vietnam's cities again echoed with explosions. But this holiday the noise was from millions of firecrackers, strung from lamp poles and trees and tossed from alleyways. The sidewalks in some parts of Hanoi were ankle-deep in shredded pink firecracker casings, evocative of fallen rose petals.

Although few Vietnamese followed the complex tactics that passed as diplomacy between Washington and Hanoi, most people did have a sense that the decades of war and deprivation were finally over, that Vietnam's isolation had ended, and that their country was about to reach its true potential.[1]

To the Vietnamese military officers and civilians responsible for resolving the long MIA dispute with the United States, however, this was not a period of optimistic expectation. Had the Bush administration seriously expected Vietnam to suddenly *discover* multiple sets of American MIA remains, and thus provide free grist to the American activists' vitriol mill? In any event, the PAVN and the Politburo firmly believed that Vietnam had made the last major initiative by providing the rich lode of documents and photographs through the Swamp Ranger back channel. It was now up to the new Clinton administration to take the next meaningful step: lifting the trade embargo and preparing for full diplomatic relations.[2]

Ted Schweitzer watched these developments with mounting pessimism. On an almost daily basis, his contacts in the PAVN probed him for insights into seemingly incomprehensible developments in the new Clinton administration. Experienced Vietnamese officers realized that any American president would have to enjoy the trust and confidence of the large military establishment in the United States in order to complete the reconciliation with Vietnam. But Clinton seemed strangely hell-bent on alienating the American military through a series of gratuitous slights and insults. When Clinton raised the obscure gays-in-the-military issue during his first encounter with the press following his election, the Vietnamese had asked Schweitzer about the significance of this matter.[3]

"Beats the hell out of me," Schweitzer had replied honestly.

But in Clinton's first month as commander-in-chief, as he slipped into a near-disastrous open conflict over both the gays-in-the-military and the women-in-combat controversies with his immensely popular chairman of the Joint Chiefs of Staff, General Colin Powell, the Vietnamese watched with mounting alarm. Bill Clinton was not going to immediately lift the trade embargo, not with the Pentagon verging on open revolt.

The alarm in Hanoi deepened as Clinton slowly completed appointments to his foreign policy and national security teams. Several key players, such as Frank Wisner in the Pentagon and Winston Lord at State, were old Indochina hands who had helped form America's wartime policy. They were suspected of being crypto-enemies of Vietnam, who still harbored irredentist dreams of a non-Communist "democratic" Vietnam, a disorderly, multiparty monstrosity that was utterly anathema to the dour Tonkinese leaders in Hanoi. Accordingly, Vietnam resorted to its traditional MIA policy of cautious inaction, cloaked in the mantle of ostensibly relevant busywork.

In early March, the Vietnamese thought they saw positive signs in Washington. The National Security Council reportedly moved a sweeping interagency review of policy toward Vietnam onto a "faster track."[4]

But then the Clinton administration indefinitely postponed International Monetary Fund board meetings in which new IMF loans to Vietnam were to be approved. And leaders in Hanoi saw subtle signs that Bill Clinton, who had avoided military service during the Vietnam War, was bending to political pressure from POW/MIA activists.[5]

When the alleged accelerated policy review in the National Security Council disappeared into the bureaucracy, Hanoi retreated further into its shell of inertia. Schweitzer informed the DIA that this policy was now officially established throughout the Vietnamese government. Because the United States had made no tangible gesture toward lifting the trade embargo, Vietnam would follow a course of neither helping nor hindering the JTF/FA effort. "This does not mean a complete lack of cooperation" by Vietnam, Schweitzer wrote James Renaud, "but rather a lack of initiative on their part."[6]

Schweitzer's back-channel effort was stymied. He had been on the verge of locating the remains of an F-111 crew whose plane had crashed in shallow water in November 1972. The aircraft, flown by Captains Ronald D. Stafford and Charles J. Caffarelli, rested on the bottom in only eight meters of water, close inshore to the barren beach near the mouth of the Ben Hai River that marked the old Demilitarized Zone. The official American crash coordinates for this wreckage were inaccurate. But the Vietnamese knew exactly where the wreckage lay. PAVN divers had found the aircraft intact. But the PAVN was unwilling to attempt recovering the skeletal remains of the crew, ostensibly because the plane had crashed still carrying its bomb load.[7]

Schweitzer knew, however, that the true reason for their reluctance lay in the new Vietnamese policy of stalling any initiative until the United States lifted the trade embargo. When he pressed his contacts to make a good-faith effort in leading the JTF/FA to the sunken F-111, they said, "This is not a good time."[8]

THE ATMOSPHERE OF tense limbo following the dramatic events of the fall was not eased by the release of the Senate Select Committee on POW/MIA Affairs final report. Although the committee had conducted the most rigorous investigation of the issue since the Vietnam War, the report was quickly attacked by both radical activists and more moderate groups.

Committee members and staff had anticipated the wrath of the more strident activists such as Joe L. Jordan, the executive director of the small but rabid National Vietnam P.O.W. Strike Force.

People like Jordan did not have massive support, and when they did receive national publicity, they often squandered the opportunity through wild accusations and self-aggrandizing bombast. For example, one of Jordan's newsletters ("A Vietnam Veteran Speaks Out on the POW/MIA Issue") began:

I am a heavily-decorated Vietnam Veteran. I flew 147 Combat Missions North of the 17th Parallel. I was one of the lucky ones who made it home. If a SAM Rocket had been a few inches

closer, I would be what is referred to as a POW/MIA. I volunteered for three tours of duty in a unit with a very high casualty rate.[9]

This rambling discourse is signed "Joe L. Jordan, Da Nang 67–68."[10] From this information it is reasonable to assume that Jordan was a combat aviator assigned to the Da Nang air base in 1967 and 1968. However, excerpts of Jordan's military record obtained under the Freedom of Information Act from the National Personnel Records Center (NPRC) in St. Louis indicate that Jordan, a communications technician with a naval intelligence squadron, spent less than six months at the Da Nang air base, all in 1968.[11] Under the "Decorations and Awards" section of this records excerpt, Jordan is listed as earning a National Defense Service Medal and two Navy Air Medals, but no decorations for combat valor.

The citation for Jordan's second Air Medal notes that he was a member of a "special unit flying in fixed-wing aircraft with Fleet Air Reconnaissance Squadron ONE engaged in combat operations in Southeast Asia between February and May 1968."[12] However, his assignment was for "combat-support," not strike missions. Jordan's NPRC military record lists no Navy Combat Action Ribbon and no Navy Combat Aircrew Ribbon.

There is no record that Jordan's unit suffered the heavy combat casualties in Vietnam that he claims, although one of the unit's planes was lost to a North Korean fighter in April 1969.[13]

Retired Navy Captain Byron Wiley, who commanded Jordan's squadron before the Vietnam War, described his claim of being a "heavily-decorated" combat veteran as "outrageous." Wiley stated that the unit's policy was not to expose communications technicians with knowledge of cryptographic equipment to capture. Hence, the "combat" missions that Jordan describes with such breathless detail were probably flown in safe orbit patterns over the Tonkin Gulf.[14]

Jordan's hyperbole, however, was not limited to self-promotion. He seemed to pride himself on launching vitriol at anyone in a position of authority who challenged his group's bizarre conspiracy theories about Indochina POW/MIAs. In one of Jordan's newsletters addressed to DIA Director Lieutenant General James Clapper, Jordan began, "Dear General Clapper, I just wanted to write you today and tell you what a real scumbag and piece of garbage you are." Jordan added, "You are a liar, a Communist, a traitor and a betrayer of everyone who ever served in the U.S. Armed Forces."[15]

In a long series of vicious attacks on the Senate select committee in general and Senator Kerry and Frances Zwenig, committee staff director, in particular, Jordan often resorted to sordid vituperation. He called Zwenig "Mata Hari of the 1990s" and accused Kerry of sipping "French wine at the Officers Club in the [Hanoi, PAVN] Citadel."[16] (There is no wine of any kind at the PAVN officers club; the only alcohol available there is Hanoi draft beer.)

Therefore it was not surprising when Jordan continued his attacks on the Senate select committee leadership.

But when the American Legion launched a well-organized effort to discredit the Senate select committee in the eyes of its millions of members, it was clear that the committee's major findings were unpalatable to many American veterans.[17]

This was unfortunate. Although the committee effort had not been perfect, the investigation had probed the issue with much more vigor than any previous inquiry. And the committee's findings, although not the stuff of headlines, were based on tens of thousands of investigative hours and hundreds of sworn depositions.[18]

These findings included the "possibility of survival, at least for a small number" of American POWs after Operation Homecoming. But the committee found no evidence that any had survived to the present day. Further, the committee found no evidence of a conspiracy to cover up POW/MIA information from the families or the public.[19]

The committee's final report was tamer than the often acrimonious testimony and internecine struggles among members and their staffs. For example, when testimony indicated that the Nixon administration might have knowingly abandoned live POWs in Indochina, Henry Kissinger countered with testimony calling such charges a "flat-out lie." Kissinger also accused members of the committee of "fishing for something that could be embarrassing" to him and the Nixon administration.[20]

And when the committee vigorously investigated some of the more egregious private POW rescue fund-raising activities, supporters of these groups on the committee staff waged a rear-guard action to prevent the committee from moving forward with their recommendations that the Justice Department start a criminal fraud investigation of these groups.[21] Committee Vice Chairman Senator Bob Smith was reportedly the leader of the efforts to curb the request for a fraud probe of politically well-connected private fundraisers. His efforts were described as vigorous.[22]

This acrimony continued beyond the end of the public hearings in December 1992. For example, when the activists' principal advocate on the committee, Senator Smith, launched a counterattack on his colleagues who believed only a few POWs survived the Operation Homecoming repatriations, the DIA (at the behest of Senator Kerry) almost immediately parried. Smith delivered an ill-advised, but seemingly plausible list of 324 "still unaccounted for" MIAs "who may have survived in captivity."[23] Much to Smith's embarrassment, the DIA analysis that committee members distributed to the public and press showed the number of errors the list included. The remains of five of the 324 MIAs named on Smith's list had already been repatriated. And more than half of those named were known to have died in their loss incidents, or casualty records indicated there was little chance of survival.[24]

In this list, Smith's staff noted under the entry for Major Dean A. Pogreba: "Supporting data from Select Committee deposition points toward shoot-down and possible capture of Pogreba in China." That was an obvious reference to the bizarre deposition of retired General Thomas Lacy.

Instead of establishing Smith as a credible dissenting expert, the ploy of disseminating this flawed list of possible surviving POWs severely undercut his credibility. He was reportedly outraged at the DIA's swift rebuttal.[25]

(Smith's lingering animosity came to a head in June 1993 when he formally requested that Attorney General Janet Reno investigate "potential federal criminal violations," specifically perjury and mail fraud, by members of the State Department, the Defense Department, and the DIA. Among those named on the list were DIA officers thought to have helped discredit Smith's initiatives during the committee hearings.[26])

THE SUSPENSION OF Vietnamese government cooperation in early 1993, coming as it did after the extravagant optimism of the previous autumn, was not well received by the JTF/FA. Some elements within the organization apparently saw the General Political Directorate as the instigators of this hard-line policy, when in fact the PAVN was probably just the tool the Politburo had chosen to implement it. Persons unknown within the JTF/FA now counterattacked through selective leaks to the news media. Unnamed "U.S. officials familiar with the MIA search" told William Branigin of the *Washington Post* that, contrary to American policy of not paying for information on MIAs, Ted Schweitzer had "paid Vietnamese authorities handsomely" for up to 4,800 photographs allegedly obtained free from Hanoi's Central Military Museum. Further, these sources told Branigin, "Most of the same photos were available to the public at the Vietnam News Agency archive in Hanoi for far less money than Schweitzer paid."[27]

Although the article contained accurate elements, it was grossly misleading. The photographs that Schweitzer paid "$250 a frame" for were not from the Vietnam News Agency, but had come from the museum and the Blue Files in the Ministry of Defense. These included previously unpublished pictures of dead MIAs, such as that of Major Joseph Morrison. This article caused immediate consternation in Hanoi. The General Political Directorate quickly blamed Robert Destatte and Garnett Bell, their old "intelligence officer" nemeses, as behind the leaks to Branigin.

"If they want to employ tactics against us," Colonel Dai stated, "we will counterattack."[28]

Major General Thomas Needham, JTF/FA commander, made several trips to Hanoi to press the Vietnamese to break the logjam during this period.

But these missions only exacerbated the problem. Instead of dealing with Colonel Dai and the PAVN's General Political Directorate, Needham continued his former contacts with Ho Xuan Dich and the VNOSMP. Colonel Dai, now verging on paranoia, viewed Needham's actions as a carefully contrived insult. Dai saw the American military MIA investigators as conspiring with enemies of the PAVN within the Vietnamese government.[29]

The result of all this unfortunate intrigue was the complete suspension of any meaningful progress toward resolving MIA cases. Although the JTF/FA tried to put the best face on this stalemate, there was little that could be done to pressure the Vietnamese into the true cooperation they had so solemnly promised in October and November 1992.

Instead, ceremony took the place of substance. One of the most elaborate of these rituals was the repatriation of seven sets of skeletal remains tentatively identified as "Caucasian/Negroid," and thus possibly those of American MIAs. The ceremony took place on the apron of Noi Bai Airport on February 8, 1993. A U.S. Air Force C-141 jet transport—piloted by an attractive young redheaded female captain, to the amazement of the assembled Vietnamese —landed to disgorge an honor guard from the four American services. While the Vietnamese watched with a mixture of solemn interest and bemusement, the trim young American troops transferred each of the seven small wooden containers to a large polished aluminum air-transport coffin, draped the coffin in the American flag, and rendered full honors. The ceremony took over an hour to complete. This was an obvious demonstration that the American military cared deeply about recovering the remains of fallen comrades. But it is unlikely that the Politburo was moved by this ceremony.[30]

When asked by Henry Kamm of the *New York Times* if Vietnam's cooperation had indeed been adequate, Lieutenant Colonel Jack Donovan, the Hanoi JTF/FA detachment commander, replied: "Vietnam at this time is increasing the level of cooperation. They are bending over backward to help us."[31]

But six days later on March 30, 1993, when Donovan met privately with Ted Schweitzer, Donovan complained bitterly that "his documentation work had ground almost to a complete halt and he had seriously considered pulling one team out of Saigon because of no cooperation." Donovan told Schweitzer he was surprised by this lack of cooperation and that he could not understand why the Vietnamese were behaving in this manner.[32]

In effect, the resolution of the MIA issue had again reached a rigid stalemate.

Traveling the country on what eventually proved a fruitless quest for MIA remains in the hands of retired PAVN officers and unnamed overseas Vietnamese, Schweitzer came to realize the danger of the stalemate continuing much longer.

Vietnam was being rapidly transformed into a rapaciously market-oriented society, in which humanitarian concerns such as the resolution of both America's and Vietnam's MIA issues meant little. He heard the term *Tu San Do* for the first time from Vietnamese military and civilian contacts. This translated as "Red Capitalists," and was an amalgamation of commonly used phrases meaning Communism, private property, and red. The *Tu San Do* were mainly younger people who had not fought in the American war. They cared nothing about politics; indeed, they found in Vietnam's vestigial police state an apparatus of corrupt, underpaid bureaucrats who could easily be manipulated by bribes. Making money and accruing property were now laudable goals.[33]

Many of the most successful Red Capitalists were younger party members, including some in the military and the Ministry of the Interior. Their free-market ethos had spread to older generations, who might have worked selflessly to resolve the MIA issue in order to help their country win reconciliation with America. By the spring of 1993, however, Schweitzer warned the Pentagon that any such altruism was no longer possible. "Those Vietnamese who do possess knowledge of our MIAs, or those who possess the actual remains, are simply not going to give their possessions to us for free. This is the reality here. There is no longer much hatred toward us here. That is not what is holding up the return of the remains. It is 'Red Capitalism.' "[34]

Soon, he predicted, whatever remained of government authority—a composite of fear, patriotism, and a sense of civic duty—would be so diluted by free-market profit motives that America would have lost any chance of collecting organized POW archives or recovering significant numbers of MIA remains. "Selfish" individuals in the VNOSMP, among PAVN veterans, and in the disparate General Political Directorate archives and houses of tradition, would simply pack up whatever documents or remains they had and hide them as a nest-egg hedge against inflation to be sold to the Americans at a later date.

(Vietnam's policy toward the repatriation of French remains from the First Indochina War underscored Schweitzer's warning. In 1991 France was paying Vietnam $7 million a year to maintain French war cemeteries. Vietnam then contacted the French government to announce that, due to land shortages, these cemeteries were being closed. France could either purchase the exhumed remains on a "per-kilo basis" or they would be "dumped into the ocean." France purchased the remains for an undisclosed fee. On examination by forensic pathologists, some of these remains proved to include "animal bones" and non-Caucasians, some of whom had died after the French left Vietnam in 1954.[35])

With this rapidly changing reality in mind, the Clinton administration decided in early April 1993 to send General John Vessey on one last fact-finding mission to Hanoi before the White House reached its decision about the next critical phase of the normalization process. Specifically, President Clinton had to decide before the end of April whether to continue American opposition to International Monetary Fund development loans to Vietnam.

Japan's and America's leading European allies were already poised to lend Vietnam enough money to repay its outstanding IMF debt. If America still resisted these concessions, and was effectively outmaneuvered in the IMF by its closest economic partners, it would be the Clinton administration, not Vietnam, that was isolated.[36]

By sending Vessey, one of America's most respected soldiers, back to Vietnam as the White House point man, Clinton was hoping to deflect the increasingly personal animosity of the military that served him reluctantly as their commander-in-chief.

Vessey's specific mission was to quietly pressure the Vietnamese into turning over a truly meaningful segment of the archives that Schweitzer had explored. If Vessey was successful, the White House suggested, Clinton was prepared to respond in a "positive" manner.[37]

Once more, the scene was set for the final act of the long MIA drama.

CHAPTER 25

THE INCIDENT THAT WAS TO SPARK ONE OF THE MOST DRAMATIC AND rancorous controversies of the entire POW/MIA issue began inauspiciously. On January 2, 1993, in Moscow, a handful of American and West European researchers huddled over piles of musty documents in a drafty old limestone church on Ilyinka Street. The building housed the Center for the Preservation of Contemporary Documents, which included the archives of the former Central Committee of the Soviet Communist Party. This being the day after New Year's, the biggest Russian winter holiday, the echoing reading room was half deserted, and the few shambling archivists seemed bored and tired. Two scholars associated with Harvard University, Stephen J. Morris, an Australian, and his American colleague, Mark Kramer, were researching documents about the Soviet involvement in the Vietnam War. Sifting through the dense Communist bureaucratic language was drudge work.

But both researchers plowed ahead diligently, aware that their grant support under an agreement between the Woodrow Wilson International Center for Scholars and the Russian government was not open-ended. They had come to Moscow to do a job, and even if half the city was in bed hungover from moonshine vodka, they intended to work.

Stephen Morris, forty-four, was a skilled researcher and a bit of an academic gypsy. He had done graduate work at Columbia University, and held a variety of positions elsewhere as a doctoral candidate. A fervent anti-Communist and conservative, he was known as "combative and politically incorrect," and often ran afoul of entrenched liberals on campus.[1] On this research trip, he was searching for Soviet intelligence reports that would shed light on the true relationship between the USSR and North Vietnam during the critical last year of the American military involvement in Indochina.

Morris and Kramer were seated at the same long table when an archivist delivered a hefty cardboard folder of intelligence documents, which Morris had requested based on a description in the archive's catalogue of holdings.[2] He extracted several documents, then selected one that caught his eye because it was marked "Extremely Secret" and bore the stamp of the Soviet GRU (General Staff Military Intelligence). Twenty-five pages long, the document was dated December 1, 1972. In a two-page executive summary signed by GRU commander Lieutenant General Peotr Ivashutin, the accompanying document was entitled: "Translation of the Report of Deputy Chief of the General Staff, Vietnamese People's Army, General-Lieutenant Tran Van Quang, at the Session of the Politburo, Central Committee of the Vietnamese Communist Party, 15 September 1972."[3]

Morris had enough experience dealing with such documents to recognize the sensitive nature of this one. Even through the stiff impersonal military language of General Ivashutin's summary memorandum, Morris saw that he had found a historical record of some importance. Scanning the summary, he saw that the report discussed several sensitive areas, including South Vietnamese military leaders who had made secret contacts with the Communists, the progress being made to subvert the South Vietnamese Army after the bloody 1972 Easter Offensive, and the progress of a secret "physical extermination" campaign to assassinate "reactionary leaders" of the South Vietnamese government.[4]

Morris read the first two sections of the report closely, making numerous notes. He was certain that he was reading an accurate Russian translation of the transcript made from a tape-recording of General Tran Van Quang's actual words as he addressed the Politburo in Hanoi at a critical juncture in the Vietnam War. In September 1972, the military fortunes of the North Vietnamese were at a low ebb. Their vaunted Easter Offensive to crush the South Vietnamese had failed, resulting in heavy casualties. And Hanoi's negotiators in Paris were grappling for a compromise that would allow America to leave Indochina without giving its "puppets" in Saigon the wherewithal to continue the war. So the shockingly frank discussions of the Ba Be plan to infiltrate assassins in the South, as well as the details of the suborning of South Vietnamese military leaders, were plausible and understandable in the context of this critical juncture.

But when Morris reached page seventeen of the report, he was even more astounded. In addition to addressing the questions of subversion in the South, General Quang stated, "In accordance with direction fromthe Politburo, I will report to you today on American POWs captured on the various fronts of Indochina."[5] Noting that the POW issue "disturbs the public opinion of the whole world and the USA," Quang observed that there were conflicting opinions within the Politburo as to the best means of exploiting the American prisoners. Specifically, Quang told his "Honored Comrades" that Vietnam had purposely not revealed the total number of American POWs alive in captivity, but that he would do so at this meeting.

"The total number of American POWs captured to date on the fronts of Indochina, in other words in North Vietnam, South Vietnam, Laos, and Cambodia totals 1,205 people."[6]

General Quang's Politburo report detailed the various categories of these American POWs: 671 were captured in North Vietnam, "143 pilots" were

captured in South Vietnam, totaling 814. The report stated that other categories of captured "American servicemen in Indochina" included 283 in South
Vietnam, 65 in Cambodia, and 43 in Laos, totaling 391, and when this was
added to the 814, a grand total of 1,205 POWs was reached.[7]

Dividing the total of "624 American pilots" by rank, the report listed 7
colonels, 85 lieutenant colonels, and 183 majors. These pilots included "3
Astronauts" and "15 U.S. Air Force aces, having more [than] 4,000 flight
hours."[8] The POWs "captured in North Vietnam" included "36 special operations forces advisors" inserted in the border region between North Vietnam
and Laos.

All of these 1,205 POWs, the report stated, "are presently in prisons in
North Vietnam." There were a total of eleven of these prisons. "We used to
have 4 large prisons; however, after the American effort to free their POWs
from Ho-Toy [Son Tay] we expanded this number to eleven. Each prison
holds approximately 100 POWs."[9]

The report also detailed how American POWs were kept in separate
camps, according to rank.

"368 POWs have progressive inclinations . . . we will be able to liberate
these 368 first" once a "favorable international environment" forced Richard
Nixon to end the war. That environment included the overthrow of South
Vietnamese President Nguyen Van Thieu. Of the remaining POWs, 372 were
said to have neutral views, "their political outlook is not fully progressive,
yet not too reactionary." "The remainder of the POWs hold reactionary views
. . . all the POWs among the senior officers hold reactionary views. . . ."[10] The
report added that if the United States demonstrated concessions, including
a cease-fire and the removal of President Thieu, "both sides can begin
discussing the question of repatriating POWs to the Nixon government."
And while those discussions went forward, "we can free some more pilots
from the number who are progressively inclined." If Nixon did not take
any disciplinary measures against these men and the Nixon government
compensated North Vietnam "for the great damage inflicted on it by this
destructive war," the question of the remaining 1,205 POWs could be resolved.[11]

The conclusion of this section of the report galvanized Morris:

**1205 American POWs are kept in the prisons of North Viet-
nam—that is a large number. For now, we have officially published a list of 368 POWs, the rest are not acknowledged. The
government of the United States is aware of this, but they don't
know the exact number of POWs, or they perhaps only assume
an approximate number based on their losses. Therefore in
accordance with the decree from the Politburo we keep secret
the number of POWs.[12]**

That evening, Morris called friends in the United States to verify the exact number of American prisoners returned alive at the end of the Vietnam War. He was told that 591 American POWs had been repatriated in 1973. But the document he had just read stated unequivocally there were "1,205 American POWs presently in prisons of North Vietnam" from all the fronts of Indochina. That meant that over 600 American prisoners alive in September 1972 had not been returned during Operation Homecoming.[13]

Stephen Morris was a Soviet expert, and had never been active in POW/MIA affairs. But he did understand that this document represented a potential diplomatic and political time bomb. If the Vietnamese had callously held back 600 American POWs, then somehow disposed of them after their conquest of the South, this represented a war crime in the league of the My Lai and Hue massacres. And if the Vietnamese had held these hundreds of POWs for ransom, and the U.S. government had secretly paid for their release, this was a secret scandal of epic proportions.

Morris realized he was out of his league in this area. He intended to contact the *New York Times* with this blockbuster, as soon as he returned to New York in mid-January. On the Delta flight from Moscow to JFK, however, Morris's colleague, Mark Kramer, convinced him to first approach the government. "What if some of them are still alive?" Kramer asked.[14]

Morris agreed. Going to the government quietly might actually save the lives of some hapless POW "reactionaries" who had been languishing in Vietnamese jails for over twenty years. At Harvard, Morris contacted renowned Soviet scholar Richard Pipes and Zbigniew Brzezinski, Jimmy Carter's national security adviser, and an expert on the Soviet Union. Both men examined the photocopy of the Politburo document and pronounced it authentic. They could not judge the content's validity, but it was clear to both experts that the cover memorandum signed by General Ivashutin was genuine.

Morris met with the Clinton administration's deputy national security adviser, Sandy Berger, on February 11. Given the explosive potential of the document, Morris refused to release a copy to Berger. Morris was afraid that inevitable press leaks would provoke a closing of the Central Committee and GRU archives in Moscow. He proposed that Clinton should press President Yeltsin to fully open these archives, so that a methodical search could be made for similar documents that would either substantiate or refute the Quang Politburo report.[15]

Instead of handing over the document, Morris gave Berger a memorandum summarizing the report. Berger promised to investigate the matter and get back to Morris "in a week." Within days, the Pentagon's chief POW/MIA official, Ed Ross, contacted Morris for more information. But there were no high-level contacts from the White House. Finally, five weeks later, Berger did return Morris's calls, but only to inquire if he was certain 1,205 POWs mentioned in the report were all Americans and did not include South Vietnamese or other allied POWs. Morris insisted that the report was clear on this point. Only Americans were mentioned.[16]

During this period, the Defense Intelligence Agency's Intelligence and Operations Directorates were conducting their own confidential investigation of Morris's sensational document. The initial reaction from the wary analysts was skepticism. The assertion that 1,205 American POWs had been alive in the prison camps of North Vietnam on September 15, 1972, was nonsensical. It was known that scores of Americans captured alive had been killed or died of wounds or illness. Further, it was well documented that more than a hundred American POWs were in camps in South Vietnam at that time. Finally, the combined total of approximately 530 known surviving American POWs with approximately 700 South Vietnamese, Thai, and Taiwanese POWs captured on American-sponsored operations seemed to render a number close to the 1,205 in the Quang report. This calculation sparked the request from Sandy Berger that Morris verify the language of the report.[17]

The Pentagon was also conducting a separate investigation of this document in Moscow through the U.S.-Russian Joint Commission. The American request for the document took several weeks to pass through the Russian bureaucracy, where it met considerable resistance from the "unreconstructed Bolsheviks" in the KGB and GRU who had tried to block the earlier efforts of Task Force Russia. Finally, President Boris Yeltsin intervened and commission member General Dmitri Volkogonov presented his American counterpart, Ambassador Malcolm Toon, with a photocopy of the Quang report on April 8.[18]

Returning to Moscow, Morris was frustrated and disappointed with the seeming lack of action from the American government. He knew the ex-Soviet archives well, and had hoped that he could lead the effort to follow the investigative trail opened by the Quang report. But now he realized he was being rolled over by events. The April 10 issue of *Izvestia* broke the story in Moscow, probably through a leak from Yeltsin's inner circle. Then Morris heard that at least two American publications were ready to run with the article. To counter inaccurate speculation, or outright deception, Morris contacted Celestine Bohlen, the Moscow bureau chief of the *New York Times*. They met and he turned over a copy of the document and briefed her on its origin. The next day, her story, "File Said to Show Hanoi Lied in '72 on Prisoner Totals," ran on the front page of the *Times*.[19]

Bohlen's story was the first pebble in a media landslide that buried the optimistic prospects of pending normalization between America and Vietnam. General John Vessey was in the Bahamas fishing, trying to relax before leaving on his next trip to Vietnam on Saturday, April 16. But when a friend carried a fax copy of the *New York Times* article down to the fishing dock, Vessey realized his next mission to Hanoi would not be easy.[20]

The story dominated the front pages of America's leading newspapers that week and was prominently featured on network television newscasts. Most mainstream media took a balanced approach on the potentially sensational document. The *New York Times* noted that the Clinton administration had asked General Vessey to demand a convincing explanation for the secret Quang report. The paper balanced speculation that as many as 600 American prisoners might have been "killed, died of natural causes or remain in Vietnamese hands," with the obvious incongruities of the document, including the capture of pilots with astronaut qualification and the possibility that these 600 prisoners might have been American Asian allies.[21]

But other newspapers were less prudent. A front-page headline in the *Washington Times* read: "North Vietnam Kept 700 POWs After War." The article gave Stephen Morris prominent coverage and quoted his assertion that the Quang report was a " 'smoking gun' proving duplicity by the Hanoi government."[22]

But one of the most dramatic discussions of the issue occurred on the *MacNeil/Lehrer NewsHour* on the evening of Tuesday, April 13, 1993. In the lead Focus segment, Robert MacNeil led an examination of the document's implications among Stephen Morris, Zbigniew Brzezinski, and Henry Kissinger. Morris was adamant that the document was absolutely authentic. He stated unequivocally that the report was written by Lieutenant General Tran Van Quang as a report to the Politburo of the Vietnamese Communist Party. He added that this sensitive document made its way to Moscow through a Soviet military intelligence agent.[23]

Dr. Brzezinski backed his younger colleague, noting that the style, content, and GRU cover memorandum all evoked authenticity. Only a "complex Byzantine conspiracy" could have produced a forgery, Brzezinski said. He conceded that a few minor items, transliterations of names, or minor numbers of prisoners could be wrong, but the thrust of the document was valid.[24]

Henry Kissinger was somber during this discussion. He admitted that there were many elements in the Quang report that accurately reflected the Vietnamese negotiation position of September 1972. But he challenged the possibility that there could have been as many as 600 more surviving American prisoners than the Vietnamese released six months later.[25]

Brzezinski was less cautious in his assessment. He speculated that the Vietnamese probably did hold up to 1,205 American POWs in 1972, and that they planned to keep back a significant number to use as "further leverage" to force concessions from the United States. After the collapse of South Vietnam in the next two years, however, Brzezinski speculated, the Vietnamese Communists probably "executed those that were still living, perhaps with the exception of a small number whom they retained for continuing intelligence for technical purposes." He compared such a slaughter of prisoners to the 1940 massacre of Polish officers by the Soviets in the Katyn Forest.[26]

Even the *Washington Post* echoed Brzezinski's somber assessment. In a lead editorial on April 13, the *Post* noted that the Quang document raised the "extremely distressing question" of whether the Vietnamese Communists had held a total of 1,205 American POWs and then "finally killed the 600—destroying the evidence, so to speak."[27]

These shocking speculations by a respected scholar and a moderate-liberal newspaper reflected the generally inflamed nature of the debate. Brzezinski's dramatic comments also intensified the pressure on the Clinton White House to hold the Vietnamese publicly accountable on this issue. As Vessey prepared to leave for Hanoi, accompanied by several advisers, including the State Department's Kenneth Quinn, the Clinton administration scrambled to gain control of the issue. The White House emphasized that obtaining answers from the Vietnamese would be General Vessey's "first order of business" in Hanoi.[28]

(There can be no doubt that party, government, and military leaders in Hanoi were fully aware of the media volcano erupting in America after the release of the Quang document. These leaders received weekly editions of *Tin Tham Klao* from the Vietnam News Service. This was a restricted digest of foreign press commentary of particular interest to senior officials. Every article and news broadcast on the Quang document was reproduced in both the original and in Vietnamese translation, and circulated among a small group of key officials in Hanoi.[29])

The Defense Department (and particularly the DIA) had been blindsided by the sudden media firestorm. The DIA's initial assessment of Morris had been negative. Because Morris refused to share the photocopy of the Quang document with the Pentagon, DIA assumed it was either a fabrication or Morris's summary of it was exaggerated.[30]

And because the American government did not obtain a copy of the Quang report until April 8—after which it took several days to produce a translation and circulate it among the offices most concerned—the news media moved far ahead of the administration on the public assessment of the document. And while the media speculation boiled, DIA analysts dissected the Quang text. They quickly found blatant incongruities that raised serious doubts about the authenticity of the report's content, if not its provenance.

Although the Russian text and the GRU cover memorandum seemed to be authentic Soviet artifacts, the report itself did not appear to be valid for a number of important reasons. First, the Quang statement that 1,205 American POWs had been captured up to September 1972 and that there were "1,205 American POWs presently in prisons of North Vietnam" was clearly erroneous for the reasons noted above. A number were known to have died and over one hundred were in prison camps in South Vietnam. Further, the assertion that American POWs had been dispersed to eleven separate camps for security reasons following the Son Tay raid was known to be false. The Vietnamese had reacted in exactly the *opposite* manner after the abortive November 1970 rescue attempt. A number of outlying camps had been closed down and prisoners were consolidated into Hanoi, principally into Hoa Lo Prison, the Zoo, and the Plantation.

Although colonels were segregated within Hoa Lo Prison, lieutenant colonels and Navy commanders, as well as majors and lieutenant commanders, were not concentrated into separate camps.[31] However, younger junior officers were eventually moved to the isolated camp on the Chinese border known as Dogpatch.

The DIA assessed the report's assertion that only 368 POWs holding "progressive views" would be liberated first, and that all "senior officers hold reactionary views" and would thus not be immediately repatriated, as totally erroneous. All the senior officers alive in captivity were repatriated, some in the first Operation Homecoming exchange.[32]

This preliminary assessment was made available to General Vessey as his delegation prepared to leave for Hanoi. The DIA also began a public relations effort to undercut the exaggerated speculation surrounding the report. "There are a lot of questions we have about it," Pentagon spokesman Bob Hall told reporters. One of the biggest problems was that there was no Vietnamese original text available for analysis and comparison to similar documents. Further, intelligence experts and scholars noted that there was uncertainty whether General Quang had served as deputy chief of staff of the PAVN in 1972. Many accounts carried him as the commander of the PAVN's Military Region 4 (the B-4 Front), which straddled North Vietnam's southern provinces and the Demilitarized Zone.[33]

The Defense Department found an unexpected ally in the *New York Times*. An editorial on April 14 noted that there were "sound reasons to investigate the new document" before jumping to sensational conclusions. "Communist archives are notorious for disinformation and forgeries." And, the *Times* added, the existence of 600 additional surviving prisoners in 1972 seemed "dubious" when examined in light of the wartime casualty records.[34]

The new director of the DIA's Special Office for POW/MIAs, Robert R. Sheetz, stated publicly that the Quang report contained erroneous information. "DIA believes the number 1,205 could be an accurate accounting of total prisoners held, including American, ARVN [South Vietnamese military] and Thai POWs." But, Sheetz added, the numbers in the document "cannot be an accurate accounting if discussing only U.S. POWs."[35] Former DIA analyst Sedgwick D. Tourison, Jr., publicly announced that American intelligence had known for years from North Vietnamese documents and broadcasts that it was Hanoi's wartime policy to refer to Asian covert operations personnel as "American commandos...American spies or saboteurs."[36] Therefore, Tourison stated, the missing 600 "American" POWs referred to in the Quang document could easily have been South Vietnamese and other Asians. If this were the case, he said, the total number of POWs in the Politburo report was "not inconsistent with the known facts of 1972."[37]

(The Quang document stated that forty-seven American POWs captured on covert operations included "36 special operations forces advisers who were inserted in the border region between DRV with Laos." This is a clear reference to espionage, reconnaissance, and sabotage operations conducted by U.S. Military Assistance Command, Vietnam/Studies and Operations Group [MACV/SOG]. Both Major General John K. Singlaub and Colonel Steven Cavanaugh, who were wartime commanders of MACV/SOG, are adamant that none of their American personnel were lost during agent insertion missions along the North Vietnamese–Lao border. There were approximately fifteen American MIAs from MACV/SOG operations along the Ho Chi Minh Trail area of Laos and Cambodia bordering South Vietnam. However, both officers recall that as many as forty-seven Asian Special Operations personnel on MACV/SOG missions could have been captured further north in Laos. But Cavanaugh made it clear, "Those men were *Vietnamese*, not American."[38])

While the Pentagon was fighting this rear-guard action, activists were having a predictable field day. Their champion, Senator Bob Smith, went on record endorsing the report's accuracy. "It's an authentic document. There's no question about that." He noted that the report predicted the Vietnamese would free several POWs in order to put pressure on the Nixon administration, and that three American prisoners were freed ten days later.[39] Smith also tried to refute Pentagon assertions that wartime estimates of surviving prisoners could have been off by a gap of more than 600 men. The number of POWs cited in the Russian document, Smith told a news conference, "is essentially accurate."[40]

There were a number of historically valid facts in the Quang document. But that did not mean that the report was not a forgery. Douglas Pike, the respected director of the Indochina Archive at the University of California, Berkeley, was familiar with many ingenious and elaborate forged documents created by both sides during and after the Vietnam War. While working with the American mission in Saigon in the mid-1960s, Pike encountered just such a forged document. The U.S. government had been trying for months to retrieve an authentic North Vietnamese Army document to prove that regular Communist soldiers from the North were fighting in the South. Finally, U.S. military intelligence did find the needed document on the body of an NVA soldier killed in the Central Highlands. The document was released to the press in Washington with considerable fanfare. A few weeks later, Pike was drinking an afternoon beer on the terrace of the Hotel Continental when he was joined by an acquaintance from the South Vietnamese Central Intelligence Organization.

"How did you like our NVA document?" the Vietnamese asked, unable to hide a gleeful grin.

"*Your* document?" Pike replied, astounded.

The Vietnamese intelligence officer explained that his organization had salted five such documents on enemy dead in the hopes that the Americans would find at least one.

Years later, Pike recalled that both the South and North Vietnamese were masters at such "black" documentation.[41]

IN HANOI, NEWS of the purported Quang document struck like a thunder-clap, completely upsetting the plans for the scheduled April 18 arrival of what leaders hoped would be the final Vessey delegation before the lifting of the embargo and the restoration of diplomatic relations.

Ted Schweitzer was quickly made privy to the discussions being held at high levels of the PAVN and Politburo. His GPD contacts again wanted to use him as a back-channel reporting conduit to the American government. He learned that the Hanoi Politburo viewed the Quang document as a serious threat to relations with the United States. Accordingly, only President Le Duc Anh and Foreign Minister Nguyen Manh Cam would be allowed to comment on the document publicly. They had been charged by the Politburo to investigate the matter thoroughly and deal directly with the American delegation.

"The Russians are behind this," Colonel Dai told Schweitzer at the museum. "There will also probably be more such documents from Soviet archives," Dai added somberly.

The overall mood among General Political Directorate officers was one of anger and frustration. They told Schweitzer they knew the Quang document discovered in Moscow was a fabrication, but they did not know its exact provenance. They explained that the Quang document was at best completely "misleading," and at worst an outright forgery. They recognized that the Soviet Union had a number of penetration agents in the North Vietnamese military and government during the war. Therefore, it was not surprising that one of these agents had filed a distorted report. Further, they were not surprised that the Yeltsin government in Moscow had allowed this approach to reach a Western scholar such as Morris.

"Yeltsin is an anti-Communist," Dai explained. "He is trying to curry favor with America to win support and stay in power."[42]

Dai and his colleagues explained to Schweitzer that the Vietnamese government was assembling a number of important documents to present to General Vessey in order to prove that the Quang document was either a distorted and erroneous agent's message or a forgery.

This would not be too difficult, Dai indicated, because the Quang document was replete with errors, perhaps the product of a Russian GRU officer with an overly active imagination. "If it had been a Vietnamese intelligence officer," Dai said with a scornful smile, "at least he would have had his facts straight."

For example, Dai said, the title of the report itself, which noted that Lieutenant General Tran Van Quang was addressing the Hanoi Politburo, was incorrect. Quang had never used his real name during the war, Dai explained. All high-ranking officers used aliases and signed all documents accordingly. Tran Van Quang's alias was "Bay Tien," which meant "Seventh Child." Any document signed by Bay Tien, or which mentioned that name, referred to Lieutenant General Tran Van Quang. Dai knew this to be a fact because Quang was also a senior officer in the General Political Directorate.

Beyond this problem, there was glaring incongruity of textual style in "Quang's" purported remarks. Dai and Mui made it clear to Schweitzer that no one coming before the Politburo to address its members could have used the almost conversational tone that ran throughout the document's text. A person addressing this body would have employed lengthy and cumbersome honorific formalities, which would have been repeated throughout the address. In that the Quang document was completely devoid of such mandatory honorific forms of address—other than a perfunctory "Honored Comrades"—the General Political Directorate (who were trained to recognize forgeries) were convinced the document was a fraud.

The Vietnamese therefore knew that the source of the document had to either have been a Russian officer, or a poorly informed Vietnamese agent who had delivered false reports to his Russian case officer.

But the Hanoi government was aware of the media impact the Quang document had made in the West. PAVN officers told Schweitzer that Hanoi planned to present their own documents to the Americans that proved the Moscow report contained false information. Then, as in the past, Hanoi planned to hunker down and simply outwait the American side.

Reporting to the DIA, Schweitzer described this as Hanoi "adopting a bunker attitude."[43]

The widely publicized speculation that the Vietnamese might have executed in cold blood 600 or more American POWs held back after Operation Homecoming provoked true alarm among Schweitzer's PAVN contacts. They recognized that Communist Vietnam would be branded an international pariah if such a blatant, calculated massacre could be proven. Certainly, the United States would not soon renew diplomatic relations with Vietnam if this speculation became widely accepted as historic fact. So, with the approval of the General Political Directorate, Colonel Dai carefully detailed to Schweitzer the categories and types of American prisoners of war who had been killed or who had died in captivity.

The first category included those captured in good physical condition who were executed for disobeying commands on the battlefield—refusing to run for cover with the PAVN captors when American rescue forces appeared.

A second group were those captured wounded along the trail or in the South who were executed because they could not easily be moved.

The third group included those killed resisting capture.

A fourth category were those killed attempting escape and those who died in the jungle after escaping.

Prisoners beaten to death by peasants and rural militia formed a fifth category.

Dai confirmed Lieutenant Colonel Thi's earlier statement that an indeterminate number were also tortured to death in prison, thus forming a sixth category.

An entirely separate, seventh category of Americans killed were those executed by government order. The only men who fit this category, Dai stated, were a small number of "drug criminals" arrested after the conquest of the South by Communist forces.[44]

As Schweitzer made his careful notes, he recognized that this was the first substantive admission by any Vietnamese official that captured Americans had died from causes other than wounds or illness. If nothing else, the Quang document was forcing Vietnam to break its two decades of silence on this emotional issue.

Major Mui was even more forthcoming after Colonel Dai left the museum that afternoon. He took Schweitzer aside and spoke in clipped grave tones. Mui had a "colleague" in Hanoi who had served in Laos with the PAVN late in the war. On an undisclosed date, Mui said, ten American POWs held in a cave prison had overcome their guards and escaped into the surrounding jungle. All ten were recaptured by Pathet Lao auxiliaries of the PAVN, who returned the Americans to the Vietnamese. Mui's acquaintance was in the PAVN group that returned the American prisoners to the cave.

"Then they threw grenades into the cave and blew up the Americans," Mui said.

"They killed them?" At Mui's request, Schweitzer had stopped taking notes.

"I think so," Mui said, clearly uneasy. It was as if he were under orders to reveal this information, but found the duty almost unbearable. "I will try to get more details," Mui promised.[45]

ON APRIL 16, 1993, Ted Schweitzer went to Bangkok to brief General Vessey and members of his delegation before they flew on to Hanoi to confront the Vietnamese authorities about the Quang document. On the night of April 17, Schweitzer met with General Vessey, the State Department's Kenneth Quinn, and Ed Ross of the DIA. They told Schweitzer that the current assessment of the document was that it contained certain indisputable factual elements.

"It's not entirely a fake," Ross explained.

But "three quarters of the American public believes the document is authentic," Quinn added.

"Well," Schweitzer said, "the Vietnamese sure believe it's a forgery."[46]

General Vessey explained that the "only possible solution" to the impasse would be for the Vietnamese to give the United States enough hard evidence to refute the Quang report's major points. "Otherwise," Vessey said somberly, "it could be years before relations are normalized."

Schweitzer gave the Vessey delegation a computer printout of the notes he had made concerning Colonel Dai's revelations categorizing the deaths of captured Americans. It was clear from this report that the Vietnamese recognized the gravity of the situation and that their traditional hollow platitudes about the "humane treatment" American POWs had received would not suffice under the present circumstances.

Indeed, one of the officers noted with bitter irony, even Jane Fonda or Joan Baez might be having doubts after reading the Quang document.

Before returning to Hanoi, Schweitzer met again with James Renaud. The case officer told Schweitzer that National Security Adviser Anthony Lake had specifically tasked the DIA to have Schweitzer search whatever PAVN archives were still open to him to locate any additional document of embarrassing potential. If he found one, he was to contact Renaud immediately.

The Vietnamese had begun their own media counteroffensive before General Vessey's group arrived in Hanoi. Nguyen Xuan Phong, the director of the Americas Department of the Foreign Ministry, told the *New York Times* that Hanoi had "very strong evidence" proving the Quang document was a "clear fabrication." He said that Quang was definitely not the deputy chief of staff of the PAVN in 1972, but rather the commander of Military Region 4, a position he had held from 1966 to 1974. Although the purported Quang document from Moscow raised "suspicions from the American people," Phong said, he did not believe such a forgery would "reverse the belief that Vietnam has cooperated very well in this humanitarian issue over the fate of the missing Americans."[47]

Meanwhile in the United States, the radical POW/MIA activists were rallying behind Senator Bob Smith, who gave multiple interviews and called several news conferences to keep up the media pressure on the Vietnamese. In one interview, Smith resurrected earlier intelligence reports indicating Vietnam might have been holding American POWs as hostages in the late 1970s, to extract the payment of promised American war reparations. Smith's ally, former Congressman Billy Hendon, also referred to detailed CIA reports of a possible hostage-reparations swap.[48]

The CIA made the unusual step of formally announcing that these field reports from the 1970s were now considered unreliable fabrications.

To some longtime observers of Vietnamese-American relations, it almost appeared that U.S. intelligence was running a sophisticated good-cop, bad-cop operation on Hanoi, with Smith and his allies cast in the role of heavies, while General Vessey and his delegation appeared to be the honest brokers sincerely interested in receiving any exculpatory documents the Vietnamese could provide.

Perhaps this scenario was not valid, but nevertheless events in Hanoi developed as if it were.

As in October 1992, the April 1993 Vessey delegation was not distracted by unnecessary protocol or diplomatic frivolity. Vessey and his team met with Foreign Minister Nguyen Manh Cam, Deputy Foreign Minister Le Mai, and Ho Xuan Dich of the VNOSMP shortly after arriving in Hanoi.

Meeting in the Foreign Ministry conference room, the two delegations immediately addressed the problem of the Quang document. General Vessey noted that the document discovered in Moscow "raises some very serious questions that I will address with you, and I hope for some answers." Vessey emphasized that he had personally asked former Soviet General Dmitri Volkogonov to verify the validity of the report. "It is an authentic Russian document," Vessey said.

Speaking for the Vietnamese side, Le Mai followed the exact approach that Schweitzer had delineated in Bangkok. He called the Quang document "a concoction and a fabrication, not only against Vietnam, but against normalization between Vietnam and the United States."[49]

The Vietnamese proceeded to enumerate the glaring errors in the Quang document. Foremost was the fact that Lieutenant General Tran Van Quang was not in Hanoi, or even in Vietnam in September 1972, when he allegedly briefed the Politburo on the POW question. He had been the commander of the B-4 Front straddling the Demilitarized Zone in September 1972. There had been no Politburo meeting in September 1972. Further, the Vietnamese emphasized what the American delegation already knew: that American prisoners were not segregated by rank or degree of political "progressiveness."[50]

The Vietnamese side next presented materials that they said would refute the Quang report. Dich opened a bundle and laid out six documents on the wide table. He announced that these were important historical records that had only been "discovered" in Defense Ministry archives during the previous week, while the Vietnamese government searched for proof to refute the Quang report.

The most important document was the Blue Book (not to be confused with the Blue Files). This was a ragged, mildewed ledger with a faded blue-gray cover. The first page of the ledger was faded and water-stained, but the hand-printed Vietnamese words were legible, which translated as: "Index No. 6, Number of Americans in Prison, 39 Pages in This Document."[51]

The book was the central registry of American prisoners, recording their arrival at Hoa Lo Prison in Hanoi. The first entry on the wide, horizontal-format page, written in typically neat cursive with a fine-nibbed pen, was for August 5, 1964. The name listed for this entry was Everett Alvarez, Jr., the first American aviator shot down and captured over North Vietnam. The second entry was for Robert Harper Shumaker, the second known American POW in North Vietnam, who was shot down on February 11, 1965, and registered in Hoa Lo Prison on the same day.

The Blue Book registry continued in this manner for thirty-nine wide pages. A number of entries had been pasted over with hand-cut strips of graying white paper, some marked with the word "dead" *(chết)*. The last numbered entry on page thirty-nine was name 374, Nobert A. Gotner, an F-4D pilot shot down in Laos on February 3, 1971, and registered in Hoa Lo Prison two days later on February 5. There were twelve more names listed on this page, but not numbered, bringing the total number of entries in the Blue Book registry to 386, the last being James D. Cutter, an F-105G pilot shot down on February 17, 1972. The Blue Book contained no listings for the forty-three known captures from February 1972 through the Linebacker II campaign.

The American delegation immediately realized that the Blue Book was an extremely valuable document. Because the handwritten entries listed not only the date of shootdown, but also the date of registry in Hoa Lo Prison, some men shot down in the southern provinces of North Vietnam or in Laos were registered later than men who had been captured after them, but closer to Hanoi. And because General Political Directorate officers in the prison system were rarely in the direct communication chain with the PAVN units that shot down and captured the Americans, officials at Hoa Lo Prison had to depend on the documents accompanying a new prisoner for his date and place of shootdown. Thus it would have been difficult to fabricate an elaborate handwritten register that accurately reflected the exact arrival dates at the Heartbreak Hotel courtyard in Hoa Lo Prison for 386 American POWs.

Certainly the Vietnamese were capable of creating a forgery of this complexity, but they probably could not produce one that would stand up to the rigorous forensic analysis to which they knew American intelligence would subject the Blue Book.

The other documents Dich provided included more detailed shootdown reports from Air Defense regiments operating throughout North Vietnam and adjacent regions of Laos. Finally, Dich turned over the most detailed lists to date of U.S. POWs who had died in captivity.

The next day, General Vessey's delegation met directly with Lieutenant General Tran Van Quang. He showed them internal PAVN records that verified that he had been the commander of Military Region 4 (B-4 Front) in 1972. He also showed records that he had served twice as deputy chief of staff of the PAVN, from 1959 to 1960, and later, from 1974 to 1978, but not in 1972, as the Quang report alleged. "I was not in Hanoi at that time," Quang told Vessey. "I was never in charge of American prisoners of war."[52]

After two days of meetings, the Vietnamese and American delegations held a joint press conference in Hanoi. Lieutenant General Tran Van Quang, clearly uncomfortable with this level of media scrutiny, told the assembled reporters that he had nothing to do with the document that bore his name. "I did not write it. I tell you, never in my life have I made such a report because it was not my area of responsibility." Quang repeated that he was not in Hanoi at that time, nor was he the deputy chief of staff of the PAVN in 1972. He repeated that the document was a fabrication. When a reporter asked who might have fabricated the report, Quang snapped, "You can ask the Russian intelligence services."[53]

Reporters asked General Vessey if he now had more doubts about the authenticity of the Quang document. "Yes," Vessey replied. When asked if he accepted General Quang's version of his service record, Vessey replied that Quang's statements were "not inconsistent" with what the Pentagon already knew of his background. Then Vessey added, "I have no reason to disbelieve General Quang."[54]

The Vessey delegation left Hanoi that night, carrying with them some of the most important POW documents the Vietnamese had released since Operation Swamp Ranger.

GENERAL VESSEY MET with President Clinton and his national security advisers on April 21, 1993. The consensus of the Vessey delegation was that the Quang document was a flawed report of a GRU agent in Hanoi, reporting to Soviet control officers. The evidence the Vietnamese government had presented seriously undercut the accuracy of the Quang document. However, because the report did contain a certain amount of accurate information, it would have to be subjected to a rigorous intelligence analysis before a final determination could be made as to its accuracy and authenticity.[55]

This situation was not altogether unwelcome by the branches of the American government most concerned with extracting maximum information from the Vietnamese. Clearly the Vietnamese were becoming desperate; otherwise they would not have "discovered" the Blue Book, which contained sensitive information about American POWs who had arrived in reasonably good health at the interrogation center of Hoa Lo Prison, but were subsequently listed as "dead." If the White House kept its nerve regarding the embargo over the coming months, the United States could probably extract even more important POW information from Hanoi.

After Vessey briefed the President, White House spokesman George

Stephanopoulos said, "We're going to continue to review our relations with Vietnam, but until we have a full and complete accounting of the POWs, we can't move forward" toward normalization.[56]

At a Pentagon press conference, General Vessey displayed copies of Blue Book pages and commented on the Quang document. He said that, while the document was an authentic Soviet artifact, most of the "alleged facts" in it were not accurate. For example, he noted, American prisoners were never strictly segregated by rank, and the number of prisons was reduced after the Son Tay raid, not increased. Most importantly, the Quang document's assertion that 624 American aviators were captured inside North Vietnam was inaccurate. Casualty records showed that only 355 airmen could have survived their losses over North Vietnam as of February 1972. In the eight months between February and September 1972, another 108 airmen were lost in North Vietnam. Even if all of them survived—which he said was highly unlikely—the maximum number of such aviator POWs would have been 463.[57]

Commenting on the Blue Book, Vessey said the United States had requested Vietnam provide that document for years. Although Vessey did not comment on the intelligence bonanza the Blue Book represented, he did note the register would be carefully studied. Because it was an internal Vietnamese document, he said, it was particularly valuable.

"You could say, 'well, they lied to us,' and that's a good assertion," Vessey said wryly. "But why should they lie to themselves?"[58]

CHAPTER 26

As THE SECOND HALF OF 1993 PROGRESSED, THE CLINTON ADMIN-
istration tried to emulate the type of "prudent middle course" in its relations
toward Vietnam that the Bush administration had codified in the Road
Map.[1]

But this was not easy. Following the near debacle of the Quang document,
a suspicion lingered among the American public that the Vietnamese might
be hiding a monstrous atrocity, while the inept and credulous policymakers
in Clinton's Pentagon and State Department allowed themselves to be duped
by Hanoi. This was certainly the thrust of conservative criticism of Clinton's
Vietnam policy during the late spring and summer.[2] On the other side of
the issue, the American business community voiced its impatience over the
lack of progress in lifting the final stages of the economic embargo with
Vietnam.[3] And traditional liberal intellectuals chided Clinton for bowing to
the unreasonable pressures of the more irrational POW/MIA activists, who
were seen as pawns of hidebound conservatives determined to torpedo
improved relations with Vietnam.[4]

To his credit, Bill Clinton resisted capitulating to any of these disparate
pressure groups. By retaining the spirit of the Bush Road Map, Clinton's
administration managed to squeeze more information and remains from the
Vietnamese, while stingily responding with American concessions.

A week after General Vessey returned from Hanoi, the Vietnamese turned
over a typewritten ledger of 492 American POWs captured in North Vietnam
between August 5, 1964, and the last day of the Linebacker II bombing,
December 28, 1972. This was an obvious update of the Blue Book, which
Vessey had requested in Hanoi. Although this typewritten "List of American
Prisoners, No. 5," did not lend itself to the same type of analytical scrutiny
as the handwritten Blue Book, the new ledger did contain important information.[5]

For example, on page fifteen of the new list, the entry for Earl Glenn
Cobeil listed him as "dead: 5-11-1970." This meant Cobeil, the Air Force
captain tortured into insanity by the sadistic Cuban officer in Cu Loc Prison,
had eventually succumbed to his injuries on November 5, 1970. Receiving
this official Vietnamese confirmation of the date of Cobeil's death permitted
DIA analysts to perform verification analysis of his and other death reports

from the POW debriefings after Operation Homecoming. In effect, this official PAVN document could be used as a validator of debriefing reports.[6]

Another intriguing element of this new list was the omission of Laos shootdowns. This meant that the open listing of capture sites in Laos in the Blue Book tended to augment that document's authenticity. In the Blue Book, there is a whited-out name block, but personal data for Air Force Major Walter Stischer, a 1968 Laos shootdown and capture, for example; but his name does not appear in the later list. These omissions in the typewritten ledger also tended to support *its* particular authenticity, in that it reflected the official 1972 view that North Vietnam held no American prisoners captured in Laos.

Also, the Blue Book listed the full names of a man's wife, and also of his parents, personal information a Vietnamese forger would have been unable to obtain.

While the Pentagon was continuing to tweak Vietnam into releasing more documents, President Clinton was trying to prepare American public opinion for the inevitable endgame in which the embargo would be lifted and diplomatic relations established. To do this, Clinton had to face the divisive issue of his own antiwar conduct in the 1960s, as well as his efforts to avoid military service during the Vietnam War.

Clinton followed General Colin Powell's advice in deciding to deliver his first Memorial Day speech at the Vietnam Veterans Memorial in Washington. As predicted, a small but raucous group of Vietnam veterans—or at least men dressed in camouflage fatigues who claimed to be Vietnam veterans—put on a well-publicized protest demonstration on the sloping lawns leading to the somber, recessed black granite chevron known as "The Wall." Many of these protesters carried placards denouncing Clinton and warning of a possible sellout of live POWs in Indochina. One placard seemed to epitomize the protesters' view: "Never, ever trust a draft dodger."[7]

Clinton told his audience, "Let us continue to disagree, if we must, about the war, but let us not let it divide us as a people any longer." He promised to renew the nation's pledge to the families of the missing that America would do all it could for them. He noted that he had ordered the complete declassification of all U.S. records relating to POWs and MIAs from the Vietnam War. This was one of the few places in his speech where the President received loud applause.[8]

Meanwhile, others were keeping up the pressure on the Vietnamese. Senators John McCain and John Kerry, accompanied by representatives of American veterans groups, traveled yet again to Hanoi over the Memorial Day weekend. Once more they urged the Vietnamese to release documents known from Ted Schweitzer's Operation Swamp Ranger research to exist. On this visit, Ho Xuan Dich turned over a complete census of American and other Southeast Asian POWs held in South Vietnam between 1964 and 1972. As with the typewritten North Vietnam POW ledger, this prison camp census from the South verified the deaths of a number of missing Americans. And for the first time, the Vietnamese presented material from the Blue Files. These consisted of medical reports on over 300 POWs, some who died of injuries and wounds in captivity.[9]

But the mood of the visit was not congenial. When Dich fell back to the traditional policy line that American POWs had been humanely treated and had even received such amenities as magazines, John McCain cut him short. "I never got any magazines to read," McCain snapped. "Let's go on to the next issue."[10]

As the summer continued, the stage was set for the American response to Vietnam's latest concessions. Despite mounting pressure from conservatives and some veterans groups, the Clinton administration prepared to lift its opposition to international loans to Vietnam, which would allow Hanoi to pay off its $140 million to the International Monetary Fund, and thus gain access to much larger overseas credit markets. Conservatives saw this as the Rubicon in the embargo issue. Once Hanoi had tapped into multibillion-dollar development loans, continuing the U.S. embargo would only penalize American corporations vis-à-vis their foreign competitors.[11]

The Clinton administration officially lifted its opposition to international bridge loans to Hanoi on Friday, July 2, 1993, just before the start of the long Independence Day weekend. As expected, there was little furor in the mainstream press. This was partially due to the timing, but also to the astute preparations the White House had made in Congress. The day before Clinton's announcement, a bipartisan group of nineteen influential congressmen, including Vietnam veterans and former prisoners of war, signed a letter urging Clinton to lift opposition to the loans.[12]

But the White House soon made it clear that the administration would not lift the final strictures of the trade embargo until Vietnam had made more progress on completing the "full accounting" of American MIAs in Southeast Asia. "This is not a commercial or diplomatic issue for the President," Deputy National Security Adviser Sandy Berger told the National League of Families. "It's a moral one."[13]

DURING THIS PERIOD one of the strangest of the many bizarre American MIA groups to visit Vietnam arrived in Hanoi. Convicted collaborator, former Marine Private First Class Robert Garwood, accompanied by Senator Bob Smith and a television crew from ABC's *20/20,* spent several days in Vietnam in mid-July. The purpose of the trip was for Garwood to show Senator Smith and his delegation of activists the four sites in Hanoi and the nearby provinces where Garwood had allegedly seen groups of live American POWs in the mid-1970s, several years after all had allegedly been returned during Operation Homecoming.[14]

Bobby Garwood was one of the most controversial figures in the entire

MIA issue. He was the only American prisoner of war known to have not only collaborated with the Vietnamese Communists, but to have also "crossed over" to the enemy side and worn their uniform in combat against his fellow Americans.[15]

Garwood was a young Marine serving as a teenage driver in the 3rd Marine Division motor pool in Da Nang. He was captured driving alone near the village of Cam Hai on September 28, 1965. For the next year and a half, Garwood was a prisoner of war, moved repeatedly from camp to camp and reportedly receiving the same brutal treatment from his captors as the other Americans he was held with.

But sometime during this period, Garwood began cooperating with the enemy. After repeated indoctrination, Garwood accepted an official National Liberation Front "Order of Release" in May 1967. Under the terms of this propaganda document, Garwood declined the alleged offer to be freed and asked to join the Vietcong and continue the struggle against the American imperialists. He accepted the Vietnamese name Nguyen Chien Dao.[16] Garwood reportedly joined the Military Proselytizing section of PAVN Military Region 5. He conducted loudspeaker propaganda broadcasts near Marine positions, and guarded and indoctrinated U.S. POWs, urging them to follow his lead and "cross over."[17]

During this period, Garwood also reportedly took part in armed combat operations against American forces, a charge he later denied. But in July 1968, a Marine patrol from the 1st Force Reconnaissance Company operating out of the Phu Bai combat base encountered an enemy force near a boulder-strewn stream. In the firefight that ensued, the Marines saw an armed Caucasian in Vietcong uniform among the enemy. He was of average height with brown hair and spoke clear American English. This obvious American was wounded and was heard to cry, "Help me!" as he fell.[18]

When the patrol was debriefed, members identified pictures of Robert Garwood as the "American Vietcong" they had wounded. One of the patrol members, Paul Olenski, vividly remembers that firefight more than twenty-five years later. He remembers Garwood being hit by grenade fragments and possibly M-16 fire, and crying as he fell behind a boulder, "Help me, help me! I'm hit."[19]

(Activists who now claim Garwood was always an exploited POW and never a true defector would do well to read Zalin B. Grant's 1968 *New Republic* article, "American Defectors with the Viet Cong."[20] This account demonstrates that American military intelligence was well aware of Garwood's voluntary service with the enemy in the late 1960s.)

Garwood denies that he was in the firefight and that he was wounded at that time.

Later in 1968, Garwood was promoted to officer status in the National Liberation Front and held a rank equivalent to lieutenant.[21]

Garwood disappeared from POW camps in the South in 1969. Ten years later in Hanoi, he passed a note to a Finnish businessman requesting help in leaving Vietnam. On March 22, 1979, Garwood left Vietnam and returned to U.S. custody. He was court-martialed by the Marine Corps. In 1981, Garwood was convicted of communicating with the enemy and assaulting a fellow prisoner of war. Garwood's sentence did not include imprisonment, but he was demoted to the rank of private and dishonorably discharged with the loss of all pay and allowances.[22]

While his case was on appellate review, Garwood raised the claim that he had encountered live American prisoners of war in North Vietnam after Operation Homecoming. Garwood offered to provide details about these alleged POWs in exchange for immunity from future prosecution. The Marine Corps did not agree to his request.[23]

This was unnecessary. Contrary to later claims by activists and ill-informed writers, Garwood was thoroughly debriefed by Defense Intelligence Agency and Marine Corps intelligence officers, as well as by Congressmen Lester L. Wolff and Benjamin A. Gilman, soon after his return from Hanoi in March 1979. The DIA analyzed the Marine intelligence interview and noted that ". . . Garwood provided no information which would confirm that Americans still remain in Vietnam. Garwood has provided only rumors common during the years following the fall of Saigon and reported to DIA via other sources in the past." In a 1993 Defense Department investigation of Garwood's case, it was noted that Garwood "said that he had 'heard from the populace' that there were other POWs, but that he had *not* seen any himself."[24]

Further, other Americans who spoke with Garwood before his court martial report that he had no firsthand knowledge of live POWs in Vietnam. Mr. and Mrs. George L. Brooks, whose son was a Navy MIA in Laos, met with Garwood while his court martial was pending. They tape-recorded an interview in which they asked him if he had seen any other live Americans. "There might possibly be some men still alive in Vietnam," Garwood told the Brookses, but he made no claim that he had seen any himself.[25]

But in 1984, Bobby Garwood told journalist Bill Paul of the *Wall Street Journal* that he had seen a number of live American prisoners in North Vietnam, including men being unloaded from a boxcar at Yen Bai. Others, Garwood said, were being used as guinea pigs in psychological warfare courses being given by the Vietnamese to visiting Cuban and Palestinian groups.[26]

Garwood's sensational tale was exploited by the news media. In a December 1985 *60 Minutes* segment, it was asserted that Garwood had never been debriefed and by implication that the U.S. government was not interested in his information on live POWs. Even though the Pentagon refuted this allegation, it became an article of faith and was widely disseminated among true believers.[27] No matter how hard the Pentagon tried to quash the rumor that Garwood had not been thoroughly debriefed, it seemed to have become a central canon in the theology of the radical POW/MIA activists.[28]

Now, in 1993, Garwood, who had spent ten full years as an active collaborator and colleague of the Vietnamese Communists, was back in Hanoi trailing a U.S. senator and a television camera crew, claiming he could identify the sites where American POWs had been held after the war. The most dramatic, and "visual," to the *20/20* producers was the visit of Garwood and Smith to Thach Ba Lake north of Hanoi. There Garwood pointed out a pile of masonry rubble on a small island and explained that was where he had seen a "motel-like" POW camp in the late 1970s, which held a large number of American captives.[29]

The Pentagon immediately disputed Garwood's claim, noting that satellite imagery of that island proved the ruined structure he identified had not existed before he left the country in 1979.[30] Moreover, the Defense Department leaked information to reporter Susan Katz Keating that it had probably been activist former Congressman Billy Hendon who had photographed this rubble heap—an abandoned brick kiln—on a prior visit and coached Garwood to lead the Smith delegation to this site. (Such spent brick kilns are a common feature of the Red River Delta, where clay deposits are found.)

Reacting angrily to this information, Senator John McCain stated that the role of Billy Hendon in the whole "affair on Thach Ba Lake" should be thoroughly investigated by the Justice Department.[31]

This would have been simply one more bizarre issue had Ross Perot not sided with Garwood, citing his visit to Vietnam as a substantive reason for not lifting the trade embargo.[32]

Whatever the merit of the charges against Hendon, the often unpredictable activist reversed field once more—possibly to deflect scrutiny of his involvement with Garwood. On July 22, 1993, Hendon wrote President Clinton "to respectfully request that you lift the trade embargo against Vietnam at the earliest possible moment." This, Hendon said, was the only hope for repatriating live American POWs.[33]

The Vietnamese were not amused by Garwood's antics during this visit. PAVN officers contacted Ted Schweitzer to discuss how much influence Garwood had over the American news media and whether it was in Vietnam's interest to reveal Garwood's full role as a collaborator and Communist Party member. They claimed that Garwood had only decided to leave Vietnam after his application to become a full member of the Vietnamese Communist Party was rejected. They also repeated that Garwood had held a minor technical job with PAVN transportation units and had certainly not seen American prisoners as he claimed.[34]

However, in discussing the Garwood episode, Colonel Pham Duc Dai told Schweitzer that Garwood's former commander, a colonel named Teo, had been fully responsible for Garwood, "and the others."

(Dai spoke in French: *Monsieur Teo était le chef de Monsieur Garwood et les autres.*)

Schweitzer asked: *"Les autres?* The others? What others?"

But Colonel Dai quickly retreated, saying he had misspoken.

In Schweitzer's comments to the DIA, he noted that Colonel Dai virtually never made that kind of mistake.[35] It was certainly possible that Garwood had not been alone in Hanoi during those years after 1973. The Pentagon had been virtually certain that there had been at least two more "line crossers" in Hanoi, who like Garwood had voluntarily joined the Vietnamese Communist cause.

Once more, Schweitzer repeated his mantra, "Nothing in Vietnam is ever straightforward or simple."

FOLLOWING GARWOOD'S STRANGE return to Vietnam, Assistant Secretary of State Winston Lord led yet another delegation to Hanoi. Responding to the smoldering Vietnamese resentment that America only cared about its own relative handful of MIAs, Lord turned over a large microfilm archive of U.S. military records. The archive was an omnibus collection of after-action reports, intelligence summaries, lists of the names of dead Vietcong and PAVN soldiers, with their burial sites, and photocopies of Vietnamese soldiers' diaries, love letters, and even poems. These documents were described as containing information that would help Vietnam resolve the fates and burial sites of some of its own 300,000 MIA cases. In response, the Vietnamese promised to redouble their effort to find and repatriate American MIA remains.[36]

The most notable event during Winston Lord's Hanoi visit was his announcement that the State Department planned to assign three Foreign Service officers to Vietnam "on a temporary basis" to provide consular and economic service to the growing number of American tourists and businesspeople traveling to Vietnam. He denied that the opening of an American office in Hanoi in any way was "preparing the ground for normalization." But it was obvious to everyone that this was the case.[37]

The three American diplomats, led by middle-grade Foreign Service officer Scott Marciel, began their assignment in Hanoi on August 18, 1993. Their arrival sparked an anticipated quid pro quo reaction from the Vietnamese. Twelve days after the American diplomats reached Hanoi, Vietnam quietly turned over some of the long-sought Lao Files, the same documents they had secretly offered Senator Kerry, using Ted Schweitzer as an intermediary, nine months earlier. With the Lao Files, the Vietnamese also released more POW camp registers. There were a total of six bound volumes in this consignment. The documents included records of PAVN Army Group 559, which operated in Laos, and Group 875, which was responsible for prisoner recovery from Military Region 4 and the administration of POW camps in the North late in the war.[38]

Although Ted Schweitzer did not personally see the Lao Files, he was told they were relatively substantive, but that Vietnam had still not turned over all their Lao Files to the United States. One of the problems with these documents is that they included a number of fragmentary reports and some clearly incorrect information.

For example, one Group 559 report from a combined trail security and engineer team in Laos described finding the wreckage of an American AC-130 Spectre gunship shot down in the early morning hours of March 29, 1972, on the Lao side of the Ban Karai Pass. The handwritten message noted that the burned remains of the fourteen American crewmen were found in the wreckage.

(A February 1986 excavation of this AC-130 Spectre crash site discovered skeletal remains later identified at CIL-HI as those of nine of the fourteen men on board.[39])

A complicating factor in this case was a JTF/FA debriefing of a demobilized PAVN officer, who as a lieutenant said he had seen two survivors from this shootdown who were captured. He later saw these two POWs being dragged by ropes behind a truck, an ordeal he was sure had killed them.[40]

(Reports of such atrocities committed by both PAVN and Pathet Lao troops had been heard quite often during and since the war. In 1989, the official Lao government radio station reported that Lao Communist forces had "captured and killed several hundred pilots of the enemy aggressors." Although the broadcast did not differentiate the nationality of the pilots, the bulk of allied aviators lost in Laos were Americans.[41])

What made this latest release of documents especially significant was that they were delivered to the new Joint Document Center established at the Central Military Museum. This office was meant to become the repository of all Vietnamese POW/MIA documents. American government investigators and private citizens were to have free access to these materials at any time.

But Schweitzer realized that this ostensibly open establishment was only as valuable as the documents the Vietnamese chose to deliver to it. And these latest PAVN reports were the first substantive materials Hanoi had released for American scrutiny. Indeed, the true situation in Hanoi that summer was much different than the apparently accelerating joint cooperation suggested. Colonel Dai and other GPD officers Schweitzer encountered were strained and wary. The Hanoi Politburo had secretly decreed that the PAVN would release no more "breakthrough" documents or sensitive information through its own channels. The power struggle between Ho Xuan Dich of the VNOSMP and Colonel Pham Duc Dai of the General Political Directorate had now tilted back in Dich's favor. Dai told Schweitzer that his entire museum staff was under threat of prosecution if they provided any additional meaningful documents without the express permission of Dich and the Foreign Ministry.[42]

A dramatic example of these constraints concerned the efforts to recover the remains of the Mangino Four, the four young Americal Division soldiers ambushed and killed by Colonel Dai's unit in Quang Ngai Province in 1967. Although Dai knew the area well and could probably locate the Americans' final graves, Ho Xuan Dich refused Dai permission to accompany the joint excavation team searching for the graves. Dai explained that, if he were there when the remains were recovered, press accounts might renew the brutal story of the ambush, and thus risk reigniting anti-Vietnamese sentiment in the United States. Dai's presence would also divert favorable publicity from Dich.

"I am almost ready to believe that they do not want Mangino and the others to be found," Dai told Schweitzer somberly.[43]

This atmosphere of tension worsened after the Lord delegation visited Hanoi in July 1993. Now Dai told Schweitzer that GPD officers with access to sensitive MIA documents and remains had been threatened with physical violence if there were any more leaks. Above all, the Politburo and the Foreign Ministry intended to prevent any more sensitive material on American POWs killed after capture or executed in prison camps from reaching Pentagon investigators.

Dai warned Schweitzer that he should be extremely careful with one particular artifact that he had finally secured from the museum. It was the ID card of Sergeant Harold Bennett, an Army POW captured in South Vietnam in 1964 and executed by the Vietcong in June 1965 in retaliation for the execution of one of their officers, Tran Van Dong, by the South Vietnamese government.[44] Although Bennett's execution was a well-established incident in the war's history, Hanoi's leadership was apparently still convinced they could maintain their official denial that they had no information to verify the original wartime Vietcong statement. Despite threats of possible physical violence and rumors that his visa would be canceled, Schweitzer did carry Bennett's ID card and related documents with him on a flight from Hanoi to Bangkok in late 1993.

As the increasingly paranoid Vietnamese officials had predicted to Schweitzer, yet another potentially disastrous, smoking-gun document was unearthed in Moscow. General Dmitri Volkogonov contacted his Joint Commission counterpart, Ambassador Malcolm Toon, on September 2, 1993, and turned over three pages from the files of the Soviet GRU military intelligence. This document was in Russian and purported to be an excerpt of comments made during the Twentieth Plenum of the Vietnam Workers Party in late 1970 or early 1971. Like the Quang document, this new material was allegedly a GRU agent's report that had been translated into Russian from Vietnamese. It had been the sensational Quang "1205" report that had, in fact, spurred the search of GRU archives for similar material.[45]

The document's Russian transliteration of the name of the purported Plenum speaker was "Khoang Anya," an apparent reference to Hoang Anh, secretary of the Central Committee of the Workers Party of Vietnam. Referring to American POWs, the speaker stated:

"When we published the names of 368 American flyers, shot down and captured on the territory of the SRV [sic], opportunists began to say that this was a concession to the Americans. This is not correct. It is not a concession, but a political blow aimed at Nixon. . . . The total number of American aviator POW's in the SRV is 735. . . . If the Americans agree to withdraw all of their troops from South Vietnam, we will as a start, return to them these 368 people. And when the Americans withdraw their troops, we'll return to them the rest."[46]

This document seemed to support the inferences of the Quang report: that Vietnam had held hundreds more American POWs than it ever acknowledged, and that it planned to withhold prisoners after the cease-fire.[47] Once more, initial Pentagon analysis indicated the material appeared to be an authentic GRU intelligence report. But again, analysis found the content to be flawed. It was not thought possible that Vietnam could have held 735 surviving American POWs in December 1970 or January 1971.

Moreover, the text of the document seemed to indicate another flawed agent's report. It was unlikely that a senior Communist official would have used the term "prisoners of war" at a Party Plenum; at the time, policy dictated describing captured American aviators as "air pirates" or "war criminals." Moreover, the Vietnamese list of 368 prisoners that was delivered to Senators William Fulbright and Edward Kennedy in Paris on December 22, 1970, included the names of twenty POWs who had died in captivity. Yet the purported Hoang Anh comments stated unequivocally that 368 living prisoners would eventually be released.[48]

To no one's surprise, however, Senator Bob Smith immediately emphasized the importance of this new revelation. He called the document "dramatic and deeply troubling," and scornfully dismissed the Pentagon caveats as "pitiful."[49]

The reaction of Hanoi was also predictable. The Foreign Ministry called the report the product of "misunderstanding of information or deliberate fabrication."[50]

The Clinton administration did not overreact to the new GRU document, no doubt because the information it contained was clearly not supported in the historical record.

An analyst did not have to have extensive intelligence experience to realize that the second GRU document in effect served to refute, not support, the purported General Quang Politburo report. At first blush, the two documents did tend to support each other, and were so embraced by those who had endorsed the Quang document.[51] In fact, adding the 735 of the second GRU document to the 495 American loss incidents occurring between December 1, 1970, and September 15, 1972, a total of 1,230 was obtained, clearly similar to the 1,205 figure of the Quang document.

But a closer look undercut this equation. If there had been only 735 live "American aviator POWs" in North Vietnam in late 1970 or early 1971, then it was in fact highly unlikely that there could have been as many as 1,205 live POWs twenty-one months later in September 1972. This was because the 495 loss incidents between late 1970 and September 15, 1972, included 169 Killed in Action/Body Not Recovered cases and 119 repatriated POWs. The men in these 288 loss incidents almost certainly did not enter a secret, parallel prison system from which the mysterious 600 missing POWs of the Quang report would have had to have been drawn.[52]

While the existence of the two GRU documents, as well as certain declassified American intelligence reports of POW information from Vietnamese defectors and exiles, kept the controversy roiling, the American intelligence community had quietly refuted the most sensational allegations.

Analysts noted that the Quang report did contain plausible information about the political subversion of South Vietnam and the secret Ba Be assassination campaign. But it was the consensus of the American intelligence community that this GRU agent report contained "numerous errors and inconsistencies."[53] A careful review of casualty records (including the postwar analysis of KIA/BNR cases) determined that it would have been impossible for there to have been 669 more live prisoners in North Vietnam in 1972 than the Pentagon estimated. Further, to have remained unknown to other prisoners, this large number of POWs would have to have been held in a separate, secret prison system. The American intelligence community possessed no information "that would substantiate the inference of the '1205 Report' that a separate prison system existed."[54]

Further, it was well known that American POWs were not strictly segregated by rank into separate camps; that only ten colonels were lost during the war, not sixteen as the 1205 Report claimed, and that only four became POWs. Notably, it was part of the historic record that North Vietnam had consolidated, not dispersed, POW camps after the 1970 Son Tay raid, counter to the claims in the 1205 Report. And the report's claim that progressive POWs would be released at some future date as a trial balloon to test the intentions of the Nixon White House was patently incorrect. Three American POWs were released on September 16, 1972—the day after the purported secret speech—to American peace activists in Hanoi, a release that had been publicly announced two weeks earlier.[55]

Analysis further revealed what Ted Schweitzer had reported from Hanoi: that Lieutenant General Tran Van Quang had never used his name publicly during the war, but had relied on his nom de guerre, Bay Tien.

(One of the best analyses of the Quang document was written by Garnett Bell after he had retired from government service. He noted that the tone of the purported transcribed remarks made it unlikely that the speaker was actually addressing the Vietnamese Politburo. He also noted that, although there was intriguingly accurate information in the report, the figure of 1,205 live American POWs is improbable. Bell believes that this figure was a total of all foreign troops [including South Vietnamese and other Asian U.S. allies] who fell into Vietnamese hands. Two hundred thirty-three of the 1,205 might have survived their loss incident, as this figure approximates the "last known alive" lists for Vietnam and Laos.[56] If in fact there were 233 more live-capture POWs than Vietnam acknowledged, this figure would support the "darkest secret" assertions PAVN officers made to Ted Schweitzer.)

As to the second GRU agent report, the "735 Document," American intelligence analysis considered it a valid GRU agent's report, not a fabrication. But it, too, was replete with errors. The Twentieth Plenum of the Vietnam Communist Party Central Committee was not held until February 1972. Further, Hoang Anh, the purported secretary of the Central Committee, was responsible for agriculture, not military affairs. Careful analysis of casualty records showed that there were 388 living American prisoners in North Vietnam in early 1971 (four of these men died before release in 1973). And as others had noted, it would have been impossible to reach the total of 1,205 living POWs referred to in the Quang-Morris document beginning with only 735 POWs in early 1971, which is the contention of the second GRU document.[57]

American analysts were also reviewing earlier intelligence reports that suggested much larger numbers of American POWs were held by North Vietnam than Hanoi ever admitted. The most sensational of these reports was from a PAVN defector, a medical corpsman named Dang Tan, who rallied to the South Vietnamese cause in April 1969. Tan reported that "more than 800" Americans were held in North Vietnam in late 1967. But in all of Indochina, there were only a total of 574 POW/MIA casualties in September 1967.[58]

The other well-known former North Vietnamese official who had made sensational accusations was living in exile in France. His name was Le Dinh. In October 1979, the French newspaper *Le Matin* published an interview with Le Dinh in which he claimed to have encountered a group of thirty-three American POWs in Hanoi in 1974, a year after Operation Homecoming. Analysts from the Defense Intelligence Agency interviewed Le Dinh in Paris within weeks of the article's publication. Le Dinh was described as intelligent, articulate, and idealistic in the DIA's report.[59] A southerner from an aristocratic family, he joined the Communist cause in 1968 and was sent from South Vietnam to Hanoi where he was trained in intelligence work in PAVN headquarters and promoted to the rank of senior lieutenant. Le Dinh told the DIA he was writing a book on his wartime experiences.

Because he accurately described the Dan Hoi POW camp and sections of Hoa Lo Prison in Hanoi, his credibility was bolstered in the eyes of the DIA.[60] But he quickly strained that credibility by telling the analyst that he had attended staff meetings at which it was announced that 700 American POWs remained in Vietnam in the mid-1970s as a "strategic asset." Further, he stated that an unknown number of POWs who were "the sons of rich families" would be ransomed, not released. Additionally, some would never be released unless bartered for Soviet or Eastern Bloc spies captured in the West. Finally, Le Dinh claimed that he had personally encountered thirty-three "progressive" POWs in 1974.

When he described three of these Americans, however, his credibility slipped even further. One was said to be a Marine captain who "deserted at Khe Sanh in 1968." The two others were Marine sergeants, one Hispanic, the other black. They were said to be members of a 155mm artillery battery stationed near Khe Sanh and had been captured while "looking for fun" away from their unit. Le Dinh insisted that he had good recall of the particulars of these individuals.[61]

However, the DIA was impressed by some of Le Dinh's detailed knowledge of the North Vietnamese POW camp system. He had accurate information about some well-known American prisoners and the PAVN officers who had interrogated them. It was concluded he must have had access to the prison system during the war, as he claimed.[62]

But Le Dinh's credibility began to break down completely when he professed that he had "extra-sensory powers" that he could employ to determine the fate of any American ever lost or captured in Indochina. If he were given a photograph or a personal item of this person, Le Dinh said he could communicate with the spirit world for detailed information on the fate of the missing.[63]

Le Dinh declined to submit to a polygraph examination. He ended the interview by noting that he had already given away too much information, which he planned to publish in his book. The DIA's conclusion was that Le Dinh had "an inflated ego," and that he probably held only a minor position in North Vietnamese military intelligence.[64]

(The author conducted an independent analysis of Le Dinh's assertion that he personally encountered the three Marine "progressives" in 1974. Defense Department casualty records show that only one Marine ground-force captain went missing during the war, but he was far from Khe Sanh. No two Marine ground-force sergeants went missing on the same day, from any unit, at any time during the war.)

Nevertheless, Le Dinh has become somewhat of a cult figure among POW/MIA activists, who either have not read his DIA interview report, or who choose to ignore its more glaring inconsistencies. The lore surrounding Le Dinh continues to grow. One *New York Guardian* account described him as "a member of the Democratic Republic of Vietnam's Politburo, Colonel Le Dinh."[65]

HOWEVER, IT WAS not in the Pentagon's interest to go public quickly with a detailed analysis refuting either of the GRU documents, or the other intriguing but flawed intelligence reports. Revelation of the purported Quang report had driven the Vietnamese to release important documents such as the Blue Book and the PAVN Group 875 and 559 materials. Allowing Hanoi to stew in the juices simmering around this new intelligence report might sweat more revealing information out of Vietnam.

In fact, Vietnamese documents recovered through Operation Swamp Ranger and subsequent releases had already helped resolve a number of MIA cases. By September 1993, the Vessey 135 discrepancy list had been reduced to below eighty. But the overall official "unaccounted for" total had only fallen to 2,248. This was because the rigid American policy on status change remained in effect. Assistant Secretary of State Winston Lord spoke with frustration as he explained this policy during a discussion of the issue on the *MacNeil/Lehrer NewsHour*. In order for a name to be removed from the list of the unaccounted for, Lord said, either a live person or forensically identified remains had to be produced or "conclusive evidence why you can't fulfill either of the above two criteria" had to be furnished.[66]

And the Clinton administration knew that there were still more MIA remains "recovered or recoverable" in Vietnam than the fifty sets the SRV had turned over so far in 1993. The White House expected more concessions from Hanoi on this before the United States would respond with its own penultimate quid pro quo concession: lifting the economic embargo. By now, the Clinton Pentagon and State Department had been fully read in on Ted Schweitzer's intelligence reports concerning the ongoing practice of hoarding American MIA remains in the hands of active-duty and retired PAVN officers. For example, one of Schweitzer's reports, dated April 5, 1993, noted that PAVN hard-liners, including members of the Nghe Tinh Group such as Colonels Quan and Tich, were said to possess many sets of American MIA remains, which they withheld as much out of animosity toward America as for financial motives. Central Vietnam's Nghe Tinh Province remained both desperately poor and fervently revolutionary.[67]

With the goal of maintaining pressure on Hanoi over the MIA remains issue, the Clinton administration made another compromise step on lifting the trade embargo. The White House announced on September 13 that President Clinton had renewed the Trading with the Enemy Act, which provided for the trade embargo against Vietnam, Cuba, North Korea, and Cambodia. The notable exception in the determination document Clinton signed was to permit American companies to participate in development projects in Vietnam funded by international financial institutions, including the World Bank and the IMF. The White House announcement of this policy stated it was designed to "make clear to the Vietnamese that more needs to be done" on the MIA issue. Clinton would continue to maintain the trade embargo, "pending further progress on POW/MIA accounting."[68]

The White House specifically noted that Vietnam had produced "concrete results" in recovering and repatriating American MIA remains. Since the

Winston Lord visit in July, twenty-two sets of remains had been turned over, bringing the 1993 total to fifty. And Hanoi had "boosted publicity" for its amnesty program, "to encourage citizens to locate and turn over remains," an act that included a pledge to "reimburse expenses" that were incurred in recovering remains that "proved to be American."[69] (The official act was tacit recognition of a secret program that Schweitzer had been running since mid-1992.) This was another reference to the quiet carrot-and-stick pressure American officials were applying on groups of Vietnamese identified by Schweitzer to be holding remains. In the area of MIA documents, the White House noted that Vietnam had provided detailed shootdown reports from Air Defense Force units, including one forty-six-page report chronicling the shootdowns of 2,466 aircraft. And Vietnam had finally provided "long-requested" General Political Directorate documents (originally identified in the Red Book), "which could prove very useful in locating aircraft crash sites inside Laos, and in verifying numbers and other facts about our POWs during the war."[70]

While noting that these Vietnamese efforts were welcome, the White House announcement concluded that "the results are not yet sufficient" to merit lifting the embargo.[71]

Just as the Bush White House had slowly turned the screw on Hanoi through the fine manipulation of the Road Map, the Clinton administration was trying to practice the same policy. But Hanoi was less willing to respond as readily as they had during the flurry of dramatic events of the previous autumn. Again, the "bunker mentality" in Hanoi seemed to prevail.

THE SITUATION FROZE once more into a grim and tense stalemate. Ted Schweitzer, now in the last weeks of his final "consultancy" contract with the DIA, was gripped by pessimism. Colonel Pham Duc Dai and other officers from the PAVN's Department Two intelligence division stressed to him that the highest levels of authority in Vietnam had closed down the back-channel conduit that he had opened through Operation Swamp Ranger.

"There will definitely be no more Red Books," Dai told him one cool winter afternoon, yet again drinking tea under the lychee trees at the museum.

He added that the Blue Files would also remain "closed." "You have seen one, but that will be all."

(Ted Schweitzer and the author were shown part of the Blue File of Air Force Colonel John Flynn, the senior American POW in Vietnam. This included a copy of a letter written in Flynn's hand from his prison hospital, where he had received extensive medical treatment.)

The government of Vietnam would no longer permit any important MIA documents to be delivered to the Americans, Dai explained, troubled by this revelation. The old political operative had believed that his directorate could have been the confidential conduit through which both the United States and Vietnam would have gained. He had hoped to quietly channel all available information on captured and missing Americans to his counterparts in U.S. intelligence. In return, Dai and his colleagues had been optimistic that the General Political Directorate, which had controlled prisoners during the war, would gain the recognition of its own government—and of the American government—for resolving the MIA dispute and helping to normalize relations with their old enemy, the United States.[72]

Now, Dai told Schweitzer, the position of the Socialist Republic of Vietnam had hardened. Following the revelation of the two flawed GRU documents, the publicity-seeking visits to Vietnam of the irrational American activists, and the stubborn extension of the embargo by President Clinton, there was no longer a united policy in Vietnam to resolve the issue. Hard-liners and Red Capitalists, sensing a difficult period, had simply retreated into anonymity, taking with them their "mountain" of important documents, artifacts, and remains.

The policy of Vietnam's senior party, government, and military leaders was still to provide some visible cooperation with the Americans, while withholding a number of MIA remains and the Blue Files, which chronicled the fates of scores of dead Americans. Party leader Do Muoi had adopted a hands-off approach. He had given the party's blessing to what Schweitzer described to the DIA as "somewhat better, if rather limited, cooperation" on resolving the MIA issue. The government and military had been ordered to cooperate up to the point of providing a few individual American remains and the "occasional stray document, ID card, or photo." But this did not amount to meaningful cooperation, according to Schweitzer's PAVN contacts. "Any major new evidence or the relation of any major new body of data or knowledge," Schweitzer reported, "whether documents, photos or remains, will simply not be made public, if the leadership of the government and the Party have their way."[73]

Either the Americans would lift the embargo or they would not, Schweitzer's sources reported. The PAVN would continue to give the JTF/FA "small bits and pieces of information" and a few remains, but truly substantive cooperation had ceased, at least until the embargo was lifted—if not permanently. No effort would be made to pressure PAVN officers who were known to have hidden important MIA documents or remains. Without question, the best opportunity for unlimited cooperation had passed.

The screw had been tightened to its last turn.

THE CLINTON ADMINISTRATION played the endgame with unusual skill, given its bumbling foreign policy record. In a combined diplomatic and political campaign conducted with precision even experienced military leaders would envy, the White House expertly prepared the ground, then executed its policy decision with vigor and confidence.

In mid-December 1993, Assistant Secretary of State Winston Lord went to Vietnam again, and returned to announce that he was impressed with Hanoi's increased cooperation in resolving the MIA issue. After weathering the inevitable broadsides from MIA family groups and activists, which were generally defused by the distractions of the holidays, the administration asked its congressional allies to launch an entire armada of trial balloons. When Democratic Congressman Gary Ackerman, chairman of the House Foreign Affairs Asian Subcommittee, announced the embargo would soon be lifted, "It's just a question of timing," there were few reverberations in the House.[74]

Then a bipartisan Senate delegation, headed by J. Bennett Johnston, Jr., the powerful Louisiana chairman of the Energy and Natural Resources Committee, visited Vietnam. General Thomas Needham and the new Hanoi JTF/FA detachment commander, Lieutenant Colonel John Cray, told the senators that Vietnam was cooperating to resolve outstanding MIA cases. The next day, five of the senators, including three conservative Republicans, publicly endorsed an end to the embargo and the establishment of diplomatic relations with Vietnam.[75]

To demonstrate American resolve, Clinton ordered Admiral Charles Larson, commander of U.S. forces in the Pacific, to visit Vietnam and assess Hanoi's level of cooperation. Returning from Hanoi to Manila, Larson announced that the Pentagon's efforts to fully account for American missing in Indochina would be improved by lifting the embargo against Vietnam.[76]

No political figure of any power disputed Admiral Larson's comments. The sky above Washington was growing dark with unmolested trial balloons.

A week later, after what was described as an "emotionally charged debate" about the bitter legacy of the Vietnam War, the Senate voted by a margin of 62 to 38 to support a nonbinding resolution introduced by Senator John Kerry to support President Clinton in ending the economic embargo against Vietnam. Although the powerful American Legion voiced both disappointment and concern over the resolution, there was little other negative reaction. Even Senator Bob Smith's voice seemed subdued and resigned. He called the vote "immoral and incomprehensible," but did not resort to the type of bitter invective he had employed in the past.[77]

One week later, on Friday, February 4, 1994, President Clinton, surrounded by Vietnam veterans from Congress and the business community, announced that the United States was lifting the nineteen-year economic embargo against Vietnam. He also announced that the United States would open a diplomatic "liaison" office in Hanoi. Clinton said that this step offered "the best way to resolve the fate of those who remain missing and about whom we are not sure."[78]

The White House ceremony took place on a snowy Friday afternoon. Although there was predictable negative reaction from veterans groups and POW/MIA organizations, Clinton's action drew virtually no other media attention after that weekend.

To celebrate lifting the embargo, American businessmen threw a party at the Thang Loi Hotel on Hanoi's Ho Tay Lake. This was a suitable site for the occasion. Built by the Cubans, using Soviet prefab concrete techniques, the hotel was scornfully known as "Castro's Rat Palace" by foreign visitors. The Thang Loi, in a prime location, was scheduled to be replaced by a luxury hotel-conference center, built by a Southeast Asian consortium.

(Hoa Lo Prison was also scheduled for demolition and replacement by a luxury hotel.)

Foreign guests at the reception were obliged to pay a $10 entrance fee; Vietnamese paid nothing. Perhaps this was a subtle demonstration that, with the embargo lifted, the bottom line sacred to all American corporate comptrollers would now prevail in dealings with U.S. firms in Vietnam.

Ted Schweitzer, who was wrapping up his work in Vietnam, strolled among the guests in the drafty hotel ballroom. The prevalent mood among the American executives was relief. They had been working in a limbo in Hanoi for over a year. Under the final Bush embargo policy, U.S. firms could sign, but not execute contracts.

"It's finally over," a vice president of a construction company told Schweitzer. "This is what we've been waiting for. Now we can start making money instead of just spending it."

"Maybe so," Schweitzer said.

But he did not add what he really felt. Schweitzer had been in Hanoi longer than any other American. For years he had dealt with Vietnamese, first as a UN refugee officer, then as the administrator of a private humanitarian organization, and finally as a clandestine agent with a generous operational budget. He knew that the increasingly greedy Communist bureaucrats who controlled Vietnam's economy and society were not about to change their spots, simply because President Bill Clinton had lifted the embargo.

But the smiling Vietnamese guests, who indulged themselves with the free beer and canapés, were visibly optimistic. Everyone wanted to pump the hand of an American, to exchange business cards, and make contacts for potentially lucrative future dealing.

"Soon there will be many American companies here in Hanoi," a wiry old official of the Hanoi People's Committee told Schweitzer in staccato French. "There will be American hotels and factories."

"Peut-être," Schweitzer replied, "maybe so."

The man reminded Schweitzer of Colonel Dai, a thin, tobacco-stained veteran revolutionary who had endured endless decades of struggle. Men like them were not easy to do business with. Yet they clearly believed the embargo's end would bring planeloads of gullible American executives, lugging briefcases full of $100 bills, intent on paving Hanoi's streets with gold before the next Tet New Year's.

The embargo had ended. The long war was finally over. But Vietnam was still the place where nothing was ever simple or straightforward.

THE OFFICIAL VIETNAMESE reaction to Clinton lifting the embargo came from the Ministry of Foreign Relations. Deputy Foreign Minister Le Mai called the decision "positive and significant, a new page in U.S.-Vietnam relations."

These platitudes were predictable. But in spontaneous remarks after his prepared comments, Le Mai sounded bitter. The embargo, he said, had been a "backward policy."

Nevertheless, Le Mai told the Hanoi news conference, Vietnam would "continue to cooperate fully" with the United States to resolve the MIA issue. He said that the Vietnamese shared the "sorrow and grief" of American MIA families. Vietnam, he promised, would always regard the MIA issue as "a humanitarian one."[79]

Lieutenant Colonel John Cray of the JTF/FA echoed this mood of reconciliation. Lifting the embargo would help "the mission at hand." He added that "We believe Vietnamese cooperation is at a peak right now. I think the embargo decision will enhance that effort."[80]

Although there were still 1,647 "unaccounted for" cases in Vietnam (most ground losses in the South), from the total of 2,238 remaining for all Indochina, Cray told reporters in Hanoi that Pentagon investigators had determined the fate of every ₋missing American in Vietnam except for seventy-three.

As Schweitzer considered Colonel Cray's comments, he recognized that the officer was making the best of a bad situation. With Ho Xuan Dich now replaced by a young diplomat as the titular head of the VNOSMP, the Ministry of the Interior's A-15 Counter-Espionage Division led by a shadowy officer named Cong now controlled every aspect of Vietnam's "cooperation" with the JTF/FA. His responsibility was to provide the minimum valid information while creating the illusion of maximum effort.[81]

The policy of the Clinton administration had been forced along practical lines by reality. The State Department and the Pentagon had determined that the carrot-and-stick Road Map was no longer effective. Continuing the embargo indefinitely meant punishing American firms more than Vietnam. But, since lifting the embargo required at least a plausible perception of ongoing Vietnamese cooperation and tangible progress toward a final resolution, the best course was to announce that these conditions existed, then continue to work quietly behind the scenes for real results.

. . .

FOUR MONTHS LATER, as Ted Schweitzer was preparing to leave Vietnam, he attended another American-sponsored party. The inauguration of the new American Chamber of Commerce in Vietnam was a catered affair under the stars at the newly built Dragon Hotel on Ho Tay Lake. The Vietnamese guests were still exuberant, their optimism about Vietnam's post-embargo prospects untarnished.

But the American business executives Ted Schweitzer spoke with were blatantly pessimistic.

"Nothing is going forward as we hoped," the manager of an American real estate development firm told Schweitzer. "We've had three deals pending for over a year, but no one will sign the final contract."

The man explained that his home office was on the verge of "cutting our losses" and leaving Vietnam.

This dour assessment was echoed around the buffet tables on the hotel terrace. Not a single American executive Schweitzer spoke with had been able to finalize the contracts and agreements they had worked on so diligently during the commercial purgatory that lasted from the end of the Bush administration until Clinton finally lifted the embargo in February 1994.

Schweitzer was not surprised. Lifting the embargo had not changed the character of the Hanoi bureaucrats. Indeed, the new policy had only whetted their appetites. For the past several years—as *doi moi* spread north from Saigon—Japanese, Thai, Singaporean, South Korean, and Taiwanese firms had invested heavily in Vietnam. Bribery and corruption were the normal means of doing business for these Asian companies. Many Australian firms that trailed the Asians were also willing to expedite any commercial negotiation with well-placed bribes. Schweitzer had learned that one Australian company had just paid a $50,000 fee to obtain the final signature from a state committee, which allowed the company to start commercial operations in a province in central Vietnam.

Ravenous greed had become commonplace in Vietnam, even in rural Tonkin. Schweitzer had traveled during the past Tet holidays with Vietnamese friends to pagodas throughout the Red River Delta. They encountered peasants hell-bent on becoming rich. This rapacity even drove some poor farmers into keeping their children out of school. A boy or girl with a secondary education could earn a few thousand dong a month, the equivalent of $10 or $20, shuffling papers in a state office. But a young son or daughter who drove a small private swine herd, or kept flocks of ducks in the old water-filled craters of American bombs, could provide the family with a "Japanese" television or motorbike—in reality, cheap Chinese products made under license from Japanese firms and smuggled into Vietnam over the mountains.

Although Vietnam's economy was growing at an explosive rate of more than 8 percent a year, the population was growing even faster. *Doi moi* had unleashed a flood of money, not only in the cities but throughout the countryside. For the first time in decades, peasants could earn cash. Children were a valued commodity. The exodus of boat people that had first drawn Ted Schweitzer to Vietnam had stopped completely. But the uncontrolled exploitation of limited rural resources was already having an effect. In heavily farmed areas, where peasants tried to produce two or even three rice crops a year, complex new dike systems were disrupting the flow of streams, completely disrupting natural fish breeding. Families that had relied for generations on local fish as their only source of protein now had only rice to eat. But they did have televisions and motorbikes.[82]

And with the party and government preoccupied with exploiting the fruits of *doi moi,* there was no effective leadership to curb the excesses of this uncontrolled development. Explosive population growth was the most serious threat Vietnam faced. But Schweitzer had seen no sign of an effective government population-control program. Indeed, if left unchecked, in less than thirty years Vietnam's population would double. Already the average age in Vietnam was in the mid-teens. More than half the people had been born since the war. They looked ahead, not to the past.

Given these realities, the greed of bureaucrats in those state committees was more understandable. But the Australians' $50,000 bribe had set an unfortunate precedent. To the hard-bitten old revolutionaries in provincial and municipal People's Committees (the local Communist Party organizations), Australians were indistinguishable from Americans or French. If foreigners would pay that much for a single signature, only a fool would sign agreements free of charge.

Schweitzer had spent days trying to explain to his PAVN contacts that American companies doing business in Vietnam—or anywhere else overseas—could not operate in this manner. He went so far as to have translated the key provisions of the Foreign Corrupt Practices Act, which prevented American firms from making any payment to a foreign official for simply performing his normal duties. The normal duty of Vietnam's State Committee for Cooperation and Investment was to expedite Vietnam's commercial development. American companies could not pay for this service. Therefore the American executives sipping wine and scotch on the terrace of the Dragon Hotel were rendered as powerless as their counterparts in the JTF/FA.

Indeed, Schweitzer saw a direct negative impact of Vietnam's commercial boom on the final resolution of the protracted MIA issue. There were no secrets among the old revolutionaries, especially those in the Nghe Tinh cabal that controlled the army and the key ministries. If some sunburned Australian was willing to hand over $50,000 for one signature, what was a bona fide set of category 1 American MIA remains now worth? And what was the current value of a PAVN regimental battle report that listed the names of dead Americans and gave the coordinates of their graves on some forgotten jungle ridge in the Central Highlands?

PAVN officers had told Schweitzer that it was all well and good that the JTF/FA continued to spread its considerable largess through field investigations and the excavation of aircraft crash sites. The Americans did often find bones among the wreckage in remote areas. But the officially sanctioned payments for transportation and labor disappeared into the pockets of the Ministry of Foreign Affairs, the VNOSMP bureaucrats, and now the watchdogs of A-15 Counterintelligence.

(The financial motives of the Ministry of Foreign Affairs and the VNOSMP in continuing to back the JTF/FA investigations were well known. A National League of Families statement in December 1993 noted: "As long as Vietnam continues to benefit financially and politically from field investigations . . . Hanoi has little motivation to unilaterally repatriate [MIA] remains now being held."[83])

But the official MIA investigation did nothing for those who held the real secrets, retired and active-duty PAVN officers, who probably also retained control of the last recovered MIA remains. Officers like Colonel Pham Duc Dai, Colonel Quan, and Colonel Tich, who had enjoyed the prestige and tangible benefits of their positions as honored defenders of a Communist state, now faced a bleak future. As *doi moi* flourished and Vietnam's economy was transformed, these officers faced destitution. Most had already lost their free state housing, as the apartment buildings and old French villas their families had occupied for decades were sold to foreign investors. Certainly a pension equivalent to $9 or $10 a month meant nothing in the new Vietnam.

Schweitzer knew that the final answer to the MIA mystery would only come when America faced reality and again dealt directly with the People's Army of Vietnam—the organization that Colonel Dai had always told him "held the key" to unlock the door—just as it had during Operation Swamp Ranger.

TED SCHWEITZER'S LAST contact with Senior Colonel Pham Duc Dai was a chance encounter in the crowded parking lot of Noi Bai Airport north of Hanoi. Schweitzer had gone to complete his travel arrangements. Colonel Dai and his wife had driven out in a decrepit PAVN minibus to meet their son, daughter-in-law, and new granddaughter, who had flown up from Saigon.

"Bonjour, mon ami," Dai said, shaking Schweitzer's hand rather limply.

The old soldier looked frailer than ever, and the flesh of his face had acquired an unhealthy amberlike translucence. Schweitzer had heard that Dai had been under so much strain in the months leading up to the end of the embargo that he had been hospitalized from an undisclosed stress-induced illness. But he showed no sign of serious impairment this morning, only a general shriveling, as if the decades of danger and intrigue had finally drained away his last energy. When they had met like this in the past, Dai had always found pleasure in engaging in a brief, lively repartee in French, usually on some facet of world events. The colonel had seemed almost vain in displaying his grasp of the world beyond Vietnam. But today he was stolid, unresponsive.

Maybe they've got him drugged, Schweitzer thought. Certainly the Ministry of the Interior, whose members had been well trained in the former Soviet Union, was capable of dispensing debilitating drugs under the guise of medical treatment.

He and Dai exchanged pleasantries. But both refrained from any mention of the issue that had first brought them together, and which had linked them through all those exciting months of Operation Swamp Ranger.

The last time Schweitzer and Dai had discussed the MIA situation, the old colonel had been extremely nervous, his anxiety bordering on open fear. The situation, Dai had told Schweitzer, was "extremely grave." The Ministry of the Interior and its allied civilian ministry, Foreign Affairs, were absolutely determined to end the leaks of important documents from the PAVN. Moreover, these civilian officials, with the apparent blessing of the party, were determined to squeeze the Army back into its proper role as a subordinate institution in peacetime. Controlling the MIA issue had degenerated to a test of wills between the civilian and military power structures in Vietnam.

When Schweitzer politely asked after Major Mui and his wife, Mrs. Hang, the two PAVN officers with whom he had worked most closely during the most productive phase of the operation, Colonel Dai glanced furtively around the parking lot and mumbled a bland phrase that these officers were "working at their duties."

Then Dai excused himself, bundled his family into the minibus, and left the airport.

That was to be the last time Schweitzer would see Senior Colonel Pham Duc Dai.

This encounter reinforced Schweitzer's pessimism about the situation in Vietnam. He remained convinced, just as Colonel Dai had always stressed, that the PAVN controlled the answer to the MIA mystery. The Army had fought the war and had in many ways controlled the country those long wartime decades. It was the General Political Directorate that had ultimate control over American prisoners and it was the fighting units in the South, the Air Defense regiments, and the PAVN groups on the Ho Chi Minh Trail that had engaged the enemy and actually taken Americans captive. The Ministry of the Interior had been much weaker in those days, the Ministry of Foreign Affairs a minor appendage of the Politburo. The first four decades of Communist Vietnam's existence had been a time of armed struggle, not diplomacy.

But now the situation had changed. The civilians in Hanoi were intent on controlling every aspect of what was rightfully a military matter. Schweitzer's Operation Swamp Ranger had opened the door to the People's Army of Vietnam. Now the civilians were trying to slam it shut. He knew that the final answers in the complex MIA mystery lay at the end of the path he had charted into those dusty, mildewed archives of the Hanoi Citadel. But he had no way of predicting whether other Americans would ever walk that path in the future.

CHAPTER 27

TED SCHWEITZER STOOD IN THE OVERFLOW CROWD AT THE AMPHI-theater of the Tomb of the Unknown Soldiers. The white stone grave markers of Arlington National Cemetery marched down the green hillside, rank on rank. It was a fine May morning. Across the Potomac, the pale marble monuments of the Mall rose among the greenery. It was Memorial Day, 1994.

President Bill Clinton had just arrived to place a wreath at the white sarcophagus. The tomb's main sepulcher and side crypts contained the remains of men missing in action from World Wars I and II, the Korean War, and Vietnam. The symbolic act of interring one of the missing from each of the major wars of our apocalyptic century had been an act of closure meant to help America put that particular national trauma behind it.

But burying a missing man's remains recovered on the Vietnam battlefield at this tomb had certainly not healed the national wound the war had opened.

Indeed, the issue of Vietnam MIAs remained acrimonious for millions of Americans. And the process of "accounting" for MIA cases through the forensic examination of skeletal remains had engendered one of the most bitter ancillary disputes of the overall POW/MIA controversy.

The question had come to a head in 1985 following the joint American-Lao excavation of an AC-130 gunship, Spectre 17, crash site in southern Laos. This was the gunship on which Lieutenant George MacDonald had been navigator. His mother had been one of the first MIA family members preyed on by con men after the 1973 cease-fire. The excavation of the Spectre wreckage produced a number of bone fragments and partial skeletal remains, which were examined at CIL-HI in Honolulu. Positive identification of thirteen crew members, including MacDonald and Lieutenant Colonel Thomas T. Hart III, was made. These were difficult identifications because the bones were fire-damaged and, in some cases, badly crushed. MacDonald's identification had been partially based on distinctive dental work in a fragment of jaw. But the identification also rested solidly on common sense. These skull fragments had been retrieved from the part of the crushed cockpit's starboard side where the navigator had his station. It was inconceivable that Lao Communists would have salted MacDonald's bones in that position in the wreckage.[1]

Lieutenant Colonel Thomas Hart's widow, Anne, had legally challenged the positive identification of her husband done by CIL-HI. Her lawsuit was in litigation for years, eventually reaching the U.S. 11th Circuit Court of Appeals, which ruled that the government did have the right to use "its discretion" in identifying the remains of war victims.[2] But activists seized on this case, especially the purported use of MacDonald's "single tooth" as the means to make a positive identification. They called this "voodoo forensics." Their protests eventually forced CIL-HI to adopt much more stringent criteria for such identifications. In effect, this new rigor had made it all but impossible to identify MIA remains that were as battered and fragmentary as those from the Spectre 17 crash site.

And, ironically, other activists had since ignored the restrictive new identification requirements and lambasted both Vietnam and JTF/FA for lack of progress in recovering and repatriating bona fide American remains. The National League of Families, for example, noted that only two of the more than twenty sets of remains recovered between January and August 1993 had been "identified as Americans."[3]

But Schweitzer knew there were scores of similar partial sets of remains at CIL-HI in Honolulu that might never be identified under the stringent new criteria. Those men's bones seemed destined to lie indefinitely in bureaucratic limbo, their families doomed to the purgatory of uncertainty.

For these people, the Vietnam War might never end, the wounds never heal.

PRESIDENT CLINTON GAVE his Memorial Day address to the nation after laying the wreath. As always, Clinton was a convincing and effective speaker. And today he sounded particularly sincere. The focus of this speech was the fiftieth anniversary of D-Day, the invasion of Normandy. Unlike his address the year before, which had reopened the wounds of Vietnam, Clinton did not dwell on the potentially rancorous question of American missing in Indochina. Instead he evoked pride and patriotism by channeling national gratitude toward the World War II generation.

"Fifty years ago the world learned just what Americans are capable of," Clinton told his audience. "World War II was an era of sacrifice unequaled in our history."

Schweitzer noted that many of the people standing around him were in their sixties and seventies, the generation Clinton was praising. His words seemed to strike a resonant note with them.

And the speech concluded on that positive note as Clinton added, "Let us also hold a special place for all our living veterans. We owe them a lasting debt of gratitude."[4]

But as the President turned to leave the rostrum, a man to Schweitzer's right bellowed, "Bring 'em home," the battle cry of the radical POW/MIA activists.

The call was echoed by another activist to the left of the amphitheater, and the middle-aged woman directly in front of Schweitzer cupped her hand to her mouth and shouted something indistinct. Her husband nudged her, almost violently.

"Hush now," he whispered. "This is a cemetery."

The woman lowered her head, her face flushed with embarrassment and anger. "I don't care . . . I don't care."

The President did not acknowledge the hecklers as he walked slowly from the rostrum. The Secret Service agents in dark suits and the honor guard soldiers from the 3rd Infantry standing at rigid attention in their dress blues gave no indication they had heard the angry outbursts.

As the crowd dispersed, Schweitzer realized that there had only been three or four activists among all those hundreds of people.

WALKING ACROSS MEMORIAL BRIDGE in the bright May sunshine, Schweitzer thought of the handful of hecklers in that marble shrine.

Only two years before, President Bush would have been greeted by a phalanx of activist protesters, many flourishing their movement's flag, which displayed the black silhouette of a bowed prisoner's head overlooked by a guard tower. The flag's logo was the promise, "You Are Not Forgotten."

But today's protest was unorganized and feeble.

So much had happened in those two years. The initial success of Schweitzer's Operation Swamp Ranger had exceeded his most optimistic expectations. The Vietnamese government, spurred on by its own Army, had been obliged to lower the wall of deceit and reveal the full extent of their MIA archives. Schweitzer and his sponsors, Principal Deputy Assistant Secretary of Defense Carl Ford and Ambassador Richard Armitage, had been on the verge of gaining the "fullest possible" accounting for America's missing.

Then, President George Bush was defeated and the competing factions within Vietnam succumbed to greed and intrigue. The initiative that had begun so well ended short of complete success. But Operation Swamp Ranger had opened the door to reveal the heart of the mystery. Schweitzer was proud of all that he had managed to accomplish in the face of such overwhelming odds and resistance in both Vietnam and the United States.

Schweitzer strolled around the northern corner of the Lincoln Memorial, en route to the Vietnam Veterans Memorial—the Wall—set in a hollow among the oaks on the Mall ahead. He had planned to pay tribute to the scores of American missing whose fates he had been able to resolve in Vietnam. These men's names were etched on the black granite wall beside those of their dead comrades whose bodies had been returned from the war. Schweitzer felt a special sense of pride about Major Joseph Morrison and the others whose pictures he had recovered. At least their families now had answers to the one terrible question, "How and where had he died?"

Ted Schweitzer was musing on this when he virtually stumbled upon a row of vendor stands. He counted six open-fronted booths along the walk leading from the Lincoln Memorial to the Vietnam Wall, arrayed side by side as on a carnival midway. These were the information and sales stands of competing POW/MIA activist groups and souvenir vendors. Several were festooned with both the American and black logo flags of the movement. A few had South Vietnamese flags and the colors of the American armed services branches.

Schweitzer had never seen this gaudy spectacle. By chance, he had come to the Wall on the busiest holiday of the year, the day most favored by the activists. His first reaction was revulsion at the naked commercialism. Some booths were stacked high with expensive T-shirts, each bearing a variant of the "You Are Not Forgotten" message. A visitor could purchase framed photographs of famous MIAs such as Charles Shelton. They reminded Schweitzer of the plastic icons and votive relics sold at miraculous sites such as Lourdes or the Buddhist wats of Thailand.

There were also piles of tabloid-size activist newspapers, available free, but a modest "contribution" was encouraged. Examining these broadsheets, Schweitzer found that one claimed that live POWs remained in "subterranean" cells in Hanoi, while another offered the Laos bamboo cage venue for the abandoned men. Folding billboards were plastered with sensational photos of live POWs, including all the discredited forgeries peddled by Jack Bailey and the Asian con artists.

(Although Schweitzer did not encounter him, Joe L. Jordan, the Elmer Gantry of the POW/MIA movement, was peddling wares—MIA "intelligence" of dubious pedigree—at a "non-profit organization" concession called the Last Firebase that day at the memorial. And a phalanx of motorcyclist POW/MIA activists ["Operation Rolling Thunder"] also descended on the Wall. One of them, a surly biker named Michael Schiff, told the press he had "a lot of hatred, but I have it for very valid reasons." He said he had been a POW held "in a cage" for eight months.[5] A thorough review of all Pentagon POW records, however, showed no trace of any Michael Schiff ever having been a prisoner of war in Indochina. Perhaps he had served his brutal captivity in the same imaginary camp as Larry Pistilli.)

Stopping at one stall, occupied by a paunchy middle-aged man in camouflage fatigues, Schweitzer examined a clever offshoot of the old POW remembrance bracelet. This high-technology model bore not only the name of the MIA and the dates of his loss, but also a photogravure emblem etched into the shining metal, a ghostly image that shimmered in the sunlight like the hologram on a credit card. The man also sold reproductions of MIA dog tags. They were every bit as good as those the hucksters peddled along Nguyen Hue Boulevard and Dong Khoi Street in Saigon.

"See anything you like, sir?" the man asked, eyeing Schweitzer as a likely customer.

Schweitzer replaced the bracelet on the stack. "No, I'm just sort of looking around."

"We've got some interesting books here," the man in fatigues offered. "Information you'll never read in the newspapers."

Schweitzer knew he should leave before his anger at this naked exploitation erupted, but curiosity overcame him. "What kind of information is that?"

"The *truth,*" the man said, his voice ringing with fervor.

"You really believe there are still POWs alive over there?" Schweitzer kept his own voice neutral.

"By God, I *know* there are," the man said. "If you've got a minute, I can prove it to you." He reached for a well-worn binder with plastic-covered pages of news clippings. As the man flipped through the book, searching for some particular clipping, Schweitzer recognized press stories on the Quang document and saw two of the more famous bogus POW pictures.

"I'll be back in a little while," Schweitzer lied. "I've got to meet somebody."

The salesman leaned from the booth, flourishing the binder, like a hardworking soul saver at a revival meeting. Schweitzer looked down the long rank of booths. They were doing a good business. The T-shirts and garish POW bracelets seemed especially popular. He paused a moment, watching the animated conversations between customers and vendors, between the true believers and potential converts to the faith.

In recent years, Schweitzer and others had come to believe the POW/MIA movement in America had acquired many of the attributes of a religious cult, including a sense of solidarity under persecution and a belief in secret transcendental knowledge.

But now Schweitzer saw he was mistaken.

The movement had become much bigger than an obscure cult. Now there were schisms among the established orthodoxy and reformist sects. There were martyred saints, mystical zealots such as Mike Peck and depraved visionaries such as General Tom Lacy. Schweitzer thought of the relics of Shelton and the others for sale here. There was even a subsect of resurrectionists, convinced the sinister American government was repatriating live POWs in a top secret ransom plan and resettling these wretches through the Federal Witness Protection Program.[6]

This is not just a cult anymore, Schweitzer thought, turning to leave. *It's become a religion.*

. . .

TWO DAYS LATER, Ted Schweitzer had his last conference with the Operations Directorate of the Defense Intelligence Agency, an informal "out brief," to use intelligence jargon. But the rendezvous was hardly clandestine. He had lunch with a senior operations officer who used the work name Peter L. Bogen. They met on the deck of a crab house on Maryland's Eastern Shore, overlooking Chesapeake Bay. The bright summer weather held. Sailboats tacked and reached through the cool northwest breeze.

"Tom Clancy lives over there," Bogen said, pointing toward the colonial spires of Annapolis across the choppy bay. "He's got a big fancy house on a bluff."

Schweitzer sipped his beer. "I guess you make more money writing spy novels than you do as an actual spy."

"Every day of the week," Bogen agreed.

"Still," Schweitzer said, "we got a lot done."

"That is a fact," Bogen said. "Swamp Ranger was one hell of a lot more important than most people realized."

Schweitzer nodded. The previous winter, he had learned that Bogen and James Renaud had been awarded the prestigious Exceptional Intelligence Collector medal—"Spy of the Year," according to the sardonic Renaud—in a secret ceremony in the courtyard of the Central Intelligence Agency headquarters in Langley, Virginia. By winning this decoration, the DIA's Operations Directorate had eclipsed its competitors throughout the vast American intelligence community. That award was reserved for officers conducting operations of unusual importance under especially difficult circumstances. The medal citation specifically noted that Operation Swamp Ranger had made important contributions to America's national security.

"Was it worth all the trouble?" Schweitzer asked, recalling the months of fear and drudgery in Hanoi.

Bogen sat up straight and began enumerating the achievements of Operation Swamp Ranger.

"You bet," he said. "Before Swamp Ranger, the Vietnamese had painted themselves into a corner. They had left no way out to accommodate our legitimate need for information on the MIAs. You opened a back channel. They used you as a conduit for all the really sensitive material they could never give the JTF without an unacceptable loss of face."

Schweitzer had long suspected this, but Bogen's comments were the first official confirmation.

"And once that conduit was opened," Bogen continued, "Swamp Ranger produced several really critical results. First, you directly resolved quite a few well-known and sensitive MIA cases." He began ticking them off, rapping the lunch table with his index finger. "Morrison, Seuell, Mitchell . . ."

Schweitzer saw again the sweltering little lime-washed office in the corner of the Hanoi museum. He pictured Mrs. Hang and Mui furtively delivering their folders of documents and photographs.

"The second Swamp Ranger achievement," Bogen added, "was that it gave General Vessey the leverage he needed to force the Vietnamese into authorizing open research into their entire POW archive. Until you came along, they had insisted that their records were rain-soaked or eaten by termites. But no damn termite ever nibbled on the Red Book. You proved it, and Vessey was able to convince them they couldn't just keep repeating the old lies."

"Well," Schweitzer said, "they've opened a Joint Document Center at the museum now, but they haven't yet provided the important archives."

"That doesn't matter for the moment," Bogen said. "The mechanism is in place. The Red Book and other documents you delivered map out the extent of their archives. Sooner or later they will have to come clean."

"Maybe so," Schweitzer admitted. "But that's not going to be easy."

Bogen's enthusiasm was not dampened. "All those negotiations before Operation Swamp Ranger happened in the Ice Age. After you brought out the Red Book, modern Vietnamese history began. That was the turning point in our relations with Vietnam."

Bogen held up another finger. "Third, your operation established the degree of cooperation necessary to make the 'full accounting' that everybody's been talking about for twenty years actually possible. We know what they have now. And they know that we know. This is what good intelligence is all about, getting to the truth, cutting through the lies and propaganda."

Schweitzer watched the sailboats slice the whitecaps. Bogen's comments were certainly flattering. But Schweitzer knew the initiative he had begun with Swamp Ranger might never be completed, the way events had transpired in recent months.

"Still, Peter," he said, "there's a long way to go."

Bogen had to agree. "Sure, but at least we know the size and shape of the problem."

Before his last contract had expired, Ted Schweitzer had delineated the four categories of MIA information the Vietnamese had not yet relinquished.

He suspected and the DIA had confirmed that the PAVN Group 559 documents from Laos were hardly a complete account of operations along the Ho Chi Minh Trail. There were still hundreds of more documents in the Lao Files that PAVN intelligence had asked Schweitzer to offer to Senator John Kerry in November 1992. And until those files were released, the fate of scores of Americans still missing in Laos would not be resolved. Undoubtedly, the documents contained many of the "darkest secrets" Lieutenant Colonel Thi had discussed. Because of this, the Lao Files lay near the heart of the MIA mystery.

Then there were the Blue Files, the detailed personnel records of every American prisoner who survived capture to be admitted into the central prison system, run by the PAVN's General Political Directorate. Thorough scrutiny of these files would reveal how many of the Americans had died in captivity, and also provide information on the location of their remains.

Colonel Dai and others had also repeatedly told Schweitzer that there was a wealth of POW and MIA information in the voluminous wartime reports of all the far-flung PAVN units operating throughout Indochina. Most of these after-action reports had never been examined by American investigators. The documents primarily addressed operational matters, but many contained peripheral accounts of the capture or death of Americans, the location of American graves, and a record of where the Americans' dog tags and identity documents had been transferred.

Finally, there was the whole troubling issue of American artifacts and remains in private hands. Schweitzer's General Political Directorate contacts had made it clear that there were few if any American remains still in government hands. Most, perhaps "hundreds" of sets of remains, as Dai had told him, were held by demobilized PAVN soldiers or retired officers. And these same Vietnamese veterans had wartime diaries and maps that would reveal further information on MIA cases.

But the only way the United States was ever going to tap this PAVN veteran resource was to "involve the Army," just as Colonel Dai and the other GPD officers had insisted for months. Their plan to establish a separate investigation channel with both American veterans groups and the PAVN Veterans Association had been more than just a scheme to divert funds from the official joint MIA investigation effort. The need to "involve" PAVN veterans throughout Vietnam was based on a commonsense proposition: The men who had fought and captured the American enemy knew the fate of the missing and the location of the dead.

Schweitzer had explained the need for this approach through an analogy. Suppose, he had told the DIA, a foreign scholar wanted to research the American Civil War. Would his best approach be to work with the FBI in Washington? Of course not. The most efficient and ultimately effective way to conduct Civil War research was in military archives.

But Schweitzer recognized that—for complex reasons mired in internal Vietnamese politics—Hanoi had opted to conduct the resolution of the MIA issue through a civilian organization, not the PAVN. In that manner, Vietnam could control the pace of events and eventually accomplish its ultimate goal: gaining full diplomatic recognition from the United States, and even the protection of America's geopolitical umbrella. These were important considerations. But they ultimately had nothing to do with answering the protracted MIA mystery.

Schweitzer and Bogen finished their lunch and strolled back to the crab house parking lot.

"You know, Peter," Schweitzer told Bogen, "the only way we're ever going to get to the bottom of all this is through an Operation Swamp Ranger II."

Bogen scowled a moment, then, good operations man that he was, smiled without affirming or refuting Schweitzer's suggestion. But he clearly recognized the truth in the proposal. "Well," he finally said, "American embassies tend to be big places."

Now Schweitzer nodded. In his last official debriefing, he had outlined a follow-on operation to Swamp Ranger. Once diplomatic relations were renewed with Hanoi, he knew, a Central Intelligence Agency station would be established in the American diplomatic mission. And, if the CIA officers in that station were assigned the task of ferreting out the last secrets of the MIA mystery, they would simply have to follow the trail that Schweitzer's Operation Swamp Ranger had pioneered.

"Those embassy people will be busy," Bogen added.

"Maybe so," Schweitzer said. "But there's one thing they'll have to remember."

"What's that?"

"Nothing in Vietnam is ever straightforward or simple."

EPILOGUE

ARLINGTON, VIRGINIA

JULY 15, 1994

THE NATIONAL LEAGUE OF FAMILIES OF AMERICAN PRISONERS AND Missing in Southeast Asia and its activist splinter group, the National Alliance of Families for the Return of America's Missing Servicemen, held their annual conventions simultaneously in nearby Crystal City hotels. For two days, members of the league and alliance trooped back and forth on the stifling streets of this sterile high-rise suburb across the Potomac from Washington.

To consult with armed services casualty officers, alliance members were obliged to cross the street to the Hyatt, site of the league meeting. This was a not-too-subtle method for the Pentagon to express its quasi-official support for the older, less radical MIA family group.

League members were drawn to the alliance's convention in the second-floor ballroom of the Sheraton by curiosity. Radical activist Joe L. Jordan of the National Vietnam P.O.W. Strike Force had acquired some of the Druid Smoke photographs that the DIA's part-time stringer agent, Gene Brown, had purchased with government funds in Hanoi in 1992. Brown had apparently held back negatives of certain pictures. These he sold to Jordan for a reported payment of $10,000 plus Jordan's deep-sea fishing boat. Jordan quickly launched a campaign to recoup his outlay. He did not name Gene Brown, but called his source for the photos a "colorful gentleman married to the daughter of a senior NVA (PAVN) General."[1]

Among the blown-up photos garishly displayed at the rear of the ballroom were duplicates of several of the pictures of dead American airmen Ted Schweitzer had obtained during Operation Swamp Ranger. Showing the photographs in this circuslike manner outraged Pentagon officers who had worked for years to resolve the MIA issue.[2]

Despite the keen interest league and alliance members had in the pictures, however, neither Jordan nor his associates seemed able to explain the true provenance or significance of the photographs. In fact, the blow-up of Major Dean Pogreba's military ID card was mounted on a poster with an excerpt from General Thomas Lacy's bizarre deposition that described his imaginary encounter with Pogreba in 1989.

Another photo, which Brown purchased from the Vietnam News Service, showed an Eastern Bloc reporter (who is seen in other Druid Smoke pho-

tos) at the crash site of an American aircraft. One activist newsletter distributed at the alliance convention called this man a "Soviet intelligence officer
rifling through the belongings of a dead U.S. airman."[3] Another publication
given away in the Sheraton ballroom featured the same photograph. But
now the man was described as "an American POW with his captors."[4]

And alliance members told Kevin Foley, a *Stars & Stripes* reporter, that
the photograph of Navy Lieutenant Commander Robert Shumaker being
marched to captivity was actually a picture of Air Force Captain Dwight
Bowles, an F-105 pilot shot down in North Vietnam in 1965 and officially
listed as Killed in Action/Body Not Recovered.[5]

Joe Jordan did not seem bothered by these incongruities. Dressed in an
equally incongruous bemedaled tuxedo, he rushed about the hotel, reveling
in the attention.

Jordan's antics, however, did not enliven the alliance meeting, which was
marked by a small turnout and a distinct mood of pessimistic anticlimax.

Even retired Special Forces Major Mark W. Smith's lurid accusations that
he had proof Hanoi had recently transferred hundreds of live American
POWs to the control of PAVN units in Laos—where, he said, 572 surviving
American captives still languished—did not seem to motivate the small
audience the way such flamboyant charges once had. Smith, a former POW
and one of the heroes of *Kiss the Boys Goodbye,* also claimed that the
PAVN would soon release these American prisoners, who had suffered cruel
captivity for decades. But he refused to provide any details of the pending
prisoner repatriation, due to the sensitive nature of the situation.[6]

But it appeared difficult for even dedicated activists to accept Mark Smith's
claim that the Vietnam Communists could still hold 572 live American POWs
in Laos without the world's news media becoming aware of this blockbuster
story.

Clearly, the mood was different this summer than it had been in July 1993
when the two MIA family groups last met in Washington.

President Clinton had lifted the economic embargo of Vietnam. Washington and Hanoi had opened government liaison offices and were poised to
reestablish diplomatic relations. The MIA issue was well into the endgame.

The featured speaker at the alliance convention, Senator Bob Smith, former co-chairman of the Senate Select Committee on POW/MIA Affairs,
seemed subdued compared to Major Mark Smith. Like most of the others
who addressed the conventions, Senator Smith no longer spoke of live
POWs languishing in bamboo cages. Instead, he railed against the Vietnamese for their long history of withholding information that could resolve MIA
cases.

However, Bob Smith did place great stock in the General Tran Van Quang
1205 Politburo report, which he described as the "most important single
document we have ever obtained on Vietnam-era POW/MIAs." He chided
the American government for accepting the Vietnamese explanation that the

document was inaccurate. But Smith offered no theory as to what had become of the 600 American POWs allegedly cited by General Quang who were not repatriated.[7]

Unlike during previous alliance conventions at which Senator Smith had helped plan elaborate activist strategy, he cut short his post-speech questions and returned to the capital.

Bill Bell spoke next. Fewer than fifty people stayed in the ballroom to hear his comments, which were largely a rehash of his bitterness at being shunted aside by the JTF/FA's bureaucratic juggernaut.

After Bell spoke, there were no shouts of "Bring 'em home!" from the alliance audience.

WHILE THE ACTIVISTS hold their conventions, the Defense POW/MIA Office (DPMO), which replaced the DIA's Special Office for POW/MIAs in 1993, quietly continues to work on solving MIA cases.

But the DPMO is bound by the rigid congressionally mandated requirement that no case can be officially resolved—and a name removed from the list now numbering 2,224 still "unaccounted for Americans"—without the repatriation of forensically verified remains, or the return of a live person.

No one in DPMO, of course, considers this list a valid indicator of bona fide American missing. At the time of Operation Homecoming in 1973, more than 1,100 of these missing were known to have died in their loss incidents. And, among the other approximately 1,100 in the original MIA category, at least 400 were known to have been lost at sea or in circumstances in which survival was unlikely. Of the almost 700 remaining in the original MIA category, an indeterminate number should probably have been listed KIA/BNR, but were not.

In the twenty-two years since the cease-fire, Pentagon analysts have concentrated on a much smaller number of missing Americans, which fluctuated according to evidence, but has never exceeded 340 MIA cases. The repatriation of verified remains has reduced this unresolved count dramatically.

But even though the flow of American MIA remains from Indochina has slowed, the DPMO has been able to unofficially resolve a number of these cases based on the results of Ted Schweitzer's Operation Swamp Ranger.

Using the photographs Schweitzer obtained in Vietnam, the Pentagon has reached a final resolution of twenty-nine MIA cases by summer 1994. In all, the photographs the DIA's Operations Directorate collected in Hanoi "provided new information and documentation on 56 cases of missing Americans."[8]

Moreover, the documents Ted Schweitzer scanned have provided information that will probably help resolve dozens more MIA cases and serve to verify the fates of scores of Killed in Action/Body Not Recovered cases.

As of August 1994, the Pentagon has "determined the fates" of 140 of the original discrepancy list of 196 Vietnam MIA cases (from which the Vessey 135 priority list was drawn).[9]

It is likely that most of the fifty-seven open Vietnam discrepancy cases will have similar fate determinations—but not official resolutions—within a year.

Knowledgeable military intelligence officers believe that Vietnam can probably provide enough information to close approximately one hundred more MIA cases. But, since these cases might involve Hanoi's "darkest secret" (massacre or death under torture), it is not at all certain the Vietnamese will release this information.

It is also uncertain if Vietnam will ever keep the promise the PAVN made to Ted Schweitzer to turn over less sensitive Blue Files once diplomatic relations are reestablished.

In Laos, the situation is even less clear. However, the slow process of translating and analyzing the Lao Files, including those PAVN Group 559 reports released to date, continues. It is probable that these documents will help resolve a certain number of cases. But it is doubtful if any significant number of remains will be returned from the wilds of the Ho Chi Minh Trail. There, General Vessey's sensibility check on the likelihood of recovering remains from a remote crash site is especially relevant.

After two decades of investigation, America has been able to determine with some degree of certainty the fate of all but approximately one hundred of its men missing in Indochina, even though the official roster of those "unaccounted for" remains largely unchanged. The resolution of many of these cases has come in the past two years, thanks in a large measure to the initiatives begun by Ted Schweitzer's Operation Swamp Ranger.

But the remains of Joseph Morrison, James McElvain, and other Americans photographed dead in Communist Vietnamese custody have still not been repatriated.

The true legacy of Operation Swamp Ranger is that the American government finally understands the full extent of Hanoi's secret archives.

We now know where to look to find the answers.

But it will be the responsibility of those who follow Colonel Pham Duc Dai and Ted Schweitzer to again gain access to those secret archives.

In the harsh reality of war

The wounds that run deepest
are the wounds of uncertainty

These are the wounds that
cannot heal

—NEAL POINTER,
TEXAS VIETNAM
VETERANS MEMORIAL
MONUMENT,
DALLAS

GLOSSARY

A-1E—Douglas Skyraider, single-engine fighter-bomber, often used for Search and Rescue mission escort

A-4—Douglas Skyhawk, U.S. Navy/Marine Corps light attack jet

A-6A—Grumman Intruder, U.S. Navy/Marine Corps all-weather, twin-seat attack jet

A-7—Vought Corsair II, U.S. joint service attack jet

ABCCC—Airborne Command, Control, and Communication (post or center)

AC-47—Spooky gunship variant of the two-engine Douglas World War II vintage transport

AC-130—Spectre gunship variant of the four-engine Lockheed turboprop transport

ADF—Automatic Direction Finder radio compass

ADI—Attitude Direction Indicator artificial horizon for aircraft

agitprop—organized propaganda demonstrations, usually in Communist systems

AK-47—Russian-designed Kalishnikov 7.62mm assault rifle

ARVN—Army of the Republic of Vietnam (South Vietnam)

ASEAN—Association of Southeast Asian Nations

AWOL—Absent Without Leave

B-52—Boeing Stratofortress, U.S. Air Force heavy jet bomber

backseater—military aircrewman riding behind (or beside) the aircraft commander

Blue Book—central list of American prisoners of war registered at Hoa Lo Prison in Hanoi between 1964 and 1972

Blue Files—individual personnel records of American prisoners of war maintained by the Vietnamese

BNR—Body Not Recovered

CH-46—Boeing-Vertol Sea Knight medium transport helicopter

CH-47—Boeing-Vertol Chinook heavy transport helicopter

CH-53—Sikorsky heavy transport helicopter

choke point—military term for a narrow or vulnerable spot on a line of communication

CIA—U.S. Central Intelligence Agency

CIL-HI—U.S. Defense Department Central Identification Laboratory, Hawaii

CINCPAC—U.S. Commander in Chief, Pacific Forces

coi moi—Vietnamese, "openness"

debrief—a formal interview after a military or intelligence operation

Defcon—Defense Condition

Demilitarized Zone (DMZ)—the heavily fortified frontier between North and South Vietnam during the Vietnam War

DIA—Defense Intelligence Agency

DIA Intelligence Directorate—the analytical branch of the DIA

DIA Operations Directorate—the covert and clandestine operations branch of the DIA

DoD—U.S. Department of Defense

dog tag—military identity tag

doi moi—Vietnamese, "renovation"

DRV—Democratic Republic of Vietnam (North Vietnam)

E-3—U.S. Navy electronic reconnaissance aircraft

EB-66—U.S. twin-engine Electronic Countermeasure aircraft

ECM—Electronic Countermeasures

F-4—McDonnell Phantom II, two-seat jet interceptor, fighter-bomber, reconnaissance aircraft

F-86—Republic Sabre jet interceptor during the Korean War

F-105—North American Thunderchief jet fighter-bomber

F-111—twin-seat supersonic strategic bomber

FAC—Forward Air Controller

General Political Directorate (GPD)—the oldest branch of the People's Army of Vietnam

GRU—Soviet General Staff Military Intelligence

HH-3—Sikorsky Jolly Green Giant Search and Rescue helicopter

Ho Chi Minh Trail—North Vietnamese military supply route through the Annamite Mountains in North and South Vietnam, Laos, and Cambodia

Huey—Bell UH-1 single-engine utility helicopter

HUMINT—Human Intelligence

IAG—U.S. government Inter-Agency Group, responsible for POW/MIA matters

IMF—International Monetary Fund

JCRC—U.S. Joint Casualty Resolution Center, responsible for resolving unaccounted for casualty cases

jink—violent evasive/defensive air-combat maneuver

JPRC—U.S. Joint Personnel Recovery Center, military organization for the rescue and recovery of missing service members during the Vietnam War

JTF/FA—U.S. Joint Task Force/Full Accounting

KGB—Soviet state security organization

KIA—Killed in Action

KIA/BNR—Killed in Action/Body Not Recovered

kneeboard—narrow clipboard strapped to an aviator's leg for cockpit use of maps and checklists

Lao Files—Vietnamese Communist military records from operations in Laos

Lao Patriotic Front—Communist Lao government, also known as the Pathet Lao

MACV—U.S. Military Assistance Command, Vietnam

MACV/SOG—U.S. Military Assistance Command, Vietnam—Studies and Observations Group

MIA—Missing in Action

MiG-21—Soviet-built single-engine jet interceptor

Nghe Tinh Group—informal Vietnamese Communist fraternal group of persons born in Nghe Tinh Province

NPRC—U.S. government National Personnel Record Center

NSC—National Security Council

NVA—North Vietnamese Army

O-2—Cessna Bird-dog Forward Air Controller aircraft

Operation Homecoming—U.S. military operation to repatriate POWs in 1973

Pathet Lao—Lao Patriotic Front

PAVN—People's Army of Vietnam

PAVN Group 559—North Vietnamese military group on the Ho Chi Minh Trail

POW—Prisoner of War

PRC—People's Republic of China

Presumptive Finding of Death—U.S. Defense Department legal procedure, declaring missing casualty dead

PSTD—post-traumatic stress disorder

Red Book—index of holdings of the Central Military Museum, Hanoi

RF-4B—reconnaissance variant of the F-4 Phantom

SAM—surface-to-air missile

SAR—Search and Rescue

SRV—Socialist Republic of Vietnam, unified Vietnam after 1976

Stony Beach—the DIA's Missing in Action office in Bangkok

TDY—temporary duty

Tet Offensive—Communist military offensive in February 1968

Tu San Do—Vietnamese, "Red Capitalists"

UH-34—Sikorsky medium transport helicopter

USAID—U.S. Agency for International Development

VC—Vietcong, South Vietnamese Communist military forces

Vietminh—anti-French Vietnamese Communist military forces during First Indochina War

VNOSMP—Vietnamese Office for Seeking Missing Persons

WSAG—Washington Special Action Group

Source Notes

PREFACE

1. The term "espionage" is generally understood to mean the unauthorized, clandestine collection of sensitive information. As will be explained in detail below, Schweitzer's "book research" at the PAVN Central Military Museum was, at least technically, authorized by the government of the Socialist Republic of Vietnam. The details of Schweitzer's role in the penetration of the PAVN archives are based on in-depth interviews of him conducted in the United States and Vietnam in 1992 and 1993, unless otherwise indicated by source note.

2. "Remarks by the President After Meeting with General Vessey," Transcript, the White House, Office of the Press Secretary, October 23, 1992.

3. H. Bruce Franklin, "The POW/MIA Myth," *The Atlantic Monthly,* December 1991, p. 45. A more recent CBS–*New York Times* opinion poll found similar results: "More than half of Americans believe MIAs are alive in Vietnam." Cited on *CBS Evening News with Dan Rather and Connie Chung,* January 20, 1994.

INTRODUCTION

1. The details on Grommet Flight's November 25, 1968, mission and the subsequent Search and Rescue effort come from a variety of sources, including: the Defense Intelligence Agency (DIA) casualty file, Incident Number 1329-1-01 and 02; the U.S. Air Force Management Personnel Center Casualty File, Joseph C. Morrison and San D. Francisco; and the P.O.W. Network Database (a private electronic archive, Skidmore, MO), entries for: Morrison, Joseph C., and Francisco, San D.

2. Stanley Karnow, *Vietnam: A History* (New York: Viking Press, 1984), p. 597.

CHAPTER 1

1. Jonathan C. Randal, "No Pact as Talks Wind Up," *Washington Post,* December 14, 1972, p. A-1.

2. "The 9-Point Draft Accord," *Washington Post,* December 17, 1972, p. A-6.

3. Henry Kissinger, *White House Years* (New York: Little, Brown, 1979), p. 1445.

4. U.S. Air Force Casualty Office, Incident Number 1329-1-01: Francisco, San Dewayne, and Morrison, Joseph Castleman.

5. Neil Sheehan, *A Bright Shining Lie* (New York: Random House, 1988), p. 777. Also: Kissinger, *White House Years,* p. 1447.

6. Kissinger, *White House Years,* pp. 1445–47.

7. Major General Richard V. Secord, USAF (Ret.), *Honored and Betrayed* (New York: John Wiley & Son, 1992), p. 106.

8. Kissinger, *White House Years,* p. 1448.

9. Ibid., p. 1449.

10. *Report of the Select Committee on POW/MIA Affairs, United States Senate* (Washington, D.C.: U.S. Government Printing Office, 1993), p. 67.

11. Ibid.

12. Bernard B. Fall, "Communist POW Treatment in Indochina," *Military Review,* December 1958, p. 66.

13. *Report of the Select Committee on POW/MIA Affairs,* pp. 66–67.

14. Memorandum of Conversation with Xuan Thuy, Vo Van Sung, Phan Hien, and Henry Kissinger, Paris, August 16, 1971; Records of the Senate Select Committee on POW/MIA Affairs, National Archives, Washington, D.C.

15. News Release No. 028-94, Office of Assistant Secretary of Defense (Public Affairs), January 24, 1994, p. 3.

16. "U.S. Aircraft Losses in Southeast Asia—Aircraft Lost to Hostile Action, by Service, by Aircraft Model, by Area of Operation," Appendix III: "U.S. Aircraft and Helicopters Lost to All Causes," OASD (Comptroller), Directorate of Information Operations, Final Update, October 17, 1973, Department of Defense, Washington, D.C.

17. Department of Defense, *POW-MIA Fact Book* (Washington, D.C.: Department of Defense, October 1992), p. 4.

18. On November 3, 1969, one year into his first term, Richard Nixon addressed the nation on his Indochina policy. He appealed to the "great silent majority of my fellow Americans," asking for their support while America tried to achieve "peace with honor" in Vietnam. The return of American POWs was cited as a major component of this honorable peace. See: "Text of President Nixon's Speech," *New York Times,* November 4, 1969, p. A-5. Also see: Sheehan, *A Bright Shining Lie,* p. 735.

19. *Report of the Select Committee on POW/MIA Affairs,* p. 78. Also see: "Missing or Dead?—Some 'POW' Relatives Say They Are Misled by American Officials," *Wall Street Journal,* September 30, 1971, p. A-1.

20. *Report of the Select Committee on POW/MIA Affairs,* p. 78. Also see: Franklin, "The POW/MIA Myth," p. 45. Franklin views the postwar MIA controversy as an artificial and needless political construct. Without being specific, he implies that the Pentagon's late 1972 estimate of approximately 600 POWs was based on firm intelligence. Further, Franklin lambastes the Nixon administration for allegedly using the POW issue as a flagrant red herring to divert public opinion from its fundamentally flawed war policy. Franklin's points have a certain amount of merit. However, Franklin's position as a far-left antiwar academic—he reportedly helped found the pro-Castro Venceremos Brigade while teaching at Stanford in 1971—has undercut his credibility on the issue and opened him to attack by conservatives. See: John Corry, "The MIA Sellout," *The American Spectator,* December 1993, p. 58. Also see: Thomas W. Lippman, "POW Policy Sowed Lasting Doubts," *Washington Post,* September 24, 1992, p. A-6.

21. "The Children Have Wept Enough," *Time,* December 25, 1972, p. 34.

22. Major General John K. Singlaub, USA (Ret.), with Malcolm McConnell, *Hazardous Duty: An American Soldier in the Twentieth Century* (New York: Simon and Schuster, 1991), pp. 302–5. Also see: Sheehan, *A Bright Shining Lie,* pp. 134, 141. Sheehan specifies that no American-sponsored stay-behind agents planted during the exodus of anti-Communist refugees were able to function effectively after the late 1950s.

23. John G. Hubbell (in association with Andrew Jones and Kenneth Y. Tomlinson), *P.O.W.* (New York: Reader's Digest Press, 1976), pp. 536–38.

24. United States Military Assistance Command, Vietnam, Studies and Operations Group, 1971–72 Command History, Annex B, p. 501.

25. For an unclassified description of the resolution power of America's Keyhole satellites, see: William E. Burrows, *Deep Black: Space Espionage and National Security* (New

York: Random House, 1986), pp. 214–15; and James Bamford, *The Puzzle Palace: A Report on America's Most Secret Agency* (Boston: Houghton Mifflin, 1982), pp. 201–2, 208.

26. Hubbell, *P.O.W.*, p. 538. And, interviews, Guy Gruters, February 24, 1994; James Shively, February 25, 1994. Gruters and Shively were both POWs in North Vietnam.

27. Hubbell, *P.O.W.*, p. 584.

28. Following the release of the American POWs in Operation Homecoming, there was a White House dinner in their honor on May 24, 1973. At that dinner, Henry Kissinger reportedly confirmed that the National Security Council was aware of the camp near Lang So'n, and that the DRV might try to hold back these prisoners as hostages. Interviews, James Warner, February 25, 1994; James Shively, February 26, 1994. Warner and Shively were both POWs.

29. Kissinger, *White House Years*, p. 1449.

30. For a discussion of the uneven internal security policies of the Diem government, see: Sheehan, *A Bright Shining Lie*, pp. 186–88. Sheehan's discussion of similar corruption in the Phoenix Program is on p. 733.

31. For a discussion of the treatment of the civilian prisoners in the South and of the corruption of the South Vietnamese security services in December 1972, see: "Thieu's Political Prisoners of War," *Time*, December 25, 1972, pp. 18–19; and "Vietnam: The Other Prisoners," *Time*, March 19, 1973, p. 27.

The fact that the Vietnamese Communists engaged in terrorism through selective assassination as well as the wholesale massacre of civilians deemed to be reactionaries cannot be disputed. Neil Sheehan and Stanley Karnow, the two American journalists turned historian who have been among the most critical of America's involvement in Vietnam and subsequent military conduct during the war, are also unsparing in their condemnation of Communist atrocities, especially the massacre of an estimated 3,000 civilians during the Communist occupation of Hue during the 1968 Tet Offensive. See: Sheehan, *A Bright Shining Lie*, p. 720; and Karnow, *Vietnam*, p. 530.

32. "Dr. Kissinger's News Conference," *New York Times*, December 17, 1972, p. A-6.

33. "Nixon's Blitz Leads Back to the Table," *Time*, January 8, 1973, p. 9 (cited passages, p. 11).

CHAPTER 2

1. For the most vivid description of the Linebacker II bombing from the perspective of the airmen who flew the missions, see: Karl J. Eschmann, *Linebacker: The Untold Story of the Air Raids Over North Vietnam* (New York: Ballantine, 1989); the above quotes are from p. 92. Also: interview, Lieutenant Colonel Duncan Wilmore, USAF (Ret.), March 14, 1985.

2. For a detailed breakdown on each day's missions during the Linebacker II campaign, see: Brigadier General James R. McCarthy and Lieutenant Colonel George B. Allison, *Linebacker II: A View From the Rock*, USAF Southeast Asia Monograph Series, Vol. 6, Monograph 8 (Maxwell Air Force Base, Alabama: Air Power Research Institute, 1979), pp. 39–166.

3. Interview, Lieutenant General Hoang Phuong, Hanoi, February 17, 1993. General Phuong, the head of the PAVN Institute for Military History, was the commander of PAVN Air Defense Forces from 1970 to 1975. In this capacity, he led the North Vietnamese opposition to the Linebacker II bombing.

4. "Christmas in Hanoi," *Time*, January 1, 1973, p. 12.

5. Dana K. Drenkowski, "Operation Linebacker II," *Soldier of Fortune*, November 1977, p. 50.

6. "Raids Go On; Hanoi Says Hospital Hit," *Washington Post,* December 23, 1972, p. A-1; also: "Radio Hanoi Says Hundreds Killed," *Washington Post,* December 20, 1972, p. A-12.

7. Drenkowski, "Operation Linebacker II," pp. 52–53.

8. Kissinger, *White House Years,* pp. 1457–58. Also see: Carroll Kilpatrick, "Raids Halt; Talks to Resume," *Washington Post,* December 31, 1972, p. A-1.

9. These figures are from the official Pentagon list of POW and MIA casualties: "U.S. Personnel, Southeast Asia (and Selected Foreign Nationals)," compiled by the Defense Intelligence Agency, PW-MIA Branch, February 1, 1990.

10. Karnow, *Vietnam,* p. 668.

11. Interview, Lieutenant General Hoang Phuong.

12. Ibid.

CHAPTER 3

1. Kissinger, *White House Years,* pp. 1461–62.

2. Chapter III, Article 8(a), "Agreement to End the War and Restoring Peace in Vietnam," cited in: *Report of the Select Committee on POW/MIA Affairs,* p. 76.

3. Before January 1973, no single U.S. government office had a definitive list of all Americans unaccounted for in Indochina. Loss casualties were compiled by the separate armed services and civilian agencies involved. Men originally listed as Absent Without Leave (AWOL) or deserters were not originally carried on the loss-casualty roster of the secretary of defense. But after the cease-fire of January 27, 1973, the defense secretary's office compiled a name and loss-location list of 1,929 servicemen still unaccounted for. This included the 354 MIAs in Laos. When AWOLs, deserters, and civilians were added in, the total of 2,261 "unaccounted for" was obtained. For a more detailed description of this process, see: Memorandum from Sedgwick D. Tourison, Jr., to J. William Codinha, May 11, 1992, Records of the Senate Select Committee on POW/MIA Affairs, Working Papers of Committee Investigators. Also see: *Report of the Select Committee on POW/MIA Affairs,* p. 82.

4. *Report of the Select Committee on POW/MIA Affairs,* p. 70.

5. Memorandum, George Aldrich, Deputy Legal Adviser, Department of State, January 27, 1973, as cited in *Report of the Select Committee on POW/MIA Affairs,* p. 76.

6. *Report of the Select Committee on POW/MIA Affairs,* p. 84.

7. For a summary of the Kissinger–Le Duc Tho discussion of this point, see: *Report of the Select Committee on POW/MIA Affairs,* pp. 68–70.

Interview, General Robert C. Kingston, USA (Ret.), Alexandria, Virginia, June 22, 1993. General Kingston, who retired from the Army as commander-in-chief, Central Command, was the first commander of the Joint Casualty Resolution Center, established in Saigon in February 1973. General Kingston confirms that American remains-recovery teams were prevented from investigating crash sites on the Ho Chi Minh Trail in Laos or in North Vietnam by the "neutral" four-power cease-fire supervision commission, which was dominated by pro-Communist elements.

It also should be noted that, after the 1954 armistice, South Vietnamese president Ngo Dinh Diem prevented North Vietnamese graves registration teams from operating in South Vietnam; see: Sheehan, *A Bright Shining Lie,* p. 190.

8. *Report of the Select Committee on POW/MIA Affairs,* p. 82; and Interagency Intelligence Report, circa January 1973, quoted in Thomas W. Lippman, "POW Pilots Left in Laos, Files Suggest," *Washington Post,* January 2, 1994, p. A-1.

9. *Report of the Select Committee on POW/MIA Affairs,* p. 82.

10. Ibid., p. 87.

11. Kissinger, *White House Years,* p. 1472.

12. Bernard Gwertzman, "Hanoi Lists of P.O.W.'s Are Made Public by U.S.," *New York Times,* January 28, 1973, p. 1.

13. *Report of the Select Committee on POW/MIA Affairs,* pp. 81–82.

14. Ibid.

15. Ibid., p. 82.

16. UPI, "10 Yanks Listed as Laos POWs," *Stars & Stripes,* February 2, 1973, p. 1. The ten POWs listed were: Lieutenant Colonel Walter M. Stischer, USAF; Lieutenant Henry J. Bedinger, USN; Major Edward W. Leonard, Jr., USAF; Captain Stephen G. Long, USAF; Major Norbert A. Gotner, USAF; Captain Jack M. Butcher, USAF; Captain Charles F. Riess, USAF; and civilians Ernest C. Brace, Samuel A. Mattix, and Lloyd D. Oppel.

17. Cable from Colonel George Guay to Lieutenant General Brent Scowcroft, cited in *Report of the Select Committee on POW/MIA Affairs,* p. 83.

18. For the full text of the letter, see: "Former President Nixon's Message to Prime Minister Pham Van Dong," *Department of State Bulletin,* June 27, 1977.

19. "Kissinger's Deal with Peking," *Time,* March 5, 1972, p. 12.

20. *Report of the Select Committee on POW/MIA Affairs,* p. 85. Navy Lieutenant Ronald Dodge, shot down over North Vietnam on May 27, 1967, was photographed alive in PAVN captivity; his picture appeared in *Paris Match* later that year. Air Force Captain Samuel E. Waters, shot down over North Vietnam on December 13, 1966, was quoted in a Bulgarian newspaper; a photo of his military identity card appeared with the article. See: "Mystery of Missing GI's," *U.S. News & World Report,* June 18, 1973, p. 58.

21. Kissinger, *White House Years,* p. 34. Also see: *Report of the Select Committee on POW/MIA Affairs,* pp. 85–86.

22. "An Emotional, Exuberant Welcome Home," *Time,* February 26, 1973, p. 12. Also: "P.O.W.s, A Needed Tonic for America," *Time,* March 19, 1973, p. 19. The return of the prisoners was of such interest to the American public that the K-Mart Corporation sponsored live television coverage of the welcoming ceremonies for the ex-prisoners at American bases.

23. *Report of the Select Committee on POW/MIA Affairs,* p. 268.

24. Ibid., p. 146.

25. Hubbell, *P.O.W.,* p. 543.

26. Dara McLeod, "Defector Says Soviets Questioned POWs," *Washington Times,* November 8, 1991, p. A-8.

27. *Report of the Select Committee on POW/MIA Affairs,* pp. 425–26. Colonel Bui Tin is a historic figure. In Saigon on April 30, 1975, he accepted the surrender from the last president of the Republic of Vietnam, General Duong Van Minh.

28. Ibid., p. 432.

29. Ibid.

30. Excerpted declassified U.S. Air Force report (excerpt untitled) based on analysis of Operation Homecoming returned-prisoner debriefing reports of 322 U.S. Air Force returned POWs; document obtained under Freedom of Information Act request dated May 17, 1993, response dated April 19, 1994, p. 5, author's archives.

31. Ibid., p. 78.

32. Captain Eugene B. McDaniel, USN (Ret.), with James Johnson, *Scars & Stripes* (New York: A.J. Holman, 1975), pp. 37–38.

33. "Torture! POWs Reveal Horrible Suffering in Prisons; Say Some Murdered," from UPI and AP dispatches, *Stars & Stripes,* April 6, 1973, p. 1.

34. Hubbell, *P.O.W.,* p. 161.

35. *Report of the Select Committee on POW/MIA Affairs,* pp. 146–47.

36. Excerpted U.S. Air Force documents on Operation Homecoming debriefings, p. 51.

37. Interview, James Warner, February 25, 1994. Warner was a Navy aviator shot down in 1967 and released from captivity in 1973.

38. Hubbell, *P.O.W.,* pp. 491–99.

39. Interview, Admiral James B. Stockdale, USN (Ret.), March 11, 1993. Stockdale confirmed that he would have been beaten to death by the villagers who initially captured him in 1965 on the coast of North Vietnam had not a "civilian with a pith helmet and a police whistle" managed to restore order to the frenzied scene. Also see: Jim and Sybil Stockdale, *In Love and War* (Annapolis, MD: Naval Institute Press, 1990), pp. 102–3. Years after the war, interviews of former aviator POWs, captured at different times and at different locations in North Vietnam, confirmed that each man had been fired on while descending in his parachute. Further, the returnees reported, attacks by outraged villagers during quasi-ritual "punishment" sessions as the POWs were moved toward Hanoi often degenerated into near-massacres. Associated Press, "Kasler: Civilians Killed 100 POWs," *Pacific Stars & Stripes,* March 20, 1973, p. 1. For the account of Air Force pilot Guy Gruters's experience after capture, see: Malcolm McConnell, *Into the Mouth of the Cat* (New York: W.W. Norton, 1985), pp. 160–63.

40. Excerpted U.S. Air Force documents on Operation Homecoming debriefings, p. 51.

41. Hubbell, *P.O.W.,* pp. 567–68.

42. "Plantation Memories," *Time,* June 11, 1973, p. 23. Also: Hubbell, *P.O.W.,* pp. 596–97.

43. Interview, James Warner, February 24, 1994. Warner was Edison Miller's crewmate.

44. *Report of the Select Committee on POW/MIA Affairs,* pp. 268–69.

45. Lieutenant Colonel Gary D. Solis, USMC, *Marines and Military Law in Vietnam: Trial by Fire* (Washington, D.C.: History and Museums Division, U.S. Marine Corps, 1989), pp. 218–21. Also: "Army Secretary Defends P.O.W.'s," *New York Times,* July 28, 1973, p. 4.

46. Solis, *Marines and Military Law in Vietnam: Trial by Fire,* pp. 219–23. Also: Hubbell, *P.O.W.,* pp. 602–3; and "Plantation Memories."

47. Hubbell, *P.O.W.,* p. 596.

48. Alan Blunt, "Private Rescue Attempts," *Soldier of Fortune,* June, 1987, p. 44.

49. Barbara P. Wyatt, editor, *We Came Home* (Toluca Lake, CA: POW Publications, 1977), unpaginated, entry for Charles F. Riess.

50. P.O.W. Network Database, entry for: Riess, Charles Francis.

51. Wyatt, *We Came Home,* entry for Charles Riess.

52. P.O.W. Network Database, entries for: Oppel, Lloyd D.; and Mattix, Samuel.

53. *Report of the Select Committee on POW/MIA Affairs,* p. 146.

54. Sheehan, *A Bright Shining Lie,* pp. 195–96. Journalist-historian Neil Sheehan, hardly a right-winger, makes it amply clear that the National Liberation Front/Provisional Revolutionary Government was simply a construction of the Vietnamese Communist Party in Hanoi. He quotes Huynh Tan Phat, the secretary-general of the NLF: "Officially, we were separate [Hanoi and the NLF], but in fact we were the same thing all the time; there was a single party; a single government; a single capital; a single country." Also: "Notes on Senator Brooke, 9 April 1973," Diary of Major General John E. Murray, courtesy, General Murray, author's archives. (General Murray was American defense attaché in Saigon in 1973.) General Murray notes that the NLF-Vietcong had been decimated by 1973 and was completely dependent on the PAVN for war matériel. Also: A.J. Plunkett, "Last Known Vietnam POW Shuns Controversy," *Daily Press,* Newport News, Virginia, May 2, 1993, p. A-14.

55. Interview, James Shively.

56. Thomas M. Lippman, "Clandestine Document Assails South Vietnam on Prisoners," *Washington Post,* July 27, 1973, p. A-10.

57. "Pathet Lao Says No Truce, No American POWs," *Washington Post,* February 18, 1973, p. A-5.

58. *Report of the Select Committee on POW/MIA Affairs,* p. 87.

59. Ibid., pp. 90–91.

60. "U.S. Announces Halt in Troop Withdrawals," *New York Times,* March 12, 1973, p. 3. Also: "U.S. Orders Halt in Further Troop Withdrawals," *New York Times,* March 17, 1973, p. 7.

61. "Clearing the Mines, " *Time,* February 12, 1973, p. 23.

62. Major Charles D. Melson, USMC, and Lieutenant Colonel Curtins G. Arnold, USMC, *U.S. Marines in Vietnam: The War That Would Not End, 1971–1973* (Washington, D.C.: History and Museums Division, U.S. Marine Corps, 1991), p. 73.

63. Ibid., p. 238.

64. Ibid., pp. 239, 243.

65. "U.S. Commander Discusses Delays in Mine Clearing," *New York Times,* March 23, 1973, p. 14.

66. *Report of the Select Committee on POW/MIA Affairs,* pp. 89–90.

67. Memorandum for the Secretary of Defense, Subject: U.S. POW/MIA Personnel in Laos, March 23, 1973, courtesy Major General Richard V. Secord, USAF (Ret.), author's archives.

68. Memorandum for the Assistant to the President for National Security Affairs, from the Secretary of Defense, Elliot L. Richardson, March 28, 1973, courtesy Major General Richard V. Secord, USAF (Ret.), author's archives.

69. Kissinger testimony, September 22, 1992, *Report of the Select Committee on POW/ MIA Affairs,* pp. 101–2.

70. The Vietnamese tried to make it clear on the day the Laos POW list was released that the men were held in Laos, not Vietnam. The DRV representative even claimed that he had just received the list from the Neo Lao Hak Xat, the Lao Patriotic Front. See: John W. Finney, "Laos P.O.W. List Shows 9 From U.S.," *New York Times,* February 2, 1973, p. 1. Missionary Lloyd Oppel was born in Canada; hence the confusion between the nine identified as American citizens and the ten names on the list.

71. By May 1973, Congress also threatened to cut funding for air strikes in support of America's Cambodian surrogates fighting the Khmer Rouge. "No Carrot, No Stick," *Time,* May 28, 1973, p. 32.

72. "Notes on Senator Brooke, 9 April 1973."

73. "No Carrot, No Stick," p. 32.

74. "A Trail Becomes a Turnpike," *Time,* March 26, 1973, p. 34.

75. "Transcript of President Nixon's March 15 News Conference on Vietnam," *New York Times,* March 16, 1973, p. 22.

76. Richard M. Nixon, Address of the President to the Nation, March 29, 1973. For the full text of President Nixon's speech, see: *New York Times,* March 30, 1973, p. 6. Nixon's assertion that no American military forces remained in Vietnam was a political expedient that should be viewed within the context of the growing Watergate scandal. Hundreds of U.S. military personnel remained in the Republic of Vietnam, both officially under the provisions of the Paris Peace Accords and semiclandestinely as "temporary duty" members of units officially stationed elsewhere in Southeast Asia. (One additional American, officially listed as a POW, a CIA civilian aviator named Emmet James Kay captured in Laos after the Vietnam cease-fire, was repatriated by the Pathet Lao the next year, bringing the total returned American POWs to 592.)

Chapter 4

1. *Report of the Select Committee on POW/MIA Affairs,* pp. 95–96; also deposition of Dr. Roger Shields, Records of the Senate Select Committee on POW/MIA Affairs, pp. 509–11.

2. *Report of the Select Committee on POW/MIA Affairs,* p. 97.

3. Ibid.

4. Department of Defense, *POW-MIA Fact Book,* pp. 6–7.

5. Interview, General Robert C. Kingston, June 22, 1993. General Kingston states that his major focus of effort during his tenure as JCRC commander was the recovery of MIA and KIA/BNR remains, not the rescue of possibly live POWs still in captivity. However, he had Special Operations Forces in his command who were prepared to conduct such a rescue, if evidence of surviving prisoners was obtained.

6. Memorandum for the Secretary of Defense, Subject: U.S. POW/MIA Personnel in Laos, March 23, 1973. This Action Memorandum, drafted by then Lieutenant Colonel Richard V. Secord and Rear Admiral Thomas Bigley for Acting Assistant Secretary of Defense (International Security Affairs) Lawrence S. Eagleburger, makes it clear that, although the Laotian Communists had made little effort to account for American MIAs, the Popular Revolutionary Government and DRV had at least accounted for 70 percent of the American loss casualties who might have been captured.

7. As Congressman John Ashbrook stated at the time: "While the likelihood of these eighty-three still being alive is slight, there is no military reason for the North Vietnamese being as cruel and inhuman in this matter." See: *Report of the Select Committee on POW/ MIA Affairs,* p. 483. Also see: Thomas W. Lippman, "Documents Show Existence of POWs After Nixon Said All Had Come Home," *Washington Post,* September 25, 1992, p. A-22.

Also see: Deposition of Garnett E. Bell, Jr., Chief, U.S. Office for POW/MIA Affairs in Hanoi, November 7, 1991, p. 27, Records of the Senate Select Committee on POW/MIA Affairs. Garnett "Bill" Bell was one of the most experienced U.S. officials on the POW/ MIA issue. He worked as a Vietnamese translator in Operation Homecoming in 1973. When asked in his deposition if he and his colleagues had specific information about American POWs remaining behind in 1973, he replied: "This was just a general topic of discussion, but it was obvious that people had doubts. But no one had any concrete, specific cases."

8. Interview, Admiral James B. Stockdale, March 11, 1993; and James Warner, November 3, 1993. Stockdale and Warner were both military pilots who spent years as POWs in North Vietnam. Admiral Stockdale won the Medal of Honor for his heroism as a POW. He testified before the Senate Select Committee on POW/MIA Affairs that he believed the North Vietnamese did not maintain a secret, parallel prison system. James Warner stated in an interview that he was convinced the PAVN officers (members of the General Political Directorate) who ran the prisons in which he was captive were not competent enough to conceal a separate prison system from the American POWs. Warner, who was tortured for months in Son Tay Prison (the Zoo) during the horrible "purge" of 1969, and is currently the general counsel of the National Rifle Association, can hardly be described as an apologist for the Vietnamese Communists.

9. Interview, Melvin R. Laird, May 26, 1993. Laird was secretary of defense at the time of the Paris Peace Accords. Also see: Testimony of Garnett Bell, Defense Intelligence Agency, Investigator, Joint Task Force/Full Accounting, before Senate Select Committee on POW/ MIA Affairs, December 4, 1992, *Report of the Select Committee on POW/MIA Affairs,* p. 912.

10. Associated Press, "Little Hope Held for MIAs in Laos War," *Pacific Stars & Stripes,* April 15, 1974, p. 7.

11. *Report of the Select Committee on POW/MIA Affairs,* p. 189.

12. "Pilot Says He Was V.I.P. to Captors," *New York Times,* September 20, 1974, p. A-4.

13. "Last Known American Captive in Indochina Freed," *New York Times,* September 19, 1973, p. A-2; "Last Known POW Is Released," *Washington Post,* September 19, 1974, p. A-1; and P.O.W. Network Database, entry for: Kay, Emmet James.

14. Associated Press, "Thai POW Thinks All GIs Freed," *Pacific Stars & Stripes,* October 1, 1974, p. 6.

15. White Paper, "Background Information on PW/MIA Situation in Laos," Defense Intelligence Agency, PW/MIA Branch, August 16, 1974, Records of the Senate Select Committee on POW/MIA Affairs. These American POWs were: Navy pilot Barton S. Creed; Air Force pilot David Hrdlicka; and civilian aviator Eugene Debruin. Intelligence reports indicated that Air Force pilot Charles Shelton, once held near Samneua, had died before the others.

16. P.O.W. Network Database, entry for: Kay, Emmet James.

17. Lippman, "POW Pilots Left in Laos, Files Suggest," p. A-1.

18. Burrows, *Deep Black,* p. 215, and Bamford, *The Puzzle Palace,* p. 202.

19. The author has known this former intelligence officer for many years. He is a highly respected retired professional who has never been involved with radical POW/MIA activist groups. He has reluctantly decided to remain anonymous for personal reasons; he does not want to become embroiled in this rancorous controversy because he realizes that any rational account he gives of his experience would be distorted by the numerous factions involved in the issue.

20. Central Intelligence Agency Dispatch, September 3, 1968, from chief of station, Vientiane; records of the Senate Select Committee on POW/MIA Affairs.

21. P.O.W. Network Database, entry for: Wallace, Michael W.

22. *Report of the Select Committee on POW/MIA Affairs,* pp. 219–21. Also: P.O.W. Network Database, entry for: Bannon, Paul Wedlake.

23. *Report of the Select Committee on POW/MIA Affairs,* p. 189.

24. United States Military Assistance Command, Vietnam, Studies and Operations Group, 1971–72 Command History, Annex B, p. 501.

25. Interview, Colonel Hayden Peake, USA (Ret.), March 5, 1994. Unless otherwise indicated, all references to Peake are from this interview.

26. *Report of the Select Committee on POW/MIA Affairs,* p. 123.

27. Ibid., p. 124.

28. "Background Paper on Laos and the 'Black Hole' Theory," Defense Intelligence Agency, Records of the Senate Select Committee on POW/MIA Affairs, Records of Chief of Staff Frances Zwenig, Box RG46/No. 3. This document gives the best summary of what the U.S. government did and did not know about our loss casualties in Laos.

29. Interview, Colonel Hayden Peake.

30. Alan Pell Crawford, "The Real MIA Hoax, There's No Mystery About 'Survivors,'" *Washington Post,* July 21, 1991, p. C-1.

31. P.O.W. Network Database, entry for: Walsh, Richard Ambrose III.

32. Interview, Colonel James S. Hanke, USA (Ret.), December 31, 1993.

33. McCarthy and Allison, *Linebacker II,* p. 62.

34. Interview, General Robert Kingston. Also: Deposition of Robert Charles Kingston before Senate Select Committee on POW/MIA Affairs, May 20, 1992, pp. 130–31, Records of the Senate Select Committee on POW/MIA Affairs. For a description of the problems American Search and Rescue forces encountered on the Ho Chi Minh Trail, see: McConnell, *Into the Mouth of the Cat,* pp. 63–99.

35. UPI, "Ex-POW Tells of S. Viet 'Bataan March,'" *Pacific Stars & Stripes,* April 14, 1973, p. 2.

36. The Communists did not only deny the JCRC access to the trail. Communist forces in South Vietnam were also reluctant to allow JCRC search teams access to areas they controlled. On December 16, 1973, almost a year after the January cease-fire, a helicopter-borne JCRC team (unarmed men wearing international orange, in a UH-1 Huey helicopter with similar orange markings) was ambushed by Vietcong less than ten kilometers from Saigon. Three men were wounded, and Captain Richard M. Rees was killed. See: "Chronological Events," Diary of Major General John E. Murray.

37. Interview, Commander Frank C. Brown, USN, March 1, 1994. Brown was a Navy medical specialist at the El Toro Marine Corps Air Station south of Los Angeles in April 1975. He personally saw dozens of disheveled American refugees, some without passports or other identification, simply disappear off the base without being registered.

38. Defense Intelligence Agency, *U.S. Personnel, Southeast Asia (and Selected Foreign Nationals), Alpha and Chronological Reports,* Vol. 1 of 1, February 1, 1990 (Washington, D.C.: Defense Intelligence Agency, 1990), Chronological Order: pp. 48–50.

39. Frank Snepp, *Decent Interval: An Insider's Account of Saigon's Indecent End, Told by the CIA's Chief Strategy Analyst in Vietnam* (New York: Random House, 1977), pp. 566–67. Also: Keyes Beech, "Rites Held for Former CIA Agent," *Chicago Tribune,* October 28, 1977, p. 4.

40. Orrin Deforest and David Chanoff, *Slow Burn* (New York: Pocket Books, 1991), pp. 288–89.

41. Snepp, *Decent Interval,* p. 567.

42. Ibid., pp. 270, 355–77, 567.

43. Joseph Alsop, "Those Attacks on Kissinger," *Washington Post,* September 20, 1974, p. A-29.

44. For a concise press summary of the Vietnam trade embargo's history, see: William Branigin, "U.S. Firms Seek Access to Vietnam," *Washington Post,* July 28, 1993, p. A-13.

45. *Report of the Select Committee on POW/MIA Affairs,* p. 512.

Chapter 5

1. For a chronology of these events, see: *Report of the Select Committee on POW/MIA Affairs,* pp. 76, 513.

2. Franklin, "The POW/MIA Myth," p. 71.

3. Associated Press, "MIA Families Keep Praying," *Pacific Stars & Stripes,* January 29, 1973, p. 2; also: "P.O.W.s, Tidings Good and Bad," *Time,* February 12, 1973, p. 22.

4. UPI, "Raiders Out to Free Captives," *Pacific Stars & Stripes,* July 12, 1972, p. 3. Also: Letter from the Reverend Paul D. Lindstrom to Robert K. Brown, May 20, 1987; author's archives.

5. "Mother Says She Has Proof Son Is Prisoner in Laos," *Pacific Stars & Stripes,* September 30, 1974, p. 3.

6. "Blunt Statement Raps 'Exploitation': State Department Cautions About MIA Hopes," *Pacific Stars & Stripes,* October 4, 1974, p. 1.

7. P.O.W. Network Database, entry for: MacDonald, George Duncan.

8. *Report of the Select Committee on POW/MIA Affairs,* p. 372.

9. *Report of the Select Committee on POW/MIA Affairs,* p. 73. Secretary Habib's statement came from testimony before the Montgomery Committee hearings, July 21, 1976.

10. Deposition of Henry Kissinger, pp. 158–59, quoted in *Report of the Select Committee on POW/MIA Affairs,* p. 282.

11. Ibid., pp. 282–83.

12. Ibid., p. 284.

13. Interview, William Codinha, May 9, 1994.

14. *Report of the Select Committee on POW/MIA Affairs,* p. 285.

15. Interview, William Codinha, May 9, 1994; and *Report of the Select Committee on POW/MIA Affairs,* pp. 285–86.

16. "House Panel Declares No American Is Still an Indochina War Prisoner," *New York Times,* December 16, 1976, p. A-1.

17. Ibid., p. A-11.

18. *Report of the Select Committee on POW/MIA Affairs,* pp. 158–59.

19. *Report of the Select Committee on POW/MIA Affairs,* pp. 373, 513.

20. *Report of the Select Committee on POW/MIA Affairs,* pp. 53–54. Also: interview, Morton L. Smith, counselor of embassy for public affairs, American embassy, Manila, March 2, 1993. Smith, a career Foreign Service officer, was the commission's spokesman. He recalls that the Vietnamese specifically promised better cooperation on the MIA question if reconstruction aid could be guaranteed. Smith also recalls that the Vietnamese military who greeted Woodcock's flight at Hanoi's Gia Lam Airport were cold to the point of public rudeness because they had learned the commission would refuse to discuss war reparations.

21. *Report of the Select Committee on POW/MIA Affairs,* pp. 371–73. Also see: Department of Defense, *POW-MIA Fact Book,* p. 21. A complete list of U.S. citizens whose remains were repatriated during this period is included in "Citizens and Dependents, Captured, Missing, Detained or Voluntarily Remained in Southeast Asia, Accounted for or Unaccounted for from 1-1-61 Through 79/10/11," DIA PW/MIA Branch.

22. For a concise description of the political and military situation that sparked the Vietnamese invasion of Cambodia, see: Neil Sheehan, *After the War Was Over: Hanoi and Saigon* (New York: Random House, 1991), pp. 84–86. Also see: Douglas Pike, *PAVN: People's Army of Vietnam* (New York: Da Capo Paperback, 1986), pp. 60, 67–73.

23. Sheehan, *After the War Was Over,* pp. 15–17.

CHAPTER 6

1. Clark Norton and Howard Kohn, "One Man Against the Pirates," *Reader's Digest,* January 1986, p. 86. This "Drama in Real Life" details Schweitzer's heroism on Ko Kra Island.

2. Interview with Ted Schweitzer, Ho Chi Minh City, Vietnam, February 24, 1993. Unless otherwise indicated, information about Schweitzer's activities was obtained in interviews conducted in the United States or in Vietnam in 1992 and 1993.

3. Barbara Crossette, "Central Link in Release of Hanoi M.I.A. Photos: A U.S. Researcher," *New York Times,* October 25, 1992, p. A-10. Following this rescue, Schweitzer received commendations for bravery from the United Nations.

CHAPTER 7

1. *Report of the Select Committee on POW/MIA Affairs,* pp. 52–53, 377, 513–16.

2. Department of Defense, *POW-MIA Fact Book,* pp. 21–22. A bar graph in this publication clearly illustrates that the release of MIA remains by the Socialist Republic of Vietnam ebbed and flowed with the activities of these official delegations.

3. *Report of the Select Committee on POW/MIA Affairs,* p. 374.

4. Ibid., pp. 374–76.

5. Interview, Senior Colonel Pham Duc Dai, January 24, 1993.

6. Interviews, General John W. Vessey, Jr., USA (Ret.), July 15, 1993; and General Robert Kingston. Kingston accompanied General Vessey on six out of seven of his negotiation missions to Hanoi.

7. *Report of the Select Committee on POW/MIA Affairs,* p. 158.

8. *Report of the Select Committee on POW/MIA Affairs,* pp. 160–61.

9. Ibid., Appendix 2, Case Summaries, pp. 575–77.

10. Interview, Major General John Murray, December 11, 1993. Evidence of Shelton's, Hrdlicka's, and Debruin's deaths came from the same combination of sources cited above.

11. Interview, General Robert Kingston.

12. *Report of the Select Committee on POW/MIA Affairs,* "Vessey 135 Discrepancy Cases," pp. 578–634.

13. DIA Case Summary, Unclassified: Incident Number 1329-01-02, Morrison, Joseph Castleman, author's archives.

14. U.S. General Accounting Office Memorandum to Senate Select Committee on POW/MIA Affairs, B-249462, October 14, 1992, Records of the Senate Select Committee on POW/MIA Affairs.

15. *Report of the Select Committee on POW/MIA Affairs,* pp. 288–89; and interview, General John Vessey, July 15, 1993.

16. Sheehan, *After the War Was Over,* pp. 14–19. Sheehan chronicles the shift away from the obsolete Stalinist command economy imposed on Vietnam by party leader Le Duan after the defeat of the South in 1975.

17. ASEAN members include Thailand, Indonesia, Malaysia, Singapore, the Philippines, and Brunei. Although the American State Department habitually refers to them as free-market "democracies," only the Philippines—the poorest of these nations—has a functioning Western-style democratic system.

18. For a concise examination of the interplay between Vietnam's *doi moi* policy and its relations with ASEAN countries, see: Kenneth J. Conboy, "Seventeen Years Later, Winning the Vietnam War," Asian Study Center, Backgrounder, the Heritage Foundation, Washington, D.C., No. 123, May 19, 1992.

19. The remaining reeducation camps were closed in 1993, when the last surviving former South Vietnamese generals and political figures were freed. For a clear account of life in these camps, see: Robert G. Kaiser, "Surviving Communist 'Re-education Camp,' " *Washington Post,* May 15, 1994, p. A-33.

CHAPTER 8

1. Ted Schweitzer was not the first American to visit the Central Military Museum in Hanoi after the Vietnam War. On December 19, 1981, a delegation from the Vietnam Veterans of America led by its president, Robert Muller, traveled to Hanoi in an attempt to begin the reconciliation of American and PAVN veterans of the war. John F. Kerry, a Navy combat veteran and former antiwar activist, later to become a U.S. senator from Massachusetts, accompanied the delegation. The delegation's other stated purpose was to acquire information on American MIAs. From published accounts, it appears that the Vietnamese government crudely manipulated these young veterans and exploited their good intentions. For example, when they visited the Ho Chi Minh Mausoleum, their government escorts provided a wreath emblazoned with an inscription: "With Respect, From the Vietnam Veterans of America." Later, the group toured the nearby museum where one of the members, Michael Harbert, commented favorably on the combat prowess of the monumental MiG-21. "Look at this guy," Harbert exclaimed, counting the red stars on the fighter's nose, ". . . fourteen American aircraft this son-of-a-bitch shot down." Conservative veterans lambasted the Vietnam Veterans of America for the propaganda that accompanied this delegation. What was missed in the controversy was the fact that the officials of the Central Military Museum did not provide the visiting American veterans any concrete information on American MIAs, nor did they indicate the extent of the museum's archival records on captured Americans. See: Dan Cragg, "The Hanoi Connection—It's Time to Unplug It," *The Stars & Stripes—The National Tribune,* Washington, D.C., May 27, 1982, p. 6; also see: Dan Cragg, "The Dark at the End of the Tunnel —VVA In Hanoi, One Year After," *National Vietnam Veteran's Review,* Washington, D.C., January/February 1983, pp. 9–10. Even during the war, the PAVN used the Central Military Museum to impress foreign visitors with the futility of military intervention in Vietnam. Twice, in 1964 and again in 1970, Navy pilot Everett Alvarez, Jr., a POW, was taken to the museum and shown the displays of captured French military vehicles and artillery. His escorts even showed him his own helmet and flight suit. But what most impressed him about the 1970 visit was the fact that he was allowed to relieve himself on a "regular seated toilet" at the museum, instead of the filthy, rusty slop bucket he had used for years in Hoa Lo Prison. See: Everett Alvarez, Jr., and Anthony S. Pitch, *Chained Eagle* (New York: Donald I. Fine, 1989), p. 218. American journalist Neil Sheehan and his wife, Susan, visited the museum and were given this tour. But they were apparently not given a detailed explanation of the POW display. See: Sheehan, *After the War Was Over,* pp. 39–40.

2. Singlaub with McConnell, *Hazardous Duty,* pp. 312–13. Most knowledgeable American ground commanders in Vietnam considered the development of this sensor network, which was a pet project of Defense Secretary Robert S. McNamara, to be an expensive boondoggle. For Colonel John K. Singlaub, who commanded the MACV-SOG Special Operations Forces, the development of these marginally useful sensors was more than a minor annoyance. He had to dispatch his highly skilled Special Forces reconnaissance teams into heavily defended sections of the Ho Chi Minh Trail in Laos to collect "a variety of leaves, twigs, and seed pods" to serve as models for the sensor antennas. "With the money spent on the high-tech sensors, I could have hired and equipped battalions of Nungs [local mercenaries] whose human *sensors* would have led them to the enemy on the Trail with greater efficiency," Singlaub writes bitterly in his memoir.

3. The Department of Defense lists fixed-wing aircraft losses in Southeast Asia due to hostile action during the Vietnam War as 2,651; helicopter losses due to all causes were 4,869, with only twelve of these losses in North Vietnam. See: "Southeast Asia Statistical Summary," Department of Defense, Office of the Assistant Secretary of Defense for Information Operations, Washington, D.C., October 1973. A complete list of loss casualties that includes aircraft, ground, and sea losses can be obtained from the Defense Intelligence Agency. This document is entitled "Citizens and Dependents, Captured, Missing, Detained or Voluntarily Remained in SE Asia, Accounted for or Unaccounted for from 1-1-61 through 79/10/11," prepared by DIA PW/MIA Branch. This is the definitive government POW/MIA list as to original loss casualties and includes all American citizens and their dependents who fell into enemy hands in Vietnam, Laos, and Cambodia. The list does not note those whose remains have been repatriated and positively identified after October 11, 1979.

CHAPTER 9

1. Interview, Colonel Joseph A. Schlatter, USA, July 26, 1993. Colonel Schlatter confirmed the details of this meeting with Ted Schweitzer.

2. For an authoritative discussion of the General Political Directorate, see: Pike, *PAVN,* pp. 95–96, 136, 168, 170. Pike concisely reveals the important command role of GPD political officers, who were often mistaken as relatively powerless "political advisers," as in the Western model, by the American military. Throughout the history of the PAVN, its political officers have served as joint commanders at almost every unit level, from company up through division. The PAVN's main maneuver element during the Second Indochina War, the infantry regiment, was always dual-commanded on the operational level. And, in effect, it was the political officer who usually had the final authority.

3. The Hanoi Politburo knew exactly what it was about in approving the official names for the two struggles. By calling the anticolonial conflict the "Resistance War," Ho Chi Minh's government appealed to antifascist sentiments in post–World War II France; naming the conquest of the South the "War of Independence" was meant to evoke support in the American public. But the term was never widely used in the American media, and did not become synonymous with "The Vietnam War." See: Sheehan, *A Bright Shining Lie,* pp. 185–86.

4. These two Air Force officers later became the object of speculation concerning a possible "secret, parallel" North Vietnamese prison system in Hanoi because Admiral James Stockdale, one of the senior American POWs held in Hoa Lo Prison in December 1972, could not remember the two men being held with other American prisoners. After Stockdale testified about this in a Senate select committee hearing, the DIA corrected the record in a memorandum to the committee that showed that Sponeyberger and Wilson were held for about a week in Hoa Lo Prison after their shootdown on December 22, 1972, then transferred to the nearby Cu Loc Prison (the Zoo) until their release in March 1973. See: *Report of the Select Committee on POW/MIA Affairs,* pp. 264–65.

5. These were photos of Air Force Captain Samuel E. Waters, shot down on December 13, 1966, west of Hanoi, and of Navy Lieutenant Richard C. Nelson, an A-6 Intruder pilot lost north of Haiphong with his bombardier-navigator, Lieutenant Gilbert L. Mitchell, on March 6, 1968. Captain Waters's remains were returned following the visit to Hanoi of the Leonard Woodcock delegation; Lieutenant Nelson's remains were among several remains "discovered" by the Vietnamese government and returned to the United States in 1984.

6. This was exactly the term Principal Deputy Assistant Secretary of Defense for International Security Affairs Dr. Carl Ford used to describe the Red Book a year later. See: Bruce Van Voorst, "The Truth at Last," *Time,* November 2, 1992, p. 59.

7. Sheehan, *After the War Was Over,* pp. 19–20. Sheehan provides insights on the PAVN's early forays into the free-market economy. For a summary of the PAVN's extensive recent free-enterprise activity see: "Hanoi's Enterprising Army," by William Branigin, *Washington Post,* October 17, 1993, p. A-24.

CHAPTER 10

1. The high-level U.S. government body most affected by the frustrations of this ongoing stalemate was the Inter-Agency Group on POW/MIA Policy (IAG), which was established in January 1980 "to review and assess current efforts in policies . . . to consider future direction/policy to resolve the POW/MIA problem." The IAG included members from the Department of State, the Department of Defense, the Joint Chiefs of Staff, the National Security Council, and, in a break from tradition, a permanent member from the National League of Families of American Prisoners and Missing in Southeast Asia. See: *Report of the Select Committee on POW/MIA Affairs,* pp. 271–75.

2. Interview, General John Vessey.

3. Monika Jensen-Stevenson and William Stevenson, *Kiss the Boys Goodbye* (New York: Dutton, 1990). Also: Defense Intelligence Agency, "Talking Points, Subject: Examples of Inaccurate or Misleading Statements—*Kiss the Boys Goodbye,* by Monika Jensen-Stevenson," RG46/Taylor/No. 5, Records of the Senate Select Committee on POW/MIA Affairs.

4. Jim Sanders, Mark Sauter, and R. Cort Kirkwood, *Soldiers of Misfortune* (Washington, D.C.: National Press Books, 1992).

5. For a thorough examination of these films' genesis and impact, see: Elliott Gruner,

Prisoners of Culture: Representing the Vietnam POW (New Brunswick, NJ: Rutgers University Press, 1993). Gruner's discussion of *Rambo: First Blood Part II* is worth the price of the book.

6. DIA Case Summary, Incident Number 1329-1-02, Morrison, Joseph Castleman.

7. Sheehan, *A Bright Shining Lie,* pp. 189–91.

8. Philip Shenon, "The Vietnamese Speak Softly of 300,000 Missing in the War," *New York Times,* November 30, 1992, p. A-1.

9. See: *Report of the Select Committee on POW/MIA Affairs,* pp. 246–47, 358–59. Perot's continued interest—some would say obsession—in the emotional issue of live American POWs became the object of derision by one of his fiercest critics, conservative talk show host Rush Limbaugh. During the 1992 presidential campaign, Limbaugh mocked Perot by playing a recording of "When Johnny Comes Marching Home Again" whenever Perot's name was mentioned on the show.

10. *Report of the Select Committee on POW/MIA Affairs,* p. 375.

11. A full description of Carl Ford's participation in Schweitzer's project is found in: "Memorandum for Secretary of Defense from Carl W. Ford, Jr., PDASD/ISA, subject: Attempt to Obtain POW/MIA Files," dated 19 March 1992; declassified, author's archives. In this ten-page memorandum, Ford makes it clear that Schweitzer had unearthed "potentially invaluable" information in the Hanoi archives.

CHAPTER 11

1. I define the term "myth" in this case to be: "a story invented as a veiled explanation of the truth," as in *Webster's Third New International Dictionary, Unabridged.*

2. Franklin, "The POW/MIA Myth," p. 45; also: H. Bruce Franklin, "The Myth of the Missing: The POW/MIAs Keep the Vietnam War Alive," *The Progressive,* January 1993, pp. 22–25. The myth that American civilian and military leaders, including intelligence professionals, callously "abandoned" hundreds of our prisoners of war, known or suspected to have still been in Communist captivity, is similar to another postwar myth of this troubled century. A year after the German Imperial Army suffered military collapse on the Western Front and was forced by strategic reality to sue for peace in the autumn of 1918, Field Marshal Paul von Hindenburg told the National Assembly of the Weimar Republic that the kaiser's armies had not suffered a military defeat, but rather had been "stabbed in the back" by traitors on the home front. Although almost as sinister in its implied treachery, the bitter legend of abandoned American POWs has not had the same disastrous impact as the German myth. For a concise discussion of this myth, see: William L. Shirer, *The Rise and Fall of the Third Reich* (New York: Simon and Schuster, 1960), pp. 31–32.

3. *Report of the Select Committee on POW/MIA Affairs,* pp. 274–75.

4. "US-VN Normalization Road Map," *The Nation* (Bangkok), October 25, 1991, p. 1.

5. Ibid.

6. The phrase "mind-set to debunk," which entails the negative attributes of cynicism and apathy, has come to haunt the DIA. Ironically, it was coined by one of the agency's staunchest supporters, Army Colonel Joseph Schlatter, a member of the Military Intelligence branch, who served on a task force formed by the DIA director in the mid-1980s to review the performance of the Special Office for POW/MIA. At the time, Schlatter was relatively unfamiliar with the office's work and his criticism that its analysts were all too ready to debunk every Indochinese refugee report of live American POWs seemed to him justified. Later, when Schlatter himself led the office, he became convinced that his criticism was unfounded. As he testified before the Senate Select Committee on POW/MIA Affairs in 1992, "At the time, I felt this charge was somewhat valid. Now I state without reservation my belief that this is a bogus charge." See: Martin Tolchin, "Negative Mind-set on M.I.A.'s Charged," *New York Times,* December 2, 1992, p. A-12.

7. In February 1982, President Ronald Reagan made this statement in an address to MIA families. Over the next six years of his two administrations, he stubbornly refused to acknowledge the hollowness of this rhetoric. For a chronology of the key events of those years, see: *Report of the Select Committee on POW/MIA Affairs,* pp. 514–15.

8. Ibid., p. 152.

9. Ibid., pp. 152, 168.

10. Department of Defense, *POW-MIA Fact Book,* p. 39; and *Report of the Select Committee on POW/MIA Affairs,* pp. 170–72.

11. Memorandum for Brigadier General Shufelt, Subject: "The POW/MIA Issue," Defense Intelligence Agency, September 25, 1985, p. 1.

12. Defense Intelligence Agency, Memorandum for Brigadier General Shufelt, from Thomas A. Brooks, Commodore, USN, Subject: "The POW/MIA Issue," September 25, 1985; Records of the Senate Select Committee on POW/MIA Affairs.

13. "Tighe Task Force Review of DIA PW/MIA Analysis Center," Defense Intelligence Agency, Washington, D.C. 20301, May 27, 1986, p. 39. The task force report states: "There are those who would define cover-up differently than we have. Nonetheless, whatever definition is chosen, it is certain that this task force has found no evidence whatsoever that any American involved in the PW/MIA effort has tried to cover-up any facet of this painful business." An annotated copy of this report was provided the author by the press office of the American Legion's national headquarters. This version contains rebuttals of some of the task force findings by the DIA.

14. *Report of the Select Committee on POW/MIA Affairs,* pp. 55–56.

15. *Congressional Record,* June 25, 1981, p. 761.

16. Letter from Major General John E. Murray, USA (Ret.), to Richard L. Armitage, Assistant Secretary of Defense for International Security Affairs, February 26, 1986, courtesy of General Murray, author's archives. (General Murray was officially American defense attaché in Saigon in 1972–74. His actual assignment was senior American officer supervising the "termination" of the overt American military effort in Vietnam.) He begins the letter to Armitage: "The so-called MIAs in Vietnam may in fact be deserters or expatriates." General Murray ends the letter: "From my experience, I doubt the existence of MIAs in Vietnam, as I would doubt Martians on our planet." Also: Kingston deposition, p. 80.

17. "GI Deserters Wanting Out," *Pacific Stars & Stripes,* April 27, 1975, p. 1; and "U.S. Steps Up Airlift," *Pacific Stars & Stripes,* April 23, 1975, p. 1.

18. "Tighe Task Force Review of DIA PW/MIA Analysis Center," Defense Intelligence Agency, Washington, D.C., May 27, 1986, p. 65. Also see: *Report of the Select Committee on POW/MIA Affairs,* p. 55.

19. Kingston deposition, pp. 152–56, 162–63, 174–75. Also: Letter to Lieutenant General Leonard H. Peroots, USAF, Director, Defense Intelligence Agency, from Robert G. Kingston, General, U.S. Army (Ret.), December 12, 1986, courtesy of General Kingston, author's archives; and interview, General Robert Kingston, December 4, 1993.

20. Murray–Peroots letter, November 1, 1986. Also: fax letter from Major General John Murray, USA (Ret.), to author, December 8, 1993, author's archives.

21. Interview, General Robert Kingston, June 22, 1993. Also: Robert F. Ward, "Speakout: Perot Is Far from Being Alone in His Suspicions When It Comes to America's Missing Soldiers," *Rocky Mountain News,* June 15, 1992, p. C-11. In this op-ed piece, Ward, a Vietnam veteran, states that the Tighe Task Force "was unanimous in its conclusions that there were live Americans being held in Southeast Asia."

22. DA Form 2-1, Personnel Qualification Record, Peck Millard Arthur, obtained from Department of the Army, U.S. Army Reserve Personnel Center, St. Louis, under provision of the Freedom of Information Act.

23. Memorandum to Director, DIA, from Millard A. Peck, Colonel, Infantry, USA, Subject: "Request for Relief," February 12, 1991, Records of the Senate Select Committee on POW/ MIA Affairs.

24. Office of the Assistant Secretary of Defense, Command, Control, Communications and Intelligence, "Memorandum for Record—POW/MIA Management Inquiry" (prepared by Ronald J. Knecht), dated January 28, 1992, Records of the Senate Select Committee on POW/MIA Affairs.

25. DA Form 2-1, Personnel Qualification Record, Peck Millard Arthur, Section II, Item 17; Section VI.

26. Cathryn Donohoe, "Mike Peck's Mythic Battle," *Washington Times,* June 7, 1991, p. E-1.

27. Interview, former DIA POW/MIA analyst, June 24, 1994.

28. POW Management Inquiry Memorandum, p. 20.

29. Ibid., p. 11.

30. Interview, Frances Zwenig, December 17, 1993.

31. Mae Rhine, "Pentagon Officials Shoot Down POW/MIA Meeting with Zimmer," *The Democrat* (Flemington, NJ), March 28, 1991, p. A-4.

32. POW/MIA Management Inquiry Memorandum, p. 23.

33. Deposition of Garnett Bell, pp. 4–7.

34. Associated Press, "Some POWs Were Left in Vietnam, Official Says," *Washington Post,* November 7, 1991, p. A-38.

35. Deposition of Garnett Bell, pp. 17–19.

36. P.O.W. Network Database, entry for: McKinney, Clemie, O3/U.S. Navy Reserve.

37. Fax correspondence from Garnett Bell to American contact, April 13, 1992, author's archives.

38. Ibid.

CHAPTER 12

1. Although American petroleum companies were anxious to exploit Vietnam's rich South China Sea oil fields, which they had in fact explored prior to the fall of Saigon, there is no evidence that these companies ever lobbied for a premature resolution of the MIA issue, as some critics have charged. The author interviewed several American oil company executives on this matter in May and June 1993. They were adamant that their companies would patiently wait for the embargo to be lifted, following a proper resolution of the MIA question.

2. Statement of Carl Ford, Principal Deputy Assistant Secretary of Defense, International Security Affairs, Hearing Before the Subcommittee on Asian and Pacific Affairs, Committee on Foreign Affairs, House of Representatives, November 6, 1992, U.S. Government Printing Office, p. 27.

CHAPTER 13

1. Wyatt, *We Came Home,* entry for Ernest C. Brace.

2. Lisa McCormack, "Veteran Starves Self in Cage to Get POW Data Released," *Washington Times,* October 26, 1989, p. B-5.

3. Freedom of Information Request reply, National Personnel Records Center, St. Louis, April 4, 1990, military record of Craig Allen Ziegler, also known as Craig Allen Ploss.

4. Lieutenant Colonel Paul D. Mather, USAF (Ret.), "The MIA Story in Southeast Asia"

(Washington, D.C.: National Defense University, 1990), monograph, pp. 4-13 to 4-14. Also: interview, Lieutenant Colonel Paul D. Mather, December 31, 1993.

5. Mather, "The MIA Story," p. 4-29.

6. For a full representative sampling of the rhetoric from these fund-raising documents, see: Letter from Brigadier General James W. Shufelt, USA, Deputy Director for Operations, Plans and Training, Defense Intelligence Agency, to Honorable Stephen J. Solarz, Chairman, Subcommittee on Asian and Pacific Affairs, Committee on Foreign Affairs, House of Representatives, November 23, 1987 (U-1520/VO-PW), Records of the Senate Select Committee on POW/MIA Affairs.

7. Undated fund-raising solicitation (circa 1985), Skyhook II Project, P.O. Box 230, Old Westbury, NY 11568.

8. Gruner, *Prisoners of Culture,* p. 20.

9. Mather, "The MIA Story," pp. 4-27, 4-28.

10. For a detailed description of Bailey's deception, see: Susan Katz Keating, "Exposing a P.O.W. Hoax," *Reader's Digest,* December 1993, pp. 53–58. Also see: Scott Harris, "Portrait of a POW Hunter," *Los Angeles Times,* August 7, 1991, p. A-1.

11. Undated Operation Rescue solicitation, circa February 1991.

12. Keating, "Exposing a P.O.W. Hoax," p. 57.

13. Christopher Cox, "Anatomy of a POW Scam: The Donald Carr Case," *Boston Sunday Herald,* May 10, 1992, p. 1. For the most complete analysis of the bogus live-POW photographs in which non-Americans are reputed to be living prisoners, see: Gerard Calla, "POW/MIA Scams Cloud the Issue of Americans Missing in Asia," *Soldier of Fortune,* November 1991, pp. 46–79. Calla correctly identifies one well-known "prison camp" photo of a robust, bearded European with two hill tribesmen as portraying a Mennonite missionary in Laos. Another widely accepted photograph of a reputed live American POW that shows a pale, bearded man with downcast eyes was actually a picture of a Soviet baker at a South Pole research station that was photocopied from a Soviet magazine in Phnom Penh, Cambodia, by a group of low-level officials at the Cambodian Ministry of Foreign Affairs.

14. For a full discussion of this chain of events, see: "Analysis of Robertson-Stevens-Lundy Reporting," Office of the Assistant Secretary of Defense for Public Affairs, Washington, D.C., August 1991; also see: *Report of the Select Committee on POW/MIA Affairs,* pp. 322–24.

15. "The POW Scams," editorial, *Washington Post,* December 4, 1992, p. A-30.

16. For a full description of Bo Gritz and his colleagues, see: C.W. Patterson and G.L. Tippin, *The Heroes Who Fell from Grace* (New York: Dell, 1985).

17. George C. Wilson and Art Harris, "Mercenaries Sent to Laos Seeking MIAs," *Washington Post,* May 21, 1981, p. A-1.

18. Interview, George L. Brooks, July 1, 1993.

19. *Report of the Select Committee on POW/MIA Affairs,* pp. 219–20.

20. "Possible POW/MIA-Associated Markings in Southeast Asia," summary of CIA analysis performed in 1976, 1980, 1981, and 1992, prepared for Senate Select Committee on POW/MIA Affairs, August 10, 1992, File RG46/Taylor/No. 9, Records of the Senate Select Committee on POW/MIA Affairs.

21. Interview, retired Naval Special Operations officer, March 12, 1994. This officer was on the staff of the Joint Special Operations Command in 1981.

22. CIA Spot Report of January 6, 1981, cited in *Report of the Select Committee on POW/ MIA Affairs,* p. 220. And: "Possible POW/MIA-Associated Markings in Southeast Asia," p. 9.

23. Interview, retired Naval Special Operations officer, March 12, 1994. Also: *Report of* *the Select Committee on POW/MIA Affairs,* p. 220. The *Report* cites a declassified CIA Spot Report as a source of this information.

24. Wilson and Harris, "Mercenaries Sent to Laos Seeking MIAs," pp. A-1, A-10.

25. Mark Sauter and Jim Sanders, "POW/MIA: The Suffering and the Secrecy," *The American Legion,* March 1994, p. 18; quotation from p. 21.

26. "Possible POW/MIA-Associated Markings in Southeast Asia," pp. 10–11. Also: *Report of the Select Committee on POW/MIA Affairs,* p. 210.

27. *Report of the Select Committee on POW/MIA Affairs,* p. 212.

28. Patricia Ann O'Grady, Ph.D., "SIT DOWN AND SHUT UP!" Information sheet, distributed at the National Alliance of Families POW/MIA Forum, July 1993, pp. 4–5.

29. "Possible POW/MIA-Associated Markings in Southeast Asia," p. 2. Also: "New POW Evidence: The 'Clusters' Theory," *U.S. News & World Report,* July 20, 1992, p. 11.

30. *Report of the Select Committee on POW/MIA Affairs,* p. 212.

31. Thomas W. Lippman, "U.S. Team to Inspect Possible POW Prison in Laos," *Washington Post,* January 16, 1992, p. A-10.

32. Ibid.

33. *Report of the Select Committee on POW/MIA Affairs,* p. 315. Also see: "Bo Gritz: Hero or Huckster?" *Soldier of Fortune,* POW/MIA Special Edition, Spring 1983. The magazine's publisher, Lieutenant Colonel Robert K. Brown, was originally one of Gritz's supporters. He later became one of Gritz's most virulent critics and has done much to deflate Gritz's bloated heroic image in the Vietnam veteran community.

34. For a description of Lance Sijan's heroism, see: McConnell, *Into the Mouth of the Cat.*

35. Scott Barnes with Melva Libb, *BOHICA* (Canton, OH: Daring Books, 1987).

36. Donna DuVall and Jim Graves, "Scott Barnes: Man of Mystery," *Soldier of Fortune,* POW/MIA Special Edition, Spring 1983, pp. 34–36. By far the most colorful and often most insightful reporting on Barnes has appeared in *Soldier of Fortune,* a publication often ignored by the mainstream media.

37. Douglas Waller et al., "The Strange Tales of Mr. Barnes," *Newsweek,* November 9, 1992, p. 24. Also see: Jim Coyne, "Scott Barnes: The Flake That Changed America's Future," *Soldier of Fortune,* March 1993, p. 68.

38. Interview, Steve Gekoski, July 1, 1993.

39. Select Committee on POW/MIA Affairs, United States Senate, deposition of Scott Tracy Barnes, March 6, 1992, pp. 61–70, National Archives, Washington, D.C.

40. Jensen-Stevenson and Stevenson, *Kiss the Boys Goodbye,* and Sanders, Sauter, and Kirkwood, *Soldiers of Misfortune.*

41. Letter: From National Personnel Records Center, Military Personnel Records, St. Louis, to Vietnam Veterans Memorial Fund of Texas, August 2, 1991. This record contains a response to a query submitted under the Freedom of Information Act concerning Pistilli's record. The record clearly indicates that Pistilli never served in Vietnam and was never a POW. In addition, Army Reserve Major Pete Johnson, a member of the Pentagon's Task Force Russia investigating Soviet contact with American POWs in Indochina, confirmed that Pistilli was a bogus POW: Interview, Major Pete Johnson, USAF, September 10, 1993.

42. Mark Sauter and Jim Sanders, *The Men We Left Behind* (Washington, D.C.: National Press Books, 1993), p. 244.

43. Samuel Kim, *The American POWs* (Boston: Brandon Press, 1979).

44. Richard R. Burns, "The 'Wannabe' Syndrome: When Combat Fantasies Become Reality," *Behind the Lines,* May/June 1994, p. 48.

45. Aphrodite Matsakis, Ph.D., *Vietnam Wives: Women and Children Surviving Life with Veterans Suffering Post-Traumatic Stress Disorder* (Washington, D.C.: Woodbine House, 1988), pp. XVIII, 57.

46. Letter to the author from Aphrodite Matsakis, October 1, 1993. For a professional description of the psychological motives of phony POWs, see: Landy Sparr, M.D., and Loren D. Pankratz, Ph.D., "Factitious Posttraumatic Stress Disorder," *American Journal of Psychiatry,* August 1983, pp. 1016–19. Myths about POWs from the Vietnam War continue to grow. On November 9, 1993, the *Washington Times* ran a column noting that the dedication of the new Women's Vietnam Memorial was an appropriate time "to remember these 16 American women taken prisoner during the Vietnam War yet [who] still have not been accounted for by Hanoi. . . ." Navy Commander Frank Brown, a Vietnam veteran and one of the most knowledgeable mainstream members of the POW/MIA community, wrote the *Times* to correct the record. Of the sixteen women named, only ten were Americans; ten were released alive; four died in captivity; one escaped; and one, Joan E. Johnson, was never a prisoner. The newspaper did not print Commander Brown's correction.

CHAPTER 15

1. "A US-VN Normalization Road Map," *The Nation* (Bangkok), October 25, 1991, p. 1. Also: *Report of the Select Committee on POW/MIA Affairs,* p. 274. It is clear that the Bush administration intended to rely on the forthright implementation of the Road Map during the final two years of the President's term as the best means of resolving the MIA issue in time for the November 1992 elections. Because this approach relied on a complex sequence of events occurring throughout Indochina, the State Department chose not to divulge details of the diplomatic process. However, the administration did give unmistakable clues to the quid pro quo nature of the new relationship with Vietnam. Thus, in a March 7, 1991, letter from Secretary of State James Baker to National League of Families of American Prisoners and Missing in Southeast Asia board chairman Sue Scott, Baker stated: "Normalization of bilateral relations with Vietnam is linked to a comprehensive political settlement in Cambodia which includes a UN-verified withdrawal of Vietnamese troops; the pace and scope of the normalization process will be directly affected by the seriousness of Vietnam's cooperation on POW/MIA and other humanitarian issues." See: National League of Families newsletter, March 20, 1991, p. 4.

2. This incident is described in detail in a fax memorandum Ted Schweitzer sent the author on March 6, 1994. Other sources have discussed reports of a black American living beneath this bridge. See: Nigel Cawthorne, *The Bamboo Cage* (London: Mandarin Books, 1991), p. 299.

3. P.O.W. Network Database, entry for: Nolan, McKinley.

4. Ibid.

5. Calla, "POW Scams Cloud the Issue of Americans Missing in Asia," p. 49.

6. Letter from Michael D. Benge to Senator John F. Kerry, December 12, 1991, Records of the Senate Select Committee on POW-MIA Affairs. Michael Benge is a former civilian POW in Vietnam. In the late 1970s he worked in the Philippines and reportedly was familiar with a number of American deserters leaving Vietnam.

7. Interview, Lieutenant Colonel Fred Caristo, USA (Ret.), January 5, 1993. Caristo, a former officer with the American covert action element in Vietnam, Military Assistance Command, Vietnam/Studies and Observations Group, estimates that there are currently seventeen living stay-behinds in Communist Indochina. This estimate is shared by at least two DIA analysts interviewed for this book.

8. Ted Sell, "It's Hard to Tell When Defector Is a Deserter," *Los Angeles Times,* August

18, 1968, p. 2. Also: Phil Stevens, "No One Knows Fate of Deserters Still in Vietnam," *Navy Times,* June 4, 1975, p. 1.
9. Frank C. Brown, "The American Viet Cong," unpublished manuscript, p. 2.
10. One of the best accounts of these French stay-behinds is Roger F. Granger, "Uncle Ho's Foreign Legions," *Gung-Ho,* August 1981, p. 46.
11. Albert Parry, "Soviet Aid to Vietnam," *Military Review,* June 1967, p. 20.
12. "White House Official: Live MIAs Are Deserters," *Pacific Stars & Stripes,* July 13, 1993, p. 1.

CHAPTER 16
1. *Report of the Select Committee on POW/MIA Affairs,* p. 515.
2. This incident is confirmed in a classified DIA Memorandum for Record, by James Renaud, May 18, 1992, author's archives.
3. Fax message from Theodore G. Schweitzer III to DIA case officer James Renaud (his professional pseudonym), March 30, 1992, author's archives.
4. The details of Schweitzer's case officer's reactions to the March 30, 1992, Hanoi incident and related events were obtained during interviews with James Renaud on October 24 and 25, 1992, and on March 17, 1994. Renaud's overall estimate of Schweitzer's performance is included in a fax letter to the author, dated January 27, 1994.
5. Interview, James Renaud, October 24, 1992.
6. Fax message to Theodore G. Schweitzer III from James Renaud, April 8, 1992, author's archives.
7. Telefax message from Garnett E. Bell to author, dated September 28, 1994; transmitted September 29, 1994.
8. Norton and Kohn, "One Man Against the Pirates," p. 86.
9. Hubbell, *P.O.W.,* pp. 48–51.
10. Larry Guarino, *A POW's Story: 2801 Days in Hanoi* (New York: Ivy Books, 1990).
11. Fax message from Theodore G. Schweitzer III to James Renaud, April 3, 1992, author's archives.
12. *Report of the Select Committee on POW/MIA Affairs,* p. 381.
13. Ibid.
14. Ibid., p. 382.
15. *Report of the Select Committee on POW/MIA Affairs,* p. 516.

CHAPTER 17
1. Interview, Lieutenant Colonel Jack Donovan, USA, Hanoi, February 5, 1993.
2. Ibid.
3. For a description of the work of the JTF/FA detachment in Hanoi, see: Thomas W. Lippman, "U.S. Outpost in Hanoi Seeks Word of MIAs," *Washington Post,* November 23, 1992, p. A-15; and SSgt. William H. McMichael, "Searching for POW/MIAs," *Soldiers* (U.S. Army publication), October 1992, p. 13.
4. Department of Defense, *POW/MIA Fact Book,* p. 19.
5. McMichael, "Searching for POW/MIAs," p. 13.
6. National League of Families press release, "Status of the POW/MIA Issue: December 15, 1993," p. 1.
7. National League of Families press release, "Vietnam's Ability to Rapidly Account for Missing Americans," December 15, 1993, pp. 1–2.
8. Interview, James Renaud, March 15, 1994. Also: Neil Sheehan, "Letter from Vietnam: Prisoners of the Past," *The New Yorker,* May 24, 1993, p. 44.
9. Interview, Lieutenant Colonel Charles D. Robertson, USAF, February 5, 1993, Hanoi.

10. John Corry, "The MIA Cover-up," *The American Spectator,* February 1994, p. 28.

11. The Red Book index title, "MỤC LỤC BỘ SƯU TẬP HIỆN VẬT A BIÊN NIÊN CẤC SỰ KIỆN LỊCH SỬ," can be translated: "Index, Current Secret Report of Division A, Legally Obtained Historical Documents."

12. Karnow, *Vietnam,* pp. 276–79.

13. Fax message from Theodore G. Schweitzer III to James Renaud, April 8, 1992, author's archives.

14. Fax message from Theodore G. Schweitzer III to author, dated March 6, 1994.

15. James Renaud, Memorandum for Record, 18 May 1992.

Chapter 18

1. Interview, Senator John F. Kerry, April 27, 1993.

2. *Report of the Select Committee on POW/MIA Affairs,* p. 383.

3. There is no indication in press accounts that Senator Kerry mentioned his earlier visit to the museum as a member of a Vietnam Veterans Against the War delegation in the 1970s.

4. *Report of the Select Committee on POW/MIA Affairs,* p. 383.

5. Senator Kerry mentioned this during the select committee hearings on December 4, 1992.

6. *Report of the Select Committee on POW/MIA Affairs,* pp. 288–89; and interview, General John Vessey.

7. *Report of the Select Committee on POW/MIA Affairs,* p. 384.

8. James C. Hyde, "Robb Chases Hanoi Rock-Thrower During POW/MIA Committee Visit," *Armed Forces Journal International,* June 1992, p. 54.

9. Richard Sammon, "Open Doors but Little Evidence Greets Senators in Vietnam," *Congressional Quarterly,* May 2, 1992, p. 1147.

10. Ibid.

11. P.O.W. Network Database, entry for: Sather, Richard Christian. Sather was shot down on the afternoon of August 5, 1964, during raids on North Vietnamese torpedo boat bases near the coastal town of Thanh Hoa. His propeller-driven A-1H Spad took direct hits from antiaircraft fire and crashed into the Tonkin Gulf near the shore. His flight mates saw no parachute and heard no emergency beeper. He was declared Killed in Action/Body Not Recovered. His skeletal remains were returned in 1985 during one of the periodic releases of remains the Vietnamese Communists implemented to orchestrate their policy toward the United States.

12. Computer file message from Theodore G. Schweitzer III to James Renaud and the DIA, dated June 26, 1992, author's archives.

13. Translation provided by Lieutenant Colonel Frederick Caristo, USA (Ret.), April 26, 1994.

14. P.O.W. Network Database, entry for: Bruch, Donald William, Jr.

15. U.S. Air Force Casualty Office Incident Number 0162-0-01, Pogreba, Dean Andrew. Also see: P.O.W. Network Database, entry for: Pogreba, Dean Andrew.

16. U.S. Air Force Casualty Office Incident Number 0162-0-01, Pogreba, Dean Andrew.

17. PAVN Museum Acquisition Card No. 3805, author's archives. Translation provided by Lieutenant Colonel Frederick Caristo, USA (Ret.)

18. Biography, Brigadier General Thomas E. Lacy, USAF, Secretary of the Air Force, Office of Information, dated September 15, 1975.

19. P.O.W. Network Database, entry for: Pogreba, Dean Andrew.

20. "War Drags on for POW/MIA Kin," Newsmakers, *USA Today,* July 13, 1990, p. A-2.

21. Deposition of Brigadier General Thomas Edwin Lacy, Sr., USAF (Ret.), April 2, 1992, Records of the Senate Select Committee on POW/MIA Affairs, pp. 179–82.
22. Ibid., pp. 48–49.
23. Ibid., p. 87.
24. Ibid., pp. 158–65.
25. Ibid., pp. 175–77.
26. Ibid., p. 149.
27. Ibid., pp. 180–82.
28. Ibid., pp. 182–83.
29. Ibid., pp. 184–93.
30. Interview, attorney William Codinha, April 26, 1994. Recalling this strange deposition, Codinha stated that he found Lacy to be a completely "incredible" witness. "When pressed, General Lacy's story simply did not stand up," Codinha added.
31. Interview, Commander Frank Brown, USN, April 25, 1994. Commander Brown is a Navy officer who follows MIA affairs closely and has good contacts within the Defense Intelligence Agency.
32. Live POW Lobby of America, *The Insider,* Vol. 3, No. 12, December 1993, pp. 3–6.
33. Ibid., p. 3.
34. Preliminary Inventory: Records of the Senate Select Committee on POW/MIA Affairs, 102d Congress (1991–92), Center for Legislative Archives, National Archives and Records Administration, Last Revision, March 15, 1993, p. 3: Box 10: [Deposition] Thomas Edwin Lacy, Sr.
35. Live POW Lobby of America, *The Insider,* Vol. 3, No. 12, December 1993, p. 6.
36. Ibid., p. 4.
37. National Vietnam P.O.W. Strike Force newsletter, circa November 4, 1993, courtesy Robert K. Brown.
38. Ibid.
39. Reply to Freedom of Information Act Request, National Archives and Records Administration NA Form 13044, dated September 26, 1991.
40. Michael Van Atta, "There *Are* Live Americans in Vietnam," *The Stars and Stripes—The National Tribune,* October 31, 1988, p. 1.
41. Susan Katz, "Paramilitary Unit Plans Asia Raid to Save POWs," *Washington Times,* January 6, 1986, p. A-3.
42. Live POW Lobby of America newsletter, April 1, 1993, p. 1.
43. Live POW Lobby of America, *The Insider,* Vol. 3, No. 12, December 1993, p. 5.
44. Michael Van Atta, "Covert Action (Behind Enemy Lines)," *The Insider,* Vol. 3, No. 5, May 1993, p. 2.
45. Letter to Michael Van Atta from Charles F. Trowbridge, Jr., Deputy Director, Special Office for Prisoners of War and Missing in Action, Defense Intelligence Agency, May 7, 1993, p. 4.
46. Fax message from Warren Gray, Office of Current Operations, Department of Defense POW/MIA Office, to Malcolm McConnell, May 13, 1994. "With regard to your question, has anyone in Van Atta's group responded to our letter request for information, the answer is no." Senior Pentagon officials responsible for POW/MIA matters also became impatient with Van Atta's meddling. Edward W. Ross, acting deputy assistant secretary of defense (POW/MIA affairs), wrote Van Atta, chiding him for claiming that the Insiders had received cooperation and support from the U.S. government for their activities. Such a claim, Ross wrote, "is simply not true." Letter to Michael Van Atta from Edward W. Ross, November 1, 1993, author's archives.

CHAPTER 19

1. Contract between Theodore G. Schweitzer III and the Central Military Museum of the People's Army of Vietnam, December 6, 1990, author's archives.

2. Ted Schweitzer, computer disk message to the DIA, July 10, 1992, item no. 5, author's archives.

3. Ted Schweitzer, computer disk message to the DIA, July 15, 1992, item no. 6, author's archives.

4. Interview, Colonel John Donovan.

5. Philip Shenon, "Once Again, a Fiery Suicide Sets Vietnam Aflame," *New York Times,* October 20, 1993, p. A-4.

6. "Vietnam: Hijacker Jailed," *Far Eastern Economic Review,* March 11, 1993, p. 12.

7. Colonel Dai's assertion is borne out by wartime intelligence reports. In the U.S. Military Assistance Command, Vietnam Intelligence Bulletin, Number 10-67 (October 1967), pp. 4–5, for example, a captured North Vietnamese Army (PAVN) document is cited that instructs Communist soldiers on the disposition of Americans killed on the battlefield: "Regarding dead U.S. soldiers, all units were instructed to strip the bodies of identification papers and to secretly bury them. A list of dead U.S. soldiers was to be maintained, and whenever a VC terrorist was executed, the enemy would claim to have killed one of the listed dead U.S. soldiers."

8. Shenon, "The Vietnamese Speak Softly of 300,000 Missing in the War," *New York Times.*

9. Defense Intelligence Agency, *U.S. Personnel, Southeast Asia,* Chronological Order, p. 15. Also: P.O.W. Network Database, entry for: Laney, Billy Ray.

10. P.O.W. Network Database, entry for: Laney, Billy Ray.

11. *Report of the Select Committee on POW/MIA Affairs,* p. 289.

12. Computer disk message entry, Ted Schweitzer to James Renaud, June 5, 1992.

13. Ibid.

14. Ibid.

15. "Remains Falsely Pushed as MIAs," *Washington Times,* June 19, 1993, p. A-7.

16. Bell deposition, November 7, 1991, p. 141.

17. Interview, Lon and Gail Stickney, Hanoi, February 1, 1993.

18. U.S. General Accounting Office Memorandum to Senate Select Committee on POW/MIA Affairs, B-249462; and *Report of the Select Committee on POW/MIA Affairs,* p. 288.

19. *Report of the Select Committee on POW/MIA Affairs,* pp. 286–87.

20. Ibid., p. 286.

21. Kingston deposition, p. 58.

22. Interview, James Renaud, March 15, 1994.

23. Ted Schweitzer computer disk message to the DIA, "Comments on U.S. Remains in Vietnam," dated 930314 (March 14, 1993), point no. 4, author's archives.

24. *Report of the Select Committee on POW/MIA Affairs,* p. 289.

25. Ted Schweitzer to the DIA, March 14, 1993, points nos. 6 and 7.

26. P.O.W. Network Database, entry for: Fryar, Bruce Carlton.

27. Fax from Theodore G. Schweitzer III to James Renaud, July 24, 1992, author's archives.

28. Ted Schweitzer reported this PAVN position to the DIA through a series of computer disk messages from May 23 through mid-August 1992. These messages are in the author's archives. "As I reported on 8 July 92," Schweitzer wrote in his July 10 message to the DIA, "everything we want [on MIA cases] is here. All of the information on all of the MIAs is here either in documents in government hands or in information in private hands."

29. Ann Devroy, "Bush Cites His Patriotism, War Record in Response to MIA Families' Heckling," *Washington Post,* July 25, 1992, p. A-1; " 'Shut Up,' Bush Tells Protesters," *Miami Herald,* July 25, 1992, p. 1. Also see: Open Letter to the President from Ann Mills Griffiths, Executive Director, National League of Families of American Prisoners and Missing in Southeast Asia; advertisement, *Washington Post,* July 29, 1992, p. A-6. Former *Reader's Digest* research editor Brian Morgan attended this meeting. He clearly recalls that Bush directed his order to "shut up" at a young heckler seated in the press gallery of the conference room, not at MIA family members: "Memorandum Concerning President Bush's Remarks to NLF on July 24, 1992," from Brian Morgan to Malcolm McConnell, October 4, 1993.

30. Executive Order 12812: "Declassification and Release of Materials Pertaining to Prisoners of War and Missing in Action," July 22, 1992; *Weekly Compilation of Presidential Documents* (Washington: Executive Office of the President, Vol. 28, No. 30, July 27, 1992), p. 1303.

31. Van Voorst, "The Truth at Last," p. 59. Also: interview, James Renaud, January 11, 1993.

CHAPTER 20

1. John Corry, "The MIA Cover-up," The American Spectator, February 1994, p. 28.

2. The author and Ted Schweitzer carefully reviewed all the scanned museum and PAVN archive records obtained during Operation Swamp Ranger and confirmed Schweitzer's count of ninety-five record cards or documents listed in the Red Book index that were not scanned.

3. Ted Schweitzer computer disk message to James Renaud, September 12, 1992, author's archives.

4. *Report of the Select Committee on POW/MIA Affairs,* p. 595.

5. Ibid.

6. Biographic note on Major Lai Vinh Mui, Ted Schweitzer computer disk message, September 12, 1992, author's archives.

7. The most extensive such accusations are found in several recent books: John M.G. Brown, *Moscow Bound* (Eureka, CA: Veteran Press, 1993); Jensen-Stevenson and Stevenson, *Kiss the Boys Goodbye;* Sanders, Sauter, and Kirkwood, *Soldiers of Misfortune;* and Mark Sauter and Jim Sanders, *The Men We Left Behind* (Washington, D.C.: National Press Books, 1993).

8. Paul Lewis, "White House Is Adamant on Balkan War Crimes, Amnesty Is Ruled Out in Stern Warning," *New York Times,* November 16, 1993, p. A-16. Also: David B. Ottaway, "U.S. Presses Balkan War Tribunal," *Washington Post,* January 7, 1994, p. A-14.

9. James Sterngold, "Japan Admits Army Forced Women into War Brothels," *New York Times,* August 5, 1993, p. A-2.

10. Ted Schweitzer computer disk message to James Renaud, dated 920918 (September 18, 1992), item no. 4, author's archives.

11. P.O.W. Network Database, entry for: Dodge, Ronald Wayne; and "Ron Dodge Captured on Film," *Soldier of Fortune,* POW/MIA Special, Spring 1983, p. 63.

12. Eschmann, *Linebacker,* pp. 227–29; Jim and Sybil Stockdale, *In Love and War,* pp. 102–3; and interview, Admiral James Stockdale, March 29, 1993.

13. P.O.W. Network Database, entry for: Apodaca, Victor Joe, Jr. A number of similar refugee accounts describe massacres of American airmen in the heavily bombed southern provinces of North Vietnam. Some were perpetrated as late as 1972. For example, Navy Lieutenant Marvin Wiles was reportedly hacked and beaten to death in a village in Quang Binh Province in May 1972. It is not clear if he had already surrendered or was still attempting to evade capture. See: P.O.W. Network Base, entry for: Wiles, Marvin Benjamin Christopher.

14. Lieutenant General W.R. Peers, USA (Ret.), *The My Lai Inquiry* (New York: W.W. Norton, 1977), Vietcong propaganda broadcast, "American Evil Appears," Appendix 13-5, pp. 280–82.

15. Karnow, *Vietnam*, pp. 543–45.

16. Fall, "Communist POW Treatment in Indochina," pp. 5–7.

17. Jim and Sybil Stockdale, *In Love and War*, pp. 102–3; and McConnell, *Into the Mouth of the Cat*, pp. 161–63.

18. F.C. Brown, "Escape in Indochina," *Behind the Lines*, May/June 1994, pp. 39–41.

19. Hubbell, *P.O.W.*, p. 419.

20. P.O.W. Network Database, entry for: Bennett, Harold George.

21. Interview, Lieutenant General Hoang Phuong, February 17, 1993.

22. P.O.W. Network Database, entry for: Grubb, Wilmer Newlin; and Benjamin F. Schemmer, *The Raid* (New York: Harper & Row, 1976), p. 135.

23. Wyatt, *We Came Home*, entry for John S. McCain II; also: Hubbell, *P.O.W.*, pp. 363–64.

24. Excerpted U.S. Air Force documents on Operation Homecoming debriefings, pp. 22–51.

25. For a description of Hoa Lo Prison, see: Hubbell, *P.O.W.*, pp. 12–15.

26. Interview, James H. Warner, September 28, 1993.

27. "The 'Cuban' Program," unclassified Intelligence Summary, obtained from the Office of the Assistant Secretary of Defense/Public Affairs, in response to Freedom of Information request, January 15, 1992, p. 4, author's archives. Also see: Hubbell, *P.O.W.*, pp. 432–34, 436–37, 447–49, 543.

28. Defense Intelligence Agency, *U.S. Personnel, Southeast Asia* Part II, Chronological Order, pp. 12–35.

29. *Report of the Select Committee on POW/MIA Affairs*, pp. 698–99. Also: McDaniel, *Scars & Stripes*, p. 33; and P.O.W. Network Database, entry for: Patterson, James Kelly.

30. Memorandum for Brigadier General Shufelt from Commodore Thomas A. Brooks, September 25, 1985, Actions Tasked to DC-2, p. 3.

Chapter 21

1. For example, retired Chairman of the Joint Chiefs of Staff and Special Presidential Emissary to Vietnam on POW/MIA Affairs General John W. Vessey, Jr., USA (Ret.), stated in an interview that, although he found no credible evidence that the Soviets had exploited American prisoners in Vietnamese captivity, it would have been logical for there to have been a secret program to do so in place: interview, notes, p. 7. General Vessey's colleague, General Robert Kingston, USA (Ret.), agreed that Soviet military intelligence would have been remiss if it had not attempted to exploit American POWs for their technical knowledge: interview, notes, p. 7.

2. For an authoritative and colorful account of this involvement, see: F.C. Brown, "Soviet Cong, Ivan in Indochina," *Soldier of Fortune*, November 1985, p. 70.

3. *Report of the Select Committee on POW/MIA Affairs*, p. 431.

4. Ibid., pp. 432–33.

5. "U.S.-Russia Joint Commission on POW/MIA's Working Group Paper on Korean War POWs Released to the Public," Department of Defense POW/MIA Update, No. 4, November 9, 1993.

6. Joint Commission Support Branch, Research and Analysis Division, DPMO (Defense

PW/MIA Office), "The Transfer of U.S. Korean War POWs to the Soviet Union," August 26, 1993, p. 39.

7. Ibid., p. 5, and Appendix B, p. 57.

8. Ibid., pp. 11–15.

9. Ibid., p. 16.

10. Ibid., p. 18. Also: United States Department of State transmittal letter from Ambassador Malcolm Toon, November 3, 1993. Also see: Associated Press, "U.S. Says Moscow Held POWs in the 1950s," *Washington Post,* September 27, 1993, p. A-14; and Associated Press, "Ex-POW's Story Indicates Soviets Seized U.S. Fliers," *Washington Times,* August 22, 1993, p. 1.

11. Joint Commission Support Branch, "The Transfer of U.S. Korean War POWs to the Soviet Union," p. 11.

12. Karnow, *Vietnam,* p. 427.

13. Albert Pavvy, "Soviet Aid to Vietnam," *Military Review,* June 1967, p. 20.

14. William R. Corson and Robert T. Crowley, *The New KGB* (New York: William Morrow, 1985), pp. 341–42.

15. Serge Schmemann, "Russians Move Mountain of Files," *New York Times,* November 15, 1992, p. E-5. Also: "Those Left Behind," *Time,* November 23, 1992, p. 19. Volkogonov's evidence counters more sensational claims that tens of thousands of American and British prisoners in German camps that were "liberated" by the advancing Red Army were retained by the Soviets after World War II. See: Sanders, Sauter, and Kirkwood, *Soldiers of Misfortune,* pp. 96–109.

16. Thomas W. Lippman, "138 Reported Missing in U.S. Spy Flights: Total from '50s–'70s Missions Grows as Russians Release Data," *Washington Post,* March 5, 1993, p. A-7.

17. "On the Work of the Joint Russian-U.S. Commission," letter from Boris Yeltsin, November 5, 1992, released by the Senate Select Committee on POW/MIA Affairs, November 11, 1992, National Archives, Washington, D.C.

18. Letter from Major Peter C. Johnson, USAR, to Major General John K. Singlaub, USA (Ret.), August 25, 1993, author's archives. Johnson's Task Force Russia colleague, Major William Burkett, confirmed this "stonewalling" assessment of former Soviet cooperation with Task Force Russia during an interview on September 7, 1993.

19. Testimony of Al Graham on November 11, 1992, *Report of the Select Committee on POW/MIA Affairs,* p. 425.

20. Hubbell, *P.O.W.,* p. 161. Also see: *Report of the Select Committee on POW/MIA Affairs,* p. 432.

21. Interview, James Warner, February 24, 1994.

22. *Report of the Select Committee on POW/MIA Affairs,* pp. 432–33.

23. Accuracy in Media press release: "AIM Offers $100,000 Reward to Free American Prisoners," courtesy Accuracy in Media.

24. John M.G. Brown, *Moscow Bound* (Eureka, CA: Veteran Press, 1993). Also see: F.C. Brown, *POW/MIA Indochina 1861–1994: An Annotated Bibliography,* 3rd ed. (Hamilton Township, NJ: Rice Paddy Press, 1994), p. 6. Commenting on *Moscow Bound,* F.C. Brown notes: "While much of the pre-1960 research is solid and supported by hard documentation, the author runs into problems when attempting to support a 'Soviet connection' to the Vietnam POW/MIA issue, primarily through his reliance on previously discredited sources.... [John M.G. Brown bends] facts to fit theories instead of the other way around...."

25. Letter: From National Personnel Records Center, Military Personnel Records, St. Louis, to Vietnam Veterans Memorial Fund of Texas, August 2, 1991. This record contains a response to a query submitted under the Freedom of Information Act concerning Pistilli's record and reveals that he never served in Vietnam. Also: Interview, Major Pete Johnson, September 10, 1993. Major Johnson of Task Force Russia verified that Pistilli was never a POW and never had contact with "Russian and Chinese interrogators" in a prison camp near Vinh. Senate Select Committee on POW/MIA Affairs investigator Robert Taylor also stated that Pistilli was a "wannabe" who had no valid information on MIA matters: Interview, Robert Taylor, July 14, 1993.

26. Sauter and Sanders, *The Men We Left Behind,* p. 244.

27. Interview, Major Pete Johnson, September 10, 1993.

28. Interview, Colonel Ben Pollard, USAF (Ret.), August 9, 1993.

29. Freedom of Information request, response from National Personnel Records Center to B.G. Burkett, concerning military record of Joel Jay Furlett.

30. Jim Camden, "Veteran Takes Kids on Trip from Reality, Stories of Vietnam, POW Camps, Heroism Discounted as Fabrications," *Spokane Chronicle,* May 8, 1993, p. B-1. Also: interview, Jim Camden, September 7, 1993.

31. Camden, "Veteran Takes Kids on Trip from Reality," column 2.

32. Sparr and Pankratz, "Factitious Posttraumatic Stress Disorder," pp. 1016–19. Also see: Keith Langley and Vincent Liberto, "Factitious PTSD," *Vet Center Voice,* Vol. 10, No. 7, May 1991, p. 3.

33. *Report of the Select Committee on POW/MIA Affairs,* p. 300.

34. Interview, Chuck Schantag, P.O.W. Network, July 1, 1993. Schantag, who has been described as a dedicated and well-meaning POW/MIA activist, stated that his network has information on approximately 1,000 "Black Cowboy" MIAs captured by the enemy in Indochina who are "not named on any Pentagon list."

35. Interviews, General John Vessey and General Robert Kingston.

36. Elaine Sciolino, "K.G.B. Telltale Is Tattling, but Is He Telling U.S. All?" *New York Times,* January 20, 1992, p. A-1.

37. McLeod, "Defector Says Soviets Questioned POWs," p. A-8.

38. George Lardner, Jr., "KGB Plan 'Flopped,' Ex-Official Says," *Washington Post,* January 22, 1992, p. A-7.

39. Associated Press, "Ex-KGB Agent: I Didn't See U.S. POWs After War," *Washington Times,* January 7, 1992, p. A-4. Also: Snepp, *Decent Interval,* pp. 355–57.

40. Defense Intelligence Agency, *U.S. Personnel, Southeast Asia* Part II, p. 50.

41. Declassified government Memorandum, Subject: Jan Sejna, November 4, 1992, Records of the Senate Select Committee on POW/MIA Affairs, RG46/Zwenig/No. 4, declassified 13/12/92, p. 1.

42. Ibid.

43. Ibid., p. 2.

44. Craig W. Whitney, "P.O.W. Trade Bid from '67 Disclosed," *New York Times,* June 27, 1993, p. A-1.

45. Sanders, Sauter, and Kirkwood, *Soldiers of Misfortune,* pp. 238–40, 273. Also: Jensen-Stevenson and Stevenson, *Kiss the Boys Goodbye,* pp. 160–65, 425–30.

46. Jensen-Stevenson and Stevenson, *Kiss the Boys Goodbye,* pp. 425–30.

47. *Report of the Select Committee on POW/MIA Affairs,* pp. 227, 427.

48. Deposition of Jerry J. Mooney, Day 1, January 15, 1992, pp. 143–44, 157, Records of the Senate Select Committee.

49. Ibid., p. 144.

50. Cawthorne, *The Bamboo Cage,* pp. 62–67.

51. Letter, Barry A. Toll to Senator John Kerry, with enclosed seven-page statement, June 14, 1992; also: deposition of Barry A. Toll before Senate Select Committee on POW/MIA

Affairs, June 26, 1992, pp. 23, 38–39, 82, 87, Records of the Senate Select Committee on POW/MIA Affairs.

52. Statement, p. 4, enclosure to Toll letter; also: Toll deposition, pp. 18–23.

53. Statement, Toll letter, p. 3.

54. Ibid., pp. 3, 5; also: Toll deposition, pp. 38–39, 81–86.

55. Statement, Toll letter, p. 6.

56. Interview, Steve Gekoski, July 1, 1993, transcript, p. 1.

57. Ibid., p. 2.

58. Agent Report, DA Form 341, United States Army Intelligence Agency, Subject: Toll, Barry Allen, 902d Military Intelligence Group, Fort Monroe, Virginia, August 5, 1975, and enclosure: DA Form 2823, sworn statement executed by SUBJECT, July 25, 1975, RG46/Taylor/Box no. 7, Records of the Senate Select Committee on POW/MIA Affairs.

59. DA Form 3822-R, Report of Mental Status Evaluation, Toll, Barry A., August 6, 1975, prepared by Jacob R. Aslanian, M.D., Major MC, Records of the Senate Select Committee on POW/MIA Affairs.

60. Letter, J. Lawrence Wright to Robert Taylor, August 19, 1992, RG46/Taylor/No. 7, Records of the Senate Select Committee on POW/MIA Affairs.

61. Ibid., enclosure: Affidavit of J. Lawrence Wright, August 19, 1992, p. 2.

62. Ibid., p. 3.

63. Letter, Barry A. Toll to Bob Taylor, subject: "List of parties I related POW/MIA abandonment issue to as factor in demanding discharge from Army," July 1, 1992, p. 1, RG46/Taylor/No. 7, Records of the Senate Select Committee on POW/MIA Affairs.

64. Toll freely discussed this crime and his incarceration with Senate Select Committee on POW/MIA Affairs attorneys; see: Toll deposition, p. 18.

65. Interviews, Steve Gekoski and Robert Taylor.

66. FBI Priority telegram (65A-554) declassified from secret, from Tampa Field Office to Counter-Intelligence Office, FBI Headquarters, Washington, D.C., September 12, 1986, p. 2, Records of the Senate Select Committee on POW/MIA Affairs.

67. Sydney H. Schanberg, "POW Searchers Risk a Deal with Clinton," *Newsday,* November 5, 1993, p. 73. Harve Skaal, a MACV-SOG veteran as well as the unit's historian, refutes Toll's claim. Toll, Skaal states, was a "grunt" with the 4th Infantry Division who served a security guard at a MACV-SOG radio relay base known as Sledgehammer inside Cambodia for three months in 1969. Interview, Harve Skaal, May 17, 1994.

68. Interview, Steve Gekoski, transcript p. 3.

69. Toll deposition, p. 81.

70. David Dahl, "He Insists POWs Are Alive in Vietnam," *St. Petersburg Times,* July 26, 1993, p. A-1.

71. Taylor interview.

72. Agenda of the National Alliance of Families for the Return of America's Missing Servicemen, 4th Annual POW/MIA Forum, July 16, 1993, and July 17, 1993. In the list of speakers, Toll is referred to as a "Former Intelligence Operations Specialist who monitored POW intelligence for Nixon."

73. Interview, Major Ralph Peters, USA, Task Force Russia, July 20, 1993.

74. Interview, Major Pete Johnson, USAR.

75. Interview, Major William Burkett, USA, May 6, 1994.

76. Alexander Zuyev with Malcolm McConnell, *Fulcrum: A Top Gun Pilot's Escape from the Soviet Empire* (New York: Warner Books, 1992), p. 199.

77. Interview, Alexander Zuyev, June 10, 1993. In order to be sure that this information was accurate before the paperback version of *Fulcrum* was printed, I specifically questioned Zuyev on this point. He was adamant that the Soviet nuclear weapons officer had told him the dual-channel bomb-arming system had been obtained from American Vietnam War POWs taken to the Soviet Union.

Chapter 22

1. Interview, James Renaud, March 15, 1994.

2. DIA negotiation folder notes for Operation Swamp Ranger photographs and artifacts relating to Major Joseph C. Morrison, U.S. Air Force, author's archives.

3. Ibid.

4. DIA negotiation folder notes for Operation Swamp Ranger photographs of Lieutenant Gilbert L. Mitchell, USN.

5. DIA negotiation folder notes for Operations Swamp Ranger and Druid Smoke photographs of Major Marvin N. Lindsey, USAF.

6. P.O.W. Network Database, entry for: Wilson, William Wallace.

7. Bill Gertz, "F-111 Cockpit in Moscow May Have Held U.S. MIAs," *Washington Times,* May 20, 1993, p. A-1.

8. PAVN Museum Red Book index, p. 139; and PAVN Museum acquisition card 4926, author's archives.

9. Mike Blair, "POWs, Aircraft Given to Soviets," *Spotlight,* December 28, 1992, p. 10. Also: Cawthorne, *The Bamboo Cage,* p. 65.

10. Mooney deposition, January 15, 1992, pp. 143–44, 157. Also: *Report of the Select Committee on POW/MIA Affairs,* pp. 227, 427.

11. Photograph of artifacts from October 17, 1972, F-111 loss, author's archives.

12. Defense Intelligence Agency incident report no. 1952-0-01, Ward, Ronald Jack, p. 1.

13. Ibid.

14. Photograph of F-111 escape capsule, author's archives.

15. Computer disk message, Ted Schweitzer to DIA case officer James Renaud, September 29, 1992, point no. 3.

16. Thomas W. Lippman and Don Oberdorfer, "Hanoi Has Photos of Dead GIs," *Washington Post,* October 20, 1992, p. A-1. Also: Melissa Healy and Michael Ross, "New Data May Tell POW Fates," *Los Angeles Times,* October 21, 1992, p. A-1.

17. Details of these conversations were related to Ted Schweitzer by one of the Americans involved.

18. *Report of the Select Committee on POW/MIA Affairs,* p. 386.

19. Lippman and Oberdorfer, "Hanoi Has Photos of Dead GIs," p. A-1.

20. Ibid.

21. Computer disk message, Ted Schweitzer to the DIA (undated), circa mid-October 1992.

22. Fax message from Theodore G. Schweitzer III to author, March 6, 1994, p. 2, item no. 5.

23. Eric Schmitt, "U.S. Archivists to See Hanoi's Files on Missing," *New York Times,* October 23, 1992, p. A-6.

24. Barbara Crossette, "Reagan Officials Say U.S. Knew Americans Survived in Vietnam," *New York Times,* August 13, 1992, p. A-1. Also: Thomas W. Lippman, "Documents Show Existence of POWs After Nixon Said All Had Come Home," *Washington Post,* September 25, 1992, p. A-22; and *Report of the Select Committee on POW/MIA Affairs,* pp. 122–25.

25. Crossette, "Reagan Officials Say U.S. Knew Americans Survived in Vietnam," p. A-1.

26. "Remarks by the President After Meeting with General Vessey," Transcript, the White House, Office of the Press Secretary, October 23, 1992, p. 2.

27. "Press Briefing by General Vessey, Senator John McCain and Senator John Kerry,"

Transcript, the White House, Office of the Press Secretary, October 23, 1992. Also see: Thomas W. Lippman and Don Oberdorfer, "Bush Hails 'Breakthrough' in Vietnam War MIA Cases," *Washington Post,* October 24, 1992, p. A-15.

28. Karnow, *Vietnam,* p. 554.

29. Lippman and Oberdorfer, "Bush Hails 'Breakthrough' in Vietnam War MIA Cases," p. A-13.

30. Van Voorst, "The Truth at Last," p. 59. Also see: Barbara Crossette, "Central Link in Release of Hanoi M.I.A. Photos: A U.S. Researcher," *New York Times,* October 25, 1992, p. 10.

31. Van Voorst, "The Truth at Last," p. 59.

32. For a powerfully written description of this meeting, see: Jane Gross, "Years After a War Death, Proof Brings a New Grief," *New York Times,* November 1, 1992, p. 1.

33. Ibid., p. 18.

34. Mooney deposition, pp. 27–28; and Cawthorne, *The Bamboo Cage,* p. 34.

CHAPTER 23

1. Van Voorst, "The Truth at Last," p. 59.

2. Ibid.

3. Ibid.

4. Fax message from Ted Schweitzer to James Renaud, November 5, 1992.

5. Ibid., p. 1.

6. William Branigin, "In Vietnam, Clinton Victory Sparks Hope and Fear," *Washington Post,* November 7, 1992, p. A-14.

7. Ibid.

8. Michael Weisskopf, "Clinton Backs Early Military Retirement," *Washington Post,* November 12, 1992, p. A-9.

9. Philip Shenon, "U.S. Team in Hanoi Studies Relics of the Missing," *New York Times,* November 15, 1992, p. A-1.

10. Fax message from Ted Schweitzer to James Renaud, November 8, 1992; this is the second message sent on that date.

11. Don Oberdorfer, "In Appreciation, White House Orders Conciliatory Gestures Toward Vietnam," *Washington Post,* November 7, 1992, p. A-20.

12. Reuters, "U.S., Vietnam to Get Direct Phone Links," *Washington Post,* November 12, 1992, p. A-36.

13. Thomas W. Lippman, "Kerry Says Bush Letter Promises More Gestures Toward Hanoi," *Washington Post,* November 19, 1992, p. A-32.

14. Letter from John F. Kerry and Bob Smith, Senate Select Committee on POW/MIA Affairs, to the Honorable Trinh Xuan Lang, Vietnamese Mission of the United States [sic], November 2, 1992, archives of Theodore G. Schweitzer III. The address block of this letter is in error; it should have read "Vietnamese Mission to the United Nations."

15. Ibid., enclosures.

16. Ibid., p. 1.

17. Fax message from Ted Schweitzer to James Renaud, November 12, 1992.

18. Thomas W. Lippman, "3 Senators Press Hanoi on MIAs," *Washington Post,* November 17, 1992, p. A-27.

19. Ibid.

20. Philip Shenon, "Hanoi Backs Study to Trace M.I.A.'s," *New York Times,* November 17, 1992, p. A-9.

21. Ibid.

22. Computer disk message from Ted Schweitzer to James Renaud, September 18, 1992; and fax message from Ted Schweitzer to author: "Notes on Senator Kerry Visit to Hanoi 16–19 November 1992," January 1, 1994.

23. Schweitzer fax message of January 1, 1994.

24. The Lao Files are generally assumed to include military records from PAVN Group 559 and Group 875, units that controlled logistics and security along the Ho Chi Minh Trail in Laos. PAVN Group 559 was officially named Transportation Group 559 and was subordinate to the Rear Service Department (Logistics) of the PAVN. It was activated in May 1959 and was still operational after the last Americans were lost in Laos in 1974. For details, see: Major General Nguyen Duy Hinh, *Lam Son 719*, Indochina Monographs (Washington, D.C.: U.S. Army Center of Military History, 1979), Chapter 2, "The Operational Environment: The Ho Chi Minh Trail System," pp. 10–12.

25. Schweitzer fax message of January 1, 1994.

26. Interviews, Frances Zwenig, December 19 and 20, 1993, and September 6, 1994.

27. Interview, Ted Schweitzer and James Renaud, December 22, 1993.

28. Thomas W. Lippman, "Hanoi Gives Personal Effects of GIs to Visiting U.S. Senate Delegation," *Washington Post,* November 18, 1992, p. A-1.

29. Ibid., p. A-30.

30. Philip Shenon, "For Vietnam, Settling the Past Could Be Good Business," *New York Times,* November 22, 1992, p. E-5.

31. Don Oberdorfer, "Japan to Resume Aid to Vietnam," *Washington Post,* October 28, 1992, p. A-17; and William Branigin, "U.S. Seen as Being Under Pressure to Lift Embargo on Vietnam," *Washington Post,* November 9, 1992, p. A-14.

32. Branigin, "U.S. Seen as Being Under Pressure to Lift Embargo on Vietnam," p. A-14.

33. Ibid., p. 18.

34. Mary K. Magistad, "Chinese, Vietnamese Open Talks," *Washington Post,* December 1, 1992, p. A-31.

35. For an analysis of the Chinese military build-up during this period, see: William Branigin, "As China Builds Arsenal and Bases, Asians Wary of 'Rogue in the Region,' " *Washington Post,* March 31, 1993, p. A-21. Also: "Asia's Arms Race," *The Economist,* February 20, 1993, p. 19.

36. Barbara Crossette, "Behind Vietnam's Candor: A Fear of Being Isolated," *New York Times,* November 1, 1992, p. E-4.

37. Interview, Ambassador Ha Van Lau, Ho Chi Minh City, February 9, 1993. Also: interview, Colin Leinster, March 26, 1993. Leinster, a veteran journalist with experience in Southeast Asia, wrote on Vietnam's economy for *Fortune* in 1993; he, too, was told of Vietnam's desire to see the U.S. Navy back in Cam Ranh Bay.

38. William Branigin, "Vietnam: The Big Buildup Begins," *Washington Post,* December 6, 1992, p. H-1.

39. Thomas W. Lippman, "Bush Opens Door Wider to Vietnam," *Washington Post,* December 15, 1992, p. A-1.

40. Ibid.

41. Reuters, "Vietnam Pledges to Increase Cooperation on MIA Searches," *Washington Post,* December 19, 1992, p. A-13.

CHAPTER 24

1. The author spent eight weeks in Hanoi and Ho Chi Minh City during this period.

2. Interviews with Colonel Pham Duc Dai, Major Lai Vinh Mui, and Lieutenant General Hoang Phuong, Hanoi, January 23, 25, 28, and February 3, 6, and 11, 1993.

3. Weisskopf, "Clinton Backs Early Military Retirement," p. A-9.

4. Don Oberdorfer, "Administration Moves Toward Decision on Whether to Ease Pressure on Vietnam," *Washington Post,* March 19, 1993, p. A-48.

5. Ibid.

6. Computer disk message from Ted Schweitzer to James Renaud, March 10, 1993, "Subject: SRV Policy Toward JTF/FA."

7. Computer disk messages from Ted Schweitzer to James Renaud, March 2 and 10, 1993.

8. Computer disk message from Ted Schweitzer to James Renaud, March 2, 1993, "Subject: Caffarelli/F-111."

9. National Vietnam P.O.W. Strike Force newsletter, "A Vietnam Veteran Speaks Out on the POW/MIA Issue," February 24, 1992, p. 1.

10. Ibid., p. 3.

11. Excerpt of Navy record, Jordan, Joseph Loren, Transfers and Receipts—NAVPERS 601-12. Obtained under Freedom of Information Act request from National Personnel Records Center, St. Louis, August 20, 1993.

12. United States Seventh Fleet citation, the Air Medal (Second Strike/Flight Award) to Joseph Loran [sic] JORDAN, undated.

13. "History of Fleet Air Reconnaissance Squadron One," *The Hook,* Spring 1987, p. 28. Also: Interview, Captain Byron Wiley, USN (Ret.), August 24, 1993.

14. Interview, Captain Byron Wiley.

15. National Vietnam P.O.W. Strike Force newsletter, July 23, 1992, p. 1.

16. National Vietnam P.O.W. Strike Force newsletters, undated, circa December 1992.

17. American Legion, "The American Legion Analysis of the Final Report of the Senate Select Committee on POW/MIA Affairs and an Assessment of the Accomplishments of That Committee," February 22, 1993.

18. *Report of the Select Committee on POW/MIA Affairs,* pp. 5–6.

19. Ibid., pp. 7–11.

20. Thomas W. Lippman, "Kissinger Calls POW Charge a 'Lie,' " *Washington Post,* September 23, 1992, p. A-1.

21. Jack Anderson and Michael Binstein, "POW-MIA Panel Riven by Disputes," *Washington Post,* November 30, 1992, p. C-16.

22. Memorandum from Senator Bob Smith to J. William Codinha, August 25, 1992, Subject: "Fraud," RG46/Zwenig/No. 5, Records of the Senate Select Committee on POW/MIA Affairs. Also: Murray Waas, "Panel to Cite Fraud by POW Groups," *Boston Globe,* December 2, 1992, p. 1.

23. "U.S. POW/MIAs Who May Have Survived in Captivity," Memorandum with attachments, dated December 1, 1992, Records of the Senate Select Committee on POW/MIA Affairs.

24. "DIA Analysis of the 324-Name List Prepared by the Office of Senator Bob Smith," Records of the Senate Select Committee on POW/MIA Affairs.

25. Interview, Frances Zwenig, December 19 and 20, 1993. Also: Memorandum from Sedgwick D. Tourison, Jr., to Frances A. Zwenig, December 2, 1992, "Subject: Senator Smith's list of 324 individuals," RG46/Zwenig/No. 6, Records of the Senate Select Committee on POW/MIA Affairs.

26. Letter to Attorney General Janet Reno from Senator Bob Smith, June 29, 1993, from Senator Bob Smith press kit dated July 15, 1993. Also: Adam Clymer, "Claim of P.O.W. Cover-up Rends Senate Decorum," *New York Times,* September 8, 1993, p. A-16.

27. William Branigin, "U.S. Said to Pay Hanoi for MIA Photos," *Washington Post,* February 14, 1993, p. A-42. The article's subhead, "Deal with American Writer Illustrates Vietnam's Desire to Profit from MIA Search," was viewed by the PAVN as a direct assault on the General Political Directorate.

28. Interview, Colonel Pham Duc Dai, February 16, 1993.

29. Computer disk message from Ted Schweitzer to James Renaud, March 5, 1993, "Subject: PAVN's Retaliation Against JTF/FA."

30. Among the seven sets of remains repatriated at Noi Bai Airport were those of Air Force Captain James A. Branch, an MIA F-4 crewman shot down in 1965. Documents relating to Branch were among the first items from the Central Military Museum given to Ted Schweitzer.

31. Henry Kamm, "Hanoi Sees 'Positive Sign' from U.S. on Relations," *New York Times,* March 25, 1993, p. A-5.

32. Computer disk message from Ted Schweitzer to James Renaud, March 31, 1993, "Subject: Meeting with LTC Donovan 930330."

33. Computer disk message from Ted Schweitzer to James Renaud, March 28, 1993, "Subject: Public Opinion About PAVN," p. 2.

34. Ibid.

35. Defense Intelligence Agency Memorandum, dated 910628 (June 28, 1991), unclassified, author's archives.

36. Elaine Sciolino, "U.S. to Send General to Vietnam, Hinting a Thaw," *New York Times,* April 10, 1993, p. A-3.

37. Ibid.

Chapter 25

1. For an insightful portrait of Stephen Morris and his Moscow research, see: David Chanoff, "The Man Who Knows Too Much," *Boston Magazine,* October 1993, p. 82.

2. Thomas W. Lippman, "A Researcher's Dream Find on U.S. POWs Turns into a Nightmare," *Washington Post,* April 25, 1993, p. A-4.

3. For Morris's detailed personal description of the discovery of the Quang document, see: Stephen J. Morris, "The '1205 Document,'" *The National Interest,* Fall 1993, p. 28.

4. English translation of the "Alleged Vietnamese Report Apparently Given by Vietnamese General Lieutenant Van Quang [sic] to the Vietnamese Politburo of the Central Committee on September 15, 1972," furnished by the Office of the Assistant Secretary of Defense, Public Affairs under Memorandum for Correspondence, No. 116-M, April 14, 1993; henceforth, Vietnamese Politburo Report.

5. Ibid., p. 3.

6. Ibid., p. 4.

7. Ibid.

8. Ibid.

9. Ibid., p. 5.

10. Ibid., pp. 5–6.

11. Ibid., pp. 6–7.

12. Ibid., pp. 7–8.

13. Chanoff, "The Man Who Knows Too Much," p. 84.

14. Ibid., p. 109.

15. Ibid., pp. 109–10.

16. Ibid., p. 110.

17. Interview, James Renaud, April 13, 1993.

18. Chanoff, "The Man Who Knows Too Much," p. 110; and Department of Defense,

Office of the Assistant Secretary of Defense (Public Affairs), Interagency Intelligence Analysis: "Recent Reports on American POWs in Indochina: An Assessment," January 24, 1994, p. 1.

19. Celestine Bohlen, "File Said to Show Hanoi Lied in '72 on Prisoner Totals," *New York Times,* April 12, 1993, p. A-1.

20. Nayan Chanda, "Research and Destroy: Origins of Vietnam War POW Document Remain Obscure," *Far Eastern Economic Review,* May 6, 1993, p. 20.

21. R.W. Apple, Jr., "U.S. to Press Hanoi to Explain '72 P.O.W. Report," *New York Times,* April 13, 1993, p. A-1.

22. Bill Gertz, "North Vietnam Kept 700 POWs After War," *Washington Times,* April 12, 1993, p. A-1.

23. *MacNeil/Lehrer NewsHour,* Tuesday, April 13, 1993, transcript, p. 3.

24. Ibid., p. 4.

25. Ibid., p. 5.

26. Ibid., p. 6.

27. "The Hanoi 600," editorial, *Washington Post,* April 13, 1993, p. A-18.

28. Lawrence Jolidon, "U.S. Wants Answers on Viet Letter," *USA Today,* April 13, 1993, p. A-1; and Bill Gertz, "U.S.-Hanoi Ties Off Until POWs Accounted For," *Washington Times,* April 13, 1993, p. A-1.

29. The DIA was made aware of this foreign news digest in a computer disk message from Ted Schweitzer, "Subject: Subscription to SRV News," March 3, 1993.

30. Interview, James Renaud, April 13, 1993.

31. Hubbell, *P.O.W.,* p. 546. The four surviving American colonels were John Flynn, David W. Winn, Norman C. Gaddis, and James E. Bean.

32. Vietnamese Politburo Report, p. 6.

33. Steven A. Holmes, "Pentagon Is Wary on P.O.W. Text; Families See Proof of Lies," *New York Times,* April 14, 1993, p. A-6. Also see: Thomas W. Lippman, "Deception on POWs Indicated, File on 1972 Account by Hanoi Is Suspect," *Washington Post,* April 15, 1993, p. A-15.

34. "New Questions on the P.O.W.'s," editorial, *New York Times,* April 14, 1993, p. A-20.

35. Bill Gertz, "POW Numbers Disputed," *Washington Times,* April 14, 1993, p. A-1.

36. Thomas W. Lippman, "Asians Classified as American, POW Expert Says," *Washington Post,* April 15, 1993, p. A-21.

37. Ibid.

38. Interviews, Colonel Steven Cavanaugh, USA (Ret.), October 1, 1993; Major General John K. Singlaub, USA (Ret.), September 24, 1993. Also: Singlaub with McConnell, *Hazardous Duty,* pp. 302–5.

39. Holmes, "Pentagon Is Wary on P.O.W. Text; Families See Proof of Lies," p. A-6. The three American POWs, Air Force Major Edward Elias, and Navy Lieutenants Norris Charles and Markham Gartley, were freed to an American peace delegation on September 25, 1972. Each of the three had made a number of pro-Communist, antiwar statements and could thus have been categorized as "progressive." See: Ernest W. Lefever, *TV and the National Defense* (Boston, MA: Institute for American Strategy Press, 1974), pp. 114, 120–21.

40. Thomas W. Lippman, "POW Document Renews Bitter Arguments," *Washington Post,* April 14, 1993, p. A-1.

41. Interview, Douglas Pike, April 16, 1993.

42. A detailed description of the Vietnamese reaction to the Quang document is found in the undated computer disk message, FILE-38.DOC, from Ted Schweitzer to the DIA, author's archives.

43. Ibid., p. 2.

44. Fax message from Hanoi, Theodore G. Schweitzer III to author, April 16, 1993.

45. Telephone interview with Ted Schweitzer, Bangkok, April 17, 1993.

46. Ibid.

47. Philip Shenon, "A '72 Report on P.O.W.'s Is a Fake, Vietnam Asserts," *New York Times,* April 14, 1993, p. A-6.

48. Stephen Engelberg, "Old M.I.A. Theory Is Given New Life," *New York Times,* April 18, 1993, p. A-20.

49. William Branigin, "U.S. Gets 'Important Information' on POWs," *Washington Post,* April 19, 1993, p. A-16. Also: Philip Shenon, "Hanoi Offers Documents on P.O.W.'s," *New York Times,* April 19, 1993, p. A-13.

50. Interview, General John Vessey, July 15, 1993.

51. "TÀI LIỆU 6: DANH SÁCH TÙ BINH MỸ Tổng Cong 39 Trang." The author obtained a photocopy of the Blue Book list from the Office of the Assistant Secretary of Defense, Public Affairs, under a Freedom of Information Act request dated May 17, 1993. The translation of the index title was provided by Lieutenant Colonel Frederick Caristo, USA (Ret.).

52. William Branigin, "U.S. General Questions Alleged POW Document," *Washington Post,* April 20, 1993, p. A-15. Also: Philip Shenon, "Vietnam Report on Prisoners a Fake, Reputed Author Says," *New York Times,* April 20, 1993, p. A-6.

53. Shenon, "Vietnam Report on Prisoners a Fake," p. A-6.

54. Branigin, "U.S. General Questions Alleged POW Document," p. A-17.

55. Interview, General John Vessey, July 15, 1993.

56. Thomas W. Lippman, "Vessey Faults Russian Paper on U.S. POWs," *Washington Post,* April 22, 1993, p. A-25.

57. Ibid.

58. Ibid. Also: Steven A. Holmes, "Envoy Said P.O.W. Undermines Old Russian Report," *New York Times,* April 22, 1993, p. A-6.

CHAPTER 26

1. Comments of Winston Lord, assistant secretary of state for East Asian and Pacific Affairs, *MacNeil/Lehrer NewsHour,* September 17, 1993, transcript, p. 5.

2. "General Vessey: 'No Reason to Disbelieve' Vietnam's Denials on U.S. P.O.W.'s—What About 25 Years of Lies?" Decision Brief, No. 93-D 32, the Center for Security Policy, April 20, 1993. Also: Al Santoli, "Dealing with the Haunting Legacy," *Washington Times,* April 20, 1993, p. F-1.

3. Thomas W. Lippman, "U.S. May Ease Curbs on Vietnam," *Washington Post,* June 22, 1993, p. A-1.

4. Sheehan, "Letter from Vietnam: Prisoners of the Past," pp. 46–47. Also: Franklin, "The Myth of the Missing," p. 22.

5. William Branigin, "Vietnam Offers File on POWs; Hanoi Releases New Prison Log," *Washington Post,* April 26, 1993, p. A-13.

6. "U.S. Pilots Captured in the Democratic Republic of Vietnam," Ministry of National Defense, Democratic Republic of Vietnam, p. 15; obtained from assistant secretary of defense, Office of Public Affairs, under Freedom of Information Act request, May 17, 1993.

7. Reuters photograph accompanying "Transcript of Clinton's Speech at Memorial to Vietnam War," *New York Times,* June 1, 1993, p. A-14.

8. Associated Press, "Disagree, If We Must About the War, but Let Us Not Let It Divide Us," *Washington Post,* June 1, 1993, p. A-6.

9. Reuters, "U.S. Given MIA Material," *Washington Post,* June 1, 1993, p. A-6.

10. Ibid.

11. Orson Swindle, "Don't Let Hanoi off the Hook," op-ed comment, *USA Today,* July 1, 1993, p. A-11. Swindle, a former POW, was Ross Perot's campaign manager in the 1992 presidential election.

12. Thomas W. Lippman, "U.S. Drops Opposition to Loans for Vietnam," *Washington Post,* July 3, 1993, p. A-18.

13. Thomas W. Lippman, "Clinton to Retain Embargo on Vietnam," *Washington Post,* July 17, 1993, p. A-12.

14. Thomas W. Lippman, "Garwood Plans Trip to Vietnam," *Washington Post,* July 6, 1993, p. A-12.

15. Major Charles D. Melson, USMC, and Lieutenant Colonel Curtis G. Arnold, USMC, *U.S. Marines in Vietnam: The War That Would Not End, 1971–1973* (Washington, D.C.: History and Museums Division, U.S. Marine Corps, 1991), pp. 234–35.

16. Solis, *Marines and Military Law in Vietnam,* pp. 223–30.

17. Ibid., p. 224.

18. Zalin Grant, *Survivors* (New York: W.W. Norton, 1975), pp. 145–49. Also: "Slain Leader of Red Charge Believed to Be U.S. Marine," *Pacific Stars & Stripes,* August 2, 1968, p. 1.

19. Interview, Paul Olenski, February 21, 1994.

20. Zalin B. Grant, "American Defectors with the Viet Cong," *The New Republic,* September 7, 1968, p. 15.

21. Solis, *Marines and Military Law in Vietnam,* p. 224.

22. Ibid., p. 228.

23. Ibid., pp. 228–29.

24. "The Case of Pvt Robert R. Garwood, USMC, Final Report," Report to the Assistant Secretary of Defense for Command, Control, Communication and Intelligence, Vol. 1, June 1993, p. 55.

25. Interview, George L. Brooks, July 1, 1993.

26. Bill Paul, "Veteran's Tale: Robert Garwood Says Vietnam Didn't Return Some American POWs," *Wall Street Journal,* December 4, 1984, p. 1.

27. Jensen-Stevenson and Stevenson, *Kiss the Boys Goodbye,* pp. 350–51.

28. Defense Intelligence Agency, "DIA Evaluation of US PW/MIA Information Provided by Pfc Robert L. Garwood, USMC: Debriefing of Pfc Robert Russel [sic] Garwood on 29 March 1979," undated.

29. William Branigin, "Garwood's Vietnam Trip Revives Issue of POW 'Sightings,' " *Washington Post,* July 24, 1993, p. A-14.

30. Ibid.

31. Susan Katz Keating, "Pentagon Believes Ex-POW Was Coached About Campsite," *Washington Times,* July 22, 1993, p. A-1.

32. "Ross Perot's MIA Charge," editorial, *Washington Post,* July 22, 1993, p. A-30.

33. Letter from Bill Hendon, to the President, July 22, 1993, author's archives.

34. Fax message from Ted Schweitzer to author, May 21, 1993.

35. Computer disk message from Ted Schweitzer to the DIA, July 10, 1993.

36. William Branigin, "U.S. Team Gives Hanoi MIA Archive," *Washington Post,* July 17, 1993, p. A-12.

37. William Branigin, "U.S. Offers to Post Envoys in Hanoi, 1st in 40 Years," *Washington Post,* July 18, 1993, p. A-24.

38. Associated Press, "U.S. Given Clues to MIA Pilots," AP Online, September 10, 1993. Also: the National League of Families of American Prisoners and Missing in Southeast

Asia, "POW/MIA Agreements Between the US and SRV, February 1982–August 1993," p. 12.

39. P.O.W. Network Database, entry for: Wanzel, Charles Joseph III.

40. Interview, U.S. intelligence community source, March 11, 1994.

41. Paul Wedel, "Laos Radio Reports Hundreds of Pilots Caught, Killed in War," *The Stars and Stripes—The National Tribune,* February 27, 1989, p. 1. Also: "Laos: In Hanoi's Dark Shadow," *Time,* December 18, 1972, p. 40.

42. Computer disk message from Ted Schweitzer to the DIA, July 22, 1993, author's archives.

43. Ibid.

44. Computer disk message from Ted Schweitzer to the DIA, undated, circa August 1993. Also: P.O.W. Network Database, entry for: Bennett, Harold George.

45. Memorandum for correspondence, No. 275-M, September 7, 1993, Office of the Assistant Secretary of Defense, Public Affairs.

46. Ibid., attachment: "Informal Translation, Report of Khoang Anya, Secretary of the Central Committee of the WPV at the XX Plenum of the CC WPV at the end of December 1970—beginning of 1971," pp. II, 18. Note, in the Russian text, the term "SRV" is abbreviated "DRV," *Demokraticheskaya Respublica V'etnama,* Democratic Republic of Vietnam.

47. Thomas W. Lippman, "Document Indicates Hanoi Held Additional U.S. POWs," *Washington Post,* September 9, 1993, p. A-30.

48. Adam Clymer, "Soviet File Feeds Debate on P.O.W.'s," *New York Times,* September 9, 1993, p. A-1.

49. Ibid.

50. Reuters, "Vietnam Rejects P.O.W. Document," *New York Times,* September 10, 1993, p. A-8.

51. Stephen J. Morris, "Ghosts in the Archives," op-ed comment, *Washington Post,* September 12, 1993, p. C-3.

52. Fax message from Malcolm McConnell to General John W. Vessey, Jr., September 13, 1993.

53. The analysis of these documents is from "Recent Reports on American POWs in Indochina: An Assessment," released by the Office of the Assistant Secretary of Defense, Public Affairs (No. 028-94), January 24, 1994.

54. Ibid., p. 3.

55. Ibid., p. 4.

56. Bill Bell, "The Tragedy of American MIAs: Conspiracy or Politics as Usual?" *Air Commando News Letter,* December 1993, p. 6.

57. Ibid., p. 8.

58. Ibid., pp. 6–7.

59. Defense Intelligence Agency, Directorate for Defense Intelligence, PW/MIA Branch, "Final Report of Interviews with Le Dinh," undated, p. 1, Records of the Senate Select Committee on POW/MIA Affairs.

60. Ibid., p. 5.

61. Ibid., pp. 8–9.

62. Ibid., p. 14.

63. Ibid., p. 15.

64. Ibid., pp. 18–19.

65. Jeffery Brailey, "The POW Controversy Continues," *New York Guardian,* May 1993, p. 6.

66. *MacNeil/Lehrer NewsHour,* September 17, 1993, transcript, p. 5.

67. Ted Schweitzer computer disk messages to the DIA, April 5 and 8, 1993.

68. The White House, Office of the Press Secretary, "Renewal of the Trading with the Enemy Act and U.S. Policy Toward the Embargo Against Vietnam," September 13, 1993, p. 1.

69. Ibid., p. 3.

70. Ibid., p. 4.

71. Ibid., p. 2.

72. Colonel Dai and his colleagues' position is summarized in a series of computer disk messages from Ted Schweitzer to the DIA, beginning in July 1993 and ending in December 1993.

73. Ted Schweitzer computer disk message AAR-2, circa December 1993: "PW/MIA Situation in Vietnam Dec. 1993," p. 1.

74. Thomas W. Lippman, "U.S. May Lift Vietnam Embargo," *Washington Post,* December 31, 1993, p. A-1.

75. George Esper, Associated Press, "No Timetable in MIA Search, Senators Told," *Washington Times,* January 9, 1994, p. A-6. Also: George Esper, Associated Press, "5 Senators Ask End of Vietnam Embargo," *Washington Times,* January 10, 1994, p. A-1.

76. William Branigin, "U.S. Admiral Urges Trade with Hanoi," *Washington Post,* January 21, 1994, p. A-27.

77. Steven Greenhouse, "Senators Urge End to U.S. Embargo Against Vietnam," *New York Times,* January 28, 1994, p. A-1.

78. Ruth Marcus and Thomas W. Lippman, "Clinton Lifts Vietnam Trade Embargo," *Washington Post,* February 4, 1994, p. A-1.

79. William Branigin, "Vietnam Pledges Continued Cooperation on MIA Issue," *Washington Post,* February 5, 1994, p. A-10.

80. Ibid.

81. For a detailed description of this situation, see: National League of Families of American Prisoners and Missing in Southeast Asia, "Report of National League of Families Trip to Vietnam, Laos and Cambodia," Vietnam, March 22–24, 1994, pp. 1–2.

82. Robert G. Kaiser, "To Vietnamese, 'Times Have Never Been Better,' " *Washington Post,* May 15, 1994, p. A-1.

83. National League of Families of American Prisoners and Missing in Southeast Asia press release, "Vietnam's Ability to Rapidly Account for Missing Americans," December 15, 1993.

CHAPTER 27

1. P.O.W. Network Database, entry for: Hart, Thomas Trammell III (this entry also lists information on Lieutenant MacDonald).

2. Ibid.

3. National League of Families of American Prisoners of War and Missing in Southeast Asia, "POW/MIA Agreements Between the U.S. and SRV, February 1982–August 1993," p. 12.

4. Lorraine Adams, "Clinton Hails D-Day on Memorial Day," *Washington Post,* May 31, 1994, p. A-10.

5. David Montgomery, "Biking Veterans Provide a Roaring Remembrance," *Washington Post,* May 30, 1994, p. B-1.

6. The person generally cited in press accounts as having knowledge of this diabolical program is George R. Leard, an Air Force veteran. But when the Senate select committee deposed Leard, he adamantly denied that he had any knowledge of the secret POW return program. See: Deposition of George Russell Leard, December 14, 1992, pp. 29–32, Records of the Senate Select Committee on POW/MIA Affairs. Also see: "Secret POW/

MIA Returnee Program," National Vietnam POW Strike Force, September 9, 1993, pp. 1–2.

EPILOGUE

1. National Vietnam P.O.W. Strike Force letter to Senator Robert Smith, May 23, 1994.

2. Susan Katz Keating, "Publication of Gory Photos of Dead GIs Outrages Military," *Washington Times,* July 8, 1994, p. A-3.

3. Photo caption, *U.S. Veteran Dispatch,* July 14, 1994, p. 6.

4. Photo caption, *Washington Inquirer,* July 15, 1994, p. A-1.

5. Kevin Foley, "DoD, Families Fight over POW/MIA Photos," *Stars & Stripes,* July 25–31, 1994, p. 1.

6. Accuracy in Media, *AIM Report,* August-A, 1994, No. 23, 14, pp. 1–2.

7. Transcript, "Remarks by Senator Bob Smith to the POW/MIA Family Members," July 15, 1994.

8. Robert J. Caldwell, "A Cache from Secret Military Archives," *San Diego Union-Tribune,* July 24, 1994, p. G-5.

9. Letter to the author from the Defense Prisoner of War/Missing in Action Office, July 18, 1994.

INDEX

Malcolm McConnell,
a former Foreign Service
officer, is a
military historian
and a Roving Editor
for *Reader's Digest*.